MEDIEVAL PHILOSOPHY

Peter Adamson presents a lively introduction to six hundred years of European philosophy, from the beginning of the ninth century to the end of the fourteenth century. The medieval period is one of the richest in the history of philosophy, yet one of the least widely known. Adamson introduces us to some of the greatest thinkers of the Western intellectual tradition, including Peter Abelard, Anselm of Canterbury, Thomas Aquinas, John Duns Scotus, William of Ockham, and Roger Bacon. And the medieval period was notable for the emergence of great women thinkers, including Hildegard of Bingen, Marguerite Porete, and Julian of Norwich. Original ideas and arguments were developed in every branch of philosophy during this period—not just philosophy of religion and theology, but metaphysics, philosophy of logic and language, moral and political theory, psychology, and the foundations of mathematics and natural science.

Peter Adamson took his doctorate from the University of Notre Dame and first worked at King's College London. In 2012 he moved to the Ludwig-Maximilians-Universität München, where he is Professor of Late Ancient and Arabic Philosophy. He has published widely in ancient and medieval philosophy, especially on Neoplatonism and on philosophy in the Islamic world.

PETER ADAMSON

MEDIEVAL PHILOSOPHY

a history of philosophy without any gaps

volume 4

OXFORD

UNIVERSITY PRESS

OXFORD
UNIVERSITY PRESS

Great Clarendon Street, Oxford, OX2 6DP,
United Kingdom

Oxford University Press is a department of the University of Oxford.
It furthers the University's objective of excellence in research, scholarship,
and education by publishing worldwide. Oxford is a registered trade mark of
Oxford University Press in the UK and in certain other countries

First published 2019
First published in paperback 2022

Impression: 3

Published in the United States of America by Oxford University Press
198 Madison Avenue, New York, NY 10016, United States of America

British Library Cataloguing in Publication Data
Data available

Library of Congress Cataloging in Publication Data
Data available

ISBN 978–0–19–884240–8 (Hbk.)
ISBN 978–0–19–285673–9 (Pbk.)

Printed and bound by
CPI Group (UK) Ltd, Croydon, CR0 4YY

For my father, David Adamson

CONTENTS

Preface   xi
Acknowledgments   xv
Dates   xvii

Part I. Early Medieval Philosophy

1. Arts of Darkness—Introduction to Medieval Philosophy   3

2. Charles in Charge—The Carolingian Renaissance   10

3. Grace Notes—Eriugena and the Predestination Controversy   17

4. Much Ado About Nothing—Eriugena's *Periphyseon*   24

5. Philosophers Anonymous—The Roots of Scholasticism   31

6. Virgin Territory—Peter Damian on Changing the Past   39

7. A Canterbury Tale—Anselm's Life and Works   46

8. Somebody's Perfect—Anselm's Ontological Argument   52

9. All or Nothing—The Problem of Universals   58

10. Get Thee to a Nunnery—Heloise and Abelard   66

11. It's the Thought that Counts—Abelard's Ethics   72

12. Learn Everything—The Victorines   79

13. Like Father, like Son—Debating the Trinity   87

14. On the Shoulders of Giants—Philosophy at Chartres   94

15. The Good Book—Philosophy of Nature   101

16. One of a Kind—Gilbert of Poitiers on Individuation   107

17. Two Swords—Early Medieval Political Philosophy   114

18. Law and Order—Gratian and Peter Lombard   121

19. Leading Light—Hildegard of Bingen   128

20. Rediscovery Channel—Translations into Latin   135

21. Straw Men—The Rise of the Universities   142

Part II. The Thirteenth Century

22. No Uncertain Terms—Thirteenth-Century Logic   153

23. Full of Potential—Thirteenth-Century Physics   161

24. Stayin' Alive—Thirteenth-Century Psychology   168

25. It's All Good—The Transcendentals   175

26. Do the Right Thing—Thirteenth-Century Ethics   182

27. A Light that Never Goes Out—Robert Grosseteste   188

28. Origin of Species—Roger Bacon   194

29. Stairway to Heaven—Bonaventure   201

30. Your Attention, Please—Peter Olivi   208

31. None for Me, Thanks—Franciscan Poverty   215

32. Begin the Beguine—Hadewijch and Mechthild of Magdeburg   222

33. Binding Arbitration—Robert Kilwardby   229

34. Animal, Vegetable, Mineral—Albert the Great's Natural Philosophy   236

35. The Shadow Knows—Albert the Great's Metaphysics   242

36. The Ox Heard round the World—Thomas Aquinas   248

37. Everybody Needs Some Body—Aquinas on Soul and Knowledge   255

38. What Comes Naturally—Ethics in Albert and Aquinas   262

39. What Pleases the Prince—The Rule of Law   269

40. Onward Christian Soldiers—Just War Theory   277

41. Paris when it Sizzles—The Condemnations   284

42. Masters of the University—"Latin Averroists"   290

43. The NeverEnding Story—The Eternity of the World   297

44. Let Me Count the Ways—Speculative Grammar   304

45. Love, Reign over Me—The *Romance of the Rose*   311

46. Frequently Asked Questions—Henry of Ghent   318

47. Here Comes the Son—The Trinity and the Eucharist   325

48. Once and for All—Scotus on Being   332

49. To Will or Not to Will—Scotus on Freedom   339

50. On Command—Scotus on Ethics   345

51. One in a Million—Scotus on Universals and Individuals   352

Part III. The Fourteenth Century

52. Time of the Signs—The Fourteenth Century   361

53. After Virtue—Marguerite Porete   368

54. To Hell and Back—Dante Alighieri   374

55. Our Power is Real—The Clash of Church and State   381

56. Render unto Caesar—Marsilius of Padua   387

57. Do As You're Told—Ockham on Ethics and Political Philosophy   394

58. A Close Shave—Ockham's Nominalism   400

59. What Do You Think?—Ockham on Mental Language   407

60. Keeping it Real—Responses to Ockham   414

61. Back to the Future—Foreknowledge and Predestination   421

62. Trivial Pursuits—Fourteenth-Century Logic   428

63. Quadrivial Pursuits—The Oxford Calculators   435

64. Get to the Point—Fourteenth-Century Physics   442

65. Portrait of the Artist—John Buridan   449

66. Seeing is Believing—Nicholas of Autrecourt's Skeptical
Challenge   456

67. On the Money—Medieval Economic Theory   463

68. Down to the Ground—Meister Eckhart   470

69. Men in Black—The German Dominicans   476

70. A Wing and a Prayer—Angels in Medieval Philosophy   482

71. Alle Maner of Thyng Shall be Welle—English Mysticism   489

72. Say it with Poetry—Chaucer and Langland   495

73. The Good Wife—Sexuality and Misogyny in the Middle Ages   502

74. Sighs Were her Food—Catherine of Siena and Affective
Mysticism   509

75. The Most Christian Doctor—The *Querelle de la rose* and
Jean Gerson   516

76. Morning Star of the Reformation—John Wyclif   523

77. The Prague Spring—Scholasticism across Europe   529

78. Renaissance Men—Ramon Llull and Petrarch   536

Notes   543
Further Reading   609
Publisher's Acknowledgment   627
Index   629

PREFACE

There is, as it turns out, quite a lot of medieval philosophy. It's a huge territory to explore, even if you are not dealing with philosophy in the Islamic world or Byzantium (respectively covered in the previous and next installments of this book series). Just compare this book to earlier offerings in the series: *Classical Philosophy* included a mere forty-three chapters and *Philosophy in the Hellenistic and Roman Worlds* fifty-three chapters. That's fewer than a hundred chapters to cover about a millennium of philosophy in total, whereas in this volume telling the story of medieval thought will take seventy-eight chapters for only half a millennium, from the ninth to the fourteenth centuries. And this despite the fact that there isn't much to say about the tenth and eleventh centuries, the so called "Dark Ages"—even if there is somewhat more to say than you might think. The profusion of material may come as a surprise, given that most non-specialists would be hard pressed to name more than a handful of medieval philosophers.

But it makes historical sense. As we get closer to the present, there is simply more in the way of surviving text; from the medieval age we even have manuscripts in the original handwriting of some of the main protagonists. Furthermore, this period saw the rise of institutions that produced a staggering amount of philosophical writing, especially for use in classroom contexts. Consider that a document providing information on the members of the University of Paris just in the year 1329–30 records about two thousand individuals.[1] And these are people whose names we know! The number of extant works by unidentified authors is so large that you could produce a creditable history of medieval scholasticism by discussing nothing but anonymous manuscripts (a "history of philosophy without any names," if you will). To make matters yet more daunting, in this book we are frequently going to go beyond the world of the schoolmen. We will be discussing the philosophical contributions of men who were not masters at the schools and universities, and of thinkers who weren't men at all. Indeed one of the most exciting features of medieval thought, one particularly highlighted in this book, is the survival of numerous works by women. This makes for another contrast with the ancient world, whose women philosophers speak to us only through the intermediary of male authors.

In Chapter 1 below I set out the chronological range of medieval philosophy and begin to make a case for the broad approach I have taken to the subject, which includes topics like mysticism and natural science. So there is no need to do that here. Instead I would just like to give some brief advice about how to read the book. Ideally, you should start at the beginning and go through to the end without skipping anything (this is after all how I wrote it). Hopefully that will give you an impression of the different epochs of medieval philosophy and its evolution from one period to the next. It may be, though, that you are more interested in some philosophical topics than others, in which case you may be frustrated by the chronological rather than thematic arrangement of the material. Here, then, are a few thematic threads that could be followed through the book by reading it with gaps.

We may as well start with God. It's worth emphasizing already now that, contrary to popular belief, medieval philosophy is about much more than just theology. Many of the chapters that follow have nothing to say about religion at all. But if you are primarily coming to this material with an interest in the philosophy of religion, you might want to focus on those chapters dealing with proofs of God's existence and manner of being (Chapters 4, 8, 25, 35, 36, 48, 68), His power and knowledge in relation to human freedom (Chapters 3, 6, 7, 49, 61, 76), the possibility of rationally grasping or speaking of God (Chapters 4, 12, 29, 36, 42, 68, 69, 71, 75), or specifically Christian doctrines like the Trinity, Eucharist, and Incarnation (Chapters 13, 14, 47, 74, 76, 77). Another important topic here is the Christian value of asceticism and voluntary poverty (start with Chapter 31, but it comes up a lot, especially in discussing Franciscan thinkers, as in Chapters 29, 30, and 57). If you're inclined to think that a belief in an immaterial, immortal soul is another distinctively Christian belief, then you're actually wrong about that: it was espoused already in antiquity by most pagan thinkers. Still, you can read here about how immaterial souls and angels were conceived in Latin Christendom (Chapters 24, 33, 34, 37, 41, 53, 69, 70). To find out about what happens to the soul after death, you're best off asking Dante (Chapter 54).

If you're interested in everything I've just mentioned, go straight to Henry of Ghent (Chapter 46), because he was too.

If your interest in matters psychological runs more towards knowledge and the mind, then you may want to look at the epistemological debate between upholders of representationalism and knowledge as direct relation (Chapters 28 and 30), the illuminationist theory of epistemology (Chapters 27, 29), or suggestions of outright skepticism (Chapter 66). There is also the will, a faculty whose operation will frequently occupy our attention in this book (for instance in Chapters 3, 11, 19, 30, 46, 49, 53, 57, 61).

A medieval scholastic would at this point complain that you are going about things in the wrong order. You should really start with logic and the philosophy of language (Chapters 2, 5, 22, 33, 44, 59, 62, 65) and, once you have the basics under your belt, tackle the most prominent topic discussed under that heading, the problem of universals (Chapters 9, 10, 51, 58, 60, 65, 77). Or if philosophy of language leaves you cold and you prefer language that is more aesthetically pleasing, have a look at the chapters on literary medieval figures (Chapters 15, 32, 45, 54, 72, 78).

Once you've studied logic, you're ready for the mathematical disciplines of the quadrivium and for natural philosophy, which became increasingly mathematical in its approach as the Middle Ages developed (Chapters 15, 23, 27, 28, 34, 43, 53, 64, 77). If that's still not practical enough for you, try the branches of practical philosophy itself, namely ethics (Chapters 11, 19, 26, 38, 46, 50, 72) and political philosophy (Chapters 17, 40, 55, 56, 57, 75, 76). Also relevant here are parts of the book dealing with medieval theories of law and economics (Chapters 18, 39, 67), and attitudes towards women (especially Chapter 73 but see also the various chapters on women authors). Finally, if you are especially interested in the historical framework within which all these themes were explored, then you're probably the sort of person who'd be inclined to read the book from front to back anyway, so go with that instinct. But if you're pressed for time, broader historical developments are empha-sized especially in Chapters 1, 2, 5, 18, 20, 21, 41, 52, 55, and 77.

Whether you read the book selectively or straight through, I would consider my mission as an author accomplished if it leaves you unsatisfied. My fondest hope is that you'll be struck, even if only occasionally, by the thought that medieval philosophers had some extraordinarily interesting ideas and that you would like to follow up on what you've read here by turning to the original sources. Happily, almost all the figures covered here are at least partially available in English transla-tion. The notes to the chapters will give you references to many such translations. For anthologies of primary texts and for secondary literature, you can start by consulting the "Further Reading" section at the back of the book. Finally, I would point you towards the History of Philosophy podcast series. It included not only most of the material that became the basis of this book, but also numerous interviews with experts on a wide range of topics in medieval thought, all of it free to listen via that modern equivalent of the Averroist collective mind we call the Internet, at www.historyofphilosophy.net.

ACKNOWLEDGMENTS

One of the most gratifying things about working on this book series has been the extraordinary generosity of colleagues around the world who have shared their expertise with me. From early on I was given valuable advice about what to cover in the book and on drafts of individual chapters; also, many of these scholars agreed to be interviewed for the podcast version. I would here like to record my gratitude to the academic experts who appeared as guests on the series: Andrew Arlig, Rachel Barney, Susan Brower-Toland, Charles Burnett, Therese Cory, Richard Cross, Isabel Davis, Catarina Dutilh Novaes, Kent Emery, Russ Friedman, Stephen Gersh, Monica Green, Caroline Humfress, Mark Kalderon, Peter King, Jill Kraye, Scott MacDonald, John Marenbon, Robert Pasnau, Dominik Perler, Martin Pickavé, Giorgio Pini, Tom Pink, Christof Rapp, Andreas Speer, Eileen Sweeney, Juhana Toivanen, Sara Uckelman, and Jack Zupko, as well as fellow podcasters Sharyn Eastaugh, Jamie Jeffers, and Robin Pearson. Pretty well all of them also gave me advice that was helpful in writing the book. I am particularly grateful to Catarina Dutilh Novaes, Danielle Layne, Dominik Perler, and Giorgio Pini for general discussion of how to approach the medieval period, and to Martin Pickavé and Christina Van Dyke for invaluable comments on the entire manuscript, and for further discussion. Further advice on particular topics is acknowledged in the notes to the relevant chapters. Any mistakes or infelicities that remain are, of course, to be blamed not on these many helpful scholars but on God's providential plan for the universe.

Looking further back, I should mention the teachers who got me interested in medieval philosophy in the first place and gave me my first training in this field. They are too many to list in full but I should at least name David Burrell, Cristina D'Ancona, Stephen Gersh, Mark Jordan, John Kleiner, Michael Loux, Ralph McInerny, and Richard Taylor. More recently, I have benefited from continued collaboration with members of the King's College London Philosophy Department and from the support of my colleagues at the Ludwig Maximilian University in Munich, especially Matteo Di Giovanni, Eleni Gaitanu, Rotraud Hansberger, Oliver Primavesi, and Christof Rapp.

In producing the podcast I was ably assisted by Hanif Amin Beidokhti, Andreas Lammer, Julian Rimmer, and Bethany Somma. For the production of the book, I would like to acknowledge Fedor Benevich for his work on the index and Peter Momtchiloff for his unstinting support of the whole book series.

Finally and as always, more than thanks are due to my family: to my wife Ursula, my daughters Sophia, Johanna, my brother Glenn, and my parents Joyce and David. The book is dedicated to my father, who will especially appreciate the frequent mention of bishops.

DATES

All dates given here are AD. For dates of authors, use has been made of the biographical appendix in vol. 2 of R. Pasnau (ed.), *The Cambridge History of Medieval Philosophy*, 2 vols (Cambridge: 2010), among numerous other sources.

Philosophers and other authors		Selected historical events	
Augustine	d. 430		
Boethius	d. 524/5		
Gregory the Great	d. 604	Christian missionaries arrive in Britain	597
Isidore of Seville	d. 636	Synod of Whitby	664
		Muslim conquest of Spain	711
Bede	d. 735	Battle of Tours	732
Fredegisus	fl. 800–30	Viking raids begin in England	787
Alcuin	d. 804	Charlemagne crowned emperor	800
		Death of Charlemagne	814
Hrbanus Maurus	d. 856	Muslim invasion of Sicily	827
Gottschalk	d. 668		
John Scotus Eriugena	d. after 870	Death of Charles the Bald	875
Hincmar of Rheims	d. 882	Death of Alfred the Great	899
		Founding of Abbey of Cluny	910
Gerbert of Aurillac (Pope Sylvester II)	d. 1003	Death of Otto I of Germany	973
Abbo of Fleury	d. 1004		
Notker Labeo	d. 1022	Battle of Hastings	1066
Peter Damian	d. 1072	Submission of Henry IV to Pope at Canossa	1077
Berengar of Tours	d. ca. 1088	Toledo taken by Christian forces	1085
Lanfranc of Bec	d. 1089	*Domesday Book* compiled	1086
Constantine the African	d. before 1098/9	Death of William the Conqueror	1087

Manegold of Lautenbach	d. after 1103	First Crusade launched	1095
Anselm of Canterbury	d. 1109		
Ivo of Chartres	d. 1115		
Roscelin of Compiègne	d. after 1120		
William of Champeaux	d. 1122	Concordat of Worms	1122
Bernard of Chartres	d. 1124/6		
Hugh of St. Victor	d. 1141		
Peter Abelard	d. 1142		
Gilbert of Poitiers	d. 1142		
Gratian	fl. 1140s		
James of Venice	d. after 1147	Second Crusade launched	1147
Adelard of Bath	d. ca. 1152		
Bernard of Clairvaux	d. 1153		
William of Conches	d. after 1154		
Thierry of Chartres	d. after 1156	Charter of University of Bologna	1158
Bernard Silvestris	d. ca. 1160		
Peter Lombard	d. 1160		
Heloise	d. 1164		
Richard of St. Victor	d. 1173	Murder of Thomas Becket	1170
Hildegard of Bingen	d. 1179		
Dominicus Gundisalvi (Gundissalinus)	fl. 1162–90		
John of Salisbury	d. 1180		
Clarembald of Arras	d. ca. 1187	Capture of Jerusalem by Saladin	1187
Gerard of Cremona	d. 1187	Third Crusade launched	1189
		Death of Frederick Barbarossa	1190
Alan of Lille	d. 1202/3	Charter for university at Paris	1200
		Death of Eleanor of Aquitaine	1204
		Fourth Crusade sacks Constantinople	1204
		Crusade begins against Cathars	1209
		Founding of university at Cambridge	1209
		Church approval of Franciscan order	1210
		Charter for university at Oxford	1214
		Fourth Lateran Council	1215
		Magna Carta	1215

		Restrictions on teaching of Aristotle at Paris	1215
		Church approval of Dominican order	1215
		Foundation of university at Padua	1222
Michael Scot	d. ca. 1236	Mongol invasion of Russia	1237
William of Moerbeke	d. 1286		
William of Auxerre	d. 1231		
Philip the Chancellor	d. 1236		
Hadewijch of Brabant	fl. early–mid-13th c.		
Alexander of Hales	d. 1245	Foundation of university at Rome	1245
John Blund	d. 1248	Foundation of Dominican studium at Cologne	1248
William of Auvergne	d. 1249		
Lambert of Auxerre	fl. 1250s	Death of Emperor Frederick II	1250
Robert Grosseteste	d. 1253		
Clare of Assisi	d. 1253		
Richard Rufus	d. after 1259	Recapture of Constantinople by Greek Christians	1261
William of Sherwood	d. 1271	Condemnations at Paris	1270, 1277
Bonaventure	d. 1274		
Thomas Aquinas	d. 1274		
Peter of Spain	d.1277		
Robert Kilwardby	d. 1279		
Albert the Great	d. 1280		
Boethius of Dacia	d. ca. 1280		
Siger of Brabant	d. 1282/4		
Mechthild of Magdeburg	d. 1282		
John Pecham	d. 1292	Expulsion of the Jews from England by Edward I	1290
Roger Bacon	d. ca. 1292		
Henry of Ghent	d. 1294		
Peter Olivi	d. 1298		
Matthew of Aquasparta	d. 1302	First meeting of French Estates General	1302
Martin of Dacia	d. 1304	Death of Pope Boniface VIII	1303
Jean de Meun	d. 1305		

John of Paris	d. 1306		
Godfrey of Fontaines	d. 1306/9		
John Duns Scotus	d. 1308	Beginning of Avignon Papacy	1309
Marguerite Porete	d. 1310		
Dietrich of Freiberg	d. after 1310		
Giles of Rome	d. 1316		
Ramon Llull	d. 1316		
Thomas of Erfurt	fl. early 14th c.		
Radulphus Brito	d. ca. 1320		
Dante Aligheri	d. 1321		
Peter Auriol	d. 1322		
Meister Eckhart	d. 1328		
William of Pagula	d. ca. 1332		
Durand of St Pourcain	d. 1334	Hundred Years War begins	1337
Richard Swineshead	fl. ca. 1340–54		
Siger of Courtrai	d. 1341		
Marsilius of Padua	d. 1342/3		
Walter Chatton	d. 1343		
Walter Burley	d. 1344		
Francis of Marchia	d. 1344		
William of Ockham	d. 1347	Founding of university at Prague	1347
Thomas Bradwardine	d. 1349	First wave of the Black Death begins	1347
Gerald Odonis	d. 1349		
Richard Rolle	d.1349		
Adam Wodeham	d. 1358		
Gregory of Rimini	d. 1358		
John Buridan	d. 1358/61		
Richard Kilvington	d. 1361	Second wave of the Black Death begins	1361
John Tauler	d. 1361		
Berthold of Moosburg	d. after 1361		
Roger Swineshead	d. ca. 1365	Founding of university at Vienna	1365
Nicholas of Autrecourt	d. 1369		
William Heytesbury	d. 1372/3		

Petrarch	d. 1374	Great Papal Schism begins	1378
Catherine of Siena	d. 1380	Battle of Poitiers	1380
Nicole Oresme	d. 1382	Peasants' Revolt	1381
John Wyclif	d. 1384	Founding of university at Heidelberg	1385
William Langland	d. ca. 1388		
Albert of Saxony	d. 1390		
		Cloud of Unknowing written	1390s
Marsilius of Inghen	d. 1396		
Walter Hilton	d. 1396		
Henry of Oyta	d. 1397		
Henry of Langenstein	d. 1399	Banning of Wyclif Bible in England	1409
Geoffrey Chaucer	d. 1400	Lollard uprising	1414
Julian of Norwich	d. after 1416	Execution of Jan Hus	1415
Jean Gerson	d. 1429		
Paul of Venice	d. 1429		
Christine de Pizan	d. ca. 1430		

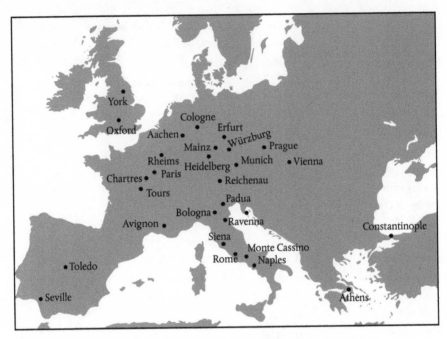

Map of Europe in the Middle Ages

PART I
EARLY MEDIEVAL PHILOSOPHY

1

ARTS OF DARKNESS
INTRODUCTION TO MEDIEVAL
PHILOSOPHY

Most periods in the history of philosophy have appealing names. Putting Plato, Aristotle, and friends under the heading of "classical" philosophy already highlights the unique role of ancient thought as the model and source for all that comes after. Authors like Erasmus and Machiavelli can bask in the positive connotations of the term "Renaissance." As for Descartes, Hume, and Kant, their importance and fame is so well established that they hardly need any help from a historical label, but they get an alluring one nonetheless: "modern" philosophy, with its suggestion that these are the thinkers who remain relevant for us today. The poor relative is medieval philosophy. This word "medieval" is useful, since it picks out the epoch in European history that we're going to be covering in this book. But there's no denying that it sounds vaguely like an insult. Neither classical nor modern but in between the two (this is what "medieval" means: "middle age"), the very word conjures up a time of social collapse, superstition, oppressive and dogmatic religious authority. Medieval philosophy is, in short, the philosophy of the Dark Ages.

Our task here is to illuminate this supposedly dark period of human thought. I'll start by highlighting some of the main figures and themes that lie ahead. First though, a brief word about what I mean by "medieval philosophy." In the previous volume of this series I covered philosophy in the Islamic world, and in so doing provided extensive coverage of Jewish thought in the medieval period, even making forays into Christian Europe when looking at figures like Gersonides. So none of that material is on the "to-do list," though characters like Avicenna, Averroes, and Maimonides will feature as influences on the philosophers we will be covering. Something else that *is* on the to-do list, but not yet, is the Byzantine tradition. In the surviving Eastern part of the Roman Empire, the medieval period saw the continued production of philosophical works in Greek, but that's a story for the next volume. So as of now, by "medieval philosophy" I mean the philosophy of Latin Christendom in the medieval period.

That gives us clear cultural and geographical boundaries for our topic. More difficult is setting chronological boundaries. As far as the starting point goes, the die is cast. Another earlier volume covered philosophy in late antiquity, and the last figure discussed from Latin Christendom was Boethius. Like Augustine, Boethius should indeed be seen as a late antique figure, not a medieval philosopher, even if both he and Augustine are often covered in university courses on medieval philosophy. Boethius died in 525 AD, so you would think I'd be kicking off these episodes with figures from the later sixth or perhaps seventh centuries. But here we do have a period that could legitimately be called a "dark age," at least as far as philosophy goes. After the collapse of the Western Roman Empire, philosophy in Western Europe collapsed too, even as it was flourishing in the Islamic world, as seen in that other earlier volume in this series.

On the other hand, the collapse in Europe was not nearly as long-lasting as usually supposed. In the popular imagination, intellectual history recovered only in the Renaissance. Here popular imagination is almost right. It's just that the recovery happened in the *Carolingian* Renaissance, that is, during the reign of Charlemagne in the late eighth and early ninth centuries. Scholars attached to his court, particularly Alcuin, renewed the study of philosophy, along with the other disciplines they called the "liberal arts." Following this rebirth, we have continuous philosophical activity in Europe right down to the present day. So, from the point of view of the historian of philosophy, you could even consider the ninth century as the true renaissance.[1] As we'll be seeing, the twelfth century has also been honored with the title of "renaissance." This is not to deny, of course, that a renaissance also happened after the medieval age. As we'll see in the closing chapters of this book, the thought of that period was far more continuous with "medieval" intellectual history than is often supposed. But there were genuinely new developments in the Renaissance too, notably the reception of new sources, especially Plato, into Latin, and more generally the self-conscious return to classical texts staged by the humanists. Still, any line dividing late medieval philosophy from Renaissance philosophy is going to be a blurry one. Mostly for convenience, I am going to draw it at the year 1400. I will however be emphasizing that "medieval" thought anticipated Renaissance and early modern thought in some ways, and in other ways survived past 1400.

So that's the terrain to be covered: philosophy in Latin Christendom, beginning with the Carolingian period around the year 800 AD and ending in 1400. It's more than half a millennium of philosophy, featuring debates within all areas of philosophy and many dozens, in fact hundreds, of significant figures. In keeping with the approach of this whole series, we'll be looking at quite a number of them, far too many even to name in this opening chapter.[2] But just so you have an idea of what to expect, let me mention a few.

We may as well begin with Thomas Aquinas. I suppose he is the only medieval thinker who you'd be almost certain to encounter in an undergraduate course on philosophy, unless you count Anselm because of the couple of pages in which he presented his famous "ontological argument" for the existence of God. There are several reasons why Aquinas is so prominent. He was among the first who grappled systematically with the works of Aristotle that were reintroduced into Latin Christendom in the twelfth and thirteenth centuries. Showing a rare gift for synthesis, he wove Aristotelian ideas together with ideas from previous medieval thought, from Augustine, and from Neoplatonism. His writings are also very readable, at least by medieval standards, composed in straightforward Latin and full of concise arguments that were designed for use in teaching contexts. In fact, as I can testify from my own experiences teaching Aquinas to students, those arguments still work quite nicely in the same context today. To this we can add the fact that he is recognized by today's Catholic Church as a leading theological authority, even promoted in recent papal encyclicals.

It would, however, be a serious mistake to think of the coming journey as a dutiful trek through dimly lit lowlands as we make our way to the solitary peak of Aquinas, followed by a swift descent back into obscurity until we reach the Renaissance. This was certainly not the way the medievals themselves saw things. Though Aquinas always had his adherents, he had his detractors too. It was only much later that he came to be seen as the indispensable medieval thinker. Centering our story on Aquinas would not only be historically anachronistic, it would also run the risk of obscuring other thinkers from this period who should have an equal claim to our attention. Take for instance Aquinas' younger contemporary John Duns Scotus, who innovated in several areas of philosophy and whose radical new understanding of necessity and contingency set the stage for later thinkers like Leibniz. Or take Peter Abelard, among the most original logicians and metaphysicians who has ever lived, and no mean contributor to the history of ethics.

Abelard is frequently seen as the first major "scholastic" thinker, but he was not the first major medieval philosopher. That title should probably go to Eriugena, an author of the Carolingian period who was unusual in being able to work with and translate Greek Patristic literature. This led him to propose a stunning, and for his contemporaries shocking, vision of God and the created world, rethinking the Christian Neoplatonism of late antiquity. Another pioneering figure was Anselm of Canterbury, best known for his aforementioned ontological argument for the existence of God—though, as we'll see, he was more than a one-trick pony. Along with these two early thinkers, let me mention two later ones from the fourteenth century: William of Ockham and John Buridan. Like Abelard, Ockham is primarily known for doing logic and metaphysics within the framework of nominalism. But also like Abelard, his work ranged more widely than that: Abelard's contribution in ethics is matched by Ockham's in political philosophy. As for Buridan, he is probably the medieval thinker whose star has risen fastest in recent scholarship. He too was a brilliant logician, and also a crucial figure in the history of medieval science.

Thus far the entries on this list of landmark thinkers have something in common: they are all men. But one exciting aspect of medieval intellectual history is the emergence of great women thinkers, like Hildegard of Bingen, Marguerite Porete, and Julian of Norwich. They are only a few of the female authors we will consider below. As in antiquity and the Islamic world, women were only rarely allowed to enter into the cut and thrust of technical philosophical debate. That's something that became common only in early modern Europe—and about time, too. But we can very easily make a case for the inclusion of medieval women in our history. They were major contributors to the medieval mystical tradition, which resonates strongly with the contemplative aspects of late ancient Platonism, or Sufism in the Islamic world. Women also played a significant role in the marriage of philosophy and medieval literature.

The next question is, what issues can we expect to see these medieval philosophers discussing? A short answer would be "all sorts." Every branch of philosophy was explored in the medieval period. But let's start with the most obvious: medieval thinkers had a lot to say about God, and religious beliefs more generally. I like to say that working on contemporary philosophy of religion is basically just like studying medieval philosophy, except not as interesting and you don't have to learn Latin. That's a bit unfair to my colleagues who do philosophy of religion, but there's some truth in it. Most of the proofs for and against God's existence being debated today were already discussed with great sophistication in the medieval period, along with such issues as divine omnipotence, the nature of miracles, the metaphysics of the afterlife, and so on. Furthermore, the medieval discussions did not simply presuppose the truth of Christian belief. Philosophers frequently offered arguments that were explicitly designed to be convincing even for a hypothetical atheist or non-Christian reader. So this aspect of medieval philosophy should interest you if you are religious, or are interested in religion, or are keenly anti-religious and want to understand the opposing side.

If you couldn't care less about religion, medieval philosophy still has a lot to offer you. Perhaps the most common and pernicious prejudice about medieval philosophy is that it was really all theology, that these thinkers talked of nothing but God and other recondite questions of faith. There are at least three reasons why this is wrong. First, the fact that a philosophical argument, distinction, or concept was developed in a theological context doesn't preclude the development from having application outside such a context. Ideas developed to explain such things as angels, grace, the Trinity, the Incarnation, or transubstantiation can be deployed outside the debate where they were first proposed. Second, this actually happened historically. A nice example would be one I have already mentioned briefly: Scotus' conception of necessity and contingency. His agenda was, in large part at least, to explain God's omnipotence. Yet his proposals constituted a giant step in the direction of our modern-day understanding of modality. When atheist philosophers do modal logic today, they are working with a conception of possibility and necessity that owes a great deal to Scotus.

Third and most importantly, medieval philosophers didn't in fact spend all their time arguing about God and theology. Especially once the medieval universities arose, with a distinction made between theological and non-theological faculties, it became standard to designate certain areas of intellectual activity as drawing solely on natural reason. As early as the Carolingian period, we find examples of philosophical debate being conducted for its own sake, without any explicit comment on what the debate might all mean for our understanding of God or the state of our souls. And like souls according to most medieval philosophers, such debates could have a life of their own. Perhaps the best example is the problem of universals. Consider giraffes. We might wonder what it is that is shared by all members of this class that makes each of them qualify as a giraffe. This would be a "universal"—in other words, it would exist in or apply to all the particular members of the class of giraffes. But do such universal natures really exist? If so, what sort of existence could they possibly possess?

While this question is not wholly unconnected to theological problems, it was treated throughout the medieval period as an issue to be solved in its own right. In general, philosophical logic and philosophy of language were the first areas to capture the attention of medieval thinkers. This can be observed already in the Carolingian age, and problems of logic and language would be uppermost in the minds of fourteenth-century figures like Ockham and Buridan. This is a striking feature of medieval philosophy, and one that might make this period of thought especially interesting for us today. Like twentieth-century analytic philosophers, medieval thinkers were deeply and centrally concerned with philosophical problems related to language. Their fascination with words was not restricted to the word of God.

Nor were theology, logic, and language the only games in town. Free will had been put squarely at the center of the Latin Christian philosophical tradition thanks to Patristic authors, especially Augustine. It stayed there in the medieval period, as the nature of choice, both human and divine, continued to be an abiding concern. Another Augustinian theme of perennial importance was the nature of knowledge. Augustine proposed in a short work called *On the Teacher* that humans achieve knowledge thanks to assistance from God.[3] For Augustine, our ability to attain truth relies on the presence within our souls of the Truth that is Christ. This so-called "illuminationist" model of knowledge continued to be popular among medievals. But it received competition when Aristotle's more empiricist approach became known. The stage was set for an epistemological showdown, which unfolded in the thirteenth century. Meanwhile, there were questions about the scope and possibility of human knowledge. We tend to assume that radical skeptical hypotheses are a distinctive feature of "modern" philosophy, emerging for the first time with people like Descartes and Hume. Yet we find such hypotheses already in medieval texts, albeit never developed with quite the systematic ambition of the modern philosophers.

Like Muslims and Jews in the medieval period, medieval Christians also generated a mystical tradition, which not only stressed the limitations of natural human knowledge but also offered a path to go beyond those limitations. Sufism and Kabbalah drew on and influenced mainstream philosophy, and the same is going to be true here. The female medieval thinkers usually come into the story about here, allowed to contribute to spiritual literature just like the desert mothers of late antiquity and the female sufis of the Islamic world. But of course this was a game men could play too, as we'll see with such figures as Bonaventure and Meister Eckhart. A lesson we've learned from late antiquity and the Islamic world applies here too: there is no sharp boundary between mystical and non-mystical authors. Bonaventure and Eckhart were both scholastics and mystics, while figures not usually classified as mystics draw on classical texts of mysticism like the works of the Pseudo-Dionysius. Good examples here would be Albert the Great and his student Aquinas.

The mystics remind us that philosophy need not be presented in dry treatises full of relentless argumentation. To tell the story of medieval philosophy without any gaps, we need to cast our net wide enough to take in literary works by Dante and Chaucer, the visionary treatises and poems of Hildegard or Mechthild of Magdeburg. If what comes to your mind when you hear the word "medieval" is besieged castles, knights in shining armor, and ladies in attendance at jousting tournaments, then most of what follows will probably come as a bit of a shock to you. Still, the ideal of "courtly love" will be relevant at points, like when we look at the *Romance of the Rose* and the debate it triggered about misogyny in medieval literature. More generally, the scholar of medieval thought needs to look beyond the obvious formats of the free-standing philosophical treatise or commentary on Aristotle, taking seriously texts like glosses written in the margins of manuscripts, or sermons and popular poems, which are often an important witness to medieval ethical ideas.

Speaking of ethics, we should not underestimate the medieval contributions in practical philosophy. The need to define sin, and to explain what is happening in humans when they perform sinful actions, led to a blossoming of reflection on ethical issues in Latin Christendom. Throughout the medieval centuries, debates also raged over questions in political philosophy. The most burning issue here concerned the rival claims to authority made by the Church, on the one side, and by worldly rulers, on the other. Should the kings and emperors of Europe submit to the commands of the popes, and if so, then on which issues? We also find fascinating medieval discussions of more specific issues in ethics and politics, for instance voluntary poverty and the circumstances in which it is just to wage war.

A final area I'd like to mention before wrapping up this introduction is natural science. Throughout this book series, we've occasionally cast an eye on the intricate connections between philosophy and the sciences, considering such areas as medicine, optics, and astronomy. Again, there's an unhelpful prejudice that lurks here, to the effect that the Renaissance and early modern periods in Europe saw advancements in the natural sciences which had been stalled ever since late antiquity, if not since Aristotle. But the medievals too engaged in science. Early scientific discussions centered on the one dialogue of Plato that was (partially) known to the Latin Christians, his *Timaeus*. A more empiricist approach to science came along later, but well within the medieval period. One of the great contributors to scientific method, Roger Bacon, lived in the thirteenth century and was thus a near contemporary of Aquinas, and the fourteenth century saw a number of authors apply mathematics to problems in physics.

So there's plenty for us to look forward to in the rest of this book. But let's begin by looking back, reminding you of the late ancient legacy that came down to the medievals, mentioning the few texts of significance for the history of philosophy produced in Latin in the couple of centuries following Boethius, and finding out how these became the seeds for the first flowering of medieval philosophy in the Carolingian age.

2

CHARLES IN CHARGE
THE CAROLINGIAN RENAISSANCE

Suppose a man writes one book chapter per week and, during the writing of each chapter, consumes three cups of coffee, each cup containing 250 ml of water. If an Olympic-size swimming pool contains 2.5 million liters of water, how many years of writing about philosophy will it take the man to drink a swimming pool's worth of coffee?[1] Ah yes, the word problem, mortal enemy of nearly every school-child, though I personally rather liked them when I was doing math as a kid (always preferring words to numbers). Whether you like them or loathe them, they go back a long way. Some of the earliest examples can be found in a text written by a man who has a strong claim to be the first significant medieval philosopher: Alcuin. He is most famous for his association with Charles the Great, usually known in English by the badly pronounced French version of that name, Charlemagne. Alcuin has been called Charles' "minister of religious affairs." He took a hand in formulating decrees issued in Charles' name, tutored Charles himself in philosophy, and promoted learning in Charles' vast kingdom, expressing the fond hope that Charles' court at Aachen might become "a new Athens."[2]

The sort of learning Alcuin wanted to promote with the benevolent support of Charles was embodied by the "liberal arts." These weren't arts that voted for left-wing politicians, not least because there was no opportunity to vote once Charles was in charge. Rather, the liberal arts were a curriculum of seven disciplines, divided into two groups of three and four. The first three arts, or "trivium" (literally, the "three ways"), included grammar, rhetoric, and dialectic or logic. The remaining four, or "quadrivium" (the "four ways"), were the mathematical arts of arithmetic, geometry, music, and astronomy. This is where the word problems come in. Alcuin's little book *Propositiones ad acuendos iuvenes*, or "Problems to Sharpen the Minds of the Young," is a collection of mathematical puzzles.[3] Some demand calculation, for instance by asking the reader to multiply and add fractions of numbers of animals. Some are more like logic puzzles: if two men marry each other's mothers and both couples have sons, how will these sons be related to one another?[4]

Alcuin's interest in the liberal arts is an example of something we tend to underestimate: the continuity between late ancient and medieval culture. We see this in the political sphere, with Charlemagne dealing with the still existing Eastern Roman, or Byzantine, Empire. We see it in law, with Roman legal codes exercising influence on medieval legal codes (see Chapter 18). We see it in religion, with theological debates fought by Augustine and his contemporaries still much on the minds of medieval churchmen. And we see it in philosophy too. Alongside Aristotle, the most dominant philosophical authorities in the medieval centuries were the two late ancient Christians mentioned above: Augustine and Boethius. Indeed, for early medieval philosophy we can hardly distinguish between the influence of Boethius and that of Aristotle. Until a more complete set of Aristotelian works became available in the twelfth century, the medievals had access only to the logical writings that had been translated into Latin and commented upon by Boethius.

Other works by Boethius—his *Consolation of Philosophy* and series of short treatises on Christian theology—alongside the writings of Augustine provided medievals with further, indirect access to ancient thought. Then there were the more obscure Latin works that bring us back to the liberal arts, notably The *Marriage of Mercury and Philology*, written by Martianus Capella.[5] It depicted the seven liberal arts disciplines as bridesmaids in attendance at an allegorical wedding, much as Boethius personified our favorite discipline as Lady Philosophy in the *Consolation*. Martianus' work was very popular in the early Middle Ages, and it was only one of several texts to bring the liberal arts to the attention of men like Alcuin.

The curriculum appeared as early as the first century BC, when the Roman scholar Marcus Varro composed a (now lost) work on the disciplines covering the seven liberal arts plus medicine and architecture. In its medieval form as a sequence of seven disciplines, it turns up not only in Martianus but also in Augustine, who was in turn drawing on late ancient Platonist sources.[6] Boethius is worth mentioning again here, since he was not only the key source for dialectic or logic, but also wrote a text on music. Then there was another author of late antiquity who was an absolutely crucial source of knowledge for medieval scholars. His name was Isidore of Seville, and his much-read work was entitled *Etymologies*.[7] As Isidore's name tells us, he lived in Seville, where he was bishop. This was in the late sixth and early seventh century, at which point the Western Roman Empire was like a man who has lost all his James Brown records: defunct. Isidore's Spain was ruled by the Visigoths, though around the time of his birth they were forced to contend with Byzantine attempts to recapture the Iberian peninsula.

Despite this, intellectually speaking, Isidore still inhabits late antiquity. The impressive range of texts he uses as sources in his *Etymologies* includes the great

Latin writers. He is especially fond of Virgil, Cicero, and Lucan, but cites a host of other ancient authors too such as Ovid, Horace, and even the Epicurean poet Lucretius. Such non-Christian figures weren't entirely unknown to Isidore's medieval heirs. There were medieval commentaries on the pagan Martianus, and on works by Virgil, Ovid, Lucan, and Horace.[8] But the medievals often relied on Isidore himself as a conduit for ancient knowledge and culture. From this point of view, his *Etymologies* could hardly have been more useful. Divided into twenty books, it begins by covering the liberal arts, before going on to the Christian religious sciences, cosmology and natural science, and finally activities like agriculture, war, shipbuilding, and food preparation.

True to its name, Isidore's *Etymologies* is structured around words. It will typically explain the meaning or (supposed) derivation of each term he discusses. He even gives us a brief account of how things get their names (§I.29). There may be some underlying rationale (*causa*), as with the word *rex*, meaning "king," which comes from *recte agendum*, or "acting correctly." Alternatively it may be a reference to the origin of a thing: the word for human being, *homo*, reflects the belief that humans came from the earth, *humus*. And no, the name of the popular chickpea-based spread "hummus" does not come from this Latin word, though Isidore would probably think it does. He's given to rather fanciful and even far-fetched etymologies, perhaps because he is less interested in actually finding the right derivation than in helping us remember the meaning. Sometimes he does get the etymology right, for instance with the words "history" and "philosophy." He correctly tells us that the former comes from the Greek *historein*, meaning "to observe" (§I.41) and that philosophy means "love of wisdom" (§II.24).

While Isidore's *Etymologies* can't exactly be described as a work of philosophy, there is quite a bit of philosophy in it. He goes through the basics of logic, echoing the ancient approach to this subject by summarizing Porphyry's *Isagoge*, followed by Aristotle's logical works. While going over these, he quotes the saying that when writing *On Interpretation*, Aristotle "dipped his pen in his mind" (§II.27). This remark would later be repeated by Charlemagne himself in the midst of a dialogue about logic with Alcuin.[9] To some extent, we can also see Isidore's whole project as a philosophical or scientific one. He is not just telling us where words come from: he is teaching us what they mean and about the things for which they stand. As he says himself, one of the tasks he is undertaking is the "differentiation" of things, by noting the features that distinguish one thing from another, as, for example, cruelty distinguishes the tyrant from the king (§I.31). All of this is reminiscent of far older philosophical works, for instance Plato, who told a similar story about etymology and its significance in his *Cratylus*, and whose dialogue the *Sophist* explored the idea that understanding something means finding its distinguishing features.

Another figure of the (very) late ancient world who loomed large in the early medieval age was Gregory the Great. He was a contemporary of Isidore's, in fact a friend of Isidore's older brother, and served as Pope from the years 590 to 604. For Alcuin and other Carolingian-era thinkers, Gregory was a major authority in theology and ethics. His most significant work is a massive commentary on the book of Job, though other works survive too, notably a set of *Dialogues* on miraculous events. His approach to the Bible emphasizes allegorical readings. Rather ironically, given that this kind of interpretation was pioneered by the Jewish writer Philo of Alexandria, Gregory claims that allegory distinguishes the true Christian approach to the Old Testament from the overly literal understanding of the Jews.[10] As for ethics, Gregory aspires to live his life in accordance with the monastic ideal pioneered by the so-called "desert fathers," like Evagrius, who joined their Christian piety to a radical asceticism.[11] Such radical withdrawal from the world is in the background here, but a more relevant influence on Gregory would have been Benedict, who lived in Italy in the first half of the sixth century. Benedict composed a "rule," or set of instructions for the monks under his supervision, which helped to shape Gregory's idea of the perfect religious life.

All these ancient figures in turn helped to shape the philosophy and worldview of the outstanding intellectual during the reign of Charlemagne, Alcuin. His view of ethics was deeply shaped by the monastic tradition, as we can see from the many surviving letters he wrote to fellow clergymen, giving advice on best practice in monastery and the personal quest for virtue. He also owed something more basic to Gregory the Great, namely the fact that he was a Christian at all. Well, that's a bit of an exaggeration, but Gregory did play a significant role in the Christianization of Alcuin's home island of Britain. He sent a mission to convert the pagans there to the true faith in the year 596, a major event in the spread of the new faith in the British Isles. With conversion came the establishment of monasteries, the centers of learning in Anglo-Saxon Britain at this time, just as on the Continent. Alcuin himself came from Northumbria, where he was able to study at one of the most significant libraries of the time at the monastery in York.

He could also benefit from another illustrious predecessor, a fellow scholar of Northumbria whose name you will certainly know if you've ever read anything about early British history: Bede. He is known mostly for his work as a historian, and Alcuin himself wrote a history of York in poetic form that makes extensive use of Bede and praises him in fairly extravagant terms.[12] But both men were the sort of all-round scholars the liberal arts curriculum was meant to produce. They contributed to theology and mathematics, and tried their hand at poetry too—the main outlet for their skill in the art of rhetoric, since monks were hardly given frequent opportunities to make public speeches or argue court cases.[13] All this activity was part and parcel of a religious vocation. Both men used their competence in mathematics to write about the correct calculation of the calendar, which had such important religious implications that major political disputes could arise over the correct date of Easter.[14]

Because of Alcuin's link to the glamorous and historically pivotal court of Charlemagne, it's easy to overlook the importance of his British background. In fact Alcuin did not spend that much of his life at the Frankish court.[15] He probably joined Charles only in 786, when he was already an accomplished scholar in his mid-forties, and thereafter returned to England for three years before returning to court. But even if Alcuin's scholarly personality was Northumbrian, the highlights of his scholarly output came through his association with Charles. In stark contrast to the disappointing political leadership back home, Charles was an awe-inspiring monarch who took a genuine interest in religious and intellectual issues. A treatise by Alcuin on rhetoric takes the form of a dialogue between himself and his king,[16] and Alcuin went so far as to call Charles "a philosopher steeped in liberal studies," granted wisdom directly by God.[17]

Here we catch a glimpse of a still emerging ideology that is going to stay with us throughout the medieval period: the idea that God appoints secular kings to rule. An interesting illustration is a set of decrees written in Northumbria in 786, quite likely with Alcuin's involvement. These emphasize the dire sin involved in regicide, pointing out that it means killing "the Lord's annointed."[18] Alcuin's devotion to Charles is also shown by the fact that he compares him to the biblical Solomon in a short work he wrote about the soul (95);[19] elsewhere he compares him to King David. There's also a hint of Alcuin's commitment to the ideal of kingship in his account of the soul itself. Alcuin proceeds on the principle that it is natural for humans to love God, and that this love is the same as our love for the good. Since it is the rational part of the soul that loves God, this aspect of the soul is its best part and must rule over the body and the rest of the soul, "as if from a throne of royal power" (74).

This wasn't mere flattery on Alcuin's part. The parallel between reason and a just ruler goes back to Plato's *Republic*, and though Alcuin couldn't have read the *Republic*, his broadly Platonist allegiances are as clear as his allegiance to Charles. He even speaks of our mind as being trapped in our body as in a prison, another image that can be found in Plato.[20] Alcuin's studies in York would have acquainted him with a number of late ancient authors with a broadly Platonic outlook, not least among them Augustine, whom Alcuin cites by name in this little treatise on the soul. He notes that he was able to read a work by Augustine while in England which was inaccessible at Charles' court (87). Among Alcuin's borrowings from Augustine is the idea that the powers of the soul form an image of the Trinity, with the three divine Persons corresponding to understanding, will, and memory (78).[21]

With his wide learning, Alcuin was useful to Charles as a tutor and court intellectual, and also as a proponent of theological doctrine. Charles saw himself as an authority in religious matters, and involved himself in a variety of religious disputes. One such dispute concerned the veneration of images, icons of Jesus and the saints. This religious practice had been forbidden in the Byzantine realm by imperial edict earlier in the eighth century, and more recently rehabilitated. Already Bede had pronounced on the issue, urging a middle path between veneration of icons and the no-tolerance policy of the Byzantine iconoclasts. Visual images may be used in worship, but not worshiped themselves. Now in Alcuin's day, a fellow scholar at the Frankish court named Theodulf criticized the resurgence of full-blown veneration of icons in Byzantium.

I mention all this for several reasons. First, it gives us a foretaste of a controversy we'll be looking at in the next volume, when we discuss Byzantine philosophy. Second, it's a nice example of the interconnected world inhabited by men like Alcuin. The Frankish elite had dealings and arguments, both political and theological, with the far-away court in Constantinople. Indeed, Charles engaged in diplomatic relations with the even further-flung court of the Muslim caliph in Baghdad. Third, it is our first case of a theological dispute that relates to philosophical concerns (there are many more such cases to come). Alcuin's Platonist outlook was a good match for Theodulf's critique of image worship. After all, we use our senses to view images, and from a Platonist point of view sensation is vastly inferior to the powers of the mind. The point is made by Alcuin himself in a letter to his student Fredegisus, when he extols the mind's understanding above the power of eyesight.[22]

Alcuin got more directly involved in another theological controversy, over a new doctrine that was being propounded by some Christians in Visigothic Spain: Adoptionism. It was a new entry in the long list of attempts to explain how Christ could have been both God and human. The Adoptionists proposed that Christ was fully God's Son insofar as he was divine, but only "adopted" by God as a son insofar as he was human. The rest of humankind is thereby given grace and saved through Christ, insofar as they share in his human nature. If this strikes you as a pretty good suggestion, then you haven't been studying your liberal arts. Alcuin wrote attacks on Adoptionism, and also outlined the controversy for a highborn woman (we are not entirely sure who) in a surviving letter. He remarks that the woman's training in dialectic will help her understand that Christ as a human cannot have been God "in name only," as the Adoptionists claimed.[23] On the other hand, he elsewhere says the Adoptionists went astray by being *too* confident in the application of reason to the nature, or rather natures, of Christ. A true understanding of this matter lies beyond our capacity for rational understanding, and as Alcuin puts it, "where reason fails, there faith becomes necessary."[24]

With his focus on the liberal arts, the Platonist flavor of his philosophy, the monastic flavor of his ethics, and his reading list—heavily dominated by such figures as Augustine, Boethius, Isidore, and Gregory—Alcuin may seem to be as much a figure of late antiquity as of the Middle Ages. But that appearance is largely deceiving. It's been estimated that as much as 94 percent of Latin literature was lost in the wake of the fall of the Roman Empire.[25] Without the copyists and scholars of the Carolingian period, it would be more like 100 percent. They did much to save authors like Cicero, Isidore, Boethius, and Virgil from oblivion. But they lived in an age where knowledge of these authors had become very rare, and was possible only because of the labors of scholars working in religious institutions. It was a very different world from the one inhabited by even late ancient Christian thinkers like Boethius. Another crucial difference was that, unlike Boethius, Alcuin had no knowledge of Greek. He could consult only the Latin texts that survived from late antiquity. In this Alcuin was typical of his time, and of early medieval philosophy in general. But in the history of philosophy, it seems that every rule has an exception. In this case, the exception came from Ireland, and his name was John Scotus Eriugena.

3

GRACE NOTES
ERIUGENA AND THE
PREDESTINATION CONTROVERSY

R eaders of the previous volume in this series will remember my sister, and know a fair bit about her already: her career as a trapeze artist, her short temper, the help she gives me writing these books, and the fact that she doesn't exist.[1] One thing I haven't mentioned about her is that she's an atheist. She is annoyed that God hasn't allowed her to exist, and has decided to return the favor. (Like I say: short temper.) Most other atheists you meet will give more conventional reasons for their disbelief. They may say that modern science has managed to account for all the features of the world formerly inexplicable without reference to a wise Creator. In light of this, we no longer have good evidence for the existence of God, or any supernatural being. Or they may invoke the notorious "problem of evil."[2] The God worshipped in the Abrahamic religions is meant to be all-powerful, all-good, and all-knowing. How then can the world be so full of suffering and evil? Why would He allow this, since He is clearly in a position to put a stop to it and, being good, would certainly want to do so?

The standard response from the theist is the "free will defense." God allows suffering and evil because He must do so, if He is to give freedom to His creatures. In giving us meaningful freedom of choice, He must give us the chance to do wrong; but doing wrong means doing evil, and causing suffering. In the Christian tradition, especially since Augustine, the origins of sin were traced back as far as the first humans. The original sin of Adam and Eve has been passed down to all their descendants, and the human condition is one of congenital weakness. As Oscar Wilde put it, we can resist anything except temptation. In particular, we can resist God's mercy, literally embodied when He became a human and sacrificed Himself for us. This act of sacrifice has held out a promise of rescue from the state of sin. But, according to Augustine, we were not thereby restored to the even more original sinlessness of Adam and Eve through Christ. Rather, humans have retained a tendency towards evil, and only a further gift of divine grace can give us the strength to be good. We cannot, in other words, merit salvation on our own power, but need God's help in order to be saved.

Whether you are an atheist or not, you will probably regard all this as theology and not philosophy. Yet the Augustinian position on grace led to agonized debate among medieval philosophers. Whatever your religious beliefs or lack thereof, your understanding of free will has been indirectly shaped by centuries' worth of reflection on this thorny theological problem. A moment's reflection of our own shows why this problem is so, well, problematic. Augustine insisted, on the one hand, that sin is the result of free will. All human sin, beginning with the original sin of Adam and Eve, is a perverted use of the freedom God has given us. This is why it is just that God should punish us for our misdeeds. On the other hand, Augustine insisted too that, born into sin as we are, none of us can avoid doing evil without God's help. To say otherwise would be to fall into the position of the rival theologian Pelagius, which Augustine attacked ferociously in the mature phase of his career.

Given the weight of Augustine's authority, medievals standardly took the Pelagian view to be heretical. So, for them it was a basic ground rule that humans need grace from God in order to be good. It is up to God, not us, whether any of us will receive that gift. But in that case, it looks as if God is like a man standing at the edge of a lake who sees a group of drowning people who cannot swim. He has plenty of life preservers on hand, but throws them only to a select few, letting the others sink to their doom. Surely we would not praise this man for saving the lucky ones, but rather accuse him of heartlessness for ignoring others he could have helped. In the same way, one might say to Augustine and the medievals who followed his lead that their God is not merciful at all. He arbitrarily and unjustly lets some of His creatures go to eternal torment when He could have given them salvation. Furthermore, on this Augustinian picture humans in the state of sin turn out to lack meaningful free will. If we aren't able to be good without God's help, then any freedom we have seems to be useless, nothing more than the ability to decide which sins to commit.

These were bullets that one ninth-century medieval thinker was ready and willing to bite. He was a monk named Gottschalk, and his signature doctrine was "double predestination." The idea is a simple one: God has decided in His inscrutable wisdom which of us will be saved and which condemned. This decision was made already before any of us were born, and there is no court of appeal. It's an uncompromising view, but one that looks pretty reasonable within the Augustinian framework I've just sketched. After all, if my salvation requires God's intervention, and if He decides *not* to intervene, then He has effectively decided that I will be damned. From this point of view, Gottschalk was simply drawing the obvious conclusion of

Augustine's teaching. Indeed, he was able to quote from the works of Augustine in support of his own position.

From another point of view, though, Gottschalk's teaching was dangerous and deviant, and needed to be stamped out. His two main critics were fellow clerics: a student of Alcuin and Gottschalk's former abbot, Hrabanus Maurus, and an influential bishop named Hincmar. Both of them worried that anyone convinced by Gottschalk would lose all motivation for being good. After all, if God has already decided I'm going to hell, then there's nothing I can do about it, and I may as well have some fun first. Even better if God has placed me among the elect, since I'm sure to keep my place no matter how many sins I commit.[3] All this was happening during the reign of Charlemagne's grandson, a monarch by the name of Charles the Bald (to get an idea of what he may have looked like, have a look at my picture on the dust jacket of this book). In the year 849, Charles intervened in the predestination debate, taking Hincmar's side in the controversy. Gottschalk was imprisoned, and his writings burnt. Here we see again, as with Charlemagne, that secular rulers could and did try to settle theological controversies, weighing in with a kind of authority not even Augustine's texts could provide.

Still, things didn't end there. Even as Charles continued discussing the problem of free will with his advisors, Gottschalk's sympathizers continued to espouse double predestination. What was needed was a more convincing account, one that would preserve the teaching of Augustine while also preserving human freedom. For this purpose Hincmar turned to the sharpest mind of the time, which belonged to John Scotus Eriugena. He hailed from Ireland, being one of numerous scholars who found their way from there to mainland Europe in the Carolingian period, presumably fleeing from Viking raids. In fact, both "Scotus" and "Eriugena" mean "someone from Ireland," so his name rather redundantly means "John Irishman Irishman." Watch out by the way that you don't confuse him with the more famous medieval thinker Duns Scotus, who was Scottish. (I've actually been in libraries where books by one Scotus were shelved amidst the books by the other.)

We know of Eriugena's presence at Charles the Bald's court by the 840s. He supposedly enjoyed a warm relationship with the sovereign. Reports to this effect are borne out by the fact that he was entrusted with the task of translating a precious text sent to the court as a gift by the Byzantine emperor, another monarch with a memorable name: Michael the Stammerer. The manuscript contained the works of the Pseudo-Dionysius, a late ancient Christian theologian strongly influenced by pagan Neoplatonism.[4] Eriugena was ideal for the task. He had facility with Greek, very rare even among well-trained scholars in the Latin West. Equally important, he had a taste for bold, speculative philosophy, which was exactly what he found in

Dionysius. The results would be fully revealed only in Eriugena's masterpiece, a sprawling philosophical and theological dialogue entitled the *Periphyseon*.

For now though, Eriugena did as Hincmar requested, producing a strident refutation of Gottschalk's theory of double predestination. It did not end the debate either, but had at least one salutary effect, by teaching Hincmar to be more careful what he wished for. That taste for bold speculation was all too clear from the arguments Eriugena aimed at Gottschalk. Hincmar was alarmed, and disowned the treatise entirely. It would eventually be condemned in the year 855, about five years after it was written, even though Eriugena was writing in support of what would turn out to be the victorious side in the debate. Two more theologians leapt into the fray to attack Eriugena, who withdrew from the controversy without further attempts to justify his stance, albeit that some of the ideas he put forward in this early treatise do reappear in the *Periphyseon*.

Eriugena would have had cause to feel bitter about the reception given to his treatise on predestination, because the most fundamental point he wanted to make was one already put forward by Hincmar and Hrabanus. If we want to be good Augustinians, we must posit an asymmetry between goodness and sin.[5] In our fallen state, we are capable of sinning but incapable of being good—for that, we need the help of God's grace. The Pelagians violated this rule by placing both good and evil within the scope of human power, and thus leaving insufficient room for grace. Gottschalk strayed too far in the other direction, by effectively making God the author of both goodness *and* sin, in that both are predestined. Neither of these views preserved asymmetry. Hincmar, Hrabanus, and Eriugena all saw this point, and explained why good and evil are different: God predestines the redemption of those He elects to receive effective grace, but He does *not* predestine the damnation of sinners.

Of course it's one thing to say these things and another to argue for them. Step forward Eriugena. He begins his treatise with a mission statement that could apply to his whole career, stating that "true philosophy is true religion and true religion is true philosophy" (§1.1).[6] He then adds some rather swaggering remarks to the effect that his expertise in the liberal arts of dialectic and rhetoric will enable him to clear up the whole predestination debate (§1.3). Eriugena even quotes some technical terms in the original Greek, advertising the unprecedented level of intellectual firepower he's bringing to this battle. By contrast, Gottschalk is routinely convicted of muddled thinking, which has seduced him into deviation from true religion. At one point Eriugena aims the philosopher's ultimate insult at his opponent, saying that Gottschalk's position doesn't even manage to be false, because for that it would have to have a misleading resemblance to the truth (§3.1). Gottschalk's position is so incoherent that it falls short of this modest goal and remains nothing but empty words.

One mistake Eriugena claims to find in Gottschalk is a confusion between God's *foreknowing* that I will do something, and His *predestining* that I will do it (§2.2, 5.1, 11.7). As Boethius had already argued in late antiquity, knowing that something is going to happen doesn't mean causing that thing to happen. Thus, God can foreknow sin without predestining it. When making this distinction, Eriugena quotes Augustine's definition of predestination as the "arrangement before time began of all that God is going to do" (§2.2). This is only one of many quotes from Augustine in the treatise, a reminder that this was not just an abstract theological debate, but an argument over how to interpret this authoritative father of the Church. In fact, there are chapters of Eriugena's *On Predestination* that consist almost entirely of quotation from Augustine, a technique Eriugena will reuse later in his *Periphyseon*, which includes long verbatim citations of Greek and Latin authorities. Such extensive quotation made more sense in the ninth century than it would today. Eriugena can't assume his readers will have access to the texts he refers to, so lengthy citation has the double goal of borrowing Augustine's authority and making the relevant passages readily available to the audience.

Yet Eriugena does offer arguments as well as quotations. He complains that, in addition to that fundamental confusion between God's knowing a thing and causing it to happen, Gottschalk has ascribed a *double* predestination to a God who is purely *one*. It's an early sign of his Neoplatonic leanings that Eriugena hammers relentlessly on this point (as at §2.6, 3.5). Gottschalk's position would require that God exercises two distinct and contrary kinds of predestination over His creation, and this is inconsistent with God's simplicity. Instead, everything that God does proceeds from one essence. You might wonder whether Eriugena's argument makes sense here. After all, he does want to say that God foreknows not just two things, but everything that will ever happen, with His single, simple act of knowledge. So why couldn't God also predestine two kinds of things, choosing the elect for salvation and the unredeemed sinners for punishment?

Eriugena has a good answer, in that his argument turns on the kind of *causation* exercised by simple things (§3.2). On Gottschalk's theory, God would be the cause of two contrary things, predestining both salvation and damnation. This is something a cause with multiple parts might be able to do. Take the humble pencil. Its business end can put marks on a page, while the eraser at the other end can take marks off a page. The reason it can have these two contrary effects is that it has more than one part. But God is not like this: He is utterly simple. Maybe, though, this isn't the only way for a cause to have contrary effects. It might act at different times. Consider a murderous doctor who saves someone's life one day by performing an operation, only to kill that same person with poison on the following day. Could God perhaps do the same, dealing out eternal life at one time, and eternal punishment at some other time? Not according to Eriugena. Again taking over ideas found in Augustine and Boethius, he thinks that God's eternity precludes change from one moment to the next. Divine foreknowledge and predestination already occurred before time even began (§2.2), and never altered thereafter. In fact Eriugena says it is misleading to talk about God's *fore*knowing, and questions whether past, present, and future tense verbs can be applied to God as they are to temporal things (§9.6). This gives us another reason why we cannot imagine God exercising two opposite kinds of causation. He would have to use both in His timeless eternity, so that we would have a simple cause doing two contrary things simultaneously. And this is clearly absurd.

Another problem with double predestination, according to Eriugena, is that it fails to preserve divine justice. If God is to issue commands to us and justly punish us when we fail to obey, then He must give us freedom rather than predetermining us to sin (§4.3, 5.8). Likewise, it would make no sense for God to reward us for doing things if we had no choice in doing them. Here, Eriugena must be careful to avoid falling into the Pelagian heresy, which gives humans not just free will but the capacity to merit salvation without any involvement from God. Of course, he refuses to go so far as Gottschalk, by making God predestine all human actions, both good and sinful. But he accepts that God does exercise predestination over some of us. He has, from eternity, decided which of us will be offered effective grace and thus obtain salvation. Here we come back to the point about asymmetry: God must get some of the credit for helping us to be saved, but none of the blame when we sin and are damned.

Eriugena's way of achieving this is to say that human freedom is exercised in both good and bad actions. In the case of bad actions, God knows beforehand that sin will occur, and after the sin has been committed, He administers just punishment. Apart from that, He stays out of it. The case of good actions is different. Here, God must step in to assist the person who is choosing freely. Divine grace is, as Eriugena puts it, "cooperative" (§8.9). Without it a person who is freely choosing to do good would be unable to succeed. Let's go back to our analogy of the swimmers. Before, I gave the impression that the swimmers were drowning through no fault of their own. But that is not how Eriugena sees things. Rather, God would be like someone on shore who has generously offered to save everyone in the water. Some of the swimmers are ignoring this and in fact making every effort to drown themselves, eagerly weighing themselves down so that they will sink. Clearly there is no obligation to save these fools against their will. Meanwhile others are doing their best to stay afloat, and gratefully accept the offer of assistance. If they get help from the man on shore, their own efforts will enable them to avoid drowning. Analogously, it is just for God to punish those who freely sin, while both free choice and grace are involved in salvation.

To this extent Eriugena was basically following the line already suggested by Gottschalk's other opponents, Hincmar and Hrabanus Maurus. Eriugena does indulge his distinctively "philosophical" style and pushes hard on points like God's utter unity. But it's really only as he develops his argument that he goes beyond what Hincmar could accept. In another premonition of his Neoplatonic leanings, Eriugena brings up the late antique idea that evil is privation or non-being (§10.2–3). This notion was already pioneered by Plotinus, and we find it in some of Eriugena's favorite authors, like Augustine and the Pseudo-Dionysius. Eriugena uses it against Gottschalk: how can God predestine or cause evil and sin, if evil and sin are nothing at all? In fact, how can God even foreknow sin, the point on which Gottschalk relied so much? There's quite literally nothing to know! Pondering this puzzle, Eriugena concludes that God knows sin the way we see darkness (§15.9), in other words by being aware of the absence of goodness or light. A further radical, and for Eriugena's contemporaries unacceptable, implication is that God does not after all directly cause the punishment of the damned. Their suffering is an evil, and evil is non-being or nothing. Eriugena understands it as a failure on the part of these souls to attain salvation and happiness (§18.9–11). God's role in this process is merely to set up a just order of laws governing the universe, under which sinners fall short of the salvation that God actively offers to others who seek His help.

4

MUCH ADO ABOUT NOTHING
ERIUGENA'S *PERIPHYSEON*

S pare a thought, if you will, for Zeppo Marx. He was the not particularly famous fourth member of the famous Marx Brothers. I trust you will be familiar with his siblings: Groucho, with his quick wit, his cigar, and his greasepaint mustache, Chico, with his piano-playing pyrotechnics and preposterous accent, and of course Harpo, the greatest silent film star after the advent of sound, and beneficiary of the best props department since Shakespeare's assistant suggested working a skull into the final act of *Hamlet*. But what did Zeppo have? A reasonable singing voice and a willingness to play straight man to Groucho. Last in alphabetical order and last in the fans' hearts, Zeppo teaches us the importance of competitive advantage. To succeed in show business, just like normal business, you need to offer something special, something that makes you stand out from the crowd.

The same point applies to the history of philosophy, as nicely illustrated by John Scotus Eriugena. In many respects he was a man of his time. Like his contemporaries, Eriugena's intellectual world was structured by the study of the liberal arts. He commented on the aforementioned allegory of these arts by Martianus Capella, probably in the course of teaching it to younger scholars. This sort of activity would not have distinguished Eriugena from other scholars of the Carolingian period, whose names are nowadays known only to experts. The Zeppo of ninth century medieval philosophy was arguably Hrabanus Maurus, who briefly appeared in Chapter 3 as an ally of Hincmar and Eriugena against Gottschalk's teaching on predestination. He also wrote an encyclopedic work called *On the Nature of Things*, carrying on the legacy of earlier chroniclers of human knowledge like Isidore of Seville.

Eriugena's competitive advantage over scholars like Hrabanus was his facility with Greek. This was not entirely unique. Hincmar's teacher Hilduin, bishop of St. Denis, already had a go at producing a Latin version of the works of the Pseudo-Dionysius. But in combination with his adventurous turn of mind, Eriugena's access to the works of Dionysius, as well as other Greek theologians like Gregory of Nyssa and Maximus the Confessor, made him the most remarkable thinker of the period. His place in history is secured by an enormous treatise to which he pointedly gave a

Greek title: *Periphyseon*, meaning *On Nature*. It takes the form of a dialogue told over five long books, featuring only two characters, a teacher and a student (*nutritor* and *alumnus*). This student is no neophyte. He is steeped in the Latin tradition, especially Augustine, and like the teacher is able to throw Greek terminology into the discussion. His role is to set problems and puzzles for the teacher to solve, often by asking for resolution of apparent conflicts between authoritative texts. He is, however, of a more conservative mindset than the teacher. Throughout the dialogue, the student is coaxed away from his traditional understanding of topics in logic, metaphysics, and theology and brought to accept far bolder, more innovative teachings based on Dionysius and the other Greek sources.

The *Periphyseon* has an alternate, Latin title, *De divisione naturae*, meaning *On the Division of Nature*.[1] The alternate title refers to a distinction set out at the beginning of the whole work, which despite many digressions provides a structure for all that will follow. It is a fourfold division of nature, which for Eriugena means "all things, both those that are and those that are not" (441a). This maximally general use of the word "nature" goes all the way back to the Presocratics, whose inquiries into the world around them were also usually given the title *On Nature*. The teacher proposes dividing all things in terms of two criteria: whether or not they create and whether or not they are created. This yields four types of thing: creating but not created, both creating and created, not creating but created, and neither creating nor created (441b). The student, apparently having already attended some classes we missed, is quick to understand what the first three types would mean. The first type is what creates, but is not created; pretty obviously this is God. The third, opposite type is also easy. That which does not create but is created will be the familiar non-divine things in the world around us.

The student is immediately able to provide the less obvious identification of the second type, that which is created but also creates. This applies to what Eriugena calls "primordial causes," which play roughly the role of the Forms in the Platonic tradition, or divine ideas in ancient authors from Philo of Alexandria to Augustine (whom Eriugena cites as an authority, 446a). On Eriugena's version of the doctrine, God first creates things within Himself by grasping them in His wisdom (552a). The things then proceed into the created world as concrete manifestations of God's intellectual understanding. This is how we get the familiar objects in the world around us, the created but not creating things of the third division. They participate in the primordial causes, just as sensible things participate in Forms in the ancient Platonist theories. Eriugena puts a distinctively Christian twist on this old idea, though. For him, the primordial causes are not just God's ideas, but are His "Word" (557a, 642a), also known as the second person of the Trinity. The begetting of the Son by the Father is thus identified with the creation of the causes of all things within God Himself.

This is more than theological window dressing. An ancient pagan Platonist could easily agree with Eriugena that ideas in a divine mind are the intelligible causes of the physical things that participate in them. But such a Platonist might stop short of Eriugena's idea that the creation of these physical things is simply the manifestation of God in the world. It would not be a stretch to see Eriugena as understanding the whole process of creation through the lens of the Christian doctrine of the Incarnation. According to that doctrine, the Son is eternally begotten by the Father, and then becomes present in the created world by being incarnated as Jesus Christ. Eriugena understands all of creation to follow this sort of two-step procedure. First, things are created within God Himself by being grasped in his Wisdom or Word, the second person of the Trinity. Then they manifest in, or as Eriugena also puts it, "descend" into, the created world itself (678d). Eriugena is even willing to say that God is in a sense creating Himself within or as the world. Here he is, as so often, taking inspiration from the Pseudo-Dionysius, who had spoken of "theophany," literally, "God's showing Himself" or "appearing" to us in the things He has created (446d).

At this point, the student in Eriugena's dialogue is like someone trying to remember the names of the Marx Brothers. He has easily managed the first three items on the list, but the fourth presents more difficulty. The student has to ask the teacher to explain what sort of nature might be neither creating nor created (442a). So far, all three of the divisions of nature have turned out to be, in some sense, identical with God: the creating Father, the created and creating Son or primordial causes, and the created manifestation that is the world. The same is true of the fourth division. For Eriugena, all created things are designed and destined to return to their divine source.[2] Of course God remains a creator, but if we think about Him as the final cause or goal for the things He has created, then we are not thinking of Him in this way. He is not source, but destination, not starting point, but finishing line.

Again, Eriugena is here taking over a traditional Platonist thesis but rethinking it in Christian terms. Late ancient Platonists thought of reality as coming forth from a single divine principle and then returning to it. This dynamic of procession and return could take many forms. For instance pagan Platonists saw the human soul as an effect of a universal intellect, and duly understood philosophy itself as the soul's attempt to return to its cause by achieving intellectual knowledge. Eriugena's version of this circular dynamic is that the emergence of things from God is mirrored by an eventual return to Him (529a). In the end, the distinctions between created things will be eliminated, as all things are received back into God. Eriugena is quick to point out that his beloved discipline of dialectic, one of the liberal arts, itself embodies this process with its procedure of division and synthesis (478d–479a), a procedure that is of course on show in the *Periphyseon* itself.

At a more theological level, the Christian story of humankind's fall and redemption fits perfectly into the Platonist pattern of procession and return. Having fallen away from God through sin, human nature is renewed and made whole again. For Eriugena this means that we will ultimately be gathered back into the divine primordial causes. This is a rather daring version of the Christian narrative of sin and redemption, since it seems to imply that everything will ultimately just become identical with God. Suggestions in this direction were already present in Eriugena's treatise on predestination, but our future unity with God emerges as a major theme only in the *Periphyseon*. It's easy to get the impression that Eriugena foresees a complete reversal of the original creation, and holds that in the end there will be nothing at all other than God. But in fact his eschatological theory is more nuanced than that. He says that things will indeed be "changed into God," but even so will preserve their own natures (451b). While this may sound paradoxical, it exemplifies a fundamental aspect of Eriugena's thought. He understands the world, now and at the end of time, to be both separate from God and the same as Him, since created beings are simply an expression of what God is.

Despite the access we have to God through the created world that is His manifestation, Eriugena believes that God in Himself remains utterly beyond our grasp. It's on this point that Dionysian influence becomes really unmistakable. Like the *Divine Names* of the Pseudo-Dionysius, Eriugena's *Periphyseon* offers a detailed exploration of the two theological paths, positive and negative, called in Greek *kataphatike* and *apophatike* (458a–b). The positive or "cataphatic" approach is to transfer to God words that are appropriate for created things. Above all, there are the many names and descriptions applied to God in Scripture. For Eriugena, these are to be taken in a "metaphorical" sense. Even highly complimentary names like "truth" or "goodness" are not to be used of God in a straightforward sense, since God is rather the *cause* of truth and goodness.

For this reason Eriugena repeats a linguistic trick first proposed by Dionysius, who added the Greek prefix *hyper-* to words when applying them to God. In English the corresponding prefix would be "super-," in the sense of "above" or "beyond." We would not, for instance, call God "essence" but rather "superessential," not call Him "wise" but rather "beyond wise," not "loving" but "more than loving" (462a–b, 521d). What Eriugena likes about this is that it combines the virtues of positive and negative theology. The surface grammar of a statement like "God is super-good" is positive. It seems to offer a description of God, assigning to Him the attribute of super-goodness, whatever that might mean. But as soon as we start to think about what that would in fact mean, we see that the force of the prefix "super-" is negative. Using it involves denying that God is good, not because He falls short of goodness but because He transcends goodness entirely. The apparently positive statement is in fact a concealed negation.

But even a purely "apophatic" or negative theology undersells God's transcendence. You can't just add negations to all the positive attributes, even sneaky negations like the prefix "super-." If you stop there, you remain within the realm of language, which is applicable to created things but not to God. Eriugena has a nice argument that God is beyond language (458d–459c). It begins from the observation that any description we can give of something will always have some other, opposing description. As soon as we use language to describe something, we imply that there is something else that has the opposed feature. If I say that Zeppo Marx looks good in a suit, then I am contrasting him with other people who don't look so good in a suit. But nothing can be opposed to God, since there is nothing else that stands alongside Him as an eternal principle. This means that not only positive predicates, but also the negations or opposites of those predicates, are going to be inappropriate to God. Eriugena refuses to take no for an answer, and urges us to place God beyond the reach of language entirely, whether that language is positive or negative.

In a remarkable section found in the third book of the *Periphyseon*, Eriugena applies his radical metaphysics to an issue that had bothered several of his predecessors: the problem of non-being or nothingness (*nihil*). Back in classical antiquity, Parmenides had proposed a radical metaphysics of his own by banning all talk of non-being, including even the non-being involved in differentiating between things. Parmenides' argument was that non-being just isn't the sort of thing one can talk or think about. So we are left with nothing but being, which must be unchanging, undifferentiated, and one. Plato conceded that Parmenides had a point, but only as concerns absolute non-being. In his dialogue the *Sophist*, he argued that we can make sense of non-being if it means difference rather than the unrestricted negation of being. If I say that Harpo is not well dressed, this just means that Harpo is different from people like Zeppo, who *are* well dressed. Centuries later, Augustine too made much ado about nothing. In his dialogue *On the Teacher* he raised the problem that if words are signs that refer to things, then we apparently need something for the word "nothing" to refer to; but that clearly makes no sense, since the word "nothing" refers to, well, nothing.[3]

Closer to the time of Eriugena, Alcuin's student Fredegisus had written a little treatise with the cheerful title *On Nothing and Darkness*.[4] Fredegisus wanted to solve Augustine's worry about the referent of the word "nothing" in light of the notion that it was God who assigned names to things. God created an object for every word He instituted, so that there are no "empty" words, words that fail to refer at all. Hence, even the words "nothing" and "darkness" do refer to existing things. Eriugena likewise approaches the topic of nothing within the context of creation. He is out to explain the meaning of the by now traditional claim that God created the universe "from nothing," in Latin *ex nihilo*.[5] When the teacher and student in the *Periphyseon* first broach this issue, there seems to be (if you'll pardon the expression) nothing to worry about. It seems that the word "nothing" in the phrase "creation from nothing" simply means the absence of all things. The point of talking of creation *ex nihilo*, then, would simply be that God did not create the universe out of anything else, like pre-existing matter (635a, 636c).

Unfortunately, things are not quite so simple. The student reminds the teacher that they accepted not just a temporal creation of bodies out of nothing, but the *eternal* creation of all things in God's Wisdom, in the form of the primordial causes. How can things be eternally made in this fashion, yet also be created from nothing? A first step towards an answer is to realize that temporal priority is not the only kind of priority. God is eternally "prior" to the things He creates by being their cause, rather than by existing before they do (639b). As we know from Eriugena's earlier discussion of the primordial causes, things are created within God and exist eternally and virtually in Him before becoming manifest in the physical universe. Upon reflection though, as far as the present problem goes, this sounds more like a step backwards than a step forwards. Aren't we now saying that the things around us were in fact created from *something*, namely the primordial causes? Well, yes (664a). So the only possible conclusion is that the phrase "creation from nothing" applies to the way the primordial causes themselves are produced by and within God. The word "nothing" simply indicates that God is beyond all being or, as Dionysius would say, "super-essential." God Himself is the nothingness from which all things come, an unknowable nothingness or "darkness" that transcends even the things He creates within Himself (681a; as we'll see later in this volume, this Dionysian theme will be taken up by authors like Meister Eckhart and the author of the *Cloud of Unknowing*).[6]

This account of unknowable darkness sheds further light on the division of four kinds of nature at the beginning of the *Periphyseon*. As the first creating and uncreated nature, God the Father is utterly transcendent, an unknowable source of the things He fashions within Himself in an act of "begetting." What is begotten within Him is the Word, which contains within it the causes of created things. So this Word is the second nature, both created and creating. Yet the second nature is still transcendent, because it lies beyond the created and not-creating third nature of the physical universe we see around us. Our language and thought are at home only with this third nature, with physical reality. This becomes clear in Eriugena's treatment of the ten Aristotelian categories, which shows how he was inspired not just by the exotic Greek texts he was able to read, but also by the works of Latin logic that were standard fare in the Carolingian period.

Of course the ancient classification which divides predications, or descriptions of things, into ten types is familiar from Aristotle's *Categories*, which was throughout late antiquity used as an introductory textbook on logic. The early medievals knew it too, thanks to the translation and commentary of Boethius. But the Carolingians were actually more interested in a different, related work called *On the Ten Categories*, because it was falsely believed to be a work of Augustine. It is a major source for the first book of Eriugena's *Periphyseon*. Under the influence of this Pseudo-Augustine, he argues that the physical objects we see around us are mere collections of accidental features, like qualities and quantities, which have been joined to the first category of substance. Yet substance itself lies beyond the things we can see and touch (489c–d). It is simple, whereas bodies are composites of these accidental features. And in fact, even though things around us have qualities and quantities—like Zeppo's handsome features and his being a certain height—the categories of quality and quantity themselves are also beyond physical things, invisible principles that have visible effects (493a). All this is fully consistent with Eriugena's metaphysical scheme, which makes the physical universe a mere manifestation or visible appearance of invisible, intelligible principles.[7] This understanding of substance and the other categories will stay with us in Chapter 5, in which we'll consider some early medieval thinkers who make even Zeppo Marx look like a household name.

5

PHILOSOPHERS ANONYMOUS
THE ROOTS OF SCHOLASTICISM

If the rise of social media has taught us anything, it's that cutting-edge communication technologies are valued for one reason above all others: we can use them to tell other people about our cats. Things were no different when the very latest in communication technology was pen, ink, and parchment. So it was that in the early Middle Ages, a scholar at the abbey of Reichenau wrote a poem about his cat Pangur.[1] Here it is, in the translation of no less a fellow poet than W. H. Auden:

> Pangur, white Pangur, How happy we are
> Alone together, scholar and cat.
> Each has his own work to do daily;
> For you it is hunting, for me study.
> Your shining eye watches the wall;
> My feeble eye is fixed on a book.
> You rejoice, when your claws entrap a mouse;
> I rejoice when my mind fathoms a problem.
> Pleased with his own art, neither hinders the other;
> Thus we live ever without tedium and envy.

The charm of the poem is undeniable, with the evident affection of this medieval monk for his faithful feline companion. It's made more touching by the fact that the poem is not in Latin but in Old Irish. The author was an Irishman, living far from home in Germany. More poignant still, we know the cat's name but not that of the poet.

In both respects, he was a typical representative of early medieval culture. There were many Irish scholars living on the European mainland in this period, enriching its culture with their expertise in classical languages and the liberal arts, as well as the occasional cat poem. We've already met the greatest of these Irishmen, John Scotus Eriugena, and we'll be meeting more in this chapter. But even more typical is his anonymity. It's sometimes jokingly remarked by experts in medieval philosophy— who are of course famous for their sense of humor—that the most prolific philosopher of the age was "Anonymous." We have hundreds of manuscripts with philosophical texts written by unnamed authors, who are unsurprisingly usually given short shrift by historians. And you can't really blame them. After all, there are many obscure figures from these centuries whose names we do know, and who are likewise waiting to be rescued from oblivion. We'll be meeting some of them in this chapter too.

One of the characteristic scholarly activities of the medieval period was commentary on earlier texts. Many surviving manuscripts are adorned by anonymous comments, or "glosses." These were written in the margins or just above the words of the main text so that one is literally invited to read between the lines. This was no act of vandalism, as it would be if you wrote in a library book today. To the contrary, we find that manuscripts were sometimes produced with glosses specifically in mind, with deliberately wide margins around the main text to leave room for them. Experts can tell a lot about these manuscripts by studying the handwriting used in them. For instance, even when a text is in Latin, tell-tale abbreviations and features of the script used may show that the scholar who copied it out was from Ireland.

Which brings us back to the contribution of Irish scholars in the Carolingian period. We know the names of many such scholars, in part thanks to a list of names written in a ninth-century manuscript. Ironically the man who recorded them is himself anonymous, while many of the Irishmen he mentions are to us nothing more than names.[2] Yet in their day they were renowned scholars. They are being listed here as the leading exegetes of earlier works by classical authors like Horace and Ovid, and earlier medieval authors like Bede. Other manuscripts show us that, exceptional though he may have been, Eriugena was far from unique. His knowledge of Greek was shared by other Irishmen working in France in the late ninth century. His countryman Martin was active at this time in the city of Laon, and I do mean active. There are at least twenty manuscripts with his handwriting in them, one of which is a glossary and grammar book for learning Greek.[3]

Two other Irish scribes, both anonymous, were close to Eriugena—in fact one of them has even been thought to be Eriugena himself. More likely, though less romantic, is that they were two unknown students of his. The scribes are known to today's scholars simply as i1 and i2. These Irish i's smiled on the philosophical ideas of their teacher.[4] They revised and added glosses to the *Periphyseon*, possibly under the guidance of Eriugena himself, and made notes on other manuscripts, including Boethius' treatise on music. In one manuscript the distinctive ideas of Eriugena are used to interpret the Bible. There's nothing to suggest that Eriugena's colleagues were outstanding philosophers in their own right, but it does show that he was not operating in a vacuum. We have here a little group of like-minded scholars gathered around one outstanding figure, who are collectively trying to understand and expound the Bible and texts of classical antiquity.

Further anonymous scholars from about this time applied Eriugena's ideas to other philosophical works. One was the abovementioned *On the Ten Categories*, another anonymous work, at that time thought to be by Augustine. A gloss to one manuscript of this treatise tries to explain a passage which speaks of Being (here the Greek word *ousia* is used) as "the most general genus." The idea here is a simple but important one. Given that you are reading this, you are, I think we can assume, a human being. You and I are members of the same species, the human species. But we are also animals, just like Hiawatha the giraffe. Aristotle called this higher-level grouping a "genus": the genus of animal includes humans, giraffes, and all the other animal species. We can go further, though. Animals fall under a higher genus of living things, which includes plants. Living things then fall under the still higher genus of bodies, which embraces not only animals and plants but also things like rocks. If we keep going like this, will we eventually get to a most general genus, a group that includes absolutely everything? According to this text and the anonymous author of the gloss, the answer is yes: everything is a "being."

Reasonable enough, you might think. After all, can you think of anything that isn't a being? It's when the anonymous commentator connects these logical ideas to theology that his affection for Eriugena starts to show.[5] Following the sort of Platonist line found in the *Periphyseon*, the anonymous author explains that this highest genus, being, is to be identified with God Himself. All created being, from rocks to plants to animals to humans, are derived from this single divine being. Another anonymous gloss adds the negative perspective of Eriugena's theology, stating that since the divine being is beyond our comprehension, it is, rather paradoxically, a kind of non-being. With these glosses, our unknown scholars are showing us that Eriugena's ideas had some impact among his contemporaries. They are also paving the way for a long-running medieval argument over the general features of things, usually called "universals." Eriugena and his colleagues seem to think that a nature found in many things, like *human*, *giraffe*, or even *being* is not just something real, but something divine, a cause for all the things that partake of it. One author of the time compared the relation between the species *human* and individual humans to the relation between the roots of a tree and its branches. John Marenbon, one of the few scholars to work with these glosses, has coined the term "hyper-realism" for this idea that a general nature is not just real but expresses its reality in the individuals that partake of it. Hyper-realism is, in effect, the logical version of Eriugena's core metaphysical teaching that God's transcendent being is made manifest in created things.

If you were to ask one of these unnamed scholars what they thought they were doing when they meticulously studied and annotated their logical textbooks, they would unhesitatingly reply: dialectic. Enshrined as one of the liberal arts, dialectic offered considerable scope for exploring philosophical issues. In the first instance it would mean doing logic. But as we've just seen, fairly innocuous logical texts could provoke forays into metaphysics and theology. So just imagine what might happen when the texts being glossed weren't so innocuous. This was the case with the *Marriage of Philology and Mercury* of Martianus Capella, whose frankly pagan contents were tolerated by early medieval readers eager to learn from it. It was simply too useful a text to be ignored, providing, as it did, a detailed discussion of all seven liberal arts. Back in the time of Charlemagne, Alcuin had described these arts as the columns that support the temple of Christian wisdom.[6] Now in the time of Charles the Bald, Eriugena was only one of several scholars writing glosses on the work.

You won't be surprised to hear that an important set of glosses on Martianus, produced even before Eriugena's, is by our elusive, yet prolific friend Anonymous. This unnamed scholar's comments were a major source for a further set of glosses by a philosopher whose name we do know, Remigius of Auxerre. It's usually assumed that such explanatory comments were added to Martianus' allegory as an aid to teaching, as I suggested with Eriugena's glosses. But there may have been more to it than that.[7] A closer look shows that the commentators struggle with apparent contradictions between Martianus and other, authoritative texts. Never mind the paganism; Martianus doesn't even agree with the standard astronomical picture endorsed by the ancients. He makes Mars and Venus orbit around the sun, rather than the earth. The glosses also discuss discrepancies between Martianus and Boethius on technical points concerning the musical scales. With glosses like these, our commentators are trying to reconcile their key sources for two of the liberal arts, astronomy and music. This suggests a more advanced enterprise than classroom teaching, even if other manuscripts (like the Greek-Latin glossary I mentioned earlier) were obviously produced for a pedagogical context.

With all this careful exegesis devoted to authoritative texts, produced within teaching contexts and by collaborative groups of scholars, we're seeing the emergence of something that historians usually call "scholasticism." The word comes from the Greek and Latin words for "school" (*skhole*, *schola*), and for good reason. Before the arrival of universities around the year 1200, philosophy was normally done in the context of the schools that were scattered throughout medieval Europe, in England, France, Switzerland, Germany, and Italy. They were sometimes supported by secular authorities, as when the courts of Charlemagne and Charles the Bald facilitated the scholarship of Alcuin, Eriugena, and their less celebrated collaborators. More often they were instruments of the Church, based at religious houses, parish churches, and cathedrals. That last setting was particularly important. Cathedral schools, a kind of forerunner of the medieval universities, would provide the context for a flowering of scholasticism in the twelfth century, the age of thinkers like Peter Abelard and John of Salisbury, who are frequently seen as pioneers of scholasticism.

But twelfth-century scholasticism did not come from nowhere. The intellectual values of the ninth-century scholars we've just been discussing were not so different from those of an Anselm or an Abelard. They too saw antique literature as a storehouse of wisdom, which needed to be preserved and explained through copying and commentary. This applied especially to Christian authorities like Augustine, Boethius, and Isidore of Seville, but pagan authors like Plato, Aristotle, and Martianus were also valued. The classical works were not followed out of blind devotion, but precisely because they were taken to represent the greatest achievements of human reason. It's worth remembering here that in the ninth century, it was actually feasible for one person to master the sum total of existing human wisdom.[8] So much had been lost in the disruptions of late antiquity and the early medieval period that a committed scholar with access to a well-stocked library could work their way through all the important texts on theology and the liberal arts.

This remained a rare attainment, to be sure. The schools that proliferated from the ninth to the eleventh centuries were not primarily intended to turn out fully rounded intellectuals. Their purpose was more modest, and more practical. In an age where nearly the entire population was illiterate, where were the functionaries of the secular government and Church going to come from? The next generation of officials, secretaries, and clergymen would be trained to read and write at the schools, under the banner of the first liberal art, "grammar." The very word comes from the Greek *grammata*, meaning "letters," and the basic purpose of grammatical training was indeed to impart the gift of literacy. As the schools became more numerous, and as competition intensified between masters trying to attract students, the schoolmen became ever more specialized and ever more likely to engage in technical disputes over dialectic and theology.

It would be nice to say that there was simply a smooth, gradual increase in school activities from the ninth century down to the blossoming of full-blown scholasticism in the twelfth. But, as usual, things are a bit more complicated, as I realized when I sat down to make a list of the philosophers I wanted to cover in this book. I had several thinkers from the ninth century and quite a few from the eleventh and twelfth, but couldn't think of a single one for the tenth century. This was to some extent the result of ignorance on my part, but I'm not entirely to blame. The tenth century was a period of considerable disruption, with extensive Viking raids and the new threat posed by the Magyars. Moving along the Danube River from Hungary, they invaded Bavaria (which is where I live, but I'm glad to report that the Hungarians I've met here have been very nice). By the year 937 the Magyars had visited destruction on wide swaths of Germany and moved into France. Finally, they were defeated by Otto, king of Germany, in 955. This period of instability contrasts sharply with what was going on in the Islamic world at the same time. The Muslim conquests had previously spread the new religion over a vast territory from Spain to the Indus River. Even more land fell into Muslim hands in the tenth century, as they wrested control of Sicily, Sardinia, and Corsica away from the Christians and even made incursions into mainland France and Italy. No wonder then that this century was a highpoint for philosophy in the Islamic world, bookended by the later life of al-Fārābī and the early life of Avicenna.

Meanwhile, what was going on in Christian Europe, philosophically speaking? Not a great deal, to be honest, but somewhat more than is commonly thought.[9] Take Abbo of Fleury, for instance. He was brought to the abbey there when very young, and returned there as a master after further training in Paris and Rheims. Abbo wrote on logic and astronomy, contributing to the study of the calendar as Bede and Alcuin had done a few generations ago. Also like Alcuin, Abbo was committed to the monastic ethic, and urged discipline upon the younger monks under his care. This led to his undoing, when he was killed by his own brethren when he tried to break up a fight among some monks at a monastery he was visiting. That happened in the year 1004, only one year after the death of a man who was perhaps the most outstanding scholar of the tenth century, Gerbert of Aurillac. He eventually became Pope, and in this role was known as Sylvester II. So he makes up to some extent for all those anonymous philosophers, having had two names. Whatever we want to call him, he had particular interests in mathematics and natural science, pioneering the use of the abacus for doing arithmetic, and building his own astronomical instruments.

Most of the scholars I've been mentioning came from or at least worked in France. But, as I say, there were schools springing up all over Europe. A particularly interesting one was at the abbey of St. Gall in Switzerland. Here there was even a female teacher of Greek, by the name of Hedwig.[10] She was the niece of Otto, the German king who defeated the Magyars. St. Gall could also boast of another well-rounded expert in the liberal arts, Notker, who was nicknamed Labeo or "the lip" because of his protruding lower lip. Notker Labeo helped the young men who came to study Latin with him by producing German translations of the core texts of the liberal arts curriculum, like Martianus' *Marriage of Philology and Mercury*, Gregory the

Great's *Moralia*, and Boethius' Latin versions of Aristotle's logic. In fact Notker interspersed the German version with the Latin original, much like the facing-page translations that are still published nowadays.

So far I've been giving the impression that any well-educated person in these centuries would have had unalloyed respect and admiration towards the sort of text Notker was making available in German. But in fact that is not the case. Though no one would have had a bad word to say about the classical church fathers, there were plenty of critics who thought that pagan literature was dangerous, especially for the minds of young Christians. Eriugena was chastized for occupying himself with Martianus rather than Augustine. When Gerbert of Aurillac was being considered for an archbishopric, an opponent to his candidacy remarked, "the disciples of Peter must not have as their teacher a Plato, a Virgil, a Terence, or any other of the herd of philosophers." In the eleventh century, Manegold of Lautenbach criticized Wolfhelm of Brauweiler for his interest in the pagan Macrobius (I mention this example mostly for the fabulous names). Even the anonymous poets were getting in on the act. One of them took time out from petting his cat to ask what good it could possibly do for Christians to read a pagan like Martianus.[11]

Yet perhaps the most famous remark about the dangers of the liberal arts was uttered by a specialist in those very arts. His name was Lanfranc of Bec, praised upon his death as a man who would have been admired by Aristotle for his skill in dialectic, and by Cicero for his mastery of rhetoric.[12] Lanfranc drew on a deep knowledge of the liberal arts in commenting on the *Moralia* of Gregory, and wrote now lost philosophical works.[13] Yet when he was embroiled in a notorious theological controversy with the scholar Berengar of Tours, Lanfranc charged: "having abandoned sacred authorities, you have taken refuge in dialectic." Like scholasticism itself, their dispute had its roots in the ninth century. Back then, a monk named Ratramnus had written an explanation of the Eucharist for Charles the Bald in which he explained that the bread and wine used in Communion are symbolic in nature. Now, in the eleventh century, Berengar took up a similar view, arguing that the bread and wine are Christ's flesh and blood only figuratively. Lanfranc disagreed fervently concerning the theological point. For him, only the appearance and flavor of bread and wine remain, but really they have been transformed into the flesh and blood "born of the Virgin."

Later on in this book, we'll return to the philosophical implications of the Eucharist. For now, let's focus on Lanfranc's approach to the issue. To him, it was simply inappropriate to use reason to understand this mysterious and miraculous transformation. Rather one should follow authoritative doctrine, and only then apply reason to defend and understand the Eucharist more deeply.[14] He was bound to disagree with Berengar, a man capable of stating "it is the sign of an eminent mind that it turns all things to dialectic."[15] Like many medieval debates to come, the clash between Lanfranc and Berengar was about the scope and place of reason in theology as much as it was about the theological issue at hand. Various thinkers will take various views on this methodological question in the centuries to come. But most will, broadly, agree with Lanfranc: reason plays a vital role in Christian doctrine, but there are bounds beyond which reason cannot go. Philosophy should thus accept a subordinate role to Scripture, comparable to the relationship between a hand-maiden and her mistress—a famous analogy devised by the author we turn to next.

6

VIRGIN TERRITORY
PETER DAMIAN ON CHANGING
THE PAST

S uppose a Roman citizen captures a bear and brings it to the capital to be used in gladiatorial combat. Before the bear has a chance to perform, it breaks loose, runs through the streets and kills an innocent passer-by. Is the person who captured the bear liable for the death? This question was discussed by Ulpian, who wrote in the early third century AD and is a major source for our knowledge of ancient law. His answer was that there is no liability, since as soon as the bear escapes captivity, it reverts to its status as a wild animal. You might assume that this must have been a response to an actual event, and perhaps it was. But legal scholars did frequently work with hypothetical examples, too, using imaginary scenarios to illuminate the fine points of law.[1] This was a practice that would have been well known to the early medieval schoolmen, because they were trained in a curriculum that culminated in theology and law. As we'll discover later, the emergence of scholasticism in the eleventh and twelfth centuries went hand in hand with the development of medieval law, which was powerfully influenced by the Roman legal tradition.

From early on in the Middle Ages, hypothetical cases were used in other areas of intellectual endeavor. Consideration of such scenarios could help to determine points of Church doctrine and to clarify philosophical issues. Suppose that a man has sex with a woman he mistakenly believes to be his wife. Has he committed the sin of adultery? Or suppose that the Devil transforms himself so that he looks like Christ. Would a Christian who is convinced by this deception and worships the Devil be committing a sin?[2] Commenting on this phenomenon, the historian of early medieval society Richard Southern has remarked that "fantasy played a part in shaping scholastic thought in the sense that extreme cases provided the best material for drawing distinctions between closely-related concepts."[3] This is a fact of no small importance for the history of philosophy. A penchant for creative hypothetical reasoning is still visible in later thinkers like Descartes, as we see with his skeptical evil demon hypothesis. Nowadays, when contemporary philosophers discuss, say, a scientist named Mary who knows everything there is to know about the color red apart from what it looks like, or the possibility of "zombies," physically identical copies of humans with no inner consciousness, they may be unwitting heirs to an originally medieval habit of mind, which in turn may have derived from Roman legal culture.

All of which should help to explain why this chapter is devoted to the question of whether God can restore virginity to a woman after she has had sex. Clearly, this is not a problem of pressing practical importance. But Peter Damian found it worth discussing, in order to contemplate the nature of God's power more generally. Again, this is typical of the medieval age. An interest in hypothetical thought experiments goes very nicely with a conviction in the existence of an all-powerful Creator. You can introduce pretty well any scenario, no matter how baroque, with the words, "Suppose that God decides to do the following..." It may seem that invoking God's power in this way is just a quaintly medieval way of getting at possibilities that we don't find in the actual world. After all, calling God omnipotent seems to mean just that He can do anything that can be done. To put this in more technical terms, omnipotence would be the capacity to bring about any possible state of affairs. From this point of view, asking whether God can do something is just a medieval way of asking whether that thing is possible. Could God create a color without a body in which the color resides? Could He create a human the size of a mountain? Could He, indeed, restore virginity after it has been lost?

But this overlooks alternative definitions of omnipotence. God may be so powerful that He can even do *impossible* things. He might, for instance, be able to create a round square, to make one plus one equal three, or make me both bald and not bald (a 50 percent improvement over the current situation). A different, opposing option would be to say that there are some things which are indeed possible, but which God cannot do. For instance, one might suppose that God cannot sin (Peter Abelard will hold this view). The upshot is that medieval discussions of God's power, and the medieval thought experiments involving God's use of that power, do tell us a lot about medieval notions of possibility. But we also need to bear in mind that the scope of God's power may be narrower, or wider, than the scope of what is possible.

We especially need to bear it in mind when we look at Peter Damian's discussion of whether God can restore lost virginity. Damian is not primarily interested in clarifying the philosophical notion of possibility. His concern is rather to understand, and above all not to disrespect, God's majesty. He approaches the issue as a theologian, indeed as a theologian with a powerful distaste for abstract disputes with no religious motivation or foundation. This led him to make some rather dismissive remarks about philosophy, for instance that he scorned Plato, Pythagoras, and Euclid, preferring the "simplicity of Christ."[4] He nonetheless played a major role in shaping the intellectual scene of the eleventh century. Damian was born in the year 1007 in the northern Italian city of Ravenna, incidentally a major center for the study of law in the early Middle Ages. Over the coming century the Normans would be extending their power throughout Europe. They would hold all of southern Italy by the end of the century, and I probably don't need to tell you that William the Conqueror successfully invaded England in 1066, though I bet you didn't know that this is the same year that Peter Damian would write his discussion on God's power to restore virginity.

In his early years Damian established himself as a teacher of the liberal arts, and may also have been trained in the law.[5] However, he retired to a monastic life, becoming prior of the Fonte Avellana monastery. Inspired by the teaching and spiritual devotion of Romuald of Ravenna, Damian took up the cause of eremitic monasticism. This means that, rather than living in a community, monks should seek isolation and live a life of individual prayer insofar as possible. Damian himself felt the tension between this aspiration and a life helping others through preaching. Ultimately he decided that living as a hermit would be a more powerful way to serve the faith. In this he was following the example set by antique figures like Evagrius, who said of the hermit: "having been separated from all, he is also united to all."[6] Damian encouraged such punishing practices as sleep deprivation and self-flagellation, tools for suppressing everything else to make room for the love of God. But he also fought for the cause of Church reform, railing against corruption and insisting on the need to banish from the Church any clergymen who were found practicing sodomy.[7] His writings on this subject are a key source for medieval attitudes towards homosexuality (see Chapter 73).

It's only one of the 180 letters we have from Peter Damian. Another (*Letter* 119) was addressed to Desiderius, a monk at the monastery of Monte Cassino, and contains Damian's discussion on restoring virginity. His point of departure is a remark made by the Latin church father Jerome, who cautioned that, once lost, virginity cannot be restored, even by God.[8] While mindful of Jerome's authority, Damian begs to differ. We should not dare to place any limits on God's power. The recipient of the letter, Desiderius, had taken a different view. He defended Jerome's remark on the basis that if God does not *want* to restore a woman's virginity, then He cannot do so (§2, 597a). Damian, who is not known for pulling any punches in his correspondence, dismisses this out of hand. If God is unable to do otherwise than He wishes, then the only things that are possible for Him are the things that He actually does. If God chooses to make it rain, then it would be impossible for Him to make it not rain.

Here Damian is setting down an initial point of great philosophical interest: there are some things which do not happen, but remain possible nonetheless. That may seem obvious. Right now you are reading this book, but could quite easily be doing something else (though I wouldn't recommend it). But maybe it isn't so obvious after all. Consider this: assuming you have read the whole book up to this page, does it remain possible that you haven't read it? It seems plausible to say that you could have refrained from reading it beforehand, but now it is too late. There are no "do-overs": what is done is done. For this reason, ancient and medieval thinkers, beginning with Aristotle, were attracted to the notion that the past is necessary. The same consideration can be applied to the present: you are reading this sentence right now, so again the die is cast, and you can no longer avoid reading this sentence.[9] This leaves only the future to be genuinely open, with different, conflicting possibilities available to us. Once the future has become the present and then the past, though, these possibilities will be narrowed down to one actual state of affairs, which is necessary in the sense that it is too late to prevent it.

Now we can see more clearly what is at stake in Peter Damian's letter on divine omnipotence. If God can restore a woman's virginity, then He can undo the past. So the past is not necessary after all. Well, *maybe* that is what it means. It depends entirely on what we mean by "restoring virginity." Rather than getting straight to the question of whether God can really change the past, Damian insists that God can make two kinds of change to the woman's condition now. He can restore her "with respect to merit" and "with respect to the flesh" (§5, 601a). The latter simply means putting her body back in the condition it was before engaging in intercourse, in other words restoring her hymen. It's quite obvious that God can do this. He can also remove the moral imperfection that, according to Damian, would be involved in the original loss of virginity. For a philosophically minded reader whose concern is solely with God's ability to change the past, all this is entirely beside the point. But it is vital for Damian's wider aim, which is to ensure that God is capable of offering redemption to humankind, that is, restoring their moral perfection. At stake here is nothing less than the possibility of the narrative of Christianity itself. To Damian, this would be a matter of considerably greater importance than clarifying our ideas about possibility and necessity. In this respect, his letter is of a piece with his other activities, such as fighting for the purity of the Church and acting as a spokesman for the virtues of eremitic monasticism. Virginity stands for the spiritual purity that he was striving for throughout his career, and its restoration stands for the cleansing of sin through divine grace.[10]

For similar reasons, Damian also dwells on the question of what it means to say that God cannot do evil or commit a sin (§3, 597b). Still anxious not to curtail God's power, Damian seeks refuge in the traditional thought that evil is non-being or nothingness, as Eriugena had done in his treatise on predestination (see above, Chapter 3). Thus, even if we say that God is unable to do sin, there is literally nothing—no positive reality—that lies beyond the scope of God's power. The discussion of the virginity question is dangerously close to being settled right here. If restoring virginity were an evil, then on that basis alone we could conclude that it is not something God could do. In that case we would never find out Damian's view on the broader question of God's ability to change the past, which would be a shame. Fortunately, Damian thinks it obviously a good thing to restore virginity. Also fortunate is that Damian does still want to tell us, not only whether a virgin can be restored physically and morally to a pure state, but also whether God can make it the case that she never lost her virginity in the first place. So far Damian has said nothing that would settle this issue. As he moves on to deal with the problem, he considers an admirably clear example that doesn't involve the theological and moral complexities of the virginity case: can God *now* make it the case that Rome never existed?

That's the good news. The bad news is that scholars are deeply divided over how to interpret the solution, or perhaps solutions, that Damian goes on to offer. I'll spend the rest of this chapter explaining some of the different interpretations. The simplest reading, and one still frequently associated with Damian, is that he takes the radical position of holding that God can do even impossible things. Even though Rome did exist, God can make it so that it never existed, thus bringing about a contradictory state of affairs: Rome both did and did not exist. Some scholars have connected Damian's (supposed) embrace of this to his (supposed) hostility towards dialectic and philosophy.[11] For Damian would be rejecting the most fundamental rule of logic, the principle of non-contradiction, which states that the same thing can never be both true and false. But this interpretation has severe problems. In this very letter, Damian actually claims more expertise in dialectic than his opponents (§7, 603c), and he also seems to deny that God can make contradictory things happen, since, if he did, he would be thwarting His own will (§10, 608d–609a).

On the other hand, Damian does clearly seem to be saying that God can bring it about that, if you will, there was no place like Rome. And a moment's reflection will show that this doesn't need to involve bringing about a contradiction. If God now makes it so that Rome never existed, He would not make Rome both exist and not exist in the past. Rather, He would replace its past existence with its past non-existence. There's nothing impossible about that, unless of course we think that the past is necessary and unalterable. Here another interpretation presents itself.[12] Damian follows Boethius' lead in holding that God is eternal in the strongest sense of not being subject to time at all (§17, 618c). This means that, even if Rome's existence is necessary from our point of view, because it lies in our past, it may not be necessary from God's point of view. He stands outside of time, surveying all things at once. For Him, then, the past is no more necessary than the future.

Given Damian's emphasis on God's timelessness, this reading has some plausibility. But it doesn't really do justice to Damian's insistence that God really can make it such that Rome never existed, *even though it did exist*. In fact he says, with his characteristic rhetorical aggression, that someone who denies this deserves to be put to a branding iron (§17, 618c). Simply alluding to the timeless nature of God's power doesn't explain how it is that both options remain timelessly open to Him. So here's a simpler idea.[13] Maybe Damian just wants to reaffirm that God retains the power to do things even when He does not do them, as we already saw with the rain example. All things are subject to God's will, and the fact that they have already happened doesn't mean they fall outside the scope of His power. If this is all Damian wishes to say, then he is in line with more standard treatments of the question in the later Middle Ages, giving us a less outrageous, but more sensible Peter Damian.

We can expand on this interpretation in light of a distinction that Damian makes between two kinds of necessity, which we might call absolute and subsequent necessity.[14] Something is absolutely necessary if it intrinsically cannot be otherwise. For instance, it is absolutely necessary that one plus one is two. By contrast, some things are necessary only on a certain assumption (§7, 603a). For instance, if we assume that you will finish reading this chapter, it necessarily follows from this that you will have read the chapter's last sentence. But your having read that sentence would not become absolutely necessary: it would remain the case that you could have refrained from reading it. It's hard to imagine why you'd stop reading now, having gotten this far, but it remains possible in itself. Applying this idea to the past, we can say that once God wills that Rome should exist, it necessarily follows that Rome must exist, given that nothing can thwart God's will. Yet Rome's existence remains merely possible in itself. God's timeless eternity remains relevant here, in that His relationship to past, present, and future events is always the same (unlike our case, where the future is open and the past and present closed). Whether we talk about Rome's past existence, the present existence of Germany, or the future existence of a nation wisely ruled by a benevolent, giraffe-loving philosopher, we are dealing with things that become necessary only if God wills them to be the case. In this sense, the past is subject to God's will in just the same way the future is. Still, God cannot will anything both to occur and not to occur, so there is no threat that a contradiction will arise.

I find this interpretation fairly compelling, but it too has potential problems. Some scholars claim to find in Damian the idea that the principle of non-contradiction itself is subject to God's will, meaning that God simply chooses to avoid bringing about contradictions.[15] If this principle itself is subject to God's will, then after all these subtle interpretive maneuvers we would be back with something like the traditional reading, that God can do the impossible. Setting this aside, though, it's noteworthy that Damian distinguishes between two kinds of necessity. About a generation later, in the same context of the question of whether God can change the past, the more famous thinker Anselm of Canterbury will make the same distinction very clearly, by contrasting *necessitas praecedens* with *necessitas sequens*: preceding and subsequent necessity.[16] It's just one example of Anselm's clear-headed approach to the problems that had arisen in the first few centuries of medieval philosophy, an approach which for some licenses calling him the first great scholastic philosopher.

7

A CANTERBURY TALE
ANSELM'S LIFE AND WORKS

Y ou will presumably be familiar with Douglas Adams, the author of *The Hitchhiker's Guide to the Galaxy*, which has almost as many jokes about philosophy in it as this book (and his are funnier). Another novel by Adams entitled *Dirk Gently's Holistic Detective Agency* is less celebrated, but has a scene in it that I like very much. The title character Dirk Gently refers to Sir Isaac Newton as "the renowned inventor of the cat flap." When it's pointed out to him that, more to the point, Newton also discovered gravity, Dirk responds that gravity was just waiting around for someone to notice it, whereas the cat flap was a true stroke of genius: "a door within a door, you see." It's put to him that this actually seems quite an obvious idea, at which point Dirk says, "it is a rare mind indeed that can replace the hitherto nonexistent with the blindingly obvious."

Of course, being extraordinarily famous for one thing, when you deserve to be famous for other things too, is not that harsh a fate. Zeppo Marx would presumably have leapt at such a chance. And it certainly wouldn't have bothered Anselm of Canterbury that he was, in this respect, the Isaac Newton of medieval philosophy. Fame was the last thing on his mind when he devised his so-called "ontological argument," a proof intended to show that the existence of God is blindingly obvious, indeed entailed by our very conception of God as "that than which nothing greater can be conceived." Anselm owes his renown mostly to this argument; yet even without it he would have a prominent place in the history of medieval philosophy. He lived most of his life in the eleventh century, dying in 1109, but helped to prepare the way for the flowering of scholasticism in the twelfth century. He was also a significant, though reluctant actor on the political stage whose life story will give us a first glimpse of a long-running battle between clerical and secular authority.

Anselm was formed by, and for the most part remained within, the sort of monastic intellectual culture that has provided the main context for philosophy ever since the Carolingian Renaissance. Like Peter Damian, Anselm hailed from northern Italy, but he moved in his early twenties to France, where he became a monk at the abbey in Bec in the year 1059.[1] Here, he encountered Lanfranc, whom we saw engaging in a dispute over the correct understanding of the Eucharist. Lanfranc was well known as a teacher of the liberal arts and must have had a significant role in shaping the intellectual outlook of Anselm, who succeeded him as the prior of Bec in 1063, later becoming abbot. He did not enjoy the duties involved in these posts, but that was as nothing compared to what awaited him. In 1093, he reluctantly agreed to be appointed archbishop of Canterbury.

His biographer, Eadmer, claims that during his investment as archbishop, Anselm actually physically resisted when William II, the king of England, personally bestowed the ring and staff upon him. The king's right to appoint bishops was at this time becoming a matter of intense debate. The 1070s had seen the eruption of the "Investiture Contest," in which churchmen resisted the claims of secular rulers to exercise authority over them. But in describing the scene, Eadmer may also have been writing with the benefit of hindsight, having a clearer understanding of the significance of this investiture ceremony, and also knowledge of the rocky relationship Anselm was to have with William.[2] They clashed over the restoration of land to the Church and other financial matters. Eventually Anselm had to go to Rome to petition the Pope for his support. He returned to England after William's death, only to go into exile again because of the Investiture Contest, which pitted him against William's successor, Henry I.

Amidst these political battles and despite his official duties, Anselm somehow managed to compose the works of philosophy and theology that stand as a landmark in the transition from early medieval thought to the intellectual renaissance of the twelfth century. (Yes, I know we just had a renaissance in the Carolingian period; between the eighth and fifteenth centuries, philosophy was reborn more often than a phoenix with a heavy smoking habit.) In many respects, Anselm's writings would be at home in the earlier period we've been examining so far. He tells us that one of his better-known works, the *Monologion*, was written at the request of his fellow monks for the sake of meditating on the divine.[3] Anselm claims that he was reluctant to set down his thoughts, and that he has done so only in humble compliance with their requests. The pastoral dimension of Anselm's career is also shown by prayers and other spiritual writings, which are rarely read by historians of philosophy but provide important context for his more philosophical writings.[4] These texts are deeply informed by Augustine, still the dominant intellectual force in monastic culture. Yet Anselm also points the way towards a major feature of philosophy in the twelfth and thirteenth century: a reliance on reason, rather than revelation and authority.

In the preface of the *Monologion* he explains that what we are about to read will, supposedly at the request of Anselm's brethren, consist of nothing but rational argument. True to his word, in what follows Anselm refrains from quoting Scripture. This approach displeased his teacher Lanfranc when Anselm sent him the *Monologion*, to ask whether it met with his approval. Though Lanfranc had criticized his opponent Berengar for trying to explicate the Eucharist using nothing but the tools of dialectic, he was certainly not opposed to the use of reason. That even he felt some disquiet at the lack of authoritative quotations in the *Monologion* powerfully demonstrates the novelty of Anselm's method. In the twelfth century, figures like Abelard will have no hesitation in relying purely on arguments that could persuade even a fair-minded Jew or atheist. Anselm was a pioneer in this regard, and though he was humble enough to submit the *Monologion* to Lanfranc, he was also confident enough in his approach that he left the treatise as it was despite Lanfranc's criticism.[5]

It was at Bec that Anselm wrote the groundbreaking *Monologion* and its sequel, the *Proslogion*, which contains the famous ontological argument. Yet at this same time, he was dealing with somewhat more traditional topics. He penned a work on grammar, the first of the liberal arts, and used his dialectical skills to address the problem of freedom's compatibility with divine predestination and the Augustinian position on grace, the issue that had led to such disputes in the time of Eriugena. Later, during his time at Canterbury, Anselm's rationalist project would take an even bolder form, as he tried to show why God not only did, but in fact had to, become incarnate (this in a work called *Cur Deus homo*, or *Why God Became Man*). Again, the preface to the work declares his method. Even if we knew nothing about Christ, we could work out for ourselves that God must become man in order to save humankind, and that otherwise the immortality for which humans are destined could never come to pass.

Behind that argument lurks a fundamental presupposition. Things in the created world can only be rightly understood in light of their purposes. To some extent, this was old news. Ever since Aristotle, nature had usually been understood in a teleological way. If you want to understand a giraffe's long neck, you have to realize what purpose is being served by its length. But Anselm, following the lead of Augustine, tends to see even apparently abstract notions in teleological terms. Consider his treatise *On Truth*. We might assume that truth is a pretty straightforward notion: a sentence is true if what it says matches the way that things are. Anselm would agree with that, but he would insist that affirmative sentences also need to be understood as serving some purpose. They are, as it were, trying to do something. Their goal is to describe the world, or as Anselm puts it, "to signify that what is, is" (*On Truth* §1). So the truth of an assertion is an example of what Anselm calls *rectitudo*, meaning "correctness," or if you prefer to stick closer to the Latin word, "rectitude."

In light of this, Anselm feels free to apply the concept of truth much more widely than we would today. If truth is the same thing as correctness or rectitude (§2, 11), it can turn up wherever rectitude is at stake. And for Anselm, that's just about everywhere. A right action is a "true action" (§5). God, being purely good and the source of all other good, is the ultimate example of something that is as it ought to be, so Anselm concludes that He is nothing other than Truth itself (§10). Moreover, we can apply this concept of truth or rectitude to the human will. Since we can will what we ought to, as when we love God, or fail to do this, as when we sin, the will can be "true" or "false." In other words, it can have or lack rectitude.

Anselm develops this idea in two further treatises which form a trilogy together with *On Truth*, called *On Free Will* and *On the Fall of the Devil*. Here he is trying to understand the sinful choices that led to the fall of humans and of Satan, a former angel who was punished for trying to usurp God's authority.[6] Like *On Truth*, these treatises are written in dialogue form. As in Eriugena's *Periphyseon*, the dialogue unfolds between a teacher and a student, with the teacher coaxing a puzzled student into understanding some rather novel ideas. At the very outset, the student poses the question that had so vexed Eriugena and his contemporaries: if we need God's grace to avoid sin, how is it that we remain free? The teacher responds by saying that freedom is not the power to choose between sinning and not sinning (*On Free Will* §1). After all, God cannot sin, nor can the angels who have been confirmed in their commitment to God after they chose obedience to Him, rather than the defiance shown by Satan.

Here Anselm is raising the question we just discussed in Chapter 6, as to whether there is anything that God cannot do. His answer is yes: God cannot will evil.[7] He can only will one thing, namely the good. But this does not make Him any less free. In fact, God's inability to choose anything but goodness makes him *more* free than a creature who can choose between good and evil (§1). This may sound perplexing, but it is easier to understand in light of Anselm's earlier definition of the will. Remember that the will is not just a power to choose, but has a purpose.[8] This purpose is, as Anselm puts it, to "preserve rectitude for its own sake," and freedom is nothing more nor less than the ability to do this. In other words, the reason we have a will is so that we can persevere in willing goodness or justice because they are good and just, rather than to win some reward or avoid some punishment (§3). Obviously being unable to sin, like God and the good angels, does not inhibit the ability to persevere in goodness. To the contrary, it ensures that the will is always used in the way it was meant to be used. In other words, an incapacity for sin actually guarantees freedom.

As humans, we face a different and more problematic situation. The first humans, like Satan before his fall, faced the choice of whether to use will correctly or incorrectly. Unfortunately, they picked wrong. We still bear the burden of this choice, being unable to persevere in goodness because we are born into original sin. To use Anselm's preferred language again, we are not in a position to "preserve rectitude for its own sake." Doesn't that mean, then, that we do lack freedom after all? Anselm argues that it does not, and his argument is a clever one. Someone could have a power to do something without being in a position to use that power. His example is eyesight (§3, 12). Suppose that I sit you down in a theater where a movie is playing, and that your eyes are in good working order. Clearly, you have the power to see the movie. Imagine though that I blindfold you. Do you now lack the power to see the movie? No, that would be the case of someone who actually lacks eyesight, that is, someone who is blind. Rather, you do have the power, but are unable to use that power until the blindfold is removed.

In the same way, even in their fallen state humans have the power to preserve rectitude for its own sake. In other words, they do have free will. It's just that they can't *use* this power in the way it was meant to be used, at least not without God's help. But that isn't to say that humans can't use free will at all. We are willing freely with every choice we make, including our sinful choices. Why, though, does sinning count as a use of free will at all, if the purpose of the will is to preserve rectitude? Well, because you can use a power without using it rightly. The medievals would say that the true purpose of sexual potency is reproduction. When people have sex merely for pleasure, then they are not using the capacity as they should, but they are still using it. Likewise, the choices of Adam, Eve, and Satan before they fell, and the sinful choices we make now, are incorrect uses of the will. Yet they are still free.

You might object to this that sinning doesn't seem to have anything to do with freedom at all. If freedom is the power to preserve the will's rectitude, how is it involved in violating that very rectitude? To understand Anselm's answer, we need to factor in another condition that he lays down for freedom of the will. No one is free to will something if they are compelled or coerced into willing it. Even the threat of guaranteed punishment can count as coercion. This is why Anselm insists that Satan could not have known the awful fate that would befall him if he defied God. If he had known, he would not only have chosen differently, but would have had no alternative but to choose differently, so he would not have been free (*Fall of the Devil* §22–4). The same goes for humans. If God acts justly in punishing us, it is because humankind sins "through a judgment that is so free that it cannot be coerced to sin by anything else" (*On Free Will* §2).

This is what the will to sin has in common with the will to preserve rectitude. Neither is coerced by any outside force. Whether the choice is good or bad, the choice is only free if it is determined by the person who is exercising their will to choose. A remarkable feature of Anselm's analysis is that, according to him, someone can even be coerced by their own motivations. When describing the fall of the Devil, he says that Satan must have had two opposing motivations (*Fall of the Devil* 13–14). One was a motivation to be just, the other a motivation to have whatever would make him happy. Justice would imply obedience to God, while Satan supposed that he would become happy by defying God. The other angels had the same pair of motivations, but chose justice over happiness (and good thing too, since Satan's choice made him far from happy in the end).

Anselm reasons that if God had given the angels only one of these two motivations, they would have been unfree in their choices. If He bestowed only the desire for justice upon the angels, God would effectively be forcing them to be obedient, which would render their choice both unfree and morally worthless. As it is, the angels did have a choice of which motivation to follow, which is why Satan could rightly be punished and the good angels rightly rewarded. The fact that the good angels can no longer sin is no hindrance to their continued moral goodness and freedom, since this is a reward for their original free choice to be obedient to God. And what about God Himself? He doesn't seem to have two motivations, one for justice and one for happiness. Rather He has a simple, single will. But that's no problem, because no one else is responsible for giving God this single motivation, as He would have been responsible for giving such a motivation to the angels. Since God's goodness comes entirely from within, there is no hint of coercion in His choice, and He remains fully self-determined and free.

With all due respect to Eriugena, I have to say that this is an unprecedentedly sophisticated and clear-minded attempt to make sense of Augustine's position on freedom. With a deft series of distinctions and definitions, Anselm has secured everything an Augustinian might want. There is the needed asymmetry between acting rightly and wrongly, in that we are unable to be good without grace but able to be evil through our own power. Yet we also remain free with respect to these choices. We can also see exactly how God remains perfectly free even without being able to do certain things that even His creatures can do (like sin, for example). These victories do not come without costs, though. In particular, we might balk at defining an apparently basic idea like freedom with the rather complicated formula "power to preserve rectitude for its own sake." But Anselm was a master at deriving powerful conclusions from such verbal formulas, as we're about to see with the case of the formula "that than which nothing greater can be conceived."

8

SOMEBODY'S PERFECT ANSELM'S ONTOLOGICAL ARGUMENT

I was planning a vacation recently, and a colleague of mine told me about this amazing island. It lies in the most temperate region of the ocean and is always pleasantly warm and sunny, untouched by hurricanes or monsoons. The beaches are a pearly white, made of sand so fine that lying on them is said to be like sprawling on a silken blanket. A gentle breeze wafts the scent of hibiscus and coconut through the air, except for one particular area frequented by people who don't like the smell of hibiscus and coconut (here it instead smells like freshly brewed coffee; no one is quite sure why). As for the islanders, they are without exception cheerful and wealthy, yet take delight in satisfying the whims of visitors, plying them with exotic cocktails and succulent food, and arranging nightly showings of Buster Keaton movies with live accompaniment by the world's leading pianists. It sounded pretty good, and I was just about to book my travel arrangements when I found out that this otherwise perfect island has one serious flaw: it doesn't exist. That's the last time I take vacation advice from a metaphysician.

In fact my colleague is not the first to imagine such a perfect island, an island which could not possibly be improved apart from its unfortunate non-existence. It appears in a famous objection, posed by a monk named Gaunilo, to a proof for the existence of God devised by Anselm of Canterbury. When even the objection to an argument is famous, you can guess that the argument itself must be pretty well known. And indeed, Anselm's so-called "ontological argument" for God's existence is probably the single most famous philosophical contribution by any medieval philosopher. It has provoked critiques, starting with Gaunilo in Anselm's own lifetime, and subsequently from such household names as Aquinas and Kant. It has also inspired later arguments for God. Proofs with the same general strategy, usually spelled out in much more rigorous fashion, have been offered for instance by Descartes, Gödel, and Alvin Plantinga.[1]

It's standard for historians of philosophy like me to complain that Anselm's argument is usually taken out of context. Students are typically asked to read only the few paragraphs where the proof is set out, ignoring the rest of the treatise in which the proof appears, Anselm's *Proslogion*, to say nothing of his previous and closely related work, the *Monologion*.[2] As we'll see in what follows, it does help in understanding Anselm's argument to look at these texts in their entirety, as well as his response to the critique of Gaunilo. But to some extent, Anselm is himself to blame for fact that people focus on the proof to the exclusion of the rest of the *Proslogion*. It comes at the start of the treatise and provides the foundation for all that follows, so the whole project stands or falls on the success of this strategy. Indeed, in the prologue, Anselm tells us that he wants to base his whole account of God on one single powerful pattern of reasoning. This will be a departure from the approach of the *Monologion*, which offered a series of independent arguments in an attempt to capture the nature of God insofar as is possible for the human mind.

What the two texts have in common is that their arguments are intended to be convincing even for an atheist, such as the "Fool" of the biblical Psalms (13:1, 52:1) who "said in his heart that there is no God" (*Proslogion* §2). This Fool is explicitly invoked at the start of the ontological argument. The idea is that Anselm's proof could bring even this person to see that God must exist. Similarly, the *Monologion* begins by asserting that the arguments to come should persuade any rational person, even one who has never heard of God or Christianity. This is a bold claim, given that Anselm is going to go on to argue not just for God's existence but for specifically Christian doctrines like the Trinity, purely on the basis of reason. Yet Anselm is far from dismissing the importance of revelation or belief through religious faith. His motto is the Augustinian slogan *credo ut intelligam*, "I believe in order to understand," an attitude also explicitly adopted in Anselm's philosophical dialogues (*On Free Will* §3). The ontological argument and the rest of the argumentation offered in both the *Monologion* and the *Proslogion* are not intended to replace faith with rational proof, as if this were something better, but to provide an insight into what exactly the person of faith already believes.

It's important to bear this in mind when looking at Anselm's various proofs for God's existence. It helps draw our attention to a feature of all these proofs: they are part of a larger project of understanding what God is like, instead of just establishing that He exists. The formula at the center of the ontological argument describes God as "that than which nothing greater can be conceived." From this formula, Anselm wants to infer not just that God exists and indeed necessarily exists, but also that He is good, powerful, just, eternal, and so on. In this respect his proof is not unlike one offered several decades earlier, but half a world away, in central Asia. The great Muslim philosopher Avicenna also devised an argument for a necessarily existing God. Much as Anselm tries to extract a wide range of traditional attributes of God from the formula "that than which nothing greater can be conceived," Avicenna wanted to show that a Necessary Existent must have such features as uniqueness, immateriality, power, and goodness.[3] This is what Anselm has in mind when he says that his *Proslogion* is going to provide "one single argument" that will yield all the results achieved through separate arguments in the *Monologion*.

The first of these far less famous arguments has a very Platonist flavor. It observes that there must be some cause for the goodness we find in the things around us (*Monologion* §1). Although goodness manifests itself in different ways, goodness itself should have the same meaning in each case. Otherwise we would have no unified idea of goodness, only a welter of different ideas that are misleadingly expressed by the same word. We need, therefore, to suppose that there is a cause of goodness, which is the source of this shared nature that we find in all good things.[4] As the cause of all goodness, this source will itself be good, indeed the most good and great of all things, namely God. Is this a persuasive argument? It is no worse than a prominent consideration in favor of the theory of Forms in Plato's dialogues, the so-called "one over many" argument. Yet Plato concluded from it that there is an abstract Form of goodness, which seems rather different from establishing the Christian God.

A similar argument in the *Monologion* (§4) begins from the humble observation that some things are better than others. Anselm's example is that humans are better by nature than horses, which are better by nature than trees. Can we imagine that the scale of goodness just keeps going indefinitely, like a scale of heat with no highest temperature? In that case, there would have to be an infinity of natures in the universe, since every nature has some nature that is better than it. But this strikes Anselm as patently absurd. So again, we can postulate a highest nature which is maximally good. And again, we may feel that Anselm owes us an argument that the maximally good thing is really God. A helpful consideration appears further on (§15), where Anselm anticipates the reasoning he will use in the *Proslogion* a few years later. If God is maximally good, as these proofs claim to show, then He must have every property that belongs to a maximally good thing. What properties will these be? Well, any property such that it is better, or "greater," to have it than not to have it. In contemporary philosophy of religion these are sometimes called the "great-making properties." For instance, it is better to be powerful than to be weak; so the maximally good thing, being maximally good, will be powerful. In fact He will be all-powerful, since it is better to have each individual power than not to have it, so He must have them all. He will also be just, merciful, wise, eternal, and so on, since again it is better to have these properties than not to have them.

Now it seems far more plausible to identify the thing established by Anselm's arguments with God. Indeed, it seems that we can grasp God's nature quite easily.

We just think of every property such that having it is better than not, and ascribe it to Him: job done. But Anselm cautions us against such a straightforward interpretation of what he is doing. He may not be a negative theologian on a par with the Pseudo-Dionysius or Eriugena, but he does deny that we can grasp God's nature fully with the finite resources of the human mind (§65). In fact you can even ground apophatic theology in the logic of great-making properties. If it is better to be beyond the grasp of human language and thought than to be graspable by humankind, then God, being maximally good, must be ineffable. How can we, nonetheless, ascribe all those other great-making properties to him?[5] In the *Monologion* Anselm offers a traditional response, that we are only using the likenesses of created things to describe him. But he already glimpses a more innovative answer: God is understood not as the best thing, or as greater than everything else, but as that than which nothing is better (§15).

As Anselm will later point out in his replies to Gaunilo's criticism, this is a subtle but crucial difference. The ontological argument would not work if we just said that God is greater than anything else (*Replies* §5). We need to say that God is that than which nothing greater exists or indeed *could* exist: "that than which nothing greater can be conceived." This leaves room for Anselm to admit that God outstrips our understanding. If He were the greatest thing we can conceive, then obviously we would be in a position to conceive of Him. But if He is that than which nothing greater can be conceived, He may to some extent lie beyond our grasp. Still, we grasp Him to some extent, just as we must to some extent grasp anything when we call it "ineffable" or "inconceivable" (*Replies* §9). Suppose I say "Five trillion is an inconceivably large number." Even as I tell you that you can't conceive of this number, I am telling you something about it, namely that it lies beyond your comprehension.

The *Proslogion* is devoted entirely to working out the implications of this idea that God is that than which nothing greater can be conceived, from which one can infer God's goodness, eternity, omnipotence, and so on. By the way, this part of Anselm's project struck his critic Gaunilo as unproblematic (*On Behalf of the Fool* §8). Unfortunately, the argument at the very beginning serves as a foundation for all that follows, and it fails to convince him. Why? Because it tries to infer the very existence of God from the formula, an application of Anselm's new trick that seems to Gaunilo too tricky by half. Yet the argument is elegantly, or perhaps infuriatingly, simple. Invoking the atheistic Fool from the Psalms quotation, Anselm says that even though the Fool does not believe in God, he will surely be able to understand the formula and shares the idea encapsulated in that formula. To put it the way that Anselm does, this thing than which nothing greater can be conceived at least exists in the Fool's mind, even if it does not exist in reality (*Proslogion* §2).

Now Anselm sets out to show the Fool that his atheistic position makes no sense. It is contradictory to suppose that God doesn't exist in reality, but only in the mind, if we understand God as that than which nothing greater can be conceived. This is because, if God existed only in the mind, it would be easy to conceive of things better than Him. Notably, we could conceive of Him as existing in reality and not just in the mind. As Anselm puts the point, "if that than which a greater cannot be thought exists in the mind alone, this same that than which a greater cannot be thought is that than which a greater *can* be thought; but this is obviously impossible" (§2). This is the same sort of reasoning used later in the *Proslogion* to prove that God is, for instance, eternal. It belongs to the very nature of that than which a greater cannot be thought to be eternal, because if it were not eternal, we could think of something better: we need just think of something that is eternal. In the same way, it is implied by the formula that the thing in question must exist, because if it didn't exist, we could conceive of something better than it. The Fool must therefore admit that God exists, on pain of contradicting himself.

Like Mr T, Gaunilo pitied the Fool, and argued on his behalf that Anselm's argument fails. He devised a number of objections, including his famous island analogy (*On Behalf of the Fool* §6). Consider, says Gaunilo, an island than which no better island can be conceived. If we supposed that this island didn't exist in reality, we would fall into the same contradiction, because a non-existing island clearly isn't one than which no better island can be conceived. Therefore, such an island in fact exists. Gaunilo's objection is a powerful one. If you can use a pattern of reasoning to prove something false, then you know there is something wrong with that pattern of reasoning. Since the version of the argument with the island apparently works just like Anselm's argument, but yields a false conclusion, we can infer that Anselm's proof must be a failure. Notice, though, that Gaunilo's island objection shows only that the reasoning used by Anselm must have gone astray somewhere, without actually diagnosing the mistake.

How might Anselm respond? We don't have to guess, because we actually have Anselm's reply to Gaunilo's criticisms, a very helpful document for understanding how Anselm thought his proof was supposed to work in the first place.[6] Obviously, to meet the objection he has to show that it makes a difference that we are being asked to think about an island, as opposed to God. The difference is that existence belongs to the very nature of that than which nothing greater can be conceived, whereas existence cannot belong to the very nature of an island. As the American military proved when they were testing atom bombs in the Pacific Ocean, an island is the sort of thing that can go out of existence. So if we find ourselves entertaining the idea of an island that can't possibly fail to exist, then we are entertaining something that makes no sense. By contrast, that than which nothing greater can be conceived is going to be something whose very nature guarantees its real existence. Anselm had already made this point in the *Proslogion* (§3).[7] That than which nothing greater can be conceived is not merely something that exists, it is something that *must* exist. It exists necessarily, because it cannot even be conceived as not existing.

I think this is a good response to the island objection. But the proof has been subject to many other criticisms. Apart from the island objection, the most well-known response is probably the one made by Kant, who argued that Anselm was wrong to take existence as a property on a par with features like justice, goodness, or eternity.[8] Existence is not just one more property that I can think of a thing as having. This is why it struck an absurd note at the beginning of this chapter when I treated the existence or non-existence of an island as a feature on a par with the whiteness of its sands or scent of its breezes. According to Kant, when I think of something, I am conceiving of it as having a range of properties. Its existence is simply the realization or instantiation in the world of something that has those properties. Whether this same objection can so plausibly be applied to the idea of *necessary* existence, though, seems to me to be an open question. Even if existence is not a (great-making) property like justice or eternity, the trait of existing necessarily might be.

But I think we don't need to deny that existence, or necessary existence, is a property in order to defeat Anselm's argument. If the way I've set it out does capture Anselm's line of reasoning accurately, then it has a more fundamental flaw. For me to say that necessary existence is included in the very nature of a thing is not yet to assert that the thing exists. Rather, it is to say that *if the thing did exist*, then it would by its very nature exist necessarily. This seems not only right, but a genuine insight on Anselm's part, and one strikingly parallel to what Avicenna had been doing just a few years previously. Anselm realized that if God is to be that than which nothing greater can be conceived, He would be the sort of thing that cannot fail to exist. But this, as far as I can see, just means that God cannot exist contingently. In other words, He can't exist while possibly not existing. From this it doesn't follow that God in fact exists. Gaunilo made this same point in a passage which should be remembered alongside his much more frequently noticed island objection: "it must first of all be proved to me that this same greater than everything truly exists in reality somewhere, and then only will the fact that it is greater than everything make it clear that it also subsists in itself" (*On Behalf of the Fool* §5).

9

ALL OR NOTHING
THE PROBLEM OF UNIVERSALS

Irving Thalburg, the producer of the Marx Brothers' movies, had a brilliant knack for show business but also a nasty habit of making people wait for him. The Marx Brothers were familiar with this habit. Once he made them wait outside his office for so long that they smoked cigars, blew the smoke under the crack beneath his door and yelled "fire!" Another time, Thalburg interrupted a meeting with them and left them waiting in his office. The Marx Brothers decided they'd had enough. When the producer finally returned to the meeting, he found them gathered stark naked in front of his office's fireplace, which they were using to roast potatoes. Thalburg laughed, had a potato, and never made them wait again. This anecdote confirms something already abundantly clear from their movies: the Marx Brothers shared an anarchic and irreverent sense of humor. Of course, that wasn't the only thing they had in common. They were indeed brothers, and thus shared the same parents; they had grown up together in the Bronx; they all hated waiting and liked a roasted potato.

In addition, there is the fact that the Marx Brothers were all humans. An obvious fact, but surprisingly hard to explain. In addition to the specific features that distinguish each of them—Chico's piano-playing ability or Groucho's quick wit—the Marx Brothers, and indeed all humans, share in the feature of humanity. We are all animals, too, a feature we have the honor of sharing with giraffes among other creatures. Philosophers call such shared features "universals," because they belong universally to all the members of a class: thus humanity belongs to all humans. But what exactly is this shared humanity? On the one hand, it seems to play an important role in the world and in our understanding of things. When we know, for instance, that all humans are rational, it seems that we are understanding something not just about you, me, Groucho, or Zeppo, but about humanity itself. What we are understanding is that the possession of humanity implies the possession of rationality. On the other hand, the idea of a universal thing that actually exists out in the world is a rather odd one. In our everyday experience, we never encounter abstract humanity or animality. We encounter concrete particular humans and animals, whom we can distinguish from the other members of their class by their special characteristics. We tell Groucho apart from another animal, like the giraffe Hiawatha, by noting that they belong to different species; and we tell him apart from Chico by noting that Groucho does have a mustache or doesn't play piano.

The difficulty of accounting for the shared features of things is called the problem of universals. Perhaps the most famous attempt to answer the problem is also the earliest attempt: Plato's theory of Forms. This theory was apparently intended to explain common characteristics like humanity or largeness by postulating a single, overarching Form or paradigm, humanity-itself or largeness-itself. And readers have traditionally understood Plato's Forms as universals. This may not be quite right, though. Aristotle points out that although a Platonic Form does play the role of a universal by accounting for shared membership in a kind of thing, it also seems to be just another kind of particular, albeit a perfect, unchanging, and paradigmatic particular.[1] In fact it was Aristotle himself who really started talk of "universals" in philosophy. Unfortunately, he left it rather unclear what sort of metaphysical status we should assign to a universal like humanity or animality.

For this reason, ancient commentators on Aristotle already engaged in detailed discussions of the problem of universals, discussions that were passed on to the medievals thanks to the translations and commentaries of Boethius. For Boethius and his medieval heirs, the starting point for discussion of this problem was the beginning of Porphyry's widely read Introduction to Aristotelian logic.[2] In a few sentences that rank as one of the most enticing but unsatisfying passages in the history of philosophy, Porphyry sketches out the questions that would need to be answered in order to solve the problem of universals (Introduction §2). We would need first to decide whether they are real or not; if they are real, whether they are bodily or incorporeal; and if they are incorporeal, whether they exist in bodies or separately. That last question was of particular importance for Porphyry and other ancient commentators who wanted to reconcile the philosophies of Plato and Aristotle, since it seemed plausible to say that Plato's Forms were indeed separate universals, whereas Aristotle apparently recognized the reality of universals but understood them to be immanent within bodies.

The exegetical problem of harmonizing Plato and Aristotle was one reason the ancient commentators were so interested in the problem of universals, but it wasn't the only reason. If you think about it, many of the things we say every day involve universals. Even when I talk about a particular thing, like a specific person, I'll often be saying that some universal feature applies to that particular. Suppose I say "Groucho is chomping on a cigar," or "Hiawatha is loping across a savannah."

Groucho and Hiawatha are particulars, but many people may be chomping on cigars, and many giraffes loping across the savannah. "Chomping on a cigar" or "loping across a savannah" are universals: they can be, and are, realized in many particular instances. Then there are sentences where no particulars appear at all, as when we say "Cigar-smoking is unhealthy" or "Giraffe is a type of animal." This explains why philosophers still worry about the problem of universals today. Until we sort out the status of universals, we cannot really say how our language gets hold of the world. None of this escaped the ancient commentators and their medieval readers, and they had still further reasons of their own to take the problem seriously. Unlike most philosophers nowadays, they followed Aristotle's lead in believing that knowledge in the strict and proper sense—the kind of knowledge involved in scientific understanding—is universal in scope.[3] So, for them, answering Porphyry's questions was an urgent task in the study of knowledge, or epistemology, as well as in philosophy of language.

Given the strictly introductory purposes of his little treatise on logic, Porphyry took the liberty of leaving his own questions unanswered. The passage thus offered a wonderful opportunity for later philosophers. By commenting on it, they could offer their own account of universals, without having to worry about contending with any theory of Porphyry's own. This led to a certain way of posing the problem that might puzzle contemporary philosophers. Because Porphyry was introducing Aristotelian logic, he was interested in universals that are the species and genera of substances. In other words, his questions were framed in terms of asking whether such items as "humanity" and "animality" are real, are incorporeal, and are separate. Though one could extend the question to non-substantial cases like "cigar-chomping" and "loping across the savannah," later thinkers taking up Porphyry's questions largely focused on sorting out the status of substantial species and genera.

Since the medievals encountered Porphyry through Boethius, they had to take account of what he had said on the issue. They had plenty to work with, because Boethius was so interested in Porphyry's *Introduction* that he commented on it twice. In the earlier commentary, he made a convincing point concerning Porphyry's list of questions, namely that his posing all three questions already implied his answer to the first two. If you answer the first question by saying that universals aren't real, you don't need to go on to ask whether they are bodily or incorporeal; and if you answer this second question by saying they are bodily, you don't need to ask whether they are separate from bodies or in them. Thus, Boethius assumed that, for Porphyry, universals are both real and incorporeal. In his later commentary, he explained why and how this is so. Universals must be real, since otherwise there would be nothing for us to know when we understand the general features of things (Boethius, *Second*

Commentary §20–2). We encounter such features in particulars, and then "abstract" or isolate them through a mental process, something Boethius compares to isolating the line that forms the edge of a body (§26). The feature we are noticing is alike in all the members of a species: Groucho, Chico, Harpo, and Zeppo are all similar in being humans. Yet it is only at the level of mental understanding that we isolate humanity as something in its own right (§31).

While this goes well beyond the intriguing list of questions posed by Porphyry, Boethius says less than one might want about the humanity that is in Groucho and also in Harpo. Is humanity one and the same thing in both of them? Or is it that we have Groucho's humanity, which is one thing, and Harpo's humanity, which is something else, but these two humanities are similar to one another? If we take the first alternative, we are committed to something that really exists out in the world and is universal. If we take the second alternative, then true universality occurs only in the mind of someone who abstracts and isolates humanity as a general concept. An analogy might help here. The first option would be like your watching the Marx Brothers movie *Duck Soup* on television while I am watching it in a cinema. One and the same movie is being viewed in two places at the same time. The second option would be like two actual bowls of duck soup made according to the same recipe. They taste exactly alike, but were made from different sets of ingredients and are two distinct meals. (Vegetarians may want to vary the example slightly, using the Marx Brothers movie *Animal Crackers*.)

In the twelfth century, philosophers working in France split over the correct understanding of universals, and more or less along the lines I've just indicated. Some thinkers, whom we can call "realists," believed that humanity is something real that exists in the world. It is present, or instantiated, every time that a human exists. Others found this impossible to accept, and insisted that everything that really exists is something particular. Historians refer to this camp as the "nominalists." The usual story you'll hear is that nominalism was pioneered by the great Peter Abelard, following ideas first put forward by his teacher Roscelin, and that the anti-realist position is called "nominalist" because Abelard and his allies held that a universal is nothing but a word or a name, in Latin *nomen*. In fact, though, things are considerably more complicated.

Let's start by considering the contribution made by Roscelin to this debate. He is often portrayed as a forerunner of Abelard's nominalism, not least by the famous Anselm of Canterbury, who mocked Roscelin for saying that universals are nothing but puffs of air. Actually, modern scholars have doubted whether Roscelin meant to stake out a metaphysical position about universals at all.[4] He did however pave the way for Abelard to some extent, by insisting on a strong contrast between language and its features, on the one hand, and the reality expressed by language, on the other hand. A nice example of this is tense. Consider the difference between saying "Groucho *smoked* a cigar," "Groucho *is smoking* a cigar," and "Groucho *will smoke* a cigar." Roscelin, Abelard, and other so-called "nominalists" were inclined to think that different sentences, with verbs in different tenses, could all refer to one and the same event. It's just that Groucho's smoking the cigar is future, present, or past from the point of view of the speaker. In this and other cases, it is dangerous to assume a diversity of things on the basis of the diverse linguistic expressions used to refer to those things. (There's a slight difficulty here in that words are themselves things. If I utter the name "Groucho," that sound I am making is a thing, just as Groucho himself is a thing. Abelard would later eliminate any possible confusion on this score, by distinguishing between the utterance in itself (*vox*), and the utterance insofar as it is meaningful, which he called *sermo*. The utterance is indeed a thing, but it is not meaningful insofar as it is a thing. It is meaningful insofar as it is a *sermo*, a signifying utterance.[5])

Along with other like-minded writers at the dawn of the twelfth century, most of whom are anonymous, Roscelin was putting forward his ideas about language in the context of grammar, the first of the liberal arts. The main authority for grammar was the late ancient author Priscian, and his work was made the subject of several commentaries at about this time. Priscian informed his readers that a *nomen* ("name" or "noun") must always signify a substance by ascribing some quality to that substance. This too brings us to the problem of universals. To what does a general noun like "human" refer? A universal substance or only particular human substances like Groucho and Harpo? We find grammatical commentaries close to Roscelin's approach saying that words have always been introduced to signify some particular substance. Only afterwards do they come to signify other, similar things.[6] Someone somewhere would have first used the word "human" and meant by it one particular human. Perhaps it was Adam referring with surprise and delight to Eve, who had just been produced from one of his ribs, and thereafter, as a matter of convention this same word "human" was applied to anything else that seemed to be similar to the first thing that bore the name of human. This does seem to head in the direction of Abelard's later, nominalist view.

Still, for an explicit formulation of nominalism we need to wait for Abelard and his critical response to those who started espousing realism about universals.[7] His target was a man named William of Champeaux, master of the school at Notre Dame and a rival of Abelard. The two initially encountered one another in Paris around the year 1100, and later led competing schools. In an autobiographical work, Abelard tells us how he refuted William's realist understanding of universals. In response, William reformulated his theory, only to be crushed again by the superior intellect of Abelard. We don't have to take Abelard's word for this, fortunately. We can judge for ourselves who had the better of the debate, because Abelard's commentary on Porphyry explains William's original and revised positions, along-side the objections that apparently forced William to change his view and then retreat from the controversy altogether.

William's original way of understanding universals as real things went as follows (Abelard, *Glosses on Porphyry* §23–7). If we consider humanity just by itself, we see that it is universal in nature. It is one and the same for, and in, all humans. Nonetheless, in various particulars humanity is joined to various features or characteristics, which William called "forms." Thus, in Chico Marx, humanity is connected to piano-playing ability and a preposterous accent, whereas in Harpo Marx it is joined to harp-playing ability, muteness, and an alarming tendency to sprint after women.[8] Without these other "forms," humanity would remain single and universal. It becomes particularized and multiple thanks to its association with such accidental features. There is a family resemblance between this proposal by William of Cham-peaux and the "hyper-realism" of the earlier Eriugena and his followers. They believed that every substance is an expression of a single, archetypal substance, much as all things are ultimately an expression of the transcendent reality that is God.

William's theory was not quite that Platonist, in that it did not assert the existence of some paradigmatic humanity separate from all individual humans. In a way, this was its chief flaw. If humanity in itself is not separate from humans, and if it is one and the same in all humans, then all humans turn out to be numerically identical with each other insofar as they are humans. In other words, Groucho, Chico, and Harpo are all actually one human being. This, at least, is the objection pressed against William by Abelard (§31–3). To point to the accidental features of things, as William did, is no help. For such accidental features depend on the individual substances to which they belong (§39). Conceptually speaking, Harpo must first exist as a human substance, and only then have such additional features as harp-playing and skirt-chasing. But insofar as he is just a human substance, Harpo will be the same substance as Chico and Groucho. A further problem is that if one and the same substance, namely universal humanity, is the substance of both Harpo and Groucho, then it will have contrary properties (§29). Humanity will be both mute and wisecracking, both harp-playing and non-harp-playing. Even the Marx Brothers' movies never involved anything quite that absurd.

Despite his name, William of Champeaux did not respond to this attack by washing Abelard right out of his hair—at least, not yet. Instead he proposed a revised account. This time the idea was to say that it is in virtue of their *agreement* in humanity that particular humans have a shared nature (§56). Groucho, Chico, Harpo—and yes, even Zeppo—are distinct people, but there is some one thing in which they agree. Or, as William of Champeaux preferred to put it, they "do not differ" in respect of humanity. Abelard easily dismisses William's tricky negative formulation: two humans do not disagree in respect of being a stone either, since they are both equally not a stone (§61). To the more basic idea that the Marx Brothers, and all the rest of us, are humans in virtue of some real thing that is humanity, Abelard replies that human is just what each person is in himself or herself (§59). This had better be distinct in each person. Otherwise, just as with the first attempt to defend realism, Harpo and Groucho will wind up being identical insofar as they are humans.

The problem, as Abelard sees it, is that William and the other realists are desperately holding on to the notion that humanity is a *thing* (*res*). In fact, though, humans are alike not in virtue of some real object in the world, their humanity. Rather, they are simply alike in all being humans (§89). And "being a human" is not a thing. It is, rather, what Abelard calls a "status" (§71), again coining a new technical term in order to clarify the situation as he sees it. A thing's status is simply some way that it is, and ways of being are not themselves things. The realists might complain that a status must indeed be a thing. My being a human is something about which we can have knowledge, and something that explains features of the world. For instance my being a human explains my being rational and alive. So how could it be nothing at all? Abelard responds with an example (§92). Suppose a slave of ancient Rome is beaten because he refuses to go to the forum. His refusing to go is a status, and it explains something, namely why he was beaten. But we are surely not tempted to say that his refusing to go to the forum is actually a thing in its own right. Rather, the man who refuses, and is beaten for it, is a thing. His refusing to go is just a status, one that he lives to regret.

This leaves the way clear for Abelard to give his own, positive account of the universal, which is that it is nothing more, or less, than a word. Universality is like the tense of a verb, an unavoidable aspect of our language that does not correspond to anything out in the world. Rather, we produce universality through a mental process of extracting some shared feature of things. In my mind, I take the four Marx Brothers and remove from them the accidental features that vary from one person to another. What I am left with is a common idea that would apply equally to any human (§103). Abelard compares this to the way painters represent the idea of a lion by depicting a single generic lion, as opposed to painting some particular lion, like the one that was killed by Hercules (§108). It is this conceptual operation, not the existence of any universal thing, that allows us to use words universally. When I say the Marx Brothers were all human, I am simply ignoring their particular features and focusing on a commonality I have noticed about them. What I am saying is true, because they do each have the status of being a human, which is not something universal. In fact "being a human" is no thing at all.

With this deft series of arguments, terminological devices, and clarifications, Abelard has set out the first explicit and sophisticated version of nominalism. It will not be the last. As we shall see, debates over the problem of universals will be confronted by later medieval thinkers, some of whom will show in greater detail how nominalism might answer possible objections, while others press the case for more refined versions of realism. But we've only begun to consider the innovative and brilliant philosophy of Abelard, which involves new proposals in philosophy of language, metaphysics, theology, and ethics. Which is to say nothing of the events with which his name is above all associated: his love affair with Heloise, and its tragic ending.

10

GET THEE TO A NUNNERY
HELOISE AND ABELARD

I'm not going to bother opening this chapter with the usual attention-grabbing example, humorous anecdote, or tribute to classic film. The story I have to tell needs no introduction, being itself a classic tale of star-crossed love. Its protagonists are Peter Abelard and Heloise, who fell desperately in love, produced a child, and married in secret. On the orders of Heloise's outraged uncle, Abelard was attacked and castrated, and he and Heloise both took up a monastic life. From Abelard's own account of this disastrous sequence of events, and from the moving and intellectually high-powered letters the two sent to one another, we know the whole story and also something of what happened next. Abelard set up a religious retreat, called the "Paraclete" in honor of the Holy Spirit (the word is derived from Greek, and means "Comforter"). He invited Heloise and some of her fellow nuns to live there, and advised them on religious questions. The two lovers are now buried together in a Paris cemetery which, appropriately to Abelard's role in medieval culture, is the resting place of both other philosophers, like Lyotard and Merleau-Ponty, and the rock star Jim Morrison.

It's a story that has been exciting the romantic imagination since the thirteenth century, when Jean de Meun worked the couple into his consummate work of courtly love, the *Romance of the Rose* (see Chapter 45). Jean also translated into French several letters exchanged between the two, as well as Abelard's autobiographical account, melodramatically but not inaccurately entitled *Historia calamitatum*, or *Story of Calamities*. Ever since, Abelard and Heloise have gone down in history as something like a real-life Romeo and Juliet. There is even a legend that when Abelard's grave was opened so that Heloise could be buried with him, his skeleton opened its arms to embrace her corpse. Predictably, modern-day scholars have reacted with skepticism, even raising doubts as to whether the documents used by Jean de Meun are genuine. Now, though, their authenticity is widely accepted,[1] which is a good thing since they offer a fascinating window onto Abelard's intellectual development and onto the personality of the brilliant Heloise. Perhaps scholars have been reluctant to accept the authenticity of the letters because the Heloise who speaks in them confounds expectation. The letters are astonishing in their frank descriptions of her own state of mind, and her refusal to accept Abelard's moralizing account of the tragedy that befell them. For some, they also suggest that Abelard's philosophy was powerfully influenced by Heloise's concerns, ideas, and interests.[2]

Even before the two met, both had established a reputation. In the *Story of Calamities* Abelard tells us that he decided to seduce Heloise in large part because of her widely admired intellect. "In looks she did not rank lowest," he remarks, "while in the extent of her learning she stood supreme."[3] He was rightly confident of his ability to win her affections, since he himself was good-looking and was already established as a scholarly celebrity for his expertise in dialectic. John of Salisbury, who would later briefly study with Abelard, wrote that he was "so eminent in logic that he alone was thought to converse with Aristotle."[4] Exploiting his renown, Abelard arranged to become Heloise's teacher. The rest is, quite literally, history. Of course, even today it remains true that skill in philosophy is a sure path to romantic success. But in the twelfth century, such skill could also attract envy and rivalry. Alongside his account of his relationship with Heloise and its consequences, Abelard also recounts his numerous conflicts with other leading intellectuals of the day. His enemies included the leading theologian and political operator Bernard of Clairvaux, and no fewer than three of Abelard's own teachers: Roscelin, William of Champeaux, and Anselm of Laon (not to be confused with Anselm of Canterbury, inventor of the ontological argument).

It would be putting it mildly to say that Abelard does not emphasize his intellectual debt to these figures. To the contrary, he portrays William of Champeaux and Anselm of Laon as jealous and incompetent. He takes evident relish in explaining how he demolished William's theory of universals not once, but twice (5), and says that Anselm's reputation was "owed more to long practice than to intelligence or memory," adding the mocking comment that his visitors left him more confused than before they had arrived (7). (To be fair, that was also true of Socrates.) The case of Roscelin is more complicated. Abelard subjects him to no similar character assassination in the *Story of Calamities*, and we know from other sources that Abelard was influenced by Roscelin's approach to logic. Modern-day scholars have called this approach "vocalism," alluding to Roscelin's insistence that dialectic deals with words and not things. With this, Roscelin paved the way for Abelard's nominalism.

Roscelin's vocalism was not offered as a solution to the problem of universals, but as the key to interpreting the works of logic that were being studied with such intensity at this time. For Roscelin, Porphyry's *Introduction* and Aristotle's *Categories* were about words, not things. This reading of the texts was anticipated already in antiquity, when it was suggested as a way of defusing potential conflict between Plato and Aristotle. If Aristotle was only talking about words in his logical writings, not making any claims about things, then it was no problem that he acknowledged only everyday physical objects as "substances" and made no mention of the transcendent objects recognized in Platonism.[5] After all, our words refer in the first instance to physical things, not to gods, immaterial souls, or forms.

Still, even if Roscelin was not espousing nominalism, his proposal could naturally lead to a position like Abelard's. Universal species and genera play a major role in the logical treatises of Porphyry and Aristotle. So if those treatises really are only about words and not things, it stands to reason that species and genera are nothing but words, as Abelard claimed. Despite Roscelin's importance in helping to shape Abelard's understanding of dialectic, Abelard turned against him as well, heavily criticizing Roscelin's teaching of the Trinity. Roscelin returned the favor in a surviving letter that excoriates Abelard's treatment of Heloise: "you taught her not to argue but to fornicate." He notes with satisfaction that by arranging for Abelard to be castrated, God justly "deprived you of that part by which you had sinned."[6]

Abelard's own account makes it clear that he was a proud, even arrogant man, and one who remained fiercely concerned with his reputation even as he was later writing down his life story. He claims that when he was castrated, his loss of face bothered him more than the loss of other parts of his anatomy (17). Though this side of his personality is not particularly attractive, Abelard's self-esteem was well founded. His works represent the high point of the study of dialectic in the early medieval period, and not just because of his innovative nominalist account of universals. Another major contribution was his account of propositions. Indeed, it would be fair to say that Abelard actually *discovered* the idea of a proposition, more or less as it is used in philosophy today.[7]

Take a common, everyday sentence like "A giraffe is in the kitchen cooking dinner." When I say this, I am making an assertion, and there is something I am asserting, namely that there is indeed a giraffe in the kitchen, cooking dinner. Abelard calls this the proposition's *dictum*, meaning "that which is said." He compares the relationship between the proposition and the *dictum* to that between a name and the thing that it names. Nowadays philosophers would call the *dictum* the proposition's "content." Now, remember Roscelin's and Abelard's point that differences at the level of words do not need to imply differences at the level of things. With this in mind, Abelard points out that the same content can be expressed in many different ways. If I say "The giraffe *cooks* dinner" or "The giraffe *is cooking* dinner," there is no difference in content, just a difference in expression. The same goes for tense, as we saw in the last chapter: if I tomorrow say "The giraffe *was* cooking dinner," that assertion will refer to exactly the same thing as my saying today "The giraffe *is* cooking dinner." It goes for grammatical mood, too, for example, if I said "The giraffe *should be* cooking dinner" instead of "The giraffe *is* cooking dinner."

Abelard makes another leap forward when it comes to the question of negating a proposition. For Boethius, the negation of the proposition "A giraffe is in the kitchen cooking dinner" would be "A giraffe is *not* in the kitchen cooking dinner." Which looks reasonable enough, and not just because giraffes are notoriously bad cooks. But it has a disadvantage. In stating this denial I seem to be saying something about a certain giraffe, namely that she is not cooking dinner. But what if I wanted to deny the proposition without talking about any giraffe at all? Abelard gives us the tools to do so, by saying that there are in fact two ways to negate a proposition. In addition to saying "A giraffe is *not* in the kitchen cooking dinner," I could say "It is *not the case that* a giraffe is in the kitchen cooking dinner." In the latter case, I am not implying that there is a giraffe who might be getting dinner ready if she weren't so lazy. Abelard calls the first kind of negation "separative," because it just denies that a predicate is connected to a subject. The second kind is called "destructive," because what is being denied is the whole proposition rather than the attachment of the predicate to the subject.

If not for his encounter with Heloise, Abelard might have continued to focus mostly on these sorts of logical issues, which dominated during his early career. Things changed once he became a monk and devoted himself to his new pastoral duties and to theological issues. The religious life may have been thrust upon him, but he made it his own. In a monastic setting Abelard was still able to teach and engage in intellectual disputation, much as he had done before. Heloise, by contrast, lamented piteously even as she took the habit, and never really reconciled herself to her new narrow and cloistered life (18). It was an ironic fate, in that Heloise had earlier disguised herself as a nun to get away from her overbearing uncle. Apparently, it was this that provoked the uncle into having Abelard attacked and mutilated, because he was under the impression that Abelard was forsaking her.

Once she really was a nun, Heloise was in a sense still in disguise, living a life of chastity but still consumed with her old desires. She tells Abelard so in letters she wrote to him in a correspondence provoked by her reading of his *Story of Calamities.* Abelard's message in that work was that the misfortunes that befell him were sent by God, to punish his lust and steer him towards a more righteous path. Heloise was having none of this. In her letters, she points out that she and Abelard were actually separated and thus chaste when disaster struck (66). In the aftermath of that disaster, Heloise has continued to be chaste in body, but not in mind. She admits that she is not able to repent sincerely, as Abelard was apparently able to do (68–9). In her first letter responding to Abelard's account of their story, we find the following, stunningly forthright passage: "If Augustus, emperor of the whole world, thought fit to honor me with marriage and conferred all the earth on me to possess for ever, it would be dearer and more honorable to me to be called not his empress but your whore" (51).

To get the full sense of what that quotation tells us about Heloise, we need to notice that it turns on a pun: the Latin word for "empress" is *imperatrix*, while the word for "whore" is *meretrix*.[8] This was a woman who could call on classical learning and perform rhetorical tricks even in the midst of impassioned lament. The same is clear from Abelard's presentation of Heloise in the *Story of Calamities*. At first, he writes about her as if she was simply an instrument of temptation, sent by God to bring about Abelard's well-deserved downfall. But he goes on to repeat the arguments she made at the time, against the idea of marrying in secret to mollify her uncle (13–14). It was a bad idea on practical grounds, for one thing. It would not make the uncle happy, and would tarnish Abelard's name (she was right on both counts, of course). Heloise also gave more principled reasons, quoting classical objections to marriage as inimical to the scholarly life: Seneca, for instance, cautioning that philosophy is a serious and all-consuming activity, which allows no room for family entanglements.

Heloise's honest self-appraisal, her refusal to renounce the value of the love she shared with Abelard, and her literary taste make her an intriguing and sympathetic historical character, and also allowed her to play a role in shaping Abelard's intellectual career. Her broad reading in classical literature, including authors like Seneca, seems to have rubbed off on Abelard.[9] Some scholars also give her a role in the development of Abelard's revolutionary approach to ethics; we'll test this hypothesis in the next chapter. Furthermore, after taking up residence at the Paraclete with her fellow nuns, Heloise requested pastoral guidance from Abelard. He composed hymns at her request, sent her letters offering rules for the sisters' conduct,[10] and answered a set of detailed questions she posed to him concerning difficulties of scriptural interpretation. Constant Mews, who has written extensively about their relationship, has commented that these questions are so insightfully posed that it's clear Heloise could have answered them herself.[11] Mews also suspects her to be the author of a poem mocking the idea that the liberal arts are an inappropriate activity for women.[12]

The liberal arts had brought the couple together, but once they entered upon their new monastic lives, both Abelard and Heloise took up the more religious disciplines of theology and biblical exegesis. Heloise was a devoted enough student of the Bible that she learned some Hebrew in addition to her Greek and Latin—a rare attainment for anyone at this time, let alone for a female scholar. The questions on Scripture she sent to Abelard represent this part of her intellectual life. As for Abelard, he is often seen as a champion of dialectic and as a devotee of the pagan philosophers, and he was indeed both of these. Yet he devoted much of his life to theological problems. Abelard's characteristic self-confidence convinced him that he could outdo scholars with long training in Church doctrine and exegesis. In a typically self-congratulatory anecdote, he relates how, as a younger man who was still a complete neophyte in the field of scriptural exegesis, he took up an obscure biblical passage and produced such marvelously insightful commentary on it that students flocked to him (7–8).

Yet Abelard did pay heed to the authoritative tradition. When his theological proposals met with condemnation and he was forced to burn his writings on the subject, he responded by changing his method instead of his mind, seeking support for his views in the church fathers. One product of this renewed interest in the tradition was his treatise *Sic et non*, which one might loosely, if verbosely, render as *On the One Hand and on the Other Hand*. The book consists of textual quotations, mostly from patristic authorities, which espouse contradictory views on a variety of questions. This may sound like an irreverent, even subversive project, reminiscent of the ancient skeptics' practice of piling up arguments on both sides of a philosophical debate in order to induce suspension of judgment. But for Abelard the compilation of disagreements was just a preliminary step towards resolving those disagreements, by showing them to be merely apparent. In another example of his sensitivity to the way that language can mislead, he cautioned against taking patristic or scriptural texts at face value.[13]

The same moral is taught by another of his triumphant anecdotes, which pits him directly against his enemy Anselm of Laon. The story goes that Anselm was outraged at a supposed heresy uttered by Abelard (21–2). Abelard said he could explain his view, but Anselm demanded that he offer authoritative support and not try to confuse the issue with rational argumentation. In response Abelard immediately, and no doubt gleefully, produced a quotation from Augustine, which confirmed his own view verbatim. Flustered, Anselm said weakly that the passage in Augustine needed to be treated with care, and that despite appearances it did not confirm Abelard's view. To which Abelard triumphantly replied that "this was irrelevant at the moment as he was looking only for words, not interpretation." You can see why Anselm of Laon was bound to despise him, and why Heloise was bound to love him.

11

IT'S THE THOUGHT THAT COUNTS
ABELARD'S ETHICS

I was recently at a gathering of historians of medieval philosophy—yes, that's the kind of jet-set, exciting life I lead—at which someone remarked that Peter Abelard was in fact not a medieval philosopher, but a modern philosopher who time-traveled to the medieval age. Indeed, when you read Abelard, you notice how easily he would fit into a modern-day department of analytic philosophers. All the traits are there: the sardonic tone, the confidence in his own sharpness of mind, the bold and original theoretical claims, and the relentless defense of those claims by anticipating and undercutting all possible objections. Like modern-day philosophers, Abelard loved to work with examples, the more vivid and thought-provoking, the better. Here are just a few, drawn from his writings on ethics. Two men want to build a house to serve the poor, but only one of them is able to do so. A servant is pursued by a lord who has lost his mind, and is forced to kill him in self-defense, even though the servant's act of insubordination will certainly bring terrible consequences. A monk is trapped in a bed with a group of affectionate women, and cannot escape sexual pleasure as a result. A poor woman smothers her own baby by rolling over on him in the night. Or, if those examples aren't eyebrow-raising enough for you, what about the men who were adamantly convinced that it was morally right for them to execute Jesus Christ?

Just as the story of Abelard and Heloise needed no introduction, so Abelard's use of examples is hard to improve upon, and I won't be replacing them with my own. In fact, I'm even more tempted than usual to tell you to put down this book and go read Abelard instead. The work I especially recommend is called the *Ethics*, or alternatively *Know Thyself* (*Scito te ipsum*),[1] and it makes use of all the examples I just mentioned. Let's start with the case of sponsoring a house to shelter the poor. I think we can all agree that this is a good thing to do. But what exactly does the goodness consist in, and where is it to be located? The answer seems obvious: the building of a poorhouse is a good thing, which is why we praise the sponsor who arranges for the house to be built. The same goes for sinful actions. If someone commits adultery, we blame him for doing so, because engaging in adultery is wrong. Apparently, then, it is *actions* that are right and wrong. So it is by performing actions that people are good or bad, righteous or sinful, praiseworthy or blameworthy.

Abelard denies this.[2] He asks us to imagine not one, but two people who want to sponsor a poorhouse (*Ethics* §97–8). Abelard doesn't give them names, so let's just call them Groucho and Harpo. They are equal in their moral zeal, their sympathy for the plight of the poor, and their desire to do something to help the indigent. Both of them decide to have a poorhouse built, but with differing results. In Groucho's case, everything runs smoothly, but poor Harpo is robbed by a thief before he can donate the money. Now Abelard asks us: do we really give Groucho more credit, morally speaking, than Harpo? The only reason Groucho has the house built and Harpo does not is that Groucho can do so, and Harpo cannot. But this seems to be a matter of luck, not of moral character.

This shows that the action, in this case sponsoring the poorhouse, cannot really be the thing we care about when we are considering right and wrong. Abelard has a battery of other examples to prove the same point. Suppose that Chico and Zeppo are judges, who both condemn men to be executed (§58). The two condemned men are guilty and deserve to be put to death, so in both cases the judgments can be considered just. However, in passing down his sentence Chico is motivated simply by the desire to make the right decision, whereas Zeppo harbors a secret vendetta against the accused, and would have sentenced him to death no matter what. Even though our two judges performed exactly the same action, it seems that Chico has done right, whereas Zeppo has done wrong. Again, we see that actions in themselves are not morally decisive. Abelard also uses the more theologically loaded example of handing over Jesus Christ to be crucified (§57). This is an action that was performed by God the Father, who allowed His Son to be sacrificed, and also by Judas, who was betraying Christ. But obviously we don't make the same moral judgment concerning God that we do in the case of Judas.

Actions by themselves, then, are neither good nor bad. So we need to look somewhere else to find right and wrong. An obvious place would be the desires and motivations that bring people to perform their actions. Think of the examples we've already considered. The reason we admire both Groucho and Harpo, it seems, is that both have the right sort of desire, namely to help the poor. It's just that, now being poor himself, Harpo can't fulfill this desire, whereas Groucho can. Likewise the reason we admire Chico the judge, but not Zeppo, is that Chico is genuinely trying to pass down the right verdict, whereas Zeppo is motivated by revenge. Again, Christians admire God the Father, but curse Judas, because they believe God gave His Son for the sake of redeeming mankind, whereas Judas was motivated by greed and resentment.

Plausible though this may seem at first blush, it is problematic to say that motives and desires are the proper objects of moral judgment. After all, can you really be blamed for having wicked desires, the sort of motivations that Abelard calls a "bad will"? Perhaps you are powerfully tempted by opportunities to overeat, betray your friends, and cast aspersions on the Marx Brothers. But we wouldn't and shouldn't judge you harshly just for having these desires, so long as you manage to resist them. In fact, Abelard goes so far as to say that it is *more* admirable to avoid sin when temptation is powerful. It's easy to avoid wrongdoing when you have no urge to do wrong, the difficult thing is resisting sins you would very much like to commit. Hence we admire those who struggle against their own bad wills and prevail more than we admire those who have no bad will in the first place (§22). Indeed, you might wonder whether someone who is lucky enough to have a good will is admirable at all. If you are simply the sort of person who gets a kick out of helping old ladies across the street and volunteering for charities, and never feels the compunction to do anything wrong, then are you morally outstanding or just fortunate?

Abelard is putting his finger on a deep philosophical puzzle here, one that is often framed in terms of a contrast between Aristotle and Immanuel Kant. Aristotle was convinced that virtuous people take pleasure in doing virtuous things and have a strong desire to do so, in part because they have the habit of acting well, and people enjoy whatever is customary for them. Kant instead is going to insist that people should act out of moral duty if their actions are to count as morally good. If they happen to enjoy virtue, that's fine, but it has nothing to do with morality. Abelard is an important forerunner of Kant in this controversy. In fact he seems to be suggesting an even more radical view than Kant's, namely that you *must* have bad desires and resist them if you are to be rightly congratulated for being virtuous. As Abelard puts it, people who are born with a tendency towards sinful lusts have been given "material for a fight, so that victorious over themselves through the virtue of moderation they might obtain a crown" (§5). Though he doesn't quite come out and say so, it seems that for him, the most admirable people would be the ones who have the worst desires, while managing to prevail in the struggle against those desires.[3]

While this aspect of Abelard's moral theory is, to say the least, open to dispute, he has an almost irresistible argument against the idea that desires and motivations make all the difference between good and bad. This is that people sometimes do wrong while acting *against* their desires (§22). As usual he offers a vivid example.

This is the case of the servant who kills his feudal lord in self-defense (§11–17). It's something he certainly would not want to do, given the reprisals that will certainly be meted out to any medieval servant who kills his lord; but he does it nonetheless, because if he doesn't, his lord is going to murder him instead. Of course, usually when people sin, they are acting on a sinful desire, but this example shows that that can't always be the case. Perhaps, then, we could say something slightly different, namely that the sin consists in *enjoying* a wrongful action. The servant example is unusual, in that his deed is committed reluctantly. Usually, though, people take pleasure in wicked behavior, and it might be this reveling in sin that marks people as sinful. But yet again, Abelard argues that this cannot be right. It's here that he gives his example of a man who has taken a sincere vow of chastity, but who is chained down and forced to enjoy sex with women (§42). (As we know from *Monty Python and the Holy Grail*, this is the sort of thing that happened from time to time in the Middle Ages.) Again, it's hard to argue against Abelard's point once he has given you the example. Clearly there is a difference between sinning and taking enjoyment in sinning (§47).

So now we seem to be stuck. If morality isn't a matter of which action you perform, nor a matter of what motivations lead you to act the way you do, nor a matter of taking pleasure in wrongdoing, then where do the wickedness of sin and righteousness of virtue reside? Abelard's answer is that they lie in *consenting* to a desire, in other words, in forming an intention to act in a certain way. Consider again the man who is chained down and forced to abandon his chastity. (Don't worry or, for that matter, get your hopes up; this won't be getting graphic.) The reason he is not to be condemned for the sinful activity that ensues or for the pleasure he gets out of it, is that he has not consented to what is happening—if he were released from his chains, he would immediately flee from this temptation. His case is entirely different, then, from that of someone who intentionally breaks a vow of chastity.

In light of this observation, we can now see that there are four stages involved in any action, whether sinful, virtuous, or morally neutral. First, we have a desire or "will" that motivates us to perform the action. We do not necessarily have any control over whether or not we have a certain desire; we may simply find that we have it. What we *can* control is whether or not we "consent" to a desire, as opposed to resisting it. Giving consent, then, is a second stage, which consists in forming an intention to act on the desire in question. Then, the action itself is a further, third stage. Just as the desire does not guarantee consent, so consent to the desire does not guarantee acting on it. Something might prevent the action from occurring, as when Harpo's poverty stops him from performing an act of charity. Fourth and finally, if one does succeed in performing the action, there will come the results of acting, which could include taking pleasure in sin. Abelard's theory, then, amounts to the claim that morality has to do only with the second stage of consent. Good and bad lie with the intentions we form, not the desires we have, the actions we perform, or the pleasure we take in them.

Like any interesting philosophical claim, Abelard's idea not only has some good arguments behind it but also some difficult objections to face.[4] The most obvious one, perhaps, is this: what makes good intentions good, and bad ones bad? The natural thing to say would be that an intention is good if it intends a good action, and bad if it intends a bad action. But Abelard is telling us that all actions are in themselves morally neutral. So it can't be, for instance, the sinfulness of committing adultery that makes it wrong to *intend* to commit adultery. Rather, it must be the other way around. Whereas Abelard's account so far has, like his writing style, been one that would not be out of place in contemporary philosophy, his solution to this problem is one that strikes a more medieval note. He thinks that sinful intentions are the ones that show "contempt for God" (§113) by consenting to desires that God wants us to resist. Conversely, good intentions are the ones that would please God (§230), though we don't hear much about these, because Abelard's *Ethics* breaks off just after the start of the second book, which was planned to cover goodness.

This does not mean, though, that Abelard is telling us that morality is just a matter of following God's commands, like certain "voluntarist" thinkers we'll be meeting later in this book. Though he doesn't say much about this issue, he seems to think that natural reason is capable of discerning good from bad, that is, of telling which desires ought to receive our consent. So he is convinced that pagans, especially pagan philosophers, were capable of virtue. And historically speaking, Abelard is right to claim common ground with non-Christian thinkers. His ethical theory is similar to that of the Stoics. They also thought that human action involves giving consent to a motivating "impression" that one ought to do something. Abelard is especially close to Roman Stoics like Epictetus, who likewise argued that the morally decisive thing is the exercise of one's power of choice, or *prohairesis*.[5] However, Epictetus argued for this by pointing to the fact that choice alone is completely under our power. Abelard, by contrast, reaches the same conclusion by showing that we do not really blame or praise people for their desires or even for the actions they perform, but for the fact that they consented to do such and such an action.

But if this is so, how do we explain the fact that we typically reward and punish people for their actions, and hardly ever because of their intentions? We send people to jail for murder, but don't imprison people for merely forming the intention to kill. If a would-be murderer doesn't even get to the stage of attempting the murder, then he is guilty of no crime at all. This seems to show that it is actually the action we care about after all. Of course, Abelard meets this objection with an example. We are to imagine a poverty-stricken woman who takes her child into her bed to keep him warm, and tragically smothers him in her sleep. Here the desire and the intention to kill the baby are very much absent; yet she might be told by a priest to do penance for what has happened (§79). Why is this? For purely pragmatic reasons, says Abelard. We want to discourage other women from doing the same thing, so we make a lesson of the woman even though she is morally innocent.

This is a good answer, I think, and it can be generalized. The reason we spend so much time evaluating, punishing, and praising *actions* is just that they are our only guides to finding out what intentions people had, even if they may be imperfect guides. Actions are public and observable, whereas intentions are not, so we must look to the things people do to find out what they chose to do. But strictly speaking, we judge them on their choices, not on their actions as such. It's also worth emphasizing that, even if actions are *in themselves* morally neutral on Abelard's theory, that doesn't mean that they are morally neutral in every respect. Rather, they become good or bad precisely by stemming from good or bad intentions.[6]

But the road to hell is, famously, paved with good intentions. What if someone does something truly appalling while intending to carry out God's will? In that sort of case, wouldn't we condemn the appalling action despite the fact that the person was doing their best to act well? Abelard discusses this problem too. In a passage that he must have known would shock his readers, he comments that those who crucified Christ were acting in ignorance, and doing what they thought was right. This, he thinks, is why Christ said "Forgive them, for they know not what they do" (§120–3, quoting Luke 23:34). Abelard even remarks that they would have been more blameworthy if they had *failed* to persecute Christ, given that they thought it was morally right to do so, because it is always a sin to fail to do what you think you ought to do (§131). Yet he still wants to say that what they did was somehow wrong. This makes most sense if we take Abelard to be thinking that intentions have to tick two boxes in order to be good. Firstly, the person involved must believe that what they are intending is right; secondly, the intention must in fact actually be right, that is, actually be what God would want (§109). Thus, his advice for those who would avoid sin is to do whatever you sincerely believe is right. In order to do genuine good, though, your belief will need to be correct.

Let's close by considering whether all this is really as pioneering as I've suggested. Was Abelard a kind of conceptual time-traveler? Just by itself, his emphasis on intention fits rather well into the landscape of twelfth-century moral theory. In particular, Abelard's enemy Anselm of Laon had already said that merely forming an intention to sin is itself sinful.[7] But Anselm also assumed that the subsequent action is sinful. What was unique, and genuinely radical, about Abelard was that he denied this, and insisted on the moral neutrality of actions in themselves. Some scholars have traced this development to the influence of Heloise, or seen it as a view held in common by the two lovers.[8] In one of her letters to Abelard, she looks back upon their earlier dalliance and says that she is both wholly guilty and wholly innocent. For, sinful though her actions were, they were done out of sincere love. At which point she adds, "it is not the doing of the thing (*rei effectus*) but the condition of the doer (*efficientis affectus*) which makes the crime, and justice should weigh not what was done but the spirit in which it is done" (notice again her use of Latin wordplay).[9]

But this does not really show agreement between Heloise and Abelard.[10] In fact thinking that it does runs the risk of underestimating the sophistication and interest of Heloise's letter. She sees her former self as illustrating the paradox that someone can do wrong precisely because of a motivation that is itself good, namely love. Elsewhere in her letters, she uses her current situation to illustrate the flip side of the same paradox: in her soul, she still yearns for Abelard, even though her outward comportment is chaste. Where Abelard insisted that good actions become good because of their good intentions, Heloise insisted that an innocent soul is compatible with exterior sin, while a tormented soul may lead an outwardly blameless life. We should not fall into the trap of thinking that Heloise's interest as a moral thinker is exhausted by the impact she may have had on Abelard. Medieval women could have minds of their own, and Heloise certainly did.

12

LEARN EVERYTHING THE VICTORINES

R eligion put the history into the history of philosophy. The pagans of antiquity by and large saw history as irrelevant to a philosophical understanding of the world. Whether you were a Platonist who saw physical things as mere images of eternal Forms, an Aristotelian who believed that the celestial bodies are moved everlastingly by a divine intellect, or an Epicurean who thought that all things result from random atomic interactions, you were offering an account of the universe's permanent state. No particular historical event figured importantly in any of these worldviews. But for Jews, Christians, and Muslims, history was central. All three faiths accepted the reality of prophecy, with the figures of Moses and Muhammad playing an especially crucial role for Jews and Muslims, respectively. The divine had manifested in the created world at certain times and places. Diehard Aristotelian philosophers who were adherents of Judaism and Islam were still able to preserve a "the more things change, the more they stay the same" attitude. They could, and did, explain prophecy as a naturally occurring interaction between immaterial principles and unusually gifted humans. The possibility of such interaction is always present and its mechanism is rationally comprehensible. It is just that it only occurs when circumstances are especially favorable.

But for medieval Christians this sort of compromise was not really available. For them the universe was a stage upon which is played the drama of humankind's fall and redemption. Already in antiquity, Christian thinkers historicized philosophical doctrines in order to fit them into this theological picture. The Greek church father Origen is a perfect example.[1] He adapted Platonism into a cosmic morality tale in which souls err and fall away from God, later returning to Him through the guidance of Christ. For the medievals, a more influential reimagining of this fall and rise was that of Augustine. He understood the universe and its relation to God in thoroughly historical terms, with the key events being the original sin of the first humans and the Incarnation and sacrifice of the Son of God. The philosophical implications were far-reaching. For medieval Christian thinkers God intervenes in, and even enters into, the world in a way that is not necessary but contingent on His will. History teaches us when and how this has occurred, so these thinkers were bound to take history very seriously.

No medieval thinker took it more seriously than Hugh of Saint Victor. For him the correct understanding of history was foundational for all knowledge, or at least all knowledge worth having.[2] It was the most basic of three approaches he described for interpreting Scripture. When taking up the Bible, one must first understand it as what we would call a "literal" record of real events. This is what Hugh calls an "historical" interpretation. One should not stop there, though. A second approach discerns a further symbolic meaning behind historical events, a type of exegesis Hugh calls "allegorical." Finally, there is what he calls "tropological" interpretation, which means taking an ethical message from the text. Hugh applies all three kinds of approach to the same scriptural material, for instance in a treatise he wrote on Noah's Ark.

On the one hand, the ark was a real boat. Hugh describes it in bewildering detail, to the point that it seems clear he was envisioning an intricate diagram, even though no such diagram is found in the existing manuscripts of his treatise. He dwells on descriptions found in the Bible, for instance concerning the dimensions of the boat, and adds details of his own, like little side compartments to allow seals and otters to swim into the sea and then return to the ark. The ark's structure is then mined for its symbolic significance, as when Hugh says that the ark had two exits, a door and a window, which represent the soul's ability to engage in practical action or to look upwards in contemplation.[3] Finally, the story of the ark teaches us a moral lesson: the flood waters that covered the earth represent the worldly desires that deluge the soul, and the ark a place we build within ourselves, safe from these desires.

Hugh produced a number of other exegetical, contemplative, and educational works, the best known of which is his *Didascalicon*, which means something like "educational handbook." Much-copied and much-read in the Middle Ages, it provides an overview of secular and religious learning aimed at budding scholars.[4] This was Hugh's natural audience, because he was head of the school at the Abbey of Saint Victor. In no small part thanks to Hugh, this institution became one of the most important intellectual centers of the entire Middle Ages. Historians even have a collective name for the scholars who taught and studied there, the "Victorines." The abbey was founded in 1108 by none other than William of Champeaux, whose realist theory of universals was twice refuted by Peter Abelard. Perhaps in reaction to his defeat at the hands of Abelard, William and some colleagues retired to an empty hermitage dedicated to Saint Victor, which was near Paris on the River Seine.

This might sound like a simple retreat, in every sense of the word. But in founding the abbey William of Champeaux was joining a reform movement that reshaped the Church in the twelfth century. In the previous century, Peter Damian had already urged that stricter discipline should become the norm in monastic settings. And despite Abelard's unforgiving portrayal of him, William was a skilled dialectician who could blend expertise in the secular arts with the sort of spiritual reform pioneered by Damian. That blend would become the trademark of the Abbey of Saint Victor. It was both a place to engage in austere contemplation and a school that produced highly trained scholars who travelled throughout Europe, spreading the reformist practices and knowledge they had acquired on the banks of the Seine.

The list of scholars who were associated with Saint Victor is effectively a roll call of the major intellectuals of the time. Hugh's students Andrew and Richard of Saint Victor took on different aspects of their master's legacy, Andrew achieving renown as a scriptural interpreter, Richard as a contemplative or mystical author.[5] Peter Lombard, author of the most influential theological synthesis of the century, also studied under Hugh (see Chapter 18). Bernard of Clairvaux had friendly relations with the Victorines, and Thomas Becket—of "will no one rid me of this trouble-some priest?" fame—was friends with Achard, the second man to serve as abbot at Saint Victor. Among all these leading lights, Hugh shined most brightly. This at least was the opinion of the thirteenth-century theologian Bonaventure, who commented on his predecessors: "Anselm [of Canterbury] excels in reasoning, Bernard [of Clairvaux] in preaching, Richard [of Saint Victor] in contemplating, but Hugh in all three."[6]

Hugh's most famous remark befits this versatility, and his attention to the educational needs of the students at the abbey. He wrote in his *Didascalicon*: "learn everything; you will see afterwards that nothing is superfluous" (§VI.3). That makes Hugh sound like the original adherent of philosophy "without any gaps." Yet the quotation needs to be understood within its original context, namely a discussion of the things a student needs to know in order to interpret Scripture. Hugh was under no illusions about the difficulty and unwelcoming nature of this task. He compared the works of the philosophers to a freshly painted wall whose inviting color conceals the "clay of error" beneath, whereas the Scriptures are more like a honey-comb, seemingly dry, yet sweet once one delves into them (§IV.1; cf. §V.2, VI.3).[7] The rigorous and comprehensive course of study described in the *Didascalicon* is designed to prepare students to do just that. Expertise in geometry, for instance, comes in handy when analyzing the dimensions of the ark.[8] For this same reason, Hugh is also quick to criticize those who pursue knowledge uselessly. He complains that in his day, there are "many who study but few who are wise" (§III.3). The targets of his lament are those who engage in learning for its own sake, rather than for the sake of understanding God and the Bible.

It is easy to dismiss this attitude as typically medieval, and not in a good way. Speaking of the cultivation of the liberal arts in the Carolingian era, the great historian Edward Gibbon wrote that "the grammar and logic, the music and astronomy, of the times, were only cultivated as the handmaids of superstition."[9] Hugh might seem to be carrying forward that same approach in the twelfth century, even as men like Abelard were pursuing what may strike us as a more enlightened and rational form of philosophy. But just as we saw that the Carolingians were considerably more sophisticated than Gibbon's quote suggests, so Hugh's attitude towards secular learning rests on a nuanced understanding of humankind. As Platonists of various religious persuasions had been teaching for centuries, we are divided between two natures, immaterial souls attached to physical bodies. Philosophy must address itself to both aspects. For Hugh our incorporeal aspect is served by theoretical philosophy, which culminates in contemplation and pure understanding, whereas practical philosophy teaches us how to engage with the bodily realm and to attain virtue (§I.5, I.7, II.1, V.6).

This twofold project was reflected in the life that Hugh and his colleagues lived at Saint Victor, with their dual commitment to scholarship and ascetic discipline. When William of Champeaux was debating the merits of founding the abbey in the first place, a colleague named Hildebert encouraged him by saying that William's previous attainments as a dialectician had made him only "half a philosopher." What was missing was strict ethical discipline.[10] Hugh provided a theoretical framework for this approach to philosophy. The reason that his *Didascalicon* became the medieval equivalent of a bestseller was that it provided a concise and clear encapsulation of the Victorine program of study. His overview of the secular sciences is fairly traditional, built around the seven liberal arts already familiar to us from the Carolingian period. He does, however, innovate by adding a list of seven so-called "mechanical" arts like fabric-making, hunting, and medicine (§II.20).

A less obvious, but deeper novelty is Hugh's interest in the very process of learning. The first stage involves wide reading and, above all, memorization (*memoria*) of what one has read. Nowadays, memorization seems to have gone out of fashion as a learning method. What's the point of having lots of information in your head when you can just look things up on the Internet? Hugh can tell you what the point is. By memorizing, we internalize what we have read, beginning to reshape the soul itself by conforming it to that which we seek to know.[11] Hugh keeps this in mind throughout his works. From the schematic presentation of the sciences in the *Didascalicon* to the richly symbolic correspondences detailed in his discussion of Noah's Ark, he is constantly trying to help his readers remember what they are reading.

Next, the educational process continues to another stage, which Hugh calls *meditatio*. An obvious translation here would be "meditation"; a better one might be "rumination." Hugh describes it as a kind of undirected procedure of pondering over what one has read and memorized (III.10). He seems to see it almost as a kind of reward for the hard work one has put into reading and memorization, speaking of the delight of the ruminative process. Finally, after *memoria* and *meditatio* comes *moralia*, which means putting one's insights into practice ethically. In another of Hugh's beloved parallels, and in this case a fairly plausible one, the three stages of learning are said to correspond to his three approaches to Scripture. History is analogous to *memoria*, the more open-ended search for allegorical interpretation is analogous to *meditatio*, and the "tropological" discovery of ethical lessons in Scripture is of course analogous to *moralia*.[12]

Hugh compares the learning process to the minting of a coin, with the malleable soul of the learner taking on the likeness of whatever it knows. It is in this sense that the mind is said to "be all things" (§I.1). There is a nice wordplay here, which works in both English and Latin. Through learning, the soul is "re-formed," just as monastic culture was being "reformed" through the efforts of the Victorines and others. For Hugh, these two sorts of reformation are individual and social enactments of the cosmic redemption that is at the heart of Christian theology. Here we come back to the Augustinian understanding of history, with its central moments of fall and redemption. When we achieve understanding and virtue, we are acquiring something that we lacked at birth. But we are also recovering something that was lost by human nature through sin. In fact, we have the chance to attain an even higher degree of perfection than the first humans ever had. Adam and Eve were created with a natural knowledge that we lack, but they never achieved the crowning perfection that comes through obedience to God.[13]

Hugh's educational theory presupposes this theological background, and also a metaphysical framework that is assumed throughout the *Didascalicon*. Like Eriugena, Hugh sees created things as images of paradigmatic Forms, called "primordial causes." These causes are like the plan that a skilled craftsman makes in his mind before producing something. Hence they are ideas within the Wisdom of God, which is identified with the second person of the Trinity (§I.1, II.1).[14] The Christian trappings of the view are not merely incidental. If the paradigms were not identical with the divine Son, Hugh could not equate growth in understanding with the path towards redemption. In fact, given his warning that knowledge is "useless" if it does not bring us closer to God, Hugh can really only justify the attempt to achieve understanding of paradigmatic Forms by associating those Forms with divinity. Still, the metaphysical picture itself is fundamentally Platonist. Plotinus and like-minded pagans would readily have agreed that philosophy is nothing more or less than, as Hugh puts it, "the pursuit of...that wisdom which is the sole primordial idea or pattern of things" (§I.4).

The ancient Platonists had been divided when it came to the question of using physical things to attain wisdom. Since we are trying to reach immaterial paradigms, the material world could seem to be at best a distraction. This seems to have been the view of Plotinus and his student Porphyry. But Porphyry's student Iamblichus, and later Neoplatonists like Proclus, held that pagan religious and magical practices could enable one to make contact with divinity through bodily things.[15] Probably none of them would appreciate the comparison, but Hugh of Saint Victor is in this respect more like Iamblichus and Proclus than like Plotinus and Porphyry. Where the Neoplatonists spoke of theurgy, Hugh speaks of "sacraments." In fact, he composed a major theological treatise entitled *On the Sacraments of the Christian Faith*.[16]

We normally associate this term with a very specific set of Christian ceremonial practices, such as marriage, ordination of priests, and, of course, the Eucharist. But Hugh uses the term more broadly, to refer to any physical thing that also has a symbolic meaning and bears the operation of divine grace.[17] If you want to see an example, just look around. Hugh considers the creation of the world itself to be a sacrament, an infusion of grace into the corporeal realm. Impressive though creation is, though, Hugh believes that the restoration of fallen nature is more difficult than creating nature in the first place. So it took God only six days to fashion the world, whereas the restoration of humankind took six ages. Yet again, there is a connection here to Hugh's understanding of history. Broadly understood, history is, quite simply, everything that has happened in the physical universe. A factual or "historical" understanding of the world is indispensable.

Still, we will never reach an understanding of nature's divine paradigms unless we also think allegorically. Hence Hugh remarks in the *Didascalicon* that things, as well as words, have meaning (§V.3). This is the occasion for another of Hugh's many slighting references to "the philosophers." With their expertise in dialectic, they remain at the level of words, which are mere representations of human concepts, whereas things that have actually existed in history are representations of divine ideas. Later medieval thinkers like Thomas Aquinas will justify philosophical inquiry by citing a famous biblical text, *Romans* 1:20: "the invisible things of him from the creation of the world are clearly seen, being understood by the things that are made." Hugh would agree to an extent, but is convinced that in our fallen state, no such inquiry can succeed on its own in bringing us to God.[18] Only the grace offered in the sacraments, and above all in the Incarnation, makes this possible. This is why he dismisses what one might call "merely philosophical," secular learning that makes no attempt to understand Scripture or to see history itself in allegorical terms.

It's fitting that someone as interested in history as Hugh was should have had a big impact upon it. It was William of Champeaux who had founded the abbey, and initiated the characteristically Victorine fusion of scholarship and spirituality. Yet Hugh was the real intellectual father of the Victorines who followed. Among his successors, Richard of Saint Victor particularly stands out. He originally came from Scotland, making him the first Scotsman to feature in this book series (and certainly not the last). As implied in that quote I mentioned from Bonaventure—Richard was the one who "excelled in contemplation"—he especially continued the allegorical and contemplative aspects of Hugh's legacy. Two of his most significant works allegorize parts of the Old Testament.[19] One is devoted to Jacob and his family, the other to an ark, not Noah's Ark but the Ark of the Covenant, the one that Indiana Jones was looking for.

Richard's treatise on the Ark of the Covenant lays out an entire theory of contemplation. Whereas Hugh speaks of this as a final stage in the mental trans-formation that brings us closer to God, for Richard contemplation itself comes in six different stages. These range from imaginative reflection on the beauty of the sensible world to the mystical attitude appropriate for things that are beyond human reason. It's common to say that this contemplative aspect of Victorine thought exemplifies a widespread feature of the twelfth century: "interiorization." It was a period when thinkers urged us to turn our gaze inward in search of divinity, and to reshape the inner self that we find there so that it reflects God's image more truly. We've just seen Hugh understanding Noah's Ark in this way. Abelard's idea that moral goodness lies in the soul's intentions, and not outward actions, is another example.

This observation is illuminating to a degree, but, like any historical generalization, should be qualified with a few caveats. For one thing, it was not really all that new. Rather, Hugh and Richard of Saint Victor were laying particular emphasis on long-standing contemplative themes in the Augustinian, monastic, and Platonist traditions. For another thing, these Victorine heroes of interiority also laid great emphasis on the beauty of nature. Contemplation can be directed outwards, as well as inwards. As we'll see in due course, other twelfth-century thinkers were even more deeply engaged in the study of nature. So this time of interiority was also a time for celebrating the exterior world as the visible manifestation of divine grace.

Finally, whatever "interiorization" we find with the Victorines was compatible with political engagement. Their monastic lifestyle echoed the so-called "Gregorian reform" led by Pope Gregory VII at the end of the eleventh century. The Victorines may have been great spiritualists, but they also traveled to other monasteries, taking on positions of leadership and trying to spread the reform movement. As the historian Giles Constable has written, this movement sought to "monasticize first the clergy, by imposing on them a standard of life previously reserved for monks, and then the entire world."[20]

So the Victorines were not just writers of the lost arks. They were morally and politically active as reformers and preachers. This is something they had in common with their powerful ally Bernard of Clairvaux. Actually, saying that Bernard of Clairvaux was merely "politically engaged" would be like saying that Indiana Jones had a fairly hands-on approach to archeology. Bernard was a central figure of the twelfth century, who not only pushed the reform agenda but also took a hand in Church politics and helped to launch the Second Crusade (unlike Indiana Jones, who, of course, was involved in the last crusade). In the history of philosophy, Bernard usually plays a more subsidiary role, featuring above all as the scourge of Peter Abelard. We have yet to delve into the nature of that dispute. Doing so will give us further opportunity to appreciate the Victorines and the subtle mind of Abelard, as we take up the most controversial topic of Christianity in the twelfth century, and most other centuries too, for that matter: the Trinity.

13

LIKE FATHER, LIKE SON DEBATING THE TRINITY

I don't know if you're familiar with Reese's Peanut Butter Cups. They were nearly invented in the nineteenth century by George Washington Carver, who is credited with the idea of peanut butter itself. Amazingly, he stopped there rather than taking the next natural step of coating a small puck of peanut butter in chocolate and wrapping the result in luridly orange plastic. If Dirk Gently is right that it takes a genius to render the previously non-existent obvious, in this case the genius in question was H. B. Reese, who devised the peanut butter cup in 1928. When I was young, they were marketed with commercials that are emblazoned upon my memory. At a cinema, a boy is eating a chocolate bar and a girl is enjoying peanut butter straight from the jar, as one does at the movies. Both jump at the horror movie playing onscreen, with the result that the chocolate lands in the peanut butter. The result? Surprisingly delicious! They turn out to be, as the 1970s tagline put it, "two tastes that taste great together."

Why I am bothering you with this? Because debates over the Trinity were the Reese's Peanut Butter Cup of medieval philosophy. Some have a taste for the rational inquiry of philosophy, others for the revelatory truth claims of religion. Many assume that the two don't mix, that they are like oil and vinegar. But they turn out to be more like chocolate and peanut butter: two tastes that taste great together. Antique Christians were convinced that they could find evidence for God's Trinitarian nature in the Bible. Augustine's *On the Trinity* devotes several books to the scriptural basis of the doctrine, which is, of course, central to Christian theology. But as Augustine goes on to show in his *On the Trinity*, the conceptual tools of philosophy can help us see how it is possible for one and the same substance to be three Persons.[1]

The core of the Trinitarian dogma is the claim that the three divine Persons differ from one another, while being the same God. But what does this mean? A first thought might be that each thing is the same as itself, and different from any other thing. This makes the Trinitarian doctrine look problematic. But further reflection will show that there are many ways of being the same or different. The Marx

Brothers were four things, so not the same as each other in every respect; yet they were the same in respect of being human. Really, the problem of universals is just the difficulty of how things are able to share this sort of "sameness." Then there is the problem of sameness over time. Am I the same as the boy who first watched those Reese's Peanut Butter Cup commercials? That boy was different in many ways: more hair, less interest in philosophy. Or what about a thing and its parts? Is a peanut butter cup the same as its peanut butter center plus its chocolate coating? It may seem so, but consider that if so, anything that loses a part would cease to be the same thing. Do I really make a peanut butter cup no longer the same thing by taking a bite out of it, or make myself no longer the same thing by trimming the little hair I still have?

Clearly, then, consideration of the Trinity can lead directly to fundamental issues in metaphysics. The same is true for epistemology. While Christians did invoke passages in the Bible to support the Trinitarian doctrine, they were also tempted to think that human reasoning can establish God's triune nature without any help from revelation. Anselm already made a case for this in his *Monologion*. In the twelfth century a number of thinkers went so far as to say that pagan philosophers had reached an understanding of God's Trinity even before the time of Christ. On the other hand, medieval thinkers frequently hasten to remind us that God lies beyond the grasp of reason. This might seem to apply especially to the mysterious, even paradoxical notion that He is somehow three despite being one, and even simple. The Trinity duly became a kind of litmus test for how far medievals thought that reason can take us in understanding God.

It was a test that Peter Abelard failed, according to Bernard of Clairvaux. When Bernard and his allies summoned Abelard to the city of Sens to face trial in the year 1141, the accusations concerned his teaching on the Trinity. Bernard wrote to the Pope about Abelard: "he is ready to give reasons for everything, even for those things which are above reason."[2] Bernard had been alerted to the offensive nature of Abelard's teaching by William of St. Thierry, who had compiled a list of his erroneous claims in theology. Abelard differentiated the divine Persons in terms of their distinctive properties, ascribing power especially to the Father, wisdom especially to the Son, and love especially to the Holy Spirit. William and Bernard took exception to the suggestion that the Persons were unequal in respect of power and wisdom. For Bernard, Abelard also placed too little emphasis on the role of grace in human redemption, seeming to suggest that Christ was merely an ethical example for us to follow. This goes well with Abelard's moral teaching, and his claim that virtue involves forming the right intentions, which lie wholly within our power. Unfortunately, at least in Bernard's opinion, it didn't go so well with

88

Christianity. Abelard was coming dangerously close to the Pelagian heresy by implying that humans can merit salvation without divine grace.[3]

Abelard refused to answer to his critics at Sens, instead appealing to the Pope, but Bernard prevailed when the Pope took his side. Abelard was excommunicated, confined to a monastery, and forced to burn his writings on theology with his own hands. Eventually Bernard and Abelard were reconciled and the Pope lifted the excommunication, but the damage was done. Abelard later recalled the episode as a humiliation worse in some respects than his earlier castration.[4] In the longer run, though, these events have done more harm to Bernard's reputation than to Abelard's. Historians of philosophy tend to see him as an anti-rationalist and pig-headed obscurantist, incapable of appreciating the subtlety of Abelard's superior mind. It doesn't help that Bernard evidently didn't bother to examine Abelard's works for himself, largely just following the accusations of William of St. Thierry. Worse still, Bernard was a repeat offender. He went on to make accusations against another of the leading philosophers of the era, Gilbert of Poitiers, and succeeded in getting Gilbert to recant some of his theological claims.

There's an important lesson here: if you want historians of philosophy to look kindly upon you, be kind to philosophers. But Bernard of Clairvaux was far more than an anti-philosopher. It's appropriate that his preaching played a role in the launching of the Second Crusade in 1146, because he was nothing if not a crusader. He was a leading member of the reformist Cistercian order, distinguished by their white clothing and strict observance. The name "Cistercian" comes from the Latin name of the city of Cîteaux, where Bernard arrived in 1112 to join a community that followed the Rule of St. Benedict. He became a critic of other orders and communities, such as the one at Cluny which was Abelard's first stop after his excommunication (he would spend the rest of his life there and at another Cluniac priory). The purpose of the austere Cistercian rule was, of course, to bring the monks closer to God. Bernard and his brethren were convinced that a rigorous, spiritual life could even provoke a direct vision of the divine, a mystical approach that contrasted sharply with the argument-based approach of the schoolmen.

Bernard's devotion to monastic spirituality, and his critique of Abelard and others for what he saw as vainglorious abuse of reason, did not mean that he was wholly opposed to the intellectual tools provided by the secular liberal arts. The historian G. R. Evans has written that Bernard was "not at the forefront of the work of the schools, but up-to-date nonetheless."[5] He had particularly warm relations with the Victorines, and himself wrote treatises of a rather "scholastic" nature, especially on the topic of free will. His criticism of Abelard grew out of opposition not to the use of reason as such, but to the unconstrained use of reason. By trying to go too far with his natural gifts, Abelard had strayed into errors. Bernard and William of St. Thierry worried that those errors might be passed on to other, simpler believers who did not have the tools to diagnose where Abelard had gone wrong.

Before we get too indignant on Abelard's behalf, we should also bear in mind that he attacked his own teacher Roscelin for, of all things, an erroneous teaching on the Trinity. Following the account of names he found in classical works on grammar, Roscelin assumed that if the divine Persons have three different names, they must be not one, but three "things." Abelard attacked this assumption, turning against Roscelin his own strategy of distinguishing the level of words from the level of things. The Persons cannot be different things, as Roscelin claimed. That would be to fall into the heresy of tritheism: a belief in three gods rather than one. Rather, Abelard argued, the Persons differ in respect of their properties, like the Father's power as opposed to the Son's wisdom. Hence the accusation Bernard leveled at Abelard that he failed to acknowledge the equality of the Persons.

But if God really is one, how can He have different properties from Himself? To deal with this question, Abelard developed a systematic account of how things are the same as, and different from, each other.[6] He wasn't the first to do this. Aristotle and his followers had already distinguished between various sorts of sameness and difference. The most obvious is being *numerically* the same. For instance you are numerically the same as yourself, so that if we are counting, we find that you are only one thing, whereas if we counted you and me we would have two things, not one. In other words, you and I are numerically distinct people, while being the same in other respects, as in form or in species, since we are both human. So far, so sensible. The problem is that in being a Trinity, God is in some sense not identical with Himself, despite being numerically one. That is, when we count how many Gods there are, we had better come up with the answer "only one." And yet God the Father is not wholly identical with God the Son.

Abelard points out, though, that it actually happens all the time that two things are numerically the same, yet somehow different. Imagine that you are holding a peanut butter cup, and somehow resisting the urge to pop it into your mouth. How many things would be in your hand? The answer, pretty clearly, is one. Yet we could differentiate (within this numerically one thing) between the peanut butter cup, on the one hand, and, on the other hand, the peanut butter and chocolate from which it is made. After all, I can say things about them that are not true of the peanut butter cup: the peanut butter and chocolate are the ingredients of the cup, whereas the cup is not an ingredient of the cup.

Unfortunately, God can't be exactly like a peanut butter cup, and not only because, being omnipresent, He wouldn't fit into the orange wrapper. It's also because, despite being three Persons, He is simple. He has no parts, nor can He be distinguished into matter and form, the way a peanut butter cup can be distinguished into its ingredients and its shape. Still, we have made a step towards understanding what must be going on with the Trinity, by showing that a thing can be different from itself. This will especially be the case with the Trinity, because the Persons are not, as Abelard puts it, "mixed" with one another the way that the properties of physical things can be. A peanut butter cup is sweet and round, so sweetness and roundness are "mixed" together in it, which just means that the sweet thing is round and the round thing is sweet. The Persons are not like this, because they actually exclude one another. The Father begets the Son and is not begotten, so the Father is not "mixed" with the Son. For this reason, Abelard is in a good position to insist that his account of the Trinity doesn't just reduce to calling one thing by three names. The difference in words really does express a difference in the thing.

Stepping back from the details of this philosophical account of the Trinity, we should pause to notice that it is indeed just that: a philosophical account of the Trinity. Abelard was boldly carrying on Anselm of Canterbury's project of applying pure reason to fundamental precepts of Christian faith. It was a trendsetting move. Critics like William of St. Thierry and Bernard of Clairvaux remarked with disquiet that, thanks to Abelard, there was a trend throughout France of engaging in rational "disputation" over the nature of the holy Trinity.[7] Supporters of Abelard stepped forward to denounce his critics in terms much harsher than those used by any modern-day historian of philosophy. Abelard's student Berengar of Poitiers delighted in mentioning Bernard's youthful indiscretions, and dismissed Bernard's major commentary on the biblical *Song of Songs* as derivative and badly written to boot.[8] (This student of Abelard's is not to be confused with Berengar of Tours, opponent of Lanfranc in the earlier debate over the Eucharist.) We also have a number of anonymous treatises preserved in manuscripts which carry on Abelard's ideas in theology as well as logic. Other anonymous authors sought to reconcile Abelard's views with the ideas found in the other main contributors to the Trinity debate in the twelfth century: the Victorines.

The Victorines took a peanut-butter-cup approach to the cultural conflict between the secular teachings of the schoolmen and the rigorous monasticism of the Cistercians. Hugh of Saint Victor was the H. B. Reese of the movement, immersed as he was in the liberal arts, while also being deeply committed to a life of spiritual devotion. When he turned his attention to the Trinity, he drew heavily on Augustine, whose *On the Trinity* described a threefold structure in human thought. The mind, its act of understanding, and its desire to understand can be distinguished from one another. Hugh observes that this same structure will appear in any rational being. Since God too is rational, we can thus extrapolate from our own trinitarian nature to God's, without necessarily needing any scriptural revelation to point us in this direction.[9] Given his carefully orthodox and Augustinian conclusions, to say nothing of his commitment to monastic reform, Hugh's rationalist approach to the Trinity provoked no hostility from Bernard of Clairvaux. To the contrary, Hugh actually contacted Bernard well before William of St. Thierry did, expressing his own worries about Abelard's teachings on various topics.

Richard of Saint Victor set out a more daring exploration of the Trinity. He carried forward Hugh's rationalism, going so far as to complain that he has nowhere been able to find sufficient proofs of this key Christian doctrine (§1.5). Richard admits that humans are incapable of knowing God fully (§1.19), but then to some extent humans are unknowable even to themselves. Somehow we are single beings composed of two radically different things, a physical body and an immaterial soul. This mysterious fact points towards a similar compatibility of unity and plurality in God (§3.9–10, 4.2, 4.10). Richard proceeds by establishing God's unity and simplicity first, and then arguing that God is nonetheless three Persons. Divine simplicity is secured by reaffirming a claim already made by Boethius: a human may be powerful or wise, but God is His power and wisdom (§2.13). Furthermore, these features are really identical to one another. Despite our use of two different words, in itself God's "power" is just the same thing as His "wisdom" (§2.18). This could be taken as a quiet criticism of Abelard, in that Richard is applying power and wisdom to God as a whole, rather than seeing these as properties that are especially appropriate to one or another divine Person (§3.7; but he does emphasize the power of the Father at §5.4).

As for the multiplicity of Persons, Richard provides an innovative account that revolves around the idea of God's love. In line with Anselm's famous formula that God is "that than which nothing greater can be conceived," we can say that God must bear the greatest possible love towards the most perfect object, namely Himself. But as Gregory the Great observed, love is ideally directed not at oneself, but at another person (§3.2). So God must love someone else, and this someone else must be Himself, since otherwise He would not be loving the most perfect object. So that gives us a God who is two Persons—we're two-thirds of the way there! Richard next makes the assumption that in perfect love, a person not only loves someone else but also desires that they love a third person (§3.11). Hence the need for the Holy Spirit: it provides the Father and Son someone that they can love jointly. Richard's assumption looks suspiciously convenient, and for all his stress on providing convincing arguments, he doesn't really make a strong case for it. Why does true love entail wanting the beloved to love some third person? I think one might come to his aid by giving the example of raising children. I don't want to imply that any romantic alliance that lacks children is defective or imperfect. But there is a unique fulfillment in the way that the mutual love of two parents is inextricably bound up with their love for that child.

Richard hastens to add that, given God's simplicity, the difference in Persons does not amount to a difference in substance (§4.9). That would lead to tritheism, the accusation Abelard threw at Roscelin. Richard avoids it by drawing a distinction between the being of a substance and what he calls its "existence" (§4.12–18). He calls attention to the *ex-* part of the Latin *existere*: in Latin, the preposition *ex* means "from." In light of this we should understand "existence" to refer not just to something's being, but to where it "came from." In the case of the Father, we have a divine Person who did not come from anywhere, as He exists in and from Himself. By contrast, the Son comes from or is "begotten" by the Father, while the Holy Spirit comes from the Father and Son jointly (§5.8). Though the entire Godhead is a single substance, the three different ways of originating distinguish the Persons from one another (§4.17, 19, 22).

Though Bernard of Clairvaux probably wouldn't care to admit it, Richard's account is not all that dissimilar to Abelard's, with the three types of existence in Richard essentially playing the role Abelard assigned to the special properties of the Persons. The Victorines also shared Abelard's fundamental aim of using unaided reason to explain this theological doctrine. This is why Hugh of Saint Victor, like Abelard, was inclined to admit that the pre-Christian philosophers had intimations of the Trinity. In particular, the medievals turned to the one Platonic dialogue known to them, the *Timaeus*. There we find Plato describing a divine creator who looks to a kind of cosmic blueprint, the Forms, which could be seen as playing the role of the second person of the Trinity, or God's wisdom. Plato's creator furthermore fashions a force of life within the cosmos, a soul of the entire universe. For Abelard this so-called "world soul" was analogous to the third Person of the Trinity, the Holy Spirit. Still, despite accusations to the contrary, neither Abelard nor his closest followers in fact went so far as to say that Plato had fully understood the Trinity.[10] The members of the so-called "school of Chartres" would not be quite so cautious.

14

ON THE SHOULDERS OF GIANTS
PHILOSOPHY AT CHARTRES

Teachers have always evaluated their students, and nowadays the students are invited to return the favor. I've taught in the United States, England, and Germany, and in all these places I have had to distribute forms at the end of each semester so my students could anonymously voice their opinion of the quality of my teaching. Students can also go onto websites to "rate their professor," and could formerly even assess whether the teacher in question was "hot." Reflecting on one's instructors is not only a modern-day activity, though. The greatest teacher evaluation in history is surely Plato's dialogues, which explore the character and techniques of Plato's teacher Socrates more deeply than any paperwork or website could hope to do. As a bonus, we learn from Alcibiades' speech in Plato's *Symposium* that Socrates was most definitely hot. The medievals too liked to comment on their instructors. For a forerunner of today's negative evaluations, just think of Peter Abelard's scathing remarks about his teachers Anselm of Laon and William of Champeaux.

And for a glowing report from the same period, we can turn to John of Salisbury. He's going to be appearing routinely in the coming chapters, since he is a richly informative source for the intellectual scene in the twelfth century, and wrote a major treatise on political philosophy, the *Policraticus*, as well as a defense of the logical arts, the *Metalogicon*. In the *Metalogicon*, John praises the effective pedagogical techniques of Bernard of Chartres (§1.24).[1] From what he says, I think Bernard's teaching would pass muster even with the discerning students of today. John mentions Bernard's sensitivity to the needs of his pupils, his focus on the essentials of the teaching curriculum, and his encouragement of dialogue in class. Bernard was surprisingly lenient with students caught plagiarizing from classical sources when they were supposed to be writing original prose in a classical style.

Another of Bernard's gifts as a teacher was that he could come up with vivid imagery to make a point. An example is his famous remark that we are like dwarves on the shoulders of giants. If we see farther than our predecessors could, it is because we are adding modestly to their mighty achievements (reported at *Metalogicon* §3.4).

Among the giants on whose shoulder Bernard of Chartres liked to perch was that master of the teacher evaluation, Plato. Bernard's philosophy was shot through with Platonism, and especially with ideas from the *Timaeus*, known in this period thanks to the late ancient philosopher Calcidius' Latin translation and commentary. An anonymous set of marginal glosses on the *Timaeus* has, plausibly, been ascribed to Bernard.[2] At the very least, these glosses reflect his approach to the text, which was so influential that he effectively rendered Calcidius' commentary obsolete. We can see this just by counting surviving manuscripts. There are almost fifty manuscripts of the Latin *Timaeus* on its own from the twelfth century, a huge increase from the handful we have from the eleventh century; yet the number of copies of Calcidius' commentary falls precipitously.[3] His popularity would recover only in the Renaissance. So it's for good reason that John of Salisbury honors Bernard of Chartres with the title "most accomplished of the Platonists of our time (*perfectissimus inter Platonicos seculi nostri*)" (§4.35).

A trickier question is whether we should honor Bernard with being the founder of a philosophical movement, a group of like-minded thinkers whom we can call a "school of Chartres." Many scholars have been happy to do so, in large part thanks to the testimony of John of Salisbury. John was not a student of Bernard himself, but he did learn from Bernard's students (§2.10). These included two major philosophers of the twelfth century: Gilbert of Poitiers (on whom, see Chapter 16), and William of Conches, who carried on Bernard's example by engaging creatively with the *Timaeus*. John also studied with Thierry of Chartres, the greatest Frenchman named Thierry until a certain striker came along to play for Arsenal. Thierry of Chartres is sometimes thought to have been Bernard's brother, and he taught another commentator called Clarembald of Arras.[4] We can also throw into the mix another Platonist philosopher of the twelfth century, Bernard Silvestris (not to be confused with Bernard of Chartres). Together, all these thinkers represent a formidable group.

If, that is, they were a group. A skeptical note was sounded decades ago by the medievalist Richard Southern.[5] He was confronting a romantic conception, indelibly linked to the surviving Western facade of the Chartres cathedral. It has carvings dating from the twelfth century which represent the liberal arts along with a group of pagan philosophers. It seems almost too good to be true: a representation of all that the school of Chartres held dear, executed in stone just when this school was at the height of its powers. But Southern argued that it is, indeed, too good to be true. He pointed out how little evidence there is that all these men, apart from Bernard of Chartres himself, actually taught at Chartres for any significant period of time, as opposed to Paris, which had already become the more important location for teaching. In the case of Thierry for instance, the most we can say is that he may have divided his time between Paris and Chartres.[6] Bernard Silvestris dedicated a major treatise called the *Cosmographia* to Thierry, but his own teaching was carried out at Tours.

A lot of ink has been spilled over this issue of geography. The real question for the historian of philosophy, though, is not where the figures of the so-called "school of Chartres" were active, but whether they actually shared a distinctive intellectual program. If we think about these figures I've named—Bernard and Thierry of Chartres, William of Conches, Gilbert of Poitiers, Clarembald of Arras, Bernard Silvestris, and John of Salisbury—we can say that they all had expertise in the liberal arts and an interest in classical literary and philosophical texts. But so did lots of other thinkers of the twelfth century. Certainly, most can be identified as Platonists. But the *Timaeus*-centered Platonist project of Bernard of Chartres and others doesn't really find an echo in Gilbert, and John of Salisbury was opposed to Platonism. His admiration for Bernard notwithstanding, John gently mocked Bernard's hope of reconciling the teachings of Plato and Aristotle: if these two great men couldn't even agree when they were alive, there isn't much hope of getting them to agree now that they're dead (§2.17).

Despite this lack of one single location or body of doctrines, there remains a kind of family resemblance among the so-called "Chartrians." It wasn't just an affection for Plato that was passed from Bernard of Chartres to a whole generation of scholars, but a certain sort of literary taste. These figures inevitably call to mind the later humanists of the Renaissance, given their close attention to the Latin text of favorite classical authors.[7] As figures like William of Champeaux and Abelard were focusing on the logical and metaphysical questions that could arise in dialectic, the Chartrians celebrated the arts of grammar and rhetoric. John of Salisbury describes how Bernard of Chartres encouraged attention to and love for the classics, Thierry of Chartres commented on Cicero's works on rhetoric, and Bernard Silvestris commented on Virgil, while William of Conches loved to quote Horace.

In keeping with their intense study of secular literature, the Chartrians often wrote in a self-consciously refined style. Admittedly, Abelard did write poetry too. But his philosophy is mostly set out in rigorous, argumentative texts that prefigure thirteenth-century scholasticism. By contrast, when the Chartrians weren't writing commentaries and glosses on classical texts, they were trying to compose classics of their own, using poetic or dialogue form. Another trademark literary technique came into play when they were reading, rather than writing. They often used the word *integumentum*, meaning a "covering" or "cloak," to express the way the surface meaning of a text may conceal its true significance.[8] With this technique, frankly pagan material could be redeemed for use in a Christian context. In his commentary on Virgil, Bernard Silvestris explains the seduction of Venus by Vulcan as a symbolic representation of the corruption of the mind by lust. A similar message is taught by the encounter between Aeneas and Dido. Virgil shows Dido perishing in flame after Aeneas leaves her, in order to show how sinful lusts burn away to mere embers once the soul resists them. As a whole, for Bernard the *Aeneid* "describes under a covering (*in integumento*) what the human spirit should do and suffer, so long as it is placed in the human body."

The same strategy could be used to save Plato from himself, as it were. Confronted with a passage of the *Timaeus* which seems to say that souls exist in the stars before coming into the body, William of Conches remarked that Plato was offering "nothing heretical, but the most profound philosophy sheltered in the covering of the words." Plato meant only that different souls are influenced by different stars during our earthly life, not that souls really existed previously in the heavens.[9] The Chartrians reserved their boldest such maneuver for another problematic idea in Plato: the so-called "World Soul." In the *Timaeus*, it is said that the divine craftsman not only gives souls to individual humans, but also grants a soul to the entire universe. The cosmos is a single living organism, a visible god that constitutes the greatest image of the intelligible realm (*Timaeus* 34a). This is problematic from a Christian point of view. It is difficult, for instance, to see how the soul of the whole universe could fall and be redeemed by Christ.

Among the Chartrians, it was William of Conches who engaged with this problem most seriously.[10] His initial solution was one that had been suggested, if not wholeheartedly embraced, by Abelard: Plato's World Soul is to be identified with the Holy Spirit, the third Person of the Trinity. As his career went on, though, William expressed uncertainty on the point. And no wonder. There were obvious objections to his proposal, such as the fact that Plato has the divine craftsman creating the soul of the cosmos, whereas the Holy Spirit is, of course, uncreated. In glosses he wrote on the *Timaeus*, William was willing to go only this far: "some say [the World Soul] is the Holy Spirit, which we now neither deny nor affirm." Bernard Silvestris was not quite so shy. For him, the pagan philosophers were simply expressing the ideas of Christian theology in different terms. Where Christians speak of the divine Son, the philosophers say "intellect"; where Christians talk of a Holy Spirit, the philosophers say "World Soul."[11]

Though this is often thought of as a distinctively "Chartrian" position, it was in fact never taught by the one thinker we know to have been based primarily at Chartres: the earlier Bernard. He never proposed identifying Plato's cosmic soul with a divine Person. In general, Bernard of Chartres was careful not to let Platonic metaphysics infringe on the unchallenged transcendence of God. We can see this from his handling of the Platonic "Forms" or "Ideas."[12] Bernard was wholeheartedly committed to this theory, but stopped short of the traditional identification of the transcendent Forms with God's Wisdom and the second Person of the Trinity. Because the Forms are created, they must be inferior or posterior to God Himself, something Bernard expressed by saying that while the Forms are eternal, they are not co-eternal with the Holy Trinity.

Bernard's explanation of these eternal Forms could hardly be more characteristic. It displays his grammatical approach to the issue and his flair for vivid metaphor. Taking the example of the color white, he compared the noun "whiteness (albedo)" to a virgin. The verb "is white (albet)" is like a virgin lying on a bed, waiting to be defiled. Finally, the adjective "white (album)" is like the same woman after having lost her virginity (Metalogicon §3.2). His point was that whiteness in itself is pure and untouched by matter. It is a separate Form, graspable only by the mind. By contrast, the whiteness we see in white bodies around us is mixed together with matter, and so available to sense perception. Bernard coined the phrase formae nativae, or "inborn forms," for the images of transcendent Ideas that appear in material bodies. The resulting picture of the world is true to the one we find in Plato's Timaeus. Bernard's divine Creator is distinct from the intelligible Forms, and fashions the physical cosmos by putting immanent images of those Forms into matter.

Though other Chartrians likewise took inspiration from the Timaeus, they did not always apply its ideas in the same way. Thierry of Chartres and his student Clarembald also appropriated Platonic ideas in their theology. But rather than distinguishing God from the Forms, they actually identified God with one Form in particular: the Form of Being.[13] This is an idea they could find in Boethius, and it will have a powerful echo later on in Aquinas (see Chapter 48). Thierry of Chartres also offered a memorable, if not particularly illuminating suggestion for how to conceive of the Trinity. He compared the three Persons in one God to the fact that $1 \times 1 \times 1 = 1$. He meant this to represent not just the way that unity can be preserved even as multiplicity is introduced, but also the equality of the Persons to one another. Again, the Chartrians' training in the liberal arts is showing here, with Thierry applying arithmetic to theology, much as Bernard of Chartres had used grammar in his metaphysics.

Reflection on the Timaeus was bound to lead to interest in another area of philosophy not represented among the liberal arts: the study of nature. Plato's dialogue does speak of a divine craftsman and of Forms, but it is above all a description of the physical universe. The Chartrians followed suit. An outstanding example is a treatise by William of Conches, to which he gave the rather surprising title Dragmaticon.[14] To the modern ear, the title calls to mind nothing so much as a cross-dressing Transformer, and medieval readers would have found it an odd choice too. William's title followed a vogue for Greek-style titles, like Hugh of Saint Victor's pedagogical bestseller *Didascalicon*. In this case William was apparently alluding to the "dramatic" presentation of the *Dragmaticon*. It takes the form of a dialogue between a philosopher and Geoffrey Plantagenet, who was at that time the Duke of Normandy. William served as tutor to Geoffrey's sons, one of whom would go on to become King Henry II of England. The *Dragmaticon* thus echoes a long-standing ideal of scholarship in aristocratic surroundings. Like Alcuin teaching Charlemagne, William offers tutelage to the duke and his family. This traditional setting for philosophy, already challenged by the activity at cathedral schools and monasteries, is about to be largely supplanted by the rise of the medieval university.[15]

William's fictionalized lessons with the duke prove, if proof were needed, that card-carrying Platonists could take a deep interest in the natural world. William adheres to the standard Platonist goal of using the intellect rather than the senses. But this is no bar to pursuing philosophy of nature, since he thinks that the fundamental principles of physical things are invisible. The four elements, fire, air, water, and earth, can never be found in nature in their pure forms. We grasp them by abstracting from the bodies we see around us (§2.2.3–8). Like Plato in the *Timaeus*, William also holds that the elements consist of invisibly small particles, indivisible "atoms." Throughout the *Dragmaticon*, the character of the duke is often the mouthpiece for authorities who apparently disagree with William's teaching. So here, when the topic of atomism comes up, the duke points out that Boethius speaks of matter as infinitely divisible, and not as consisting of indivisible atoms (§1.2.3). To this William's philosopher character responds, rather unpersuasively, that the atoms are indeed "infinite," but only in the sense that we cannot grasp their multitude with our limited minds.

Still, William insists upon his right to overturn accepted teaching if he sees fit. One mustn't run roughshod over the teaching of the church fathers, or more recent authorities like Bede, when issues of theology and morality are at stake. But the philosophy of nature is different (§3.2.3). William thinks that in physics, only "probable" explanations can be provided, and when he finds his own account more probable than that of the fathers he is not afraid to say so. A notable example comes when he rejects the traditional idea that there is water in the heavens.[16] This notion is based on a line in the Book of Genesis, where God is said to have placed the sky *amidst* the waters, so as to divide them apart. But for William, water has its natural place between earth and air. It cannot be found up in the celestial realm, which is fiery in nature. (He here accepts Plato's view on the matter, rejecting

Aristotle's idea that the heavens are made of a "fifth element" distinct from fire, air, earth, and water; §3.5.4 and 6.32.)

William's naturalist approach is also on display when he interprets the biblical statement that Eve was fashioned from a rib taken from Adam's side. In an earlier treatise called *Philosophy of the World*, which William used as a basis for the *Dragmaticon*, he had argued that both Adam and Eve were made from muddy earth. When creating Adam, God had used material with a perfect balance of elemental properties. Eve is said to be taken from Adam's "side" because she was instead made from mud lying nearby, which was not so ideal in its proportions. This typifies the "Chartrian" approach to textual interpretation. William treats Adam's rib as an *integumentum* for a true, "scientific" explanation. He corrects the surface meaning of the text in light of his conviction that all bodies are made of the four elements.

The *Dragmaticon* is full of similar proposals, explaining everything from the fact that our fingers are more swollen when we wake up in the morning to the legend that the Prophet Muhammad's tomb floats in midair, which William suspects to be a kind of magic trick involving magnets (§6.14.4, 2.6.9). In some cases, he tries to explain supposed phenomena that are in fact spurious: why it is that premature babies born in the seventh month of pregnancy sometimes survive, whereas those born in the eight month always die (§6.10.2)? In general, his ideas about female sexuality make for alarming reading. He believes that pleasure in sex is needed to conceive, which is why prostitutes rarely get pregnant. To the duke's objection that rape victims do conceive, the philosopher character responds that although the victim may not be rationally consenting to the sex act, she takes carnal pleasure in it nonetheless (§6.8.10). Obviously this is not William of Conches at his best, and in general no modern-day scientist is going to be impressed by his theories. Still, William does represent a remarkable feature of twelfth-century thought which deserves another chapter to itself: a blossoming of exploration devoted to the physical universe.

15

THE GOOD BOOK
PHILOSOPHY OF NATURE

"The faithfulness of nature to its original laws of motion, the continuance of all things as they were from the beginning of the creation, awaken a considerate mind into a quick and lively sense of the depth thereof. *Nulla litura est in libro naturae.* God never saw it necessary (as upon mature thoughts) to correct and amend anything in this great volume of the creation, since the first volume thereof."[1] These words were written in the middle of the seventeenth century by the Protestant English theologian John Spencer. The sentiment seems to fit his age, at the dawn of the Enlightenment: God does not intervene capriciously in the world, but has made nature perfect and unchanging. Spencer's polemic had contemporary political relevance, too. He was arguing against those who invoked supposedly miraculous occurrences, or "prodigies," as signs of God's displeasure with the English government.

Yet that quotation would also be right at home in the twelfth century, a time when intellectuals likewise spoke of an unblemished "book of nature." Hugh of Saint Victor, for instance, remarked that the whole of the sensible world is "like a book written by the finger of God."[2] The metaphor goes back to antiquity, and can be found in several works by Augustine.[3] It was the beginning of a long-running tradition, according to which the Bible is not the only "good book" sent by God. Nature is a further revelation of God's providential will, so it behooves the thoughtful Christian to study it, by undertaking what we would call "science," and what the medievals (and for that matter people in the seventeenth century) called "natural philosophy." This was a part of intellectual life from the very beginnings of the medieval age.[4] From the eighth century onwards, scholars like Bede, Alcuin, and Abbo of Fleury displayed expertise in the field of astronomy. The use of the instrument known as the astrolabe began around 1000 AD, a development sometimes credited to Gerbert of Aurillac. As with the more famous example of a writing system for mathematics (hence "Arabic numerals"), the astrolabe was an import from the Islamic world, where Arabic-speaking scientists were far more advanced than their Latin Christian counterparts.

The twelfth century would produce even more readers for the book of nature. It's no coincidence that this coincided with a surge of interest in Arabic scientific literature, which began to be translated into Latin at this time. That's something we'll be looking at later in this book (Chapter 20), so I won't go into it now lest, like an emperor ordering a bust, I get ahead of myself. I do however want to mention Adelard of Bath, a fascinating figure who translated mathematical works from Arabic into Latin, and wrote a set of *Questions on Natural Philosophy* in dialogue form, for which he claimed to be using his Arabic learning. Adelard overturns any lingering prejudices we might have about authority-bound, intellectually slavish medievals. In his dialogue on natural philosophy, he has one of the characters say: "I have learnt one thing from my Arabic teachers with reason as a guide, but you are led by another thing—a halter, captivated by the lure of authority. For what should authority be called but a halter?"[5] And he wasn't alone. We may remember Peter Abelard's triumphant anecdote in which he embarrassed Anselm of Laon by turning Anselm's demand for authoritative evidence against him. Equally memorable is a comment made by the theologian Alan of Lille, about whom much more shortly. He expressed his doubts about authority by comparing it to a nose made of wax: it can be bent any which way you like.[6]

The discover-it-yourself attitude of Adelard and other twelfth-century thinkers went together with another attitude liable to strike us as genuinely "scientific": a preference for explanations in terms of the regularities of nature rather than miracles. Five centuries before John Spencer, the book of nature was expected to work in a predictable fashion, ensuring the comprehensibility of the universe. This is something we can trace back further still if we look hard enough. Already in the seventh century, one of those anonymous Irish scholars we keep meeting wrote a work explaining miracles of the Bible in more or less naturalist terms. Lot's wife, it turns out, was transformed into salt when God adjusted the balance of substances in her body, and the Virgin Birth can be understood as analogous to spontaneous generation.[7] But it's really with figures like Adelard of Bath that we see an impatience with simplistic appeals to God's will. As he puts it, "there is nothing in nature that lacks a reason (*ratio*)."[8]

All very well, you might say, but like his near namesake Abelard, surely Adelard was an exceptional case: a mathematician and translator, at the extreme rationalist fringe of his age. There's some truth in that. Yet we can see many of the same tendencies in the far more mainstream group we just looked at, the thinkers who have traditionally been linked to Chartres. The naturalist approach to the Bible we saw with William of Conches was also adopted by Thierry of Chartres. In his commentary on the Book of Genesis, he states that he will be tackling this biblical text *secundum phisicam et ad litteram*, meaning that he will approach it with the tools of natural philosophy and linguistic analysis. He will not, he says, try to draw out any allegorical or moral significance from the text, which makes for a stark contrast with Hugh and Richard of Saint Victor. True to his word, Thierry's commentary trades in illuminating empirical observations, as when he compares the emergence of dry land from the seas to the way that water spread on a table top dries unevenly.[9]

But this is not to say that the twelfth century saw a wholesale abandonment of long-cherished, authoritative texts. In this respect Adelard of Bath was indeed unusual, for the emphasis he placed on observation and for his use of newly available material just being imported from Arabic. For this reason a leading French historian of this period, Jean Jolivet, has described Adelard as studying nature *sans livre*: "without a book." In other words, he no longer saw nature as something to be decoded the way you interpret a text, using the tools of the liberal arts and the wisdom of classical texts.[10] Yet it was left to more mainstream scholars, especially those who adopted the "Chartrian" approach, to produce the most elaborate and popular works of natural philosophy in the twelfth century. They took their inspiration from Latin authors of late antiquity, like Martianus Capella and Boethius. But for them the most important guide to the book of nature was Plato's *Timaeus*.

We've already seen one outstanding representative of this kind of natural philosophy, with William of Conches' *Dragmaticon*. In the rest of this chapter, I'll be telling you about two more. One is the *Cosmographia* (another "Greek" title) written by Bernard Silvestris. The other, written a generation later and influenced by the *Cosmographia*, is the *Lament of Nature* by the aforementioned theologian Alan of Lille.[11] The two texts have a great deal in common. Both alternate between prose and poetry, a literary technique already used in Boethius' *Consolation of Philosophy*. In fact, Lady Philosophy from Boethius' *Consolation* provided a model for the character of Nature as depicted by Bernard Silvestris and Alan of Lille. (We'll see both the prose-poetry form and the device of personification in a number of authors later in this book, for instance in Marguerite Porete: see Chapter 53.) They agree in their account of Nature's function: she helps to perpetuate the cosmic order by reproducing forms in matter, something Alan compares to the production of coins from unformed metal. Bernard and Alan both make a place for humankind in their narratives, too. They see humans as an image in miniature of the universe. Each of us is a so-called "microcosm" of the great cosmos that surrounds us. The main difference between Bernard and Alan is that, whereas Bernard's *Cosmographia* sticks to the cosmological themes promised by its title, Alan's *Lament* has an ethical theme. He tells of how Nature appeared before a human poet to complain of the misdeeds of humankind. She is especially outraged by sexual misdeeds, and among these, by the practice of homosexuality.

There's a revealing (in every sense of the word) detail in Alan of Lille's allegorical description of Nature. She takes the form of a ravishingly beautiful woman, with a dress upon which are inscribed depictions of plants and animals; but the dress is torn. Alan has lifted this straight from Boethius, who likewise had Lady Philosophy appearing in a garment violently ripped by unnamed attackers.[12] In Alan's *Lament*, the torn dress represents the assault on natural modesty by human evildoers (§8.24). But in his hands, the image has taken on a more complex meaning as well. He refers to her garment as an *integumentum*, the same term used by the Chartrians to describe the surface meaning of a text which hides a true, philosophical message. Indeed, just before the bit explaining Nature's torn clothing, Alan has used this same literary technique to explain why the classical poets spoke of pagan gods who engaged in sexual misconduct of their own. Such myths are only a covering, which, when unmasked, reveals a deeper meaning: the false pagan husk conceals the kernel of monotheistic truth.

For Bernard Silvestris and Alan of Lille, the concept of *integumentum* was a key to unlock classical texts and also key to their own literary productions. They unhesi-tatingly imitate the allegorical approach of late ancient authors like Martianus Capella, populating their cosmos with a whole host of supernatural figures: along-side Nature we meet such cosmic forces as Mind and Heaven, who are likewise personified and allowed to give speeches and recite poetry. A classicizing literary taste is expressed in the very names of these characters, which are often Greek rather than Latin, such as *Nous*, *Hyle*, and *Urania* (Intellect, Matter, and Heaven). At the same time, their use of allegory expresses a conviction about nature itself. Macrobius, another of the ancient Latin authors who inspired Bernard and Alan, had written that "nature does not like to show herself open and naked,"[13] which is why she is described using myth. If nature is a book, she is not like a technical treatise, but like an allegory or fable. She needs careful interpretation if she is to be read rightly as the work of God's providence.

Bernard and Alan may wrap their philosophy of nature in cunningly woven literary artifice, but their core message is clear nonetheless, especially if you know your *Timaeus*. Plato's dialogue describes a divine intellect, the so-called "Demiurge" or craftsman of the universe, who puts images of intelligible Forms into a passive "receptacle" to produce bodies. Bernard and Alan likewise explain the physical cosmos as the joint production of several principles. Bernard's *Cosmographia* begins with Nature's plea to *Nous*, or Mind. She is unhappy with the unformed, chaotic state of matter, and requests that Mind do something about it (67). Matter's own attitude about this prospect is ambivalent. On the one hand, she is described as yearning for form, an idea that can be traced back to Aristotle through the intermediary of Calcidius.[14] On the other hand, Matter is several times said to have an innate tendency towards chaos and evil, so that Mind and Nature must struggle to master her and subdue her to form (70, 117, 119). Again, this reflects the Platonic source, since the *Timaeus* states that the receptacle needs to be "persuaded" by intellect if it is to submit to order and form. Hence the universe is a compromise between the designing intention of Mind and Matter's recalcitrance.

Broadly speaking, the result is, nonetheless, a well-ordered and providentially designed cosmos. Even something as basic as the arrangement of the four elements has a purpose: potentially destructive fire is separated from earth by a buffer of air and water (72), a point also made by William of Conches in his *Dragmaticon*.[15] Furthermore, the motions of the heavenly bodies ensure that events here on earth will unfold in the way that Providence intends. For Bernard, every human is allotted a certain lifespan by the stars at the moment of his birth (98), a clear allusion to astrology, which was frequently associated with natural philosophy throughout the medieval period. (Another twelfth-century author, Daniel of Morley, remarked that "he who condemns astrology, by necessity destroys physics."[16]) In a characteristic passage, Bernard evokes once again the idea that the natural world can be read as a book: like written announcements of things to come, the stars foretold the lives of Homeric heroes, the Latin eloquence of Cicero and Virgil, and the mathematical skill of Thales (76).[17] He goes so far as to make the stars not just signs but even causes of things that happen in the world below (78),[18] albeit with the significant caveat that humans retain their freedom even in the face of "the laws of the fates and inexorable destiny" (98).

Bernard is thus very optimistic about the physical universe, which as an image and effect of the intelligible forms in cosmic Mind is a case of "the perfect coming from the perfect" (89). Yet he gives Matter considerable scope in explaining natural phenomena that seem less than perfect. Non-human animals are said to be made with somewhat less care than humans, so that they are unbalanced and more easily dominated by the elemental humors. Lions have tempers that quite literally run hot, whereas donkeys are overly influenced by phlegm, which makes them stupid (120). Humans alone are perfectly balanced in terms of their elemental makeup. But as Alan of Lille would hasten to add, this does not mean that they always behave as they should. In fact, Alan has Nature say that humans are unlike other animals in that they alone can defy her laws (§8.3).

In developing this theme, Alan shows how much his imagination has been shaped by his study of the liberal arts. As I mentioned, the misconduct that especially concerns Nature is sexual deviance, above all homosexuality. The poem takes an unexpected and repugnant turn when Nature rails against same-sex relations, which she compares to a grammatical mistake (§1).[19] Heterosexual sex is like a well-formed sentence, whereas homosexual sex is like using the wrong gender for a word in Latin. In English, an analogous (albeit non-gendered) metaphor might be combining a singular noun with a plural verb. Even by the low standards of the long, squalid, and, of course, still ongoing history of unconvincing attempts to say why homosexual love should be worthy of condemnation rather than celebration, Alan's remarks are fairly preposterous. But they do reveal something about him as an author. The evocation of grammar in this context shows that here, in the second half of the twelfth century (his *Lament* was written in the 1160s), the liberal arts retain their fundamental role, even in the context of natural philosophy. If you see nature as a book, then why not apply the arts of linguistic analysis to understanding the world around you? Nature is a myth that needs interpretation and also has rules and norms, as language does. Supposedly "unnatural" sex breaches those norms, and is thus akin to a solecism in speaking or writing. No self-respecting medieval scholar would want to be accused of that.

16

ONE OF A KIND
GILBERT OF POITIERS
ON INDIVIDUATION

Having grown up as an identical twin, I've always been fascinated by the problem of individuation: what makes two things of the same type different from one another? As children, my brother and I were constantly confronted with adults who seemed to have difficulty with this concept. We hated being called "the twins," as if the two of us were entirely interchangeable, and I still bear a grudge against a teacher who was going through an attendance list one morning and called out, "the Adamsons?" as if neither of us could be present without the other. But you don't have to be a twin to find the question philosophically interesting. Consider again that other set of siblings, the Marx Brothers. It was usually quite easy to tell them apart, except when Groucho and Harpo were performing the mirror scene in *Duck Soup* (do yourself a favor and look it up online). But what exactly made them four distinct individuals? This is the flip side of the problem of universals, where the challenge was accounting for the humanity that belongs to Groucho, Harpo, Chico, and Zeppo. Now we're asking, not how it is that they all belong to the same species, but how it is that they come to be four separate members of that species. We can also pose the question in this way: how or why is humanity *divided* into Groucho, Harpo, me, and my brother, the way that the genus animal is divided into many species, like human, giraffe, and elephant? Ancient and medieval philosophers did pose the question like that, and added that particulars cannot be further divided in the same way. This is why the particular members of a species are called "individuals," and why the difficulty of accounting for the whole phenomenon is called the problem of individuation.

You might think that giving a solution is easy. All we need to do is find any feature that belongs to Groucho and doesn't belong to Harpo. That feature will distinguish Groucho from Harpo, and hence "individuate" him: Groucho wears a greasepaint mustache and Harpo doesn't. This may be a promising first step, but it's no more than that, because we are not just asking why or how Groucho is distinct from Harpo. We want to know how it is that Groucho is distinct from *all* other humans, what makes him the individual that he is and no other. And as even the merest acquaintance with silent film will tell you, there have been more than a few humans apart from Groucho who wore greasepaint mustaches. The same applies to other properties that could help us pick Groucho out from the crowd, or from his brothers. Groucho was brilliant at wisecracking, but so was W. C. Fields; he smoked a cigar, but so did Fidel Castro; he later hosted a game show on American television, but so did Wink Martindale.

Just as with the problem of universals, late ancient and medieval philosophers thought about individuation within the framework of Aristotelian logic. Which instrument from Aristotle's conceptual toolkit might unlock this particular difficulty? We can immediately rule out the genus and species as candidates for individuating factors. It obviously is not by being an animal or a human that Groucho becomes distinct from all other things, because there are plenty of other animals and humans. For that matter, suppose Groucho were, in fact, the only existing human, like Adam just after having been created, or perhaps as the only survivor of a disease that strikes down everyone in its path apart from wisecracking game show hosts who smoke cigars and wear greasepaint. If Groucho were the only human in existence, then humanity might seem sufficient to individuate him. But even then, there would be problems. We really want Groucho to be individuated not just from all the other things that exist presently, but from all the other things that ever have existed or will exist. So even if he were the first human, like Adam, or the last one, like the sole survivor of an apocalypse, we would need to say more to explain what makes him unique. Indeed, we might even want a guarantee that he is distinct even from other *possible* humans, humans that do not exist but quite easily could (like the sister my brother and I do not have).

This line of thought may push us in the direction of solutions suggested, though not fully worked out, by Porphyry and Boethius, the two ancient authors who exerted the most influence on medieval discussions of the problem.[1] Both of them hinted at what we might call an "accidentalist" theory of individuation. By this I mean the idea that the accidental features of a thing make it the individual that it is. The idea of an "accident" is standard Aristotelian fare. It just means any feature that belongs to a thing, but not in virtue of the thing's species membership, so that it can survive as the kind of thing it is even if the feature is lost.[2] Thus Groucho's cigar-smoking is accidental to him, because he remains a human when he's not smoking a cigar, or even if he quits smoking cigars entirely. By contrast, his being alive is essential, not accidental, since he can no longer exist as a human without being alive.

Now, we've already seen that an accident like cigar-smoking is not up to the job of individuating, since other humans also smoke cigars. But what if we took *all* the accidental features together? There may be other cigar-smokers, and other game show hosts, but there aren't likely to be any other cigar-smoking game show hosts who are named Marx, wear round glasses, and get mentioned posthumously in philosophy books. Indeed, it seems quite plausible to think that no individual possibly *could* share all the features of another individual. This is what Porphyry must have been thinking when he remarked, "things are called individuals because each of them consists of characteristics, the collection of which can never be the same for anything else."[3] Boethius knew this passage well—as we've seen, he commented on Porphyry's introductory logical work twice—and sometimes spoke as if he agreed with the idea.

On the other hand, it may seem superfluous to appeal to *all* the properties of something, if we could point to just *one* property that nothing else shares, or could share. Boethius made suggestions in this direction too. What if we just referred to the place occupied by something at a given time? That would pick out Groucho very nicely, assuming that nothing else can be exactly where Groucho is when he is there. Alternatively, and rather more mysteriously, Boethius alludes to a special kind of property which belongs to only one person. Using the example of Plato, he says this property would be called "Platonity." It would be a quality that relates to Plato the way that "humanity" relates to human. This quality, he says, "belongs only to one man, and not to just any man, but only to Plato."[4] The idea does have its appeal, not least because, applied to our favorite example, it would give the world the new and delightful word "Grouchocity" (the capital of Freedonia?). Also it's clear that, to the extent that we can make sense of a property like this—the property of being Groucho or Plato—it can be possessed by only one thing. But this will need to be filled in with a lot more detail if it is to provide a truly illuminating account of individuation.

Step forward Gilbert of Poitiers. Distinguished from most of his peers, if not actually individuated, by his unusually sharp intellect and skill in dialectic, Gilbert was a student of Bernard of Chartres and held the office of chancellor at Chartres in the 1130s, in addition to teaching in Paris. So Gilbert is yet another representative of the group we have been, with some trepidation, calling the "school of Chartres." His solution to the problem of individuation departs from the "accidentalist" strategy that had been sketched in Porphyry and Boethius, and adopted by many medievals up to and during the time of Gilbert. Medieval proponents of the accidentalist solution included Thierry of Chartres, who was another student of Bernard, and Thierry's own student Clarembald of Arras. Despite the popularity of the accidentalist theory in the early medieval period and the weight of authority that supported it, Gilbert had good reasons to be skeptical. Just to restate the basic idea, the accidentalist realizes that nothing can be individuated by essential features, since these are shared by all other members of the same species. Groucho is rational, but so are Harpo, my brother, and every other human that ever has existed or will exist. Instead, we should look to accidental features. Groucho has accidents also found in other humans, but it could never happen that some other human has *all* the same accidents. Alternatively, we can point to an accident of Groucho's that nothing else could have, such as his place. One problem with this account might not bother us so much today, but would be seen as deeply troubling in a medieval context: incorporeal things like God and angels have no place. Indeed, God has no accidents at all. Yet incorporeal things can be individuals. So the accidentalist account is at best incomplete. We'll have to come up with a separate way to individuate immaterial beings.

Another difficulty is that accidents are usually possessed only temporarily. Indeed, we said that accidental features are precisely the features that a thing can lose while surviving as the thing it is. How can Groucho be the individual that he is because of his place, given that he can move around? How can he be individuated by a whole set of features that includes cigar-smoking and wisecracking, when he can give up cigars and imitate Harpo's vow of silence? If you think about this, you begin to suspect that the accidentalist strategy gets things backward. Substances like humans, giraffes, trees, and rocks do not depend on their accidents in order to be the substances that they are. To the contrary: Groucho's accident of cigar-smoking can only exist thanks to Groucho, because this accident is, as Aristotelians would say, "predicated" of him.

This is just as true of place as it is true of any other accident. For Aristotle and his followers, something's "place" is, strictly speaking, the boundary of whatever is containing it, for instance the limit of the air surrounding Groucho. If Groucho were to vanish, this boundary would vanish too, and in this sense, it is dependent on him. So how can it do the job of individuating Groucho? The same applies to other accidents. As Boethius pointed out in his commentaries, Aristotelian logic recognizes not just individual substances like Groucho but also individual accidents, like the cigar-smoking that belongs to him and no one else. This instance of cigar-smoking is individual because it belongs to him. But in that case the accidentalist story is circular: Groucho is supposedly individuated by his accidents, but his accidents only get to be individual because they belong to him and no one else.

At the root of all these difficulties is a fundamental confusion.[5] The accidentalist account is plausible because we do in fact use accidents to tell things apart. We tell

Groucho apart from Harpo by noticing that he is, for example, the one with the cigar, not the one with the blond wig. But that doesn't mean that accidents really account for the distinctness between things. How could they, if accidents depend on those very things? This would be like saying that the Marx Brothers movies are funny because people laugh at them. It's true that these two things go together: funny movies do provoke laughter, and we can tell that a movie is funny from the fact that people laugh at it. But it's because the movies are funny that people laugh, not the other way around. In the same way, it may be true that we only find particular accidents, and unique collections of accidents, in individual substances. This is why we can use accidents to tell substances apart. But that is a matter of epistemology, not metaphysics. Or to put it another way, accidents show us *that* things are individual, but they don't explain *why* things are individual.

Gilbert of Poitiers' novel approach to the issue is going to avoid all these problems.[6] His solution involves some technical terminology, which does not necessarily make his views easier to follow. He contrasts "what something is (*id quod est*)" with "that by which it is what it is (*id quo est*)." Groucho is a human, but is what he is though humanity. The same distinction can be made for accidental features: a cigar-smoker is what he is by virtue of cigar-smoking. Effectively, this just boils down to the distinction between a thing and the features that characterize it. Next, Gilbert says that only a substance, and not its characterizing features, can be individual. Groucho is an individual, but his humanity, his cigar-smoking, and his wisecracking are not. Instead, they are what Gilbert calls "dividuals." By this he means that these features can be found elsewhere too: cigar-smoking is "divided" among Groucho, Fidel Castro, and all the other cigar-smokers.

Now here comes the clever part. As Boethius taught us, Groucho's cigar-smoking is not to be confused with Fidel Castro's. Nor do Groucho and Harpo have the same humanity. Rather, humanity appears twice in them, and four times if you add Chico and Zeppo too. In each of the Marx brothers, in each of the Adamson brothers, in every human, there is a humanity which belongs only to that individual human, while also being "similar" or "conforming" to other instances of humanity. It is the fact that humanity can be exemplified over and over like this that leads Gilbert to deny that one single instance of humanity can be called an "individual." An individual is, as we would expect, something non-repeatable. Nonetheless, the humanity in Groucho is "singular," as Gilbert puts it, because it is his humanity and no one else's.[7]

These points put Gilbert in a position to make sense of Boethius' suggestion about Grouchocity. Grouchocity will be the entire collection, or as Gilbert says, the "total form," of Groucho's features. Together, the singular features "coalesce" or "cohere" into an individual (Gilbert uses the Latin verb *concrescere*, meaning "grow together"). Though each member of the total form is a "dividual," in that a similar property may be found elsewhere, you are never going to find *all* the properties exemplified anywhere else. While this may sound reminiscent of the accidentalist view, it is really very different. Gilbert actually treats the essential and accidental features of a thing as being on a par, at least as far as individuation goes.[8] All of them are possessed as singular features, and serve as parts of the total form that guarantees individuality.

Also, unlike his predecessors and contemporaries, Gilbert does not confuse the question of what makes something individual with the question of how we know something is individual. He sees clearly that accidents merely *show* us that one individual is distinct from another, without *making* it be distinct (*non facit, sed probat*).[9] His firm grasp of this point is itself shown by his including not only the present features of a thing in the total form, but also all the thing's past and future properties. Obviously, we are not currently able to know a thing's future properties, so they can play no practical role in helping us distinguish one individual from another. (Imagine how useless it would have been if, when people couldn't tell me and my brother apart as children, our mother had said "Peter is the one who will be a philosopher, and his brother is the future art historian.") Metaphysically, though, future properties are important, because they enter into the totality of singular characteristics which collectively guarantee the thing's individuality. This also solves the problem about things changing over time—losing the features that supposedly individuate them, according to the accidentalist account. According to Gilbert, it is the total form that individuates, and it includes all the properties the thing has over its whole existence.

As an added bonus, Gilbert now has a nice story to tell about that other, more celebrated difficulty, the problem of universals. We arrive at a universal by noticing the similarity between singular characteristics, for example the four instances of humanity in the four Marx Brothers. But, Gilbert insists, everything that really exists is singular. Universal humanity, freed from connection to any individual human, is only a conceptual construct. Still, it guides our thought in a useful and accurate way, since each human really does possess his or her own singular humanity. On this score Gilbert is fairly close to Abelard's nominalism. We can also guess what he might say to the obvious complaint that he is just helping himself to the idea that Groucho's humanity, cigar-smoking, and so on are "singular." Is he assuming too much here? After all, what we wanted to explain in the first place is how it comes to be that there are single things in the world, and not just universal things. To this Gilbert can reply that there are no universal things: nothing can exist without being singular. If Groucho is a cigar-smoking human, then his cigar-smoking and humanity must be real. So they must be singular.

Gilbert of Poitiers' subtle account of individuality shows that good philosophy could be done within the apparently unpromising context of commentary upon centuries-old logical works. One should not be misled by that context, though. Gilbert's aim was not just to explain authoritative works of logic, or even to devise a powerful and original account of individuality. The whole time, he had his eye on related theological issues.[10] His theory enables him to say very clearly what it means for God to be simple. Whereas all other individuals have total forms made up of many characterizing features, God is what He is through a single, simple form called "divinity." This is one of the doctrines for which Gilbert, like Peter Abelard, was attacked by Bernard of Clairvaux and his allies. When he was put on trial in 1147, with the Pope himself being asked to judge on the question of Gilbert's heresy, the very first accusation was that he taught that God is distinct from the form or nature of divinity.[11] Gilbert came out of his ordeal better than Abelard did, since he was cleared of the charges after a "confession of faith" was drawn up which was acceptable both to him and to his critics. And he later had a small measure of revenge upon Bernard of Clairvaux. When the great man held out an olive branch by suggesting a meeting to read through some theological texts together, Gilbert suggested that he would be better served by learning some beginners' level material from the school curriculum.

With Gilbert of Poitiers, we've almost finished with the scholars connected to the so-called "school of Chartres." But there's one important member of this group who remains to be considered: John of Salisbury. He briefly studied with Gilbert in Paris, and is among our most important sources of information on philosophy in the twelfth century. Not only that, but John was one of the first medieval thinkers to write a treatise dedicated specifically to political philosophy. To set the stage for him, though, we'll have to look at the historical political context, and especially a famous controversy that pitted secular authority against the Church.

17

TWO SWORDS
EARLY MEDIEVAL POLITICAL
PHILOSOPHY

R anking Roger, lead singer of the ska band the English Beat, is not exactly known
for incisive commentary about the history of political thought. This is, after all,
the man who gave the world such lyrics as "You move your little feet, you rock to
the beat...I see you 'pon the street, you look so sweet, I see you with your dancin'
feet." Yet he also sang the words "two swords slashing at each other only sharpen
one another," and you could hardly ask for a better ten-word summary of early
medieval political life. The image of "two swords" was frequently used in the debates
of the time. It was drawn from a passage of the New Testament that has no obvious
relevance to politics. It comes in the Book of Luke (22:38), just after the description
of the Last Supper and Christ's prediction that Peter will deny him three times. Jesus'
disciples are gathering weapons and say, "Behold, here are two swords," to which he
replies, "It is enough." A widespread medieval interpretation of this text took the two
swords to refer to the spiritual authority of the Church and the secular rulership
exercised by kings or emperors. Presumably this is what Ranking Roger had in mind too.

We tend to think of the Middle Ages as a time when the Church exercised
suffocating, unchallenged control over all aspects of society. But if anything, the
rise of the Church as a powerful institution created an unprecedented situation
where there was not just one, but two possible supreme authorities.[1] In ancient
Greece and Rome, pagan religious institutions were largely integrated into political
life; just consider the fact that Julius Caesar's career included a stint as high priest of
Jupiter. Even after the advent of Christianity, religious standing continued to be
closely tied to political sovereignty, with both Western and Eastern emperors
intervening in theological controversies, calling church councils, and appointing
bishops. But the Church already began to acquire a degree of autonomy in late
antiquity. Bishop Ambrose of Milan successfully faced down two emperors in the
late fourth century.[2] It was a foreshadowing of the famous public humiliation that
would befall Emperor Henry IV in the year 1077, forced to wait barefoot in the snow
as he begged for absolution from Pope Gregory VII.

That was the most notorious episode of the so-called Investiture Contest, which saw the swords of Church and empire slash at each other over several generations, leading thinkers of the eleventh and twelfth centuries to sharpen their theories of political legitimacy. The seeds of the conflict go back at least as far as the ninth century, when the two swords were wielded by the same man: Charlemagne. This, at least, was the view of his court philosopher Alcuin, who understood the text from the Book of Luke to refer to his emperor's mission of combatting both heretics within the Church and pagans outside it.[3] Yet Alcuin did recognize different spheres of action for Church and emperor. Speaking to a priest on behalf of Charles, he wrote: "our job is the defence of the Church and fortification of the faith; yours to aid our warfare by prayer." Elsewhere, he said that "the secular and the spiritual power are separated; the former bears the sword of death in its hand, the latter bears the key of life in its tongue."

With these remarks Alcuin was echoing the ideas of Pope Gelasius, who did much to shape early medieval conceptions of political life. In an oft-quoted letter written to the Eastern emperor Anastasius at the end of the fifth century, Gelasius affirmed the legitimacy of imperial power, but insisted that the Church is supreme in questions of religion (§3). In this neat picture, which is sometimes called political "dualism," kings and emperors have ultimate responsibility for and power over worldly affairs, while popes and bishops deal with spiritual matters. But the neat picture was already beginning to blur in the Carolingian period. Charlemagne's father Pepin sought and received the sitting Pope's approval to seize kingship in 751 (§6), and Charlemagne himself was anointed as emperor by Pope Leo on Christmas Day in the year 800. It was not necessarily the stocking stuffer Charlemagne was hoping for. Indeed he subsequently claimed he would never have entered the Church had he known what Leo was planning (§9–11). If his regret was sincere, then it was perhaps because he understood all too well the implication that imperial authority was for the Pope to give—and therefore to withhold, should the Pope deem it suitable.

Under Charlemagne's grandson Charles the Bald, this idea of ecclesiastical primacy was explicitly articulated by Bishop Hincmar (we met him in Chapter 3). He pointed out—and points don't get much more pointed than this—that royal power is conferred by religious consecration, whereas religious authority depends on no royal stamp of approval.[4] History seemed to be on his side. Charles the Bald was anointed king of Aquitaine by a bishop in the year 848, just the first of a series of Frankish kings to be symbolically legitimized by the Church in this way. Unfortunately for Hincmar's theory, though, even the highest positions in the Church were often filled at the whim of a secular monarch. In the eleventh century, the German emperor Henry III found it expedient to install a pope of his choice so that the pope could reciprocate by crowning him. He was simply extending the logic of a long-standing practice, whereby kings and emperors would select the men who served as bishops within their realms.

It's here that we come to the term "investiture," which gives the Investiture Contest its name. It seemed only reasonable to the early medieval monarchs that they should be able to appoint bishops, not only because of the religious aura historically attached to their royal position but also because of the considerable worldly implications. A medieval bishop, after all, would control land and other wealth; they could even control military forces. So selecting a bishop was as much a political appointment as a spiritual one. Before long, though, this practice of "lay investiture" would give rise to conflict between the most powerful men of Europe. It began in earnest in the later eleventh century, as part of the reform movement sweeping across the European clergy, triggered in part by debates over the practice of simony, in which Church offices were effectively bought and sold.

Many monastic figures railed against simony (including familiar names like Abbo of Fleury and Peter Damian), but few wanted to go so far as a certain cardinal named Humbert. He drew a close link between simony and lay investiture, complaining that men could become bishops by bribing the secular authority, with the decision then being rubber-stamped by the Church (§20).[5] Humbert was even willing to say that a bishop who paid for his office was a bishop in name only, so that any priest he then ordained was not really a priest either and thus could not administer the sacraments. There's an echo here of a late antique controversy involving Augustine. He had refuted the Donatists, who claimed that a priest in a state of grave sin cannot effectively perform sacraments. Augustine denied this, in part because of the alarming consequence that every Christian would somehow need to verify the state of his or her priest's soul. For similar reasons, Peter Damian and others rejected Humbert's position.

But the problem was admitted to be a real one, and under the pontificate of Gregory VII (which lasted from 1073 to 1085 AD), the Investiture Contest was like an inexpertly poured beer: it came rapidly to a head. Gregory had a great zeal for reform and an equally great zeal for strengthening the papacy. It's no coincidence, for example, that Berengar's interpretation of the Eucharist as merely symbolic was condemned under Gregory. This was part of a larger quest to establish Rome as the supreme arbiter in matters of doctrine. Gregory's push for centralizing Church power in the papacy meant reigning in the bishops, and asserting dominion over them. And how could he do that if bishoprics were in the gift of secular rulers? On the other hand, look at it from the point of view of a king or emperor, such as

Henry IV. The loss of control over the bishoprics would be a huge blow, in practical and symbolic terms. So it was all but inevitable that Henry and Gregory would come into conflict.

In the popular imagination, the central event of their contest of wills is Henry's capitulation, begging for forgiveness in the snow after Gregory excommunicated him (§33–4). But this was in fact a mere tactical surrender on Henry's part, which helped him win the wider war. Once Gregory did absolve him, Henry was able to consolidate his political position in Germany, and ultimately to depose Gregory as Pope. The Investiture Contest was not over, though. It would finally be resolved when the next German emperor, Henry V, reached an agreement with Pope Calixtus II. We know this agreement as the Concordat of Worms (§44). The broad outlines of the reconciliation were already proposed by Ivo of Chartres, an expert on canon law who had studied with Lanfranc of Bec and associated with Abelard's despised teacher Anselm of Laon.[6] Ivo saw clearly the key problem, which was the fact that a bishopric combined both worldly and spiritual authority. Returning to something of the spirit of Gelasius' "dualist" political theory, Ivo suggested that kings should still bestow land and any other temporal gifts upon a would-be bishop, but the Church would also need to confer religious office on the candidate (§40). Effectively, both sides would thus have a veto.

What we're seeing here is the emergence of the idea that political authority can be distinctively secular, with religious standing being reserved for the Church. Of course, the idea was emerging slowly, and very incompletely. Kings were being deprived of control over spiritual affairs, but their own standing continued to be linked intimately to religion. The Carolingian monarchs were said to "be king by the grace of God (*rex dei gratia*)," a formula already used by Isidore of Seville. And though they were said to hold the sword of earthly force, which one can see as a step towards the modern idea of the state monopoly on violence, there was the significant caveat that kings and emperors should always wield this sword in defense of the Church. For this reason, those authors who polemicized on behalf of the kings sought to de-emphasize the secular nature of royal authority.

As so often in this period, some of our best examples come in works of unknown authorship. The so-called "Anonymous of York" set forth the boldest claims for kingly privilege. Anonymous put all his emphasis on the king's holiness, going so far as to argue that even in Jesus Christ, kingship was more important than priesthood (§37). The rival view was advanced by propagandists who supported the primacy of the papacy. A particularly interesting author from this camp was the fabulously named Manegold of Lautenbach. He lived through the highpoint of the Investiture Contest and wrote in favor of the claims of Pope Gregory VII, arguing that the Church can rightly depose an earthly ruler who fails to live up to the necessary moral standards (§38), whereas papal authority is not invalidated by moral failures in the man who holds the office (notice that he here adheres to Augustine's anti-Donatist position). For his pains Manegold was imprisoned by Henry IV.

Manegold of Lautenbach is especially noteworthy because he drew a direct connection between the royalist position and the study of philosophy. In a treatise attacking a royalist opponent named Wolfhelm, Manegold produced one of the most bitter anti-philosophical works of the early medieval period.[7] He grudgingly admitted that the philosophers sometimes got things right, as with their teachings on virtue (ch.22), which is only to be expected since they are using the God-given power of reason. But philosophers too are merely human, and so are bound to go astray. Inevitably, then, their views are a mix of true and false (ch.1). Writing at the close of the eleventh century, Manegold makes for a vivid contrast with authors of the century to come. Though he admires Plato above all others (ch.2), as many twelfth-century thinkers will, he unhesitatingly identifies errors in Plato and dismisses out of hand the notion that the Platonic dialogues might refer obliquely to the holy Trinity (ch.8). Even before the burst of interest in natural philosophy in the twelfth century, he is already warning that inquiry into the physical world comes at the expense of religious concerns (ch.20). He also reminds the reader that all natural laws are subject to revision by miracles, remarking gleefully that these have been so frequent that nature can hardly have any confidence in herself anymore (ch.22).

The Concordat of Worms was reached in the helpfully memorable year of 1122.[8] But this did not usher in an age without political thought. To the contrary: the first major medieval work devoted to political philosophy was written later in the twelfth century by John of Salisbury, who wrote so admiringly, albeit at second-hand, about the teaching methods of Bernard of Chartres.[9] John's own list of teachers was second to none in this period: he studied with Peter Abelard, Gilbert of Poitiers, William of Conches, and Thierry of Chartres. From the tradition of scholarship associated with Chartres, he inherited a love for classical literature, so much so that he's been called the "best-read man of the twelfth century." And he was no amateur when it came to political life, either. John left the cloistered world of the schoolmen for the rough and tumble of Church politics. He applied for a post with the Archbishop of Canterbury in 1147, armed with a letter of introduction from no less a personage than Bernard of Clairvaux. He spent the next twelve years as an ambassador for the Church, rubbing shoulders with the Pope and somehow finding time to write his two main works: the Metalogicon, an impassioned defense of the logical arts from certain unnamed critics, and the work relevant to us here, the Policraticus.[10]

John's wide reading is on show throughout the *Policraticus*, as he draws on Cicero, shows unusually good knowledge of Aristotle for the time, and quotes such ancient writers as Horace and Virgil.[11] He constantly illustrates his points with examples from classical history, much as Machiavelli will do several centuries later, and has a good eye for the amusing anecdote, as when he repeats Cicero's wry remark about a man who served as Roman consul for only one day: "so vigilant was he, that he never slept during his term of office" (§7.25). John also cites at length from another supposed source, a letter to the Emperor Trajan written by the historian and philosopher Plutarch (§5.1). But it seems almost certain that he has only invented this letter as a mouthpiece for his own ideas. These include an extended comparison of society to a unified organic body, with the ruler as its head, the senate or advisors of the ruler as the heart, the treasurers as the stomach, the soldiers and tax collectors as the hands, and the lower classes as the feet (§5.2; also at, for example, §4.8, 6.1). While this sort of metaphor did appear in antiquity,[12] John gives it unprecedented and vivid detail, as when he says that the functions of the lower classes are so manifold that society has more "feet" than a centipede (§6.20).

Like any good philosophical analogy, John's comparison has important implications. If the whole of society is like a single organism, then each of its parts is intended to contribute to the welfare of the whole. Echoing themes already found in Plato's *Republic*, John insists that each member of the society must carry out his proper function if the society is to flourish (§6.22). This applies even, or rather especially, to the ruler. John recognizes the unchallenged authority of the ruler, who is an image of God upon earth (§4.1). But this does not mean that the ruler is somehow outside of the social body as a whole. Rather, as its head, the true king or "prince" is one who looks to the good of all the members, and he is subject to the laws just like anyone else (§4.1, 8.17). Again as in Plato, the benevolent ruler has a kind of perverse twin, the malevolent tyrant, who instead uses his position for selfish gain: an image of Satan, rather than of God.

John's political theory takes a startling turn when he expresses approval of tyrannicide, that is, the murder of such an evil king.[13] He arrives at the topic in a rather roundabout way, in the course of talking about flattery at court. Such behavior is normally condemnable, but flattery of a tyrant may be excused as a necessary expedient. John then adds that we're surely allowed to flatter such a ruler, given that we're even permitted to slay him (§3.15). After dropping this bombshell, John says little more on the topic. He does later mention a series of classical tyrants who got their comeuppance, sometimes by being murdered. But he seems far less aware of the potentially explosive nature of his teaching here than later readers were, for instance Fidel Castro, who cited John in a defense of his actions in the Cuban revolution!

Some readers have inferred from this that John was not really making a practical or political recommendation, but simply pointing out that tyrants tend to get murdered, and their murderers excused. On this reading, his remarks are (yet again in the spirit of Plato) just part of a wider case that the true king prospers in this world and the next, whereas the tyrant is inevitably miserable (§8.21). But upon closer inspection, it seems that John is serious about permitting tyrannicide. It's just that he severely limits the practical implications of this permission. For one thing, a king-slayer motivated by justice should wait to be sure the wicked ruler will not mend his ways. Even then, he may not go back on an oath to the king, which would eliminate many potential assassins in a feudal context, nor may he violate religious obligations in carrying out the murder. The whole idea is to act as an instrument of divine justice, so the last thing you should do is act against God in the process of eliminating the tyrant. In the end, John suggests, it's probably best just to pray for God to deal with the tyrant rather than taking matters into one's own hands (§8.20). Furthermore, John sees tyranny as a more widespread phenomenon. It's an evil character type that can be found among private citizens, who are to be dealt with by the rule of law rather than vigilante justice, also among priests. Ecclesiastical tyranny is the most harmful of all, because the priests look to our salvation rather than our worldly welfare (§8.23). Yet one may not exercise violence against this kind of tyrant, because of the sanctity of the clergy.

Ultimately, John is more interested in the ideal case where things go well than in the cases where tyranny undermines the unity and prosperity of society. That happy outcome requires virtue on the part of both ruler and clergy.[14] But like Manegold of Lautenbach, John thinks that moral failure can undermine a secular ruler's legitimacy, whereas this is never the case with a pope. Here John taps into a rich vein of political thought, which holds that an unjust ruler is not just an unfortunate cross to be borne, but in truth no ruler at all, whether or not anyone is in a position to do something about it. (Remember the etymology provided by Isidore of Seville, who related the Latin word for king, *rex*, to the word *recte*, meaning "correctly" or "with justice"; see Chapter 2 above.) With his focus on justice and his insistence that even the king is subject to the law, John was a man of his time. The twelfth century was not just an era of resurgent philosophy. It was also a time of law, with legal scholars doing what John was doing: turning back to antiquity for inspiration, and adapting classical ideas for their new situation.

18

LAW AND ORDER
GRATIAN AND PETER LOMBARD

Twelfth-century intellectuals have a lot to answer for. It was at this time that scholasticism began to flower, before blossoming fully in the thirteenth century. So for several leading thinkers of the early modern era, it was here that the rot set in. Men like Descartes and Hobbes quietly borrowed from scholasticism, while loudly denouncing its shortcomings. That attitude still persists today, so that the word "scholasticism" stands for an inflexible body of authoritative doctrines which only left room for philosophers to engage in pointless distinction-mongering. But these accusations are largely unfounded. While exploring the roots of scholasticism, we've seen remarkably open-minded writers engaging in controversies over fundamental theological and philosophical issues. In this chapter, I'll call two further witnesses for the defense: Gratian and Peter Lombard. Far from parroting an unquestioned and monolithic body of teachings, these two central authors of the scholastic tradition exposed and creatively reconciled tensions in the authoritative canon.

Both of them hailed from northern Italy, which along with Paris was an early center for scholasticism, especially with regard to law. The resurgence of legal activity began in the later eleventh century, when the *Digest* of Roman law assembled under the Eastern emperor Justinian was being read in Italy. In the twelfth century, the city of Bologna in particular became the place to be for ambitious young lawyers, and Gratian seems to have been active there in the first half of the century. His masterful compilation of law circulated in different versions during his own lifetime, and it hasn't been possible to determine the date he wrote it, though we know it appeared at some point in a twenty-year span from 1125 to 1145. It's usually called the *Decretum*, but the title that Gratian gave it is more revealing: the *Concordantia discordantium canonum*. This shows that Gratian's goal was not simply to lay down the law, if you will, but to bring discordant legal texts into agreement.

Towards this end, he supplied thousands of quotations from a wide range of sources, including Latin and Greek church fathers, earlier church councils, and letters written by popes. He was following in the footsteps of earlier compilers, a notable example being Ivo of Chartres, whom we just met in the context of the

Investiture Contest. Ivo is not exactly a household name, but perhaps he should be, given that he was both an early proponent of the solution accepted in the Concordat of Worms *and* a forerunner of Gratian. It's important to note that Gratian and Ivo were talking mostly about *church* law, not secular law. So Gratian's *Decretum* is not about general problems of property, contract, or criminal law. Rather it deals with issues that arise in ecclesiastical contexts: what to do about misbehaving priests, or the range of powers that belong to bishops. He has much to say about the appointment of clergy, as well he might, given the context of the Investiture Contest.

Gratian improved on earlier canonists like Ivo by being more comprehensive, but his real innovation was his ambition of bringing the legal tradition into agreement with itself. In addition to quoting from earlier texts, he adds bridging passages and comments (*dicta*) to explain the relevance of the material and resolve apparent conflicts. His favorite author is Augustine, and as anyone who has read him will know, Augustine alone could serve as an abundant source of apparent inconsistencies. An important precedent for Gratian's harmonizing approach was Peter Abelard's treatise *Sic et non*. But Abelard, in characteristically provocative fashion, simply juxtaposed conflicting passages and left the job of reconciliation to the reader. Gratian's *Decretum* is like a legal version of *Sic et non* with an answer key.

The result was a work that became canonical in every sense of the word, attracting more than one hundred commentaries before the century was out.[1] When universities began to appear in places like Bologna, Paris, and Oxford, Gratian's work provided a textbook for students. Some observers worried that law was outstripping theology as a subject. As bright young men flocked to become lawyers, one contemporary complained that "Bologna grows fat while Paris shrivels,"[2] reflecting a widespread perception that northern Italy was the home of law, Paris of theology. Gratian's *Decretum* would be supplanted as the key legal compilation in the mid-thirteenth century. But he is still quoted liberally by philosophers like Thomas Aquinas, and in that period remained important to later experts in canon law like Accursius.

The *Decretum* touches on a number of philosophical issues, sometimes in passing and sometimes at greater length. The best example is the opening sections, which take up questions about the nature of the law itself. What is it? Under what circumstances does it have force? How are we to identify the sources on which to base church law, in particular? He begins by telling us, "the human race is ruled by two things, namely by law (*ius*) and customs. Natural law is what is contained in Scripture (*in lege*) and in the Gospel" (§1).[3] Gratian then adds that the so-called "golden rule," Christ's exhortation to do to others as we would have them do to us (Matthew 7:12), is an expression of this natural law. This is a big moment, since it's the first time that we're encountering the concept of natural law, which will play a major role in later medieval and early modern philosophy (see below, Chapter 39).[4]

We may immediately feel wrong-footed, though. The phrase "natural law" conjures up the idea of a set of rules that we should all be able to access with our inborn reason. Gratian seems to agree, since he will go on to say that natural law emerges along with "rational creatures" and never changes thereafter (§5). But if natural law has to do with reason, and not revelation, then why draw such a strong link between natural law and Scripture? Of course, Gratian is writing about church law, so he wants to stress that Scripture does indeed have a distinctively legal kind of authority. But he does not seem to be saying that the deliverances of natural law can *only* be reached by turning to Scripture. Nor does he think that everything found in Scripture is part of the natural law (§6). Rather, he's doing what he does best, by emphasizing agreement, in this case between natural and religious law. His example is well chosen. The golden rule may be found in the New Testament, but it is also something that humans could grasp without the benefit of revelation. Even then, God would be part of the story. After all, human reason itself is a divine gift, as far as Gratian is concerned. Thus, heathens too are drawing on a heavenly source when they discover and follow the natural law with no help from the Bible.

Alongside the natural law, there is what Gratian calls "human law" (§1, quoting Isidore of Seville). This means any law set down by a human authority, whether secular or ecclesiastical. In addition, there are all the requirements and guidelines that fall under the heading of "custom." How, then, does custom relate to human and natural law?[5] One thing is clear: no human law or custom has force if it contravenes the natural law. Suppose it is part of the natural law that children should respect their parents. If so, then we cannot be obligated to mistreat our parents just because some king lays down a supposed law directing us to do so, or (less hypothetically) because we belong to a society where the old are routinely scorned by the young. So the natural law sets boundaries for human laws and custom. There's plenty of room within these boundaries, though, which is why there can be so much variation between various human laws and various customs, without any departure from natural justice.

More difficult is the question of how customs interact with human law. Gratian tries to strike a delicate balance here, as he juxtaposes texts that seem to give priority to custom with others that emphasize the authority of written laws. He reasonably points out that laws are pointless if they contradict deeply ingrained social practices (§4). Had he been alive in 1920s America, Gratian would not have been surprised that Prohibition failed to produce a teetotal population. Custom also gives us rules to follow when human law is silent. On the other hand, Gratian is a great supporter of centralized authority, especially the authority of the pope. He strongly supports the Church's side in the Investiture Contest, declaring lay investiture as invalid. His compilation of church doctrine is itself an attempt to strike a blow for law against custom. With a book like Gratian's, the popes and their emissaries would find it easier to insist that local church authorities around Europe were (almost literally) singing from the same hymn sheet.

These issues about the nature and sources of legal authority are the most obviously philosophical ones in the *Decretum*. But there are many more, sometimes raised only in passing, as when Gratian mentions that there is one circumstance where we may be permitted to violate natural law: when we are faced with an exclusive choice between two evils (§13). Interestingly, a gloss on this passage gives as an example the Jews whose conscience told them they must crucify Jesus. As Abelard pointed out, they were (this time, literally) damned if they did and damned if they didn't. Murdering Christ was a sin, but neither would it have been right for them to violate their own moral conviction. Gratian also offers influential remarks on another issue: the question of when Christians can justly partake in war (see further Chapter 40).[6] He sets down two basic requirements here, namely that the war be declared by a legitimate authority and that the war be undertaken for reasons of defense or redressing an injury, and for the sake of justice rather than revenge.

At first this sounds rather restrictive. Armies would be unleashed only in response to the wrongful aggression of others. But when Gratian discusses the sorts of wrongdoing that could justly provoke a declaration of war, he states that all enemies of the Church are fair targets. This was no idle point, given that the First Crusade had been launched in living memory, at the end of the eleventh century, with the Second Crusade coming up shortly after Gratian wrote the *Decretum*. Another problem he faces is narrower and has to do with the role of clergy in war. Priests are forbidden to shed blood; yet it was common for them to go on campaign, with the Crusades again providing a good example. Supposedly, one bishop avoided the difficulty by electing to use a mace rather than a sword in battle! Gratian's solution is slightly less creative: clergymen may help wage war in an advisory and spiritual capacity, but not do any fighting themselves.

Gratian was not the only systematizing thinker of the twelfth century to hail from northern Italy. Indeed, he was not even the most famous. That honor must go to another man, whose geographical origin is clear from his very name: Peter Lombard. He wrote a massive treatise on theology, whose broad approach was much like the one Gratian took in the *Decretum*. Apparently conflicting authorities were quoted, with Peter Lombard explaining how the conflicts could be resolved. His masterpiece is the *Sentences*. The English version of the title may seem rather generic.

One imagines a cover blurb: "If you liked Peter Lombard's first two books, the *Letters* and the *Words*, you'll love his *Sentences!*" But actually the Latin title *Sententiae* refers to the authoritative opinions he is quoting. In any case, here's how influential it was: I could spend the rest of this book talking about nothing but texts responding to the *Sentences*, and still do a pretty good job of covering medieval philosophy without any gaps. It became standard for theologians to cut their teeth by commenting on the work. This could be the occasion for path-breaking philosophy when the commentaries were written by such luminaries as Thomas Aquinas, Duns Scotus, and William of Ockham. The practice would become so well established that we still find Martin Luther commenting on the *Sentences* in the early sixteenth century. His personal copy, with extensive annotations, still exists today.[7]

It's only with Peter Lombard that we finally see the full emergence of something many would assume was an ever-present feature of medieval intellectual life: a systematic and complete presentation of Christian theology. Abelard and Gilbert of Poitiers had ambitions in this direction, and Peter drew on both of them. But the most thorough single work of theology prior to his *Sentences* was Hugh of Saint Victor's *On the Sacraments*.[8] All these men were active in Paris. So it's no coincidence that Peter came there early in his career, bearing a letter of introduction addressed to the Abbey of Saint Victor by none other than Bernard of Clairvaux, whose endeavor to live a godly life apparently involved achieving omnipresence in the history of this period. Peter may even have studied with Hugh of Saint Victor personally. But in his *Sentences* he dropped Hugh's distinctively "historical" approach and adopted a more "logical" or conceptual structure.[9] Peter also helped his readers by equipping his text with features we'd take for granted today, but which were not so obvious at the time, such as a table of contents, detailed chapter headings, and even dots to indicate where direct quotation of other texts begin and end, the way we use quotation marks.[10]

Like Gratian, Peter Lombard wants to demonstrate that the apparent differences between authoritative texts mask a deeper underlying agreement. The approach is summed up in the nifty Latin expression *diversi sed non adversi* ("diverse, but not opposed"). On some particularly difficult topics, though, Peter simply set out different theological positions without trying to harmonize them or decide between them. One such case was the Incarnation. From all the many topics covered in the *Sentences* I've chosen to discuss this one, not only because it is an important theological issue but also because Peter's remarks on it occasioned some criticism amongst his readers.[11] The question had already been thoroughly explored in late ancient Christian philosophy.[12] Christ was both fully human and the incarnation of the second Person of the Trinity. But how can one person be both fully human and fully divine?

Peter approaches the question much as the late ancient authors had done, by asking about the relationship between two natures in Christ (§5.1.1). But his immediate points of reference are more recent. He discusses three positions on the question, which recall the theories of the Incarnation defended by Hugh of Saint Victor, Gilbert of Poitiers, and Peter Abelard. All three shared a basic assumption about human nature, namely that every human has an immaterial soul and a material body. Since the soul seems to be much more like God than the body is, it may seem natural to assume that Christ's divine nature had to do especially with his soul. And indeed, Peter Lombard remarks that divinity became united to Christ's flesh "through his intellect" or rational soul (§2.2.1). On the other hand, Christ's divinity should be somehow joined to his entire human nature, and human nature does include the body. How then was divinity joined to both body and soul in Christ?

The first answer, inspired by Hugh of Saint Victor, is that the body and soul were both "assumed" by the divine nature (§6.2.1). This avoids the difficulty of leaving Christ's body outside his divinity, but threatens to eliminate the human nature entirely. The second view, which is that of Gilbert of Poitiers, takes more or less the opposite approach by saying that divinity is a third, distinct thing in Christ added to body and soul (§6.3.1). Here there's no danger of eliding Christ's humanity, but it's difficult to see how Christ will be a single, unified person; divinity and humanity would be juxtaposed rather than fused. Indeed, you might even wonder how on this view we have one rather than two persons in Christ, and the whole point was to understand how a single person can have two natures. Finally, there is the third view, based on Abelard. This time the idea is to start with the divine Person, and imagine it taking on human nature in a more accidental or extrinsic way, like someone putting on a set of clothes that he can later take off (§6.4.1).

Peter Lombard is too modest to pick from among these options. He simply documents the strengths and weaknesses of all three views, without endorsing any of them. Oddly, he was later taken to task for embracing one idea that he seems to reject pretty decisively in the *Sentences*, namely that Christ's human personhood is "nothing" whatsoever. If it were, then his humanity would constitute a further Person alongside the second Person of the Trinity. The judgment that in Christ the human person was nothing has been called "Christological nihilism," which I mention mostly in case any readers are in a religious heavy metal band and looking for a good album title. There are some hints that Peter may have taught this view in private,[13] but, as I say, he does not endorse Christological nihilism in the *Sentences*. More generally, the *Sentences* was mostly accepted as being not just acceptably orthodox but the ultimate guidebook to Christian theology and its textual sources. Hence its long career as a basis for commentaries, which gives the work a central role in the history of philosophy.

Of course, Peter Lombard was setting out to write about theology, not philosophy. But like Gratian, he touches on many philosophically important topics, some of which are familiar to us from entirely non-theological contexts.[14] Indeed, the debate over the Incarnation we've just been discussing has a variety of philosophical implications. Any solution depends on a theory of human nature, and a view on the question of how natures or essences belong to particular things; it connects to questions about parts and wholes too. Another nice example of the philosophical interest of the *Sentences* comes along later in the third book, when Peter is discussing Christ's possession of the virtues. This leads him to inquire into the nature of faith, hope, and charity. In this context, he asks whether perfect charity is compatible with treating some people better than others (§29.2.6). Modern ethicists still wonder whether we are justified in preferring to promote the welfare of our own friends and family as opposed to, say, strangers in other countries who are poverty-stricken and need our help much more than our intimates do. Admittedly, in the *Sentences* the question comes and goes quickly. But that very brevity invited later authors to have their say on this and other philosophical issues Peter had raised, producing more than a few sentences of their own.

19

LEADING LIGHT
HILDEGARD OF BINGEN

When I was a graduate student at the University of Notre Dame, a joke was doing the rounds. Notre Dame is playing football away at Boston College, and the two coaches are chatting before the game. The BC coach asks whether the Notre Dame coach would like to know the result beforehand. "How's that possible?" asks the Notre Dame coach, and his colleague says, "Just follow me." He goes to a payphone and feeds in ten dollars in quarters, then dials and hands the phone to the Notre Dame coach. A deep voice says, "This is God. What would you like to know?" The coach asks about the result of the game, and God says, "You're going to lose by a field goal." When the game is played, the prediction proves true. The following season, BC is playing the return game at Notre Dame. The two coaches meet again, and agree to try to find out the result ahead of time. They go to a payphone and the Notre Dame coach slots in a single quarter. The BC coach says, "Only 25 cents?" "Sure," says the Notre Dame coach, "from here it's a local call."

The point of the joke is presumably to exalt the home of the Fighting Irish at the expense of their fellow Catholic school, Boston College. But I enjoy it in a different, rather more ironic way: it exposes the preposterous notion that God, assuming He exists, would be more strongly tied to one university than another. I say it's preposterous, but probably not everyone back at South Bend would agree. This is, after all, a region that used to refuse to set its clocks ahead in spring like the rest of the country, instead sticking to what the locals liked to call "God's time." But for me, the notion that God arbitrarily chooses certain people or places for His favor is downright medieval. I don't mean that as an insult, of course, but as a genuine historical observation. Actually the idea goes all the way back to antiquity. In one of his more puzzling pronouncements (which is saying something), Aristotle remarked that the divine mover is located at the periphery of the cosmos, a line which occasioned many attempted explanations by later commentators.[1] The phenomenon of prophecy, meanwhile, was common currency among the Abrahamic religions. And prophecy was usually understood as God's choosing certain humans to be granted special knowledge. Hence many ancient thinkers and nearly all medieval ones accepted the possibility that God manifests Himself in specific places or to specific people.

But it's one thing to believe this, another to be confronted with someone who claims to have experienced such a manifestation. That's what happened to (here he is yet again) Bernard of Clairvaux in the year 1146, when he opened his mail and found a letter from a woman named Hildegard of Bingen (3–5).[2] Amidst fulsome praise for Bernard, the letter contained some disconcerting claims. Hildegard wrote that she had been having visions, in fact experiencing them since childhood. She had long kept them secret, but was now asking Bernard what to do about it. Characteristically, though, Hildegard had already decided what to do. Five years earlier, a particularly vivid vision had unlocked for her the inner meaning of Scripture. After confiding in a trusted monk named Volmar, she had begun to compose her first major piece of writing, called *Scivias*—the title apparently abbreviates the Latin *Sci vias Domini*, "Know the ways of the Lord."[3] So Hildegard was by this time preparing to reveal herself to the world, just as God had revealed Himself to her. Bernard and other church authorities undertook to investigate her claims and Hildegard's gift was accepted as true. Henceforth, she would be not the obscure head of a convent in the Rhine valley, southwest of the city of Mainz. She would be the "sybil of the Rhine," a visionary whose fame spread across Europe, like Joan of Arc but with a pen instead of a sword—and we know which of those is the mightier.

When Hildegard wrote to Bernard, she was already well into in her forties, having been born just before the turn of the twelfth century. According to her own account of her childhood, which is quoted in one of the admiring biographies written after Hildegard's death, she was already visited by what she called the "living light" at the age of 3 (190). She began to display what one can only call magical powers, for instance by foreseeing the pattern on the coat of an as yet unborn calf. As a reward for this adorable act of clairvoyance, Hildegard was given the calf as a present. Her parents could afford it: they were well-to-do. But they didn't do all that well by Hildegard. At the age of 8 she was entrusted to the care of a woman named Jutta, who brought Hildegard with her to a convent attached to the monastery of Disibodenberg. Hildegard would remain here for decades, living a life of solitude but managing to acquire some degree of education thanks to Jutta and later the monk Volmar. She would later withdraw with her sisters to a new location some distance away, a decision which would annoy just about everyone concerned, apart from Hildegard herself. But she usually got her way.

In this she was, of course, unlike most twelfth-century women. But then, not too many twelfth-century women had direct communications from God, or would have been in a position to write about such communications. (It will become more common in the thirteenth and fourteenth centuries, as we'll be seeing in due course.) As if that weren't enough, Hildegard wrote on scientific topics, particularly medicine, with descriptions of the properties of plants, animals, and gemstones placed in a setting reminiscent of the works on natural philosophy composed by her contemporaries. Speaking of composing, she also wrote words and music for liturgical use—scores for these pieces have survived and they are frequently performed by early music groups. These compositions are quite unusual for the period, which is unsurprising, given that, as one of her correspondents gushed in a letter written to Hildegard, she had undertaken no prior study of music (181).

In her own day and in modern times, Hildegard has often been treated as a kind of idiot savant, a mere conduit for the inspiration that flowed through her. Yet her three main works all present intense descriptions of the visions she had enjoyed, followed by highly articulate discussions of the theological and philosophical meaning of those visions. The obvious inference is that Hildegard was both an intense visionary and a highly articulate theologian and philosopher. So you can't blame me for being suspicious when her medieval biographers emphasize her simplicity at the expense of her learning, celebrating the blazing divine light that dwelt within Hildegard rather than paying tribute to her intellectual firepower. But I have to admit that this attitude began with Hildegard herself. She said that the entire content of her writings was revealed to her by the living light: not only the visions, but also the interpretive passages in which she makes sense of them. Her intimate understanding of the Christian textual tradition, and even of books by "certain philosophers" (192), was not the result of study but simply another manifestation of her gift.

This aspect of Hildegard's intellectual profile is bound up with the most basic and yet most remarkable fact about her: she was a woman. From what we have seen so far, medieval philosophy was an exclusively male pursuit, practiced in the boys' club contexts of monasteries and schools. The coming of the universities at the turn of the thirteenth century is going to introduce many changes, but gender diversity will not be among them. If Hildegard and her writings were taken seriously, indeed recognized as sources of deep wisdom, it was precisely because that wisdom was understood to be not her own. Hildegard herself said as much. Anyone who picks up her writings expecting to find a proto-feminist will be alarmed at the frequency with which she emphasizes her lowly status as a mere woman, "formed in the rib" of Adam (31). Her ideas, she seems to suggest, would count for nothing if they had not been dictated to her by God Himself. In a letter she wrote to her contemporary Elisabeth of Schönau,[4] Hildegard claimed to be nothing but a "vessel built by God for Himself and filled with his inspiration" (79).

Yet a comparison of these two women reveals that Hildegard was extraordinary even among medieval women mystics. Where Elisabeth had to rely on her brother to write down her visions, Hildegard boldly wrote her own treatises—and in Latin, the language of intellectual culture, rather than in German.[5] Then, there is Hildegard's confident interpretation of her own visions. After you've read Hildegard, you'll probably remember above all the imagery. *Scivias* begins by describing how she saw a mountain "the color of iron," upon which was seated a vast man glowing with light and sprouting two wings, while a small child stood at the foot of the mountain, its face obscured by light pouring forth from the man above (132). But do press on to read her explanation of the imagery, which tells you that the man is God, the mountain His created kingdom, and the child, the humble person who is suffused with grace. Hildegard is not sharing with us a report about some inscrutable "trance" state. The visionary image serves as a *text* that stands in need of interpretation, like the text of the Bible, and it is paired with an authoritative exposition that only Hildegard can supply. Indeed her works frequently slide from exegesis of the visions to exegesis of biblical passages, and back again. So even though Hildegard is often described as a "mystic," her works are full of discursive, explanatory prose.

Likewise, Hildegard is far from disdaining rationality as a feeble and inadequate mode of understanding. To the contrary, she speaks frequently and positively of human reason, which she identifies as the third and highest part of the human being, along with body and soul (173). She sees vice as a failure of rationality (145), and reason as our instrument for reaching God (95). But reason does need to know its limits and accept guidance from faith. Hildegard makes this clear on the rare occasions when she alludes to the masters of the schools in her day, usually critically. Her attitude here is close to that of Bernard of Clairvaux or William of St. Thierry, who encouraged Bernard to persecute Peter Abelard.[6] Hildegard complains that the schoolmen were motivated by desire for fame rather than wisdom, and blames them for failing to root out heretics like the Cathars (who, she remarks in a particularly wince-inducing moment, are "worse than the Jews"[7]).

Were these accusations based on actual acquaintance with scholastic teachings? Hildegard's works touch on a wide range of philosophical and theological issues, so she frequently has the opportunity to imply such acquaintance. And imply it she does. To mention just a few examples: she refers to the "understanding and will" as twin powers of the soul (7); she speaks of God creating natural things like a smith forming things from bronze (14), much as authors like Bernard Silvestris spoke of nature "coining" things from matter; she distinguishes God's foreknowledge from His creative activity (176); she assumes Augustine's idea that evil is non-being.

With her typical flair she adds to that idea a wonderful image, saying that evil first emerged when Satan fell and stretched out his hand to grasp at the nothingness through which he was plummeting (94). Her works on physical topics are also full of recognizable, if occasionally somewhat idiosyncratic, appropriations of standard medical learning. She teaches for example that gemstones contain inner heat, having been formed by warmth in the earth, which accounts for their beneficial healing powers (107).

But Hildegard's most remarkable confrontation with scholasticism is a letter she addressed to the Parisian master Odo of Soissons. He had written to her to ask her opinion about Gilbert of Poitiers' idea that divinity is a property distinct from God Himself. As usual Hildegard begins by stressing her humble position. She is not "imbued with human doctrine" but depends on God for guidance. Yet she is far from hesitant in answering his question. She well understands Gilbert's point, and thinks he is laboring under the misconception that human words can be applied to God.[8] Like other critics of Gilbert, she argues that his teaching would compromise divine simplicity. Divinity is therefore to be identified with God, and in fact nothing whatsoever can be added to Him, in adherence to the rule that "whatever is in God is God" (22).

Surely though, God's light didn't descend all the way from heaven just to tell Hildegard that Gilbert and his scholastic colleagues were stepping out of line. Didn't the visions grant her insights that were unavailable in any other way? Actually, it seems not. One of the stranger aspects of her writings is that, though the accounts of the visions are very strange, the ideas she extracts from them with the help of the living light aren't particularly strange at all. Far from giving her a unique way of understanding God, the light frequently tells her that God is beyond her grasp, just as He is beyond the grasp of all other humans (17, 133, 148, 153). Divine transcendence is, of course, anything but an unusual idea, even if one can count on Hildegard to express it in an unusually memorable way: the knowledge of humanity is like a mountain rising up towards God but the summit of that mountain is God's own knowledge, which remains hidden from view (159).

Similarly Hildegard's exegetical remarks, whether directed to her own visions or to Scripture, often juxtapose historical, allegorical, and ethical interpretation, something familiar to us from Hugh of Saint Victor.[9] Her cosmology too is not unlike what we find in other natural philosophy of the time. There are occasional unfamiliar elements, as when she describes the cosmos as having an egg-shaped rather than spherical form. But this seems to be intended mostly for symbolic effect,[10] with the shape of the egg representing the initial simplicity of humankind broadening into understanding with revelation, and then constricting to a time of great tribulations as the world approaches its end (92). One of the key themes we found in Bernard Silvestris and Alan of Lille was that the human is an image in miniature of the universe, a so-called "microcosm." This is a favorite theme of Hildegard too. She writes that "the human being contains the likeness of the heaven and earth within" (12; cf. 95). In a more detailed application of the same idea, she sounds a bit like John of Salisbury comparing society to the human body: the heavenly firmament is analogous to the head, with the planets being like our eyes, the air corresponds to our hearing, and so on down to the earth, which is like the heart (105).

This is, of course, not to say that Hildegard's writing is banal or derivative; far from it. It is to say that what is really philosophically revolutionary about her writing is not so much what she believes but the way she writes about her beliefs. She speaks with an authority that no philosophical argument could ever provide, because when she speaks, it is actually God we are hearing. The overall effect is as if an Old Testament prophet were proclaiming the philosophical teachings of the day. This is particularly important when it comes to the area of philosophy that is perhaps most dominant in Hildegard's writings, which is ethics. Again, her ethical teaching itself is nothing revolutionary. She praises virtue and scorns vice, and for her, as for so many Christian authors, virtue is love of God instead of the world. But no other author of her time, and few of any time, express this core idea with such a powerful combination of imagery, poetry, and stagecraft. And I do mean stagecraft. Hildegard's *Scivias* includes a play written to be performed by her sisters in costume, in which they acted the parts of the virtues, the vices, and the penitent soul who is trying to improve her lot (53–62). This raised both eyebrows and hackles. An abbess who gives us a late entry in the fierce competition for best name of the twelfth century, Tengswich of Andernach, wrote to Hildegard criticizing the impropriety of such goings on.

The practical implications of Hildegard's epistemic and moral certainty are evident from her dealings with church authorities. Consider a letter she wrote to the Archbishop of Mainz, who would have been the leading ecclesiastical official in her area. Hildegard had been instructed to allow one of her nuns to depart in order to take up a post elsewhere. Unhappy with this decision, Hildegard did not hesitate to pull rank on the archbishop, speaking on behalf of "the clear fountain"—that is, the voice of God—to say that the "legal pretexts brought in order to obtain authority over this girl are useless before God, for I am the height and the depth, the circle and the descending light" (51). In other words, back off. Of course Hildegard is not saying that she herself outranks the bishop. The first-person pronouns in that passage represent God, not her. But given that she claims to speak for God, she can effectively speak with higher authority than any cleric.

Yet Hildegard did not see herself as standing outside the Church's authority. Towards the end of her life she became embroiled in the worst controversy of her career. She was instructed to exhume the body of an excommunicated man buried in her graveyard, and refused on the grounds that the man had recanted before his death. Rather than digging up the grave, she dug in her heels, and once again invoked the moral certainty granted to her by her visions. She did not yield even when her convent was punished by being forbidden to indulge in music, as painful a sanction as one could imagine for Hildegard. Nonetheless, she did work through proper channels to get the decision reversed rather than simply engaging in outright defiance.[11] So we cannot consider Hildegard a rebel, exactly. But she knew her own mind and knew that her mind was aligned with that of God. It's easy to imagine that, admidst the admiration she received from her contemporaries, there was also a good deal of disapproval and frustration, if not envy. Chastizing letters like the one from the abbess Tengswich of Andernach were presumably only the tip of an iceberg.

If she was met with mixed feelings in her own time, Hildegard provokes little but admiration today. I'd like to illustrate one more reason why, which is simply the beauty and power of her writing. Here is one of her verses:

> Love
> abounds in all,
> from the depths exalted and excelling
> over every star,
> and most beloved
> of all,
> for to the highest King the kiss of peace
> she gave.
>
> *Caritas abundat in omnia*
> *de imis excellentissima super*
> *sidera*
> *atque amantissima in omnia*
> *quia summo Regi*
> *osculum pacis dedit.*

Whatever we make of her purported gift of divine vision, it's clear that Hildegard had a gift for writing. For this, for her humble, yet imperious personality, and for her inimitable fusion of powerful imagery and philosophy, if pressed, I might name her as the most fascinating figure we've covered in our look at the twelfth century. At the very least I'd put her in the top three, along with Abelard and Heloise. Notice that the majority of that list is female—so much for the notion that medieval philosophy was a boys' club.

20

REDISCOVERY CHANNEL
TRANSLATIONS INTO LATIN

I know you'll find this difficult to believe, but I can, on occasion, be somewhat pedantic. When American friends invite me somewhere by asking, "Do you want to come with?" it's all I can do to keep myself from shouting back, "The preposition 'with' takes an object!" Fortunately I've read a lot of Stoicism, so I can usually manage to restrain myself and say, "Sure, I'd love to come with...*you*." In their ironic way, the gods of grammar have arranged for me to live in Germany, where I can now annoy others by committing solecisms of my own on a regular basis. But that doesn't mean I don't get annoyed myself. Probably the worst thing is the way younger Germans unnecessarily use English words. My pedant's hackles rise faster than the stock price of a helium manufacturing company when I hear them use verbs like *downloaden, dancen,* or *managen.* Sometimes Germans even use English words and phrases that actual English speakers would never say, like *Handy* for a cell phone, *Smoking* for a tuxedo, and worst of all, *Partner Look* to describe two people who happen to be dressed the same.

But I can't really enjoy gloating about the parlous state of the German language, and not only because, if I did, the most suitable English word to describe my emotional state would be "*Schadenfreude.*" It's also because so much of the philosophy I love goes in for the same sort of linguistic borrowing. If you read through medieval Arabic translations of Hellenic scientific works, you'll come across plenty of examples, with Greek words simply transliterated in Arabic, as when they call "imagination" *fanṭāsiyyā.*[1] A few centuries later, when medieval scholars in turn began to translate from Arabic into Latin, it was a case of *plus ça change, plus c'est la même chose.* One of the first Latin translators was Adelard of Bath, and he scattered Arabisms through his works, sometimes providing an explanatory gloss for the reader. When discussing the outermost sphere of the cosmos, he wrote in Latin script the word *almustakim,* which reflects the Arabic [*al-falak*] *al-mustaqīm,* and helpfully added, *id est rectus:* "that is, straight."[2]

If that still leaves you puzzled, you're probably in the same state as most of Adelard's readers, who had no way of seeing behind the Arabicism to the true meaning. That didn't stop them from trying, though. When Thomas Aquinas was reading another treatise derived from Arabic, he came across the phrase "the first cause is not *yliathim*." You can almost see him scratching his head in confusion, before deciding that this strange word must reflect the Greek word for "matter," *hyle*, which would make sense, given that the first cause or God indeed has no matter. A good guess, then, but wrong. In fact *yliathim* is another Arabicism, based on the word for "shape" or "form." What Aquinas was reading was in fact a statement of God's transcendence: "the first cause has no shape," that is, no determination or attribute.[3] Meanwhile, other coinages from Arabic were becoming common currency in the works of Aquinas and others. The Latin technical terminology of the thirteenth century often reflects terms they inherited from the Arabic-speaking philosophers like Avicenna. To give just two examples, any medieval philosophy scholar will be familiar with the word *intentio* and the phrase *dator formarum*, which correspond respectively to Avicenna's *maʿnā* and *wāḥib al-ṣuwar*. These mean, respectively, the content of a thought in Avicenna's theory of the soul, and the "giver of forms" in his cosmology, which emanates souls and other forms into pre-prepared matter to produce the substances we find in nature.

Such details of vocabulary are glimpses of a wider process. As Greek and Arabic works became available to the medieval Latin reader, philosophy itself was revolutionized. This was one of the two historical developments that had the greatest impact on medieval philosophy as we move forward into the thirteenth century; I'll leave you to guess at the other until Chapter 21. Aquinas and his contemporaries lived in an entirely different intellectual world than Anselm or even Peter Abelard, who was active only a century earlier. The late ancient sources who had exercised so much influence in early medieval philosophy, like Boethius and especially Augustine, remained vitally important. But they were now joined by Muslim philosophers like Avicenna and Averroes, who had been made abundantly accessible in Latin. The most important philosophical source of all was one who had still been known very incompletely in Abelard's day. This was, of course, Aristotle. The coming century of Latin medieval thought will be dominated by the project of absorbing these new sources and integrating them with what had come before, even as some rejected the new texts as a dangerous source of heresy.

Much like the earlier Greek-Arabic translation movement, the Latin translations began with practical disciplines, rather than going straight for metaphysics or works on the soul. Already in the tenth century, Gerbert of Aurillac may have picked up some of his mathematical knowledge thanks to travels in Spain, then part of the Islamic world. When the first major medieval translator came along in the eleventh century, his specialty was medicine. This was Constantine the African, who brought books from Tunisia to Salerno and produced the *Pantegni*, a Latin version of an Arabic medical work.[4] It would be one of the most important sources for the *Dragmaticon* of the Chartrian thinker William of Conches. It was from Constantine's translation that William took the idea that there were several psychological faculties seated in the brain,[5] an idea soon to be reinforced for Latin readers when they read it in Avicenna's work on the soul.

All this was only a small foretaste of the philosophical and scientific feast that would be dished up to the Latin-speaking world in the twelfth century. The first course was served by Adelard of Bath. I choose the word "course" advisedly, since his focus on mathematics seems to have been motivated by a concern with the course of study we know as the liberal arts. His Latin version of Euclid's *Elements*, based not on the original Greek but on an Arabic translation, filled a gap by supplying a standard work on geometry. The success of his project is shown by the existence of a manuscript from the same time period, where Adelard's rendering of the *Elements* is found together with works by Boethius on music and arithmetic, thus providing a primer on the quadrivium.[6] Like many medieval translators, Adelard wrote scientific treatises of his own too, which brings us to a bit of a puzzle. Obviously he was acquainted with Arabic scientific literature—he translated some of it—so it seems we should believe him when he says that in his original writings he is drawing on "Arabic learning (*Arabum studia*)." Yet scholars have failed to identify his sources. So is this just a bluff? Perhaps not. Adelard may mean that he studied with another scholar who spoke Arabic, and is referring to personal oral instruction rather than literary sources.[7]

Certainly in this period scientific and philosophical learning was sometimes shared from one culture to another through face-to-face contacts. Instead of depending on the medieval version of interlibrary loan, as happened earlier when Eriugena was able to get his hands on Greek manuscripts sent to France as a gift from the Byzantine emperor, the translations mostly emerged in places and times where Latin-speaking Christians had access to native speakers of Greek or Arabic. The best example is the most important center for Arabic-Latin translations: Toledo.[8] It fell into Christian hands in 1085, though it would be several decades before Christian scholars arrived and took advantage of the presence of Arabic-speaking colleagues. At least some of these scholars came to Toledo specifically in search of otherwise unavailable texts. For instance, Gerard of Cremona, one of the greatest of the Toledan translators, went there to find Ptolemy's *Almagest*. After his death, Gerard's students wrote of how he was motivated by pity for readers of Latin, who had so little access to the literary riches available in Arabic.[9] Another translator in Toledo at the same time was Dominicus Gundisalvi, whose name you'll also see as Gundissalinus. Between the two of them, Gerard and Gundisalvi rendered numerous works by Aristotle, and by Muslim and Jewish authors too, into Latin.

A particularly intriguing translator also active in Toledo is one who called himself Avendauth. He is usually thought to be none other than Abraham Ibn Daud, a Jewish Aristotelian philosopher.[10] It was thanks to him that readers of Latin could peruse one of the works of the Islamic world that exerted most influence in the thirteenth century: Avicenna's treatise on the soul. Avendauth nicely illustrates the point about personal scholarly contacts. In the preface to his translation of Avicenna, he tells us that he would read out the text "in the vernacular (*vulgariter*)" to Gundisalvi. This probably means that he was reading it out in Arabic, though some have suspected a process of double translation, with Avendauth reading it in a vernacular Romance dialect and Gundisalvi in turn translating on the fly into Latin.[11]

Moving along to the next generation of translators, among the successors of Gerard of Cremona and Gundisalvi was Michael Scot.[12] (That's two, for you Scots who are keeping count of countrymen.) He translated Aristotle's writings on zoology from Arabic in Toledo, before traveling to Rome and then joining the court of Frederick II of Sicily. He carried on the Toledan project of uncovering what Gundisalvi once called the works "hidden in the secret places of the Greek and Arabic languages," with a particular devotion to Aristotle and his greatest commentator: Averroes. I get goosebumps when I consider that Averroes' own lifetime overlapped with the first translations done in Toledo. Even as he commented on the Arabic Aristotle down in southern, Muslim Spain, the Toledans were translating Aristotle from Arabic up in northern, Christian Spain. Michael Scot was in turn active in the first decades of the thirteenth century, so just following Averroes' death in 1198. He was not the sole translator of Averroes into Latin, but was responsible for the majority of his commentaries.

Averroes' works had a massive impact on the study of Aristotle in Latin. For one thing, they helped to make Aristotle himself available, since Averroes' longest commentaries quoted the Aristotelian text bit by bit before commenting on them. The *Metaphysics*, in particular, was for some time known in Latin only in the version that Michael Scot produced while translating Averroes. Although translations based on the Greek quickly overtook these Arabic-Latin versions, Averroes never fell out of favor as the medievals' primary guide to Aristotle. His ideas concerning the eternity of the world and the human intellect will occasion bitter dispute, and the controversial movement sometimes called "Latin Averroism" will be a going concern well until the Renaissance. Still, the radical Aristotelians we call the "Averroists" and their detractors did agree on one thing: they all saw Averroes primarily as an Aristotelian philosopher. Those who rejected his ideas did so not because he was a

Muslim, but because his commentaries revealed a conflict between Aristotle and Christianity, or (as Thomas Aquinas argued) because his commentaries in fact misrepresented Aristotle to make it seem that there was such a conflict.

I've just mentioned that Michael Scot was present at the court of Frederick II of Sicily, which brings us to the fact that the translation movement was not wholly Toledan. Frederick was a great admirer of Arabic culture and had extensive ties with the Islamic world. In one case, he sent a set of questions on mathematics to the Ayyubid sultan; Frederick had the endearing habit of practicing diplomacy by means of intellectual posturing. His questions were passed on to a Muslim scholar named Kamāl al-Dīn Ibn Yūnūs, who was also the teacher of two scholars present at Frederick's court, a Christian translator and astrologer called Theodore of Antioch and a Muslim named al-Urmawī. Through these contacts, knowledge about figures like Avicenna and al-Fārābī would have been brought to Sicily.

The Islamic world was not the only culture in possession of the scientific treasures coveted by Latin Christians. There was also the Byzantine realm, where many antique philosophical texts were still available in the original Greek. Indeed, our present-day access to Greek philosophical texts is almost entirely thanks to the Byzantine manuscript tradition. By the twelfth century, the Eastern Roman Empire was a shadow of its former glory, reduced in size and power in the wake of the Muslim conquests. But Constantinople could still offer unparalleled access to Aristotle and other Hellenic authors. Among the translators who began to exploit this, the most important for our story was James of Venice, who was in the Byzantine capital in 1136 along with two other Italian translators. James was single-handedly responsible for a massive increase in the amount of Aristotle available in Latin, with new versions of several logical works, and treatises on natural philosophy.

James of Venice worked with Greek texts, but had something in common with his colleagues who translated from Arabic: absolute fidelity to the source text. Whichever language they were working with, the translators would try to render each word in the source text into Latin, even preserving word order insofar as they could. So medieval scholars had to get used to a kind of "translationese," reading texts full of phrases that would be natural enough in Greek or Arabic but that seemed very strange to the Latin ear. Not everyone appreciated the effect. As a well-read aficionado of classical literature, John of Salisbury was appalled by James of Venice's version of the *Posterior Analytics*. He said blame must lie with the translator or with scribes who had made errors copying the Latin text, and certainly not with Aristotle himself, a judgment John might have revised if he ever had the somewhat dubious pleasure of reading Aristotle in Greek.[13] This helps to explain why Latin readers turned to thinkers from the Islamic world, like Avicenna and Averroes, for help in understanding Aristotle. Still, the translators knew what they were doing. Their method was born out of reverence for the Greek and Arabic originals. As one translator remarked, "He should be condemned who, when he translates a book… does not blush to take away from the author what he had labored over, and to usurp that material for himself."[14]

This highly literal technique had been used in the Greek-Arabic translation movement too, though some Arabic translators adopted a more natural style. In the case of the Latin translations, the technique continued to be used for generations to come; it would be criticized and abandoned in the Renaissance. We still see it with the greatest translator of the thirteenth century, William of Moerbeke, who from 1260 to 1280 undertook to produce new versions of just about all of Aristotle. His translations supplanted the earlier ones, such as those by James of Venice, and became the basis for the sophisticated Aristotelian philosophy of the late thirteenth and fourteenth centuries. Another figure to build on earlier achievements was Robert Grosseteste, who we'll be covering in his own right in Chapter 27. For now, I'll just mention that he commented on several Aristotelian treatises and produced a popular translation of Aristotle's *Nicomachean Ethics*, though not the first Latin version of that treatise. An earlier one was already achieved in the twelfth century by Burgundio of Pisa, who also translated the Greek theologian John of Damascus. Thanks to Burgundio, John of Damascus would become a major authority for Christian doctrine in Latin Christendom, just as he was in Byzantine Christianity.

In one spectacular case, the translations from Arabic and Greek came together to expose the complicated history of the *Book of Causes*, translated by Gerard of Cremona. The Arabic work he worked from had a different title: *Book of the Pure Good (Kitāb fī l-Maḥḍ al-khayr)*. It was in turn a selective adaptation from the *Elements of Theology*, a systematic presentation of late ancient Platonism from the pen of one of its greatest exponents, Proclus. The Latin *Book of Causes* was a popular work, receiving a commentary from no less a scholar than Albert the Great. An association with the name of Aristotle no doubt helped it achieve wide success. But then William of Moerbeke translated the original source from Greek—that is, the really original source, Proclus' *Elements of Theology*. Thomas Aquinas explained the situation in his own commentary on the *Book of Causes*,[15] and compared the Latin version to what William had found in Proclus. For good measure he also brought in a further source, the Pseudo-Dionysius. All in all, it was a remarkable feat of textual criticism, only slightly besmirched by his guess about the provenance of that strange word *yliathim*, which was made in this same commentary.

It's going to take me much of the rest of this book to chart the full impact of the new texts; for now I just want to mention just the biggest and most obvious point.

The influx of works by Aristotle, Averroes, Avicenna, and others led to a new understanding of what philosophy is in the first place. The translators had initially sought merely to fill gaps in the liberal arts curriculum, but the arrival of Aristotle changed things out of all recognition. We already see this beginning to happen in Toledo, where a short work on the philosophical curriculum by al-Fārābī was translated and then used to help in deciding what else to translate.[16] By the mid-thirteenth century, the sequence of philosophical works required for "arts" students at the universities of Paris and Oxford was thoroughly Aristotelian, and in fact had more in common with the curriculum of fifth-century Alexandria or tenth-century Baghdad than with that of Carolingian or even twelfth-century France.

The difference already began with logic. In the very early medieval period, Latin readers lacked even access to Boethius, but his versions of the initial writings in Aristotle's *Organon*, or logical treatises, came into wide use in the twelfth century. Then the translation movement completed the *Organon*, which meant that medievals could now study the *Sophistical Refutations*, inspiring them to work on pseudo-arguments and argument technique more generally, and the *Posterior Analytics*, where Aristotle laid out his theory of scientific demonstration. The resulting changes were profound. Even a very well-informed twelfth-century thinker like John of Salisbury could proclaim solidarity with the moderate skepticism of Cicero, according to which we must often content ourselves with merely probable beliefs.[17] That favorite text of the twelfth century, Plato's *Timaeus*, fit nicely with this approach since its cosmology is presented as a mere "likely account" of the universe. The average thirteenth-century scholastic will be having none of this. He has read the *Posterior Analytics* and knows that philosophy is meant to consist of valid syllogistic arguments grounded ultimately in certain first principles. Aquinas (admittedly, not exactly an average scholastic thinker) will even claim that theology is a special case of an Aristotelian demonstrative science.

Furthermore, the *Posterior Analytics* and other newly translated works made it abundantly clear that a good Aristotelian should be empirical in studying the created world. As we've seen, the twelfth century can boast numerous treatises on natural philosophy, especially by the thinkers in the orbit of Chartres. But these authors were engaged in a literary exercise more than an empirical one, building on the ideas of the *Timaeus*. Without the newly rediscovered Aristotle, it's unthinkable that we could get a thirteenth-century thinker like Roger Bacon, who developed remarkable new ideas about how science might be grounded in sense experience. As for the institutional context in which these new developments largely unfolded—well, that's the second of the two most important developments I mentioned earlier in this chapter.

21

STRAW MEN
THE RISE OF THE UNIVERSITIES

With the huge influx of scientific and philosophical literature we've just discussed, an educational ideal of the early medieval ages drifted out of reach. No longer would it be possible for any one person, no matter how intelligent and industrious, to master all available human knowledge.[1] Ironic then, you might think, that it was at just about the same time—in the late twelfth and early thirteenth centuries—that we see the rise of the medieval universities. The very name "university," after all, seems to promise the opportunity of comprehensive education: it is a place where you can study all things. But as it turns out, that is not what the medieval word meant. The term *universitas* had nothing to do with universal knowledge, nor for that matter did it refer to a place. This is not to say that the medieval university had nothing in common with our modern-day institutions. On the contrary. A list of the customs and practices that still survive from medieval universities could include the wearing of academic gowns, the division of teaching staff into faculties and of teaching sessions into lectures and seminars, the observing of summer holidays, the provision of student housing, the hazing of first-year students, examinations, endowed chairs, the awarding of bachelor's and master's degrees, and such administrative terms as chancellor and rector. Also, medieval university students drank a lot.

Yet the fact that we still use the word "university" can be misleading. Originally, *universitas* just meant a group of people who banded together for collective action. It was applied to many groups, not only scholarly ones. When the medievals called the scholars at Bologna, Paris, or Oxford a *universitas*, it was because those scholars had joined forces, at first to seek informal protection of their interests from the Church or secular governments, and then later to seek recognition as legal entities. It was only much later that these groups acquired buildings for teaching. Typically, masters would instruct their students in private rooms, such a room being called a *schola* or "school." At the University of Paris many of these rooms were on the "Street of Straw," so called because the students sat on bundles of straw during class. Instruction in these "schools" had already been the practice for generations, which is why we've been talking about "scholastics," "schoolmen," and so on as we've looked at the twelfth century. What changed with the universities is that the students and masters came together to form politically and economically powerful blocks. This enabled them to win the support of kings, bishops, and popes, and also to annoy those same authorities with their demands, their unlawful behavior, and their alarming independence of mind.

In this sense, the universities were simply a development out of the schools of the preceding generations. But the difference was more than one of size. Up through the twelfth century there had been two major institutional contexts for philosophy, the monastery and the schools. In a monastery, the emphasis was on personal moral development and the philosophical teaching that went on was part of a pastoral relationship between master and student. Hence the intensely personal, intimate tone of works by monastic thinkers like Anselm. The schools, by contrast, were oriented towards expertise in the liberal arts, and characterized by competition between masters who sought to draw fee-paying students. It's in that context that we must understand the bitterness between Peter Abelard and William of Champeaux: intellectually, their feud was about the status of universals, but personally, it was about who could claim the title of sharpest mind in Paris. Bernard of Clairvaux's attempt to bring Abelard, and later Gilbert of Poitiers, to heel is often seen as a manifestation of tension between these two institutional settings. Bernard represented the monastic ethos and wanted to subdue the creeping secularism and arrogance of the upstart schoolmen.

One might take the emergence of the universities as a clear victory for Team Abelard. But in fact, they sought to preserve the moral framework of monastic life alongside the liberal arts curriculum. Such moral traits as discipline and modesty were considered as important for the student as the knowledge they would acquire. In theory, at least, such moral features were even considered in the process of awarding degrees. Student instruction also continued to have a religious setting. Admittedly, most of the dozens of universities that sprang up around Europe in the Middle Ages did concentrate on the liberal arts and the disciplines of medicine and law. But the two universities that were most important in the history of philosophy were Oxford and Paris, and at both, theology was the culminating discipline of the university, with the arts treated as a more basic preparatory level of study. Bonaventure, one of the greatest professors at Paris, remarked that the arts were like the foundation of a house, medicine and law like the house's walls, and theology like the roof at the top.[2]

Another difference between the universities and the earlier schools was simply the higher degree of organization implied by the term *universitas*. Such practices as the wearing of specific clothing (hence those academic gowns) and the use of official seals on documents were outward manifestations of the corporate nature of the university. Not all the universities had the same kind of organizational structure, though. There were many differences of detail from one university to the next, but the main contrast is between the arrangements at Paris and at Bologna, whose size, fame, and early foundation made them the two models that others would follow. Bologna came along first, having emerged as a major center for law already in the twelfth century. The University of Paris can be roughly dated to the turn of the thirteenth century. It would be associated above all with theology, carrying on the tradition of the great Parisian theologians among the schoolmen at Saint Victor and in nearby Chartres. So it's no coincidence that it was Bologna that gave us Gratian, and Paris that gave us Peter Lombard.

Beyond this intellectual difference, there was a contrast of constituency. Bologna was really a corporation founded by students. For them the university was a means to improve their bargaining position against their own masters. Collective action meant they could force masters to, for example, pay a fine if a lecture was missed, started late, or taught inadequately. (If the Internet had already existed then, Bolognese students would certainly have invented the Rate My Professor website.) By contrast, the Paris model, which was adopted also at Oxford, had the masters joining together as a university to offering a program of studies to young students. And I do mean young. Scholars would begin their studies at the faculty of arts at the tender age of 14. The majority of them would never even attain a degree, satisfying themselves with a basic grounding that could launch them on their further careers. This is another important contrast between medieval universities and the ones we know: these great centers of learning were to a large extent offering what we would think of as a high school education.

The fact that most of the students were teenagers helps to explain why they were so strong-willed and, to be frank, badly behaved. They were scholars, but they weren't necessarily gentlemen. Many complained about the debauchery of these supposedly morally upstanding young men, and some of the biggest disputes involving universities in the thirteenth century erupted when the students came together to show solidarity for a fellow scholar who had, say, committed murder. The reason the confederations of students were so powerful was that they could threaten to vote with their feet if the town or other authorities failed to capitulate in such a case. This happened more than once in medieval times. The university at Cambridge was indirectly born when students left Oxford in protest at the hanging of students in reaction to a killing committed by one among their number. Similarly, the University of Vicenza was set up by students who withdrew from Bologna.

Decamping like this, or simply going on strike, served as a powerful threat in any dispute. Masters depended on teaching students for their livelihood, and the cities too benefited economically from the presence of such a large number of students. Perhaps no one benefited more than the local taverns.

In fact, two of the most significant events concerning the University of Paris in the thirteenth century involved arguments over a bar bill. The first came in 1200, when a student beat up an innkeeper after arguing with him over payment, and the town authorities reacted by killing several students. In protest, the university went on strike, forcing the king to take sides: he backed the university and offered it a charter outlining its new rights. Medieval universities didn't have sports teams, but they went in for rematches nonetheless. Almost thirty years later, another dispute over a bill led to riots, another police intervention, and then a strike of no less than three years, which ended when the authorities once again gave in to student demands. Students didn't actually *have* to open negotiations over their rights by beating up innkeepers, though. Bologna had already been given royal backing in 1158 when a more peaceful appeal to Frederick Barbarossa led to his placing the scholars there under his protection. However the rights were acquired, to be a student at these major institutions of learning was to enjoy a significant degree of legal protection. In Paris, a university student could only be arrested if he was caught in the very act of committing "homicide, adultery, rape ... or at a scene of bloodshed with a club, rock, or weapon."[3]

Amidst all this murder, rioting, whoring, and political brinksmanship, the universities did manage to put on a few classes. So what was the medieval version of the "student experience," as today's institutions like to put it? The first thing to realize is that each student had a relationship with one particular master. In fact, in Paris it was laid down that no one could be considered a student without such a relationship.[4] To "matriculate" was to be entered into the list of students attached to the master. This was a matter of legal importance, since it was how each student secured access to the rights that the university had managed to win for itself. Having matriculated, the student would be instructed by the arts faculty for the rest of his teenaged years. The first degree he could attain would be the bachelor's, or *baccalaureus*. Despite attempts to suggest that this term came into Latin from the Arabic-speaking world, it seems to be of older provenance and to refer originally to a wreath worn on the head of an initiate. At this stage the student could himself instruct younger students, while working towards a master's degree of his own.[5] You'll notice, by the way, that I keep referring to the student as "he." Women were not admitted to study at the university. So female intellectuals of the thirteenth and fourteenth centuries (and there were some, as we'll be seeing) were educated outside the university system, either in a convent as Hildegard of Bingen had been or through private tutoring in the aristocratic class.[6]

As he progressed through the course of study, the student would be instructed largely by means of "lectures." The word "lecture" comes from the Latin *lectio*, meaning that an authoritative text was *read* by the master for the benefit of the students. The so-called "ordinary" lectures on standard texts were the bread and butter of the arts teaching and took place first thing in the morning. Masters could also read texts outside the usual curriculum in "extraordinary" lectures. Furthermore, "reading" could be done in two different ways. The master could either offer an exposition of the text in the form of a running paraphrase or depart from it a bit more by posing a series of problems about it, in so-called *quaestiones*. The same kinds of teaching were already used in the twelfth-century schools: Gilbert of Poitiers refers to them.[7] A further kind of teaching was the "disputation." This was an event where two (hopefully) well-prepared students would argue on either side of a point, with the master coming in at the end to adjudicate the issue. The most free-wheeling kind of teaching at the university would have been the "quodlibetal disputation," the word *quodlibet* meaning "whatever you like." Here the idea was that the audience could raise any question for debate, with the master again giving an answer in conclusion. Occasionally, though not usually, the questions raised were intentionally trivial or silly: if a person is born with two heads, should he be baptized once or twice?[8]

This was one of the practices that was mocked by later critics of scholasticism, who liked to depict the activities of the university as strictly authority-bound and mired in absurd minutiae. But, in fact, all these modes of teaching gave the masters opportunities to put forward new, and at times daring, ideas. This could be true even with the ordinary lecture taught as straightforward exposition. But it's more obvious with the other types of teaching. Standard texts could offer a jumping-off point for innovative philosophical ideas, especially when lectures were put in the form of questions. A good example would be Duns Scotus' pioneering metaphysical theories, which were advanced in lectures on that standby of the theology curriculum, Peter Lombard's *Sentences*. In the context of an extraordinary lecture, meanwhile, masters were by definition traveling off the beaten path in their choice of material.

Then there were the disputed questions, which are worth dwelling on in a bit more detail.[9] Textual reports of a disputed question will include the cases put for and against a given proposition, followed by the master's response and then replies to the initial arguments *pro* and *contra*. Often the master would answer the question at hand not with a flat "yes" or "no," but by showing the true solution to be rather more subtle. The arguments on both sides might invoke a wide range of authorities:

everyone from Aristotle to Augustine to Avicenna and Averroes, or even occasionally an author whose name didn't start with A (Isidore of Seville, perhaps). The upshot was that a series of disputed questions on a given topic could provide an evaluation of the whole history of ideas on that topic, along with nuanced attempts to reconcile the different authoritative views and original positions staked out by means of finely drawn distinctions. Good examples of the genre are Aquinas' disputed questions *On Truth* and *On Evil*. Here we see the full flowering of the dialectical seeds planted by Abelard in his *Sic et non* and then by Gratian and Lombard. We can now also see why so many works of medieval philosophy take the form of expositions or disputed questions. They were simply records of teaching, set down by the master himself or as a report by students who were present. Even writings not grounded in an actual teaching session would often display the same structure, the most famous example being Aquinas' *Summa Theologiae*.

So that's how the students would be taught. The next question is what the students would be taught. And in the thirteenth century, questions didn't get more disputed than this. Certainly some texts were uncontentious. In theology the basic textbook became Lombard's *Sentences* with further lectures on the Bible, and no one was going to complain about that. The debates rather concerned the arts faculty syllabus, which provided the reading list for the majority of students, who were also the youngest and most impressionable participants of the university. As the name "arts faculty" implies, the basic structure was still the old trivium of grammar, rhetoric, and dialectic, at least at first. But as the works of Aristotle became available, there was heated controversy about which of them should be read. There could be little objection to pursuing the "old logic" that had already been known before the translation movement, with its works by Aristotle and Boethius. But what about Aristotle's works on natural philosophy and his *Metaphysics*? These were full of problematic teachings. Among other things Aristotle seemed to depict the human as a mortal being whose soul was a mere form of the body, suggesting that an afterlife is impossible, and also to argue that the universe had always existed rather than having been created.

An initial salvo in this intellectual battle was launched in the second decade of the thirteenth century. Statutes laid down at Paris in 1215 banned teaching of "the books of Aristotle on metaphysics and natural philosophy or on summaries of them."[10] Of course, the implication is that masters had been doing exactly that. The ban, of course, had no effect elsewhere. Aristotle continued to be read in Oxford, while a new university at Toulouse boldly advertised the possibility of studying the natural philosophy that was now blacklisted in Paris. Nor did the ban do much to blunt the Parisians' interest in this cutting-edge Aristotelian material. As we'll be seeing, much of the philosophical action in the first half of the thirteenth century continued to revolve around the interpretation and assimilation of Aristotle. By the middle of the century, the process was complete. In the 1250s a new curriculum was set down in Paris, which actually *required* the reading of numerous works by Aristotle on natural philosophy and psychology, as well as his *Metaphysics* and *Ethics*.[11] Henceforth, philosophical education in Latin Christendom was going to mean what it had meant in late antiquity, and what it meant in the Islamic world (until Avicenna emerged as the central philosophical figure to whom all others must respond). It was going to mean the study of Aristotle.

Though our interest is, of course, with the universities as a setting for philosophy, we should remember that the universities were not institutions of philosophy, not even in the more inclusive medieval sense of the term "philosophy." As we've seen, Bologna, which was the most important university alongside Paris, specialized in law. Conversely, some disciplines that did belong to the study of "philosophy" in the broad, medieval sense were *not* studied at the universities, at least not as part of the standard curriculum. The mechanical arts had been included by Hugh of Saint Victor in his catalogue of the arts, but apart from medicine these did not feature in the course of study at Paris or Oxford.[12] A more striking absence was the whole second part of the liberal arts curriculum, that is, the mathematical disciplines of the quadrivium. These were pursued at universities, but would remain excluded from ordinary lectures.

What about the crowning role of theology, at least in the system observed in Paris and Oxford? Did it cast a long shadow over the secular disciplines pursued by the arts masters? As with a good disputed question, it isn't possible to give a simple yes or no answer. For one thing, students and masters in the theology faculty might also teach in the arts faculty, so the university was not clearly divided into two constituencies of theologians and arts masters. Nonetheless, theology professors did worry that their colleagues in the arts might be drawn into what they disdainfully called "curiosity" about logic or the natural world. It was an updated version of the complaints that, in the previous century, men like Bernard of Clairvaux had directed against men like Abelard. This tension will come to a head in the 1270s with two rounds of condemnations in Paris which sought to bring the arts masters and other Aristotle enthusiasts to heel (Chapter 41).

A further complication was that there was, after all, a way in which the university masters split into two different constituencies. (As Abelard knew, with every *non* comes a *sic*.) The influence of two mendicant orders, the Franciscans and Dominicans, would be increasingly felt at Paris as the thirteenth century wore on. They would cause much annoyance among the "secular" masters who did not belong to these orders. Mendicants sometimes refused to join in collective action on behalf of the university; they refused to study or teach in the arts faculty; and perhaps worst of all, they took jobs away from ambitious secular masters. It's a tension we'll need to bear in mind when we look at the condemnations of the 1270s and the debate between the Dominican Thomas Aquinas and the arts master Siger of Brabant.

PART II

THE THIRTEENTH
CENTURY

22

NO UNCERTAIN TERMS
THIRTEENTH-CENTURY LOGIC

Whatever you think of Bill Clinton's performance as US President, you cannot deny that he would have made an excellent scholastic philosopher. Admittedly, the monastic lifestyle might have presented him with some difficulties. But Clinton was able, in the midst of a cross-examination, to come up with the line "It depends upon what the meaning of the word 'is,' is." Clearly, this is a man who would have been right at home in a medieval disputation. Clinton's ease with such fine distinctions was acquired through his training in law, another reason to think he would have found the medieval university a congenial setting. But the medievals who really got to the bottom of the meaning of the word "is," and quite a few other words into the bargain, were those who taught and wrote about logic.

Our look at the newly translated philosophical sources and the rise of the universities has prepared us to understand developments in the thirteenth century. So rather than giving you an introductory chapter on the period, in this and the next several chapters I'll be offering a tour through several branches of philosophy and how they were pursued in the early thirteenth century. It was a time of great intellectual upheaval, as ideas from those newly translated sources reshaped all philosophical disciplines. Nowhere was the impact of these sources more immediate or far-reaching than in logic. The result was the greatest period of development in this discipline between the invention of logic by Aristotle and the work of Gottlob Frege in the nineteenth century.[1] Of course, logic had been a standard part of the curriculum for centuries already, in the guise of "dialectic," one of the arts covered in the trivium. And Aristotle had already been central to the study of dialectic during the twelfth century. So the change was not a sudden rediscovery of Aristotelian logic as such. It was rather the expansion of the logical works now available, and the increase in the number and sophistication of logical textbooks and commentaries. To mark this distinction, the medievals themselves referred to the Aristotelian texts that had long been available in the translations of Boethius as the "old logic (*logica vetus*)," whereas the works that had become available more recently were called the "new logic (*logica nova*)." It may seem perverse to call equally ancient things "old" and "new," but as Bill Clinton might put it, sometimes it depends upon what the meaning of the word "new" is.

We can already observe the process of recovering Aristotle in John of Salisbury, that "most well-read man of the twelfth century." Along with his pioneering political treatise the *Policraticus,* John composed another work with a Greek-style name: the *Metalogicon.*[2] At the outset of the work he announces that he is taking issue with a man he calls "Cornificius." The gesture is a typical sign of John's antiquarian literary taste: Cornificius was a critic of Virgil, whose name is being borrowed for the occasion. Whatever the identity of the opponent behind this name, he didn't like the arts of the trivium.[3] He dismissed dialectic as pointless, probably because of the poor teaching he received. John describes how classes would become so consumed with pedantic complexity that participants would bring along a bag of peas, counting them out one by one to keep track of multiple negations (§1.3). "Cornificius" was thus led to adopt the contrary view that whatever is useful in the study of language and argument can be learned quickly and easily. Against him, John argues passionately that the arts of the trivium are anything but trivial. Without grammar, one cannot use words properly; without rhetoric, one cannot use them eloquently; without dialectic, one cannot pursue philosophy itself.

John still represents a twelfth-century mindset, as is clear from his interest in authors like Virgil and Cicero, his frequent allusions to Martianus Capella, and his praise of the thinkers of Chartres as the greatest teachers of the age. Yet he's acquainted with a wider range of logical works than those used by, say, Bernard of Chartres. He explains the usefulness of the whole of Aristotle's *Organon,* including the so-called "new logic": this included the *Prior Analytics,* which systematically surveys the types of valid syllogism, the *Topics,* which studies the techniques of argumentative disputation, and the *Sophistical Refutations,* which offers a diagnosis of misleading, invalid arguments (§4.1–4, 23). These are the works that are going to revolutionize logic among thirteenth century thinkers, who will take to heart John's declaration that no one who fails to master the *Analytics* can call himself a logician (§4.2).

Before the student of logic can proceed to the syllogistic arguments of the *Analytics,* though, he will first need to learn about the parts of arguments. These parts will be the individual premises of syllogisms and, even more basically, the terms that appear in those premises. If our syllogism is "Giraffes are ruminants, all ruminants have four stomachs, therefore giraffes have four stomachs," then the first premise is "Giraffes are ruminants," and it includes the terms "giraffe" and "ruminant." This way of understanding the study of logic was established in antiquity, when it governed the interpretation of Aristotle's works on logic.

His *Categories* was thought to address the topic of individual terms, while his *On Interpretation* deals with whole propositions. The *Prior Analytics* would complete the job by looking at how one should put together propositions to form valid arguments, and for good measure the *Sophistical Refutations* shows how *not* to do this. All of this was a perfect fit for the new universities in Paris, Oxford, and elsewhere. Since students were so often asked to participate in disputation, it was urgent that they master the skills and rules of argumentation. That included being able to spot bad argumentative moves made by your opponent, which is where the study of sophistical arguments came in.

There's a chicken-and-egg problem here. Were the schoolmen so interested in logic because of their educational culture or did that culture only develop because of the availability of Aristotle's entire logic? There is truth in both alternatives. Disputation was already a feature of twelfth-century education, but thirteenth- and fourteenth-century logic reached new heights of technical sophistication thanks to the encounter with Aristotle. In the first half of the thirteenth century, progress was made especially in understanding individual terms. For this reason, the logicians of this period are credited with devising what is called "terminist" logic. This is not to say that their writings dealt only with terms, just that it was on this topic that they made their most innovative proposals. Two particularly important early terminists were William of Sherwood and Peter of Spain. Active in the 1230s and 1240s, they both wrote overviews of logic with substantial sections devoted to the analysis of terms.[4] Somewhat later, their work was taken up and further developed by Nicholas of Paris and the author of a text called simply *Logica*, which is ascribed to Lambert of Auxerre though its authenticity isn't certain. Especially the textbook by Peter of Spain will be used by later writers like John Buridan.

Some of the advances made by the early terminists were practical ones, which enabled them to do advanced logic without the use of quasi-mathematical symbols or quotation marks, neither of which were in use at this time. Like any natural language, Latin grammar frequently allows for ambiguity. The sentence *omnis camelopardus homo non est*, for instance, can mean "Not every giraffe is a human" or "Every giraffe is not a human." To avoid such problems, our logicians simply laid down the artificial rule that "not" affects what comes directly after it in a sentence.[5] Another, slightly more colorful example would be a mnemonic device devised by the logicians to help them recall the main properties of syllogistic arguments. A set of clever nicknames was given to the syllogistic moods, with each vowel in the name having a significance.[6] For instance the three "a"s in "Barbara" indicate that the first premise, second premise, and conclusion of the relevant syllogism all involve affirming something universally, as in "All giraffes are animals."

As I've said, the more substantive proposals made by the terminists have to do with the individual terms that appear in the propositions that can serve as premises and conclusions in a syllogism. Aristotle's logic dealt with what is called "categorical" logic, from the Greek *kategorein* which means "to predicate" one thing of another.[7] In other words, he was interested in propositions like "Socrates is human," where the predicate "human" is ascribed to the subject Socrates. Of course, we can also say that a predicate fails to apply to a subject, as when we say "Hiawatha is not human." (Another reason Bill Clinton would have made a good medieval logician: he was expert at issuing categorical denials.) Back in the twelfth century, Abelard had already pointed out the difference between merely formulating such a predication and actually asserting it. His theory of *dicta* ("things that can be said") played a role in his nominalist position on universals, but it was more basically a point of logic. A *dictum* such as "Hiawatha's being a giraffe" does not yet assert that Hiawatha actually is a giraffe. To do that, you must deploy the verb "is," or in Latin *est*: "Hiawatha *is* a giraffe," or if you prefer, *Hiawatha camelopardus est*. Logicians then, as now, called this verb a "copula."

One thing we can see from this example is that not all the terms in such a proposition are "categorical," that is, standing for a subject or predicate. Rather, we must add another kind of term, a copula, in order to have an assertion at all. And there are many other terms that play a non-categorical role in propositions. If I say "Every giraffe is an animal," or "Bill Clinton is no longer President," the words "every" and "no longer" seem to be modifying either the terms of the proposition or the way that the predicates are attached to the subject. We might say that such terms come "along with" the subject and predicate. Indeed, this is what the medievals did say. Alongside "categorematic" terms that refer to the subject and predicate of the proposition, they recognized "syncategorematic" terms, adding the prefix *syn-*, which means "with" in Greek. This vocabulary was actually borrowed from grammar, showing yet again the interplay of the three arts of the trivium.

Much of the technical discussion in terminist logic involved syncategorematic terms. Take, for instance, the so-called "modal" terms "necessarily" and "possibly."[8] If I say "Giraffe is necessarily animal," is "necessarily" functioning as an adverb that modifies the whole proposition? Or does it only modify the predicate, so that I am ascribing to giraffe the property "necessarily-an-animal"? That might seem like a pointless question, but it is actually crucial. If "necessarily" is attached to the predicate and not the copula, then the proposition as a whole is being asserted as merely true, and not as a necessary truth. In which case I won't be able to use this premise in an argument to prove other necessary truths, because you can't infer a necessary truth from a mere truth. In this case, the terminists held that the necessity does apply to the whole proposition. It's perhaps not surprising that a word like "necessarily" would give rise to such difficulties. But the terminists found that even the copula needed careful thought. Bill Clinton was right: it isn't so obvious what the meaning of the word "is," is. If I say "Giraffe is animal," does that refer to some one existing giraffe like Hiawatha, who is an animal? Does it mean that all the presently existing giraffes are animals? Does it mean that all past, present, and future giraffes are animals? Or perhaps even that there is a conceptual connection between "giraffe" and "animal," such that my claim would be true even if there are never any giraffes?[9]

You can pose more or less the same question concerning the apparently more straightforward categorematic terms. What exactly is the function of a single term like "giraffe"? Does it allude to one specific giraffe I have in mind, like Hiawatha? Or to all the giraffes that exist? To the ones that exist now, or also in the past and future? Or could it refer even to possible, but never really existing, giraffes? In fact, it seems clear that one and the same term "giraffe" can function in all of these ways. For this reason, the terminists distinguished between what a term means and how it functions in a given proposition. They called its general meaning its "signification."[10] Following suggestive remarks in Aristotle, signification was defined with reference to communication between a speaker and a listener. The signification of the term "giraffe" is either the concept in my mind that I'm trying to convey to you when I say "giraffe" or the concept that arises in your mind when you hear me say it.[11] The concepts in our minds in turn signify things out in the world, for instance Hiawatha in the giraffe enclosure.

Yet as we've just seen, I don't need to have any particular giraffe in mind when I say "Giraffe is animal." So the terminists devised a theory about what they called "supposition."[12] A term "supposits" for whatever it stands for in a given proposition. So the term "giraffe" has only one signification, but many possible suppositions. No ingenuity was spared in distinguishing supposition into its types and subtypes. Most generally, the terminists recognized three types, which were called personal, simple, and material supposition. Personal supposition is when a term supposits for a thing or things in the world. Despite the name, the thing doesn't need to be a person. The word "tower" might for instance supposit for the Eiffel Tower or the Leaning Tower of Pisa, which do both have a lot of personality as towers go, but still aren't persons. Our authors further distinguish between types of personal supposition, in order to clarify which giraffes I am referring to when I say "giraffe." I can use the word to refer only to one giraffe, like Hiawatha, and then I am using "discrete" supposition. Equally, I can use the same term to refer to all giraffes, which is "distributive" supposition. But what if I am not referring to any giraffes in particular, but just to the basic concept of "giraffe"? In that case, I am using what the terminists called "simple" supposition. William of Sherwood's example is "Human is a species." Obviously, this isn't a case of personal supposition at all, since it isn't as if Bill Clinton or any other human is a species. In addition to personal and simple supposition, the third and final type is illustrated by propositions like "Human has five letters." Here I am referring neither to particular humans nor to the species human, but to the word itself. The terminists express this by saying that I am employing neither personal nor simple supposition, but "material" supposition. Nowadays we could simply make this distinction using quotation marks: a human doesn't have five letters, but "human" does.

What is the point of all this? Most basically, the terminists were trying to keep track of what we are and are not committing ourselves to when we say things. Among other things, this enables us to avoid making fallacious inferences. As they again spared no ingenuity in pointing out, many fallacies are invalid because they use the same term twice, but with two different kinds of supposition. This was something already recognized in antiquity, albeit with much less systematic rigor. For example Augustine warned against the following tricky argument:[13]

> You are human
> Human is made of two syllables
> Therefore you are made of two syllables

This would be an example of a fallacy that arises because one moves from discrete personal supposition to material supposition. The first premise is about you, the second premise about the word "human." In this case, spotting the mistake is pretty easy, but the terminists explored more difficult cases too. For instance, how can it be true to say "Pepper is sold here and in Rome" if there is no particular peppercorn that is sold in both Munich, where I am now, and in Rome? Various solutions were offered here, for instance by saying that the proposition involves a special kind of "unfixed" simple supposition.[14]

Supposition theory wasn't only a tool for avoiding mistakes. It also provided a context for arguing over numerous important philosophical issues. Notably, we can now recast the problem of universals as one about the supposition of terms. If I say "Red is a color," what is the term "red" suppositing for, and why is my statement true? It is tempting to say that "red" here has simple supposition and thus refers to the universal *red*; the reason it is true is that the universal red is a real thing, and is a color. Of course, this interpretation would be unacceptable to those thinkers who, in the tradition of Abelard, insisted that nothing real can be universal. Thus, in the fourteenth century, the nominalist John Buridan is going to argue against distinguishing simple and material supposition. Since the universal is actually just a name, saying something like "Human is a species" or "Red is a color" is actually a statement about the word "human" or the word "red."[15]

The work of the terminists also raised problems that belong to what we would nowadays call philosophy of language. Take the question of how a term comes to have the supposition that it has. A novel and philosophically exciting feature of the terminist theory is that a term's supposition is a function of the proposition in which that term appears. Adding syncategorematic terms can change the supposition of the term. Suppose I take the proposition "Giraffes are tall" and add the word "always," to get "Giraffes are always tall." I thereby extend the scope of (or as the medievals said, "ampliate") the term "giraffes," so that it supposits for the giraffes that exist in the past and future, and not just for the ones that exist now. Conversely, if I add the word "blue" and say "Blue giraffes are tall," I "restrict" the term "giraffes" to only those giraffes that are blue. The reason this is exciting is that it suggests a general theory about language: what determines the supposition of a term is its *context*. This suggestion was debated in the thirteenth century. Some logicians, especially in Oxford, thought that supposition was indeed always a function of context. Others, especially in Paris, held that each term has a "natural" supposition all by itself, which can be altered by its context to produce what they called "accidental" supposition.[16]

A final thing to note about logic in the first half of the thirteenth century is that, despite their focus on terms and predications, these authors realized that they needed to go beyond what they could find in Aristotle. Here, there was indirect influence from Stoic logic, mostly via Boethius. The Stoics had not added much to Aristotle's pioneering work on categorical syllogisms, but had explored other kinds of inferences, including those involving "if-then" statements.[17] Just like the late ancient Aristotelians, the medieval logicians were loath to admit that Aristotle had dropped the ball when it came to these inferences. Instead, they tried to show how Aristotelian logic could be extended to handle them, thinking of an "if-then" statement as a "molecular" proposition made up of two "atomic" statements, both of which are predications. When I say, "If Hiawatha is a giraffe, then she is tall," the "if" and "then" simply link two predications: "Hiawatha is a giraffe" and "Hiawatha is tall." This can be handled easily enough within the terminist system by treating "if" and "then" as syncategorematic terms, and then giving appropriate truth conditions for the molecular propositions that involve them. They did something similar with the more basic problem of propositions that seem to involve no predication at all.

A statement like "Hiawatha runs" would be analyzed as a concealed predicative statement, "Hiawatha is running."

I could go on, but will leave it there, along with the promise that we have much more to expect from medieval logic. First though we're going to discover that thirteenth-century philosophy can stake a claim to achievements in other philosophical areas, a claim that is, unlike Bill Clinton, unimpeachable.

23

FULL OF POTENTIAL
THIRTEENTH-CENTURY PHYSICS

If someone asked you to summarize the place of medieval philosophy in the history of Western science in only two sentences, you could do worse than to say, "In the medieval period, science was based largely on Aristotle. Early modern thinkers had to free themselves from Aristotelianism to launch the scientific revolution." On the other hand, you could also do a lot better. Of course, any two-sentence summary of a whole philosophical age is likely to be misleading. The only perfect one that comes to mind is "Medieval philosophy is really interesting. There's this great book about it that I'm reading at the moment." But it's particularly misleading to portray the medievals as backward-thinking Aristotelians. True, they did devote considerable effort to understanding Aristotle's newly available works on natural philosophy and related material from the Islamic world. But they were not backward-thinking. Some of the new ideas that emerged in early modern science have their ultimate roots in commentaries on Aristotle's *Physics*, composed beginning around the middle of the thirteenth century. Some of these innovations were put forward by that shadowy, multifaceted thinker we have come not to know, but to love anyway: Anonymous.

If we wanted to enumerate the deficiencies of the ancients' natural philosophy, their cosmology would be a good place to start. The universe is not in fact a perfect sphere, containing nested smaller spheres that serve as seats for the planets, with the earth sitting still in the middle of the whole system. We now know that the sun does not circle the earth, but the other way around, although we continue to speak of "sunrise" and "sunset," which is a good thing, since those words are needed to put on productions of *Fiddler on the Roof*. Alongside this incorrect description of the physical cosmos, Aristotle also bequeathed to posterity a well-entrenched theory of fundamental physical principles like motion, time, and space, or rather place. Thirteenth-century commentators on the *Physics* are not going to challenge the earth-centered cosmology, but they are going to make productive suggestions about the principles of natural philosophy.

Their suggestions were not necessarily intended as innovations. To the contrary, they were often put forward as explanations of what Aristotle himself meant to say. But the commentators didn't just want to get Aristotle right: they wanted to show that what he said was itself right. Better to give an implausible interpretation of his text that credits him with a true theory than to give a more convincing reading of his words that has him making a mistake. If all else failed, they were willing to depart from Aristotle's teachings when these couldn't account for the phenomena we see around us. Thus, the medievals brought to bear observations from the natural world in their commentaries. Consider, for instance, the difference between throwing a feather and throwing a baseball. (Non-American readers may wish to substitute a different, culturally appropriate example. British readers might imagine throwing a cricket ball, Germans a potato dumpling.) Why is it so much easier to throw the baseball than to throw the feather, so that the same amount of force will cause the baseball to fly a considerable distance, but the feather to float harmlessly to one's feet?

It turns out that this is a very difficult question for Aristotle to answer.[1] In fact, he is hard pressed to explain the motion of projectiles at all, since he generally explains motion and change in terms of the influence of a mover on something that can move. In his jargon, the mover "actualizes" the movable thing's "potential" for motion or change. He applies this analysis not just to spatial motion, but other kinds of change, like making something hot. That would indeed be a nice example for his theory. If you put a baseball next to a fire, the heat of the fire will actualize the potential hotness of the baseball, in other words warm it up. Likewise, if a group of people are pushing a broken-down car along a road, they are actualizing its potential for motion. If actuality is bestowed by a mover, though, why does change continue once the mover is no longer exerting any influence? The baseball does stop heating up as soon as it's taken away from the fire, as Aristotle's account would expect. But the car may continue to roll briefly after the people stop pushing it. And if you throw the baseball, its motion occurs almost entirely while it is no longer in contact with your hand. So what is causing it to keep moving? What determines the distance it flies before dropping to the ground?

Like a clumsy bartender, Aristotle was grasping at straws as he tried to provide an answer. He suggested that the medium through which the projectile is moving is somehow responsible for keeping it in motion (*Physics* 8.10, 266b–267a). When you throw the baseball into the air, the baseball displaces the air, and it is the motion of the *air* rather than your throwing arm that keeps the ball moving forward. A strike against this theory is the aforementioned fact that it is often easier to throw heavy things than light things. So long as you displace the air with the same amount of force, shouldn't any object move through the air in the same way? This point was made by Richard Rufus of Cornwall, thought to be the author of one of the most interesting commentaries on the *Physics* written in the first half of the thirteenth century.[2] Rufus taught at the universities in Oxford and Paris, serving first as a master in the arts faculty at Paris before joining the Franciscans. He wrote commentaries on Aristotle already in the 1230s, making him one of the earliest masters to engage seriously with these works. Rufus' account of projectile motion is reminiscent of the one proposed by the ancient Christian commentator on Aristotle, John Philoponus.[3] Rufus thinks that when you throw the baseball, you give it what he calls an "impression." The baseball's natural inclination would be to simply drop to the ground. But thanks to the impression made when you throw it, the baseball temporarily and "unnaturally" moves towards home plate instead, pushing air out of the way as it does so. The distance it will travel if unimpeded by a bat or catcher's mitt will be determined by how powerfully it has been impressed, with the impression wearing off as it travels. This also explains why it is easier to throw baseballs than feathers. The baseball is heavier, so that you have to exert more force on it when you throw. Hence the impression made upon it is more powerful.[4]

So far, we've been talking about the physical mechanics of motion. But if you think about it, motion is also rather perplexing from a metaphysical point of view. This is because it seems to exist only *over* time, rather than *at* a time. At any moment during the time the baseball is getting cozy and warm by the fire, it only ever has one given temperature. And at any instant while a thrown baseball is hurtling through the air, it only has one position. How are these temperatures and positions glued together, as it were, into a single, fluid change or motion? The question was raised by the Pre-Socratic thinker Zeno of Elea, a follower of Parmenides.[5] He argued that an arrow in flight is not moving because it is at rest at each time during its supposed flight. This was another puzzle that engaged the attention of medieval commentators. They looked at it from a typically Aristotelian point of view, by asking how motion relates to the scheme of ten categories. But we can think about the problem from a less technical perspective, by simply asking how motion or change relates to the property that will be reached by the end of the motion or change.

How, for instance, does the heating of the baseball relate to final condition of the baseball, which is to be hot? And how does the flight of a thrown baseball relate to the position it will have at the end of that flight? The Muslim commentator Averroes had given an answer to this question, when he was discussing Aristotle's remark that there are four kinds of change: something can alter in respect of its place, its quality, its quantity, or its very substance.[6] Averroes took this to mean that a motion in respect of a quality, for instance, is nothing more than that quality in an incomplete state. For instance, when the baseball is being warmed up, it is on the way to being hot, so we can just think of its status at any one time as incomplete hotness. In other words, the change involved in heating is nothing more than a series of stages of heat.[7]

When the medieval commentators began studying the *Physics*, they frequently read their Latin version of Averroes alongside it. Helpful a guide though Averroes may have been, he was often criticized in the Latin commentaries. These have been studied by Cecilia Trifogli, in a book surveying the remarks of no fewer than ten commentators who worked in Oxford in the middle of the thirteenth century, all but two of whom are anonymous.[8] As in the earlier medieval period, unidentified authors continue to play a significant role in the development of philosophy. One of these commentators complains that Averroes' idea of motion as an incomplete property is itself incomplete. Each stage in the motion or change, for instance each degree of heat in the increasingly warm baseball, is a product of change just as much as the degree of heat achieved at the end of the heating process. This means we'll need a separate motion to explain each partial change along the way. Besides, the commentator adds, some changes aren't gradual. When a substance like an animal comes to be, it does so "all at once" and not part by part. Despite these criticisms, a theory of motion inspired by Averroes is going to be put forward by another commentator on Aristotle in the following decades, whose name is not only known but renowned: Albert the Great. He proposes that we can think of a change as being just the same form as the one that will exist at the end of the change, but with potentiality mixed in. Across time, the change "flows" towards its final result, with the form becoming progressively more actual at each moment.[9]

These metaphysical difficulties about motion have to do with the fact that it is, as the commentators put it, a "successive" entity. Motion or change exists bit by bit across time, rather than all at once (*simul*). Considering how puzzling the commentators find this, it's no surprise that they also find time itself puzzling. And they aren't the only ones. Aristotle had raised a whole series of problems about time in his *Physics*, and another main source of inspiration for the medievals, Augustine, had wrestled with the topic in his *Confessions*.[10] Both of them wondered whether we can even say that time is real. The doubt is similar to the one we saw concerning motion. Just as a motion unfolds across time and so is never entirely present, so does temporal duration seem to lie outside what presently exists. After all, the past is already gone, the future is yet to come, and the present moment has no duration of any magnitude but is an undivided instant. We often compare temporal duration to spatial magnitude, talking about a "long" or "short" time the way we might talk about a long or short distance. But actually space is very different from time: the distance between pitcher's mound and home plate is all present at once, whereas the time it takes the ball to travel that distance is not.

One way to solve this problem is to give up on time's real existence outside the mind. It is we who measure changes in the world by tracking their temporal duration, so that time is really a phenomenon of the soul rather than the physical world. Aristotle flirted with this idea, saying that there can be no time without soul,[11] and Augustine also made time a feature of our mental life. For the thirteenth-century commentators, though, it was once again Averroes who represented this skeptical view about time's existence. In his *Physics* commentary, he pointed out that Aristotle's famous definition of time as a number of motion implies that time is mind-dependent. The motion is really out there, but the numbering only happens in your head. This doesn't mean that time is wholly fictitious, though. The motion in the world does have the *potential* to be numbered, so there is a basis in reality for the mental process of assigning a time to the motion, like when a fastball is measured as taking exactly 0.4 seconds to reach home plate.[12] Against this Richard Rufus, followed by anonymous authors, argues that Averroes has confused number with *counting*. The 0.4 seconds that it takes for the ball to reach home plate really is the number of the motion, whether or not anyone counts it. That number is already an actuality, and the only sense in which it is potential is that the number may or may not be measured or counted, for instance by someone with a speed gun.

The problem of number arises again in discussions of infinity, another topic discussed in Aristotle's *Physics*.[13] The standard Aristotelian view here is that nothing can be actually infinite, but there can be potential infinities. For instance, you cannot have an infinitely big body, but you could have a body that is increasing indefinitely in size while always remaining finitely large. Of course, the ban on actual infinities will have to be abandoned if we are to get to developments in modern science, and especially mathematics. So it's noteworthy that our medieval commentators begin to argue for the possibility of actual infinities in physics. They still don't want to say there could be an infinitely large body, but they do recognize a kind of infinity even in a body of limited size. As Aristotle himself said, any body can at least in principle be divided, and subdivided, without limit. The ancient atomists were wrong to think that you would ever reach a smallest body that can no longer be cut.

The question, then, is what we should say about the divisions that can be made in a given body. Let's imagine slicing a baseball in half, then in a quarter, then an eighth, and so on, like taking apart an orange with an indefinitely large number of segments. On the face of it, this sounds like a standard case of potential infinity. There are indefinitely many segments you can get out of the ball if you have a sharp enough cutting tool. But think again about the case of time. We decided that the number of time is actual in the world, and what is potential is the counting of that time. Couldn't we likewise say that, even if divisions made in the ball are potential, the *number* of potential divisions is actual? According to this view, defended by some of the commentators, infinity would be a real feature of number outside the soul. Other commentators disagree, holding that the number of divisions becomes actual only when you do some dividing (whether it is with a knife or by imagining divisions in your mind). At the bottom of this dispute is an ambiguity in the concept of infinity. Is infinity an unlimited magnitude? Or is it just the notion of being indefinite, as when you can at each stage make an even smaller division than the last division you made?

We've now considered medieval discussions about motion, time, and infinity, three of the four principles of natural philosophy discussed by Aristotle. The last of them was place, and in this case too Aristotle's account raised serious problems. His canonical definition tells us that the place of a thing is the inner surface of whatever contains that thing.[14] Suppose that I were to plunge a baseball into a pitcher of water—after all, what good is a baseball without a pitcher? In this case, the place of the baseball would be the surface of the water that surrounds it, while the place of the water would be the pitcher, or rather the inner surface of the pitcher where it touches the water. Aristotle considered and dismissed a rival theory, namely that the place of each thing is the three-dimensional extension occupied by that thing. On this view, the place of the baseball in the water would be a spatial region exactly the size of the ball itself. This region was previously occupied by water, but when the baseball is plunged into the pitcher it displaces some of the water and quite literally takes its place.

Even though Aristotle explicitly rejected this idea of place as extension, commentators found it attractive because it could help resolve tensions within Aristotle's physics. For one thing, he thought that there are "natural places" for the four elements. Earth is trying to get to its proper place at the center of the cosmos, and fire to the outer edge of the realm below the celestial spheres, which is why earth falls and fire rises. Pretty clearly, these natural places are not containing boundaries; they sound more like regions of space. Then there was the problem of the place of the universe itself. For Aristotle, there is nothing outside the spherical cosmos, not even empty space. So there is no further body containing the cosmos, to provide it with a place. Absurdly, it would seem that the universe is nowhere at all.

Yet again the commentators turned their ingenuity to solving these problems.[15] Regarding the place of the cosmos, they engaged with an ingenious solution suggested by Averroes. Since nothing contains the outermost sphere of the cosmos, we can in this exceptional case say that its place is provided by the center point of the whole universe, around which the sphere is rotating. Strike three for Averroes, according to some of our commentators. This solution would make the earth prior to the heavens in explanation, which is inconsistent with the heavens' superior role in Aristotelian natural philosophy. They devise substitute accounts, for instance that the place of the outermost heaven could be its own outer surface. As for the place of more everyday objects like baseballs, they suggest that we might be able to find a compromise between Aristotle's definition and the idea that place is extension. After all, the containing boundary of a body defines a three-dimensional region within itself, which is exactly the extension occupied by the body.

By the middle of the thirteenth century, then, considerable progress was being made in natural philosophy concerning topics we still associate with "physics": cosmology, motion, time, infinity, and space or at least place. But for Aristotle and his medieval followers, natural philosophy included much more than this. They took "physics" to include the study of plants, animals, and human nature itself. Such living beings all have a principle that gives them life, which is what Aristotle meant by "soul." On this topic too, thirteenth-century philosophers wrestled with the ideas they were finding in Aristotle and in works of the Islamic world.

24

STAYIN' ALIVE
THIRTEENTH-CENTURY
PSYCHOLOGY

Unlike Bill Clinton, George Clinton—who founded the 1970s funk bands Parliament and Funkadelic, and is no relation as far as I'm aware—would probably have made a terrible scholastic philosopher. A more natural place for Clinton in the history of philosophy would have been late ancient Neoplatonism, given that Parliament recorded a song called "Everything is on the One." Still, Clinton had the appropriate qualifications to teach at a medieval university. He did after all bear the title "Doctor Funkenstein." It would have been good fun to see the medieval arts masters devoting a disputed question to the definitions offered in the 1970 Funkadelic song "What is Soul?" "We find in Aristotle that soul is the form of the body that has life potentially," they might have said. "But to the contrary: it is stated on the album *Maggot Brain* that 'soul' is a ham hock in your cornflakes."

In fact, medieval theories of soul were never quite that funky. But they are liable to strike us as odd nonetheless, unless we have a thorough understanding of the sources that influenced those theories. As we've been seeing, thirteenth-century philosophers had access to an unprecedented range of texts, which came down to them from very different traditions. Reading a treatise on the soul from the early part of the century can be a bit like attending a Parliament-Funkadelic concert: there are plenty of ideas on display, but the overall impression is rather chaotic. One of the most sophisticated authors of the time was William of Auvergne, who wrote a lengthy treatise on soul, which tries to reconcile traditional Augustinian ideas with material from Aristotle and Avicenna. One scholar has commented that the upshot is "a quagmire of apparent contradictions, inexact analogies, unfinished arguments, and a capricious and inconsistent use of technical terms."[1]

To the extent that this is a fair judgment, it's not because William or other early thirteenth-century philosophers were slavishly following their sources without noticing the contradictions between them. They were selective and discriminating in their use of previous material, and willing to criticize some of their most influential predecessors. William stresses at the outset of his treatise that he will not simply rely on the authority of Aristotle (§1.1).[2] Later, he says pointedly that one must often disagree with Aristotle, even if his views should be welcomed when they turn out to be true (§2.12). When it came to the question "What is soul?" one particular problem was as obvious as a ham hock sitting in a bowl of cornflakes. Aristotle had indeed defined the soul as the "form of the body," or as the body's "perfection (*entelecheia*)." He went on to present the soul as a set of faculties, most of which are exercised through the body. This makes a certain amount of sense, if you think of soul first and foremost as a principle of life. It meant that Aristotle could ascribe souls to plants and animals, as well as humans, plants leading a life restricted to the functions of nutrition and reproduction, while animals display further capacities for self-motion and sensation. If the soul is the body's form, though, then how could it exist independently from body? If it cannot, then the prospects look dim for a key tenet of Christianity, the survival of soul following bodily death.

Of course, it wasn't only Christians (and while we're in a 1970s mood, the Bee Gees) who had a vested interest in stayin' alive. In late antiquity, Plotinus had criticized Aristotle's definition of soul precisely on the grounds that it would make soul dependent on body.[3] Following Plato, he saw the soul as a substance in its own right, which is immaterial and has only a temporary relationship to the body. Christians could find the same attitude in ancient religious authorities like Augustine. On the other hand, Christians had reasons not to go too far in a Platonizing direction. Their religion centered on the incarnation of God, and was committed to the eventual resurrection of the body in paradise. So it was awkward to admit that the body is nothing but an incidental and unwelcome accretion onto the soul. The upshot was that medieval authors had not only an exegetical problem about what to do with Aristotle's definition of soul, but also a philosophical problem: how to preserve the human soul's exalted status as an immaterial substance, while still saying that one human person is a union of soul *and* body?

The problems did not end there. For Aristotle, the soul has a whole range of different powers, ranging from the lowly faculty of nutrition, which we share even with plants, to the distinctively human capacity for intellectual thought. How then to show that there is unity, this time not between soul and body, but within the soul itself? If your distinctively human part is your intellect, it might seem that your lower powers would be incidental to you, no part of who or what you really are. One might even wonder whether humans have a plurality of souls: one for thinking, a second for the functions we share with animals, and a third for the functions we share with plants. This brings us back to the aforementioned question of the afterlife. Clearly the lower powers of nutrition, reproduction, sensation, and self-motion can only be exercised through the body. So upon the death of our bodies, it would seem that if anything at all can survive, it will be the intellectual part of the soul. This may again encourage us to see your intellective part as the "real you." But in that case, what would be the point of your once again taking on a body at the resurrection?

I've already mentioned the obvious authority figures of Aristotle and Augustine. But for discussions of the soul in this period the most important authority was Avicenna. We've just seen how Averroes' ideas provided an inspiration and foil for authors writing about physics in the first half of the thirteenth century. In psychology, that is, the study of soul (from the Greek *psyche*, "soul"), Avicenna was even more influential, to the point that his importance at first outstripped that of Aristotle.[4] The earliest example of this tendency is in a work on the soul by Dominicus Gundisalvi, one of the translators who worked at Toledo in the twelfth century. He quotes liberally from Avicenna, while making only sparing use of Aristotle. In the early thirteenth century, we find something similar with the Oxford arts master John Blund, who did not die until 1248 but was already lecturing on Aristotle around the turn of the century. He too turned to Avicenna for help in understanding the soul.

An expert on the Latin reception of Avicenna, Dag Hasse, has written that, if Blund's writing on the soul reflects actual classroom discussion, then the textbook must have been Avicenna's *On the Soul* and not Aristotle's.[5] Blund recognizes the challenge presented by Aristotle's original definition of soul as the form of the body, and embraces Avicenna's solution, namely that the soul does exercise its powers through the body, but its relation to body is merely accidental (§15). Blund connects this with a methodological question: which branch of philosophy studies the soul? Insofar as the soul is studied through its incidental relation to the body, it falls under the purview of natural philosophy (*physica*). But insofar as one studies the soul in itself, one is doing metaphysics (§17). Then comes a remark that may overturn our expectations about medieval philosophy, though these expectations have been overturned so often by now that they are as dizzy as the stage manager at a Parliament-Funkadelic show. Blund asks whether the soul isn't a subject studied in theology. Yes, he replies, but only as concerns the soul's reward and punishment. The question of what soul actually is has nothing to do with theology (§22).

What we discover when we tackle the properly philosophical issue of the soul's nature, then, is that it is incorporeal. Blund shows this with a proof that indirectly goes all the way back to Plato and his dialogue on the immortality of soul, the *Phaedo*. (Whatever happens to your soul, at least your best arguments may live on well after your death.) Like Plato, Blund argues that if soul is the principle of life, then being alive is intrinsic to soul. So it is no more susceptible to death than a triangle is susceptible to having angles that fail to add up to 180 degrees (§317; compare *Phaedo* 106b–d). As an immaterial thing, the soul is simple as well as immortal, notwithstanding its numerous faculties, which form a unity within it the way that species are unified within a single genus (§40). On the other hand, only the rational aspect of the soul survives after the body's death, since it is the aspect whose power can be exercised without using the body at all.

At this point, we might wonder when the theologians are going to burst through the door, insisting that they want to have a say after all. They may complain that Blund is making the soul sound very much like God: simple, immaterial, and eternal. How, then, is it that the rational soul falls short of divinity? Blund doesn't consider this question as such, but he would have a good answer ready. Though the soul is simple in comparison to the body, it is in some sense composed of multiple aspects or parts. Blund applies to the soul a distinction taken from Boethius, contrasting being or substance in itself with the particular nature or essence that belongs to that substance. It is one thing for me simply *to be* and another for me *to be a human*. A soul too exists as a substance which takes on a nature, in this case the nature appropriate to souls. To this minimal extent, it fails to be completely one (§330).

This idea, that even an immaterial substance like the soul may be constituted from more than one thing, is going to play a major role later medieval thought. For instance, some thinkers will say that it is thanks to some sort of composition that angels are distinct from God (see Chapter 70). Only God alone is perfectly simple. He is pure being, with no qualifications or specifications added. In this earlier period, the same basic idea is often expressed with the apparently rather paradoxical claim that incorporeal things are made of both form and matter. Obviously, the matter of something like a soul or an angel cannot be like the crude matter of bodies, but even an angel or soul does have matter. Here we can detect the influence of another thinker from the Islamic world, in this case a Jewish one, the eleventh-century philosopher Ibn Gabirol.[6] He put forward a doctrine that attracted both admiration and condemnation from Latin medieval thinkers. We know his theory under the name of "universal hylomorphism," which sounds a bit like it could be a Parliament-Funkadelic song (who, I think it is not entirely inappropriate to observe, released a track called "Funkentelelechy," which could in turn be the soul of a German radio operator). Ibn Gabirol's idea was that everything, apart of course from God Himself, is composed from both matter and form. Among other advantages, this would ensure that only God is perfectly simple.

Where John Blund gestured towards Ibn Gabirol's theory, and other authors such as Philip the Chancellor and Roger Bacon embraced it outright, it was firmly rejected by the aforementioned William of Auvergne.[7] He was a dominant figure on the philosophical scene until his death in 1249, serving as the Bishop of Paris from 1228. Towards the end of his life, he wrote a lengthy treatise on the soul, which he included as part of an even more massive treatise collecting his thoughts on a range of theological topics.[8] As this context suggests, he does not follow John Blund in confining himself to a philosophical, as opposed to theological, treatment of soul. To the contrary, he immediately announces in a prologue that the natural philosopher cannot know that the soul is created in God's image, a belief that had inspired Augustine's treatment of the human mind in *On the Trinity*.[9] William borrows heavily from Augustine, but Avicenna remains a powerful influence here too.

One of William's borrowings from Avicenna is precisely to insist that soul is something substantial, rather than being only an accidental form of the body (§1.5). In a phrase that will appear in other medieval treatments of soul, William states that the soul is a *hoc aliquid*, or "this something," Aristotle's expression for an independent and self-subsisting individual (in Greek *tode ti*). This is why other thinkers made soul a compound of matter and form, to ensure that it is a "this something." But William thinks soul is a special kind of individual, which is free from matter. To prove this he again makes use of Avicenna. He argues that if soul is capable of thinking about a simple and immaterial object of the understanding, then it must itself be simple and immaterial (§2.10). With this statement Avicenna already seems to be in the background, but the more obvious debt comes when William tells us to imagine a human in midair without anything available to his senses (§2.13). This is Avicenna's famous "flying man" thought experiment,[10] although William draws from it a slightly different conclusion. Avicenna asked us to recognize that the flying man would be directly aware of the existence of his own essence or self, even without any sensory input. By contrast, William simply observes that the flying man will be capable of thinking. It is apparently only by noticing that he is thinking that the flying man knows that he exists. Thus, William does not connect the thought experiment to Avicenna's innovative proposal that every human soul has permanent self-awareness, which is more fundamental in our mental life than any act of thinking or sensation.[11]

Yet William does lay great emphasis on the soul's guaranteed knowledge of itself. In a passage that evokes Augustine, while also prefiguring a famous passage of Descartes' *Meditations*, William argues that the soul could never know that it does *not* exist, because the soul's knowing anything presupposes that it *does* exist (§1.4). Moreover, to deny the existence of soul in the impressively functional human body would be like seeing an expertly steered ship and denying that it has a helmsman (§1.7). To his credit, William anticipates the objection that may leap to

mind for the modern reader: some machines are capable of very impressive functions despite being lifeless and without soul. William's version of the objection
considers a water clock. He says that this is no counterargument at all, because
human intervention is needed to set up the water clock and keep it functioning
properly (§1.7). He also singles out for criticism Alexander of Aphrodisias, the most
important late antique commentator on Aristotle. William is appalled by Alexander's suggestion that the soul could somehow emerge from, and hence depend on,
the physical states of the body. This must be wrong, because the soul is superior to
the body, and the better can never be generated by the worse. Besides, William adds,
the soul is a substance, so it cannot just be an accidental side effect of bodily
composition (§5.3–4).

Whereas Alexander appears only as a whipping boy, Avicenna seems to provoke
a more mixed response. Not only does William like Avicenna's idea that the soul has
guaranteed access to itself; he also agrees with John Blund and Avicenna that the
soul's relation to body is purely incidental. In fact, the body is nothing but an
external tool for the soul, like a musician's instrument, or like a house or even a
prison in which the soul finds itself for now but can eventually leave (§3.11). On the
other hand, William keeps an eye on the doctrine of the resurrection, insisting that
humanity consists in both body and soul, not only soul (§1.2). He chastizes Avicenna
for saying that the soul needs the body in order to be to be singled out as the
individual soul that it is, and continues to depend on the body for this individuating
function during its earthly life (§2.1).[12] William is further annoyed by Avicenna's idea
that the soul is given to the body by an intellectual celestial being distinct from God,
the so-called "giver of forms (dator formarum)" (§5.2). Rather, it is God Himself who
creates each soul directly, as an individual substance which is already differentiated
from other souls.

One interesting stretch of William's treatise concerns the question of how exactly,
and when exactly, the soul comes to be in the body. William is particularly
concerned with the advent of the rational soul, since it is only upon its arrival
that the embryo can really said to be a human. This happens not at conception, but
on the forty-sixth day of pregnancy (§4.4). Prior to that, the lower soul parts may
already be present, which causes William difficulties along the lines mentioned
above. If the developing infant can have a vegetative or animal soul without the
rational soul, then do these souls remain distinct throughout the human's life? If so,
then each of us is walking around with two or even three souls. Perhaps George
Clinton has that much soul, but for the rest of us it seems unlikely. William's
solution to this problem, if you can really call it a solution, comes in the shape of
a metaphor. When God finally gives the rational soul to the embryo, the lower souls

are absorbed into it like dimmer lights being swallowed up in a much brighter light (§4.3). That's not particularly persuasive, but William does make the more telling point that we can't just say there is a distinct soul for each power or faculty that a person possesses. Within sensation alone there are five powers (sight, hearing, etc.) but no one would say that sensation involves five souls. Just as one and the same person can fulfill various governmental offices, so one soul can be responsible for various functions (§3.6). If you'd prefer a groovier example, just think of how George Clinton was able to be the presiding genius for both Parliament *and* Funkadelic.

William levels one final criticism at the previous tradition, which is worth mentioning because of the resonance it will have later on. He observes that the rational soul has, in addition to its intellectual power, also a power of choice, what Augustine called the "will." Sadly, Aristotle and his followers in the Islamic world paid little or no attention to this crucial human capacity (§3.7). William even seems to say that the will can operate independently of the judgments of intellect. This would make him an early proponent of what has come to be called "voluntarism," something we'll be discussing extensively later in this book.[13] But here we are leaving the study of the soul and getting into the area of ethics. That's an area I do want to get into shortly, but first we're going to need a bit more metaphysical background.

25

IT'S ALL GOOD
THE TRANSCENDENTALS

In writing this book, I'm making an effort to spare you the technical jargon that typically festoons philosophical prose. I assume that you don't really want to fight your way through the sort of phrases I confront all the time in my day job, like "internalist epistemic theory of justification" or "jointly necessary and sufficient conditions." But with the medievals it's constantly tempting to introduce technical terminology, because they did this so often themselves, usually making conceptual breakthroughs by regimenting language so as to capture fine distinctions. In some cases what may seem a case of mere scholastic hair-splitting has survived to become a standard instrument in the toolkit of today's philosophers. An excellent example is the contrast between "extensional" and "intensional," which we're going to find useful in what follows.

The basic idea is that you can think of or talk about one and the same thing, or group of things, in more than one way. The aforementioned George Clinton was the leader of the soul-drenched, jazz-organ-infused 1970s band Funkadelic and also the leader of a more disco-leaning group called Parliament. Hence, if you are thinking about the leader of Funkadelic and I am thinking about the leader of Parliament, what we are thinking about is "extensionally" identical. We are in other words thinking of the same man out there in the world, George Clinton. Yet our thoughts are "intensionally" distinct. Thinking about the leader of Funkadelic is not the same as thinking of the leader of Parliament, even if it turns out that they are one and the same. They must be different, since someone could realize that George Clinton led Funkadelic without realizing that he led Parliament. Another frequently used example, which, as it happens, also involves organs, is that the extension of the phrase "animals with hearts" is the same as the extension of the phrase "animals with kidneys," because all animals with hearts have kidneys and vice versa. Still, these phrases obviously mean different things and are thus intensionally distinct.

The medievals achieved unprecedented clarity on this point and deployed it in innovative ways. But it was already suggested in Aristotle's *Metaphysics* in a passage which states that unity is "convertible" with being, even though unity and being are somehow different (1061a). Anything that is, is one thing, and vice versa. So what is and what is one are extensionally identical even though they would appear to be intensionally distinct concepts. Now, the *Metaphysics* was one of the many texts that came to be read by scholastic philosophers in the thirteenth century after being unknown during the early medieval period. Once the medievals began to study the work, this passage really caught their attention.[1] Aristotle did have a point, after all. How could anything exist without having some kind of unity? Even something that is nothing more than a scattered bunch of other things, like a crowd, is still one crowd. It must have some degree of unity; otherwise we wouldn't be entitled to refer to it as something that is.[2]

Which brings us to the transcendentals, which are nothing less than the properties or features that apply to *all* existing things. Being and unity are both transcendentals, since everything that is has being and is one, as we've just seen. There are other examples, notably "true" and "good." Aquinas also includes "thing" and "something," which sound less redundant in Latin than they do in English: *res* and *aliquid*. As we'll see later in this chapter, "beauty" was also sometimes considered to be a transcendental property. But medievals discovered more besides these, and in fact you can quite easily make your own transcendentals at home. To take a rather trivial example, nothing can be both round and square, so all existing things have the property of not-being-a-round-square.

The transcendental that first attracted serious attention in the thirteenth century was goodness.We can see this in William of Auxerre, a master of theology at Paris in the decades following the founding of the university (not to be confused with William of Auvergne, whose views on the soul we just discussed). He took up a question that had been raised by Boethius in one of his theological treatises.[3] Why, asked Boethius, are all things that exist good? William accepted Boethius' answer, namely that God is a purely good cause, so everything He creates winds up being good too. For this reason, to be and to be good are one and the same thing. Reading Boethius or William of Auxerre on this issue, one may feel like someone who's turned up late to a play and missed the first act. Who ever said that everything that is, is good? What about natural disasters, cancer, and most of the disco music that wasn't produced by George Clinton? The world seems to be chock-full of terrible things, so how can anyone say that all things are good?

The answer lies with a late ancient Platonist doctrine about goodness which found a welcome reception in Augustine and Boethius and was then widely accepted by the medievals.[4] According to this doctrine nothing can *be* at all without having some share in goodness. This is not to say that everything is perfect. To the contrary, only God is perfect. Still, even evil things must somehow share in goodness or they could not be at all. This understanding of evil as relative non-being forms a background assumption for the whole discussion of transcendentals, and explains why goodness is always included alongside unity and truth as coextensive with being. This leaves us with a more subtle question, which William of Auxerre leaves unanswered. Can it be true to say that being and being good are in some sense *one and the same*? William himself admits that this is problematic. After all, one thing can be more good than another, but it seems that one thing cannot *be* more than another.[5]

A solution would be provided by Philip the Chancellor, another theologian of Paris and a contemporary of William of Auxerre, with both dying in the 1230s. Philip was a significant figure in the life of the university in the first third of the century, because he served as Chancellor at the cathedral of Notre Dame for about twenty years. Philip's decisive contribution to the theory of transcendentals came in a treatise called *De bono*, meaning *On the Good* and not, as you may have been hoping, that the work is a prophetic tribute to the lead singer of U2. Like William of Auxerre, Philip the Chancellor was strongly influenced by Boethius, and he accepted the doctrine that being and good are convertible. But unlike William he also made use of the materials from Aristotle and the Islamic world that had recently become available in Latin. In fact, Philip nicely illustrates the dynamic we've been seeing throughout early thirteenth-century philosophy, with newly translated texts being used to make progress on difficulties that had already been faced by earlier generations.

Thanks to his exposure to Aristotle and the resources of terminist logic, Philip was able to explain more precisely the relationship between being, goodness, unity, and truth. We can formulate the puzzle more precisely by framing it as a dilemma. If being is the same as unity, truth, and goodness, then aren't these further notions pointless or, as the medievals put it, "nugatory"? "Unity," "truth," and "goodness" would be mere synonyms of "being." Saying that "All things that are are good" would no longer be an ambitious claim about metaphysics and God's creation, but a mere tautology, on a par with such empty observations as "It is what it is" or (as 1970s soul singers liked to say) "Everything is everything." On the other hand, if saying that "A thing is" does have a different meaning from saying that "A thing is good," then goodness must somehow differ from being. That would suggest that Boethius was wrong, and that it isn't necessary that whatever is, is good.

Philip the Chancellor's solution is that being, unity, goodness, and truth are indeed the same, but only *extensionally*. They are however different in *intension*. He makes this point using the vocabulary of thirteenth-century logic: "though they are convertible with respect to the extension and scope of their supposits, the good goes beyond being conceptually (*ratione*)."[6] We see here how important supposition theory could be in contexts beyond logic. To say that two different terms "supposit" for the same thing means that the two terms refer to the same object or objects out in the world. But this doesn't mean that the two terms have the same signification. To go back to our former example, the terms "leader of Parliament" and "leader of Funkadelic" both supposit for George Clinton, while meaning something entirely different. Supposition theory provided the tools clearly to express this fact, and Aristotelian theory of language could offer a deeper explanation of the phenomenon.[7] For Aristotle, words signify concepts in the mind, while concepts signify things in the world (*On Interpretation* 16a). So we use different words to lead the mind to different concepts, which may turn out to apply to one and the same thing, in our example George Clinton. Likewise, "being" and "unity" are distinct concepts; yet both apply universally to everything that there is.

This is a good start towards an account of the transcendentals, but it seems there is more still to explain. The terms "being," "unity," and so on clearly have a much closer, more intimate connection than other words that are intensionally different while being extensionally the same. It seems that whatever falls under being *must* also fall under unity, goodness, and truth, which isn't usually the case with intensionally distinct, yet extensionally identical entities. George Clinton may be the leader of both Parliament and Funkadelic, but he could retire and pass leadership of the two bands to different people, perhaps Fred Wesley and Bootsy Collins. Then, the titles would become extensionally as well as intensionally distinct. Or, as the medievals would say, the terms "leader of Funkadelic" and "leader of Parliament" would come to supposit for different things. With the transcendental terms this cannot happen. Why not?

Again, Philip is ready with an answer. Although the other transcendental terms introduce a conceptual change from the basic idea of being, they do not add much. Being "the leader of Funkadelic" is a positive designation that brings with it certain legal and financial rights, as George Clinton has often been eager to point out. By contrast "unity" adds only something negative to being, namely the absence of division. This idea that the other transcendentals add *negative* characterizations was also used in a text written jointly by another Parisian theologian, Alexander of Hales, and some of his collaborators, especially John de la Rochelle. However, Alexander and John added that the transcendentals could also allude to the way that being *relates* to other things. For instance, the reason that being is convertible with truth (something that may have been puzzling you since I mentioned it) is that any case of being can be understood, that is, can be related to the intellect. Likewise, the good is being insofar as it relates to our will or faculty of choice.[8] These ideas will be taken up by the most famous exponent of transcendental theory, Thomas Aquinas. He states explicitly that when two things differ only conceptually, this is because they are distinguished only by virtue of negations or relations.[9]

That's how the transcendentals differ from one another. What do they all have in common? Well, the reason they are extensionally the same is that all of them apply to everything that exists. The medievals had a more rigorous way of putting this point, which will explain why these concepts are called "transcendentals." Where Parliament-Funkadelic transcended the boundaries of musical genre, and often of good taste, the medievals' transcendentals transcended the categories. These were, of course, another inheritance from the Aristotelian tradition. Substance, quantity, quality, relation, and the rest were taken by the scholastics to constitute ten classes of being. On this understanding of Aristotle's categories, "being human" really is what it sounds like: a way of *being*, in this case a kind of being that is appropriate to substances, since humans are substances. By contrast, the being that belongs to blue is a qualitative sort of being. The transcendentals are not like this. They cut across all the categories, applying just as much to a substance like a human as to a quality like blue. Just as each human that *is* is *one* human, so each instance of blue that *is* is *one* instance of blue.

This trans-categorial status gives the transcendentals both their name and their philosophical importance, but it raises some further problems. Within the Aristotelian logical framework adopted by the scholastics, we understand concepts by finding definitions. And we define things by dividing a large class into a smaller subclass, as when we say that human is the sort of animal that is rational. But with the transcendentals that obviously won't be possible. You can't understand being as a certain, specific kind of something or other, because everything that there is has being. We grasp the categories as divisions within being, but cannot grasp being itself in a similar way, since it isn't a division of any more general class. Of course, that applies to the other transcendentals too, as unity, truth, and goodness all apply to everything. How then should we try to define them?[10]

The answer is, basically, that we can't. The best we can do is somehow to characterize them, for instance by explaining that unity means being insofar as it lacks division. This isn't a proper definition but does convey what we might mean when we talk about unity, and also why it is different from being—intensionally different, of course, not extensionally different. If you press the point by asking how we would *learn* about such general concepts, the scholastics will suggest that you go read one of the texts that has been made available in the recent Latin translation movement. This time they will point you not to Aristotle but to Avicenna. He argued that concepts like being are "primary intelligibles." They are immediately available to the mind, and we do not learn about them on the basis of anything else. Authors like Thomas Aquinas are happy to accept this, and even cite Avicenna by name when explaining the idea.[11]

As a result the transcendentals are more than just important notions in thirteenth-century metaphysics. They actually define what metaphysics *is*, since it can be understood as the science of the first and most general concepts that we have.[12] Which, you won't be surprised to hear, is going to raise even more problems. A rival conception of metaphysics would make it the science of the most fundamental *causes* of being, rather than the most general concepts, which would bring metaphysics very close to theology. Aristotle's *Metaphysics* muddied the waters instead of clearing them up, since some parts of that work seem to undertake a general study of being, while other parts stage an inquiry into the first causes of all things. Any attempt to bring the two projects together would inevitably lead us to ask whether the transcendentals really do apply to *everything* in the same way. Can we apply the notions of being, unity, and goodness to God in the same way as we apply them to created things? These concerns are going to lead to intense disagreement in the later thirteenth century, as we'll see later (Chapter 48).

The transcendentals also play a role in another area of philosophy entirely, namely aesthetics. The medievals did not recognize this as a sub-discipline of philosophy on a par with physics, ethics, or metaphysics. Yet they did talk about beauty, which some authors—including Alexander of Hales and his colleagues— wanted to include in the list of transcendentals. Some scholars have sought to find the same idea in Thomas Aquinas. But in passages where Aquinas enumerates the transcendentals, beauty is not included.[13] And with good reason. Elsewhere, Aquinas tells us that to be beautiful is to be good in a certain way. Beauty is the tendency of goodness to be *pleasing*. So beauty would relate to goodness much as goodness relates to being. In a sense, then, it might count as a transcendental in that its extension is just as wide as that of goodness, which in turn is just as wide as the scope of being. But it is unlike the other transcendentals in that it involves a relational feature of goodness, rather than of being.

Aquinas' remarks on beauty stand in a long tradition, which (like the conception of evil as non-being) can be traced back to Augustine and ultimately to pagan Platonism. In this tradition, beauty was defined in terms of symmetry and order, which were in turn seen as manifestations of divine reality in the physical realm.[14] God, in other words, is ultimately and perfectly beautiful, something expressed in a famous line of Augustine's *Confessions*, "Late have I loved you, Beauty so old and so new."[15] If you consider a work of art such as the cathedral at Chartres, you can see how this spiritual, dare I say transcendent, understanding of beauty might be put into practice. But what about a work of art like the classic Funkadelic album *Let's Take it to the Stage*? Part of what makes it enjoyable is its ridiculousness, its irreverence, its roughness around the edges. You might suppose that in the Middle Ages aesthetic tastes ran exclusively towards the cathedral end of the spectrum. But as it turns out, the medieval artistic sensibility could be pretty funky. When commenting on the appeal of poetry or visual artworks, medieval authors often emphasized the play of contradictory features, like sweetness and bitterness in food. Audiences enjoyed incongruity and parody, and did not insist that beauty should somehow convey a transcendental goodness present in all created things. To the contrary, they were comfortable with the idea that beauty was merely skin-deep. In fact, Isidore of Seville related the Latin word for beauty, *pulchritudo*, to the word for skin, *pellis*.[16]

While the medieval philosophers do not much acknowledge this dimension of aesthetics, Aquinas does emphasize the *relational* nature of beauty. Just as truth is being as related to the mind, so beauty is goodness as related to our capacity to feel delight. This fits with the dynamic nature of aesthetic experience, which always depends on an interaction between artwork and audience. Philosophers were also open to the idea that beauty is, if not superficial or "skin-deep," then at least characteristically bodily in nature. They were, after all, devoted to a religion based on the incarnation of the divine in a human body. For this reason somewhat less intellectualist thinkers, including Aquinas' contemporary Bonaventure, gave great weight to sensation and used vividly physical metaphors as they described our journey to know God. For the most powerful of examples, we need only think back to the visions of Hildegard. For authors with this frame of mind the beauty of nature, or of a work of art, could have a role in spiritual life precisely because these things appeal to the senses.

As I've said, the case of beauty shows that the theory of transcendentals was not only about metaphysics. If I may indulge in one more technical expression, the transcendentals have what philosophers would nowadays call a "normative" dimension. It is not only being or unity that has universal scope, but also goodness and, according to some authors, beauty. For the thirteenth-century scholastics existing things do not just call us to know about them, but also to value them. As they would put it, things make a claim on our will as well as our intellect. But how should we respond to and understand the goodness of these things, and what is our place within the world of goods? These are the questions we'll be tackling next.

26

DO THE RIGHT THING
THIRTEENTH-CENTURY ETHICS

I'd like you to imagine that you're riding the London Underground at rush hour, and that you have managed to get a seat. You notice a woman with a swollen belly standing right nearby. Being an outstanding and admirable human being, you hasten to offer her your seat. As it happens, another passenger standing next to you turns out to be a philosopher. She also turns out to be one of those rare philosophers who is actually socially outgoing (I did say you'd have to use your imagination). She asks you why you offered your seat to the pregnant woman. Probably, you'd shrug and say that it was obviously the right thing to do. The philosopher, being a philosopher, might reply, "Sure, but that doesn't explain why you did it. People fail to do the right thing all the time." To which you would presumably say something to the effect that it would not have felt right to continue sitting there while someone in greater need was forced to stand. Your conscience would not have allowed it.

This answer would strike the philosopher as intriguing, especially if she happened to have an interest in thirteenth-century moral theory. Medieval thinkers devoted careful attention to the phenomenon of moral conscience. Some of them saw it as playing precisely the role just suggested. It is conscience that leads you actually to perform the action you take to be good, rather than just understanding that it would be the right thing to do and then doing something else. As the medievals would put it, conscience somehow involves the power of *will*, and not just the power of reason. The idea that humans have such a power, the faculty of will, was not a medieval invention. The concept emerged in late antiquity and played a major role in the writings of Augustine.[1] Its prominence in the Augustinian tradition explains why William of Auvergne was indignant and puzzled to find it receiving so little attention in the works of Aristotle and philosophers of the Islamic world (Chapter 24). This is typical of the situation that gave birth to thirteenth-century ethics. As in other areas of philosophy, new translations were making new ideas available, and these needed somehow to be reconciled with long-traditional doctrines and authorities.

In the case of ethics, the most important new arrival on the scene was, appropriately enough, the Ethics—that is, the Nicomachean Ethics of Aristotle. It would
however take a few additional decades before the confrontation with Aristotle could
fully emerge, because his Ethics was not rendered into Latin in its entirety until the
late 1240s. Until that time, only the first three of the ten books of the Ethics were in
circulation, in a translation probably executed by Burgundio of Pisa.[2] Incomplete
access didn't stop the scholastics from trying to understand what Aristotle was
saying. A handful of commentaries on the Ethics survive from the first part of the
century. As usual, they are mostly anonymous. The commentators had plenty of
other material to make up for the unavailability of the last seven books of Aristotle's
Ethics. They brought to the text all the traditional ideas of Augustinian ethics as well
as other new sources, like Avicenna.

Among Avicenna's bequests to the Latin philosophers was his claim that the soul
is two-faced. It has one relation to the body, which is inferior to it, and another
relation to a principle superior to it.[3] For Avicenna, the superior principle would
have been a celestial intellect, but the medievals could easily adapt his point by
saying that the soul's two faces look down to the body and up to God. When they
turned to Aristotle, the commentators saw that they could use this idea to expound
his understanding of happiness. The first book of his Ethics explains that happiness
must be something self-sufficient and complete, or perfect. For Aristotle this goal
could be achieved by living a life of virtue, both practical and intellectual. Here was a
chance to invoke the two faces. A life of practical virtue demands that the soul pay
heed to the body, whereas the perfect intellectual life means that the soul focuses on
contemplating God.

In spelling out the details of these two lives the early commentators wind up
straying rather far from their source material.[4] The last book of Aristotle's Ethics
praises the life of contemplation as the most happy of all, but our commentators
couldn't yet read this final book. So when they likewise give contemplation first
prize as the most perfect life, they must be getting the idea from somewhere else, for
instance from Avicenna.[5] They also describe contemplation as a sort of mystical
union with God, which would be totally foreign to Aristotle. It will not be until the
commentary of Robert Kilwardby that this tendency is corrected. When it comes to
the practical side of things, the divergences are even more striking. Aristotle
envisioned the excellent man as leading a life of civic engagement, his virtues
displayed by fighting bravely in war, participating in government, and showing
generosity to friends. The commentators instead reflect the ascetic impulse that
began in ancient Christianity and lived on in medieval monasticism. They see
practical virtue primarily as the soul's resisting bodily desire, with each soul

attempting to bring itself closer to God rather than to join in action with fellow humans. Moreover, they dismiss virtue in this life as inadequate for true happiness. Only the prospect of an afterlife together with God can satisfy Aristotle's ambitious criteria.[6]

This may all sound like a "theological" distortion of Aristotle's *Ethics*, such as we might expect from medieval commentators. But this is the thirteenth century, when the scholastics are increasingly distinguishing between the remit of theology and the remit of philosophy, with Aristotle, of course, personifying the philosophical side of that contrast. So it is here. The commentators talk of two complementary approaches to ethics. For Aristotle and other philosophers, virtue is a matter of hard-won habit acquired through moral education and repetition of good actions. Theologians don't deny the existence of such habitual virtues, but they add that God "infuses" us with another kind of virtue, a tendency to prefer good to evil. This tendency survives in us even in our current fallen state of sin. I see a parallel here to another thirteenth-century debate in the field of epistemology. Some thinkers of the period (like Bonaventure) believe that humans have knowledge through illumination from God. Others (such as Aquinas) instead emphasize the role of sense experience, adopting Aristotle's broadly empiricist approach. Similarly in ethics, the theological line is that we should open ourselves to God's assistance, whereas the "philosophical" or Aristotelian stance is that we need to improve through experience.

The inborn tendency to choose the good, which we would call moral conscience, is discussed not so much in the commentaries on Aristotle as in commentaries on the *Sentences* of Peter Lombard.[7] In a characteristically concise and authority-strewn discussion, Lombard had asked why the will does not always steer us towards what is good (91). He cited the Latin church father Jerome, who referred to a "spark of reason which could not be extinguished even in Cain" (93). This more or less set the terms of the debate. On the one hand, we have a "spark" within us that urges us to be righteous; on the other hand, we nonetheless fall into sin. Both are everyday features of our moral life and both stand in need of explanation. The passage that Peter Lombard cited from Jerome supplied another ingredient. There the medievals could find a Greek-derived term, which they wrote as *synderesis*.[8] It isn't far wrong to think of this as a kind of innate ethical conscience, except that the thirteenth-century authors routinely distinguish between *synderesis* and conscience (*conscientia*).

Before we get into the mechanics of *synderesis* and conscience, let's go back to your imaginary conversation with the philosopher on the Tube. Initially you told her that it just struck you as obviously right to give up your seat to the pregnant woman. The philosopher pointed out that there is a difference between seeing that one ought to do something and actually deciding to do it, perhaps even *wanting* to do it. Our feelings of obligation and remorse seem to play a role here. The medievals speak of the "murmurings" of guilt we experience when we do something wrong. Are these murmurings helping us to realize something, to form knowledge about good and bad? Or are they instead helping to motivate us, giving us a kind of push towards what we already know to be good and a desire to do it? From a medieval point of view, the question here is whether conscience and the "spark" of *synderesis* have more to do with reason or with the will. If they are connected especially to reason, they must be intended to help us to *know* the good. If they are connected to the will, they are meant to help us *choose* the good.

An early treatment of this problem can be found in the treatise *On the Good* by Philip the Chancellor, the same text that introduced us to the topic of transcendentals. (Which, I can't resist pointing out, is a great example of why it is worth doing the history of philosophy without any gaps. Most likely you'd never heard of Philip the Chancellor before, but he turns out to have played a pivotal role in the history of both metaphysics and ethics.[9]) Philip's view is that *synderesis* is a "disposition," in other words an inborn tendency, and one that straddles the divide between reason and will. It is superior to our power of reasoning, and should instead be called by the more exalted name of "understanding" (101). Philip seeks to have his cake and eat it too, presenting *synderesis* as a power that produces both motivation and knowledge. It is a "supreme moral power,"[10] not only because it has this overarching influence upon us, but also because it can never go wrong.

The catch is that *synderesis* isn't enough, because it only guides us to very general moral precepts. When you select a specific action that you take to be good, you have gone past *synderesis* and come to what Philip calls "conscience." Conscience is engaged when your base-level sense of right and wrong, which is given by *synderesis*, is supplemented by the power of choice so that you make up your mind to do something specific here and now. Even well-meaning people can go wrong at this stage, something Philip illustrates with an example we've seen before in Peter Abelard. The people who put Christ to death were acting, as we might put it, in good conscience (104). Philip puts it by saying that their *synderesis* was in good working order. It allowed them to see that someone who pretends to be the Son of God should be executed. Their mistake, fallible as they were, was to think that Christ was indeed a mere pretender and therefore someone who fell under this general rule. We can change our example on the Tube slightly to provide a parallel case. Suppose you give up your seat to the woman with a sympathetic smile at her bulging belly, but she's not pregnant after all, just overweight, and when she realizes why you've offered your seat, she is mortified.

This kind of situation, where someone unwittingly does something bad—you know, like offending someone on public transport, or putting to death the Son of God—is also raised in Bonaventure's commentary on Peter Lombard's *Sentences*. Specifically, he asks whether people should always try to follow their conscience (114–15). His answer is an unqualified yes, which is remarkable given that scholastics hardly ever answer a question with an unqualified yes. You should never do something you believe to be wrong, nor should you fail to do something you believe to be right. But following your conscience isn't a moral "get out of jail free" card. It doesn't excuse you from moral blame when you get things wrong. As Abelard already pointed out when he discussed the example of Christ's killers, people following deeply and sincerely held beliefs can still do terrible things. The upshot is that if you want to do what is good (what is "pleasing to God," as Bonaventure puts it), you need to satisfy two conditions: you have to believe that what you're doing is right, and it actually has to be right.

This is compatible with what Philip the Chancellor said about the same issue, though Bonaventure's discussion is more detailed and illuminating. When it comes to the role of reason and will in conscience, though, Bonaventure has a view that is rather different from Philip's. He exploits what is by now a traditional distinction between *synderesis* and conscience to give due weight to both rational belief and motivation.[11] For Bonaventure, conscience operates at two levels. First, it gives us a sense of general moral rules, about which we can never be wrong. These rules, he suggests, could be equated with the natural law (116). Second, conscience is also involved in determining how to apply those rules, and, as in Philip, this sort of "applied conscience" can go astray. For Philip the unerring and general grasp of moral precepts was the function of *synderesis*, but Bonaventure has reserved another role for this power. For him *synderesis* is precisely the motivational power that pushes you to do what your conscience has judged to be right.

Let's go back one more time to our imaginary example, and imagine that it is Bonaventure who struck up a conversation with you on the Tube (let's also imagine that you speak Latin). He would say that when you realized you should give up your seat, this was because you used your conscience to understand the general rule that people in need should be given assistance. A further use of conscience determined that this woman is in need, because she looked to be pregnant. However, it is *synderesis* that made you downright eager to give up your seat and that would murmur with recriminations in your soul if you failed to do so. In other words, it would help move your will towards the right choice. So conscience is an intellectual power, a tendency to form beliefs, whereas *synderesis* has to do with what Bonaventure calls the "desiring part of the soul" (116).

For Bonaventure and many other medieval thinkers, intellectual judgments about the good could remain idle if we did not have some distinct power to explain why we are actually motivated to act on these judgments. But many other medieval thinkers would disagree. Those who adopted a more Aristotelian line can be called "intellectualists." They tended to think that the will simply follows, and puts into action, the judgments reached by practical reason. Their idea is that believing something to be good already involves having a reason to do it, so that judgments about right and wrong have motivational force built into them. It would probably have been impossible for the earliest commentators of the thirteenth century to develop a reading of Aristotle along these lines, because their access to the text was so partial. But when the whole *Nicomachean Ethics* came into circulation in the middle of the century, the opportunity was there, and it was taken by Albert the Great.

Albert was the first master to lecture on the complete *Ethics*, in the year 1249 and in the city of Cologne. The student who took the notes on these lectures was a young Thomas Aquinas. We'll get into Aquinas' views on these matters in Chapter 38. For now I just want to glance at Albert's way of understanding *synderesis*. He is happy to make it a faculty for knowing something, along the lines just sketched, rather than a faculty for desiring or wanting something. So he gives it more or less the function that Philip the Chancellor had assigned to *synderesis*: it is the power to grasp general ethical precepts.[12] The difference is that it is no longer an overarching power that governs both reason and will, but a source of rules we use as a basis for moral reasoning. What *synderesis* gives you is akin to the first principles that we use in the non-practical sciences. A convenient, though slightly anachronistic analogy might be the axioms of geometry or arithmetic.

This is only one respect in which Albert shows himself to be a more faithful Aristotelian than earlier commentators on the *Ethics*. Like them, he continues to see contemplation of God as the sole source of perfect human happiness, something Aquinas too will accept. But Albert makes space for genuinely civic virtue in his ethical teaching, on the basis that this sort of practical goodness is an important step along the way to ultimate beatitude, because it prepares the soul for contemplation. As I've said, Albert's more profoundly Aristotelian approach was only possible because he was able to read the whole of the *Ethics*. So some of the credit should go to the man who produced that complete Latin translation from the Greek original. Important though this contribution was, it would be a gross injustice to see this translator as nothing but a transmitter of texts. He was a philosopher in his own right and also a pioneer of scientific inquiry, notably concerning the subject of light. His name was Robert Grosseteste.

A LIGHT THAT NEVER GOES OUT
ROBERT GROSSETESTE

Metaphors exercise a stronger influence in philosophy than most philosophers would probably like to admit. Whole political theories have been grounded in the comparison of the state to a human body, as we saw with the *Policraticus* of John of Salisbury. Philosophy itself has often been described metaphorically, as when the Stoics drew an analogy between its three parts of ethics, physics, and logic and the yolk, white, and shell of an egg, or the fruit, trees, and surrounding wall of an orchard. In our own day, misguided parents who discourage their children from studying philosophy modify the Stoic image, suggesting that philosophy may be more like a natural fertilizer sometimes used in orchards. But no metaphor has been a more constant or influential feature in the history of philosophy than the comparison of knowledge to eyesight. It plays a role not just in major philosophical works like Plato's *Republic*, but even in our very language. To realize something is to "see" it, and you can "perceive" that something is true. To make a nice point in an argument is to offer an "observation," while accurate anticipation of future events can be called "foresight."

The same was true in ancient Greek. Our word "theory" comes from the Greek *theoria*, which means "viewing" or "beholding" but was used by Aristotle to refer to philosophical contemplation. Even the Greek word for "intellect," *nous*, relates to a verb of seeing, *noein*. The medievals were enthusiastic users of this metaphor, not least because it went so nicely with another analogy between God and light. This too has Greek roots. The Neoplatonists frequently said that their first principle generates all other things like a source of illumination spreading forth its rays. Authors of the Abrahamic traditions carried on the tradition. In the Islamic world, the metaphor was central to the Illuminationist philosophy of the twelfth-century thinker Suhrawardī,[1] while Christians could read in the book of John that "God is light" (1 John 1:5), an image developed by patristic authors like Augustine and the Pseudo-Dionysius.

The next step is pretty obvious: if God is light and knowledge is vision, then perhaps God is the light that enables us to have knowledge. That is the fundamental thesis of what has come to be called the medieval theory of divine illumination.

It is based on one of Augustine's favorite metaphors and also captures his idea that we can only achieve knowledge thanks to Christ's presence as an "inner teacher" in our souls.[2] So, naturally enough, it is often seen (there's that visual metaphor again) as a distinctively Augustinian aspect of thirteenth-century thought, contrasted with an Aristotelian theory of knowledge on which humans come to know things through sense experience. Where Aristotle proposed a "bottom-up" epistemology built on sensation, the Augustinians insisted that something as exalted as knowledge can only come from the very top, that is, from God. The implications of the dispute are far-reaching. The Augustinian theory suggests that the best way to achieve knowledge might be to withdraw from the world and meditate or contemplate, in hopes of opening oneself to divine light. The Aristotelian model would instead encourage us to go out into the world and investigate, in order to activate the mind's potential for understanding.

But as so often, the neat contrast gets messier the more closely you look at it. Aristotle himself used the light metaphor in an influential and inscrutable passage which compares a mysterious and unidentified "maker intellect" to the light that makes eyesight possible (*On the Soul* 5.3). Already in antiquity, Alexander of Aphrodisias—certainly no Platonist, and too early to be an Augustinian—identified this intellect with God. Meanwhile, we find pioneers of the divine illumination theory emphasizing the need for what they call *experimentum*, which is not "experiment" exactly, but does mean sensory experience of the physical world around us. One such pioneer was Robert Grosseteste. He gave light a central role in his philosophy, invoking it in his account of knowledge and also in a breathtakingly original cosmology.

Most of the major thirteenth-century philosophers were active in the second half of that century, but alongside Philip the Chancellor, Robert Grosseteste is an exception. He died in 1253, having served as Chancellor of the University of Oxford (these were good decades for chancellors) before being consecrated as Bishop of Lincoln in 1235.[3] On that basis you might conclude that we're dealing here with a distinctively English thinker, and Grosseteste was certainly an important figure for the development of philosophy at Oxford. There is a scholarly controversy lurking here, though, since some have proposed that Grosseteste must have received an intellectual formation in Paris.[4] Wherever he was initially trained, he wasn't content to stop learning. In the early 1230s, when he was already into his sixties, he decided to study Greek. His motivation was probably above all theological: he wished to read the New Testament in the original.[5] He was able to draw on the assistance of Greek-speaking scholars, who had begun to travel in Europe more frequently following the Crusaders' sack of Constantinople in 1204. Remarkably, he not only mastered the language but went on to execute translations of key philosophical works, including Aristotle's *Nicomachean Ethics* and *On the Heavens*. He also consulted and translated Greek commentaries on these works from the late ancient and Byzantine periods.

We may be reminded of the ninth-century translator and philosopher Eriugena. Like him, Grosseteste even translated writings of Dionysius. But philosophy in the thirteenth century almost always meant studying the works of Aristotle, and Grosseteste was no exception. When he tells us that knowledge involves illumination from God, he is commenting on that key work of Aristotelian epistemology and scientific theory, the *Posterior Analytics*.[6] Confronted with Aristotle's pronouncement that we have demonstrative knowledge of something only when we know its cause, Grosseteste says that he couldn't agree more, and he likewise endorses the doctrine that knowledge must be universal in character. Illuminationism comes in when he explains how we are able to have such knowledge.

Universals, Grosseteste explains, appear at numerous levels of reality. They exist in physical things around us as their forms, in the heavens, and in the minds of angels—that sound you hear is the nominalist Peter Abelard turning in his grave next to Heloise. Finally and most importantly, universals exist in God's mind as the eternal, paradigmatic "reasons" of things.[7] That other sound you hear is Aristotle turning in his grave, as Grosseteste says that the theory of demonstrative knowledge found in the *Posterior Analytics* can work only if we posit these rather Platonist-sounding divine ideas. They are the source of all created things, and you did say, didn't you Aristotle, that we can only know things by knowing their causes? Still, we shouldn't get carried away in emphasizing the perversely anti-Aristotelian nature of Grosseteste's commentary. He is one "illuminationist" who is totally committed to Aristotle's idea that knowledge is grounded in sensation. Admittedly, he does offer a distinctively theological reason for this, namely that in our fallen state we cannot just know things in God's light. Instead we must engage in laborious empirical study to make up for our weakness as knowers.[8] But as Grosseteste puts it, "knowledge comes to us via the senses, but not thanks to (*gratia*) the senses," for no knowledge would be possible without the illumination provided by the divine light. Even people who know nothing of God are, unbeknownst to themselves, grasping truths in the light of God's reasons.[9]

I should head off a common misconception at this point, which is that theories of divine illumination always involve simple acts of awareness, inexpressible in language and perhaps even mystical in character. This is certainly not Grosseteste's view. Though he sometimes talks as if we grasp simple essences in God's light, he more usually mentions that light in explaining our grasp of complex propositions.[10]

Otherwise, he could hardly integrate this theory into a discussion of Aristotelian demonstration. Divine illumination grounds the certainty of syllogistic arguments. When we use such an argument to offer a demonstration, our minds come a bit closer to the mind of God, who, of course, permanently understands the causes or "reasons" of everything. It is, however, important to Grosseteste, as it would be for a more mystical author, that in the ideal case we have a *direct* illumination from God. That is the situation of the blessed in the afterlife, who will enjoy a grasp of God "without mediation." On this point, he is willing to voice a rare explicit disagreement with Dionysius, whose relentless emphasis on divine transcendence ruled out the possibility of a direct vision of God. Instead, Dionysius had proposed that souls in heaven get only a representation of what God may be like in Himself, like people who didn't get to go to Woodstock and have to content themselves with watching documentaries about it.

Interesting though Grosseteste's translations and commentaries are, it is his little treatise *On Light* that is most likely to, as the Woodstock generation would have put it, blow your mind.[11] It's only a few pages long but these are among the most innovative pages of philosophy written in the first half of the thirteenth century. The work treats of light not in the context of the study of human eyesight, or for that matter human knowledge; instead, the gist is that the entire cosmos is quite literally formed from light. Light begins at a single point and then disperses itself through space as far as the outermost sphere of heaven, which is the most pure and perfect body, primary matter which has received primary form (95–6), said primary form being light itself. At this outermost limit of the universe, body is at its most subtle. The universe contains a series of concentric celestial spheres below which are found less subtle bodily constituents, namely the four Aristotelian elements, of which the densest is earth.

Obviously, Grosseteste is here trying to understand the Bible's statement that God began to create by saying "Let there be light" (Genesis 1:3). But that isn't the only source for his spectacular proposals. Firstly, there is his understanding of the mechanics of light. It's crucial to his theory that each point of light has a natural tendency to spread out in all directions (13–14). This principle was first set out in the Arabic tradition by al-Kindī and then taken up by the great Ibn al-Haytham, the first scientist to come close to a true understanding of human eyesight.[12] Grosseteste probably did not know Ibn al-Haytham, who was translated into Latin too late for him to read, but he read optical works by al-Kindī as well as a treatise by him called *On Rays*, which tries to explain a wide range of physical and magical phenomena by appealing to the influence of rays. Another figure lurking in the background is Ibn Gabirol, proponent of universal hylomorphism. Grosseteste takes from him the ideas that light is form and that the extension of form carries matter along with it.[13] For, as Grosseteste states not once but twice, the form of light cannot exist without matter (10–11, 30). This explains why a *material* universe should arise from the natural dispersion of light.

As far as modern scholars have been able to discover, though, Grosseteste's use of mathematics to explain this dispersion seems to be all his own. His idea is that as it extends outwards, light is "multiplied" into three dimensions. This requires infinite expansion, even though Grosseteste retains the traditional cosmology of Aristotle according to which the universe is finite and spherical in form. Light is infinitely multiplied in a different sense, because it is through this sort of multiplication that point becomes line, line becomes surface, and surface becomes three-dimensional solid. Grosseteste considers a point to be a "part" of a line, and smaller angles to be "parts" of a larger angle (81–4). As light is multiplied through the three dimensions, ratios arise between different spatial magnitudes. All of which is more exciting than it sounds. On standard medieval assumptions about infinity, what Grosseteste is proposing would be impossible. One infinity cannot stand in a definite ratio to another by being its double or triple. He rejects these standard assumptions, giving the example of all the numbers, which are twice as numerous as just the even numbers (43–6). On the modern-day understanding of infinity Grosseteste is wrong about that particular example. Yet the modern-day mathematician would agree with him that some infinities are larger than others. This is what is meant by saying that one infinite set has a larger "cardinality" than another, for instance the irrational numbers compared to the rational numbers.

Of course, for Grosseteste mathematics is only a means to the end of explaining God's creation. Actually he never explicitly mentions God in *On Light*, but it has been plausibly suggested that Grosseteste was led to ponder the notion of infinity by reflecting on the boundlessness of God's mind.[14] We can also see him as trying to capture what other thinkers of his time were approaching through the idea of transcendentals (Chapter 25).[15] If God is light and all things in creation are somehow fashioned from light, then light is a unifying principle for all things. Light is metaphysically fundamental and required for knowledge too, so we may compare it to the transcendentals of being and truth. Grosseteste himself connects light to another property sometimes counted as transcendental, namely beauty.[16] Just as light alone has the natural tendency to diffuse itself, so it alone is intrinsically beautiful. That is why the most beautiful body in the universe is the outermost celestial sphere, a pure fusion of light with primary matter.

Given his fascination with light and his emphasis on empirical observation of the world around us, we may wonder what Grosseteste had to say about actual eyesight.

So in conclusion let's turn to his ideas on optics, focusing on the intriguing phenomenon of rainbows.[17] He wrote a work dedicated specifically to this topic, which rejects Aristotle's account and makes the superior proposal that the rainbow effect is created by the refraction of sunlight through a cloud. This idea was adopted and adapted a generation or so later by Roger Bacon.[18] Bacon agreed that light is being refracted to produce a rainbow, but not by the cloud as a whole. Rather, it is the individual droplets of water in the cloud, with light bouncing off them as if from innumerable tiny mirrors.

Grosseteste's explanation of the rainbow tells us something about his approach to science in general.[19] On the one hand, the science of optics is grounded in pure mathematics. By modeling light rays and their reflections as lines and angles, mathematicians since Euclid had long been applying the tools of geometry to mirrors and shadows. On the other hand, a mirror reflection, the casting of a shadow, or a rainbow is a physical phenomenon. Grosseteste and after him Roger Bacon appreciated this, and were not content just to propose geometrical models. They invoked empirical evidence for and against various possible models. It's on this basis that Grosseteste argues for *refraction* of light rays rather than mere reflection. Still, there has been quite a bit of controversy about how much credit we should give Grosseteste for developing new techniques in empirical science. At one end of the spectrum, A. C. Crombie published a book in the 1950s with the provocative title *Robert Grosseteste and the Origins of Experimental Science*. At the other end, the leading recent scholar of his thought James McEvoy tartly commented that Grosseteste "was too bookish to be bothered experimenting."[20]

While that may underrate his contributions to empirical science, it would be going too far to say that Grosseteste did anything so grand as invent, or anticipate, the experimental scientific method. His idea is rather that, with God's light making the world intelligible to us, we can reach scientific understanding simply by observing. As remarked above, this is the real meaning of his term *experimentum*, which should be translated "experience" or "observation," not "experiment." Grosseteste's methodological innovations lie more with the use of mathematics in physics, which does foreshadow later developments (see Chapter 63). But it would be rash to draw general conclusions about experience and science in the thirteenth century without first discussing one of Grosseteste's greatest admirers, a man who lavished praise on the Bishop of Lincoln and took more from him than just an explanation of rainbows.

28

ORIGIN OF SPECIES
ROGER BACON

Around the turn of the thirteenth century, a young man from the town of Assisi, in the center of modern-day Italy, informed his father that he wouldn't be going into the family business. In fact, he wouldn't be going into any business at all, unless you count caring for lepers and preaching to birds as a business. The young man's name was, of course, Francis. By the time of his death in 1226 he had started a movement that would transform Christianity across Europe. The followers of Francis of Assisi were the Franciscans, just one of several mendicant orders which emerged in the thirteenth century. The term "mendicant" refers to the fact that they were sworn to poverty and survived on charitable donations alone. The members of mendicant orders, sometimes called "friars," posed a challenge to the established Church. Their devotion to a life of humility and poverty served as an unspoken (and sometimes spoken) rebuke to the wealth of bishops and the worldly entanglements of popes. A clash was inevitable. As we'll see in Chapter 31, it came in the form of agonized debate over the mendicant ideal of absolute poverty.

More surprising is the role that the Franciscans came to play in the medieval universities and, thus, in the history of philosophy. Francis of Assisi himself was no scholar. He led a life of simplicity without the adornment of book-learning, which could so easily lead to pridefulness. Some of his followers felt disquiet at the meeting of scholasticism and mendicancy: the Franciscan Brother Giles remarked pithily that "Paris destroyed Assisi." But the history of Franciscan schoolmen is as old as the history of the Franciscan Order itself. Already during Francis' lifetime the friars began to take instruction in church doctrine and theology from "lecturers." Robert Grosseteste was not himself a member of the order but did serve as the first lecturer to the Franciscan friars in Oxford. There he may have met, if not actually taught, Roger Bacon, one of three outstanding Franciscan thinkers who are going to be occupying our attention in the next several chapters, after which we will turn to the Dominicans. (Later on we'll be meeting two more Franciscan luminaries, Duns Scotus and William of Ockham.)

Bacon takes our story on directly from Grosseteste, carrying on his intellectual project by expanding on his idea of a science founded in "experience"[1] and by exploring the problems of light and vision that drove Grosseteste's innovative cosmological speculations. He also admired Grosseteste's activity as a translator, valuing his productions much more highly than those of more famous contributors to the translation movement, such as William of Moerbeke.[2] Grosseteste was one of the few contemporaries who managed to earn Bacon's respect. Another was Adam Marsh, a student of Grosseteste whose lectures Bacon was able to attend in Oxford. Bacon was also a student and master at the University of Paris, where he encountered such heavyweights as Alexander of Hales and William of Auvergne. Having shuttled back and forth several times between Paris and Oxford, Bacon had a deep familiarity with the scholastic culture on both sides of the channel.

He was not impressed. Alexander of Hales, he noted, represented an older generation which still lacked access to the full range of works in natural science and metaphysics, because translations were not yet available or because their study was banned in Paris.[3] Earlier luminaries like Gratian, Peter Lombard, and the Victorines had been unaware of the philosophical riches that would be unearthed in the translation movement.[4] They might thus be forgiven for their inadequate grounding in the sciences. But there was no excuse for Bacon's own contemporaries who were failing to engage with the Aristotelian tradition as Bacon himself set out to do. Because he was so disappointed by most of the Latin translations he could consult, and because he was doubtful that any translation can capture the full meaning of an original text, Bacon devoted himself to the study of languages. He mastered Greek and Hebrew and encouraged others to do the same.

Above all he implored the church authorities to make "science based on experience (*scientia experimentalis*)" fundamental to the university curriculum. He made his pitch in a series of works addressed to Pope Clement IV in the 1260s. These were written at the explicit invitation of the Pope, which gave Bacon an exemption from his order's rule against publishing works for wider circulation.[5] The result was a frenzy of scholarly activity, intended to demonstrate the utility and acceptability of the *scientia experimentalis*. Discoveries made in natural philosophy could put theology on a sound foundation, and for that matter assist in just about every area of human endeavor, from statecraft to warfare. In one astonishing passage Bacon proposes the possibility of building chariots that can power themselves, a flying machine like a bird but with artificial wings, and instruments for diving to the bottom of rivers or the sea.[6] To persuade us of the viability of the last scheme, he mentions how Alexander the Great had himself lowered in such a device to do some deep-sea exploring, a legend also recounted by the Muslim historian Ibn Khaldūn, who found it much harder to swallow.[7]

Though he was an imaginative enough man to look forward to the invention of the car, plane, and submarine, Bacon spent most of his time looking to the past. He was convinced that the ancients were more advanced in the sciences than the men of his own age. Not so much the ancients in general, as Aristotle in particular. For Bacon, Aristotle was one of the few who have achieved a complete or nearly complete understanding of philosophy. No one has matched the insight achieved by the earliest biblical figures such as Adam and Noah, and by Solomon, who was the first to revive science after a period of oblivion. Later there was another revival thanks to the Greeks, culminating in the work of Aristotle. Here Bacon hastens, like many a late ancient Christian, to say that Hellenic science was all borrowed from the Hebrew tradition. Bacon believes that after Aristotle only Muslim thinkers have come close to the same level of understanding; he especially admires Avicenna.

In his quest to take a place of his own in this pantheon of greats, Bacon emphasizes again and again the indispensable role of sense experience.[8] He admits that human souls may possess some sort of innate knowledge, but we have no access to it because of our fallen and bodily state. We are effectively born as blank slates, and unless we are fortunate enough to enjoy a direct illumination from an angel or God, we are on our own. We must learn through close observation of nature and other personal experiences. Knowledge achieved in this way (per experimentum) is better than knowledge achieved through abstract proof (per argumentum). Bacon applies this even to mathematics. It is one thing to follow the logic of a proof for the first proposition of Euclid's Elements, another to have the intuitive insight provided by a visible diagram that accompanies the proof.[9]

Bacon is above all renowned for his application of mathematics to natural philosophy, discussed below. But he was a multifaceted thinker who made innovations in a whole range of fields. A fine example is his work in the philosophy of language. Given Bacon's philological activities and his extensive training in the logical arts, it was natural for language to become one of his abiding interests. And given his irreverent and creative mind, it was natural that he would take an unusual approach. He pays particular attention to what we might nowadays call "semiotics," the study of signs. Though he mostly has language in mind here, street signs and even the noises made by animals count as signs as well. Here Bacon is taking up a theme explored in the works of Augustine,[10] even though, unlike fellow Franciscans such as Bonaventure, Bacon does not really see himself as an Augustinian. In fact, he tries to persuade us that he developed his own ideas about signs without even consulting Augustine's works.

Bacon holds that significant language is conventional in nature.[11] The meaning of our words is entirely artificial, in contrast to natural signs like the barking of a dog (§7–8).

Language is thus a tool that we fashion for ourselves. Indeed words can only have meaning when they are used by someone who has the intention to signify (§1). In the first instance this will be the person who first used a word to signify some existing thing, the word's meaning being set by the intention of this original name-giver. Whoever first applied the word "bacon" to cured pork determined that this word signifies cured pork. Since language is entirely conventional, though, others are free to take the same word and use it differently. This gives rise to the possibility of equivocation. If I use the word "bacon" to refer to cured meat, but you use it for a thirteenth-century philosopher and scientist, we are using the word with two entirely different meanings.

Bacon—the philosopher, not the cured meat—thinks that equivocation is a complex phenomenon which none of his predecessors managed to explore fully. It comes in different types, which may be closer to or further away from the "univocal" use of a word. Using a word univocally means using it in exactly the same way on two occasions, as when I offer you bacon for breakfast and then later ask if you'd like bacon for lunch too (§37). Furthest from this univocal use is applying the same word to something that exists and then something that doesn't exist. This is because the existent and the non-existent can share nothing in common at all: the distance between them is "infinite" (§38; cf. §141). This claim is a bit puzzling. You'd think that the name "Roger Bacon" which was used during his life to refer to him can still be used now that he is dead in exactly the same way without any equivocation at all. But Bacon's remarks on the non-existent fit with his idea that the original name-giver always seeks to signify some existing thing. Once the thing no longer exists, the act of signifying cannot possibly be the same.

From here Bacon goes on to provide a list of types of equivocation, from most to least equivocal. There is the use of words to signify two things that have a relation. The classic example here is "healthy," which can be applied both to a person and to the sort of food that helps a person to be healthy, like fresh vegetables. An example from the other end of the caloric extreme might be "bacon bits," a rather alarming and certainly unhealthy offering found in many American salad bars. These stand in some kind of relation to real bacon, though perhaps only the manufacturers know exactly what that relation is. Another form of equivocation occurs when the same word is used to refer to both a genus and a species (§41). I might talk of bacon generally at one time, and Canadian bacon at another. Finally, the slightest form of equivocation is when a word is used with the same meaning but different grammatical form. I'm not able to illustrate this with bacon, but Bacon himself points out that it works with eggs: in Latin, the word *ovum* means "egg" in both the nominative and accusative cases (§43). Given that he is analyzing language and not doing theology, Bacon only occasionally touches on the implications of all this for talking about God. Unlike many medieval thinkers, he's confident that we can in fact use language to refer to God (§21). He suggests that this may be achieved through a relation or "analogy" between God and the things He creates (§40), an idea we will see again in later thirteenth-century thought (Chapter 48).

Speaking of seeing, let's now turn to a more famous aspect of Roger Bacon's thought: his theory of light and vision. As I've said, he here continues the efforts begun by Robert Grosseteste. Where the latter's natural philosophy traced all things back to the propagation and multiplication of light, Bacon is conversely going to explain light in terms of a more basic set of physical principles.[12] The word at the heart of his natural philosophy is "species." This is potentially confusing, because we've so often seen the word in the context of logic, as when species is contrasted with genus. Originally, though, the Latin word *species* means the outward appearance of something, and that's somewhat closer to the way Bacon is using it. A good English rendering might be "effect." Bacon's idea is that natural things influence the world around them by imposing a "species" or "effect" on other things; hence his official definition of species as "the first effect of any natural agent" (§1.1, 28–9). A basic example might be fire, which affects nearby bodies by giving them the species of heat.

For Bacon this mechanism underlies all physical interaction. Sound is a species produced by vibration (§1.2, 12–14), so that the excitement of particles involved in frying bacon impresses a sizzling noise upon the air and subsequently your organ of hearing. Then, when you taste the bacon, the "species" is the taste that is communicated to your tongue and thus to your sense faculty. Illumination (*lumen*), of course, is the propagation of a species from a light source (*lux*). Though species like these, which are available to our outer senses, are the most obvious cases, Bacon's theory can be applied more widely. He alludes to Avicenna's example of the sheep that perceives hostility in the wolf and agrees with him that a faculty called "estimation" in the sheep receives the species of the wolf's hostility (§1.2, 79–81).

Bacon denies that, in producing species, things are somehow sending out parts of themselves which would be lost, like the sheets of atoms thrown off things in the visual theory of ancient atomism. Strictly speaking, species are not "emitted" at all (§1.3, 8–9). Instead, the influence of the natural agent causes a potentiality to be realized in the thing it affects (§1.3, 51–2). This can occur only through direct contact. So if a light source is to illuminate a visible object, it needs first to actualize the potential illumination of the air that is immediately surrounding it. This illuminated air then affects the air next to it, and so on, until the species of illumination is realized in the visible object. The same is true for the propagation or, as Bacon calls it following Grosseteste, the "multiplication" of any species (§2.1, 11–13). For this reason, Bacon thinks that all natural action requires a medium. It would be impossible in a void (§4.1, 109–26). Thus, for vision to occur, there needs to be air or some other transparent medium between the light source and the lit-up visible object, and also between the object and the viewer.

Even though the medium is absolutely required for the multiplication of species, it also inhibits the transmission of the natural effect by offering resistance (§4.1, 19–20). This is one reason why the influence becomes less pronounced as one gets further away from the original source. You feel less heat from a frying pan if you take a step away from the stovetop. Then, too, the mere process of being successively multiplied causes a gradual weakening of influence (§6.1, 18–20; §6.4, 25–9). This may remind us of the ideas put forward by earlier thirteenth-century physicists like Richard Rufus (Chapter 23), who proposed that a force impressed on a moved body will "wear out" by itself, in addition to being impeded by the air or other medium through which the projectile moves.

Bacon's theory is especially well suited to explaining the propagation of light, and he does apply it especially in that context. He confronts the age-old question of whether we see by sending something out from our eyes, like visual rays, or by receiving some influence that comes to the eyes from the visible object.[13] His answer: both, of course, because all natural things influence their surroundings. By this rule the sense organ too must cause a multiplication of species, even if it also receives the species of what it sees (§1.5, 68). It may seem superfluous that the eye should actively do something to its environment as well as being affected by a species coming from the object. But Bacon thinks there is empirical evidence to support his two-way theory. The fact that cats' eyes gleam in the dark shows that they are sending out visual rays, while the afterimages of bright lights that we see after we turn away from those lights shows that our eyes have been affected.

For all of this Bacon is drawing on the visual theories of the Muslim scientist Ibn al-Haytham, whose works he studied with great care. He played a major role in the transmission of Ibn al-Haytham's theories in Latin Christendom, to the point that Bacon's version of those theories will remain the standard account of eyesight until Kepler in the seventeenth century.[14] But his ambition to situate optics within a more general natural philosophy shows the influence of another source from the Islamic world, a text called *On Rays* and ascribed to the early Muslim thinker al-Kindī.[15] This treatise invokes the mechanism of "rays" to explain light and vision, other natural influences like sound, and above all the more occult powers involved in astrology and magic. Bacon's "multiplication of species" is an updated version of the same theory. He tends to agree with al-Kindī that the natural philosopher should take an interest in astrological and magical influence. He is also an enthusiastic believer in the science of alchemy.

We need to be cautious in approaching this aspect of Bacon's thought, where he explores what we would nowadays call "pseudo-science." When he uses the word "magic," it is always because he wants to draw a distinction between the fraudulent claims of magicians and his own "science of experience." Experience demonstrates that stars do exert an astrological influence, but we should not follow al-Kindī and others who went so far as to say that the stars actually determine all future events. Astrology can provide only probable conjectures and is at its most reliable when predicting general phenomena like weather patterns. Similarly, when it comes to alchemy, we need to base our practice in experience. For Bacon this means understanding that bodies are composed from four fundamental ingredients, the so-called "humors." Alchemy is the art that studies and learns to manipulate these ingredients and their effects. It was, of course, standard medical theory that human and other organic bodies are made up of the humors, but Bacon is unusual in applying the scheme to non-organic things like minerals and metals.

He has an almost obsessive interest in the possible applications of this theory, especially in the use of alchemy and medicine to prolong the span of one's life. In a passage that brings together many of his scientific interests, Bacon explains how to produce an elixir of longevity. First, get an alchemist to make you a mixture which is perfectly balanced in its humoral properties. Next, have an astronomer tell you the propitious moment in terms of astral influence. Finally, ask a specialist in geometrical optics to set up mirrors so that they will focus the astral rays on the mixture, transmitting the "celestial virtue" into it.[16] If you are lucky enough to find yourself in Paris or Oxford in the thirteenth century, you'll only need to find one specialist to carry out all these tasks: Roger Bacon himself.

But something must have gone wrong, because Bacon did not live an extraordinarily long life. Nor did his astrological investigations help him to avoid misfortune in his later years. In the late 1270s, he was caught up in a church crackdown on deviant philosophical teachings, including, among other things, condemnation of belief in magic. Bacon's frequent diatribes against the insufficiently scientific practices he called "magic" were probably intended not only to mark the boundaries of proper method, but also to shield him against precisely such condemnations. If so, they didn't work any better than his experiments with longevity, and he found himself imprisoned briefly for his unorthodox teachings. Nowadays, he gets a warmer reception. Despite his flirtations with the occult, he has (like Robert Grosseteste, but with considerably more plausibility) been hailed as a pioneer in experimental science, a worthy forerunner to a man who shared both his name and his scientific attitude, the Renaissance thinker Francis Bacon.[17]

29

STAIRWAY TO HEAVEN
BONAVENTURE

It would be so convenient if figures in the history of philosophy actually fell neatly into the boxes we use to keep them straight in our heads. You would have your liberals and conservatives, your idealists and your materialists, your empiricists and your rationalists. But often as not, philosophers defy such easy categorization. No contrast is older or more familiar to the historian of philosophy than the one between Platonism and Aristotelianism; yet Aristotle borrowed more than a few ideas from Plato, and I'm on record as saying that Plato was not a Platonist.[1] So you should already have been suspicious when I said that in covering thirteenth-century scholasticism, I'd be looking in turn at the Franciscans and then the Dominicans. Were these two orders really associated with opposing philosophical approaches or doctrines?

The traditional answer would be yes, and the traditional basis for that answer would be the contrast between two of the era's greatest thinkers: Bonaventure and Thomas Aquinas. Bonaventure, a Franciscan, stands for a mystically tinged theology and skepticism concerning the secular offerings of philosophy. He steers by the star of Augustine, about whom he wrote, "No question has been propounded by the masters whose solution may not be found in the works of this Doctor."[2] Aquinas, a Dominican, represents the Aristotelian side of the debate, aware that theology is needed to complete the teachings found in the philosophers but eager to make full use of those teachings nonetheless. The contrast is epitomized by their rival conceptions of human knowledge. Bonaventure promotes Augustine's idea, already revived by Robert Grosseteste, that human knowledge is possible only thanks to an illumination granted by God. Aquinas instead places his trust in our senses, following the Aristotelian line that we can abstract general knowledge of the world from our perceptual experiences.

The contrast seems to be confirmed by other members of the two orders. Bonaventure had Franciscan followers like his student John Pecham, who became Archbishop of Canterbury and in turn taught Matthew of Aquasparta. Both agreed with Bonaventure on many points, not least the requirement for divine illumination in human knowledge. In recognition of this group, one book devoted to the illumination theory has gone so far as to say, "in this crucial period, the Franciscan school at Paris and the Augustinian current of thought became for all practical purposes one and the same."[3] Among the Dominicans, meanwhile, Thomas Aquinas' own teacher Albert the Great was among the most outstanding exponents of Aristotle in the thirteenth century and Aquinas' contemporary Robert Kilwardby did pioneering work commenting on Aristotle's logic.

But as I've already hinted, simple contrasts rarely tell the whole story. Dominican scholasticism cannot just be equated with Aristotelianism. Albert's thought was shot through with Platonist themes, citations of Augustine appear regularly in the pages of Aquinas' works, and Kilwardby is notorious for his involvement in condemnations aimed *against* the excesses of Aristotelian philosophy. As for the Augustinian side of the contrast, when we talked about Grosseteste and his embrace of the illumination theory, we found him presenting that theory in the context of commenting on Aristotle. Among the Franciscans, in Roger Bacon we've just seen a very different approach to philosophy than the one pursued by Bonaventure.

As for Bonaventure himself, though his admiration for Augustine is unmistakable, his ideas incorporate Aristotelian philosophy within a larger vision. This strategy is encapsulated in a short treatise of his entitled *Retracing the Arts to Theology*.[4] It surveys the arts and philosophical sciences and shows that the image of the divine is present in even the meanest of them. The project is in the spirit of Hugh of Saint Victor, who, as you may recall, earned special praise from Bonaventure as excelling in reasoning, preaching, and contemplation (§5, cited above in Chapter 12). Hugh did not consider the so-called "mechanical" arts beneath his notice and neither does Bonaventure, who sketches the purpose of such activities as farming, hunting, and weaving (§2). Even these arts are a "light" given to us by God, though merely an "external" light, because they involve us with things outside ourselves. Every human enjoys the gift of two further lights within his or her own nature: the "lower" light of sensation and the "inner" light of philosophy. Crowning them all is the light of grace, which offers salvation. But all four lights are given by God (§1).

Bonaventure also detects images of the divine within all these arts. When a blacksmith makes a horseshoe, he tries to fashion something that represents as well as possible the idea of a horseshoe in his mind, in an unwitting imitation of God's creation of things through the divine Word (§12). Even when we look at something, the visual image we receive is a so-called "similitude" begotten by whatever it is we're seeing, just as God the Son is begotten by God the Father (§8). Parallels of the same sort are discovered in the various philosophical sciences. When he comes to logic, Bonaventure takes his cue from the Aristotelian account of words as representing mental concepts. He points out that linguistic signs make our ideas known in physical form, that is, in the sounds we make when we talk. Just so was the divine made known in the Incarnation (§16).

What does all this show, other than that Bonaventure has mastered the Augustinian art of finding Christian motifs in even the unlikeliest places? At least two things. One is that the other arts can be considered to be "handmaids of theology" (§26), a famous phrase with roots in antiquity.[5] Anyone thinking that philosophy or the other "lights" given to humankind may be incompatible with theology had better turn up the dimmer switch and think again. Far from being in tension with theology, the other arts are to be *used* by theology. This too can be traced back to Hugh of Saint Victor, who admonished his youthful students to "learn everything," because all knowledge may help in understanding Scripture. Bonaventure is saying something more, though. For him the "lights" of the arts, sensation, and philosophy show that we have been created in God's image, and every use of these lights is an imitation of divinity. The parallels Bonaventure draws may seem far-fetched, but they are backed up by his explanation of how created things come to have the limited degree of reality they possess. In this short work, that explanation is only sketched: the causes or "reasons" for things that we find in matter are mere images of what Bonaventure calls "ideal reasons (*rationes ideales*)," which are found in God Himself (§20).

We might go so far as to say that created things are nothing more than *signs* of divine reality, much as a linguistic sign represents the meaning intended by the person who uses the sign. You listen to someone's words to know what they have in mind. Similarly, we can seek to understand the divine mind by investigating created signs in the world around us. Thus do the building blocks of terminist logic become symbolic elements supporting the serene edifice of Bonaventure's theology. He would never consider philosophy to be an error or sin, so long as the philosopher keeps sight of the overall goal. This very work *Retracing the Arts to Theology* practices what it preaches and shows the philosopher how to proceed. Bonaventure postulates divine exemplars of things, another idea with late antique roots. But in his hands the theory itself shows that pagan philosophy was bound to remain incomplete, and that Christians who pursue philosophy purely for its own sake are engaging in a futile exercise, and displaying mere "curiosity." To study the world for its own sake is to concentrate on the created image at the expense of the divine reality.[6]

All of this might lead us to expect that Bonaventure would use the illumination theory above all to explain our knowledge of God. True understanding would consist in simply beholding His light in the form of the divine exemplars. But for Bonaventure this is a prospect we may anticipate only in the afterlife. In this life we will always fall short of a direct grasp of God. This point emerges in one of

Bonaventure's most informative treatments of the issue, the fourth of a set of disputed questions on the subject of the knowledge of Christ.[7] He chose this as the first topic he would take up after becoming ordinary master in 1253–4. The selection of theme may indicate the influence of Alexander of Hales. He was the contemporary whose ideas had the greatest impact on Bonaventure, who studied with Alexander after his arrival in Paris from his native Italy in the 1230s. Bonaventure admired his master greatly, and spoke of his own ideas as little more than dutiful exposition of those that Alexander had put forward. The admiration was mutual, with the teacher saying of his illustrious student that "in him, Adam seemed not to have sinned."

Now, a scholastic discussion of Christ's knowledge may sound like a pretty unpromising place to look for an account of human epistemology. But for these theologians Christ was fully human and fully divine, and in his former aspect he fulfills human nature perfectly. Thus, Christ gives us an example, indeed the one and only example in this earthly life, of a person who enjoys the full remit of possible human knowledge. To focus on His manner of knowing is thus to explore the ideal human cognitive state, something we might (with numerous caveats to avoid anachronism, to say nothing of heresy) compare to the Stoics' idea of a perfect sage who would never make a mistake. This explains why the fourth question in Bonaventure's series actually has nothing directly to do with Christ's knowledge. Instead, it asks whether it is generally the case that humans attain certainty through illumination from the divine exemplars.

Where Grosseteste explored the illumination theory while commenting on Aristotle, Bonaventure reveals the true lineage of the idea by kicking off his disputed question with no fewer than nine quotations from Augustine. The format gives him ample opportunity to do this, because it is standard to quote authoritative sources and produce arguments on both sides of a question before resolving it (see Chapter 21). In this case, we get thirty-four points in favor of the illumination theory (115–26) and twenty-six against (126–32). After then offering a "response" that sets out his own positive answer (132–7), Bonaventure concludes by answering the negative considerations one by one (137–44). Again, this is totally standard for the format, as is the fact that Bonaventure does not just say "Yes, we do know in the light of the divine exemplars," but takes this opportunity to refine the proposal and indeed to unfold a whole theory of human knowledge.

Though this theory requires that the divine exemplars are somehow involved in each case of human knowing, Bonaventure stridently denies that the exemplars are the *only* factor involved by being the direct objects of our thought (132–3). If they were, then we would enjoy a vision of God already in this life every time we attain knowledge. That would leave no room for improvement, which is unacceptable, since our state in paradise or when granted a special revelation surely has to be better than the state of everyday knowing. Still, the exemplars must be involved somehow, every time anyone knows anything. This case has already been made in the initial series of arguments in favor of the proposal, which were taken from Augustine and others. You'll be relieved that I am not going to tell you about all thirty-four of them. Instead I'll reduce them to two groups of considerations, having do, on the one hand, with the things that we know and, on the other hand, with our situation as knowers.

Concerning the objects that we know, Bonaventure sounds like many a Platonist when he demands that nothing can really be *known* unless it is unchanging (118, 121). There is a hint of Aristotle here too. He stipulated that only necessary and eternal truths are truly knowable. For the Platonists, for Aristotle, and now for Bonaventure, we cannot take ourselves to *know* that something is true if it may stop being true at some point. Thus, created things in the sensible world cannot be the true objects of our knowledge, because none of them endures forever. And what about us as knowers? Here Bonaventure and the sources he has quoted argue that our minds are simply too limited to achieve genuine knowledge by their own power. How can a limited mind come to grasp the unlimited (122), as when we come to understand number, which is potentially infinite? How can creatures who are fallible by nature enjoy knowledge, which is infallible? The mismatch between imperfect knowers and the perfection of knowledge can be overcome only if some other perfect principle is involved, and that principle is provided by divine illumination (121).

We can bring the whole line of argument together by referring to the key word in the title of Bonaventure's disputed question: how is it that humans achieve *certainty*? Only if there is no hint of unreliability on either side, in the subject or in the object. The things we know must be guaranteed to be permanently knowable, and our act of knowing must be guaranteed to grasp the truth about those things. Speaking of truth, Bonaventure repeats an argument from Augustine to the effect that God must be involved in our knowledge, since knowledge is always true and God is nothing other than the Truth itself (115). We can see here that the theory of illumination connects to the now familiar doctrine of the transcendentals. God is the source of being and truth for all created things, so when we know them, we are indirectly knowing Him. It's another way of making the point we found in *Retracing the Arts to Theology*, that all things are mere signs of divine reality.

But we need to be careful here. All the talk of unchanging objects may lead us to think that the divine exemplars are the very things we know, insofar as we get to know anything. As I've already said, though, Bonaventure insists otherwise. In the "response" at the center of the disputed question, he explains that we never know the divine exemplars, at least not in this life. Rather, we know created things as images of the exemplars. The talk of "illumination" is not meant to suggest that we are beholding God's ideas like lights flashing in our mind's eye. Rather we are knowing about created things *in the light of* the exemplars. The metaphor does not have God playing the role of a brilliant lamp into which we are staring, but of a lamp that is making other things visible so that we can see them. Bonaventure describes it with somewhat less metaphorical (but not entirely literal) language by saying that the exemplars serve as rules or standards (*regulae*) for the things we know (134). When we know that giraffes are ruminants, it's as if we are implicitly comparing created giraffes to the divine idea of a giraffe, with the comparison allowing for certain knowledge rather than mere belief. The exemplars provide a perfect standard in the light of which we can judge. But something else is needed too. We must enjoy an encounter with some actual created giraffes, or there will be nothing for the divine light to illuminate. To this extent, like Grosseteste before him, Bonaventure could retain Aristotle's point that human knowledge draws on sense perception.

The broad lines of Bonaventure's teaching were explicit and emphatic enough that his followers, notably John Pecham and Matthew of Aquasparta, also embraced the theory. But they added various refinements of their own, among which I'll mention just one. Pecham notes that some of our concepts seem to be so immediate that we grasp them with no prompting from sense perception. The transcendentals would be such primary concepts. They therefore constitute an exception to the general rule that sensation is needed as a second source for knowledge alongside the divine exemplars.[8] Pecham and Matthew of Aquasparta are also somewhat more careful in distinguishing between the grasp of simple concepts and whole propositions, the difference between understanding plain old *giraffe* and understanding a complex truth like "Giraffes are ruminants." It seems that Grosseteste mostly had propositions in mind when he first started to develop the illumination theory. But by the time we get to Bonaventure and especially his followers, we are seeing the theory applied to both kinds of knowledge.

I don't want give you the impression that the understanding and acquisition of knowledge was the final goal of Bonaventure's writings. To see that it was not, we can do no better than to turn to his most celebrated treatise, the *Journey of the Mind to God*.[9] In this work Bonaventure makes many of the same points we've already discussed, for instance that created things are mere signs or traces (*vestigia*) of God (§2.1). The illumination theory also emerges at several points, as when Bonaventure says that God provides the rule by which we understand things, as if we make our judgments in accordance with immutable laws (§2.9), or that since the human mind is changeable, it cannot know unchanging things without help (§3.3). But like *Retracing the Arts to Theology*, the *Journey of the Mind to God* places the illumination theory and philosophy itself within a more general and ambitious context.

It is a contemplative work full of numerical correspondences and other symbolic images, yet another reminder of the Victorines. Where they had analyzed the various features of Noah's Ark, Bonaventure stays closer to home by dwelling on a vision enjoyed by his fellow Italian and the founder of his movement, Francis of Assisi (Prologue §3 and 7.3). Francis beheld an angel with six wings, which for Bonaventure symbolize six steps in our journey towards God. We begin with created things understood as the traces of God and proceed up to the Trinity itself by way of an analysis of the human soul. As in his other works, Bonaventure does give normal, non-theological knowledge its due. Philosophy allows us to understand the workings of our own souls, which, as we know from Augustine, has a threefold structure that mirrors the divine Trinity (§3.1, 3.5). But we should leave this mode of thinking behind when we come to contemplate the Trinity itself. At this stage Scripture must play the role that philosophy played before (§4.5). Ultimately Bonaventure is true to his Franciscan roots. For all his deft scholastic distinctions and his care to retain at least some of Aristotle's teachings, philosophical knowledge is not his goal. Or rather, even if philosophical knowledge is his goal, it is not his final goal. Just as bodies and the mind are a kind of "ladder" to God (§1.2), a stairway to heaven, if you will, the real meaning of philosophy is found when we discover that it too is a trace of the divine. As Bonaventure says (Prologue §4), there should be no speculation without devotion, no observation without exultation, and no knowledge without love.

YOUR ATTENTION, PLEASE
PETER OLIVI

Here's a riddle, which I've only just made up: what do you sometimes not pay when you want to, and at other times pay without trying? The answer is "attention." Attempting to focus on something and failing to do so is the most familiar of experiences. You might be reading a reasonably priced and handsomely packaged book about the history of philosophy and find that your mind wanders. If so, don't feel bad. It happens to me all the time. I might be reading up on, to take another randomly chosen example, thirteenth-century Franciscan philosophy, only to realize that my eyes have been drifting across the same page for several minutes without my taking in any meaning. At other moments we are able to pay attention to things without any effort. We are often aware of things without being *consciously* aware of them. Suppose that you're at a crowded party, focusing on a conversation with one person, and then halfway across the room someone else says your name. Your ears will prick up and you'll notice you've been mentioned. Evidently you have been monitoring the hubbub of voices in the room without even realizing it.

Given how common these experiences are, you'd think they would have attracted the interest of philosophers from the very beginning. But that isn't really the case. There were some discussions of awareness and attention in late antiquity; Plotinus even gave the example of failing to concentrate when you're reading.[1] The topic becomes truly central, though, in the medieval thinker Peter Olivi.[2] Born in southern France in the late 1240s, Olivi entered the Franciscan Order at the tender age of 12. He studied at Paris and had the opportunity to learn from Bonaventure, who was by then minister general of the order. Olivi seems to have expected that he would become a master at the university but this ambition was thwarted after a heated rivalry between Olivi and another young Franciscan named Arnauld Gaillard. Probably thanks to their mutual recriminations, neither was allowed to pursue the higher studies at Paris needed to become master of theology. It wouldn't be the last dispute of Olivi's career. He was a provocative and challenging figure, known above all for his insistence that voluntary poverty was central to the mission of the Franciscan Order. Other enthusiasts for this ascetic approach rallied around Olivi, seeing him as a great spiritual leader even as others within and outside the order saw him as a troublesome radical. Olivi's orthodoxy was questioned but he ultimately managed to persuade the order that his teachings were acceptable. In 1287 he was even appointed as the lecturer to the Franciscans in Florence; he died eleven years later in his native France.

Olivi would probably be surprised to find himself praised as an innovative philosophical mind, or to be highlighted at all in a book on the history of philosophy. His vocation was that of a theologian and his writings are dedicated to commentary on the Bible and to defense of his strict interpretation of the Franciscan way. When he offers explicit remarks about philosophy, these are largely dismissive, though one should bear in mind that by "philosophers" he means those who follow Aristotle. In one frequently quoted passage Olivi's penchant for sarcasm is on full display, as he responds to an argument of Aristotle's by saying, "Aristotle argues for his claim without sufficient reason, indeed with almost no reason at all. But without reason he is believed, as the god of this age."[3] Olivi sneers at those contemporaries who are willing to follow Aristotle's authority wherever it leads rather than engaging in the philosophical reflection needed to improve on Aristotelian doctrine. And improvement was needed, in Olivi's view. We are after all talking about a pagan idolator who defended such abominable teachings as the eternity of the world.

Olivi's lack of allegiance to the Aristotelian tradition freed him to make new philosophical proposals that can be almost startling in their anticipation of themes from the early modern period. Of course, Olivi isn't the first theologian we've seen stray into philosophical territory. Nor is he the first to do so in the context of commenting on that mainstay of thirteenth-century scholasticism, the *Sentences* of Peter Lombard. It's above all here that he sets forth some of his most original ideas, in the form of a critique aimed at Aristotelian views on the human soul. Here he's carrying on a discussion that began in earlier thirteenth-century writings, concerning Aristotle's definition of soul as the form of the body (see Chapter 24). In addition to the obvious difficulty that this could imply the soul's dependence on the body, thus precluding its immortality, there was a puzzle about whether we can really understand humans to have only one form. Olivi's contemporary Thomas Aquinas insisted that this is exactly what we should think. For Aquinas, the person is a single substance whose unity is provided by one and only one form, which is the person's soul.

Olivi rejects this idea. Actually, that's putting it mildly. What he really says is that Aquinas' view is "a brutal error" that is "contrary to reason and dangerous to the faith."[4] It may be true that *some* powers of the soul are tied to the body in the way Aristotle suggests. The soul gives us powers of digestion, reproduction, sensation, and movement, and Olivi admits that the use of such powers requires the body. But the rational soul cannot be a bodily form. This higher soul has powers that are manifestly incorporeal, in particular the capacities for thought and free choice, so how could it have such an intimate relationship with the body? In order to explain how we humans can have such radically different powers, ranging from the lowly processes of nutrition to the exalted exercise of freedom and intellective thought, we should simply give up on the idea that each of us has one and only one form. Instead, we possess a plurality of forms which give us a variety of capacities. Taken in its entirety, the human soul is simply an aggregate or collection of these different powers, all of them parts of a greater whole.

This conclusion frees Olivi from any concern that the soul may be unable to survive without the body, or that its relation to the body would render it unable to exercise a power of choice exempt from the necessity that attaches to physical things. The rational soul is a stranger to corporeal things, something Olivi at one point memorably captures by proposing that the soul's being in a body would be like wine being contained in a chamber pot.[5] But as Aquinas would be quick to point out, Olivi's theory of multiple forms in a single human has a big disadvantage too. It threatens to undermine the unity of the soul and thus of the person. Olivi seems to be suggesting that each of us is not one but at least two substances, an immaterial rational soul hovering above an embodied being that is made up of form and bodily matter. But, in fact, this isn't how he sees things.

Instead, the soul is already a substance in its own right, with no dependence on the body at all. It does have matter, but the soul's matter is incorporeal or "spiritual," an idea used by Philip the Chancellor and Olivi's fellow Franciscans Roger Bacon and Bonaventure. The soul's matter unifies the multiple powers and forms that make up the single soul. The physical body too is included in the unified person. The lower soul is responsible for sensation and other tasks realized through the body, so we should admit that it is unified with the body it is using. The higher, rational soul lacks this sort of connection to the body, but it is unified to the lower soul because the two souls share the same spiritual matter. Thus, even though the rational soul has no direct relationship to (never mind dependence on) the body, it forms a unity with the body indirectly or "transitively." It is unified to the lower soul and the lower soul is in turn unified to the body.[6]

All of this is, I think, profoundly un-Aristotelian, which, of course, would bother Olivi not one little bit. In Aristotle's writings on the soul we are told that it is the human *person* who performs the various psychological functions *through* the soul. Your soul is not a separate thing in its own right, never mind a separate thing whose most important part is only indirectly related to your body. By contrast, Olivi insists that the soul itself is the subject of our most important psychological activities. This is evident from his treatment of free will. Here we're again anticipating a central dispute in later medieval philosophy, which is usually framed as a clash between two ways of explaining free actions, called by modern scholars "intellectualism" and "voluntarism." As we saw, the basic idea of the intellectualist position is that human choice is prompted by some belief or understanding of the best thing to do. The voluntarist, by contrast, wants to say that a free choice consists in a sheer act of the will. Our choices may somehow be influenced by our beliefs but ultimately the explanatory buck stops with the faculty of will, not the faculty of reason.

To some extent this sharp contrast is like a Swedish communist's favorite dish: a red herring. The so-called "voluntarists" typically provide a role for reason in human choices, while the so-called "rationalists" do acknowledge the need for a faculty of will.[7] Still, there is at the very least a strong difference in emphasis between an author like Olivi, who looks forward to the voluntarists of the fourteenth century, and Thomas Aquinas. He is usually seen as an intellectualist, not least by Olivi himself, who is no more impressed by Aquinas' views on freedom than by his rival's views on the unity of soul. For now it will be enough to explain Olivi's complaints without asking whether he represents Aquinas' ideas fairly. As Olivi understands it, the intellectualist explanation of choice would have the will being moved passively by reason. Suppose I believe that my readers will be entertained by the occasional use of puns, and come up with a wince-inducing wordplay like the one at the beginning of this paragraph. Having formed the (admittedly rather dubious) belief that it would be a fantastic idea to include the pun in this book, I choose to do so and type it out on my computer. The intellectualist thinks my will is just carrying out the determination of my reason, like an executive branch of government whose sole task is to implement rulings laid down by a legislative branch.

But this seems wrong, says Olivi, or rather with characteristic asperity he calls it "insane." The whole point of the will is that it *initiates* choice. It is, therefore, the will that makes the decision, and the most that reason can do is to give it advice. The will is not passive with respect to beliefs or reason, but active. It moves itself rather than being moved by another part of the soul. There's a connection here to Olivi's ideas about the higher soul. One of his main purposes in isolating the thinking and willing soul from the body is that bodies are incapable of this kind of self-initiating activity which is not moved by anything else. A stone can't just get up and roll on its own. It needs some other cause to set it in motion. By contrast, humans are self-movers, and according to Olivi, if we are searching for the source of this spontaneous action, we should look to the will's irreducible capacity for choice, not to reason's ability to perceive things as choiceworthy.

Olivi's emphasis on the soul's active nature finds its most unusual and philosophically fruitful expression in another area of his psychology: his account of perception. Again, the best way to appreciate his view is to start with the position he's attacking. It's one we're familiar with, since we've just seen it put forward by Roger Bacon. According to him perception occurs when a so-called "species" reaches the perceiver from an object. This could be a sound, a smell, or something more sophisticated like the hostility of a dangerous animal. But philosophers talking about perception usually focus on the case of vision, so let's do the same. In honor of the hero of this chapter, please imagine that you're seeing a green olive. Bacon's explanation of how the visual experience occurs is that a green object will affect the air surrounding it by imparting the species of green to it. This species is then passed on or "multiplied" through one part of the air after another. When the effect gets to the air touching your eye, the species is received in your eye and this causes you to see green.

A pretty plausible theory, you might say, and even one that is in broad terms true. But Peter Olivi thinks it suffers from two fatal weaknesses.[8] The first is that, whatever it means for the so-called "species" of green to turn up in your eye, the presence of that species in the eye cannot be identical with, or even give rise to, a perception in your soul. Immaterial things can certainly influence physical things, as when your soul commands your hand to reach out to take an olive out of a bowl, but the reverse is not the case. Bodies cannot affect anything incorporeal. That's the first problem with the species theory, one that would, of course, only impress someone who shares Olivi's assumption that bodily states cannot affect an immaterial soul.

The second problem, however, involves fewer metaphysical presuppositions. In fact, it is a brilliant, though not necessarily unanswerable objection, which will have echoes in early modern philosophy in debates over the empirical basis of knowledge. Olivi observes that, according to the species theory, what you would be aware of when you see a green olive is not actually the olive. It is the species of green in your eye. This might explain why you see green, but it can't explain why you see the green olive. At best you would be accessing a *representation* of the green olive. But this is clearly false, at least according to Olivi. Unless you're looking at a picture of something or its image in a mirror, you don't see only a representation or species of the thing you see: you see the thing itself. What Olivi is proposing here is an early version of what is nowadays called "direct realism," a theory of perception that avoids invoking representations of the objects of perception in favor of the claim that we perceive things without any intermediary.

Of course, merely denying representationalism isn't giving a positive explanation of how perception does work. Olivi does offer a positive account, but not one that is particularly explanatory. It again ties in with his claims about the rational soul, and especially the will. We saw that Olivi wanted to insist on the active and self-initiating nature of the soul in the case of willing, and the same is true here. What really bothers him about the species theory is that it makes us passive as perceivers, much as the intellectualist theory of choice made the will passive. Against this Olivi insists that perception is no more passive than the will. To perceive an olive I must actively do something: I must attend or pay attention to the olive. In fact, Olivi even uses the word *attencio* to describe the phenomenon.[9] He also uses the evocative language of "imbibing" or "drinking in" what is perceived. Less metaphorically, but still somewhat mysteriously, he speaks of the soul's *aspectus*, a kind of orientation or direction of focus that we bring to bear on things when we attend to them.[10] Olivi gives an illustration of his point that is not unlike Plotinus' case of the mind wandering when one tries to read. He asks us to consider someone sleeping with his eyes open. If there is light in the room, the sleeper's eyes should be physically affected by his surroundings, just as they are when he is awake. So the sleeping person should see, if seeing is a purely passive process, as the species theory demands. But in fact, sleeping people don't see anything, because their souls are at rest and not attending to the things around them.

I should note that Olivi doesn't rule out that the eyes are somehow affected by their surroundings. To the contrary, he admits that they are, as is clear from Roger Bacon's observation that we continue to see afterimages of bright lights after we stop looking at them. Olivi's claim is rather that the physical effects in the eyes or other sense organs do not *cause* sensation. The soul perceives simply by attending to the things to which it has access. And there's another possible misunderstanding we should avoid. Olivi is not claiming that we have to be giving something our full and undivided attention in order to perceive it. If you're reading this book while a bowl of olives is on the table in front of you, you may be seeing the bowl without, as we might say, really paying attention to it. But according to Olivi this shows merely that the soul's active attention comes in degrees. It can be entirely absent, as in the sleeping case, or it can consist in the kind of basic, background awareness of our surroundings that we have as we go about our waking lives. He would no doubt have loved the example of overhearing your name at a party, since it suggests that your soul is actively monitoring the environment all the time, always ready to give particularly close attention to whatever seems salient and interesting.

Who has the better of the debate between Olivi and the representationalist? It's hard to say, given that philosophers of perception today still argue over a version of the same question. The biggest challenge for Olivi and other direct realists is probably the difficulty of accounting for perceptual error, as when you take a green olive to be a black olive because you are seeing it in a smoky restaurant. For a representationalist this is no problem. It's just a case where something is represented without total accuracy, like seeing an object in a discolored photograph. For a direct realist like Olivi it's harder to explain, since he wants to insist that you are seeing the olive itself, with no filtering representation to explain distortion of the experience. He could, however, appeal to the fact that even as we directly see the olive, we are also directly seeing smoke between the eye and the olive. Our overall experience combines these two perceptions to give us the impression of a black olive instead of a green one. Furthermore, his theory does seem more plausible when we consider normal perceptions that represent things as they really are. It certainly doesn't *seem* to us that we perceive things through a screen of representative images.

I would add that in his own historical context Olivi's position was appealing for reasons that may no longer seem so compelling today. His contemporaries would have agreed with his assumptions about the immateriality of the soul. They would have admitted that immaterial things like souls and for that matter God are able somehow to relate to, and even act upon, the physical world. If my immaterial soul can make my arm move, then why can't my soul also "reach out" to something that is across the room in order to see it? Yet there's a danger for Olivi here too. Once we start thinking along these lines, we see that the real mystery is why an immaterial soul should be restricted to perceiving only the things that are related to its body in appropriate ways. Why can't I see behind my head, if it is my soul's attention that makes the difference and not the way the objects in front of me are affecting my eyes? Olivi's solution would seem to be that our bodies do restrict the scope of our awareness in this life. Remember that the power of sense is in the lower soul, and thus tied to the body. In the afterlife we will not be so restricted, but will have a more general and unimpeded apprehension of things.[11]

Olivi's ideas about the soul, and especially about perception, have won him admiration from historians of philosophy. But the just plain historians know him above all for a different reason, one mentioned at the beginning of this chapter: his central role in one of the central religious debates in the late thirteenth century. It was a contest with ethical and political, as well as theological dimensions. Olivi became the standard bearer for one side in that contest, fiercely defending an ideal of deliberate poverty which for him constituted the core of the Franciscan way of life. And as if these stakes weren't high enough, he set the ideal of poverty within an apocalyptic view of history, according to which the Franciscans had arisen just in time to prepare humanity for its final days.[12]

31

NONE FOR ME, THANKS
FRANCISCAN POVERTY

The medievals would, I think, have been puzzled by our phrase "poor as a church mouse." Not that mice in general had it good in the Middle Ages, but if any mouse at the time was well off, it was probably the mouse who lived in a church. Extraordinary amounts of wealth were held by the Church at this time, thanks to centuries' worth of donations from secular rulers who wished to express, or at least be seen to express, piety. The census of the Domesday Book, compiled in 1086, shows that at this time 26 percent of land in the area surveyed belonged to church institutions, as compared to only 17 percent for the royal family.[1] Indeed, the ecclesiastical hierarchy was in large part just an extension of the nobility, with many a well-born son being parked in a monastery or other religious setting because he was not the first in line for inheritance. If you want to see just how wealthy the Church was, go to the British city of Lincoln, where you can still see the "Bishop's Palace," in part built right around the time that Robert Grosseteste was bishop there. Even a glance at this imposing structure will be enough to confirm that medieval bishops were not so much church mice as big cheeses.

Then came Francis of Assisi. In the sort of gesture pioneered by such ancient heroes of ascetic Christianity as Antony the Great, Francis abandoned a life of material comfort to devote himself to charity. He lived in deliberate poverty, and the rule of his order demanded that his followers do the same: "Let the Friars take nothing for themselves as property (*appropriem*), neither house, nor place, nor anything else."[2] The Franciscan movement called Christians to greater religious commitment, by preaching and by offering themselves as examples of humility and piety. The friars seemed to be everything that the powerful, complacent and wealthy Church was not. Yet as the order expanded and swelled from a small band of spiritual insurgents to a major religious movement, it became an established institution in its own right. How could an organization with links across Europe, with buildings and libraries, with a constant flow of income from charitable donations, be staffed by men who owned nothing and were not even allowed to handle money? The Franciscans' success threatened to undermine their mission of imitating the humility of Francis.

Here lay the seeds of a bitter dispute over the practicality and permissibility of deliberate poverty, which unfolded over several decades in the late thirteenth and fourteenth centuries. Critics argued that the Franciscans and other mendicants, notably the Dominicans, were engaged in a counterproductive enterprise, with poverty actually undermining their ability to help the poor and teach religion. Given the obvious and unflattering comparison between the riches of the established religious hierarchy and the ostentatious penury of the Franciscans, we might expect that such criticisms came from bishops and popes who worried that their authority was being undermined. But the earliest critics of the mendicants' vow, who came forward in the 1250s, were motivated by a different political context and one that will be all too familiar to today's professional philosophers: university infighting, especially over the filling of academic positions.

We can trace the trouble back to a man who has been flitting in and out of our story, Alexander of Hales. We first saw him as the leader of a group of masters who wrote on the transcendentals, then as the teacher who inspired the young Bonaventure. But if you remember just one thing about Alexander, let it be that he was the first Franciscan to hold a chair at the University of Paris. He already held a chair of theology when he decided to join the order in about 1236. Since the Dominicans already held two other chairs, this gave the mendicants control over three out of twelve chairs in theology at Paris.[3] That alarmed the so-called "secular" masters, who resented the loss of these posts to the friars. (I say "so-called," because many of these "secular" masters also took holy orders and could even be priests; remember that many of them worked in the faculty of theology. Still, the term is often applied to masters who were not mendicants, following the medieval Latin use of *seculares*.[4]) The secular masters were also stung by the mendicants' refusal to show solidarity with them, for instance by failing to join in a teaching strike in 1229.

The rivalry found expression in objections to the mendicants' vows, with a first significant critique coming from the Parisian master William of Saint Amour. He would have cause to regret his intervention, once he was condemned in 1256 after the mendicants presented evidence of William's supposedly heretical teachings to the Pope. Before his downfall he made a number of points against the vow of poverty, and after his condemnation these were echoed and extended by another secular master, Gerard of Abbeville.[5] To some extent their case rested on plain common sense. The mendicants claimed to be devoted to the care of the poor and would donate their worldly wealth to charity upon joining the order. All well and good, argued William and Gerard, but really effective assistance to the poor requires careful acquisition and management of resources. Charity is a lifelong calling, not something best shown with one spectacular act of self-abnegation.

From this point of view, the development of the Franciscan Order to a well-established organization with considerable material assets was advantageous; but it was hypocritical for the friars to present themselves as rootless beggars at the same time. Another accusation was that the mendicant ethos was effectively a revival of the ancient Manichean heresy, which despised the things of the physical world. Humility is well and good, but the refusal to own any possessions at all constituted a degradation of the human, who is after all unique among creatures as being fashioned in the image of God. But the most intriguing anti-poverty arguments were those that drew on the legal traditions we surveyed in Chapter 18. The writings of canon lawyers like Gratian and the legal *Digest* of Justinian were invoked on both sides of the controversy.

To see why these texts were relevant we need to understand better how the mendicants themselves described the legal status of the buildings they lived in, the clothes they wore, the books they read, the food they ate, and so on. They appealed to a distinction between "ownership (*dominium*)" and "use (*usus*)." The basic idea is quite simple. Suppose that you mislay this book before finishing it and borrow a copy from a friend (if you have no friends who want to read the book, you may want to buy two copies, or find new friends). You have physical possession of the second copy and are free to use it for as long as your friend allows, but you don't "own" it. Likewise, the Franciscans understood their apparent possessions in fact to belong to someone else, namely the Church as a whole, as represented by the Pope. A Franciscan friar with a place to live, a small library of books, and enough food in storage for the coming week would consider all these things to belong to someone else, even though he is making use of them.

Plausible though this rationale may seem, in the long run it would be a hostage to fortune. It depended on the Pope's acknowledging that he did own the order's property. When in the fourteenth century the Pope turned against the mendicants, the legal justification was potentially undermined. In the shorter run, the distinction between use and ownership presented a tempting target for secular critics. They argued that we may be able to apply the contrast to things like buildings and books, but not food and other items that are consumed in being used. In theory every time they had dinner, the friars were "using" food that belonged to someone else. But are you really only "using" something you don't own if you destroy it in the process?

The mendicants may have been poor, but they offered a wealth of arguments in favor of their vow. Numerous Franciscans and Dominicans wrote on the subject, including Thomas Aquinas. I am, however, going to concentrate on Bonaventure and Peter Olivi, since we have already made their acquaintance. As minister general of his order, Bonaventure was bound to get involved with the issue. Part of his task was to define the implications of the vow more precisely. A treatise addressed to other Franciscans, which may have been written by Bonaventure, answers questions that had been posed about the bounds of acceptable conduct. A friar may own no clothing apart from two tunics, and is allowed to patch one of his tunics to keep it in usable condition. So would he be allowed to sew his two tunics together, treating one as a "patch" for the other, enabling him to wear two layers in winter?[6] Pretty clearly, the friars who asked such questions were not enthusiastically embracing the rigors of asceticism. But when you consider how cold Paris can get in the winter, you can't blame them for asking.

As we'll see shortly, Peter Olivi will have no patience for this sort of half-hearted approach, but Bonaventure was inclined to take a more moderate line. Above all, he could hardly define the strictures of poverty in such a way that the institutional mission of the order would be undermined, given that he was the head of that institution. Even though he often criticized hypocrisy and backsliding among his fellow friars, he was seen as a moderate within the poverty debate in contrast to the more zealous Olivi. In a vigorous response to the secular critic William of Saint Amour, Bonaventure argued for the coherence and legitimacy of the Franciscan way of life.[7] He highlighted the spiritual dangers of wealth, which draws us away from God and towards the things of the body. Voluntary poverty is the most powerful way of taming one's desires, comparable to the vow of chastity undertaken in the monastic life. And if, as everyone admits, perfect chastity is better than lesser forms of sexual restraint, how can one deny that perfect poverty is best? Ownership is inextricably bound to sin. In fact, it became a feature of human life only after the fall from grace. In a state of perfected nature things would be shared by all.

Yet Bonaventure tempers this potentially radical, even communist attitude by admitting that mendicancy is not the only way to live a good and Christian life. One objection lobbed at the mendicants was that they were ironically committing the sin of pride, flaunting their poverty with a quite literally "holier than thou" attitude. Appropriately for a mendicant, Bonaventure begs to differ. Even if poverty is the most perfect life, one need not condemn all other lifestyles as wicked. Imperfection is not the same as sin. Just take the less radical sort of poverty found among monks. They may fall short of the perfect self-denial shown by mendicants, because they do own things in common with one another; yet the monastic life is clearly an admirable one. On the other hand, it's important to Bonaventure that the original exemplars of Christian conduct did embrace unqualified poverty. These exemplars were, of course, Christ and his Apostles. A heated debate within the larger poverty debate concerned passages in the Bible that seemed to conflict with the mendicant ethic. It's mentioned in passing that the Apostles carried purses (John 12:6,

Luke 22:36), something Bonaventure was forced to explain away after William of Saint Amour pointed to it as proof that Christ and his companions handled money.[8]

But, as with William's polemic, the most philosophically fruitful aspect of Bonaventure's defense concerns economic theory. His challenge was to show how the mendicants could indeed use what looked very much like "property," given that they owned nothing. He was in a strong position when it came to something like books, which were expensive to produce and thus counted as something of a luxury item.[9] The mendicants' use of books might be compared to the way that children in our own time are given textbooks to use for the duration of the school year. They don't own the books but merely use them, and the school can take the books away from the children at any time. For Bonaventure this was a point of not just moral but also legal significance. The mendicant has no standing in the law as concerns the things he uses. He cannot sue someone in a dispute over property and must give up the things he uses at the command of the real owner, namely the Church. This account can even be extended to things consumed in use, like food. The consumption occurs with the permission of the owner and involves no legal right of ownership. As William had done, Bonaventure draws on traditional ideas about law stretching back to antiquity. The position of the mendicant is like that of minors or the insane, who in Roman law could dispose of things that are legally owned by a parent or guardian.[10]

Bonaventure's intervention in the debate was a decisive one. Pope Nicholas III embraced his ideas and in 1279 wrote a papal bull confirming the Franciscans' position, in which he drew directly on Bonaventure's ideas. This added a new and rather surprising aspect to the whole dispute. To us the mendicant movement looks like a rebuke to the established Church, but for a while at least it was the mendicants who could claim papal backing. The alliance between the Church hierarchy and the friars would erode in the subsequent decades, though. In the 1320s the shoe was on the other foot, or at least it would have been if the Franciscans wore any shoes. At that time Pope John XXII issued declarations in explicit criticism of the mendicants' legal theory. By then secular masters like Henry of Ghent and Godfrey of Fontaines had chipped away at Bonaventure's carefully laid legal justifications.[11] If the mendicants are like minors or the insane, they can't even legally receive gifts, which makes it impossible to give them alms. Aristotle's authority could also be invoked against the mendicants, since he was clearly against the ethos of poverty. His *Ethics* emphasizes the need for wealth as a component of the good life, if only because it enables us to show generosity towards others.

As for the Franciscans' claim that they could coherently abandon all ownership of goods, the secular masters responded that this is, in fact, impossible. Everyone must at least be guaranteed the basic means of subsistence. This is why one may be excused for stealing food if one is starving to death. Godfrey of Fontaines introduces the idea of "natural ownership," a kind of inalienable right so fundamental that one cannot even give it away voluntarily. I'd like to dwell for a moment on how extraordinary this is: we're seeing the emergence of the notion of a basic economic right. Of course, that is not to say that Godfrey is developing a systematic theory of human rights, but it is a significant step along the way to such theories, something we would scarcely have expected to find within the context of a politicized debate over religious asceticism.

The secular arguments damaged the Franciscan case, but the friars' cause was arguably harmed still more by poverty zealots among their number who demanded a more radical approach than the one defended by Bonaventure. The main protagonist here is Peter Olivi, who set the theme of poverty within an apocalyptic view of history.[12] For him, Francis of Assisi was the "angel of the sixth seal" from the Book of Revelation, whose role was to usher in a new and final age of the world. His followers, the Franciscans, were tasked with preparing all of humankind for the end of days, and their utter poverty played a crucial role in this enterprise, since it allowed them to serve as moral exemplars. Like Bonaventure, Olivi vigorously refuted criticisms of mendicancy. But he also turned his fire against other Franciscans, who among other things had argued that renunciation of ownership was only implied by their vow rather than included within it.

No, insisted Olivi. Renunciation is at the very core of the Franciscan life, and it is of central importance that it grows out of a vow. By taking this vow, the friar performs an act of "infinite" self-discipline. Indeed it is doubly infinite. Not only is he giving up all right of ownership, but the promise has no time limit, which means that it binds his actions indefinitely into the future. Only with this sort of absolute and endless commitment can a human gain infinite merit.[13] This may make Olivi sound like an extreme and unattractively doctrinaire moral theorist. That's certainly what his opponents thought. They worried that on Olivi's view a mendicant would be in constant danger of mortal sin, since enjoyment of even one luxury in a moment of weakness would violate the sacred vow. Yet when it came to the actual practice of what was called "poor use (usus pauper)," Olivi showed flexibility. He understood that it would be impossible to give general rules covering all possible circumstances, and encouraged Franciscans to consult their own conscience when considering difficult cases. Here we may detect a connection to the idea put forward by Bonaventure and others, that an in-dwelling sense of morality called conscience or synderesis plays a fundamental role in ethical life (Chapter 26).

Olivi had many supporters in the order, who were attracted less by his tolerant approach to individual decisions than by his firm insistence on the centrality of poverty in the Franciscan way of life. These followers formed a camp within the mendicants, fervent in their asceticism and expecting the end of days. But Olivi's uncompromising stance also earned him enemies and led to him being censured in 1283. His apocalyptic views set zealous mendicancy on a collision course with the papacy. Though he did not name names, he suggested that the end days would feature the appearance of an antichrist pope. He also hit the churchmen in their apostolically approved purses, asserting that even bishops could and should give up their extensive assets and embrace the mendicant way. Then after his death, Olivi was celebrated as a great spiritual figure by some, even as others condemned him as a heretic. The zealot camp within the order would eventually face papal suppression, with four friars being burned alive for their intransigence in 1318; a year earlier, Pope John XXII had written in some exasperation that while "poverty is great, unity is greater."[14]

There was at least one thing that the papacy found even more unnerving than men like Francis, Bonaventure, and Olivi who chose to live in utter poverty: women who did the same thing. A sign of the Church's disquiet is that it took decades for the papacy to give its approval to the "form of life (forma vitae)" proposed by Francis of Assisi's colleague Clare of Assisi. Founder of the "Poor Clares," she followed in his footsteps—without wearing shoes of course—by embracing a life of manual labor, hardship, charitable work, and voluntary poverty. As Elizabeth Petroff has commented, "These goals were disturbing enough in a male order, but in a female order they were unheard of."[15] Like the mendicant orders, the Poor Clares' lifestyle was an implicit critique of the aristocratic ways of the traditional clergy. Unlike the mendicants, the Poor Clares also demonstrated that women too were strong enough to live with nothing. And as we'll see next, they were not the only community of women to claim a place for themselves within the history of medieval spirituality.

32

BEGIN THE BEGUINE
HADEWIJCH AND MECHTHILD
OF MAGDEBURG

By now you probably feel you have a good understanding of what philosophy was like in the thirteenth century. It was often highly technical, marked as it was by the use of new logical tools. Though theology was the highest science, philosophical problems were often pursued with less reference to religious doctrine than to Aristotle and other works made newly available in Latin translation. And, of course, it was undertaken at the newly founded universities, by men who were usually clerics and always wrote in Latin. Now forget all that. We're about to see that, at this same time, philosophical works were written outside the university context, by women, without using Aristotle or the new-fangled logic, and in vernacular languages instead of the Latin of the schoolmen. The protagonists of this story will be Hadewijch and Mechthild of Magdeburg. Hadewijch's dates are uncertain, but she lived in the first part of the thirteenth century. Mechthild was born in about 1208 and died in about 1282 at the convent of Helfta.

They were extraordinary figures, though not entirely unique. Among the thinkers we've met so far, the obvious comparison is Hildegard of Bingen. But, the occasional use of a German word notwithstanding, she wrote in Latin, as much a part of her claim to authority as the visions she claimed to have received from God. As for figures yet to come, we won't have to wait until the Renaissance to meet other women and men who wrote in vernacular languages. Around the turn of the fourteenth century there will be the daring philosopher-mystics Marguerite Porete and Meister Eckhart, who wrote in French and German respectively (Chapters 53 and 68). A less obvious, but still illuminating comparison would be Eckhart's near contemporary Dante Aligheri, who famously wrote his *Divine Comedy* in Italian (Chapter 54). As he will himself note, Dante had access to educational and political opportunities that were closed to women like Hadewijch, Mechthild, and Marguerite. But like them, he was working outside the institutional framework of the universities. So it was not only mystical authors who could contribute to medieval philosophy without being schoolmen.[1]

Still, mysticism did offer unprecedented opportunities for literary achievement in the thirteenth century, and it's no accident that the medieval women whose words and ideas have survived were usually mystics or spiritual authorities. A leading scholar of medieval mysticism, Bernard McGinn, has spoken of a "democraticization" of Christianity that began in the early thirteenth century, in which access to God was gradually conceded to ordinary believers as well as the powerful representatives of the Church.[2] Hadewijch would have belonged to the first generations experiencing that change. Yet there had been female writers before, even setting aside the exceptional case of Hildegard.[3] All the way back in the Carolingian period a woman named Dhuoda had written a manual of advice for her teenaged son, which mixes prose and poetry, a literary strategy we know from Boethius and his imitators in the "school of Chartres." That's a running theme: the works of Mechthild and Marguerite also alternate verse and prose sections. Moving forward to the tenth century, we can mention the German nun Hrotsvitha, an author of considerable literary ambition who (like Hildegard) wrote poetry and plays, drawing on ancient exemplars like Terence. Hrotsvitha even evokes Lady Philosophy, whose dress provides some of the threads she has woven into her own writing: a witty inversion of Boethius' image of Philosophy in a tattered dress that has been torn by the ignorant.[4]

Hrotsvitha and Hildegard might be seen as the female counterparts of philosophers who wrote in a monastic context, like Anselm and the Victorines. In the thirteenth century the universities emerged as an alternative institution in which philosophy could flourish, but these were not open to women. There was, however, another option, the one exploited by both Hadewijch and Mechthild: the Beguine movement.[5] Though the Beguines were not nuns, they did cohabitate, remain unmarried, and commit themselves to lives of devotion. They also performed charitable works. This led them to be far more socially involved than nuns, who were quite literally cloistered in their convents. The outward engagement of the Beguines made the movement controversial, as did the "grey zone" they inhabited as religiously committed women who had taken no vows that would seclude them and hence justify their autonomy in the eyes of the Church.[6] They were refused permission to preach or to live as mendicants as the Franciscans and Dominicans did. The predictable excuse was that such activities could lead to the wrong kind of intercourse between the Beguines and laypeople. Instead the Beguines typically supported themselves by working with textiles, and pursued a more subtle form of outreach, not least by writing to fellow Beguines and other intimates. With these restrictions in place, the movement was given papal approval in 1216. This didn't put an end to the disquiet: in the middle of the century Gilbert of Tournai complained that the Beguines introduced novel doctrines and were indulging in dangerous "subtleties."

All this was the context for the work of Hadewijch, who came from the Low Countries, where the Beguine movement first emerged. Unfortunately, we know next to nothing about her life apart from what her writings themselves contain.[7] They make clear that she was a spiritual advisor to her fellow Beguines, but also that she became estranged from her group after being accused of unorthodoxy (she laments her separation from them at *Letter* 26). A manuscript of her works says she came from Antwerp, but that notice was written centuries after her death, so it's far from reliable. Still, you can be confident in naming her as a philosopher from what is now Belgium, in case you're ever asked to name one during a trivia contest. She wrote in Dutch and in several genres. We have a series of letters from her pen, probably addressed to a young Beguine. Then there are fourteen "visions," reminiscent of those recorded by Hildegard of Bingen, as well as poems in two different styles. It's not certain whether all these texts are actually by Hadewijch, with particular controversy concerning some of the poems.

With Mechthild the textual situation is in one sense more straightforward. She has left to posterity a work in seven books called *The Flowing Light of Divinity* (*Das fließende Licht der Gottheit*), and there is no worry about its authenticity.[8] But it is problematic in a different respect, because the original version is lost. We have instead a Middle High German translation of Mechthild's Middle Low German, executed in the 1340s, and in a partial Latin version. If you know modern German, the fourteenth-century translation hovers just on the edge of the comprehensible, like Chaucer for speakers of modern English. Though we're better informed about Mechthild's life than that of Hadewijch, we don't know as much as we'd like. We do know that she was encouraged and assisted by her confessor Henry of Halle and that she wrote the final book of the *Flowing Light* at Helfta as a blind old woman, depending on the assistance of the nuns there (§6.64). The title is announced by Mechthild herself, or rather was announced to her by God, as she relates in a prologue to the entire work. Here she also tells us to read the *Flowing Light* nine times if we hope to understand it.

It is of, course, remarkable that women were in a position to write such ambitious texts in the thirteenth century, and equally remarkable that men helped them to do so, and later copied and translated their works. It would, however, be a mistake to reduce the historical and philosophical interest of Hadewijch and Mechthild to the mere fact of their gender. A better way into their thought is something I've already highlighted: they composed their works in vernacular language.[9] To write in Dutch or German was to stand outside the hierarchy of authority and learning, and to stand outside that hierarchy offered the chance of critiquing it. Mechthild in particular was stern in her denunciation of corrupt priests. At one point she steals a march on her fellow vernacular poet Dante by recounting a vision of clergymen in hell. She saw them being punished for their worldly sins by having their souls plunged in fiery water; devils fished them out with claws instead of nets, deposited them on the shore, skinned them alive, and boiled them for supper (§5.14; see also §3.8, 6.21).

Self-satisfied schoolmen are likewise skewered by Mechthild. After being warned that her daring book may wind up being burned, she receives a vision from God who assures her that "no one can burn the truth" and that Mechthild's book symbolizes the Trinity. The physical parchment is the incarnation of the Son, the written words the divinity of the Father, the spoken words the Holy Spirit. When Mechthild humbly replies that she is no "learned holy man (geleret geistliche man)," she is told that many clever men have wasted their gold on schooling that did them no good, and that "learned tongues shall be taught by the unlearned mouth" (§2.26; see also §3.1). It is not the schoolmen but Mechthild who is allowed to drink from the stream of God's spirit, just as the floodwaters fall on the high peaks but gather in the low valley. Mechthild does not need the education offered by the masters at the universities, as her master (meister) is God (3.14). Elsewhere she blames those who do have book learning (wise von lere) but refuse to "give themselves over to the power of naked love" (§2.23).

That brings us to the central theme in the work of Mechthild, and of Hadewijch too: love. For this, both use the word minne, which they take from the vernacular literary tradition of "courtly love." This allows our authors to play on the ideal of unrequited love familiar from medieval romances. Whereas these stories and poems often depicted a man pining for an unobtainable woman, Hadewijch and Mechthild assume the lover's role, assigning to Christ or the entire Godhead the role of the elusive beloved. There is something of a paradox here, with our authors claiming special access to God, yet speaking constantly of their utter estrangement from him. The paradox may be resolved by noting the fleeting nature of mystical experience and the inability of the mystics to enjoy that experience on command. When they sit down to write, they are recalling moments of exalted intimacy, having come back down to earth. It's this that makes their use of the motifs of courtly love philosophical. The talk of minne is among other things a way of articulating the experience of the special kind of knowledge afforded to the mystic, followed by the sudden loss of that knowledge.[10]

Let's consider how Hadewijch, taking a thread or two from Lady Philosophy, weaves together eroticism with epistemology. She may be a mystic, but is not at all opposed to rationality. In her letters she speaks often of the virtues of "reason (*redene*)," encouraging her reader to promote rationality above desire and pleasure (*Letters* 4, 24) and depicting it as an unerring guide sent by God (*Letter* 14). It is by following her own reason that Hadewijch has been able to achieve union with God (*Letter* 29). But if this is not anti-rationalism, neither is it cold intellectualism. Reason must "abandon itself to love's wish, while love consents to be forced and held within the bounds of reason" (*Letter* 18). A similar message can be taken from Hadewijch's visions. In another echo of Boethius' Lady Philosophy, one of these visions speaks of the soul's encounter with "Queen Reason," who is described as wearing a dress covered with eyes that represent knowledge (*Vision* 9). Reason requires the guidance of love, which crowns the eyes of knowledge. At the conclusion of the vision Hadewijch leaves reason behind to be embraced by love. The Dutch word *redene* does double-duty for "reasoning" and "speaking." In moving on to love Hadewijch is thus leaving behind language as well as reason, as she enjoys an intimate, inexpressible encounter with the divine.

Such encounters are as temporary as they are intense. Hadewijch makes bold use of sexual imagery to describe this special kind of knowledge, drawing not just on the literature of courtly love but also on the Song of Songs. In one particularly stunning letter she quotes from that most erotic book of the Bible and speaks of the soul as a bride longing for the divine beloved, whose arms are outstretched, his lips ready to kiss those of the lover and to satisfy all her desires (*Letter* 22). Usually though, she strikes a more desolate note. The moment of union is like lightning followed by the thunder of estrangement from God (*Letter* 30). In moments where her soul is bereft, she realizes her utter unworthiness and unpayable debt. No poet of courtly love can outdo Hadewijch when it comes to lamenting for the absent beloved. Many of her own poems are devoted to this theme and feature lines like "more numerous than the stars in heaven are the griefs of love," or "the suffering that can only be known by him who sincerely forsakes all for love, and then remains unnourished by her" (*Poems in Stanzas* 17 §3; 15 §2). Hadewijch also speaks of what she calls "unfaith," a kind of exquisite despair in which one is overcome by love, yet convinced that it is unrequited (*Letter* 8). Like the knight suffering in silence while his lady is blissfully unaware, the soul can only wait for God to take some notice of it.

This swooning, poetic language evokes the paradox of mystical knowledge, which is the most certain and exalted form of knowing when it occurs but arrives unbidden and vanishes just as suddenly. Hadewijch draws our attention to the superior status of these visions and also their transience. She often tells exactly what day a given vision came to her (typically it's on a religious occasion, like Pentecost). She may achieve nothing less than direct sight of God's face (*anschijn*) only to lose it after a brief time (*Vision* 6). Reason serves as the initial guide; then love takes the soul into the bridal chamber; but once there the soul can only await her lover in hope. What Hadewijch is describing has much in common with Neoplatonic theories of knowledge, especially those of a Christian variety, which tended to depict God coming to the soul rather than the soul ascending under its own power. Hadewijch also has a metaphysical theory to back up this theory of knowledge. She believes that our souls were created eternally in God as divine exemplars and that mystical vision (or part of it) is coming to behold one's true, original self.[11]

In Mechthild's *Flowing Light* we find many of the same themes worked out with even greater detail. The work contains scenes of frank sexuality, with the soul depicted waiting in bed and "lovesick" as she hopes for the arrival of her betrothed (§1.3) or as naked so that there is nothing between her and God (§1.44). Modern-day feminist interpreters have drawn attention to the way Mechthild includes the body as part of the relationship of *minne* between herself and God. It's been argued that the patriarchal values of medieval society were being subverted in the *Flowing Light*.[12] This was an age when women were often seen in terms of their sexual and bodily nature. Mechthild responded by valorizing physicality and making it a means to union with God rather than a hindrance, even if the body may also appear as an "enemy" to the soul (for more on this idea, see Chapter 74 below). At the same time gender roles may be switched, as when Hadewijch and Mechthild make themselves the lover and Christ the beloved, or a woman author may present herself as a soul who is neither male nor female.

We should however note that many of the same points could be made with reference to male authors. In mystical writers like Bernard of Clairvaux we can find some of the same erotic imagery, and male philosophers often expressed surprisingly fluid ideas about gender, for instance by wondering whether we will still be distinguished as men and women when we receive our resurrected bodies. Besides, the valorization of the physical is built into standard Christian theology thanks to the doctrines of the Incarnation and the Eucharist. For precisely this reason, as feminist readers of Mechthild have pointed out, she gives a central place to the Eucharist in her thought. In the thirteenth century this tendency may have been congenial to the interests of the Church, given worries about the Cathar heresy which blossomed in southern France. Since the twelfth century the Cathars had been promoting a kind of renewed Manicheanism, which disdained the body and even denied that Christ had become fully incarnate as a human. In such a context it was actually in line with the values of the Church when the Beguine mystics gave their bodies a positive role to play in spiritual life.[13]

So, as I said at the outset, we should not read Hadewijch and Mechthild solely, or even chiefly, through the lens of their gender. We should, instead, recognize them as representing and creatively responding to wider trends in medieval society and mysticism. You may object that their ostentatious humility was inextricably bound up with their femininity. Just think of Hildegard of Bingen's constant refrain that, as a "mere woman," she was a suitable vessel for God's words. Some men of the period took a similar view. William of Auvergne suggested that mystical visions were more often given to women because their souls are more impressionable.[14] And certainly there is a rhetoric of passivity in these thirteenth-century Beguines. They do not present themselves as mere mouthpieces for God, as Hildegard often did. But Mechthild is quick to assure us that she did not seek out the favors given to her (§4.2), while Hadewijch makes it clear that her visions come when God wills, not when she wishes.

Yet neither of them seems to think that their humble status is primarily a matter of gender. Rather, their claims of unworthiness are bound up with the economy of redemption. One of the most striking chapters in Mechthild's *Flowing Light* consists of the following single sentence: "Nothing comes as close to the greatness of almighty God as the sinful greatness of my own wickedness" (§5.10). This is the theological side of Hadewijch's "courtly love" theme of resignation and unfaith: as the lover suffers in her wait for the beloved, she is vividly aware that she deserves nothing better (*Letter* 8). Mechthild similarly returns again and again to the idea of estrangement or abandonment (*verworfenheit*). For her the greatest form of *minne* is the one that abandons all expectation that the beloved will arrive, the "love that lets go of love" (§2.23). This is the frame of mind that leads Mechthild to say, not once but twice, that she would "as soon die of love" (§2.2, 2.4). In a characteristic paradox, Mechthild finds a kind of joy in this very despair. At the end of a lengthy dialogue between the soul as bride and God, who remains aloof from her, she captures the thought in a rhyming couplet: "The deeper I sink, the sweeter I drink" (§4.12). Hadewijch and Mechthild know the ecstasy that comes with beholding God, but they also depict the exquisite pain of not knowing when they will be given a chance to behold Him again.

33

BINDING ARBITRATION
ROBERT KILWARDBY

As a wise man once said, "the solution to a problem with Aristotle is always more Aristotle." Well to be honest it wasn't actually a wise man: it was me, talking about Maimonides' ethics.[1] But, as a philosopher, I am at least *striving* to be wise. And it's only to be expected that Maimonides, and any other medieval philosopher, would strive to answer objections to Aristotelian philosophy by using the resources of that philosophy. Of course, fighting fire with fire is a high-risk strategy, which in the case of Maimonides led to the burning of his works. Again, we might think, this was only to be expected. Just as philosophers of the Middle Ages were committed Aristotelians, so there were medieval critics who wanted to commit the works of philosophers to the flames. In addition to the burning of Maimonides' writings carried out by Christian authorities at the behest of Jews, there were decrees by the Christian Church condemning certain philosophical doctrines as unacceptable. Most famous is a condemnation laid down by the bishop of Paris in 1277, which will be the topic of Chapter 41. In the very same month a similar edict was made at the University of Oxford by Robert Kilwardby, the archbishop of Canterbury.

On this basis alone it seems easy to fit Kilwardby into our pattern. In an age when philosophers chafed against and were constrained by anti-philosophical authority, Kilwardby was on the side of the anti-philosophers. He would represent the latest attempt to stem the Aristotelian tide that had been rising throughout the thirteenth century, in hopes of preserving a more traditional Augustinian approach. On this telling, he was the Augustinian foil to his fellow Dominican Thomas Aquinas, who was a thoroughgoing Aristotelian and perhaps even a prime target of Kilwardby's act of censorship in Oxford. Kilwardby would thus be an intellectual ally of a man like Peter Olivi, whom we saw sneering at his contemporaries for seeing Aristotle as the "god of this age" and instead favoring the opinions of Augustine, as Olivi understood them (Chapter 30).

But if scholastic philosophy teaches us anything, it's that we should question stark oppositions and seek to draw our distinctions more finely. So it is here. Kilwardby spent decades as a student and master in both Paris and Oxford before becoming archbishop of Canterbury in 1272. He wrote works of Aristotelian logic, natural philosophy, and ethics, writings that would influence Albert the Great, certainly no one's idea of an anti-philosopher. If we want to understand Kilwardby, it's far better to start with this extensive body of writings than with his decision to prohibit certain philosophical teachings at Oxford. In these writings, we do find Kilwardby saying that Augustine was "much more sublimely enlightened than Aristotle, especially in spiritual matters."[2] But we also find that he is keen to establish agreement between these two great authorities, insofar as he can, so that his own teachings emerge as creative compromises.

Kilwardby's credentials as a faithful Aristotelian can be established easily enough by considering his contribution to logic and grammar, which were no less fundamental for him than for other university schoolmen. Far from questioning Aristotle's teachings, he applies ideas taken from other areas of Aristotelian science to these arts of the trivium.[3] In particular he uses concepts from natural philosophy to explain language and philosophical arguments. His grammatical writings are based on the ancient linguistic theorist Priscian, not Aristotle. Yet Kilwardby explains the function of a verb by referring to Aristotle's ideas about motion, while a noun in the nominative case stands for a substance that is undergoing or carrying out a motion. He is also at pains to present grammar as a "science" in the Aristotelian sense. This is no easy task, since Aristotelian sciences are supposed to be general or universal, whereas the study of grammar would seem to be specific to whatever language it is you are analyzing: one grammar for Latin, another for Greek or English. Kilwardby is, of course, aware of the differences between languages, yet nonetheless insists that there are some features common to all languages, for instance that they all have nouns and verbs.[4]

More striking still is what he does with logic. Nowadays few philosophers would see a close connection between logic and physics. But Kilwardby thinks it is useful to take the four-cause theory of Aristotle's natural philosophy and apply it to syllogistic arguments. The efficient cause of a syllogism is the person who forms it, while its final cause or purpose is, of course, to produce knowledge. Kilwardby also thinks of syllogisms as having material and formal causes.[5] Basically, the matter of a syllogism is the terms that appear in the premises, while the form is the way that the terms are arranged. Consider an everyday syllogism like: "No giraffe is able to roller-skate; only things able to roller-skate are able to compete in roller derby; therefore no giraffes are able to compete in roller derby." Here the terms are "giraffe," "able to roller-skate," and "able to compete in roller derby," while the form is "No A is B; only B is C; therefore no A is C."[6] All the elements that the medievals called "syncategorematic" features of the syllogism, such as negation or modifiers like "necessarily" and "possibly," belong to the form and not the matter. Now this is quite interesting, because still today we talk about logic being "formal." So Kilwardby's view may seem to be a step towards the more abstract and even mathematical conception of logic that philosophers work with today.

Kilwardby's contributions to philosophy of language and logic are also significant for a more basic reason: he got there before most of his contemporaries. He wrote the oldest commentary on Priscian's grammar that we can date and was also one of the first to comment on the newly translated logical works by Aristotle. He did all this during his time at Paris, before joining the Dominicans in 1245 and returning to his native England, where he would turn his attention to more theological topics. In the 1250s, he was still working on problems within Aristotle's natural philosophy. He devoted one set of disputed questions from this period to the much-debated topic of time, which we saw puzzling earlier thirteenth-century thinkers like Richard Rufus and the anonymous commentators on Aristotle's *Physics* (Chapter 23).[7]

Here we have a good opportunity to test Kilwardby's allegiance to Augustine as opposed to Aristotle, since Augustine's *Confessions* is famous for proposing that time exists only in our minds and not in external reality.[8] Kilwardby does cite this opinion (§4), but can't bring himself to accept it. One reason for thinking that time is unreal would also apply to motion. Like time, motion exists only stretched across past, present, and future, and the past no longer exists, while the future does not yet exist. Yet Kilwardby assumes that no one will want to say that motion is unreal, so neither should we say this of time (§6). Instead, both motion and time should be thought of as "successive" entities that exist precisely by coming into being and elapsing. Time relates to successive motion as its quantity, much as spatial extention is a quantity for bodies, with the significant difference that spatial quantity remains fixed, while temporal quantity is "transient" (§18). So if there is any mind-independent or "subjective" aspect of time, it is not the quantitative measure of motions out in the world. Instead, it would be our own measurements of time which render it "determinate" by dividing it into minutes and hours (§77). But even this is not presented as a way of saving Augustine's position. Instead, Kilwardby uses the point to explain Aristotle's claim that we know time by counting or "marking off" a motion (*Physics* 219a).

So far we're building up a picture of a man who seems unlikely to condemn Aristotelian philosophy. But Kilwardby's actions in 1277 will become more explicable once we've talked about his views on the soul.[9] Like many of the other thinkers we've met from the thirteenth century he accepted an apparently paradoxical idea first put forward by the Jewish thinker Ibn Gabirol, though Kilwardby never mentions him and may not even have known the ultimate source of the theory.[10] The idea is that even spiritual beings like the soul have matter; only God is truly immaterial. Paradoxical though this sounds, one can give a powerful argument for it. Matter was one popular answer to the long-running question of what makes something an individual (see Chapter 16). Whereas the nature of giraffes is something held in common by Hiawatha, Harold, and all other giraffes, there is only one particular bit of matter that makes up Hiawatha, while Harold is made of another bit of matter. If it's matter that "individuates" things in this way—something that Kilwardby believed for at least part of his career—then spiritual things too must have matter. Otherwise, how could your soul and mine be distinct individuals?

Kilwardby took this idea to be faithfully Augustinian, and even associated the tendency of matter to take on form with Augustine's talk of "seminal reasons,"[11] an idea that Augustine had in turn borrowed from the Stoics. Still, when Kilwardby uses the idea to explain the human soul, his expertise in Aristotelian logic is on full display. In this logical system there is no idea more fundamental than the relation of genus to species. The most general genus of things is substance, and this genus is divided, subdivided, and sub-subdivided into ever more specific classes. Thus, we may say that there are bodily as opposed to spiritual substances, living bodily substances as opposed to inanimate ones, animals as opposed to plants, and humans as opposed to giraffes. We've already seen Kilwardby bringing together natural philosophy with logic and he does so again here. He thinks of matter as having the potential or power to take on all these forms, from the most general form of substance down to the most specific form of rationality, which is distinctive of humans.[12] So you have not just one but many forms: one that makes you a substance, another that makes you a physical body, another that makes you a living being, another that makes you an animal, and finally the form that makes you a human.

It may already be obvious what this has to do with the soul, especially since we've seen a very similar set of ideas in Olivi. For him and for Kilwardby the soul is not just one simple form. The lower psychological powers, the ones responsible for giving you life and the ability to move and engage in sensation, are forms distinct from the rational soul, which is what makes you a human. Meanwhile the soul in its entirety is nothing but the conjunction of all these powers. When humans are first forming as embryos, the powers are added sequentially. This is an idea we saw already in William of Auvergne (Chapter 24), but with a crucial difference. For William each form was effectively replaced or swallowed up when newer, more sophisticated forms arise in the fetus, something he compared to a brighter light engulfing a dimmer light. Kilwardby instead compares the process to a geometrical construction, where a triangle is added to a trapezoid to form a pentagon. There is more at stake here than a choice of metaphors. Kilwardby is trying to convey that the powers or forms in the soul remain distinct, a conclusion for which he gives both philosophical and theological arguments.[13] Philosophically, it's clear to him that the many abilities we exercise as living beings, from digestion to thought, require numerous different powers and not just one. Theologically, Kilwardby worries that if there is only a simple rational soul in a human, then the human that was Christ could not in fact have been the *incarnation* of God, but only an immaterial, divine spirit with a loose connection to a body.

In holding that our soul consists of a plurality of forms or powers, Kilwardby flirts with a danger we noted when looking at Olivi. If this theory is correct, then won't the unity of my person be compromised? My rational soul will be associated with the lower parts of my being, but it will be a distinct entity that floats free of the rest. To avoid this Kilwardby cites Augustine: the soul joins to the body in order to fulfill its desire for knowledge about all things.[14] And unlike a giraffe who dreams of rolling around the rink, the soul can achieve its desire, thanks to what Kilwardby calls its "unibility," that is, its innate tendency to form a unity with the body.[15] But why does the soul need to be united to the body in order to have knowledge? Because Kilwardby is enough of an Aristotelian to think that most of our intellectual understanding depends upon the experience of the senses.

In the contest between Augustinian theories of illumination and Aristotelian ideas of empirical science he predictably takes a conciliatory, middle position. Knowledge of some things, like mathematical truths, the soul, and God Himself, is implanted within the soul from birth. But for everything else we need to explore the world using sensation, a topic that provides the occasion for yet another compromise theory. We saw that for Peter Olivi sense organs, such as the eyes, are affected by their surroundings; yet the physical changes in these organs have no role in the soul's sensory awareness. Instead, the soul is aware of things by simply extending its attention to them. Olivi thus rejected views like that of Roger Bacon, according to which sensation occurs precisely when a representative "species" of a sense object is registered in the eyes.

Kilwardby splits the difference.[16] On the one hand, he agrees with Olivi that a mere bodily change cannot affect the soul. On the other hand, he thinks the sense organ must play a greater role than Olivi would allow. Otherwise, things would not need to be physically present in the right place, suitably illuminated, and so on if we are to see them (§78). His idea is instead that when the image of a sense object is present in the organ, the soul can "assimilate" itself to that image. It does so by actively making a further image for itself, an image of the image in the sense organ.

When I see a giraffe, an image is present in my eyes, but the mere reception of this image is not seeing. For me to see her is for my soul to fashion a further likeness of her "in and from itself" (§81–2, 85). Olivi would be ready with an objection here, namely that if the image in the sense organ is being used as an intermediary in this way, then my soul is not actually perceiving the giraffe, but rather an image of the giraffe. But Kilwardy insists that in grasping a suitably exact likeness of a thing, I am in fact perceiving that very thing (§103). And perhaps he's right about this. If you were looking at a photograph of your mother, you probably wouldn't hesitate to say that you were seeing, or looking at, your mother.

On this and other topics Kilwardby presented himself as being like a good roller skater: expert in balancing acts. Where we would probably say that his theory of sensation is neither Aristotelian nor Augustinian, he insisted that it exposed the hidden agreement between the two ancient authorities (§113). Which brings us finally to the mystery of why this conciliatory man used the power of his office as archbishop to prohibit philosophical ideas. The works I've been discussing were mostly written twenty years or more before the 1277 ban. Perhaps his views drifted towards intolerance as he aged and rose within the church hierarchy? We may hope for old age to bring wisdom but often as not, it just brings grumpiness. A look at the thirty theses Kilwardby actually prohibited tells a different story, though. About half of them concern issues in grammar and logic,[17] but the most central issue was one that had long been of interest to Kilwardby: the unity of the soul. The masters of Oxford were forbidden to teach that, in human embryos, the lower souls are extinguished when the higher soul arrives, or in general that the powers of the soul are all explained by virtue of a single form.

It's often been suspected that Kilwardby's target was none other than the recently deceased Thomas Aquinas. Yet Kilwardby's attempts to explain and justify his prohibition show that he actually didn't have Aquinas in mind.[18] What Kilwardby wanted to stamp out was the idea that the soul is a single form, something that had been asserted by William of Auvergne and others such as John Blund. Aquinas took an even more extreme view than them. He thought that a human is a composite of body and soul, and that this *whole composite* has only one form. Kilwardby later stated that this view was unknown to him when he laid down the prohibition, adding that he didn't really understand it. He had been arguing against people with the far more reasonable, yet still in his view false, view that humans have numerous forms: the single form that is the soul, plus some more forms that belong to the body. When Aquinas argued that a human has only one form in total, which determines the features and powers of both body and soul, he was adopting a stance so radical and unfamiliar that Kilwardby hadn't even thought to ban it.

We may care less about who Kilwardby was trying to blacklist and more about the black mark against his own name. After a career devoted to careful arbitration between Augustinian and Aristotelian teachings Kilwardby sought to make that arbitration a binding one. In so doing he unwittingly wrote his own epitaph. He has gone down in history as an enemy of Aristotelianism, alongside the bishop of Paris, Stephen Tempier. But this is unfair, as we can see if we take note of the differences between the Oxford ban and the one in Paris. As Kilwardby himself stressed, he was only prohibiting the *teaching* of certain doctrines, not condemning them as heretical, as was done in Paris. And unlike bishop Tempier, Kilwardby was himself a philosopher. His ban came backed with rational as well as theological arguments. This was not an attempt to crush philosophical inquiry but an attempt to stop masters from teaching their students things that were demonstrably false. Obviously, this isn't to praise or excuse Kilwardby's actions, just to say that it would be a mistake to conflate the situation in Oxford with that of Paris, or to reduce Kilwardby's entire career to the prohibition.

34

ANIMAL, VEGETABLE, MINERAL ALBERT THE GREAT'S NATURAL PHILOSOPHY

An old joke that always makes me laugh: "What do Alexander the Great and Winnie the Pooh have in common? Their middle name." The same goes for the subject of this chapter, who has something else in common with the both of them. Like Alexander, he had a close working relationship with Aristotle, while like Winnie the Pooh, he was interested in exploring the animal world and went so far as to undertake a personal inspection of beehives. Nor did he restrict his research to zoology. Indeed, there was little or nothing in the universe that escaped his interest. Aptly he was known as the "universal doctor" and already honored in his own time with the title *Albertus Magnus*, Albert the Great. The admiration was however not quite universal. Roger Bacon believed he was, if not a bear of very little brain, then a master of very little training. Albert "heard no philosophy and was not taught by anyone," and was one of many authors to write in Latin who was misled by the poor standard of translations into this language, having no facility in Greek or Arabic.[1]

There is a grain of truth in these harsh judgments, in that Albert did not enjoy the sort of education Bacon would have seen as indispensable for work in natural philosophy.[2] He hailed from Lauingen in Swabia, though his career would later give him a particularly strong connection to Cologne. Born around the turn of the thirteenth century, Albert joined the Dominican order as a young man, by which time he was living in Padua. His student experience did not include training in the cutting-edge Aristotelian philosophy so valued by Bacon. Albert's precocious interest in the natural world had to be satisfied largely through independent investigation and observation. He would not come to Paris and be exposed to the intellectual currents of university life there until the 1240s. Nonetheless, he was deemed an outstanding enough mind to be made the first Dominican master of theology at Paris, which makes him the counterpart of the Franciscan master Alexander of Hales.

During his time at Paris, Albert acquired a student whose name would eventually eclipse his: Thomas Aquinas. Though the two would not see eye to eye on every issue, Albert's intense interest in Aristotelian philosophy was certainly passed on to his illustrious student. In fact Thomas accompanied Albert to Cologne in 1248 and was the one to write down the notes on Albert's lectures on Aristotle's *Ethics*. In response to requests from fellow Dominicans, Albert then undertook an ambitious project. He would write about the entirety of Aristotelian natural philosophy, dealing with everything from the principles of physics to more specific topics like the heavens, animals, plants, and even minerals. Albert thus took up Aristotle's natural philosophy in its full scope and ambition, something that had not been done (except in the Islamic world) since Aristotle's own colleague Theophrastus. His career in the Church flourished along with his intellectual activities. In 1260 Albert was appointed bishop of Regensburg, a beautiful city located on the Danube. Sadly, he did not relish his duties and persuaded the Pope to accept his resignation. He first joined the papal Curia but eventually found his way back to Cologne, where he would spend his final years, dying in 1280, by which time he'd outlived his most famous student by six years.

Among his various projects, Albert's investigations in botany deserve special praise, because, as he noted himself, the ancient tradition gave him relatively little to go on.[3] There was a work called *On Plants*, falsely ascribed to Aristotle but actually by Nicholas of Damascus; there was ancient literature on agriculture; and there were medical writings on the uses of certain plants. Albert was obligated to supplement this rather meager material with observations he'd made himself. But he would have done so anyway. He was as committed as his critic Roger Bacon to the centrality of experience in natural philosophy. All our knowledge is grounded in sensation and one can reach the universal truths envisioned in Aristotelian philosophy only on the strength of individual observations. Even when it came to something as humble as plants, Albert was not going to be satisfied with anything less than full blown science. His own work *On Plants* emphasizes that he does not share the medical doctor's practical aims; he wants to put the philosophy back into this branch of natural philosophy.

That meant understanding real branches, along with all the other parts of plants. He also carefully distinguished between kinds of plants, while admitting that the dividing lines between types can be blurry, and sought to identify the essential and accidental parts of each plant type. Thorns for instance are mere accidental growths, whereas other parts of a plant belong to its very nature. Albert discerned parallels between plant parts and animal parts. Plant sap is a source of warmth for the organism, like blood in animals, knots in trees play the role of digestive organs, and wood is analogous to flesh, whereas bark is like skin.[4] The features that distinguish the various species of plant—Albert lists about four hundred of them—can often be explained in brute material terms. The shape of a leaf will be caused by the proportion of watery and earthy constituents in the plant matter, with wetter ingredients causing the leaves to spread out as water does. A role must also be given to the heavens, which have a particularly powerful effect on vegetation, because plants are so simple. Here Albert would be thinking of such phenomena as seasonal crop cycles.

That appeal to celestial influence is a pervasive feature of Albert's natural philosophy. He wrote treatises about the heavens and was convinced that the celestial bodies exert tremendous influence over the generation of plants, animals, and humans. Monstrous births and deformities are a good example. They result from matter's failure to take on the nature of an animal or human properly. (Since it is matter that is to blame, these monstrosities do not detract from the universality and certainty of natural philosophy.) Often matter refuses to cooperate because the heavens have worked some malign influence. As usual, Albert also mentions his own experiences on the topic, reporting on deformed births which he puts down to astrological causes, and on conversations he had with midwives about the phenomenon. Albert mentions the case of a pig born with the head of a human, something that could not be explained through normal biological functioning and thus must be put down to heavenly influence.[5] Which shows that Albert had something else in common with Winnie the Pooh: an interest in piglets.

And speaking of pork products, also with Roger Bacon, given that he too was an enthusiastic believer in astral influence. Indeed, in the later medieval and Renaissance tradition, alchemical and astrological treatises were spuriously ascribed to Albert and he was even said to have taught alchemy to Bacon! But actually Albert did not stray too far from Aristotle in the direction of the so-called "occult" sciences. In his authentic works he dismissed the claims of alchemy, agreeing with Avicenna that alchemists can only produce something that *looks* like gold.[6] Characteristically, he cited his own experience. He repeatedly tried firing a golden metal produced by an alchemist and found that it broke down into dross instead of melting as it ought to. As for astrology, he did allow for the possibility of such feats as predicting lifespan on the basis of a birth horoscope. But usually he invoked the stars in what we would see as more "scientific" settings.

This is well illustrated by his treatment of the rising and possible shifting of the seas.[7] Albert was aware of claims that the oceans and seas had changed location over time. There was very convincing evidence for this, such as the discovery of an ancient ship's rudder buried deep under now dry ground. Of course, the phenomenon is a genuine one, but the explanation offered for it was false. It was proposed that changes in the position of the stars over long periods of time brought about the shifting of the seas. Albert disagreed, arguing that the cycles of the planetary movements are regular, so that we should see the seas moving progressively across the earth as centuries go by, something that would certainly have been noted in recorded history. On the other hand, he admitted that floods (like the one that deluged the whole earth in Noah's day) are caused by the heavens, and in particular by astral conjunctions. Then, there is the evident phenomenon of the rising and falling tide. Again, and this time correctly, Albert put this down to the influence of the moon. He even claimed that the moon causes tide to rise like a magnet pulling iron, which is remarkably close to the truth. Unfortunately, he then added a more detailed and entirely spurious explanation, namely that the moon is causing vapor under the water to expand, which makes the sea level rise.

Another of his treatises on natural philosophy deals with minerals, which he divides into stones and metals; it's in this context that he makes his skeptical remarks concerning alchemy.[8] You might think that, here, the role of the heavens would be minimal. But in fact Albert thinks that stones are formed precisely when celestial influence causes earthy matter to condense, which always requires the admixture of at least some moisture to hold the stone together. Metals, by contrast, are produced through the concentration of vapor that has escaped from within the hollows of the earth. Albert also retails some rather fanciful claims about minerals, speaking of their healing properties and other effects we might deem magical, a belief also held by his fellow German thinker Hildegard of Bingen and many other contemporaries. But, as ever, Albert draws impressively on his own experience. He may, for instance, be the first author to note the poisonous effects of mercury.

You may be wondering how Albert had the opportunity to observe nature so carefully, since you're probably imagining him holed up in a university scriptorium or Dominican house. But, in fact, it was precisely his life as a Dominican that gave him the chance to see the world up close. As a mendicant, he always undertook his travels on foot. Given the many cities in which he lived and worked, that meant a lot of walking: he was a peripatetic philosopher in every sense of the word. Albert didn't just keep his eyes open while on the road, but made active inquiries, as with his interviewing of midwives and testing of fake gold. He did the same when it came to the animal world, inspecting the hives of ants and bees and even having himself lowered down a rock face to examine an eagle's nest.[9] As with plants and minerals, Albert was a pioneer in revisiting the topic of zoology, a major interest of Aristotle's that had been largely dropped ever since. (Again, with the exception of authors of the Islamic world, like Avicenna.[10])

Naturally enough, the animal that most interested Albert was the human. He discussed human nature in various places, including a dedicated treatise called simply *On the Human Being* (*De homine*).[11] It combines a detailed philosophical consideration of the soul's relation to the body with theological speculations concerning Adam and Eve, all arranged in the form of disputed questions. As usual, Albert draws extensively on Aristotle, while also paying due respect to the opinions of Augustine and other church authorities. But the most decisive influence on his theory of soul is Avicenna. Albert follows him by outlining two ways of thinking about the soul (58; see also 12). On the one hand, there is Aristotle's idea that the soul is the form of the body, in the sense that it is the body's act or perfection (46). On the other hand, there is the soul considered as a substance in its own right which can even survive bodily death.

As observed a generation earlier by John Blund (Chapter 24), these two perspectives belong respectively to the physicist and the metaphysician (36). In physics or natural philosophy we grasp the soul through the activities it manifests in the body. In metaphysics we understand soul as it is in itself, rather than approaching it through its effects. The contrast is borrowed most immediately from Avicenna, but echoes a long-standing Platonist approach to human nature according to which our true selves are immaterial and immortal, even if they have acquired an intimate relationship with corruptible bodies. Albert is enough of a Platonist to say that the human as such is nothing but intellect (*homo inquantum homo solus est intellectus*). On the other hand—this is scholastic philosophy, so there's always an "on the other hand"—Albert doesn't want to go too far in this Platonist direction. In particular, he resists the idea that the soul has only a casual or accidental relation to the body. To avoid this he rejects Plato's theory that the soul already existed before birth and emphasizes the soul's essential tendency or "inclination" to join a body. This, in fact, is what distinguishes the human soul from an angel, which has no such inclination (56).

Albert also rejects a popular argument in favor of the substantiality of the human soul. We've seen that many thirteenth-century thinkers followed Ibn Gabirol in holding that all created things, including the soul, consist of both matter and form. This would have the significant advantage of making soul a "this something (*hoc aliquid*)," as the scholastics put it. Anything that combines matter and form would be a substance in its own right, even if the matter at stake is "spiritual" matter. Albert associates this idea with Plato as well as Ibn Gabirol. Against both of them he insists on a more Aristotelian way of looking at things. The soul does have potentialities and powers, and needs the body to exercise many of these. But we should not confuse potentiality with materiality.[12] So while it's true that all things other than God have powers which they may or may not use, this does not mean that the soul or angels have matter. In fact, Albert will even admit that insofar as the soul is conceived as a form, it remains incomplete without its body. For, as a form, it is nothing but a source of bodily activities, like nutrition or sensation. It does need the body as an instrument to carry out those activities and realize its potential, and when the body dies, the opportunity to do this is lost (104). Yet the soul survives because it is a substance in its own right. Its activities are destroyed, while it lives on, like a blacksmith who can survive the destruction of his anvil and hammer.

By demoting the lower functions of soul to mere activities realized in a body, Albert can avoid embracing a notion we've found in Olivi and Kilwardby, namely that there is a plurality of forms in every single human. Like Aquinas after him, Albert instead insists that the soul is a single substance and act (104). Early in his career he claimed that the whole human soul arrives in the body as a unity bestowed directly by God. This would mean that the generation of human souls is totally unlike what happens with other animals. Whereas the soul of a giraffe would emerge from material causes, human souls would come from outside the physical realm entirely (*ab extrinsico*). As Albert began to read more deeply in Aristotelian zoology, though, he became dissatisfied with this story.[13] His new view was that the lower part of the human soul emerges from the matter provided by a pregnant mother, with form coming from the father, just as in other animal species. Yet the power of intellect still needs to be given to the human directly by God. So you got your sense faculties and your ability to digest food from your parents along with your eye color, but you got your mind from God.

Despite this double origin, Albert continues to insist that the soul is a single form and not a collection of forms enabling us to perform different activities. To the objection that a single form could never produce such varied results, Albert can respond that the variety results from the disparate nature of the body. Soul uses a subtle "spirit" pervading the entire body as an "intermediary (*medium*)," through which it expresses its activities in that body (164). These activities are then further diversified by the bodily organs. This is a pattern of thinking that arises repeatedly in Albert: a single cause can give rise to many different effects by using various recipients as intermediaries. Consider once again his theory of celestial influence. Albert thinks the planets affect our lower world by means of light, but he also knows that bodies like the moon get their light from the sun. So why don't we always just see the same sort of effects that would be produced by sunlight, instead of finding that the different heavenly bodies have different effects? For instance, the moon supposedly has a particular effect on moisture, according to astrological theory, which is why it is closely connected to the tides. The reason is that the light of the sun is absorbed by the moon and takes on a special lunar character, before being passed on to the seas or an unfortunate pig embryo. As we now see in Chapter 34, Albert uses the same kind of account in a more exalted part of his philosophy. When he comes to explain how a simple God could give rise to such a bewilderingly complex world, he suggests that God's effect is nothing other than simple being, which is diversified by the essences of the things God creates.

35

THE SHADOW KNOWS
ALBERT THE GREAT'S METAPHYSICS

D o you believe that all things in the universe, in their bewildering, seemingly infinite variety, derive from only one single cause? If so, you're in good company. It might just be the very oldest idea in the history of philosophy. It emerged in Mediterranean culture with Pre-Socratics who proposed that all things arise out of some fundamental constituent, perhaps air, water, or, as Anaximander proposed, the "indefinite." At around the same time, the authors of the *Upaniṣads* in India were tracing all things to the single reality that is *brahman*. Yet objections to the idea are almost as antique as the idea itself. As Aristotle pointed out, some Pre-Socratics preferred to introduce two or more causal principles, like Empedocles' Love and Strife or the Atomists' infinite, indestructible particles. Aristotle thought they were on the right track, because a single cause would remain inert, having nothing to act upon. In fact, even two principles wouldn't be enough, since they would cancel each other out.

In late antiquity, though, all philosophers accepted that the universe derives from one cause, with the pagan Neoplatonists identifying this cause as the One or Good and the Jews and Christians, of course, seeing the God of their Scriptures as the almighty Creator of all things. Still, like an offer of marriage from a Montague to a Capulet, the proposal continued to cause trouble. Philosophers worried less that a single cause would remain entirely inactive, as Aristotle claimed, and more that such a cause could only have one effect. The Neoplatonic First Principle and the Judeo-Christian God were claimed to be perfectly simple, and how can a perfectly simple thing generate a multiplicity? Only indirectly, claimed the Neoplatonists. Their One would produce only one effect, which would form a link in a causal chain stretching down all the way to our physical realm. We might expect thinkers of the Abrahamic faiths to abandon this scheme in favor of direct creation of each thing by God. Many thinkers of Judaism, Christianity, and Islam did precisely that. But those with a greater commitment to the Hellenic heritage adhered to the rule "from one thing only one thing can come," in Latin *ab uno non nisi unum*.

It's a motto that became notorious in both the Arabic and Latin spheres. In the Islamic world the theologian al-Ghazālī attacked Avicenna for his adherence to the "from one only one" rule, making it one of the central polemics of his *Incoherence of the Philosophers*.[1] In Paris the rule would appear on the list of banned propositions in the 1277 condemnation. Yet it struck some philosophers as intuitively plausible, or even obvious. One of them was Albert the Great. We've just seen that his commitment to Aristotelian natural philosophy was unprecedented in the medieval era. When it came to metaphysics, he was equally committed to ideas from the late ancient Platonist tradition. It would I think be fair to say that Albert is the most Neoplatonically inclined medieval thinker we've met since Eriugena all the way back in the ninth century. Neoplatonic ideas reached him from a variety of authoritative sources, which presented a united front endorsing the "from one only one" motto and its corollary that God uses intermediaries to fashion the universe.

For starters there was Avicenna. We've seen him exerting influence in the Latin sphere starting in the twelfth century, especially regarding the soul. But Albert drew more deeply on Avicenna than others had done, as we can see from his exposition of Aristotle's *Metaphysics*, which refers constantly to Avicenna.[2] Then, there was that favorite source of Eriugena's, the Pseudo-Dionysius. Albert commented on his works in lectures that were recorded by Thomas Aquinas, who would go on to write his own commentary on Dionysius' *Divine Names*. Since Dionysius was covertly drawing on the ideas of the late ancient Platonist Proclus, this too helped push Albert in a Neoplatonic direction. Finally, there was an even more indirect route through which Proclus was smuggled into Latin Christendom: the *Book of Causes* (*Liber de causis*). It is a partial translation of Proclus' elegant and axiomatic presentation of Neoplatonist philosophy in his *Elements of Theology*. The Latin *Book of Causes* was based on an Arabic paraphrase translation produced in the ninth century. It acquired considerable authority because it was thought to be a work of Aristotle himself. This is basically what Albert believed, though he saw it as an excerpt of a work by Aristotle. Albert thought the excerpting was done by a Jewish author called "David," probably meaning the translator Ibn Daud (Avendauth; see Chapter 20).[3]

True to its name, the *Book of Causes* recognizes a multiplicity of causal principles. But true to the Neoplatonic tradition that spawned it, the work arranges these principles in a chain that descends from a highest, single, and simple cause. Like Plotinus, Proclus called it "the One." The work of reconciling this teaching with Abrahamic belief already began in the Arabic translation, which speaks of the First Cause as "Creator" or simply "God."[4] This Creator is first of all the cause of being, followed by intellect, soul, and finally the world accessible to sense perception. The subsequent principles serve as intermediaries transmitting the Creator's influence to the next level down in a cosmic version of pass the parcel. In keeping with the "from one only one" rule, the being that is created immediately by God is said to be one and simple and to take on diversity only because it assumes the form of intellect.

All of this chimed well with Avicenna. He too had made an intellect the first effect of God and let it be an intermediary between God and the rest of creation. Avicenna gave Albert a further piece of the metaphysical puzzle with his distinction between essence and existence. According to this Avicennan teaching, the nature or essence of each created thing leaves open whether or not that thing exists. This is why such things need causes in the first place. They are insufficient to account for their own existence and need help from some external influence if they are to be brought into being. By contrast, God's essence guarantees, or even is identical to, His own existence.[5] This is what it means to say that God exists necessarily, whereas all other things exist contingently: in itself, each of them could have failed to exist, and exists only because of the chain of causes that goes back to God.

Albert is broadly happy with this picture, but is more reluctant than Avicenna to say that existence is bestowed by God only indirectly.[6] He would like to say that when God creates being, He is creating the being of all things. But how to secure this while still obeying the maxim "from one only one"? The answer is simple: the being produced by God is in itself one but becomes complex and diversified precisely when it joins to the essences of created things, as Avicenna described. In a further borrowing from his Neoplatonic sources, Albert compares God to a flowing fountain or shining light, with being as a single stream or irradiation which is received by many things. The Neoplatonists and Avicenna held that God produces an intellect and uses it as an intermediary to create other things, but Albert doesn't want to separate God from creation in this way, so he resorts to a cunning bit of exegesis. When he reads in the *Book of Causes* that "intellect" comes from God before anything else, he seizes on the word used in the Latin translation, which is *intelligentia*. This not need mean a cosmic "intellect." It could just mean an intellectual concept, an idea. This is precisely what it does mean, according to Albert: the *Book of Causes* is telling us that the first *concept* produced by God is being, and it is a concept that applies to all things.[7]

With this move Albert has managed to bring teachings of late antiquity, heavily filtered through Arabic transmission, into line with an idea of his own time: the transcendentals. As we saw in Chapter 25, the scholastics in the thirteenth century had developed a theory according to which some concepts, such as being, truth, goodness, and unity, apply to all things. Albert's story explains why this should be so. As Avicenna said, God has being through His very essence, so it stands to reason that being must be His sole effect. Being is then received by everything that derives from Him, which, of course, means everything other than God Himself. For this reason Albert insists that, among the transcendentals, being is the most primary. Goodness, unity, and truth always come along with being; as we saw before, they are "extensionally identical." But this is only because we can add more specific notions to that of being, like the fact that a certain being is "undivided," which is all we mean when we say that something is "one."[8]

The essences of created things restrict being in a more specific way. When a giraffe comes to be, its essence "contracts" being into the act of existence appropriate to being a giraffe. And here Albert does think that intermediaries are needed in order to explain how being is received in such a limited and diminished way (with all due respect to giraffes, needless to say). Like shadows which dim the reception of a brilliant light, other causal factors besides God are needed to explain the particular and limited form of being that turns up in each created thing. Here Albert's metaphysics makes contact with the natural philosophical themes we looked at in Chapter 34. Each giraffe comes from its mother and father through a process whose details are known best to the giraffes themselves, and there is also a role for the heavenly bodies. But none of these lesser causes accounts for the sheer being of any created thing. When excited and appreciative zoo visitors exclaim, "Thank God there are giraffes!" Albert would say they are getting things just right.

All of this gives us a new perspective on his work in zoology and the other physical sciences. Like earlier medievals with an interest in nature, Albert would have seen science as a way to appreciate God's handiwork and generosity. Every animal, plant, and stone is a reflection or "vestige" of God's being. This doesn't mean, though, that the natural philosopher has to meditate on God even as he dissects a plant or has himself lowered down a cliff to learn about the breeding habits of eagles. There's even a sense in which this would be inappropriate. As Albert puts it in one striking passage, "When I am discussing natural things, God's miracles are nothing to me."[9] It is another science that undertakes to grasp things insofar as they are related to God: theology.[10] Harder to distinguish are the remits of theology and metaphysics, since the latter discipline does investigate how being and the other transcendentals flow forth from the divine first principle. Everything we've been discussing in this chapter so far would count as metaphysics, from Albert's point of view, not as theology. The difference is that theology is supposed to orient the practitioner to love and enjoy God as opposed to just understanding Him as a cause. Thus, Albert says that, for all the scientific insight Aristotle offered us when it comes to the created world, he has not given us what we need to achieve salvation. When we do theology, we approach even the created universe with a different and more exalted approach, one that aims at beatitude rather than worldly understanding.

Ultimately, and I do mean ultimately, the beatitude towards which theology strives is available only in the afterlife. After bodily death those who achieve salvation will get to see God "face to face," as it says in the Bible (1 Corinthians 13:12). Each of us is a mere shadowy image of God's light. But once beatified, as they used to say on the radio in the 1940s, the shadow knows. In the thirteenth century it was a matter of considerable controversy how exactly to understand such knowledge. As with the "from one only one" principle, church condemnation was brought to bear on the issue. In 1241 William of Auvergne, in his capacity as the bishop of Paris, required theologians to admit that the blessed souls see nothing less than God "in His very essence or substance (in sua essentia vel substantia)." Anyone who refused to admit this would be subject to excommunication.

But it's one thing to admit this and another to explain how it could be so. On the one hand, various respected authors could be found saying that God exceeds our grasp even in paradise. These included Augustine, whose authority was as unimpeachable as a man with a lethal fruit allergy. Yet, as we've been seeing throughout this chapter, anyone who has read some Aristotle and the Book of Causes can attain at least an incomplete understanding of God even in this life. What exactly is added to this when we behold Him in the afterlife? Albert's answer is to take seriously the idea that the knowledge of God available to the blessed is a kind of vision, one whose functioning is comparable to normal eyesight.[11] For Albert, when we see something, we do so by receiving a "species" from the viewed object. So here he agrees with the sort of view put forward by his nemesis Roger Bacon, which was rejected by Olivi and Kilwardby. Especially for Olivi, eyesight cannot take place by virtue of an image or species because we would then be perceiving a representation of something rather than the thing itself. For Albert, though, we perceive the thing through the representation when it arrives in the eye.

This is not quite how things work when we see God. Albert wrote about the issue throughout his career, beginning early on in the years just after William of Auvergne's 1241 condemnation. To make sense of the obligatory thesis that we do see God "face to face," Albert admitted that there is no species involved in seeing God. There is no representation that would serve as an intermediary between the soul and God, because no representation is needed. Albert quotes Bernard of Clairvaux on this point: "Why would it be necessary to have a ladder for someone already holding the sun?" Instead, we are talking here about a direct confrontation between the soul and God's "face," which, as William insisted, means the divine essence itself. Yet Albert also wants to preserve Augustine's claim that God's infinity transcends our mind. Characteristically, he makes use of an Aristotelian distinction, in this case the one between knowing that something is the case and what something is. The blessed will see that God is before them but not attain a full understanding of what God is in His essence.

Elements of Albert's solution will reappear in the treatment of the beatific vision we find in Albert's student, Thomas Aquinas. Both of them speak of a so-called "light of glory" which God infuses into the soul. Here we may think of the tradition of explaining human knowledge by appealing to divine illumination. Though this is associated more with figures like Grosseteste and Bonaventure than with Albert, he too gives a place to illumination in his epistemology.[12] We do not receive forms as direct emanations from God, or for that matter from a celestial intellect, as Avicenna claimed. Yet, as Bonaventure suggested, neither is abstraction of ideas from sensation sufficient. We need the light of divine truth to strengthen our minds if we are to achieve the scientific understanding to which Albert dedicated his life. The light of glory in heaven strengthens us further, allowing for a knowledge of God that would be impossible in this earthly life. Aquinas too explains the beatific vision in terms of a "light of glory," but draws on other philosophical resources to explain it, including some taken from the Arabic tradition. Something similar happens with his portrayal of theology itself. He agrees with Albert that it is a science, but finds a new way to integrate the theologian's endeavor into the Aristotelian hierarchy of knowledge.

36

THE OX HEARD ROUND THE WORLD
THOMAS AQUINAS

Albert the Great was a keen eyed observer of talent, as well as nature. His classes were attended by a young man of quiet disposition who was, shall we say, big-boned. The other students called him "dumb ox." But Albert was impressed and, so the story goes, remarked that this dumb ox would "one day produce such a bellowing that it will be heard throughout the world." And so it has proved. Thomas Aquinas would become the most famous medieval philosopher, to the point where he almost needs no introduction. In this chapter, I'm going to introduce him anyway, by looking at his life, his works, and his approach to the vexed question of how Aristotelian philosophy could be made compatible with Christian theology.

Like most of the thirteenth-century thinkers we've met, Aquinas plied his trade in a university setting and wrote (no doubt even thought) using the scholastic method. Born in the mid 1220s, he came from a wealthy family in Naples.[1] He was first educated at the Abbey of Monte Cassino. Bonus points if you remember that name: Monte Cassino was also the home of the recipient of Peter Damian's letter on restoring virginity, covered back in Chapter 6. Aquinas didn't need to have his virginity restored. A famous anecdote has his brothers seeking to dissuade him from signing up to the Dominican order and sending a prostitute to show young Thomas what he'd be missing out on. Aquinas simply chased her away. Like most students of the age, Aquinas was only a teenager when he began his university training, in his case at the University of Naples. He joined the Dominicans in the early 1240s over his family's creatively expressed objections and escaped from their influence when he moved to Paris in 1244. His further studies also brought him to Cologne, where he worked with Albert the Great, but it was in Paris that he became a master of theology in 1256, inaugurating the first of two stints there. At other times we find him working at Dominican priories in Orvieto, Rome, and back in Naples, before dying in 1274 while en route to a council at Lyons.

Given that he lived to be only about 50 years old, Aquinas' output was prodigious. His most famous work the *Summa theologiae* (hereafter cited as *ST*) is a sprawling text which remained unfinished at death but still contains three sizable sections, with the second subdivided into two parts. And it was only the third of three synoptic works that covered the whole of theology, the first being his commentary on the *Sentences* of Peter Lombard, written, as was standard, upon his taking up the post of master at Paris, the second being his *Summa contra gentiles*. There's some debate about what, if any, title Aquinas himself gave to that work and how it relates to the *Summa theologiae*.[2] The *contra gentiles* of the traditional title would mean *Against the Non-Christians* and it has been read as a manual for use in converting Muslims and Jews in Spain. But, if so, it seems odd that Aquinas devotes so much space to arguing for ideas Jews and Christians would readily have admitted, such as the existence of God.

Perhaps the *Summa contra gentiles* was rather an attempt to show how Christian belief can be placed on rational foundations, a project of at least as much interest for Aquinas' fellow Christians as for representatives of other faiths.[3] Only in the fourth and final book does Aquinas turn to aspects of the Christian religion that cannot be established by rational argument, like the doctrine of the Trinity. The work is also noteworthy in that it simply lays out arguments one after another, rather than using the "disputed question" structure of the more famous *Summa theologiae*. With this structure the *Summa theologiae* imitates classroom disputation, though in a streamlined or idealized fashion. Aquinas also held a number of actual disputed questions that have been recorded for posterity, with each question containing a large number of arguments for or against the various theses being considered. The *Summa* is different. It is divided into numerous "questions," each of which contains a number of "articles," and it is within the articles that the disputed question structure comes to the fore. Each article usually mentions only a small number of "objections," mostly drawn from authoritative sources, before citing another such source against these objections (introduced by *sed contra*: "on the other hand"). This is followed by a response in Aquinas' own name. Finally, he gives answers to the objections, to the extent that these are not already obvious from his response.

The cited authorities are carefully chosen. Aquinas uses them to show how Christian sources like Augustine, the Greek church fathers, and the Bible itself can be integrated with Aristotle and other philosophical sources like the Muslim thinkers Avicenna and Averroes and the Jewish Maimonides. Platonist sources are also important for Aquinas. He continues to use the *Book of Causes* even after realizing that it is based on Proclus rather than Aristotle, and is also powerfully influenced by the Pseudo-Dionysius. It's even been suggested that the whole *Summa* has a structure inspired by the Neoplatonic theme of "procession and return," beginning from God as the First Cause of all things and then following the path that leads back to Him through the virtues and the grace offered by Christ.[4] Alongside the three *summae* and his sets of disputed questions on topics like virtue, truth, and evil, we have Aquinas' commentaries on books of the Bible and on works of Christian and non-Christian Platonism, including two treatises by Boethius, the *Divine Names* of the Pseudo-Dionysius, and the *Book of Causes*. Finally, he followed his teacher Albert's example by writing several commentaries on Aristotle.

As this choice of subjects already suggests, Aquinas saw no unbridgeable chasm between reason and religion. Such a harmonizing view was, of course, as typically medieval as knights in shining armor and alarmingly low standards of sanitation. From rationalists like Abelard to mystically leaning Augustinians like Bonaventure we've found widespread agreement that Aristotle and other philosophers could be reconciled with the Christian faith. But Aquinas proposes a new way of conceptualizing this relationship. He clearly defines the difference between theology and philosophy, a methodological distinction that reflects the division between the theology and arts faculties within the universities. We see this in a commentary written during his first period in Paris and devoted to Boethius' *On the Trinity*.[5] It does not cover most of the text and, in fact, doesn't really reach the part about the Trinity, instead lavishing attention on Boethius' remarks concerning philosophical method. Aquinas' commentary explains Boethius' meaning line by line but then steps back to consider the issues at stake by raising a number of difficulties, which are handled using (what else?) the disputed question structure.

Already in the prologue to his commentary Aquinas points to a difference between the method of philosophy and that of theology. Where the philosopher begins with things in the created world and proceeds to God, the theologian goes the other way around. But the difference is more than direction of travel. The philosopher moves along the lower road of natural reason. He must base himself on what he can glean from the senses, since all natural reasoning must have recourse to experience of the physical world. Many, even most, of Aquinas' contemporaries would have said that even this sort of reasoning depends on an illumination from God. We've seen how Bonaventure among others thought such illumination was indispensable for the certainty of a philosophical demonstration. Aquinas disagrees. The "light of reason" is derived from God, but is given to us automatically when we are created as humans. For the most part, no further assistance is needed. The human intellect is itself active and can "illuminate" the images it derives from the senses so as to understand them. It is only when we try to understand such supernatural mysteries as the Trinity that an additional light must be added (*Commentary on Trin.* Prologue; Q1 a2 *sed contra*; Q1 a3 resp) (Q1 a1 resp.).

Not that God is entirely out of bounds for the philosopher. Several times Aquinas cites what may be his very favorite line from the Bible: "the invisible things of Him are clearly known from the creation of the world, being understood by the things that are made" (Romans 1:20). Aquinas takes this to indicate that the philosopher can indeed know God, but only indirectly. Natural reason approaches God as the cause of created things (Q1 a2 resp), rather than grasping Him in Himself, as we hope to do in the afterlife. The philosopher cannot offer demonstrations that divulge God's essence, if only because things are demonstrated on the basis of their causes, and God has no cause. The Trinity provides a good example. In Himself God is indeed three-in-one. But we can never come to know this naturally, because with our inborn resources we grasp God only as a cause, and it is the whole Godhead that creates things, not only one or the other divine person (Q1 a4 resp, Q32 a1 resp).

Nonetheless, philosophy can offer several services to religion (Q2 a3 resp.). It can help the Christian to refute false criticisms of religious doctrine, the task known as "apologetics." And it can offer a deeper understanding of something accepted on the basis of faith. It should be underlined that this does not mean *proving* the articles of faith. These are believed on a voluntary basis thanks to another, supernatural "light" infused within us by God during this life, which is what Aquinas understands faith to be (Q2 a2 resp, Q3 a1 resp). Rather, Aquinas has in mind the sort of procedure used by Augustine or Boethius, as when Augustine used philosophical tools to show us that the inner workings of our own mind give us some inkling of God's trinitarian nature. A final task for philosophy is establishing what Aquinas calls the "preambles" of faith, things that pave the way for religion but are accessible to natural reason. Among these none is more central than the very existence of God. Aquinas is adamant that even if the philosopher cannot demonstrate *what* God is, he can demonstrate *that* God is. In general we always understand *what* something is in light of its causes, but God has no cause; He can be grasped only by reasoning to Him from His effects (Q1 a2 ad obj 2).

For further light on all this we can do no better than to turn to the beginning of the *Summa theologiae*. As the title implies, this is nothing less than a comprehensive study of theology, and Aquinas begins by explaining the nature of his enterprise. Theology is a science in the Aristotelian sense. That is, it offers demonstrative proofs based on unshakable first principles. The difference between theology and other sciences is that the theologian's principles are not discoverable by unaided human reason. How, then, can theology be a science at all? In answer, Aquinas reminds us of a teaching found in Aristotle's *Posterior Analytics*: one science can take over as principles things established in another science. The study of optics might require the principle that parallel lines never meet, which is shown in the higher science of geometry. Likewise, the human science of theology takes its principle from a higher science, namely the self-understanding of God Himself and the understanding that the blessed have of Him in the afterlife (ST Q1 a2 resp).

Here it helps to know that the Latin word *scientia* is a bit more flexible than our word "science." Like Aristotle's Greek term *episteme*, it can mean a branch of knowledge, like optics or theology, but it can also mean "knowledge" or "understanding." Thus, it is natural for Aquinas to say that God's *scientia* provides the principles of the sacred *scientia* that is theology, the way that one human *scientia* grounds another by demonstrating its principles. Whether we are speaking English or Latin, though, we may worry that no article of faith could ever be the basis of a rational science. We typically assume today that faith is antithetical to reason. Faith is belief that one embraces on the basis of authority, or by a sheer act of will, or just because one was brought up in a religious family. It is, in other words, the sort of belief that involves the *absence* of rational justification.

In a sense Aquinas could agree. He admits that in this life, humans have no direct access to the certain truths that ground theology. Those truths are as certain as truth comes, since we are talking here about nothing less than God's own knowledge. The theologian is like the optician who doesn't understand geometry, who we might say takes it as "a matter of faith" that parallel lines won't meet in the end. Likewise, the theologian operates with perfectly certain principles, without himself understanding why they are certain. This is, of course, unlikely to satisfy the atheist, but Aquinas isn't talking to atheists: he's talking to fellow Christians, in fact to students of theology. We should bear this in mind as we turn to the next topic of the *Summa*, namely the existence of God. Aquinas told us in his commentary on Boethius that the philosopher can use natural reason to prove that God exists, though not to understand what God is. Thus, we might expect the proofs Aquinas offers here to be intended as knock-down demonstrations.

If so, we're apt to be disappointed. In a set of famous arguments, often called the "five ways," Aquinas describes five routes to establishing that God does in fact exist (ST Q2 a3 resp). These are some of the most thoroughly discussed arguments in the history of philosophy, and if all that discussion has shown anything, it is that the arguments need a lot of help if they are to be made watertight and convincing. For this reason I tend to sympathize with readers who see the five ways in the context of theology, as Aquinas understands theology. Remember that philosophy offers various services to the theologian. These include proving certain preliminary points, which could certainly include the existence of God. But philosophy can also help us to understand things we already accept on the basis of faith, and you can be sure that these would most definitely include the existence of God. So it may be better to think of the five ways as offering the theologians a set of rational approaches for thinking about God, even if they are also intended to work as proofs. This could help to explain their relative sketchiness and the various holes one can easily poke in the argumentation. As Aquinas scholar Rudi de Velde has put it:

> what [Aquinas] is saying is like this: although there are several objections to the assumption that God exists, which should be taken seriously, we Christians firmly hold...that God is existent. Now, granted that this is true, as we believe it is, let us then try with the help of arguments found in the philosophical tradition to show how the human mind may be led to an understanding of this truth.[6]

Yet it is also important that Aquinas thinks we can and should try to prove that God exists. It is not simply obvious or, as he puts it, "known through itself (*per se notum*)" that this is the case (Q2 a1). This is one of those places where Aquinas is signaling his departure from the mainstream. Most thirteenth-century thinkers followed Augustine, who held that it is simply incoherent to argue that God doesn't exist. A typical Augustinian argument to this effect was that God is truth, and it is self-defeating to deny that there is truth: to do so you'd have to say that it is true that there is no truth (Q2 a1 obj 3). This sort of reasoning had been used by Anselm, who was, of course, responsible for an even more famous attempt to show that God's existence simply cannot be denied. This was his ontological argument, which Aquinas interprets as trying to establish that God's existence is self-evident (Q2 a1 obj 2). For Aquinas the argument fails, because it concludes from what must be the case in our minds to what must be the case in external reality. Though Aquinas does put his finger on a feature of the argument that makes people uncomfortable, I don't think it is a good objection. After all, the whole point of the ontological argument is to move from our idea of God to God's real existence. Aquinas simply rules this out as an illegal kind of inference. This amounts to stipulating that the ontological argument doesn't work rather than pinpointing where exactly the flaw in Anselm's reasoning might be.

If God's existence is not self-evident, how should it be established? On the basis of sense perception, of course, since it is on the basis of the visible created world that the invisible must be known.[7] Each of the five ways duly takes its departure from a feature of the world of sense experience. Take the first of the ways. It argues that every motion depends on some cause which moves it. That mover might in turn be moved, as when I move a stick that moves a rock. But the chain of movers cannot go on forever, since without a first unmoved mover the chain of movers could never begin. Thus, there is a first mover which, Aquinas blithely adds, "everyone understands to be God." You see what I mean: the argument has more holes than the plot of a movie about the invention of Swiss cheese. How do we know that something can't move itself, as when I get up from the sofa to fetch a drink from the kitchen? And why isn't it possible to have a chain of moved causes, each of which is moved by the previous cause, into infinity?

Or take the third of the five ways, which is probably the most mystifying. Here Aquinas asks whether it could be the case that all things are merely possible or contingent. No, because a contingent thing can fail to exist. So, if all things are contingent, then at some point everything would have failed to exist. But that is absurd, because if everything had been non-existent in the past, then nothing would exist now. It follows that not everything is contingent. Instead, there must be a necessary being, and, again, this is what everyone understands to be God.[8] The argument looks almost painfully bad, especially the bit where he infers that if each thing could fail to exist, then at some point all things must fail to exist. Aquinas may be assuming as an unstated premise something called the "principle of plenitude": that every genuine possibility is realized at some point.[9] If it is genuinely possible for all things to be non-existent, as surely it is if each thing individually can be non-existent, then at some point this must happen.

As for why he might just assume the principle of plenitude without saying so, we might suppose he is depending on Aristotle's endorsement of the principle. Or perhaps he'd have us turn to Avicenna, whose own more elaborate proof of the necessary existent is lurking in the background. A similar game can be played with the first way. In that case we might seek answers in Aristotle, who is the inspiration for Aquinas' argument, or elsewhere in Aquinas, by looking to his theory of action to see why absolute self-motion is impossible.[10] Of course, we might also use our own ingenuity to improve the argument; plenty of Thomas' admirers have done so. But a more sensible reaction might be to assume that the student is familiar with these types of argument from studying their Aristotle and Avicenna and is just being reminded of several philosophical approaches to God that can be invoked in the rest of the *Summa*. To quote another Aquinas scholar, Brian Davies, "the purpose [of the five ways] is to set the ball rolling, not to bring the game to an end."[11]

37

EVERYBODY NEEDS SOME BODY
AQUINAS ON SOUL AND
KNOWLEDGE

I haven't actually checked and am not sure how to go about doing so, but I'd be willing to bet that there is as much scholarship devoted to Thomas Aquinas as to the rest of medieval philosophy put together. He's also the only medieval philosopher you're likely to study in a typical undergraduate philosophy degree. So I was rather surprised at what happened when I sought advice from several colleagues as to what I should cover in this book. I had a sketchy table of contents already, which included quite a few chapters devoted to various aspects of Aquinas' thought, much as I've done in previous volumes with figures like Plato, Aristotle, and Augustine. My expert advisors told me this was unnecessary and even misleading. The most exciting scholarship is nowadays being devoted to other thinkers like Scotus and John Buridan. And it would be a distortion to give so much attention to Aquinas, who was in many ways unrepresentative of medieval philosophy in general and the late thirteenth century in particular. Doing the history of philosophy without any gaps means dealing with many important thinkers who are not famous. With Aquinas, have we now reached a famous thinker who is not important?

As Bill Clinton might say, it depends what the meaning of the word "important" is. In the modern era Aquinas has attained unparalleled significance for the Catholic Church. His centrality was recognized in an encyclical in 1879 and reaffirmed by Pope John Paul II in 1998. Philosophers both Catholic and not have recognized him as a thinker with innovative and fruitful teachings on the relationship between reason and religion, legal and political philosophy, the theory of action, epistemology, and many more topics besides.[1] While his writings are not marked by the rhetorical elegance of a Plato or Augustine, they do have a wonderful clarity that invites philosophical reflection. His Latin is pretty easy too, which doesn't hurt. Still, there is a sense in which it is wrong to treat Aquinas as the *most* important medieval philosopher. The people of his time and in the generations following his death would have identified him as only one significant theologian among others, and certainly not as one whose opinions elicited universal agreement.

His was an age during which Augustinianism continued to be dominant, even in the Aristotle-steeped world of the universities. In comparison to figures like William of Auvergne, Grosseteste, Bonaventure, or Robert Kilwardby, Aquinas can be considered to be something of a radical Aristotelian. Some of his views attracted indignant, even uncomprehending reactions. Of course, Aquinas himself would have rejected the label of "radical Aristotelianism." Indeed, he attacked colleagues in Paris who were more radical still, the so-called "Latin Averroists" (see Chapter 42). The very heat of his invective against them may stem from his realization that he could all too easily be lumped in with these Averroists. Like a left-wing politician excoriating the excesses of Communists, Aquinas clashed with the Aristotelian extremists in hopes of emerging as a moderate.

For corroboration we need look no further than the 1277 condemnations of Paris. Unlike Kilwardby with his Oxford ban, the bishop of Paris Stephen Tempier does seem to have had Aquinas in his sights. The Dominicans leapt to the defense of their fellow friar and began building the case for his rather early canonization in 1323. There are other signs of his high standing in the eyes of his contemporaries, such as his prominent appearance alongside other theologians in Dante's *Paradiso*.

But if one wanted to name the thirteenth-century thinker whose ideas had most influence in the following century, then Duns Scotus, Henry of Ghent, or for that matter Albert the Great would be at least as plausible choices as Aquinas. His emergence as the indispensable thinker of the Middle Ages was gradual and owes something to Renaissance authors like John Cabrol, the fifteenth-century author of a work called *Defences of the Theology of Thomas Aquinas*, or later in the sixteenth century the great exponent of Aquinas, Cardinal Cajetan.

All of which leaves me in a quandary. On the one hand, I assume readers will want to learn about Aquinas, and I want to take advantage of the massive and sophisticated body of literature on his thought. On the other hand, I don't want to give him disproportionate coverage, for the reasons just mentioned. The solution I've hit on is to compare his views to those of other thirteenth-century thinkers. This will help to put him in context and allow us to discover how ideosyncratic his ideas really were. I'll begin with the area of Aquinas' thought where he was most out of step with his contemporaries: his views on human nature and knowledge. Happily, we're well prepared for this discussion by previous chapters. We've seen how prevalent it was to suppose that the human soul consists of numerous forms, and that many philosophers of the time made human knowledge depend on "illumination" from God. On both issues Aquinas would depart from the consensus.[2]

He's having none of these plural forms you'll find in other theories of soul; or rather, he's having only one of them. The functions of human life proceed from the single form that he identifies as the rational human soul. To some extent this is just good Aristotelianism, at least as far as Aquinas is concerned. Every substance has a single substantial form and each human soul plays that role for the human who possesses it. Many forms belonging to me would be accidental, like my baldness, my modest height, or my location in Munich. But my rational soul provides me with all the features and capacities that are essential to me as a human being. Proponents of form pluralism found it incredible that just one form could produce such a wide variety of effects. When you order pizza, it would be responsible for everything from moving your body to the front door when the delivery arrives, to calculating the tip, to digesting the pizza after it's been consumed, to making your heart continue beating, however much of a struggle that might be given all the pizza you've been eating lately. Aquinas thinks this pluralist objection confuses the need for many *forms* with the need for many *powers*. Just one form can bestow many capacities on a substance, so long as the substance has many different parts for exercising those capacities (*DQS* 11 ad obj 20). The presence of one and the same soul helps your heart to beat and your stomach to digest, because your heart and stomach are such different organs.

Like a reliable pizzeria, Aquinas' theory delivers what it promises, by securing the unity of the soul where form pluralism would give us only an aggregate or "heap" (*DQS* 11 resp). What we loosely refer to as lower "souls," responsible for things like digestion and sensation, are mere capacities within the single form that is the rational soul. Thus far he is endorsing the position that Kilwardby will condemn at Oxford. Aquinas wants to go further still, though. He insists that the soul is the only *substantial* form to be found in each human. It is predicated directly of prime matter, rather than coming on top of lower-level constituents that are themselves substances (*DQS* 9 resp). Thus, there would be no actual elements, like fire and earth, in the human body, because, if there were, the substantial forms of fire and earth would be present. And that would undermine the unity of the human substance.

While the claim is a bold one, it isn't quite as crazy as it may first seem. Though Aquinas does not want to admit that there are any further full-blown substances within each person, he is happy to admit that the human has *parts* like blood, bones, heart, and brain. Indeed, the soul itself is such a part (*ST* 1 Q75, a1). The distinction between "distinct part" and "distinct substance" may seem subtle, but for Aquinas it's crucial. Many scholastics believed that the soul is one substance and the body another substance. They liked this idea because it made obvious how the soul could survive the body's death, something expressed by the popular analogy of a pilot in a ship who can simply disembark and go on his way when the journey is at an end. But for Aquinas this is unacceptable, because the soul would have a merely accidental relation to the body (DQS resp 1). If the soul were a second substance in the bodily substance, some third intermediary principle would be needed to bind these two substances together (DQS resp 6), whereas it was supposed to be the soul itself that unifies the human.

Powerful though these considerations are, Aquinas' view faced more stiff opposition than the hero in a zombie movie. Bonaventure's student John Pecham was just one figure who insisted on form pluralism, condemning the Thomistic doctrine in 1284, a decade after Aquinas died. Another posthumous attack came from William de le Mare, whose Correction of Brother Thomas argued that a plurality of substantial forms could still constitute a unified soul if they worked together in a coordinated fashion. This critical treatise by William actually took aim at no fewer than 118 different teachings of Aquinas. Written in the late 1270s, it provoked a defense from Aquinas' fellow Dominicans, so that the debates over Aquinas' orthodoxy began within just a few years of his death.[3]

One area where Aquinas' theory has surprising implications is the development of the human embryo. Given that the Catholic Church is well known for insisting that a fully human life begins at conception, it's intriguing to find that the Church's most canonical thinker doesn't think anything of the sort. Instead, Aquinas believes that the presence of a rational soul requires the presence of organs that can carry out its functions. Since this is lacking at early stages of fetal development, only the lower nutritive or plant-like functions are present at first. They are succeeded by the functions of the sensory and motive powers and finally by the advent of the distinctively human rational soul. The lower functions also have a different source than the powers of reason. They are brought out of the material provided by the parents, whereas the rational soul can be given only by God and so is created directly in the embryo at some point during gestation. With the arrival of each new kind of soul the previous form is destroyed or "discarded," to be replaced with a new single and unified form, which, however, retains the powers available to the previous forms that were in the embryo (DQS 11 ad obj 1). As you might expect, scholarly ingenuity has been devoted to reconciling this teaching with that of the modern Church. The generation of a fetus is in some sense a continuous process, and at the very least Aquinas will want to say that the early embryo has the potential to become the human that will actually develop some weeks later. So there's some prospect of harmonizing the two positions or at least minimizing the tension between them.[4]

Everything we've seen so far can be understood as Aquinas' way of explaining the Aristotelian definition of soul as the form of the body. So seriously does he take this definition that he's now left with a serious problem: how can the soul be immortal? If the soul is not accidentally related to body as a pilot is related to a ship, but is the substantial form of that body, responsible for even such humble and obviously physical processes like digestion, how could it possibly still exist in a disembodied state? Aquinas comes dangerously close to denying that it can do so. He thinks the soul's condition after death is unnatural to it and that the soul will be unable to exercise many of its powers in that condition. In a way that's good news, since it gives him a sound basis for insisting on the need for eventual bodily resurrection, which is, of course, standard Christian doctrine. But he still needs to persuade us that the soul can somehow avoid vanishing between the moment of bodily death and the future time when it gets its body back.[5]

Here he points to Aristotle's claim that intellectual thought is a purely immaterial process requiring no bodily organ. Were it seated in an organ, the mind's processes would be particularized and thus unable to engage in general, universal thinking (DQS 14 resp, ST 1 Q75 a2). And if the mind can engage in its distinctive operation without using the body, then it can survive the death of the body.[6] But Aquinas seems to be trying to have his pizza and eat it too. On the one hand, my mind must act without my body in order to think universally. On the other hand, my mind is only *my* mind because it is a power of my soul, and my soul is only my soul because it is tied to my particular body (DQS 2 resp). This is a point on which Aquinas really needs to insist. Unlike some of the radical Aristotelians who were active in Paris around the same time, he absolutely rejects the proposal of Averroes that there is only one intellect for all of humankind, befitting the universality of intellective thinking. Instead, the mind borrows the individuality of the soul, which is in turn individual because it is the form of one individual body. This explains an obvious fact which Aquinas never tires of invoking against Averroes: when a person thinks, it is that person, and not anyone else, who is thinking (see further Chapter 42).

Furthermore, even if thought itself is an immaterial process, Aquinas insists that the body plays a vital role in human knowledge. He takes very seriously another remark of Aristotle's that thinking always requires a "phantasm" or imaginary representation (ST 1 Q85, a1, following Aristotle, On the Soul 3.7).[7] If you had never encountered pizza you would be unable to imagine or represent it to yourself, and that would mean, tragically, that you couldn't think about it at all. It may seem that thinking about pizza in general, picturing the pizza you are hoping to have later, and actually seeing and tasting a particular pizza are rather similar processes. But Aquinas thinks there is a big leap from seeing or imagining pizza to thinking about pizza. Non-human animals can do the former quite readily; just think of what a dog does when the scent of freshly delivered pizza reaches its nose. But animals can't think universally about pizzas or anything else, according to Aquinas. They are incapable of the immaterial grasp of an intelligible form freed from all particularity, particularity that is present even when you are imagining or remembering pizza, since you are then grasping one particular image, a process that, unlike intellection, does depend on the body.

How do we manage the trick of universal thought where other animals cannot? It's here that other thinkers like Bonaventure would invoke divine illumination. According to them it is our imperfect access to the exemplars in God's mind that lends perfect intelligibility and certainty to our highest thought processes. It's traditional to contrast that illumination theory, which has its roots in Augustine, with the hard-nosed Aristotelian empiricism of Aquinas. But Aquinas agrees with the illumination theory to some extent. He too thinks something further is needed in order to transform the particular images of sensation, imagination, and memory into the universal ideas present in our minds. This something extra is the agent intellect. Again he here takes issue with many of his predecessors, especially thinkers of the Islamic world like Avicenna, who postulated a single agent intellect that activates thinking in the individual minds of particular humans. No, says Aquinas: it is true that some principle is needed to confer actual intelligibility and universality on our representations of things, but that principle is within the human soul (DQS 15 resp, ST 1 Q79 a3). Each of us is created by God with our own agent intellect, a "natural light" that we carry within us and that we can use to illuminate the images of things we have encountered in the world around us.

From the point of view of his contemporaries, this could seem a rather feeble gesture in the direction of agreement with Augustine. Aquinas was duly subjected to further criticism, for instance by yet another Franciscan, a student of John Peckham's named Roger Marston.[8] He insisted that illumination was needed from outside the soul. The agent intellect is not a psychological power but nothing less than God Himself. From a more sympathetic point of view, though, Aquinas may seem to be striking a balance between the illumination theory and a more extreme form of empiricism. He thinks that humans are born with everything they need to think abstract, universal thoughts, yet denies that such thoughts require nothing more than the particular images we glean through sensation. As for the charge that he is cutting God out of the story of human knowledge, this is easy to rebut. After all, the natural light that dwells within each of us was given to us by God when He infused our rational souls into our developing bodies.[9]

We've now seen what Aquinas has to say about the metaphysics of soul and the process by which we achieve knowledge, and in Chapter 36 we discuss his attempt to situate naturally acquired knowledge within theology. What we haven't yet learned is this: why is it so important to have knowledge anyway? It's so important, Aquinas would say, that it is one reason we are given bodies in the first place. We won't be able to understand the role of knowledge in the good human life without talking more about that good life. And that will mean tackling the question of what Aquinas understands by happiness, which is for him, as for Aristotle, the central concept in ethics.

38

WHAT COMES NATURALLY
ETHICS IN ALBERT AND AQUINAS

Down through the ages, there haven't been many things upon which philosophers agreed. But nearly all of them have been willing to admit that Socrates was a pretty great guy. Seen as a paragon of virtue in antiquity, he was still admired in medieval times, especially by such boosters of classical philosophy as Peter Abelard. Nor was Socrates the only hero of pre-Christian times. There was Cato, who heroically killed himself when Julius Caesar destroyed the Roman Republic. Dante duly praised Cato in his *Convivio* and placed him among the saved in his *Divine Comedy*. Likewise, the fourteenth-century English thinker Robert Holcot allowed that Socrates was saved and given eternal life. These posthumous tributes show how difficult some medievals found it to accept that Christians had a monopoly on virtue. But from a theological point of view, this was rather inconvenient.[1] How did Socrates and Cato manage to be so virtuous given that they were pagans who lacked belief in the Christian God and lived too early to receive Christ's offer of grace?

Augustine's view on this matter was a strict one: though pagans may on occasion *seem* virtuous, their virtue is in fact false. For their actions, no matter how admirable they may seem, are not directed towards the true goodness of the Christian God. In his *City of God*, he argued at length that the courage, integrity, and justice displayed by famous Romans were grounded in the wrong motives. Even Cato's suicide was a prideful act, undertaken out of resentment against Caesar. Following Augustine's lead, medievals often distinguished the apparent wisdom and virtue of pagans from the real wisdom and virtue of the followers of Christ. John of Salisbury, himself quite a booster of ancient culture, qualified his praise of Socrates and other ancient philosophers with the remark "All reason fails without faith; only those who worship Christ are wise."[2]

Why would Augustine and his successors have taken such an extreme stance? One factor may have been the need to ward off Pelagianism, the view that humans can be saved without the need for grace, a view deemed heretical in the wake of Augustine's thunderous denunciations (see Chapter 3). If Socrates was genuinely virtuous without even being a Christian, then surely Pelagius would have been right to say that it is possible to merit salvation using nothing more than our natural resources. Yet one could admit the possibility of pagan virtue while avoiding Pelagianism. It is one thing to say that everyone will, if left to their own devices, sin at some point or other, another to say that no one can *ever* be truly virtuous on *any* occasion without God's help. So we need to seek a deeper explanation of the medieval denial of pagan virtue. The Augustinian position was not based on simple opposition to Pelagianism, but on the conviction that God is the source of all goods in human life and the ultimate goal of all good human action. This is why we see early medieval thinkers giving God at least part of the credit for every case of human virtue. In that indispensable textbook of the medieval universities, the *Sentences* of Peter Lombard, we read that "virtue is a good quality of mind...that God alone works (*operatur*) in us" (§2.27.1.1).

There's a parallel here to the Augustinian theory of knowledge. We've seen how medieval proponents of the "illumination" theory argued, again following Augustine, that God must be somehow involved every time a human achieves genuine understanding. Likewise, on the ethical front, divine help was needed if humans were to be capable of genuine goodness. It was often said that virtue is "infused" into the human by God, much as the mind is illuminated with knowledge by the divine light. A good example is Philip the Chancellor, whose ethical views we discussed in Chapter 26. He shows his Augustinian credentials by suggesting that all real virtues come from God. Natural "virtue" such as was possessed by the pagans would not be virtue in the true sense of the word.[3] Philip also calls this natural kind of moral excellence "political" virtue because it is expressed in our this-worldly life and in our dealings with other people, rather than having to do with our relationship to God. For Philip even the so-called "cardinal" virtues of courage, temperance, prudence, and justice have to be infused by God and not naturally acquired, if they are to be virtues in the true sense of the word. Meanwhile, the best examples of virtue are the so-called "theological" ones of faith, hope, and charity.

This position had the advantage of agreeing with Augustine and Peter Lombard, two of the pillars that supported early thirteenth-century scholasticism. But it had disadvantages too. For one thing, it seems frankly implausible. Are we really to believe that Socrates was not showing real courage when he unflinchingly drank the hemlock, that not a single decision reached by pagan judges had ever been truly just? For another thing, there was Aristotle. As we also saw in Chapter 26, it took a while for his *Nicomachean Ethics* to become available in a complete Latin version. Once it did, the medievals were confronted with Aristotle's lengthy and sophisticated explanation of how virtue is acquired through moral education, which leads to the cultivation of good habits.[4] How could his readers continue insisting that true virtue must be infused, and never acquired through natural means? It would be like discovering how your parents go about buying and wrapping your Christmas presents, yet stubbornly maintaining that the presents are really brought by Santa Claus.

Albert the Great was the first thirteenth-century thinker to engage seriously with the whole *Ethics*, teaching lectures on the basis of Robert Grosseteste's translation. He also composed another, shorter exegesis of Aristotle's *Ethics*, plus a free-standing work entitled *On the Good*. In these works Albert sought to reconcile Aristotle with the Augustinian moral worldview of his predecessors.[5] As if that wasn't tricky enough, he also had to reconcile tensions within Aristotle's own ethical teaching. Notoriously, the *Nicomachean Ethics* lavishes attention on the practical virtues, explaining that they are dispositions to choose the ideal mean between extremes, dispositions that we acquire through training and repetition. Yet in the final book Aristotle adds that pure contemplation is to be preferred to virtuous practical activity. Is he telling us to spend our time doing philosophy *in addition* to being practically virtuous? Or telling us to forget practical virtue if circumstances allow, and spend all our time contemplating?

As we've just seen in our examination of his metaphysics, Albert does think that humans achieve perfect happiness or "beatitude" through a kind of contemplation. It is a contemplation available to us in the afterlife, when the blessed will behold God "face to face." That is impossible in our current earthly life. But we can start working towards that goal in the here and now: like Santa, God knows who has been naughty or nice and he will reward the deserving. In this sense Albert's teaching conforms to what we've found in earlier medieval ethics. No less than Peter Lombard and Philip the Chancellor, he tells us to be good for goodness' sake. Perfect virtue requires that when we perform good actions, we are striving to reach the perfect good, which is God Himself. Albert here exploits an idea that was often emphasized in medieval guidelines for administering the sacrament of confession: whether an action is sinful or not, and to what extent, depends on its circumstances.[6] It may seem that helping old ladies across the street is always good. But if you help an old lady across the street because you want to impress the married person you are hoping to seduce, you aren't being virtuous. Likewise, our conception of life's ultimate end makes a difference to the goodness of our actions. If we just seek worldly virtue, that's less perfect than if we seek God.

Albert still admits that worldly virtue is a kind of happiness, even if it is a lesser one. Where Augustine said that only "false virtue" was available to the pagans of Rome, Albert thinks that even a pagan can become genuinely, if imperfectly virtuous. For pagans too can acquire the so-called "political" virtues through the process of habituation described by Aristotle. Furthermore, the happiness of contemplation can be achieved in this life. Such earthly contemplative happiness trumps the happiness of acquired political virtue, though it falls short of the perfect beatitude of the blessed in heaven. The upshot is that Albert's ethics envisions three possible degrees of human happiness, lying respectively in the life of practical virtue, the life of philosophical contemplation, and ultimately the beatific vision. The first two were already described by Aristotle in his *Ethics*, but the third is known only in Christian theology. Ideally, the lesser kinds of virtue and happiness are stages on the way to ultimate beatitude: acting virtuously towards our neighbors is a kind of preparation and stepping stone towards blessedness.

This nuanced theory, drawing together ideas from both Aristotle and the Augustinian tradition, was itself a preparation and stepping stone towards the more celebrated ethics of Thomas Aquinas. With Albert, he holds that our ultimate happiness can lie in the beatific vision alone. No created thing can satisfy the human will, because no matter how good a created thing may be, it is good only by participating in God's more perfect goodness (*ST* 1.2 Q2 a8 resp).[7] On this point Albert and Aquinas agree with their fellow Dominican Robert Kilwardby. He too emphasizes the difference between the mere "felicity" in this life and the full happiness or "beatitude" available in the afterlife.[8] But, as in other areas of his philosophy, Kilwardby leans more towards the traditional Augustinian teachings. For him all philosophical speculation is justified by its contribution to our moral development, whereas Albert, following Aristotle, made contemplation an end in itself, and one that surpasses the life of practical virtue. Characteristically, Aquinas splits the difference. He agrees with Albert that contemplative vision is our ultimate end, but adds the more Augustinian point that the vision of the divine essence involves not just knowledge of God, but also love, and the delight one has in beholding Him (*ST* 1.2 Q3 a4 resp).[9]

Yet Aquinas was keenly aware of the tensions between Aristotelian and Augustinian ethics, as is abundantly clear from a set of disputed questions that he devoted to the topic of the virtues.[10] His attempt to resolve those tensions begins with the very definition of virtue. He asks whether virtue is correctly defined as "a good quality of mind by which we live rightly, which no one misuses, and which God works in us without our help" (*DQV* 1 a2). This definition was offered by Peter Lombard as a summary of Augustine's teaching on virtue, and in the face of such authority Aquinas can hardly deny that it hits the mark. So he goes on to agree with the definition, adding just one apparently innocuous remark: the definition would still be accurate without the last phrase about God working virtue in us without our help. That part of the definition applies only to infused virtue, not to the kind of virtue we acquire by developing our natural capacity for goodness. Aquinas is not sliding into Pelagianism here. He would stoutly deny that natural virtue is enough to merit salvation and hence ultimate happiness. But the fact remains that virtuous acts can be performed, and virtuous character cultivated, with no special help from God.

When we speak of such "natural" virtue, we do not mean that a virtuous character is born in us by nature, as if babies came into the world already honest, courageous, and generous. Babies do, however, come into the world with a natural ability to acquire these traits (*DQV* 1 a8 resp). Acquiring them takes training and practice, which is why parents coach children to perform the right kind of action repeatedly until it becomes, as we might aptly put it, "second nature." Aquinas' explanation of this point is a wonderful example of his writing method. He is trying to steer a course between Augustine and Aristotle, and is honest enough to quote precisely the most awkward passages for his solution. Thus, he admits that Augustine seems to deny the possibility of natural virtue: "The life of all those without faith is sin ... wherever knowledge of the truth is lacking, there virtue is false even if one's behavior is excellent" (*DQV* 1 a9 obj 2).[11] Since Aquinas believes, following Aristotle, that we can indeed acquire virtue naturally through habituation, he has to defuse this quotation. He does so by replying tersely (and unconvincingly) that such Augustinian remarks were meant to apply only to the higher virtues that lead us to true beatitude.

In the next article Aquinas tacks back in the other direction. Now he asks whether virtue is *always* naturally acquired or can also be infused by God. Of course, he thinks it can be infused, despite evidence in Aristotle to the contrary (*DQV* 1 a10 obj 1). But it is too simple just to shrug and say that there are two kinds of virtue which arise in different ways. For one might wonder, if we can acquire some virtue naturally, why is this not enough? Why is divine infusion also needed? Aquinas poses the objection in the terms of traditional ancient ideas about virtue. Acquiring good dispositions means that our will is guided by sound rational judgment, rather than by the lower appetites for such things as pleasure and wealth (*DQV* 1 a10 obj 6). The catch is that there's more to the good life than eating moderately and being generous with your money. Nor is it enough to fight bravely for your country, be kind to your friends, and do all the other things that naturally virtuous pagans like Socrates or Cato were able to manage. Naturally acquired virtue is like the bus that takes you to the airport: it does get you somewhere, but not to your ultimate destination. In the journey of life, that destination is God, and it is the theological virtues of faith, hope, and charity that enable us to order our choices to that most final of ends. A higher virtue like charity does not supplant natural virtue. It rather *perfects* the limited virtues we can acquire through our natural resources.[12]

What could Aquinas say to a pagan, or atheist, who says they are happy to settle for a life of natural virtue? Simply that they cannot hope to be truly happy that way. We are born with not only a disposition to acquire earthly virtue but also a natural yearning that can be satisfied fully only by the supreme good which is God. Like the airport shuttle, human nature points beyond itself, having the built-in resources to pursue and attain limited good, but also the purpose and desire for unlimited good. It's no good objecting that we can know God even in this life, so that a taste of the supernatural is already available to us in the here and now. Remember, all our knowledge is grounded in sensation, and on that basis we can only reason to the existence of God, not to an understanding of what He is in His essence (ST 1.2 Q3 a6, a8). This may still seem to paint a rather rosy picture of naturally acquired morality. Aquinas doesn't seem to be coming anywhere close to Augustine's condemnation of pagan courage and justice as "false virtue." Yet Aquinas would add a more damning point of his own: on Aristotle's own conception a virtuous person is someone who has the habit of discerning and choosing the good. The well-behaved atheists and pagans aren't just falling short, but making a colossal error, one with moral and not just abstract philosophical implications. For they are failing to discern and choose God, the greatest and most perfect good of all.

One could still, with some justice, say that Albert and Aquinas frame Christian happiness in a rather Aristotelian way. For both, contemplation in this life is better than virtuous practical action,[13] and for both, the beatitude that some will attain in the next life centers on an even better sort of contemplation. The salvation we are promised through grace looks suspiciously like the theoretical activity celebrated in the last book of Aristotle's *Ethics*. Yet one can with equal justice say that Aquinas works Christian values into the fabric of Aristotelian ethics. A nice example is his handling of the virtue of courage.[14] He follows Aristotle in thinking of the courageous person as the one who can face danger, especially death, with steadfastness. But this is praiseworthy only if one faces danger for the right reason. His favorite example of courage is the strikingly Christian one of the martyr who endures torment and death for the sake of his faith in God, whereas for Aristotle the paradigm case was fighting bravely in war. This also helps to explain a feature of Aquinas' ethics that I haven't mentioned yet, which is that the virtues we can acquire naturally, like courage and justice, can *also* be infused by God. We might imagine God bestowing courage on a martyr who is faced by a gruesome death, without the martyr having had the long moral education needed to produce this virtuous character trait naturally.

The significance of the two alternative sources for virtue, natural and divine, may be clearer if we go back to the parallel I drew at the start of this chapter between morality and knowledge. It's a parallel that Aquinas draws too. He points out the similarity between thinking that all knowledge is granted by divine illumination and thinking that all virtue is infused by God (*DQV* 1 a8 resp). In both cases Aquinas moves away from the strict Augustinian position common in his day. Knowledge and virtue can both be acquired, with some difficulty, as the realization of naturally inborn capacities. But in neither case is it enough to have what comes naturally. Natural reason is enough for philosophy but not enough for theology; the life of natural virtue is better than nothing, yet infinitely inferior to true happiness. As we'll see in Chapter 39, the same pattern plays out in another area of his thought. With his famous and influential conception of natural law, Aquinas once again seeks to give credit to human nature where it is due.

39

WHAT PLEASES THE PRINCE
THE RULE OF LAW

The most famous thirteenth-century political document was not written by any philosopher. It is, of course, Magna Carta, forced upon King John by the English barons in the year 1215. Its influence has been far-reaching, its symbolic importance hard to overestimate. To give just one example, the American state of Massachusetts, where I grew up, adopted a seal in 1775 showing a man holding a sword in one hand and a copy of Magna Carta in the other.[1] Though many of its provisions are so dated as to be irrelevant to us today, people still point to its thirty-ninth chapter, which guarantees due process of law for all freemen. This is a hint at its philosophical significance, which lies above all in its attempt to constrain the king himself by requiring him to submit to the law. Nowadays, we take it for granted that our leaders are subject to the law, even if we can't take it for granted that they will always follow the law. In the medieval period, this was not so obvious. Kings naturally promoted an ideal of absolute sovereignty and saw themselves as the source of the law rather than as being subject to it. Yet they were rarely in the position to wield unfettered military and political power, with no concern for the consent of other political players within their kingdoms. Their supremacy was challenged on battlefields, in the drawing up of documents like Magna Carta, and in the writings of intellectuals.

As we know from our earlier discussion of Gratian and other legal theorists (Chapter 18), medieval ideas of law were inspired by the Roman tradition. When it came to the question of how law relates to political authority, the medievals turned to Ulpian's *Digest* of the law code gathered under the Emperor Justinian. There they could read that "what pleases the prince has the force of law" (§1.4.1), and also that "the prince is not bound by the law" (§1.3.31). These passages seem abundantly clear: a ruler's authority is expressed not just with the sword but through the authorship of legislation, and, as the author of the law, the ruler stands above it. But there are two kinds of people who can be trusted to find surprising interpretations of abundantly clear texts: medieval commentators and lawyers. So just imagine what was possible for medievals who wrote legal commentaries! One such author, active in the thirteenth century, went by the rather splendid name Accursius. He ingeniously suggested that when the *Digest* says "the prince is not bound by the law," this means simply that the prince has the freedom to revise old laws and make new ones.[2] In his actions, though, he is bound by the laws that are currently on the books.

This is not to say that legal theorists always sought to constrain the sovereignty of the ruler. Something else we know from our look at Gratian is that medieval legal ideas developed within two parallel spheres: church law and secular law. It is in the area of church law that we see the first dramatic moves in the direction of absolute sovereignty. This may seem surprising, but remember that the Church had its own power hierarchy, its own laws, and vast material wealth. At the top of that hierarchy there was a single figure, the Pope. Using terms first applied to Roman rulers, the Pope was said to be a "living law" or the one who holds "all laws within his breast." The early thirteenth-century canon lawyer Laurentius Hispanus waxed enthusiastic about the Pope's right to reconstitute law, with his will the sole source of legal legitimacy.[3] In principle a bad pope could be put on trial and deposed by other officeholders of the Church. Obviously, some remedy would be required if the papacy were held by someone with heretical views, for instance (a topic we'll take up again in Chapter 57). But in practice the popes were relatively unchallenged, to an extent that could only be envied by their secular counterparts.

Attitudes towards medieval kings and emperors were shaped not just by the Roman legal tradition, but also by the legacy of Germanic political affairs—where the monarch was sometimes actually appointed by the most powerful lords—and the feudal arrangements that arose in the earlier medieval period. This gave rise to the expectation that a king should consult with his nobles and represent their interests. To some extent this was a matter of sheer practicality. The king could not wage war or keep the peace without the cooperation of the men who could deliver the soldiers, and his coffers would be full only if wealth flowed up the feudal chain. Unpopular kings could find their freedom to rule curtailed, as John found out. There were intellectual justifications at play too. If the king was subject to the law, this was because the law is laid down for the sake of ensuring the "common good" of the community and the ruler should always be pursuing that good. The point was put nicely by another thirteenth-century legal author, an Englishman known as Bracton: "the law makes the king ... there is no king (*rex*) where will rules rather than law (*lex*)."[4]

The underlying idea here is that the king's legitimacy depends in part upon the goodness of his rule. When we think of medieval political affairs, the phrase "divine right of kings" frequently springs to mind. Indeed, kings did claim that they were selected to rule by God himself. But there is a flip side to this coin. If the earthly king rules at the pleasure of God, then perhaps it is really what pleases the divine King that has the force of law. The idea that the cosmos is providentially *governed* or *ruled* by God goes back to antiquity.[5] We may detect some survival of this idea in our modern talk of "natural laws," which hints at a legislator behind the regularities of the universe. And that may in turn put us in mind of one of the most famous political ideas of the thirteenth century: the natural law. In a work written jointly by the Parisian thinkers gathered around Alexander of Hales, one of the authors (probably John de la Rochelle) actually compares the natural law to the law of nature. A law of nature applies to all created things. To use an anachronistic example, this would be something like the law of gravity. By contrast the "natural law" is relevant only to rational creatures.[6]

This "natural law" could be seen as a test of political legitimacy: the ruler who governs in accordance with it is a true king; the one who does not is nothing but a despot who deserves to be deposed. But what exactly does it mean to speak of natural law? By far the most famous medieval treatment is that of Thomas Aquinas. Indeed, his name is so indelibly linked to natural law theory that you could be forgiven for thinking he invented it. But he didn't. It has ancient roots, and was already invoked by Gratian. He gave the example of the Golden Rule—"Do unto others as you would have them do unto you"—as a precept of the natural law, and thirteenth-century thinkers regularly give the same example. Authors like William of Auxerre gave the natural law a central role in ethics: all virtue stems from it because it disposes us to choose what is good. It underlies basic ethical rules, such as that one should not kill or steal, two evident implications of the Golden Rule.

In William we find a more controversial application of the natural law, one that will become increasingly resonant as debates unfold over the mendicants' vow of poverty.[7] He asks whether the private ownership of property is in accordance with the natural law or not. On the one hand, it would seem not: humans naturally look to that common or shared good which is also the goal of the good ruler. On the other hand, if we take seriously the idea that the natural law tells us not to steal, we must conclude that natural law recognizes right of ownership, since you can't steal what doesn't belong to anyone. His solution is that the natural law, just like humanly legislated or "positive" law, must adapt to circumstance. In a state of innocence there would indeed be common ownership. But one consequence of sin is the need to allow and defend private ownership. For fallen humans are so greedy and competitive that without this measure society would collapse into violence.

You may notice that the natural law seems to have a close connection to what the medievals called *synderesis* (Chapter 26). This is our inborn urge to want what is good, comparable to our modern-day notion of moral conscience. Neither this nor the concept of natural law can be found in Aristotle. But here's something else that should never be underestimated: the ability of Albert the Great and Thomas Aquinas to weave un-Aristotelian ideas together with ideas from Aristotle. In this case Albert proposed that *synderesis* can be seen as providing not so much an urge for what is good, as principles for practical reasoning.[8] In so doing he provided the background for Aquinas' celebrated treatment of law in his *Summa Theologiae*.[9] Like Albert, Aquinas appeals to the traditional idea of *synderesis* and gives it a rather intellectualist spin. It is simply our inborn tendency to accept the precepts of the natural law. The most fundamental precept of all is simply that one should do good and avoid evil (*ST* 2.1 Q94 a2 resp: *bonum est faciendum et prosequendum, et malum vitandum*). This is the underlying principle at work whenever we deliberate about practical affairs, whether in our own individual actions, in a family setting, or at the political level.

Of course, we face difficult choices and challenges in all these spheres. How far can such a general injunction take us? Suppose you're wondering whether your child is ready to be given an allowance, or how heavily to tax cigarettes, or whether to legalize euthanasia. In such situations being told to pursue the good and avoid the bad, or for that matter to do unto others as you'd have them do unto you, isn't particularly useful. And in fact, even though Aquinas suggests that we reason from the principles of natural law to specific practical decisions, he almost never spells out how that would work in practice. It may, therefore, be better to think of *synderesis* and the natural law as the source of our ability to reason about practical matters, and our tendency to go for whatever seems best, rather than as providing a set of rules to follow when we are deliberating.[10]

But why does Aquinas describe all this in terms of "law"? Why not talk of moral "conscience" instead, as did other thirteenth-century authors? The answer lies with Aquinas' ambitious undertaking to integrate the natural law within a whole legal theory. For him, law is defined as "a certain dictate of reason for the common good made by him who has the care of the community, and promulgated" (Q90 a4 resp). That's a bit of a mouthful, but each part of the definition seems reasonable enough. Laws have to do with rationality, since they serve as principles and reasons for action; laws have the goal of securing the good for the whole group, or "community," subject to them; laws derive from a legislator, the one who oversees that community; and a law must be made known to those subject to it, or "promulgated." In the case of the natural law the legislator is God Himself and it is promulgated when its precepts are implanted in each human mind (90 a4 obj 1). As the term "natural law" suggests, we have it from our very nature, getting it "for free" so to speak. This doesn't mean that people always adhere to the natural law, sadly, because humans do not always follow practical reasoning, as when they are overwhelmed by their irrational desires (Q94 a6 resp).

So that's why natural law qualifies as a type of "law." But it is only one of four kinds of law recognized by Aquinas. The supreme law is what he calls "eternal law," which is nothing but the principles by which God governs the whole universe. Eternal law touches all things, even if they are inanimate or irrational, not because things like stones or giraffes consciously try to put God's law into practice but because they fall within His providential oversight (Q93 a4 resp). The natural law exists only within us as rational creatures, being our way of participating in this most general, eternal law. Natural law is thus the "impression of the divine light" in us (Q91 a2 resp and repl obj 1). Fundamental though it is for our ability to reason about the good and bad, the natural law is still not enough. It is merely natural and cannot suffice to help us find our way to our ultimate, supernatural end. For this reason God also gave us the "divine law" in the form of revelation (Q91 a4 resp). In some cases this may even seem to trump or overturn the natural law, as when God commanded Abraham to kill his own son, an action that seems to fly in the face of all the dictates of practical reason (Q94 a5 repl obj 2).

Then, finally, there is the kind of law that normally springs to mind when we think of legal affairs: the laws passed by kings and other legislators. Aquinas calls this "human law." Again, we might wonder why it is needed. Can't we just apply our inborn ability to reason, relying on our tendency to follow the natural law? Unfortunately not. Human laws are laid down with a view to securing the benefit of a whole community, not just an individual. Again, law secures the common good of that community.[11] Human laws will differ from one community to another, because their circumstances are different (Q95 a2 repl obj 3). Though every community is working from the same ultimate starting points, they naturally reach different conclusions depending on their situation. If you are ruling a nation of gluttons, you might pass laws against fast food, which would be unnecessary in a community made up of more moderate eaters. Given that all humans have the lamentable tendency to sin as well as the tendency to seek out and choose the good, every community is going to need some laws that are compulsory (Q95 a1 repl obj 1). That's part of what makes a law a law, and not just a suggestion for best practice.

With all this Aquinas is doing as Aristotle had done before him, forging close links between ethics and politics. Political legislation is guided by the same principles that ground ethical deliberation, with human laws being simply a determination of the natural law as applied to the circumstances and needs of a given community.[12] Good human laws aim to bring all members of the community along towards virtue by preventing them from sinning and, more positively, by offering them enforced training (*disciplina*) in virtuous behavior (Q95 a1 resp). The reason we outlaw murder isn't simply to prevent people from getting killed, though that is surely part of the point. It's also to ensure that our community is full of people who would not even consider committing murder. Law does accomplish its objectives especially through the threat of punishment, but if all goes well, those who are subject to the law will internalize its values and cheerfully act in accordance with those values. When you go through life without murdering people, it's hopefully not because you're afraid you'll get caught, but because that's just not how you were brought up.

One might wonder how Aquinas can apply this analysis of human law to cases of unjust legislation. For once the answer is simple: he doesn't. An unjust law is strictly speaking no law at all, but simply a form of coercion (Q95 a4 resp; 95 a2 resp). Since it lacks a grounding in the natural law and fails to promote the common good, such a law lacks legitimacy. In one of the more inspiring cases of the perennial relevance of medieval philosophy, Martin Luther King Jr. appealed to this idea in his *Letter from a Birmingham Jail*. Speaking of segregation laws, he wrote: "An unjust law is a human law that is not rooted in eternal law and natural law. Any law that uplifts human personality is just. Any law that degrades human personality is unjust."[13] Of course, Aquinas' writings on law did not aim to incite readers to civil disobedience. When he considers the question of whether one should ever break the law, he focuses on good laws rather than bad ones and asks whether it could ever be right to break a good law. Yes, says Aquinas, but only in the case of an emergency (Q95 a6 resp). His example is that though the gates of a city should not be opened during a siege, you might break this rule to let a group of the city's defenders retreat back inside the walls. In less pressing circumstances one should seek to change the law instead of simply defying it. Furthermore, we should be reluctant to change laws, since that always comes with the cost of undermining custom and stability, even if the intended change is for the good (Q96 a2 resp).

Just as only just laws are truly laws, so for Aquinas the true ruler is the one who aims at the common good. This is the difference between the true king and a tyrant. At least, this is what it says in a treatise on political rule which was addressed to the king of Cyprus and is ascribed to Aquinas, though it is not clear how much of it is from his pen.[14] It does bear the hallmarks of his Aristotelian approach, justifying the state by appealing to the idea that humans are "political animals," and portraying democracy as a defective kind of government in which the lower class (in Greek, *demos*) is in charge of the state.[15] This treatise also seems to invoke something like the natural law when it tries to justify the whole concept of monarchy—as you would, if you were writing to the king of Cyprus. The author argues that, just as there is a single bee that rules each colony, so a single man should rule the state, as also the one God governs the universe.

There are some problems squaring these remarks with Aquinas' remarks about politics elsewhere. In the *Summa theologiae* (*ST* 2.1 Q105), he endorses Aristotle's support for a so-called "mixed" constitution, which he thinks can also be found in the Old Law of the Hebrew Bible. The mixed construction also bears some resemblance to the limited monarchy often seen in the medieval period, which is presumably no coincidence. Under this arrangement there is indeed a single ruler but his governance is mediated through other officers, for instance judges. The ruler could be anyone, and he adopts his special role as the representative of all the people, even as his power is shared out among subordinates. Aquinas proclaims that "A government of this kind is shared by all, both because all are eligible to govern, and because the rules are chosen by all." While this may sound as if Aquinas wants to constrain what could otherwise be unshackled regal authority, he does say that the prince is subject to the law not because it can compel him, but only in the sense that he should voluntarily follow it (*ST* 1.2, Q95 a5).

Despite that passage about the bees, for all his talk of natural law Aquinas does not usually make direct appeals to nature when he is talking about how we should arrange our practical affairs. A notorious exception is his remark that homosexuality is shown to be wrong by the fact that even non-human animals mate with the opposite sex (Q94 a3 repl obj 2).[16] Normally, though, Aquinas doesn't seem to think you can simply "read off" moral precepts from observations about the natural world. This has led to a controversy about how exactly he thinks the natural law works.[17] Is the idea that humans have certain natural and essential functions, from reproduction to contemplation, and that the natural law declares to be good anything that will promote these functions? Or is it simply that reasoning about the good is a natural, inborn tendency, and that Aquinas thinks that this establishes the universality and inevitability of such reasoning? Nowadays many moral philosophers are opposed to the whole notion of natural law, because it seems to imply that certain actions are good to us because they are "natural." This idea may seem sinister, given that it could be used and indeed has been used to forbid such things as homosexuality and contraception. It may also seem downright silly: is it wrong for me to travel by plane, since it is unnatural for humans to fly? On the alternative interpretation of Aquinas, none of these problems arises. The "natural" part of the natural law is just supposed to mean that part of being human is having a tendency to prefer, and use reason to pursue, the good.

It's hard to tell which interpretation is correct, in part because Aquinas is rather sparing in his examples of what does and does not immediately conflict with the natural law. The medievals did not invoke the natural law to solve tricky moral problems, but to explain deeply held and fairly basic attitudes that nearly all of us share. But then it's easy to draw controversial conclusions from uncontroversial starting points. Take, for instance, the topic of warfare. When he was itemizing the precepts of the natural law, the jurist Gratian included on his list the idea that "violence should be repelled with force." This looks like permission to wage war in self-defense—something most of us today would find reasonable enough. But we're talking about philosophy in medieval Christendom, and didn't Christ tell us to turn the other cheek? How, then, could Christian intellectuals give a rationale for the state's use of violence? Let's find out.

40

ONWARD CHRISTIAN SOLDIERS
JUST WAR THEORY

July 15, 1099, is a date that lives in infamy. It was on this day that the warriors of the First Crusade succeeded in their mission of wresting the Holy City of Jerusalem from the hands of the Muslims. What followed was slaughter on an almost unimaginable scale. Thousands of Muslims and Jews were put to the sword. Christian sources on the massacre state that ten thousand people were killed in the Temple of Solomon alone: "the slaughter was so great that our men waded in blood up to their ankles." You might say, what else would you expect? Medieval Christian knights were hardly going to show mercy to non-Christians. But consider another infamous date: April 12, 1204. In this climax to the shameful sequence of events known as the Fourth Crusade, Christian warriors who were supposed to be trying to recapture the Holy Land sacked the capital city of the Byzantine Empire. A three-day spasm of murder, rape, and destruction followed, from which this greatest of the medieval Christian cities would never really recover. Surely, though, the Latin Christians wouldn't do this sort of thing on their own territory? Sadly, they very much would. Only five years later, on July 22, 1209, the city of Béziers in southern France was sacked in the crusade against the Cathars. Not only the Cathar heretics sheltering inside, but the entire population of the city, were put to death. According to legend, the papal legate overseeing this horrific event instructed the soldiers, "Kill them all, for God will know His own."

Of course, medieval Christians had no monopoly on horrific cruelty in the name of religion, in that or any other period. But the Crusades seem somehow special because of their flagrant hypocrisy. We read in the Book of Matthew that Christ instructed his followers to "turn the other cheek" and for good measure stated that "all they who take the sword shall perish with the sword" (5:39, 26:52). How could the atrocities perpetrated by the Crusaders be justified within a Christian worldview? Well, obviously they couldn't, and in fact the sacking of Constantinople and massacre at Béziers were seen as shocking by many contemporary Christians. Yet there was widespread agreement among medieval Christians that the Crusades were morally justified, even obligatory. More generally, intellectuals of the period gave careful thought to the question of war. The pacifist sentiments of Christ notwith-standing, there were circumstances in which Christians could and indeed should take up arms. Despite the religious context, medieval discussions of "just war" can seem eerily familiar, as when we find them wondering whether the use of "ultimate weapons" can ever be justified (though they meant by this crossbows, not atomic bombs) or what legal conditions need to be satisfied before war can justly be declared.[1]

To justify war you first have the general problem of reconciling violence with biblical teachings. As the main character of the recent movie *Calvary* puts it: "The commandment 'thou shalt not kill' does not have an asterisk beside it, referring you to the bottom of the page, where there's a list of instances where it is okay to kill people." Some early Christian intellectuals were inclined to agree. The Latin church father Tertullian suggested that no Christian should engage in warfare, while the Greek father Origen said that believers should fight in good causes but only with prayer.[2] But the decisive influence for the medievals came, as so often, from Augustine, who argued forcefully that violence can often be justified. The important thing, to Augustine's mind, was the *intention* that leads one to engage in warfare or other violence. Though peace is our ultimate goal, even in the midst of war, we are permitted to break the peace temporarily in order to combat and to punish sin, to defend the faith with arms as well as words.

So the medievals generally assumed that war is sometimes justified. How, though, to determine exactly when and how wars can be fought justly? To answer this question they looked to the Roman legal tradition. Isidore of Seville summed up the legal standpoint on war as follows: "A war is just when, by a formal declaration, it is waged in order to regain what has been stolen or to repel the attack of the enemies."[3] This passage was quoted prominently in Gratian's *Decretum* (§2.23.2.1) and thus set the template for pretty much all medieval discussions of war. At the heart of Isidore's definition is the idea that you are always allowed, morally speaking, to defend yourself and your property. This is part of the natural law. Of course, this doesn't mean that whenever you or your property have been attacked, you should immediately retaliate with violence. If someone steals one of your books—even a particularly beloved book like this one you are reading—you shouldn't go over to their place and exact some vigilante justice. You should call the police.

So the medieval legal thinkers were hardly going to encourage people to take the law into their own hands. Violence in general and war in particular were justified as a last resort, to be used when legal measures could not be brought to bear. An obvious case would be an imminent physical assault on your person. In such a case you have permission to fight back, since there is no time to call in the proper authorities. Similarly, if a king's territory is invaded, he may legitimately unleash his armies to protect his realm. In either case the violence used against the aggressor is a substitute for the legal sanction that would be imposed if circumstances permitted. Legitimate violence by private citizens or the state has thus been called an "extraordinary legal process" by Frederick Russell, who quite literally wrote the book on medieval theories of war.[4]

In a real courtroom setting the punishment must fit the crime, and our legal authors likewise stressed that legitimate violence must be proportional. If someone slaps you in the face, you are not morally required to turn the other cheek, but that doesn't mean you're allowed to kill him. Sometimes what counts as "proportional" is not so easy to determine. If you're assaulted by an unarmed person and you have a weapon, can you use it? Even more difficult is to say how armies should conduct themselves in war.[5] As with the example of being slapped in the face, the fact that a war is justified doesn't mean that on the battlefield anything goes. The medievals' notions of acceptable military conduct were shaped by ideals of chivalry as well as by the legal tradition. So they worried about the use of powerful but ungallant weapons like crossbows, about the even more ungallant use of deception and ambushes, and about the common practice of despoiling captured cities. A confessional manual written by Johannes de Deo in the middle of the thirteenth century offered advice concerning these issues to soldiers who feared that they might fall into sin while on campaign.

A look through more theoretical literature would have been discouraging to such worried warriors. No less an authority than Peter Lombard judged that any soldier would be bound to sin, while the more optimistic Hugh of St. Cher said that the rare individual might manage to serve as a soldier with a clean conscience.[6] Yet theologians were sometimes remarkably permissive in their attitudes about conduct in war. Unsurprisingly, there was general agreement that heretics could justly be slain. Augustine himself had argued that charity towards sinners could sometimes involve killing them. More surprising is permission for unintentional killing of faithful Christians who might be mixed in with the heretics.[7] This isn't quite "Kill them all, for God will know His own," but a medieval knight probably wouldn't be able to tell the difference. Remember, though, Augustine's point that warfare is justified by the good intention of those who declare the war and fight it. If your aim is really to punish and prevent sin and to restore peace, that in itself should preclude many of the actions we would today call "war crimes."[8]

A soldier who took this point seriously was bound to wonder what he should do if he was called to serve in an unjust war. Could there be any such thing as a medieval conscientious objector? We may again be surprised to find that the answer is yes. The Dominican writer Roland of Cremona stated that soldiers who were being dragged into an obviously immoral military endeavor should refuse to participate.[9] Yet there was a powerful counterweight to this tendency, namely the medieval relation between vassal and lord. Since a vassal was sworn to give military service to his lord, any refusal to do so had grave moral as well as practical consequences. Furthermore, authorities like Augustine taught that war leaders had the moral responsibility for unjust wars, effectively absolving the front-line soldiers from the overall sinfulness of the conflict. The general advice to the medieval warrior was, then, just to follow orders.

All of this should make it clear that the medieval Church was not in the business of trying to stamp out warfare. But, of course, the Church went further than that. Bishops and popes sometimes encouraged and, in the case of the Crusades, actually launched wars. Here we arrive at another key question: on whose authority can war justly be waged? Clearly a medieval peasant was in no position to declare war, but plenty of feudal lords had knights and foot soldiers at their disposal. There were also those recognized as kings and, at the top of the secular power structure, the Holy Roman Emperor. In parallel to that structure was the Church, with the Pope playing a role analogous to the emperor's; again, we should recall that the Church had extensive landholdings and the ability to flex its own military muscle. In short, there were plenty of people who were in a position to start serious trouble. Who actually had the right to do so?

Different legal authors took different views on the matter. One of the most important commentators on Gratian's *Decretum*, an Italian canon lawyer named Huguccio, suggested that only a secular "prince" can wage war justly.[10] But just war requires rightful authority, and no medieval author could deny that there is one authority that outranks all others: God's. Hence all agreed that the wars fought at God's explicit command (as recorded, for instance, in the Old Testament) were thereby justified. From here it was only a short step to seeing the Pope as having legitimate authority to declare war, since the Pope is God's representative on earth. A war launched by the Church could even be seen as a version of the war of self-defense: it would quite literally be fought in defense of the faith. We can find this sequence of thought in Gratian and many of his followers. A particularly clear case was Hostensius, a canonist who was tireless in his efforts to justify the "supreme authority" of the Pope in such matters, something Russell memorably describes as "high theory in the service of low cunning."[11]

Hostensius and like-minded lawyers supplied the intellectual rationale for the Crusades, arguing that the Pope was entitled to incite them and also that he could offer genuine absolution of sins for those who took the cross. But how could this be squared with the idea that just wars need a just cause? The Crusades would seem to be a clear case of an unprovoked and offensive war, not a case of self-defense. One possible rationale was that Islam itself, as an apostate religion, was an attack on the Christian faith: reason enough to fight against Muslims wherever they might be found. But this was not the usual justification. Even Huguccio recognized that Islamic states could exercise legitimate sovereignty.[12] Instead, the *casus belli* or legal justification for war was that the Muslims were occupying the Holy Land, which Christians saw as rightfully theirs to control.

The upshot is that the Crusades were seen as satisfying all the standard medieval criteria for just war. It seems clear that they would thus have found approval with the medieval thinker most famous for his views on just war theory, Thomas Aquinas. I've been trying to show over the past several chapters that Aquinas needs to be understood within his historical and intellectual context, and this is never more true than when reading his remarks on warfare. His comments are famous and influential, but surprisingly brief. They take up a single question, with only four articles, in the *Summa theologiae* (ST 2.2 Q60). Nor is what he has to say very original; he's largely in agreement with the Augustinian legal tradition. One book on the topic goes so far as to say, "Aquinas' direct teaching on war is slight and unoriginal. Derived more or less wholesale from Augustine and Gratian, it is abstract and theoretical, and inspired by no personal emotion or thought."[13] But that's a bit harsh, because there are several ways in which his discussion is a milestone in just war theory.

Aquinas brings his characteristic clarity and nuance to the issue. He identifies three criteria by which wars are justified: they must be fought with legitimate authority, for a legitimate reason, and with the right intention (Q60 a1). This checklist could withstand philosophical scrutiny even today, and Aquinas makes interesting remarks about each item on the list. Regarding authority, he points out that the reason a private person cannot make war is that he can instead turn to a higher authority. This makes clear an assumption that underlies much of the medieval theory of war: figures like princes, emperors, and popes have the authority to declare war precisely *because* there is no legal authority above them to whom they might turn in order to settle disputes. On the issue of just cause, Aquinas connects the usual ideas about self-defense and rectification of injustice to Aristotelian political philosophy. Wars are just when they are waged to defend the "common good," the same goal rulers should have in view when they are making laws.[14]

Finally, there is the third criterion of good intention. It's here that Aquinas' most philosophically fruitful idea comes in. It's called the "doctrine of double effect." The classic text on this is found in his treatment of a question that we've seen to be closely related to the topic of just war: is it all right to kill an attacker in self-defense (ST 2.2 Q40 a7)?[15] Aquinas says yes, and reasons as follows. It may be that you use force against an attacker solely with the intention of protecting yourself and kill the attacker in the process. The fact that you didn't intend to kill him makes this case very different from one where you deliberately murder somebody. The difference is indeed so large that it excuses you from moral (as well as legal) blame. In general, we may be justified in performing actions even if they have unwelcome side effects, and the justification turns at least in part on the fact that we don't intend those side effects.

Aquinas doesn't say a lot about this, nor does he raise it in the context of discussing war, but the relevance is clear. In declaring a war, you pretty well guarantee that soldiers on both sides will be killed; yet you do not intend these deaths. In specific military situations, too, double effect comes into play. A much-discussed case is bombing an area with a civilian population in order to accomplish a legitimate military goal like destroying a weapons factory. You may be permitted to do so, despite predicting that you'll cause civilian deaths, because killing those civilians is not your goal but an inevitable and unwelcome side effect. Double effect is also frequently invoked in medical contexts. When a doctor amputates a limb, her goal is saving the patient's life, and even though it will obviously result in the loss of the limb, that is not the doctor's intention.

Persuasive though such cases are, the doctrine of double effect turns out to be very difficult to formulate and defend with total precision.[16] For starters, it may seem to give us far too much moral license. Couldn't I just excuse any horrendous consequence of my actions by saying that the consequence isn't one I intended? We wouldn't be very impressed if a government bombed an entire city in order to kill a single terrorist and then said that the massive loss of life was just a regrettable side effect. But this objection relies on a misunderstanding. Proponents of the doctrine of double effect, like medieval just war theorists, are careful to warn that our actions must be "proportionate." In that case, though, why do we need the idea of double effect at all? We could just say that a responsible agent should weigh up all the foreseeable consequences of her action, both welcome and unwelcome. If the action will produce, all things considered, the best outcome among all the things she could do in her situation, she should perform that action.

The response to this, I think, would be that the doctrine of double effect is designed for people who don't like to think this way. The idea that you can weigh up all the good and bad consequences, striving to get as beneficial a mix as possible, is characteristically utilitarian, a way of thinking that could in principle license you even to engage in torture and Crusade-style mass murder so long as the consequences are good enough. The double effect theorist is more likely to be someone who thinks that some kinds of action are simply never permitted, at least if they are chosen directly. Taking another person's life would be an obvious example: murder is a line you just shouldn't cross. The problem is that sometimes we find ourselves in tragic situations where the best available option involves crossing one of these lines, and the doctrine of double effect would explain why doing so is morally excusable. The unwanted result is not something you intended, but something you simply couldn't avoid. As Aquinas says, it is only "accidentally" related to the action you chose to perform (ST 1.2 Q20 a5).

This explanation of the motive for double effect helps explain why it has been so important in contemporary Catholic thought. Notably, the doctrine has been used to explain why even abortion opponents could approve of a life-saving operation on a pregnant woman that will incidentally lead to the death of the fetus. Obviously, this is a rather contentious example that I don't propose to discuss at greater length here. But I will mention that, even in less contentious cases, there are further objections for the doctrine to overcome. Why should our intentions make so much moral difference? Isn't the decisive thing, rather, what you can reasonably be expected to foresee as the result of what you do? Then, too, it seems that any action can be described in various ways. The historian says, "The Crusaders went on a mass killing spree, slaying Cathars and Christians alike," where the Crusaders themselves would say, "We eliminated heresy from the bosom of the community, and sadly a few devout Christians got killed in the process." From this perspective double effect looks like an invitation simply to justify your action by describing it in the best possible light.

PARIS WHEN IT SIZZLES
THE CONDEMNATIONS

G iven that you're still reading this book after forty chapters, you're presumably at least open to thinking that medieval philosophy might be interesting or, even better, thoroughly convinced that it is very interesting indeed. Sadly, not everyone agrees. Prejudice against it derives above all from the assumption that thinkers of this period were constrained by the iron shackles of theology. Any green shoots of genuine innovation or free thought would have been trampled by the Church before they could blossom, leaving us with a dreary succession of unoriginal scholastics. Of course, we know by now that this would at best be a crude exaggeration, since there were plenty of heated debates amongst the scholastics themselves, to say nothing of philosophy outside the university setting. Still, there were clearly restrictions on the freedom of thought in medieval Christendom.[1] In the twelfth century Peter Abelard ran into trouble for his theological teachings, as well as his love life. Around the turn of the thirteenth century the crusades in southern France against the Cathars showed just how far the Church was willing to go in its efforts to stamp out heterodoxy. Of course, that was not really a dispute over philosophical ideas, but it may have influenced the development of philosophy. The concept of the transcendentals may have developed in part to emphasize that all of creation is good, not an arena in which good and evil principles clash, as the Cathars believed.[2]

If we're looking for the effects of persecution and censorship on medieval philosophy, then one event in particular looms above all others: the condemnations issued at Paris by the city's bishop, Stephen Tempier, in 1270 and 1277. It was not the first intervention in the intellectual life of the university. Restrictions had been placed on the works of Aristotle earlier in the thirteenth century, though these were ultimately abandoned in favor of a curriculum based on a full range of Aristotelian writings. Tempier's condemnations were rather different. He enumerated specific condemned teachings, in 1270 a brief list of ten propositions and then in 1277 a much longer list with 219 articles.[3] In neither case was anyone explicitly named as having taught the condemned articles, though the 1277 articles were preceded by an introductory remark which complained that the errors on the list were being discussed in the arts faculty at the University of Paris. Also, two manuscripts of this longer list have notes in the margin that do name names. Both refer to a certain Boethius, who is not, of course, the famous thinker of late antiquity who wrote the *Consolation of Philosophy*, but Boethius of Dacia. One of the two notes also singles out Siger of Brabant. As we'll see, these figures are at the center of modern-day assessments of the condemnations.

Tempier was not alone in being alarmed by the activities of masters and students of arts in Paris. In the late 1260s Bonaventure had identified certain philosophical teachings as "heretical," singling out three in particular: determinism, the eternity of the universe, and, worst of all, the notion that all of humankind shares one single intellect.[4] In *The Seven Gifts of the Holy Spirit* Bonaventure compared these three doctrines to three beasts of the Apocalypse. In another treatise on the days of Creation, he added as a fourth heresy the idea that happiness is attainable in this life, and complained that some of his contemporaries were turning the wine of theology into water by mixing in pagan teachings.[5] His critique of the arts masters was echoed by the two leading Aristotelians of the time, Albert the Great and Thomas Aquinas. We have the record of a correspondence in which Albert was asked to pass judgment on thirteen propositions, ten of which are identical to the articles condemned in 1270. He duly explains why each of the suspect teachings is erroneous. In that same year Aquinas wrote a work attacking the idea named by Bonaventure as being particularly heinous, namely Averroes' view that we all share one single mind. Then, there is a treatise called *Errors of the Philosophers*, which is ascribed to Aquinas' student Giles of Rome, though its authenticity is doubted. It names and shames philosophical authorities, including many from the Islamic world, for their unacceptable doctrines. Aristotle too comes in for criticism. He is not to be blamed for failing to endorse the truths of faith, since these may have been beyond his ken, but for falsely asserting things contrary to the faith when reason should have enabled him to know better.

The theologians, it would seem, were presenting a united front against provocative philosophical ideas. Their apparent goal was to rein in the arts faculty, where heretical doctrines were at best being openly discussed in front of the young students, and at worst actually being endorsed on the authority of Aristotle. But the exact sources of the controversy at Paris have themselves been a matter of controversy among modern-day scholars. The standard line is that some of the arts masters were indeed willing to follow Aristotle and Averroes wherever they might lead. Siger of Brabant and Boethius of Dacia have been called "Latin Averroists" and "radical Aristotelians," notorious especially for their views on the intellect and the eternity of the universe. They are typically contrasted with Aquinas, who emerges as a moderate figure positioned between the intolerance of Stephen Tempier and the excessive rationalism of the Averroists. Aquinas, and Albert before him, sought to cure radical Aristotelianism with the antidote of less radical Aristotelianism. Albert claimed that the cause of the heretical teachings was in fact that some Parisians were ignorant of true philosophy, and deceived by sophistical arguments.[6] Similarly, Aquinas' treatise against the unity of the intellect did not content itself with showing the incompatibility of the theory with religion. He showed that Averroes' teaching conflicts with common sense and, above all, offered an unconvincing interpretation of Aristotle. So here we see Albert and his student Aquinas trying to rescue Aristotle from his overly fervent supporters.

Unfortunately, this version of the story is far too simple, and indeed subject to qualification on pretty much every detail. We'll see in Chapter 42 that the intellectual position of the so-called "Latin Averroists," and, indeed, the very idea that there was such a group, is a matter of fierce debate. As for Aquinas, you'd have to go to an advanced yoga class to find a more complicated position. His treatise on the unity of the intellect shows that he wanted to distance himself from the arts masters, albeit without going so far as to name his chief target, who was probably Siger of Brabant. Yet it seems likely that the condemnations targeted Aquinas along with the arts masters.[7] Though his teachings weren't included in the earlier 1270 list, perhaps because of his eminent standing in Paris, the far longer condemnation in 1277 does take aim at numerous ideas that can be associated with Aquinas, including his controversial position that each human has only a single substantial form. And that condemnation was issued on the third anniversary of Aquinas' death, which may not be a coincidence. Furthermore, in the days following the condemnation, Bishop Tempier pursued an inquiry against Aquinas' student Giles of Rome, who was accused of making unacceptable statements in his commentary on the *Sentences* of Peter Lombard. The result was that Giles was prevented from teaching theology at Paris.

Later witnesses were certainly under the impression that the 1277 condemnation was directed towards Aquinas as well as the arts masters. In his survey of Aquinas' errors William de la Mare eagerly pointed out that some of these errors already appeared on Tempier's list. Almost two decades after 1277 Aquinas' admirer Godfrey of Fontaines urged the sitting bishop of Paris to overturn Tempier's condemnation.[8] He pointed out that Tempier and his commission had been so sloppy that the list contains internal contradictions, and decried the way that it besmirched the excellent teachings of the great Aquinas. Godfrey did not get his wish, though. The condemnation stayed in force and was still invoked against much later figures, including Pico della Mirandola in the late fifteenth century and even Galileo in the early seventeenth century.[9] Since it had been issued on the authority of the bishop of Paris and not the Pope, there was some debate about its general application. Could its force "cross the sea" to affect teaching in England, for instance? Pico satirically added that if Tempier's authority couldn't reach across the English Channel, then neither could it reach over the Alps to apply to him in Italy.[10]

If there is debate about the exact target of the condemnations, it is also unclear exactly what effect it was intended to have. As I've already suggested, Tempier seems to have been outraged by the mere *discussion* of the heretical theses, whether or not anyone actually accepted them. He speaks in the prologue to the 1277 articles of the fact that the arts masters were discussing these propositions in class, as if there were any room for debate about them. He threatens not just the masters with excommunication but also any student who hears a master defending such theses and fails to report it.[11] After this dramatic opening we might be expecting that the condemned theses would involve rejecting core tenets of Christianity. That may be true in some cases, like the proposition that God only moves the cosmos rather than actually creating it (art. 25). But many of the issues seem rather obscure or technical. The condemnation forbids teaching or declaring that "forms are divided only through matter," and that the subject and object of knowledge are a single substance (art. 110 and 144). You'd have to be a well-trained scholastic to understand most of the theses, never mind believe them. Indeed Tempier was assisted by a commission of expert theologians, including Henry of Ghent (on whom, see Chapter 46).

This, along with Tempier's opening allusion to activities in the arts faculty, suggests that condemned articles were based on actual teaching sessions at Paris, perhaps the "reports" of disputations set down by students.[12] Individual articles often seem quite innocuous unless you understand the broader context in which the articles were discussed. Let's take the example just mentioned, the proposition that form is divided only through matter. The issue here is one familiar to us from our look at the twelfth-century thinker Gilbert of Poitiers (Chapter 16): how is it that each individual comes to be the particular individual that it is? We saw Gilbert struggling to explain this and considering a range of possible answers. In the thirteenth century, under the influence of Aristotle and thinkers from the Islamic world, like Avicenna and Ibn Gabirol, a consensus emerged. Each thing is made an individual by its matter. Thus, the four Marx Brothers are the same in form, essence, or species, because they are all humans. The reason they are distinct individuals is that they are made of four different parcels of matter, which is how it can be that Groucho is over here smoking a cigar while Harpo is over there chasing women, while Chico is betting on the horses.

All fine and good, but what if we are dealing with things that have no matter? There's no problem about God, since there is only one of Him. But what about angels? They are spiritual beings, yet supposedly quite numerous.[13] For much of the thirteenth century this posed no difficulty. It was widely agreed that even spiritual things have some kind of matter, which can be invoked to explain what differentiates one angel from another. But Aquinas questioned this consensus. For him all matter is spatially extended, so angels cannot be made of matter. How then does it happen that there is more than one angel? Following the logic of his metaphysical commitments with complete consistency, he assumed that each angel is unique in species. In other words each angel is a distinct type of thing: the difference between the angels Michael and Gabriel is like the difference between humans and horses. Of course, there are lots of humans and lots of horses, which is how there could be more than one Marx Brother and how there could be horse races for Chico to bet on. But this is because humans and horses are made of matter. In the case of angels, by contrast, each is quite literally one of a kind. Aquinas' position is apparently condemned in the 1277 list, which forbids the teaching that "God cannot multiply individuals of the same species without matter" (art. 42) and, as already mentioned, that form is divided only through matter (art. 110). I say "apparently," because Aquinas actually didn't take himself to be denying that God lacks the *ability* to make more than one angel of the same type. His point was that it is just incoherent to suppose that there are two distinct immaterial things of the same species. For God to make two angels that are the same in species would be like His creating a round square or dry water.

Let's finally turn to the most important question of all: never mind what the authors of the condemnations were hoping to achieve; what effect did they *actually* have? Did Tempier succeed in crushing the spirit of innovation at Paris and elsewhere, or did his actions achieve nothing, or even backfire, as so often happens with censorship? A case for the last option was mounted by the historian Pierre Duhem. He suggested that Tempier unwittingly helped to pave the way for the rise of modern science by condemning certain ideas of Aristotelian science that actually needed to be rejected if progress was to be made. While Duhem's version of this thesis is now usually seen as an oversimplification, there is still a plausible argument to be made in favor of his basic idea.[14]

The argument centers especially on the idea that God has the power to do things that are *naturally* impossible, even if He cannot bring about actual contradictions (art. 17). As the medievals would say, God has the "absolute power" to do anything whatsoever, as long as no inconsistency results. In particular, the condemnations require everyone to admit that God can create more than one universe (art. 27), and that He can move the vault of the heavens away from its present location by moving it in a straight line (art. 64). So what we're imagining here is that the spherical universe could be just one of several such universes, or that our universe is simply shifted, say, a mile to the left. As the latter proposition mentions, the offending philosophers who denied God's ability to move the cosmos had given a reason why it would be impossible. In order for Him to do this, or to create another cosmos, there would have to be empty space or void beyond our universe. Otherwise, there would be nowhere to put the second universe and nowhere for our universe to move when God shifts it.

Of course, Tempier and his commission were not claiming that God actually does these things. But they did believe—and were demanding that others admit—that God *could* do it if He wanted. This was a real blow against Aristotelian science, which was wholeheartedly committed to the impossibility of void. But it can also be taken as an unintentional blow in favor of scientific progress, since, of course, void is in fact possible. We find thinkers after 1277 accepting the possibility and even actual existence of void, and even mentioning the condemnation as they do so. But let's not act like the universe if it were shifted one mile to the left, and get carried away. Fourteenth-century thinkers were developing new ideas in physical science for a number of reasons, and they may have cited the condemnation just as a convenient support for views they would have developed anyway on the basis of independent considerations.

Leaving aside these specific issues of natural philosophy, what can we say about the effects of the condemnation more generally? There's little doubt that church authority was brought to bear against some specific thinkers. I've already mentioned Giles of Rome as a victim of persecution, and don't forget that Roger Bacon was even imprisoned for his teachings. Peter Olivi was another theologian who ran afoul of the Church. Of course, it's hardly news that thirteenth-century Europe was not a high point in the history of free speech. But 1277 marks something more specific: an institutional effort to thwart the pursuit of philosophy *independently* of theology. To quote Luca Bianchi, a scholar who has written extensively on the condemnations, "Tempier was not so much interested in distinguishing philosophy from theology, but in subordinating the one to the other."[15] If we think of philosophy as an autonomous discipline that should be allowed to follow reason wherever it leads, then philosophy does seem to have been hampered by the condemnations. This is shown by the fact that later arts masters like John Buridan will refuse even to discuss certain topics because they are the affair of the theologians and not the philosophers. His circumspection may have been inspired by the critical reception given to his predecessors in the arts faculty, the so-called "Latin Averroists."

MASTERS OF THE UNIVERSITY
"LATIN AVERROISTS"

" **A** foolish consistency," wrote Ralph Waldo Emerson, "is the hobgoblin of little minds." Yet perhaps no one is large-minded enough to speak and behave with complete consistency, whether foolish or not. Many people lead double lives that positively require them to engage in doublethink: the anarchist who makes her living as a policewoman, the marriage counsellor who cheats on his wife, the geology professor who is a biblical literalist on Sundays. Philosophers normally hold themselves to a higher standard, though. Any philosopher who is caught out maintaining two mutually contradictory propositions can be expected to give up on one or both of those propositions, not just out of embarrassment, but because consistency is a ground rule of proper reasoning. Least of all would we expect to find medieval schoolmen embracing inconsistency, having been trained in logic from a young age.

How strange then that modern scholarship has ascribed a rather flagrant version of doublethink to the most convinced rationalists of the late thirteenth century, Siger of Brabant, Boethius of Dacia, and whichever other masters of the Paris Arts Faculty followed their lead. Supposedly, Siger and Boethius endorsed a doctrine of "double truth." They thought that one and the same question might receive two true answers, one provided by the rational arguments of Aristotelian philosophy, the other by Christian faith. Aristotle has proved the world to be eternal; yet we know through faith that it was created in time and from nothing. Aristotle's greatest commentator, Averroes, has shown that there can be only one immaterial intellect for all humankind; yet Christian faith requires that we survive as distinct individuals after the death of our bodies. As arts masters, Siger and Boethius were effectively professional philosophers and couldn't easily retreat from doctrines that were proven in Aristotle and Averroes. Still, they were Christians, and unwilling to give up on the belief in creation or an individual afterlife. What solution could be more elegant than saying that both sides are correct, despite contradicting one another?

Contemporaries were apparently convinced that these so-called "Latin Averroists" or "radical Aristotelians" did embrace double truth. The prologue of the 1277 condemnations complains about members of the arts faculty who believed that some things "are true according to philosophy but not according to the Catholic faith, as if there were two contrary truths and as if the truth of Sacred Scripture were contradicted by the truth in the sayings of the accursed pagans."[1] Then, there's Thomas Aquinas. In a treatise attacking the views of certain unidentified masters he called "Averroists," he remarked that one such master—probably Siger of Brabant—"thinks that faith is of things whose contrary can be necessarily concluded," so that "faith is of the false and impossible" (§123).[2] But with all due respect to Aquinas, these are hardly unbiased sources. The idea of double truth was obviously useful as an accusation. But was it really advanced as a positive doctrine by either Siger or Boethius?

Nowadays scholars are unanimous in saying no. Double truth is deemed to be a figment of earlier interpreters' imagination.[3] But that doesn't mean that Siger and Boethius were untroubled by *apparent* contradictions between Aristotelian philosophy and Christian faith, to say nothing of the sanctions they might face if they openly embraced the former at the expense of the latter. It would seem that Siger in particular moderated his stance in response to Bishop Tempier's first condemnation.[4] Before 1270 he unabashedly embraced problematic doctrines on the strength of philosophical argumentation. After 1270 he didn't exactly give up on those doctrines but he did become increasingly cautious in talking about them. His writings contain regular warnings that he is merely reporting the views of the philosophers, not asserting them in his own right (*recitando*, not *asserendo*). Siger emphasizes that he himself accepts the teachings of faith, whatever the philosophical arguments might say.

Let's look at a specific example, the one highlighted by Aquinas in the treatise he wrote attacking so-called "Averroists." The Averroists include, as you would expect, Averroes himself. In his final and longest commentary on Aristotle's treatise *On the Soul* Averroes made the striking, not to say bizarre, claim that all humans share one single intellect. Bizarre or not, he had good reasons for saying this.[5] When both you and I understand something, we are understanding one and the same thing. If we've both taken a class on giraffe biology, we wouldn't expect you to have got your head around one nature of giraffe while I have come to grasp some other nature of giraffe. Rather, we should both know about the same nature. But, in that case, what could possibly differentiate your understanding about giraffes from mine?

I just said that you "got your head" around giraffes, but according to Aristotle and Averroes after him, your head has nothing to do with it. The intellect has no organ, and though you might use your brain to imagine giraffes competing in roller derby or remember giraffes you have known and loved, you do not use your brain or any other part of your body when you engage in genuinely intellectual understanding of giraffes. The mind that grasps the nature of giraffes has no special connection to your body, because its activity is purely immaterial. But, as we've seen throughout this book in various discussions of individuation, without a relationship to matter it would seem that there is no way for multiple things to be distinguished one from another. We are forced, then, to say that there is only one act of understanding that grasps the nature of giraffes. When you and I complete our course on giraffeology, we have both come to engage in this single act of understanding, the activity of a single mind. The reason that you and I enjoy the exquisite *experience* of knowing all about giraffes, where other people do not, is that our sensations and memories are being used as the basis for a universal act of understanding about giraffes. The universal intellect is getting no help from the giraffe ignoramuses, so they don't get to share in that experience.

I dare say you aren't convinced, and, if not, you're in good company. Aquinas found this whole theory to be about as plausible as a giraffe on roller skates. He opens his treatise on the unity of the intellect by saying that the Averroists clearly contradict the teaching of the faith by denying that we can live on after death as individually distinct souls (§2). He won't even bother insisting on this point, since it's so obvious.

Instead, he wants to show that the Averroists are also contradicting Aristotle. Despite his extensive and respectful use of Averroes' commentaries in other writings, here Aquinas condemns him as "not a Peripatetic but the perverter of Peripatetic philosophy" (§59). Of course, you don't need Aristotle to realize that the notion of a single shared intellect is absurd. For it is clear that an act of understanding belongs to one particular human and not all humans (§62). Still, it is worth explaining where the Averroists have gone wrong, just to make sure everyone understands that their doctrine is indeed a departure from true Aristotelianism.

Aquinas thinks the error is rooted in the way Averroes and his followers emphasize the mind's independence from the body. Once we see that the mind does somehow depend on the body, we have a good reason to say that your mind is different from mine, namely that it depends on your body and not my body. Now, Aquinas agrees with Averroes that the mind has no bodily organ (§26). This is stated clearly in Aristotle and, besides, Aquinas himself holds that we can keep using our minds after bodily death. However, the mind is only one power or capacity of a single soul, which is the form of the body, as Aristotle also says clearly. Aquinas accuses the Averroists of violating this teaching by making the intellect completely different from the human soul (§§7, 17, 63). For them it's as if we are beings with a soul and body who then occasionally get access to a free-floating mind, like many computers accessing the same online content or, as Aquinas less anachronistically says, many people somehow seeing through a single eye (§88).

The irony, as we know from previous chapters, is that it is not the Averroists but rather Aquinas who holds an unorthdox position on this score. Most thirteenth-century thinkers did believe that the highest part of the soul, the part responsible for the activities of intellect and will, is a separate power or substance distinct from any forms that are seated in the body. So, when Siger defended such a "pluralist" idea about the soul, he was simply agreeing with mainstream scholastic ideas. Of course, it was far less mainstream for him to press on, following in the wake of Averroes, and point out that in that case there will be nothing to differentiate one separate intellect from another. We just saw in Chapter 41 that one of the propositions condemned at Paris was that there cannot be many immaterial things of the same kind, like angels, and saw too that Aquinas himself could have been the target of this condemnation. He thought that each angel must be unique in species, since it would otherwise be impossible for one angel to be distinct from another.

So, when Siger started suggesting in the 1260s that Averroes' idea of a single intellect wasn't so crazy after all, he was himself being far from crazy. Siger was simply combining a standard idea about the nature of the human mind, namely that it is independent from body and distinct from any bodily form, with a principle that even Aquinas admitted, namely that anything with a truly immaterial nature must be unique. But Siger was hardly going to endorse these ideas publicly after the 1270 condemnation. Instead, his final discussion of the intellectual soul begins by insist-ing that he will be "seeking the mind of the philosophers in this matter rather than the truth." He does go on to explain the case for the Averroist theory, but also presents arguments in the other direction, and concludes by admitting that he is unsure how to resolve the issue.

Especially with that last admission of uncertainty, Siger might be responding to the condemnation and indeed to Aquinas' attack on him by adopting a less assertive position. He may have written these words at around the time of a 1272 statute adopted by all the arts masters in Paris in which they sought to distance themselves from the rationalism that so provoked the bishop and such theologians as Aquinas and Bonaventure. In the statute the arts masters officially declare that they will steer clear of issues that are, so to speak, "above their pay grade," because they fall under the purview of theology not philosophy. Furthermore, they promise to refute any philosophical teachings that might be in tension with the faith. It has been suggested that Siger and Boethius of Dacia may have been in full agreement with this statute. But, in fact, it seems unlikely that even the chastened Siger of the mid-1270s would have been entirely happy with the form of words used by the masters.[6] For he does not, unlike the statute, go so far as to speak of "false" philosophical teachings. Instead, Siger's considered view would seem to be that competent philosophical reasoning can lead to beliefs forbidden by faith. Though we should not be convinced by such reasoning, neither should we expect that we can find a flaw in the arguments. Rather, this is just a sign of our own limitations, limitations that affected even so great a thinker as Aristotle—who was himself only human, as Siger remarks.[7] One might say, then, that for Siger philosophy can, at least on some more difficult topics, reach only provisional results. These results need to be checked against and potentially corrected by faith, because philosophy is not always in a position to rectify itself.

This is subtly different from the attitude we find in the other so-called "Latin Averroist," Boethius of Dacia. To get the traditional reading out of the way first, we do not find any straightforward "twofold truth" theory in Boethius either. To the contrary, he staunchly upholds the ban on self-contradiction that is such a fundamental presupposition of Aristotelian logic.[8] What Boethius has to say about conflicts between philosophy and faith is inspired by a different aspect of logical theory: the autonomous activity of individual sciences. Aristotle occasionally remarks that a given argument or issue is or is not germane to a given science. When a mathematician thinks about triangles, he doesn't need to worry about the material from which triangular things are made, and it is not the job of the natural philosopher to consider abstract metaphysical issues. In Boethius' hands this idea licenses a strikingly autonomous conception of philosophy. The philosopher must proceed on the basis of natural reasoning and, insofar as we are doing philosophy, we shouldn't question the deliverances of this reasoning. In fact, we should even deny anything that conflicts with our scientific principles, for example that a dead person could return to life. But any arts master can also take off his philosopher hat and assume the role of a pious believer. With his Christian hat on he will readily admit that God can and does do things that could never be brought about by natural causes.

This line of thought emerges most clearly in Boethius' treatise on the eternity of the world, which clearly explains the Aristotelian case against an absolute creation of the universe from nothing.[9] Natural philosophy denies that any change can arise out of nothing, since change is always the realization of some preexisting capacity for change (42). Also, there can be no first motion, since every motion requires an antecedent motion to set it off (49). Of course, Christians know that it is indeed possible for motion to begin, and for change to come from nothing at all, as when God created the world. But divine creation is a supernatural act and thus beyond the ken of natural philosophy. As Boethius puts it, "Whatever the philosopher denies or concedes *as* natural philosopher, this he denies or concedes from natural causes and principles" (52). However nice it might be if we could show rationally that creation from nothing is possible, this sadly can't be done. It is foolish to insist on rational proof for things that can't be proven within the framework of natural science (36). Instead, the philosopher should content himself with explaining what can and cannot happen naturally, letting the theologian concern himself with what might be supernaturally possible for God.

Boethius' solution to the conflict between reason and faith does allow for the kind of doublethink mentioned at the beginning of this chapter. Consider the geologist who is also a strict creationist. She might say that she isn't really being inconsistent, but just taking two different points of view on the question of where the universe came from. During the week she pursues an answer using the tools of science, and on the weekend she accepts a wholly different explanation on the basis of faith. This may seem irrational; yet Boethius would say it is anything but. To the contrary, it makes space for the purely rational endeavor that is science. There is no conflict between reason and faith and, in fact, there cannot be such a conflict, since the philosopher readily admits that he is not speaking of what is the case "absolutely" but only of what follows from the principles of his science (52).[10] The implicit message is that the bishop of Paris and the theology faculty should back off and let the arts masters get on with their business of expounding Aristotle, an autonomous enterprise with its own ground rules. It poses no threat to the faith, since faith involves stepping outside or rising above the discipline of rational science.

Put this way, Boethius' proposal doesn't sound particularly shocking, and indeed it wasn't. Consider one remark he makes: "When someone puts aside rational arguments, he immediately ceases to be a philosopher; philosophy does not rest on revelations and miracles" (65). The sentiment may sound familiar, since we saw Albert the Great saying almost the exact same thing: "When I am discussing natural things, God's miracles are nothing to me" (Chapter 35). We can find anticipations of Boethius' strategy in even more mainstream thinkers of the earlier thirteenth century, like the Paris theologian Alexander of Hales. Writing well before the contentious debates of the 1270s, Alexander stated that "Those philosophers who wished to prove that the world always existed proceeded only from the principles of natural philosophy."[11] If Aristotle and his followers denied creation, they did not do so in absolute terms (*simpliciter*) but only because they were speaking as natural philosophers.

So why all the fuss? A division of labor between the theologian and the philosopher had seemed reasonable in Paris only a generation before. Now, in the 1270s, it is tendentiously being presented as an admission that reason and faith reach two contradictory truths, amidst accusations of error and heresy. To understand why, we need to distinguish between two groups of critics. On the one hand, there were men like Bonaventure and Bishop Tempier. They had no time for the subtle qualifications offered by Siger and Boethius. The caveats of the so-called "Averroists" may have been sincere, but the fact remained that they were teaching teenaged university students how to prove the eternity of the world and unicity of the human intellect. Like Socrates' jurors, the Parisian authorities saw this as an open-and-shut case of philosophy corrupting the youth. An aggravating circumstance could be added to the charge sheet. In Chapter 41, I mentioned in passing that Bonaventure complained about contemporaries who thought happiness can be achieved fully in this life. While this complaint might apply to Albert the Great and Aquinas, both of whom recognized a limited form of earthly happiness, it makes more sense as an attack on the so-called Averroists. Boethius wrote a work called *On the Supreme Good* which unhesitatingly takes the intellectual perfection of the philosophers to be the greatest aim of humankind.[12]

Very different, on the other hand, were the concerns of more philosophically minded critics of the arts masters, like Albert and above all Thomas Aquinas. Their worry was that the "Averroists" were bringing philosophy itself into disrepute. As you'll hopefully recall from Chapter 36, Aquinas had his own way of understanding the relationship between natural reason and theology. For him the two cooperate by making distinctive and valuable contributions to a unified body of demonstrative science. Human reason is augmented with the addition of new principles taken from revelation, but reason is never corrected or overridden by faith, as Boethius would have it. For Aquinas reason does exactly what Aristotle promised, establishing necessary conclusions on the basis of indubitable first principles. It would be a pretty poor necessary conclusion that comes with a footnote saying that it actually only holds when we are wearing our philosopher hats.

In a sense Aquinas' goal was the same as the one pursued by Siger and Boethius. All three sought to make space for pure rational inquiry within the institutional framework of the university. Siger and Boethius attempted to do so by carefully qualifying their philosophical claims. Siger, stung by the condemnations, framed his exegesis of Aristotle with warnings about the limited competence of human reason. Boethius admitted that natural reasoning can always be trumped once supernatural phenomena are taken into account. But these were rather precarious ways to secure an autonomous role for science. Much better would be to show that science establishes truly reliable conclusions, without having to worry that these conclusions can be shown to admit of exceptions or just be outright false from the standpoint of faith.[13] This was Aquinas' solution. He went so far as to integrate theology itself into a thoroughly Aristotelian picture of human knowledge, enthroning it as the new queen of sciences, which both draws from and contributes to rational inquiry. In this respect, Aquinas was a more radical Aristotelian than either Boethius or Siger.

43

THE NEVERENDING STORY
THE ETERNITY OF THE WORLD

We saw in Chapter 21 that medieval universities had a lot in common with today's universities. No wonder then that philosophers of the Middle Ages also had a lot in common with today's philosophers: a penchant for university intrigue, occasional despair over the behavior of their students, and an obsessive interest in particular philosophical issues. In some cases those issues are the same, as with philosophy of mind, free will, logic. In others the abiding concerns of the medievals have fallen out of fashion. One of those is the eternity of the universe. Immanuel Kant still took this problem seriously enough to discuss it in his *Critique of Pure Reason*, which poses an "antinomy of pure reason" concerning the infinity of time and space. Nowadays the advance of modern science has taken it pretty firmly off the agenda. How different things were in the thirteenth century, when it seems that every significant thinker felt obligated to address the issue. But isn't this rather strange? After all, these philosophers were confident that they knew the right answer to the question of whether the universe has always existed. No, it hasn't: it was created with a beginning in time by God. So why spend so much time debating the issue? Besides, not much seems to be at stake here. If God is infinitely powerful, then surely He could have decided to create an eternal world. If He decided to create a temporally finite universe instead, what philosophical significance could this possibly have?

Quite a bit as it turns out, and for two reasons. The first is that, if you were making a list of points where Aristotle disagreed with Christian doctrine, this would appear at the very top. In several works Aristotle made his belief in an eternal universe abundantly clear. In a painful irony, he even used it as a premise in proving the existence of God, arguing that an immaterial divine mover would be needed to cause an infinite motion. So it was difficult, though, as we'll see, not impossible, to deny that this represents a direct clash between Aristotelianism and Christianity. The second reason is that there is more here philosophically than meets the eye. Aristotle and many later philosophers had seen a firm link between eternity and necessity. For them something that always exists cannot fail to exist. So asking whether the universe has always existed could seem tantamount to asking whether it had to exist, in which case God had no choice but to create it. By the same reasoning, if you could prove that the universe is *not* eternal, that would prove that it did *not* have to exist. And this would seem to imply that some cause beyond the universe was responsible for creating it. The happy result would be that you could prove the existence of a creating God by demonstrating the impossibility of the world's eternity.

This helps to explain the proliferation of arguments for and against eternity among Latin Christian thinkers and among the Greek- and Arabic-writing philosophers who influenced them. Appropriately enough, faithful followers of this book series may have the feeling they've been reading about this problem forever. The neverending story goes back to late antiquity when John Philoponus insisted that Plato's *Timaeus* had to be read as denying the eternity of the world, a result much to his satisfaction, given that he was a Christian who believed that the universe is created.[1] Pagan Platonists like Proclus and Simplicius by contrast insisted that Plato could be read as agreeing with Aristotle. The dispute passed into the Islamic world, where some relevant works of Proclus and Philoponus were translated into Arabic. Here, there was still some interest in reconciling Plato with Aristotle, but the chief issue came to be the compatibility of Greek thought with Islam and Judaism.

In the Islamic sphere most philosophers and theologians rejected the eternity thesis, often on the basis that an eternal world would need no creator.[2] But the terms of the debate changed when Avicenna showed a way to affirm both the createdness and the eternity of the universe. He explained that if something is "contingent," that is, in its own right capable either of existing or of not existing, then it would need an external cause to make it exist. Contingent things will exist only if God, the Necessary Existent, renders them existent. Yet for Avicenna divine creation must be eternal, precisely because God is the Necessary Existent. He is necessary in all respects, so whatever He does He does necessarily, and that includes causing the universe to exist. This whole theory was subjected to a searching critique in al-Ghazālī's *Incoherence of Philosophers*, but that work was received into the Latin medieval tradition rather late. In another painful irony, the Latin Christians in fact saw "Algazel" as a staunch ally of Avicenna because he also wrote an exposition of Avicenna's ideas called the *Aims of the Philosophers*. It was translated into Latin much earlier and taken to be an expression of al-Ghazālī's own views, whereas it was in fact mere preparatory groundwork for the critique of Avicenna presented in his *Incoherence*.

Another influential text was the *Guide of the Perplexed* by the Jewish philosopher Maimonides. After a nuanced and balanced assessment of arguments for and against eternity Maimonides concluded that philosophy cannot decide the issue. The universe might be eternal or it might not. The only way we can know for sure would be if God were to reveal to us whether or not He created the world with a beginning in time, which is exactly what He has done in the Bible. In Latin Christendom the best known stance on eternity is (as so often) that of Thomas Aquinas. He takes over Maimonides' solution of declaring a draw between the rational arguments for and against an eternal world, with the contest settled only by faith. He even follows Maimonides' inspired, if not particularly persuasive attempt to show that Aristotle was not so convinced about eternity after all. Both of them refer to a passage from Aristotle's work on dialectical argumentation, the *Topics*, which mentions this as a particularly difficult and debated question. Aquinas and Maimonides take this as a hint that Aristotle knew the question could not be resolved with complete certainty.[3]

With these two moves borrowed from Maimonides, Aquinas sought to take some of the heat out of the eternity debate. Neither the proponents nor the opponents of eternity could prove their case, and Aristotle's authority would be preserved in the bargain. The whole question could be removed from philosophy's "to-do" list as one whose resolution falls outside the remit of reason. Aquinas saw himself as occupying the reasonable middle ground. On the one hand were more strident Aristotelians who thought that philosophy does provide knock-down arguments in favor of eternity. It was clear that at least the Muslim thinkers Avicenna and Averroes fell into this category, even if Aristotle himself didn't. On the other hand, there were fellow Christians who were equally convinced they could prove that the world has existed for only a limited time.

A good example of the latter approach can be found in Aquinas' fellow theologian at Paris, Bonaventure. In yet another irony—that's three so far, if you're keeping track—Bonaventure shows more confidence in the power of reason to settle the issue than the supposedly far more rationalist Aquinas. In several of his writings, including his commentary on the *Sentences*, he argues that an eternal universe is impossible.[4] Obviously, he does not want to suggest that God has insufficient power to create such a universe. Rather, the problem is on the side of created things. His central idea is simply to reject Avicenna's supposed insight that something could be both created and eternal. For Bonaventure this is just a contradiction in terms. Creation means bringing something to be "from nothing (*ex nihilo*)." If God genuinely creates something, then it must be preceded by nothingness. Bonaventure assumes that the philosophers who believed in eternity were not so stupid as to miss this point. Their mistake was falsely supposing that God performs His works the way a created cause would by bringing things to be from preexisting matter or potentiality, like a carpenter who makes things out of wood, or fire which transforms fuel into flames. On this misconception the universe would at least have to come from eternally preexistent matter, if not actually being eternal in the finished form that we see.

To this core idea Bonaventure adds a battery of further arguments. For one thing, he thinks that an infinite period of time cannot already have elapsed so as to reach the current instant. For another, even the Aristotelians would admit that it is impossible for an infinity of things to exist actually and all at the same time. But this is exactly what would happen if the universe were eternal. Just consider the souls of all the humans who have lived. If there have always been humans and if human souls survive death, by now we would have gotten to an infinite number of souls. Bonaventure connects this point to that other central dispute concerning philosophy in the 1260s and 1270s, the unicity of the intellect. As we've just seen, there was intense debate in the late thirteenth century over Averroes' claim that all humans share only one single mind. Bonaventure observes that if this were true, Averroes could avoid admitting that there is an infinity of souls. There would only be one eternal mind for the whole human race rather than an infinity of rational souls continuing to exist after the deaths of their bodies. The two heretical doctrines of an eternal world and single intellect are thus the Hansel and Gretel of Averroism: they go astray hand in hand.

If you're in the mood for one more irony, you'll be glad to hear that consideration of the human species could also be used to argue in favor of the eternity of the universe. The point here has nothing to do with the survival of souls, but the question of where humans come from. I won't get into the messy details here but will go so far as to remind you that people are generated by other people (see further Chapter 73). Or, as Aristotle put it in one of his pithier lines, "man comes from man and the sun" (*Physics* 194b13). But if each human has been generated by another human, there must be an endless string of humans all the way back into the past, so the world must be eternal. This argument appears in a treatise about the eternity of the world ascribed to Siger of Brabant.[5] Believe it or not, Siger actually raises the example of which comes first, the chicken or the egg. His answer is that every egg is preceded by a chicken, to infinity. About time we got an answer to that question.

Siger does not make so bold as to claim that the universe really is eternal. He contents himself with presenting the argument and then saying, in one of those remarks that so infuriated his contemporaries and so intrigues modern-day scholars, that he is simply presenting the opinion of Aristotle without endorsing it. Still, the treatise was sufficiently provocative that Henry of Ghent took up the argument in one of his disputed questions. He raised the possibility that there could be disastrous, cataclysmic events after which species might need to be "restarted," as it were. If all the chickens are wiped out in a flood, then we'll need to get some new eggs somewhere. The solution could lie in spontaneous generation, which for Aristotle and the medievals was a genuine phenomenon. But there's a problem, as Henry points out. Aristotle accepted that you can get things like flies and worms from mud or rotting flesh, but denied that more complex, so-called "perfect" animals can arise in this way.

Avicenna was notorious for claiming that even humans can generate spontaneously, at least in theory, but few medieval thinkers agreed with him. In fact, this was another of the propositions condemned in 1277. So we are not going to escape the need for an infinite series of humans by supposing that humans can be spontaneously generated. Besides, Henry adds, even if this were possible, the resulting infant would die from lack of care if no other humans were around. Of course, he doesn't draw the conclusion that there have always been humans. We're talking about a key member of the commission that drew up that 1277 condemnation, which also included the thesis that the universe is eternal. Instead, Henry says that God directly created the first members of each species among the higher animals. Their seed became the basis for all subsequent members of the species. If you want an omelet, you have to break a few eggs, but if you want an egg, God first has to create a chicken.

Many of these same arguments reappear in Aquinas' various discussions of the eternity question. In addition to a short treatise devoted specifically to the problem, he takes it up in both the *Summa theologiae* and *Summa contra gentiles*, as well as a set of disputed questions he wrote on the power of God.[6] Throughout, he consistently adheres to the position I already described. Arguments for and against eternity are listed but always found to fall short of providing real proof, though Aquinas allows that the arguments against eternity tend to be more persuasive. But he doesn't just point out the flaws in the various arguments. He shifts the terms of the debate, focusing on the question of whether *any* created universe could be eternal rather than the question of whether *this* universe we actually live in is eternal. This is well illustrated by his reaction to the infinite souls argument that so excited Bonaventure. Aquinas effectively dismisses it as irrelevant. He observes that God could have created a universe with no humans at all (*Aet.* §12). The prospect of infinite human souls is no obstacle to God's creating an eternal world if it is in His power to create a world that has no souls in the first place.

What about Bonaventure's more central claim that if God is to be a genuine creator, He must create "out of nothing" and therefore with a first moment in time? Never one to pass up an opportunity to make a crucial distinction, Aquinas points out that the phrase "out of nothing" is ambiguous. It could mean, as Bonaventure wanted, "from a situation where there was nothing." But it could also just mean "not from something (*non ex aliquo*)," in the sense that God needed no matter to form a world, in other words nothing whose potential for being a universe needed to be realized (*ST* 1 Q46 a1 repl obj 6). Aquinas even goes so far as to cite Avicenna for the idea that eternal creation could be "from nothing" in this sense.[7] He would also agree with Avicenna that when philosophers establish God as a principle who "comes before" all other things, the priority in question has to do with causation and not time. God is "before" the world because it depends on Him, not because He existed before the world did (*Aet.* §7). Aquinas is surprisingly sarcastic about Bonaventure's view. He remarks that some of his contemporaries have been amazingly sharp-eyed, able to spot an inconsistency between createdness and eternity when even Augustine was unable to do so (*Aet.* §8–9). He also points out that if God really could have created an eternal world, those who say otherwise are unintentionally disparaging His infinite power (*Aet.* §3).

While Aquinas is especially severe in his rhetoric against Bonaventure and like-minded Christian theologians,[8] he does also expose the flaws in philosophical arguments for eternity, including arguments found in Aristotle. One of the most prominent of these had been an appeal to the nature of the heavens. The heavens are, according to Aristotelian cosmology, made of indestructible stuff, the so-called "fifth element." And many philosophers thought that if something cannot be destroyed, then neither can it be generated. Aquinas retains as much as he can of the Aristotelian view by saying that the heavens are indeed immune to change, though they depend on God for their very existence. Their permanent, unvarying nature presupposes that God has already brought them to be and given them that very nature. Incidentally, Aquinas' teacher Albert the Great found a nifty way to press Aristotle's ideas about the fifth element into the service of creationism. Since the heavens are indeed incapable of being generated naturally, Albert says, they can only have come into existence by being created supernaturally![9]

Aquinas' overall strategy obviously seeks to eliminate any direct clash between philosophy and Christian teaching. But there is a further insight underlying his position. He follows Boethius (the late ancient one, not Boethius of Dacia) in holding that God alone is eternal in the special sense of being *timeless*. This means that an eternally created world would still fall short of God's sort of atemporal eternity (*Aet.* §10; *ST* I Q46 a2 repl obj 5).[10] What makes the created world non-divine is not, in other words, the fact that it has only been around for a certain amount of time. It is that it is subject to time at all, and, of course, that it is dependent on God for its very existence. Neither of these features requires the past existence of the universe to be finite. Again, this tends to take the heat out of the debate. Whether the universe has always existed or not, its temporal existence shows its inferiority to the timeless God who created it.[11]

Given the bitterness with which Aquinas attacked his more radical Aristotelian contemporaries, and the fact that Boethius of Dacia is thought to belong to this group, it's a bit of a shock to read Boethius' own treatise on the eternity of the world.[12] We asked in Chapter 42 whether this text shows Boethius adopting a "double truth" theory, and decided the answer is no. Now we can see that Boethius' position is in fact very close to that of Aquinas. He insists that the natural philosopher cannot pronounce with any finality on the question at hand, precisely because this philosopher does not reckon with supernatural causes. Boethius' handling of individual arguments also recalls Aquinas' treatment of those same arguments. He too gives short shrift to Bonaventure's idea that genuine creation must mean bringing something to be *after* it was nothing, and likewise comments that the heavens' immunity to generation and destruction has to do only with natural causation. Boethius even cites that passage from the *Topics* to prove that Aristotle considered the eternity question too difficult to resolve with any certainty.

This is another nail in the coffin of any straightforward contrast between Aquinas and the so-called "Latin Averroists." We've seen that Aquinas had real disagreements with Boethius and Siger but also had more in common with them than he would gladly have admitted. He shared their admiration for Aristotelian science, and in a sense he was more staunch in its defense. Unlike them he refused to admit that proper philosophical reason can *ever* lead to incorrect conclusions. Nonetheless, he agreed with Siger that human reason has its limitations. Better to admit that an issue cannot be settled rationally than to admit an irreconcilable clash between philosophy and Christian doctrine. And with good reason: in the thirteenth century, if Aristotle was seen to be contending against religion, there was only going to be one winner.

44

LET ME COUNT THE WAYS
SPECULATIVE GRAMMAR

Some ideas seem so appealing, so obvious, that they appear again and again throughout the history of philosophy. One of them is that language corresponds to the world. From Parmenides, who banned non-being from his metaphysics because it cannot be spoken, to Wittgenstein, whose *Tractatus Logico-Philosophicus* proposes that propositions are like pictures that "show" reality, it seems that philosophers have never stopped trying to understand how this correspondence might work. And for good reason. A true sentence is one that describes things as they really are. Thus, if we want to understand reality—and we're philosophers, so, of course, we want to do that—an obvious way to make progress would be to analyze language. The fact that language accurately represents the world suggests that the parts and structures of language somehow mirror the parts and structures of reality.

Consider a sentence like "The giraffe roller-skates." If this is true, it seems irresistible to think that the world is arranged in much the way the sentence is. You have a concrete entity, the medievals would say a "substance," namely the giraffe, and you have the action the giraffe is performing, namely roller-skating. The grammatical contrast between subject and verb parallels the metaphysical contrast between the substance and the action. On the other hand, there also seem to be features of language that don't hook up with reality so well. What would be the real things that correspond to words like "if" and "not," to say nothing of phrases like "my non-existent sister"? In light of this we might decide that language's purchase on reality is somewhat more tenuous or at least more complicated.

If you want to know just how complicated, you can do no better than to read discussions of language produced by university masters towards the end of the thirteenth century. This was the heyday of what is called "speculative grammar." It may seem odd that philosophical questions would be raised in the context of doing grammar. Chances are that you haven't been asked to think much about grammar since you were a child, and that was the usual medieval practice too. The word comes from the Greek *grammata*, meaning "letters." Studying grammar was at first quite literally a matter of "learning your letters," that is, learning to read. (This is why the late antique pagan philosopher Simplicius chose to insult his rival John Philoponus by calling him "the grammarian"; he was effectively calling him a mere schoolmaster.[1]) But already in antiquity it came to include more sophisticated discussions of language. In a medieval setting grammar was one of the three disciplines of the trivium, along with rhetoric and logic ("dialectic"). This meant that the masters of the arts faculty, where the trivium was taught, took a professional interest in grammar and connected it to their other philosophical interests. This, in a nutshell, is how grammar became "speculative."[2]

Of course, grammar had been part of the trivium before the rise of the universities, even since antiquity. But conceptions of grammar became more ambitious in the thirteenth century. This was, as usual, because of Aristotle. Once they were able to read the full range of his logical works, especially the *Posterior Analytics*, the masters were led to wonder whether grammar would really qualify as a full-blown "science" in Aristotle's sense. The arts masters were desperate to say that it would, given the central role of grammar in their university careers. But there was a problem. Aristotle states clearly that a science must establish universal truths, whereas grammar seems always to study a particular language. The arts masters were teaching Latin grammar but, of course, knew that there were grammars for other languages. They even noted and worried about such things as Latin's lack of definite and indefinite articles, an apparent defect relative to Greek.

Variation between languages also casts doubt on the idea we were just exploring, that there is a neat correspondence between language and world. Grammatical structures differ greatly from one language to another, but it isn't as if there is one reality for the French and another for the English. (Okay, maybe that's a bad example, but you know what I mean.) The grammarians were not to be dissuaded, though. While they admitted that many features of Latin or of any other language are "accidental," they insisted that some features must be shared by all languages. It would be these "universal" features, which are essential to language as such, that are studied in grammar as a properly scientific enterprise. For instance, in Latin the word for "giraffe" is *camelopardus*, whereas in German it is *Giraffe*. It tells us nothing about real giraffes that the German word is etymologically related to the English word, while the Latin word is not. But it does tell us something about giraffes that, in all three languages, the word in question is a noun. A giraffe is a substance and nouns typically pick out substances.

Well, actually, it's more complicated than that. The authoritative source for medieval grammarians was the *Institutes* of the sixth-century author Priscian. A measure of its popularity, and of the importance of grammar in medieval education, is that there are more than one thousand surviving manuscripts of this work. When Priscian gets to defining the noun, he says that it signifies not just substance but also quality.[3] Which makes sense. There are other nouns that could pick out a giraffe, including her proper name "Hiawatha" and such words as "animal" or "thing," to say nothing of nominal phrases like "tallest resident of the zoo" and "All-Savannah Roller-Skating Champion 2016." When we say "giraffe," we are signifying a substance only insofar as it has the particular quality, indeed the particularly wonderful quality, of being a giraffe.

This line of thought is at best implicit in Priscian himself. But in the works of the thirteenth-century grammarians it becomes as explicit as an adult-rated movie. Indeed, the idea that words signify in different ways or "modes" is the basis for the name that was given to some of the speculative grammarians in this period: "modists (*modistae*)." The modists were distinguished by their conviction that grammar does indeed have the rank of a universal science and by their decision to dedicate whole treatises to the subject of the "modes of signification (*modi significandi*)."[4] We have already gotten to know one of the earliest figures usually considered as modists: Boethius of Dacia, one of the so-called "Latin Averroists." There was also his countryman Martin of Dacia, who like Boethius wrote around 1270. Their ideas were taken up and further developed by figures whose lives and work stretched into the fourteenth century, including Radulphus Brito, Thomas of Erfurt, and Siger of Courtrai (not to be confused with the other "Averroist" Siger of Brabant, though he did also write about grammar). There also survive a number of anonymous treatises that apply the modist approach. So this was a significant and widespread movement in the late thirteenth and early fourteenth centuries.

The core idea of modism is that our ways of talking express our ways of thinking and that our ways of thinking in turn express the ways things are. Thus, we have a distinction between three types of "modes": the modes of signification, which belong to language, the modes of understanding (*modi intelligendi*), which are the ways we grasp reality, and finally the modes of being (*modi essendi*).[5] It's vital to the modists that each thing out in the world really does have multiple modes of being, since otherwise there would be no basis in reality for the various ways we can think and talk about a given thing. Hiawatha is only one single giraffe but I can refer to her in an almost indefinitely large number of ways: as giraffe, as animal, as beautiful, as tall, as running, as a running joke. These ways of speaking latch onto her "modes of being," the various ways that she genuinely is. When I think of her prodigious stature and speak of her as "tall," I am talking about her insofar as she possesses the accidental attribute or "property (*proprietas*)" of tallness. When I, instead, think of her as a giraffe and call her by that name, I am talking about the "mode of being" that she shares in common with other members of her species.

The modist theory makes it sound as though our concepts somehow intervene between language and reality. Does a word like "giraffe" or "running" really signify Hiawatha, or only my thought of Hiawatha? This question was one of those disputed ones.[6] Some authors insisted that words must refer to or "signify" concrete things like a particular giraffe. But many modists, such as Martin of Dacia, insisted that language does signify concepts, at least in the first instance. To signify something, you have to have it in mind. Your words express your thoughts rather than the thing itself. On the other hand, your concept is about the concrete thing in the world. This means that language can still signify the real thing via mental concepts. If I say "Here comes a giraffe," what I am fundamentally doing is communicating a thought. But since my thought is itself about something, namely the oncoming giraffe, my words do incidentally say something about the world.

Of course, not all the noises we make signify. We sometimes sneeze, grunt, or just speak nonsense. The terminist logician William of Sherwood gives an example that would be at home in a Harry Potter novel: *buba blicatrix*. For the medievals, sounds made by non-human animals would fall mostly or entirely into this category of (literally) insignificant noise.[7] How then does a mere sound (*vox*) come to acquire meaning? Only through an act of the mind, which imposes a certain meaning on a certain sound.[8] This is what the grammarians call the *ratio significandi* or "signifying relation." Once this is added, we have something more than a sound: we have a meaningful verbal expression (*dictio*). But even this is not enough, since one and the same *dictio* can be used in different ways. This would be particularly obvious to speakers of Latin, where case endings can be added to indicate whether something is the subject of a verb, the object of a verb, an instrument, or what have you. Hence the expression for "giraffe" in Latin takes a different form when I say "The giraffe sees (*camelopardus videt*)" than it does when I say "I see the giraffe (*video camelopardum*)." We can even indicate one and the same thing with different parts of speech. The modists liked the example of pain. I can refer to it using the noun "pain," the verb "hurt," the adjective "painful," or even the interjection "ouch!"

The grammatical differences are there to mark further acts of the intellect, whose various modes of understanding correlate with cases and parts of speech. When I mean to refer to the pain in my toe, I use a noun; when I describe how it is making my toe feel, I use the adjective; when I want to let you know that you're standing on my foot, I use the interjection. Once the "mode of understanding" is marked at the level of language, we have what the grammarians called a *pars orationis*, a word as it would actually appear in a real sentence. The grammarians like to say that with this sort of expression we are signifying one thing *as* another, as when I signify a pain as something that is hurting me right now. When all goes well, the mode of signification reveals a mode of understanding that actually fits the way the world is, in other words, grasps a real thing under one of its modes of being. My toe really hurts; the thing out there really is a giraffe, and it really is seeing something, or being seen, or standing on my foot.

But sometimes all does not go well. There's a difference between saying something meaningful and saying something true. The grammarians recognize this too, and in fact their theory makes it easy to explain. Suppose you say to me, "Giraffes are ugly." I understand you just fine but I also know that you're saying something false. The good news is that you have successfully used language to convey to me what you are thinking. The bad news is that you are thinking about giraffes in a way that doesn't correspond to the way they really are. More puzzling for the modists were cases where language doesn't look as if it even *could* correspond to the world under any mode of being. To what does the word "nothing" refer, or the word "matter," assuming, as the medievals did, that matter is pure potentiality? Again, the role of mental concepts could come to the rescue here. By negating concepts that do refer to reality, the mind is capable of forming notions of potentiality, nothingness, or privation, even though no such absences really exist outside the mind.[9] This solution could also be used to handle "empty" words like "centaur" or "chimera." These signify concepts that are only figments of the mind with no correlate outside in real being.[10]

Then, there are the linguistic expressions that don't even pretend to signify anything, those words like "if" and "not." This is pretty much the group of Latin words that are "indeclinable," in other words those that get no nominal, adjectival, or verbal endings. The grammarians tended to see them as serving a merely auxiliary function. It was even claimed that they are properly speaking "not part of language."[11] In other cases a term might be a mere substitute for a fully formed *pars orationis*; a good example is the pronoun, like "he" or "it." Obviously, you can't know what a pronoun refers to without the help of context.[12] In general the grammarians are prepared to admit that context is vital in understanding the way that a given word functions in a given sentence. We can see this as a legacy from the terminist logicians who, as we noted in Chapter 22, sometimes argued that the supposition or referent of a term might be established by the context in which the term is used.[13] But the grammarians go further, emphasizing that speaker and listener are engaged in a cooperative enterprise. The speaker tries to make his meaning clear and the listener seeks an interpretation of his words that will make sense. This is one reason our attempts to communicate aren't tripped up by the many ambiguities found in natural languages.[14]

But some ways of using language are bound to cause philosophical controversy. One case that gave the grammarians trouble was the apparently innocent word "whiteness."[15] The standard modist story here would be that there are various "modes of being" picked out by forms of the word "white." There is the adjective "white" that is applied to a substance qualified by the accident of whiteness, there is the process of acquiring such an accident, which we call "whitening," and then there is the accident itself, which is the "whiteness" in a substance. But can't I also use the word without thinking of any white thing in particular? It's this usage that seems to be at stake when I say something like "I don't look good in white" or "White is the opposite of black." Sentences like these can clearly be true, but what are they about? While some were prepared to admit that whiteness is something out there in the world, Boethius of Dacia was reluctant to do so. For him this is another case where a word refers to a mental concept, in this case an abstract generalization produced by the mind based on experiences of particular white things.

A similar problem concerned terms like "human," "giraffe," or "animal." On the one hand, these can name individual things out in the world like Groucho Marx and Hiawatha. On the other hand, they are the names of species and genera, which are found in many things, because not only Groucho is a human, but also Harpo, Chico, and all the rest of us. This led the grammarians to weigh in on the problem of universals.[16] Among the modists, perhaps the most innovative view was that of Radulphus Brito. At first his solution may seem like Boethius of Dacia's idea about whiteness. Radulphus appeals to the "mode of understanding" and explains that the mode relevant to genera and species is the one that responds to the similarity between, for instance, one human and all other humans. However, he insists that this mode of understanding is grounded in the nature of the external things. So Radulphus is adopting what we might call "moderate realism" concerning universals. Our universal ideas are not mere figments, like our ideas of chimeras or centaurs, nor are they mere abstractions like Boethius' whiteness. When we think of the human species, we are attending to humans *as* they are alike to one another and not only *as if* they were alike to one another. We can also signal to other people that we have in mind whatever is common to all humans by adding the word "every," which is what we do in order to make a universal statement like "Every human is an animal."

Radulphus' solution is classic modism. It distinguishes between the levels of language, concept, and reality while positing an intimate connection between the three levels. Of course, that connection isn't always present. We do talk about chimeras and even say things that are meaningless or (horror of horrors) ungrammatical. But the whole point of modism is to reveal how the connections work when things go well. Still, we can see easily how the tools of speculative grammar could be turned in a more skeptical direction. If you think that universals have no basis in reality, you might argue that phrases like "every human" express only modes of understanding and not modes of being. You might emphasize the arbitrariness of language and of the mind. In short, you might think less like a thirteenth-century philosopher and more like a fourteenth-century philosopher.

But we're still not quite ready for the fourteenth century. We have yet to cover the two most important scholastic thinkers to come along in the generation after Aquinas and Bonaventure, namely Henry of Ghent and John Duns Scotus. First, though, I want to remind you that it wasn't only the schoolmen who were thinking about philosophy in this period. Since we've been thinking in this chapter about language, I thought it would be a good time to have a break from university life, and look at a work of vernacular literature that has much to say about philosophy, even though historians of philosophy haven't had much to say about it in return.

45

LOVE, REIGN OVER ME
THE *ROMANCE OF THE ROSE*

L ooking for a romantic gift for that special someone? I highly recommend that
you do not get them a copy of the twelfth-century treatise *On Love* by Andreas
Capellanus, because your intended sweetheart is going to have misgivings about
your liaison once he or she reads the first page. Here Andreas explains what love is,
namely "a certain innate suffering caused by seeing, and thinking too much about,
the shapeliness of someone of the opposite sex."[1] And, of course, he has a point. We
all know, from the lyrics of pop songs, if not from personal experience, that to love
is to suffer. There's the fear of possible rejection and the agony of actual rejection;
there are the pangs of longing when the beloved is absent, replaced by anxiety and
befuddlement when the beloved is present. Just ask Pat Benetar, who proclaimed
that "Love is a battlefield," or Billie Holiday whose hard won expertise on this matter
led her to proclaim that "You don't know what love is until you've learned the
meaning of the blues." The J Geils Band went further still: "I've had the blues, the reds
and the pinks. One thing for sure: love stinks."

Somewhat more poetic, though a little more encouraging, is the definition of love
found in the *Romance of the Rose*. "Love is a mental illness afflicting two persons of
opposite sex . . . it comes upon people through a burning desire, born of disordered
perception, to embrace and to kiss and to seek carnal gratification" (67).[2] But, like a
first date, this passage should be approached carefully. For starters you'll notice that
it is just a reworking of the earlier definition given by Andreas Capellanus. This is
typical of the *Romance of the Rose*, a poem built largely of other literary materials.
Being a well-read expert in the amatory arts, the author Jean de Meun strips his
sources of their Latin and reclothes them in French, having his way with them in the
process. In this case he does, however, go further than Andreas, by saying that love
is actually a kind of illness (*maladie*).

To further complicate matters, it isn't exactly Jean who is responsible for ravish-
ing his literary model in this way. At this point in the poem the voice is not the
author's own but that of Reason, one of the many personifications and emblematic
characters who populate the *Romance of the Rose*. When Reason compares love to an

illness, it is part of her overall effort to show that we should not allow the irrational passions of love to rule over us. We should never give in to such an excess of emotion that we would experience suffering as a result of our affection. Clearly Reason doesn't know the meaning of the blues. As for Jean de Meun himself, he doesn't necessarily see things in such black-and-white terms. He allows the voice of Reason to have its say but not to have the last word. Other characters will weigh in with their own ideas about love and the erotic before the poem is out.

For all its exuberance and prodigious length, Jean's contribution is a doubly modest one. He expressly draws on earlier sources, above all the *Art of Love* by the Latin poet Ovid, the ancient philosopher Boethius' *Consolation of Philosophy*, and the *Complaint of Nature* by Alan of Lille.[3] So dependent is he on these and other texts that he feels free to blame them for any untruths to be found in his own poem (235). Furthermore, Jean's exuberant and inventive recycling of these Latin works is itself offered as the completion of a poem started by another man. As Jean tells us himself, in a characteristically perplexing and ironic passage midway through the poem, the *Romance* was begun by a certain Guillaume de Lloris (162). Jean even takes the trouble to tell us how much time elapsed between the work of the two authors—about forty years—and to identify for us the last line that was written by Guillaume. That line comes only about four thousand lines into a work which, in its completed form, contains almost twenty-two thousand lines. Thus, more than four-fifths of the work is by Jean.

We know nothing about Guillaume de Lloris apart from what is divulged by the poem itself, which isn't much. Jean is writing at about 1270, so if Guillaume wrote forty years earlier, then we can date him to around 1230. He is a classic exponent of the "courtly love" poetic tradition, which we saw inspiring the Beguine mystics Hadewijch and Mechthild of Magdeburg (Chapter 32). Thus, Guillaume expresses the idea of romantic love as utter devotion (34) and depicts the agony experienced when the beloved is unattainable, going so far as to say that "No pain can equal that suffered by lovers" (38). What drew Jean to this particular text is a matter of speculation. My guess is that it was not only the standard themes of courtly love that attracted him but also Guillaume's self-aware literary artifice and his display of good literary taste.

Guillaume presents his poem as the recounting of a dream. He finds himself in a garden populated by personifications of the psychological and practical considerations that arise in a love affair. Pleasure, Courtesy, Fair Welcome, and the God of Love himself are all described, as are the forces that thwart seduction like Jealousy, Evil Tongue (*malebouche*), Chastity, Fear, and Shame. Guillaume dreams of himself pledging loyalty to the God of Love in the terms of a vassal speaking to a lord.

In the greatest obsession with a rosebud you'll find outside of *Citizen Kane*, he adopts the role of a besotted Lover who longs to possess a beautiful rose growing in the garden. To do so the Lover must call on the forces of love to help with his seduction and lay siege to the defenses arrayed to protect the flower's innocence, including a symbolic fortress built around the rose. Pat Benetar was right: love really is a battlefield. For a medieval reader the dream setting would recall a different cultural touchstone, Cicero's *Dream of Scipio*, which was commented upon by Macrobius. Just to make sure we don't miss the point, Guillaume refers to Macrobius at the very outset of his own poem. For Jean, the most self-conscious of writers, it might also have been intriguing that Guillaume often comments on his own efforts as a writer, as when he frequently apologizes that words are inadequate to describe what he saw in the dream (for example, 15, 22).

Intriguing or not, Guillaume's four thousand lines by themselves wouldn't have earned a place in this book. But Jean de Meun brings a philosophical sensibility to his completion of the poem. He trained at the University of Paris, and made more traditional contributions to our subject.[4] One imagines him winking at the reader when he says in his poem what a great service it would be if someone would translate Boethius' *Consolation* from Latin into the vernacular. Jean himself would go on to produce a French version, and also to translate the exchange of letters between Peter Abelard and Heloise (as mentioned in Chapter 10). As for his continuation of the *Romance of the Rose*, it's one of the most important works of medieval literature in any language and has much to say about philosophy. Jean peppers his poem with parodic allusions to scholastic practice and vocabulary, as when his characters accuse one another of sophistry or challenge one another to produce definitions and proofs in support of their claims about love. He also refers to many philosophers by name, from Plato and Aristotle to Avicenna and Abelard. Then, there is more substantive philosophical material, which Jean makes accessible to his French audience by including it in his poem: a direct translation of a passage from Plato's *Timaeus* (294), and an extensive summary of Boethius' ideas about the necessity of the future (266–74).

He also takes a stand on issues that had divided philosophers in the medieval period. The intellectual tumult of the twelfth century seems still to be very much alive for Jean. One of his main sources is Alan of Lille; he is fascinated by the story of Abelard and Heloise and, as we'll see shortly, by the whole topic of castration; and he weighs in on the twelfth-century debate as to whether Plato had already grasped the Trinity, his answer being no (295). A more contemporary note is struck by a vicious attack on the mendicant movement and its vow of self-imposed poverty. Jean hides behind—but not far behind—another symbolic character to make this attack, namely False Seeming (*faus semblant*). This character is introduced to argue that a successful seduction often involves a bit of economy with the truth. False Seeming advises rubbing onion juice into the eyes to make for a convincing display of lovestruck weeping (114). Then comes one of the many digressions that actually seem to be Jean's main purpose in writing his continuation of the *Romance*. Speaking on behalf of the mendicants, False Seeming boasts of the cunning hypocrisy that makes it possible to amass wealth while acquiring a reputation for abstemious piety: "We pretend to be poor, but we have everything while having nothing" (180).

Though Jean's poem is thus not short on allusions to scholastic culture, it is a good deal more entertaining than anything produced by the schoolmen. By turns ironic, self-righteous, provocative, violent, funny, crude, elegant, and obscene, the *Romance of the Rose* is quite frankly a hell of a lot of fun. Medievalists agree, because it allows them to play their favorite game of "spot the allusion." Nearly every one of the secondary works I consulted while doing the research for this chapter triumphantly pointed out previously unnoticed parallels to classical or medieval texts used by Jean.[5] Of course, detecting such resonances would also have been part of the fun for a well-read medieval audience. But if the fun is in the allusions, the action is with the poem's central theme. Guillaume already announces that the poem contains "the whole art of love" (3) and Jean continues with at least the pretence that we are being offered instruction, and fair warning, in affairs of the heart. The narrative depicts the challenges that face lovers and the means by which these challenges can be overcome. A series of benevolent symbolic personifications, including one simply named "Friend (*ami*)," appear to give the central character advice on how to win his rose.

But this is no mere instruction manual. Jean seems to be trying to say something about love in general, about its correct place in human life, or perhaps the place it is inevitably going to occupy whether correctly or not. What, then, is his message? Here interpretations differ. One traditional idea is that there is a sharp contrast between Jean and Guillaume. Where Guillaume was indeed a "courtly" author, Jean is, for all his learning, earthier and more "naturalistic." He celebrates the simple pleasures of sexuality, finding both joy and comedy in this innate human drive. On this telling Jean could be allied with the so-called "Latin Averroists," seen as "secular" in his endorsement of the purely natural.[6] Indeed, some of the speeches in the *Romance* suggest that Jean sees sexual activity in light of a tacit theory of natural law. He emphasizes that, to speak in the words of another piece of popular music, "Birds do it, bees do it" and so we humans too may as well fall in love.[7] Other readings situate Jean in a more distinctively Christian and theological frame of reference. On this interpretation, his satire is intended to warn us against excessive interest in purely physical delight, which is a consequence of our fallen nature.[8]

It's no wonder that such disagreements should emerge, because both points of view and more besides are present in the poem. A range of characters are allowed to express various ideas about love, and at great length. The speeches are written with such conviction that they may seem to speak for Jean himself; yet the speeches don't agree with one another. We are warned that the speeches will be "wise or foolish (*sages ou foles*)" but not told which ones are which. This feature of the *Romance* has been leading readers into their own disagreements for a long time. Several later medieval readers, including Christine de Pizan, got involved in a debate over the poem (the so-called *querelle de la rose*, further discussed in Chapter 74). Christine complained of the misogyny that is indeed a striking feature of Jean's work, as in a horrific passage where a jealous husband speaks of beating his wife into submission. Another famous Jean, namely Jean Gerson, agreed with Christine that the poem was liable to lead its readers into lechery. To these complaints a defender of Jean de Meun named Pierre Col responded that the poet simply "made each character speak according to his nature…It is wrongheaded to say that the author believes women to be as evil as the Jealous Man, in accordance with his character, declares."[9]

Of all the speeches in the *Romance*, the most decisive for our assessment of Jean's true attitude towards sexuality is the one given by Reason during her second appearance in the poem. Guillaume had already included a scene in which Reason advises against pursuing a love affair. In short order she was rebuffed by the character of the Lover (47). Jean reprises the scene and gives it a far more detailed treatment. Where Guillaume devoted seventy-five verses to Reason's point of view, Jean gives her more than three thousand![10] As you might expect, Reason's main objection to passionate love is that it is irrational. This does not mean that there is no proper role for sex in the good life, because sexual activity is required if the human species is to live on, a point emphasized later in a further speech by Genius, a character and theme borrowed from Alan of Lille.[11]

The Lover is no more impressed by this second more long-winded appearance from Reason than he was by the first. When she names Socrates as a paradigm of rationality, he responds, "I would not give three chickpeas for Socrates" (105). On the whole, he observes that "Whenever Love spied me sitting listening to the sermon, he took a spade and threw out of my head by one ear whatever Reason had put in the other" (71). This looks like grist for the mill of the theological reading. In our fallen state, we are incapable of listening to the call of reason and giving sex its proper value.[12] Where we should feel natural desire, we are carried away by unrestrained lust. If Reason really is speaking for Jean, then she is calling us *not* to act like the hero of courtly love romance but like the man Augustine was striving to be: one who, as Reason says, loves all humans generally rather than becoming obsessed with just one particular human. The Lover's failure to do so is meant not to be inevitable but instructive.

It's hard to know Jean's true intention, though, because it is unclear whether Reason is an instrument or target of his satire. A case in point is one of the most memorable passages of the whole *Romance*.[13] In the course of her argument Reason has alluded to the classical legend according to which Saturn was castrated and his testicles thrown into the sea, resulting in the birth of Venus. The Lover reacts by castigating Reason for her use of the word "testicles *(coilles)*" where she might have employed a suitable euphemism (106). Reason responds that, as Plato taught, language is for communication. Towards this end she has herself made appropriate words for the things created by God, so that there can be no objection to her using frank language (108). The Lover remains unmoved, albeit without indicating how many chickpeas he would or wouldn't give for Plato. What are we to make of this? Any plausible answer needs to look ahead to the very end of the *Romance*, a section that is climactic in every sense of the word. The Lover finally manages to achieve his objective and his deflowering of the rose is veiled in only the thinnest of allegorical veils. The Lover compares his labors to those of Hercules, as he struggles to force his "staff" through a narrow passage to reach into a reliquary, and so on (333). It's been well remarked of this passage that it shows how euphemism "may in fact be at least as obscene, and much more pornographic, than plain speech."[14]

We have to assume that Jean was well aware of this when he composed the rather unromantic conclusion of his *Romance*. So we may be rather skeptical of the Lover's confidence in the power of evasive language. His objection to Reason's speech might better have been directed to its matter than to its form. Once you've decided to speak of gods castrating one another, your choice of words is almost beside the point. Indeed, the Lover could have called on a formidable range of allies if he sought to press this objection. Augustine and Macrobius, and before them Plato, had expressed disquiet with such myths.[15] But Reason would be prepared for this complaint too. When the Lover advises her to use a euphemistic "gloss" to cloak her meaning if she absolutely must bring testicles into the discussion, Reason replies that we should use an interpretive "gloss" to uncover the deeper meaning of the myth.[16] Like the Platonist authors of the supposed "school of Chartres" (Chapter 14), Reason speaks of the surface of a myth as a "covering *(integumentum)*" that conceals deeper philosophical meaning (109).

So there are indeed good reasons to suppose that, in this scene and others, the character of the Lover does not speak for Jean. He is not held up for adulation but as an example of the addled state into which love can lead us. His fixation on improper language would go hand in hand with his own improper obsession with private pleasure. Where he should love all humankind and appreciate nature as God's creation, the Lover thinks only of his rose. In other words his problem is that he is not a philosopher. This is borne out, at least to some extent, by what happens when Nature herself appears as a character. In passages based closely on Alan of Lille's *Complaint of Nature*, Jean has his personification of Nature extol the well-ordered design of the cosmos and especially the heavens. She digresses to several philosophical themes, including an explanation of the darker patches on the moon as being made of more transparent material than the rest (260; the explanation is in agreement with Albert the Great). Amidst all this cosmic harmony it is only humans who violate the correct order with their sexual immoderation.

But reading the *Romance of the Rose* is like attending a disputation at the medieval university, in that there's always an "on the other hand." In this case Nature herself is made to imagine and describe some rather unnatural scenes, as when she talks about what would happen if animals could learn to reason and speak (274).[17] Besides, earlier in the poem more disreputable characters have been allowed to state that it is only "natural" for humans to engage in sex outside the bounds of marriage. Women, we are told, are naturally attracted to all men and not only one husband (217). Jean's poem contains lofty philosophical praise of nature, but also shows that a "natural" sexual ethics could be not so much high-minded as below the belt. Again one might take him to be critiquing those who are content with the merely physical or natural. This would be satire in the aid of a theological message. But to my mind the interpretations that seek to enlist Jean on the side of naturalism or of supernaturalism miss the rather obvious point that he is staging a dialogue *between* these points of view, and at least as much for our enjoyment as for our edification. Why should we expect the intellectual tensions to be resolved rather than displayed and explored? The *Romance of the Rose* is not a philosophical work disguised as a poem about love. Rather it is a poem that is in love with philosophy, but hesitates to get into a committed relationship.

FREQUENTLY ASKED QUESTIONS
HENRY OF GHENT

W e've now seen how misleading it is to think of Thomas Aquinas as the definitive thinker of the late thirteenth century, never mind of medieval philosophy in general. Sure he was original, brilliant, and very influential. But his staunch commitment to Aristotle made him idiosyncratic, if not quite as controversial as some colleagues at the Paris arts faculty. A figure who might better personify the intellectual climate in these decades is Henry of Ghent. Of course, he's far less famous than Aquinas; I recently asked someone whether they had ever heard of him and got the response, "Well I've heard of Henry and I've heard of Ghent, but not Henry of Ghent." Yet he was a major figure in his time. Though he was born earlier (in about 1217, Aquinas in 1224 or 1225), Henry's long stint as master of theology came after Aquinas' death in 1274, running from 1276 until just before his death in 1293. For evidence of his standing as a leading and more mainstream intellectual, we need only recall the 1277 condemnations. Where Aquinas may have been one of the targets, Henry of Ghent was on the commission that advised the bishop on the list of banned teachings.

With Henry we also have a leading exponent of the format that dominated philosophical writings of the thirteenth century, the disputed question. His extensive writings are largely in this form, and have been gathered into one large theological treatise (called either his *Summa* or *Quaestiones ordinariae*) and a series of fifteen further collections of questions on various issues (*Quodlibeta*). In this sprawling body of work Henry touches on all the contested issues of his day. He is often thought of as a champion of Augustine's ideas and cast as an Augustinian critic of Aquinas.[1] But we won't understand Henry well if we think of him just as a foil for Aquinas. Henry too was an original and synthetic thinker, eager to draw on the authority of Aristotle as well as Augustine, and on any number of other sources from the theological, philosophical, and legal traditions.

It was, furthermore, Henry, more than Aquinas, who would set the agenda for the last towering figure of late thirteenth-century thought, John Duns Scotus. This, despite the fact that, as Scotus himself complained, it can be hard to pin down

Henry's ideas because he says different things (*diversimode loquitur*) in different places about the same topics.[2] His views seem to have evolved over time, and the very form of his writings means that you can find Henry tackling pretty well any philosophical issue but not so easily discern the coherence or thrust of his thought as a whole. Rather than forcing his varied and voluminous output into a simple framework or choosing just one problem that he discusses, I'm going to touch on a whole range of questions addressed by Henry. This will incidentally give us a nice survey of some key philosophical issues as we get ready to turn to Scotus and then the very different context of the fourteenth century.

Question 1: Henry was a theologian. Does that mean he wasn't a philosopher?[3]

On this point Henry agrees with Thomas Aquinas that theology is a science, and one with an intimate relationship with philosophy. Henry condemns the pursuit of the liberal arts or other rational sciences for their own sake as mere "curiosity" but commends the use of philosophy towards a higher goal. This goal is, of course, God, who is ultimately pursued in practical sciences like ethics because He is the highest good (81, 111, 120), and also in theoretical sciences like natural philosophy or metaphysics because He is the ultimate cause of all things. Philosophy can thus be very useful, as long as one has already accepted the truths of the Christian faith in advance (116). This is an important constraint, because philosophy on its own is liable to reach conclusions that would be overturned from the perspective of theology. One reason for this is that philosophers consider only what Henry calls "proximate" causes, which may be trumped by the ultimate cause that is God. He alludes several times to the example of Hezekiah, taken from the Bible (2 Kings 10:1–10). Hezekiah was on his death bed, and doctors and philosophers would have predicted his imminent demise by looking to the natural causes at play. Yet God chose to heal him (56, 139–40, 212). Thus, as we read in another book of the Bible, does God make foolish the wisdom of this world (1 Corinthians 1:20).

Still, philosophy can help us understand religious doctrines more fully. As far as Henry is concerned, it is better to grasp something with certainty on the basis of reason than without certainty on the basis of faith (113). This may sound a bit surprising, coming from a medieval theologian. Surely the truths of faith are as certain as it gets? Yes, of course. But, and this is less surprising coming from a medieval theologian, we need to make a distinction here. Unshakeable confidence through faith is possible but is given only to a lucky few (62). In themselves religious truths, like God's having created the world or His having a trinitarian nature, are perfectly certain, but most believers are less than absolutely sure about them. As Henry puts it, the certainty on the side of the believer may differ from the certainty of what is believed (61, 201–2). This is a distinction we could apply to non-religious cases too. Imagine that you've worked out a complicated mathematical proof. Assuming the proof's conclusion is indeed true, it is in itself perfectly certain. But you, the mathematician, may still be unsure. You can't rule out that you made a mistake along the way.

Like Aquinas, then, Henry situates theology within a system inspired by Aristotle in which higher sciences provide the principles for lower sciences, with theology at the top. Henry is happy to claim agreement with "the philosophers" insofar as they too make the study of God the highest science (110). This is part of what philosophers call "metaphysics." We can even say that metaphysics is a "first science" because it studies primary concepts like being.[4] Still, metaphysics is part of human philosophy, which studies things in themselves, whereas theology studies things in relation to their divine source (55). That makes theology, not metaphysics, the highest and most authoritative of all sciences. Here Henry disagrees with Aquinas, who had suggested that theology is subordinated to an even higher science, namely that of God Himself. This proposal prompts a scathing response from Henry. He remarks that Aquinas apparently didn't understand what it means for one science to be subordinate to another (85). Divine knowledge is not made up of discursive arguments that can provide premises to be used in the demonstrations of a lower science. So it is a crass mistake to integrate God's understanding of Himself into the scientific hierarchy.

Question 2: While we're on the subject, what is knowledge anyway?[5]

Here Henry had a choice to make. He could go for an Aristotelian model of knowledge according to which we use our senses to learn about the world around us and then abstract our concepts from these experiences. Or he could adopt a more Augustinian theory on which God illuminates the mind. Other thirteenth-century thinkers had emphasized one of these two accounts without entirely rejecting the other, with Bonaventure highlighting the need for illumination, Aquinas the contribution of sensation. Characteristically, Henry goes for both. He describes our initial attempts to achieve knowledge along more or less Aristotelian lines. We form rough concepts in our minds on the basis of our sensory experiences. The mind has to do some work here, constructing its abstract notion of, say, a giraffe on the basis of numerous encounters with giraffes. In some cases we can immediately arrive at such a concept without having to depend on sensation, as with a fundamental or primary idea like "being" or "thing."

Either way, Henry calls the concept a mental "word (*verbum*)."[6] This is going to be important in a more theological area of his thought, since he thinks that we can understand the second person of the Trinity or the "Word of God" as the product of God's intellectual thinking.[7] But also, if concepts are "words," this makes it easier to see how thoughts connect to language. When you utter a word like "giraffe," you are simply expressing the concept or mental "word" of giraffe that is in your mind. As we form mental words, we are, of course, trying to understand the nature of the things we are encountering, to grasp the very essence that makes something a giraffe. That isn't something we can achieve simply by forming a concept, though. Since we are limited creatures, our ability to apprehend natures is also limited. Henry compares the initial concepts we form to seeing a book in dim light, such that you can tell there are letters written there but not what they say.[8] How then can we see things in, so to speak, the full light of day?

This is the cue for Henry to turn to the second option, the Augustinian illumination theory. The human mind can achieve certain understanding of true essences with help from God. But Henry doesn't think that God simply sends the essence into your mind the way that Avicenna's "Active Intellect" emanates forms into the human soul, like Star Trek characters beaming down from a spaceship onto a planet. Instead, Henry dares to boldly go where someone had already gone before. Like Plato, he asserts that true knowledge can be had only in the light of perfect exemplars, which God created as models for the things we find around us in the physical universe. These exemplars are the "very natures and essences of the things."[9] By aligning our initial concepts with them, we can avoid all error and guarantee a successful end to the scientific enterprise.

Question 3: What was that thing just mentioned about having an immediate grasp of the concept of being?[10]

Here we have to mention Avicenna again. A signature doctrine found in his writings has to do with the core notions of metaphysics: the so-called "transcendentals," those features that belong to absolutely everything, like unity, truth, and, of course, being (Chapter 25). Avicenna thought that the idea of being, or of a "thing" (shay' in Arabic, res in Latin), is so basic that we cannot be extracting it from our experiences of the world. Rather, it is known primarily or immediately. Henry agrees, and seizes the chance to forge another link between philosophy and theology. Since God is the highest being and the source of all being, we are already (in the dim, imperfect way possible for us with our natural resources) grasping God as soon as we get hold of this primary concept. The vague understanding of being that is immediately available to us mirrors the transcendent being of God, which is indeterminate not because it is vague but because it is infinite. Of course, this doesn't mean that all humans are aware that they have an innate knowledge of God. It takes philosophical work to see that our idea of being, which is so fundamental that we usually don't even articulate it to ourselves, is in some way a crude intuition of the divine.

Question 4: This has all been pretty abstract and metaphysical so far. Does Henry have anything to say about more concrete issues, for instance in ethics?[11]

Henry has something to say about almost everything, so the answer is definitely yes. My favorite example is his discussion of whether it is morally permissible for a condemned prisoner to escape in order to save his own life. Henry says that the prisoner should go right ahead and escape if the opportunity presents itself. He appeals to the natural law, according to which every human has the right and even the responsibility to maintain the link between soul and body. This is not to say that the judge who condemned the man was acting unjustly, since the judge does have the right to put him to death. But it is to say that the criminal retains an inalienable right to self-preservation. For the same reason Henry says it is morally acceptable to steal food if the alternative is starvation. On the other hand, it's not that anything goes when you are trying to save your own life. Since the judge, or the state, owns things like the prison cell's bars and the shackles, the prisoner would transgress if he destroyed these things in a bid for freedom; needless to say, it would also be wrong to injure or kill the guards. Still, the prisoner can escape with a clear conscience if he is left unattended and can just walk out without doing any damage, something Henry compares to the fact that you're allowed to stroll through someone else's field if no one has bothered to put a fence around it.

Question 5: What is the relationship between the intellect and the will?[12]

I'm so glad you asked, because with this final question we come to a pivotal contribution by Henry and one that paves the way for Duns Scotus' more famous treatment of human freedom. The issue has been a recurring one throughout the medieval period, with early figures like Eriugena and Anselm wondering how humans can be free if they need God's grace to avoid sin, and Peter Abelard locating moral responsibility in human intention on the grounds that intention is something over which we have free control. In the late thirteenth century the debate has come to focus on two powers within the soul, the intellect and the will. There is a division of labor here. Intellect is tasked with determining the best thing to do in any given situation, and on this basis will forms a volition to act. Henry says that this makes will superior to intellect, since the intellect has only an advisory capacity, whereas will has the executive function. He thus compares the intellect to a servant who goes before a master bearing a lamp to help the master see (29).

But there's an obvious problem here. If the intellect tells the will what it ought to do and the will always chooses accordingly, then how is the will free? It seems to be constrained, not by God's grace or any other external factor, but by the rational processes going on in the intellect. Consider again our prisoner deciding whether to escape. As it happens, he's read Henry of Ghent's disputed question and agrees with Henry's reasoning. He duly concludes that it would be right for him to escape. Since he now thinks that, all things considered, this is the best thing to do, all that remains for his will to do is ratify that belief by deciding to act upon it. In other words, the will would just rubber-stamp the decision already made by intellect and set action in motion. That way of looking at things could be called "rationalist" or "intellectualist." Aristotle gave medieval authors a big push in this intellectualist direction, since he depicts human choices as the outcome of practical reasoning.

Aquinas is often seen as taking Aristotle's lead.[13] He, of course, insists that the will is free; yet it seems that for him, the will cannot act directly against the intellect. What it can do is influence the intellect, for instance by instructing it to direct its attention to certain considerations rather than others. It's an all too familiar phenomenon, as when you rationalize about why it would be a great idea to watch *Star Trek* instead of reading some Henry of Ghent ("I really ought to relax first," or "It will provide me with good analogies to use when I explain Henry's ideas later"). For Aquinas, freedom really belongs to intellect and will together. They act in concert to discern and choose whatever seems good. Henry sees this as an underestimation of the power of the will. For when the will chooses, it is moving *itself*, not being moved to choose by the intellect.[14] It treats the outcome of rational deliberation in the intellect as a proposal and is always free to reject intellect's advice. This must be so, because if intellect could actually bring the will to move, it would render the will unfree (50).

It may seem that Henry has gone too far here: why bother deliberating at all if the will is just going to ignore the conclusion you reach? His answer takes the form of a metaphor. The counsel of the intellect creates a kind of "weight" in the will, meaning a propensity to do one thing rather than another (61). This disposes the will to make a certain choice, but without constraining it so that it must make that choice. This may seem rather unsatisfactory. It seems that Henry makes freedom consist in the will's capacity to defy good advice from intellect. This would be rather ironic, since Henry agrees with Anselm that humans have been given freedom for a very specific purpose, namely so that we can choose what is good (70). Really Henry just wants to ensure that when the will does choose rightly, it is choosing freely. If it only ever has one option, the one recommended by the intellect, then it would not be free. This availability of multiple options is going to be a key issue for Scotus too: together he and Henry will lay the seeds of voluntarism.

47

HERE COMES THE SON
THE TRINITY AND THE EUCHARIST

L ewis Carroll's *Through the Looking Glass* contains a scene in which Alice, in
discussion with the White Queen, says that she can't believe impossible things.
The Queen responds, "I daresay you haven't had much practice. When I was your
age, I always did it for half-an-hour a day. Why, sometimes I've believed as many as
six impossible things before breakfast." From which you might infer that the White
Queen would have felt quite at home in the Middle Ages, and not just because she
was royalty. Medieval philosophy is notoriously intertwined with Christian theology, and some Christian doctrines may seem to involve embracing the impossible.
In modern times, philosophers have sometimes taken this to be a great virtue. The
nineteenth-century Danish thinker Søren Kierkegaard put the notion of the "absurd"
at the center of Christianity, arguing that we should not and indeed cannot rationally accept the idea of God's incarnation as a human. It can be believed only by faith.

The medievals were far more inclined to think that reason goes hand in hand with
faith. By this stage I've hopefully managed to disabuse you of any notion that
medieval thinkers spent all their time thinking of nothing but faith, ignoring the
deliverances of natural reason. For that matter, when they did think about theology,
they often took a highly rationalist approach. Now, though, we're going to look at
issues that posed a particularly stern test for that approach. We won't live up to the
example set by the White Queen; I for my part have already had breakfast, and we
will be trying to wrap our minds around only two *apparently* impossible beliefs.
These are the Trinity, the doctrine that God is one and simple, yet three Persons,
Father, Son, and Holy Spirit, and the Eucharist, the doctrine that bread and wine can
turn into the body and blood of Christ.[1] However hard these things may be to
believe, medieval thinkers insisted that they are not in fact impossible. Thomas
Aquinas, Henry of Ghent, Duns Scotus, and others pushed reasoning to its limits in
order to show that the Trinity and Eucharist are indeed possible and even to a large
extent rationally comprehensible. This led them to investigate topics of more
general interest like philosophy of mind, the metaphysical status of relations, and
the connection between substances and their properties.

Of course, Christian thinkers had already been using philosophy to grapple with these matters for a long time. We saw that in the eleventh century a bitter dispute erupted in which Lanfranc of Bec attacked Berengar of Tours for holding that the Eucharist is merely symbolic in character, and that in the twelfth century Abelard and others convinced themselves that pagan philosophers like Plato had intuitively grasped the Trinity (Chapters 5 and 14). These discussions lived on in the memory of later medieval thinkers. Aquinas, for instance, refers to Berengar's position as a heresy (*ST* 3 Q75 a1). But when it came to the Trinity, they took their cue above all from an even earlier author: Augustine. In his *On the Trinity* he suggested that we can glimpse something of God's trinitarian nature in the working of our own minds.[2] When we think about something, there is a three-way relationship between the object of our thought, the act of thinking about that object, and the will (or, as Augustine puts it, "love") by which the mind directs its thinking towards that object. Despite this complex inner structure, the mind remains a single immaterial entity. This is an image of the way that God can be simple, yet a Trinity of Persons.

This theory had great appeal for the medievals. Could it be found in an authoritative church father? Did it offer the opportunity for subtle exploration of the human soul? Did it show how philosophical reasoning could support a central dogma of the Church? The answers were like the endgame in a chess match: check, check, and check again! We duly find Aquinas and Henry of Ghent presenting and refining Augustine's account by applying the theory of mind that was current in their own day.[3] The Latin translations of Aristotle and Arabic philosophical works encouraged thirteenth-century thinkers to adopt what we might call a "faculty-based psychology." By this I mean not that the scholastics worked in the arts and theology faculties but that they thought about the soul in terms of a range of powers or faculties. In this case the relevant faculties were the intellect and the will, associated respectively with the begetting of the Son and the production of the Holy Spirit ("spiration").

As Aquinas explains, the relation between the Father and Son is one of intellectual understanding. The second Person of the Trinity is "begotten" when God grasps Himself intellectually (*ST* 1 Q27 a2). In general, when the mind understands something, it forms a "word," which may actually be verbally uttered but may just remain in the intellect—what Aquinas calls an "interior word" (*ST* I Q34 a1; in Chapter 46 we saw the same idea in Henry of Ghent). This is pretty handy, since the Bible speaks of a *logos* or "word" who is God's Son, incarnated as Christ (John 1:1, "In the beginning was the word, and the word was with God," and 1:14, "the Word became flesh and made his dwelling among us"). But God will not be just two Persons: He will be three. This is because will is distinct from intellect or, to put it another way, because loving something is distinct from understanding it. Since God does love Himself—as well He should, since He is the highest Good and thus the most lovable thing—we have a further act which is associated with the production of the Holy Spirit. And by the way, the Holy Spirit is produced by an act of will that involves mutual love between the Father *and* the Son (*filioque*). This point was made already in the twelfth century by Hugh of Saint Victor. Now it is emphasized by Henry of Ghent as a way to refute the theory of the Byzantine Greek theologians, who had the Spirit proceeding from the Father alone.[4]

In applying this psychological analysis Aquinas and Henry need to steer between two heresies, Arianism and Sabellianism. Arius held that God is three substances and not only one, while Sabellius denied real plurality among the Persons (*ST* 1 Q31 a2). Against Arius we can say that God is truly one, because even in humans, never mind God, there is no difference in substance between intellect and will. Against Sabellius, we can say that God is truly three, because there is obviously a difference—what Aquinas calls an "opposition"—between the intellect and what it understands, or the will and what it loves. In this respect the Persons have a sort of genuine multiplicity that does not arise from God's other attributes. There is no opposition between, say, God's power and His wisdom, but there is a difference between Father and Son, because the Father begets, whereas the Son is begotten (*ST* 1 Q30 a1 repl obj 2; Q39 a1 repl obj 1). Furthermore the act of intellect must accompany and precede the will.[5] You have to understand something before you can direct your will towards it. Even if I effortlessly and inevitably desire almond croissants as soon as I think about them, the two acts are different and my thinking about them is presupposed by my desiring them. This is why there is an order of procession among the Persons, even though the Persons remain one in substance and therefore equal to one another.

At the core of this philosophical explanation of the Trinity is the idea of a relation. Still today, when philosophers want to talk about relations, they're apt to give the example of the relation of paternity that holds between a father and a son. In late antiquity Boethius had already proposed understanding the Trinity using Aristotle's views on relations.[6] But do we want to go so far as to say that the trinitarian Persons just *are* relations? Well, if we're Aquinas, that's exactly what we want to do. In created things, relations are accidents that belong to the things that enter into the relation. Consider, if you will, the Marx Brothers. Harpo is Groucho's brother, but Harpo is not the same thing as a relation of brotherhood. In God, though, things are different. According to Aquinas, when we talk about God the Father, we are alluding to a relation of paternity to God the Son. This is, however, not an accidental property that belongs to God, the way Harpo's brotherhood belongs to him accidentally. Rather, in God the relation of paternity just is the divine essence (*relatio autem in divinis non est sicut accidens inhaerens subiecto, sed est ipsa divina essentia: ST* 1 Q29 a4).

Some thinkers of the next generations adopted Aquinas' approach without necessarily following him on every detail. These included Giles of Rome and Godfrey of Fontaines.[7] But others, including Henry of Ghent and several Franciscans including Duns Scotus, found themselves doubting Thomas.[8] These critics were more than happy to make use of the "psychological" analysis of the Trinity based on God's acts of intellect and will. Yet they found it incoherent to say that talk of trinitarian Persons is nothing more than talk of relations arising from God's self-understanding and self-love. Instead they saw the Persons as having more fundamental ("personal") properties that underlie such relations. The Father is distinguished by his primacy as the divine Person who is unbegotten and ungenerated (or, to use the technical term, "innascible"). Aquinas alludes to this proposal; it was already put forward by his contemporary Bonaventure.[9] But he rejects it on the basis that it is a purely negative way of characterizing the Father (*ST* 1 Q33 a4). It would be like saying there is nothing more to being tall than not being short.

Aquinas' rivals were not short of objections they could press against his theory. Scotus pointed out that relations presuppose the things that enter into the relation. Conceptually speaking, there must in some sense be a Father and Son "before" the Father can be related to the Son, just as I can't be taller than you unless you and I both first exist (and even then, given my modest stature, it's rather unlikely).[10] Henry of Ghent, meanwhile, argued that a relation has no reality over and above the thing that enters into a relation.[11] It just means considering one thing "in respect of (*respectus*)" another. Harpo's relation of brotherhood to Groucho is not another real thing in addition to Harpo. It is Harpo who is real, and we say he is a brother simply because we are considering him in respect of Groucho. If this is right, then Aquinas' view could collapse into Sabellianism. For, if the Persons are only relations, and relations are nothing real, then Aquinas is failing to distinguish the Persons from one another at all.

On the other hand, there was the danger of distinguishing the Persons from one another too sharply, and thereby straying into the Arian heresy. The goal, then, was to show that the distinction of Persons is more than a merely "notional" distinction like that between me and the author of this book or between Harpo and Groucho's brother, without saying that the Persons are entirely separate things, as Harpo and Groucho are. It was in part to solve this difficulty that Scotus introduced what he called a "formal distinction."[12] The idea is that we sometimes make a distinction within a single thing, where the contrast is genuinely grounded in features or aspects of that thing. The two aspects would always be found together, but would have different definitions and can even be imagined as appearing in isolation from one another, although in fact they never do. We might say that one thing is formally distinct from another if it is not separate, but separable in principle. What would be an example? Scotus mentions several cases, one of which is the difference between intellect and will. Though they have different functions and definitions, they are simply faculties or operations of one and the same soul, so that they are not really two separate things. Hence will is never found without intellect or vice versa, since every intellectual being is also capable of voluntary choice; yet we could in theory imagine an intellectual being that has no power of will. Of course, it's no coincidence that he chooses the example of intellect and will, precisely the powers mentioned in the psychological account of the Trinity. And, of course, the Persons of the Trinity too are formally distinct.

This is a particularly clear case of theological speculation spurring philosophical ingenuity. The same thing happened in debates over a second theological topic, the Eucharist. As with the Trinity, one could easily risk courting heresy by offering philosophical explanations of the Eucharist, but our schoolmen didn't let that stop them. They eagerly tried to explain how exactly wine and bread can really, and not just symbolically, as Berengar had claimed, become the blood and body of Christ. Clearly, this is a miraculous event and not one detectable to the senses; the host still looks like bread after it has changed to the body of Christ. Thus, it is obvious that we know about it from Scripture rather than natural reason. (The main scriptural authority is Luke 22:19, where Christ breaks bread and hands it to his disciples saying, "This is my body which is given for you.") Once you assume by faith that this transformation really happens, philosophical puzzles arise, and it is here that reason comes in.

Actually there are far too many puzzles for me to discuss here.[13] How can the body of Christ be in more than one place at a time? How can it be in a place that is too small for it? What happens when consecrated wine goes bad and turns to vinegar, or consecrated bread goes moldy? All these questions and more were debated by the scholastics. I will just focus on the most fundamental problem, namely the nature of the change involved in the Eucharist. If you're like me before I did the research to write this chapter, you probably think there is a standard view that would have been held by all medieval thinkers, summed up by the word "transubstantiation." As the word implies, in Eucharistic change the entirety of one substance would be replaced by the entirety of another substance. I imagine you'll be as surprised as I was to learn that the word "transubstantiation" seems to have come into Latin discussions of the Eucharist only in the middle of the twelfth century, and that the substance-to-substance conception of the change was very controversial.[14]

Like several other controversial theses, this one was held by none other than Thomas Aquinas. He argued forcefully that it is not enough for the host's matter to be preserved and gain nothing more than a new form, as some other theologians claimed. That is what happens in natural change. Transubstantiation is something more miraculous, made possible only by divine power. Both the matter and the form of bread are transmuted into the matter and form of the body of Christ—not annihilated and replaced, but really transformed (ST 3 Q75 a3 repl 1). We can draw a rough parallel here to Aquinas' ideas about the Trinity. In that case he proposed that, in God, relations can be identical to an essence rather than additional to it. Now he proposes that we can have one whole substance becoming another, and that this can be a real change, even though nothing persists, not even prime matter. In neither case could we know that this is true through philosophy. Yet in both cases we can use philosophy to say rigorously what is happening and show that it is not impossible.

As with his position on the Trinity, Aquinas' explanation of the Eucharist did not garner unanimous support. Giles of Rome, usually rather close to Aquinas' approach, diverged from him on this issue. He said that matter is in its essence preserved through the change, even if no particular portion of matter survives from the bread to the body.[15] Scotus was even more critical. He argued that the body of Christ, which is in heaven, having ascended to the Father, simply acquires a new external relation by which it becomes present on the altar. This is a strange kind of presence, in which the parts of what is present are not in the different parts of the place where it is present (it's not that Christ's foot is pointing towards one end of the altar and his head pointing to the other end). Instead, the whole of the body is present to every part of the place on the altar.

There's another obvious question to ask about Eucharistic change: how is it that the features of the bread survive even when the bread does not, since it has (in whatever way) become the body of Christ? It still looks and tastes like bread, not like human flesh. Aquinas makes yet another bold proposal, namely that accidents can survive in the absence of the substances to which they belong. Of course, this usually doesn't happen. Harpo's sense of humor, his ability to play the harp, and his relation of brotherhood to Groucho all perished along with him when he died. But, again, that is the natural way of things. Once God is involved, the survival of accidents on their own is indeed possible. We can even see rationally that this is possible. God is capable of creating the flavor of bread indirectly, by creating bread and allowing the bread to sustain the accident of its flavor in existence. And whatever He can do indirectly, He can surely do directly.

This provoked disagreement from a philosopher who is usually thought of as being more of a rationalist than Aquinas himself, Siger of Brabant.[16] Siger did accept that God can change bread into the body of Christ while leaving the accidents unchanged. But he denied that we can use philosophical arguments to prove that this is possible. This is one of those occasions where we must admit that human reason has severe limitations. Just as our unaided minds devise arguments to show that the universe must be eternal, and are hard pressed to see what could be wrong with these arguments, so the natural resources of philosophy would rule out the possibility of a surviving, separate accident. This is for the same reason we saw before when looking at Siger, namely that the philosopher must reason on the basis of natural laws, which, of course, lay down that accidents depend for their survival on the substances that have those accidents. No bread and wine means no flavor of bread or wine, from the philosopher's point of view. The theologian has a different point of view, from which he can admit that the flavor or color of bread can survive without the bread. But Siger did not prevail in this dispute. As we move on to consider Duns Scotus and various thinkers of the fourteenth century, we will see philosophers eagerly exploring the implications of a power that can, quite literally, do anything that can be done.

48

ONCE AND FOR ALL
SCOTUS ON BEING

We began our tour through the world of thirteenth-century philosophy by citing a classic philosophical remark: "It depends upon what the meaning of the word 'is,' is." Those who recall the political debates of the 1990s will have no trouble identifying this as a quote from Bill Clinton. But historians of philosophy might rather think of a far earlier debate. Among medievals there was a heated controversy over the meaning of "is." Does "being (*esse*)" have only one meaning or many different meanings? Usually we have no difficulty answering this sort of question. The word "bill" is obviously used with a number of different meanings. It could be the first name of a former President, the business end of a duck, or what the waiter hands you at the end of a business lunch. Aristotle explained at the beginning of his *Categories*, the work on which philosophers from late antiquity through the Middle Ages cut their teeth, that words are used "equivocally" when they are applied with such different meanings. If, on the other hand, a word is used on different occasions with the same meaning, I am using that word "univocally." Thus, when I apply the word "human" to Bill Clinton and to Aristotle, I am using it as a "univocal" term.

Why, then, did the medievals worry whether the word "being" is used equivocally or univocally? Most historians of philosophy will tell you that the problem first emerged in the late thirteenth century, with Thomas Aquinas and Henry of Ghent defending the "equivocal" theory of being, and John Duns Scotus a "univocal" understanding. But that's because most historians of philosophy haven't read the previous volume in this book series. As shown there, a controversy over this very issue had already emerged in the Islamic world. Muslim philosopher-theologians writing in Arabic anticipated the views we find in Christian philosopher-theologians writing in Latin like Aquinas, Henry, and Scotus. Some of the clever philosophical moves usually taken to be inventions of the Latin schoolmen were actually reinventions. Particularly striking are the parallels between arguments given by the so-called "subtle doctor," Duns Scotus, and the no less subtle Fakhr al-Dīn al-Rāzī, who lived about a century earlier.[1]

This is no coincidence. Scotus and Fakhr al-Dīn were not reading one another, but they were provoked by the same source: Avicenna. We've been seeing that his works were highly influential in Latin translation; among Islamic intellectuals of the twelfth and thirteenth centuries his influence was even greater, to the point that he assumed the central role played by Aristotle in Latin scholasticism. It was in any case a distinction of Avicenna's that triggered both debates over the meaning of being. He contrasted the essence of a thing with that thing's existence.[2] The idea is a pretty plausible one. On the one hand, you have the question of what something is by its very nature, on the other hand, the question of whether it exists. Actually these two questions are already distinguished by Aristotle (*Posterior Analytics* 89b). What Avicenna added was the point that essences are almost always neutral with respect to existence. He gave the example of a triangle. You can study the nature or essence of a triangle and learn all sorts of things about it, for instance that its internal angles are equal to two right angles. But nothing about the nature of triangle tells you whether or not it exists. So if a triangle does exist, this must be because some other thing, like a child doing geometry homework, has come along and made it exist. This same point will apply to the child too, of course. She is a human, and if you think about what it means to be a human, you'll see that humanity involves many things, such as being alive, being rational, or being an animal, but not just plain being. So the child too must be brought to exist by some outside cause. Avicenna added that there is, however, one essence that is not like this, the essence of that which *necessarily* exists. This necessary existent is, of course, God. He exists through Himself, by His very nature, so that He cannot fail to exist and exists without needing a cause.

The essence-existence distinction was eagerly taken up and just as eagerly debated by Muslim thinkers, and the Christians independently followed suit. Already William of Auvergne made use of it in the first half of the thirteenth century.[3] But the most famous example, as usual, is Aquinas. It forms the core idea of his early work *On Being and Essence*.[4] The Avicennan background is not difficult to detect. Aquinas cites him on the very first page for the idea that existence and essence are immediate concepts of the mind, not ideas we need to reach through some indirect process of reasoning. He also applies Avicenna's triangle test to demonstrate the difference between essence and existence: I can know what something is without knowing whether there is any such thing.[5] For Aquinas, this shows that the contrast counts as what the scholastics liked to call a "real" distinction. In other words, essence is really distinct from existence, rather than something's essence and something's existence being two different points of view we take on the same thing out in the world. His follower Giles of Rome agreed and in fact took the point even further than Aquinas probably wanted to go.[6] He compared the combination of essence and existence to the relation between the matter and the form of a physical substance. Just as matter is a separate principle that receives form, so essences are distinct in themselves and then receive actual existence. The essence serves to puts limits or boundaries on being, whereas in God being remains infinite and unlimited.[7]

What does all this have to do with Bill Clinton's puzzle about the meaning of "is"? Well, let's consider again how Avicenna's distinction might apply to God. Or rather let's consider the possibility that in God's case, it does *not* apply. We might suppose that God's existing through His very essence means that, in Him, there is no essence apart from existence.[8] We might even go so far as to say that He just *is* being or existence. But if this is so, then it looks as if God has being of a very different sort than the being we find in, say, Bill Clinton. The existence that is God is not the same as the existence which was given to Bill Clinton when he was created. This forces us to say that there are at least two kinds of existence. On the one hand, there is divine existence, which is necessary and identical to God's very essence, and, on the other hand, there is created existence, which is contingent and distinct from the essence of the created thing. We can reach the same result without appealing to the unusual case of God. If, like any self-respecting scholastic, you have read your Aristotle, you know that for him "being is said in many ways" (a repeated refrain in his *Metaphysics*, as at 1028a). Aristotle would seem to think that the being of a human is different from the being of a duck. An Aristotelian will also be tempted to think that the independent being of substances like humans and ducks is different from the dependent being of accidental properties, like the color of a duck's bill or Bill Clinton's determination to get a bill through Congress.

On this basis Aquinas was led to the conclusion that being is indeed used equivocally. It means one thing when applied to God, another when applied to creatures. Yet he didn't think that this was a case of *pure* equivocation, like the completely different senses of the word "bill." Instead, language is applied to God and to creatures in different, yet related ways. Again, this is good Aristotle. He too had said that, though being is said in many ways, it is one of those terms that is applied to one primary case and then some other secondary cases. A classic illustration is the term "healthy." Its primary use is when we apply it to a healthy person, but we can also say that food or medicine is "healthy" because it contributes to the health of the person. Here we are dealing with a particular kind of equivocal use, which is called "analogy." Aquinas uses the theory of analogy to explain how various perfections are ascribed to God. Just as "healthy" is said primarily of the healthy person, so "good" is applied primarily to God, who is the cause of good and is perfect goodness itself (*ST* 1 Q13 a6 resp).[9] The same analysis can be given in the case of being. God is not just any old existing thing, but the source of existence for all other things. He is, in fact, being itself (*esse ipsum*).

Aquinas' approach has various advantages. Most obviously, it splits the difference between making God too transcendent and not transcendent enough. We don't want all the words we use for created things to be applied to God in a purely equivocal way. If that were the case, these words would have utterly different meanings from the ones they have when used normally. These other meanings would remain utterly mysterious, given that we can reach knowledge of God only on the basis of created things. If, on the other hand, we applied terms to God univocally, we would be putting Him on a par with created things. Analogy avoids both problems. Another advantage is that Aquinas avoids violating divine simplicity. If God is truly simple, then His various traits, like goodness and mercy, cannot be really distinct from one another, and this shows that we must be using the words "goodness" and "mercy" rather differently in His case. After all, I can call a created thing good without meaning that that thing is merciful. The identity between God's essence and His existence is another aspect of God's simplicity, and a way in which He differs even from other immaterial things like souls and angels.[10]

Though the analogy theory and the essence-existence distinction make for a good pairing, they don't have to come together. In the generation of Scotus, a theologian named Godfrey of Fontaines accepted that we apply language to God analogically. Yet he launched a powerful attack against the essence-existence distinction, targeting its formulation by Aquinas and especially Giles of Rome.[11] While Godfrey accepts that we can think about things either in terms of their essences or as existing things, he denies that this is a real distinction in the things themselves. Instead, it is a distinction of the sort we saw when looking at speculative grammar. If I think or speak of a duck's essence or a duck as existing, I am just using two different modes of signifying the same thing. This no more implies a real difference in ducks than it would if I used the adjective "beautiful" when saying "Ducks are beautiful" and then the noun "beauty" in saying "Ducks have a beauty rare even among waterfowl." Besides, the real version of the distinction runs afoul of obvious difficulties. If, as Giles of Rome claimed, essence is something distinct that receives existence the way that matter receives form, then essence would already have to exist before it receives existence the way that matter may already exists before taking on form. This is clearly absurd. But what about Avicenna's triangle argument, that we can understand what something is without knowing whether it exists? To this Godfrey replies that we can only know things when they do in fact exist. We never grasp such mysterious, ontologically neutral essences; our knowledge is directed towards real things.[12]

We're almost ready now to look at Scotus' solution, but not quite. While Aquinas, Giles, and Godfrey are an important part of the background, there is another author to whom Scotus replies most directly. This is Henry of Ghent. Henry's position on these matters is similar to that of Aquinas, but with a few twists. He too thinks that being is applied to God and to creatures by way of analogy. This is connected to the way we come to know God. As we saw in Chapter 46, Henry takes inspiration from Avicenna's proposal that being is a primary concept of the mind and infers that all of us have a kind of indistinct awareness or intuition of God, who, as the doctrine of analogy would suggest, is nothing other than pure being. Henry also accepts the distinction between essence and existence. But he concedes that, as Godfrey stressed, the two are always found together. There is no such thing as essence without existence, so that the difference between them is weaker than between two really distinct objects like, say, two individual ducks. Yet neither are essence and existence fully identical. They are, says Henry, "intentionally distinct." This is a step in the direction of Scotus' notion of a "formal distinction," a kind of middle ground between a real distinction and a distinction that is merely the product of our minds.[13]

Indeed, Scotus himself apparently wanted to understand the difference between essence and existence as a formal distinction. Actually, he doesn't say much about this. It's been commented that Scotus "has not given the issue much sustained attention, and it is not close to the heart of his metaphysical thinking."[14] When he does mention it, though, he seems to see it as a formal distinction, like the difference between the Persons of the Trinity. Just as Avicenna said, it is no part of what it means to be a duck that the duck must exist. So we can distinguish between the essence of a duck and its existence. Yet, as Henry admitted, there are no duck essences that don't exist. To the contrary, any real essence is always found together with existence. So, even though we these two aspects of the duck are not identical, they are only formally, not really, distinct.

Something to which Scotus has definitely given sustained attention, and that is very much at the heart of his metaphysical thinking, is the univocity of being. He uses several clever arguments to support his position.[15] One—by his standards, relatively straightforward—argument is the following. Scotus agrees with Aquinas that natural knowledge of God must be built on our experience of the created world. So, to grasp that God is a being, we need to extend a concept of being that we got from created things and apply it to God.[16] Hence, it must be the *same* concept, and the term "being" needs to be used with the same meaning. Another somewhat more complicated rationale goes like this. We can apply the notion of being to God without realizing that God is infinite, necessary, purely actual, or whatever else makes God's being so different. Plenty of people admit that God exists without understanding that He exists necessarily or is infinite. So, clearly, we begin by applying the normal notion of being to Him and then *add* infinity, necessity, and so on. It is these added features that make God so special. It's not by virtue of just existing or being that He transcends created things.

Speaking of transcending, Scotus' claim that being is univocal has a lot to do with the by now familiar concept of the transcendentals (see Chapter 25). Just by way of reminder, the transcendentals are features that belong to all things, both divine and worldly, such as unity, goodness, truth, and, of course, being. Scotus takes this very seriously and assumes that these features do indeed transcend all divisions within reality. Everything is a being; then it's a further question what kind of being. When we divide being into types, we are actually applying another, more complicated transcendental feature. Not everything is finite, nor is everything infinite, but everything is either-finite-or-infinite. The same point goes for necessity and contingency. Everything that exists, exists either necessarily in itself or only contingent upon some cause. These pairs of properties divide being, with God on one side and creation on the other. With this Scotus is rejecting Henry's idea that we are obscurely grasping God when we form our immediate idea of being. For Scotus, being is univocal. Our general idea of being applies to everything that is, and is thus no more appropriate to God than to anything else. If you want to grasp God, it isn't enough to talk about being. You have to be more specific about what kind of being you have in mind. Only once you take your idea of being and add such features as infinity or necessity are you getting closer to grasping Him, since only God is an infinite being and only He necessarily exists.[17]

We said that Aquinas' analogy theory has several advantages, but the same is true of Scotus' univocity theory. One has to do with the nature of the enterprise we're engaged in here, namely metaphysics. Scotus borrows another idea from Avicenna here, saying that metaphysics is the study of being in general.[18] And every science needs a single object of study. Experts in waterfowl study creatures, all of whom are equally and in the same sense waterfowl. In the same way, if metaphysics is a properly unified science, the metaphysician needs to be able to study being wherever it turns up, whether in God or in creatures, in substances or in accidents, and to mean the same thing by "being" in each case. The general contrary properties like necessary-or-contingent and infinite-or-finite will also fall under this science of metaphysics. This is because jointly each pair covers everything that has being, and metaphysics is the general study of all beings.

The fact that Scotus has borrowed so much from Avicenna does not, of course, detract from his importance as a thinker. For one thing, he stole from the best. For another, he develops Avicenna's ideas considerably. His sophisticated defense of a univocal conception of being was unprecedented in Latin Christendom, even if it is reminiscent of the sophisticated defense of the same idea that Fakhr al-Dīn al-Rāzī had put forward some generations earlier in central Asia. That precedent should, however, alert us to a different problem. In the Islamic world Avicenna's strong association between God and necessity had attracted a good deal of criticism from al-Rāzī and others. Most were prepared to agree with Avicenna that God must exist through Himself, that He is the necessary existent. But few were prepared to admit that God is necessary in every respect. Doesn't God enjoy the same sort of freedom we do, or rather a far greater degree of freedom? But, then, how is divine freedom compatible with His necessary existence? Reflection on this issue leads Scotus to a radical philosophical breakthrough, as he develops an innovative and influential theory of contingency.

49

TO WILL OR NOT TO WILL
SCOTUS ON FREEDOM

*H*amlet, Act 3, Scene 3. We find the Prince of Denmark doing what he does best: hesitating. He has an apparently perfect opportunity to revenge his father's murder at the hands of his uncle, Claudius, having found him alone praying. Hamlet has Claudius at his mercy but then realizes that killing him now might be *too* merciful. If he slays Claudius while he prays for forgiveness, then Claudius will go to heaven. "Am I then revenged," asks Hamlet, "to take him in the purging of his soul, when he is fit and season'd for his passage?" He decides to wait for a better opportunity. "And thus," as Hamlet elsewhere remarks, "the native hue of resolution is sicklied o'er with the pale cast of thought, and enterprises of great pith and moment with this regard their currents turn awry, and lose the name of action." I could hardly have put it better myself.

And we've all been there. Well, perhaps not quite in this situation. But we've all been uncertain how to act, or certain how to act but uncertain whether the time for action has come. At such moments we feel vividly that we have a genuine power to choose whether or not to act. Hamlet is not like a Greek tragic hero, carried inevitably forward by his own character, by the tide of events, or by the will of the gods. He is a quintessentially modern tragic hero, blessed (or perhaps cursed) with the power and responsibility to shape the present and the future. He must choose whether it is right to kill or not to kill, whether to be or not to be. As philosophers nowadays would put it, these choices seem to be characterized by the presence of alternative possibilities. Hamlet can kill Claudius as he prays or refrain from doing so. Both paths are open to him and he must choose which one to follow. For some philosophers we can count ourselves as free *only* when such alternative possibilities are available. Freedom is not simply doing what you want. If you cannot avoid performing a given action, you are unfree with respect to that action, whether you want to perform it or not.

Of course, the idea that freedom involves open alternatives was not invented by Shakespeare. Its long history can perhaps be traced back ultimately to Aristotle. In *On Interpretation* (19a) he points out that if everything were necessary, it would make no sense for us to engage in deliberation. Yet Aristotle also gave philosophers a powerful reason to be suspicious about the idea of genuinely open possibilities. In the same passage he suggests that whatever is happening right now in the present moment is necessary.[1] If this is right, then at the very moment Hamlet passes up the chance to kill Claudius, his not killing Claudius is necessary. And this makes a certain amount of sense. How could it still be possible for Hamlet to strike even as he is in the act of withdrawing, saying "Up, sword, and know thou a more horrid bent"?

To get to the modern day notion of simultaneous, genuinely open possibilities we are going to have to make a few subtle distinctions. In particular we are going to have to turn to a man who specialized in such distinctions, John Duns Scotus. We've already met him engaging in debates over the Trinity and arguing for the univocity of being. But now I'd like to introduce him properly. I'm treating him as the last of the great thinkers of the thirteenth century, even though his life spanned the thirteenth and fourteenth centuries, as did his thought, responding as it did to Henry of Ghent and others while also setting the agenda for numerous thinkers in the age to come.[2] Born in Scotland (hence "Scotus") in the 1260s, he wrote many of his works right around the turn of the century, lecturing on Peter Lombard's *Sentences* in Oxford in the year 1300 itself. These lectures are a leading example of the way that the standard task of teaching the *Sentences* could be an excuse for theologians to put forth their own views. He then had two stints at Paris, where he became a master of theology before dying in Cologne in 1308. His works are full of newly coined terminology, brilliant argumentation, novel philosophical notions, and tortuously complex reasoning, making them a thrilling, yet challenging read.

His earliest important work consists in those lectures on the *Sentences* given in Oxford (the *Lectura*). We have a revision of these lectures (the *Ordinatio*) from his time in Paris, as well as student notes on his Parisian lectures on the *Sentences* (the *Reportatio*), along with other philosophical and theological works, including a commentary on Aristotle's *Metaphysics* and a treatise on God (*On the First Principle*). More information can be gleaned from other sources, like additional notes produced by Scotus' secretary, William of Alnwick. The upshot is that Scotus has left a wealth of material for us to study. Yet this material is often confusing, because of layers of revision and the fact that we are often reading only reports of what he said. We also find Scotus rethinking his positions as his career goes along.

His views on freedom and the will offer a good example. He seems to have changed his mind about the nature of possibility and also the role of our intellect in forming our choices.[3] Here Scotus is reacting especially to Henry of Ghent, for whom the intellect has only an advisory capacity, with the will serving as the supreme power within the human soul (Chapter 46). On this reckoning it is Hamlet's will alone that determines the choice not to kill Claudius, even if it is taking the advice of Hamlet's intellect that slaying Claudius just when he is at prayer isn't the best way of exacting revenge. The early Scotus is reluctant to give the will sole responsibility and makes intellect and will cooperative causes in forming choice. But he comes to adopt a more purely voluntarist view like Henry's, which is the understanding of human action we usually associate with Scotus.

Like Henry and unlike Aquinas, the mature Scotus insists that the will is not moved to make its choices by intellect. Rather, it simply moves itself. With this he is rejecting a basic tenet of Aristotle, who had argued that self-motion is impossible—part of his argument tracing all motion to the single, ultimate mover that is God.[4] Scotus scornfully dismisses this idea, stating that the impossibility of self-motion is "not a first, no, not even a tenth principle."[5] Still, Scotus seeks to base his theory on Aristotle—this is scholastic philosophy, after all—and is especially persuaded by Aristotle's idea that rational powers are distinguished from natural powers by their capacity to select either of two contraries. The idea here is that a merely natural cause gives rise to only one effect. Fire always heats things up and never cools them down. By contrast, a so-called "rational" power can do either of two opposed things, as when Hamlet decides whether to kill Claudius or not.

Scotus argues on this basis that only the will is truly "rational," because only will can choose from either of two alternatives.[6] The intellect is, instead, a "natural" cause, more like fire. It can only form beliefs based on the available evidence. Thus, Hamlet judges that killing Claudius while he prays will allow him to go to heaven. He's wrong about this by the way. Shakespeare allows us to enjoy the irony of Claudius saying, just after Hamlet departs, that his prayers are ineffective: "My words fly up, my thoughts remain below: words without thoughts never to heaven go." Right or wrong, though, Hamlet's intellect must reach the judgment that seems most compelling. Yet he remains free to choose however he wills on the basis of this judgment. As Scotus puts it, if the will "had no power over the opposite in that very instant and at the time when it is actually determined to something, then no effect that is being actualized would be contingent."[7] Freedom is not about judging or not judging. To will or not to will: that is the question.

To be capable of this sort of freedom, the choice we make needs to be contingent rather than necessary, that is, we are going to need genuinely open alternatives to choose between. To show how this could be so, Scotus is going to have to produce a definition of possibility that was not dreamt of in Aristotle's philosophy.[8] Before Scotus it was common to assume that merely possible, or "contingent," things are simply the things that happen sometimes, but not always. And fair enough, you might say. It seems right that necessities are always true, while impossibilities are never true. Thus, it is eternally the case that one plus one equals two, eternally false that one plus one equals three. Contingent things, by contrast, might be the case but need not be. It's possible for me to sit and for me to stand. This is how it can be that you'll occasionally find me standing, though usually you'll find me sitting since that's the posture I adopt for reading about philosophy. Notice that, on this reckoning, genuinely possible things do need to happen at some point. If something is never the case, then, according to the traditional Aristotelian view, it is impossible. Also, as we already said, in this way of thinking the past and present are no longer contingent. They are necessary, since it is too late to do anything to change them.

Scotus explicitly rejects this whole way of thinking. He says, "I do not call 'contingent' everything that is not necessary or not eternal. Instead I refer to something the opposite of which is possible even at the very moment it actually exists or occurs."[9] That's actually a pretty straightforward explanation by Scotus' standards, but let's unpack it a bit. On the traditional conception of contingency only the future was open. As Hamlet stalks the hallways of Elsinore looking for Claudius, it is still open for him to kill or not. But once he finds Claudius and chooses to spare his life, the die is cast: it's not possible for him to kill Claudius while not killing Claudius. Scotus' breakthrough is to insist that it *does* remain possible for Hamlet to kill Claudius even as he refrains from doing so. This is because possibility or contingency is not defined in terms of what happens or doesn't happen. It's defined in terms of what *could* happen, whether or not it does in fact happen.

That sounds circular. But it isn't, because Scotus has a brilliant way of explaining precisely what we mean when we say that something could be the case even when it isn't. The contingent is just that which implies no contradiction. Scotus puts the point in terms of "repugnance." The reason a round square is impossible is that the terms "round" and "square" are incompatible with, or repugnant to, one another. Scotus offers the example of the chimera, a mythical beast made of parts of a lion, snake, and goat. Since these animal natures in fact exclude one another, the chimera cannot exist. Possible things are possible because they involve no such repugnance or incompatibility. As Avicenna pointed out, neither do such things *need* to exist. There is nothing about the essence of a lion, snake, or goat that guarantees the existence of lions, snakes, or goats. And the same goes in the case of actions like Hamlet's. There is no impossibility entailed by killing Claudius at prayer, so it remains possible for Hamlet to do so, even as he is deciding it would be better to catch Claudius later, when he is in a state of sin.

This conception of possibility is often hailed as Scotus' greatest contribution to philosophy. And not without reason, even if, as usual, we have to admit that the groundwork was laid by previous thinkers. For Scotus the most important inspiration here was yet again Henry of Ghent.[10] He already proposed that some things that are genuinely possible are never realized.[11] What makes them possible is that they are conceived as possibilities in the mind of God. I don't have a sister, but I could have had one. For Henry what this means is that God understands that He could have created her. Now it may seem that there is a big difference between Scotus and his predecessor on this score. Henry argued that things become possible because God thinks about them as things He could create, whereas Scotus says that things are possible in themselves, just by virtue of not involving any "repugnance" or intrinsic impossibility. But we can find Scotus talking the way that Henry did. His approach is especially close to Henry in his early works, but he always seems to retain the idea that possibility is somehow grounded in God's creative power.[12]

So is Scotus' position on possibility like a chimera, stuck together out of incompatible parts? No, and to see why, we need (of course) to draw a distinction. Repugnance or incompatibility belongs to things by their very nature. Chimeras are intrinsically impossible and lions intrinsically possible. But for lions to be possible, God has first to think of them as something He can create. Thus, we should distinguish between a "first moment" and "second moment" in the order of nature. In the first moment God thinks "Here's something I could make: a lion," which Scotus, following Henry, describes as the creation of lions in "intelligible being." In the second moment, lions are in themselves possible because they lack internal contradiction. This possibility is not something God needs to bestow on lions, nor does God need to do any extra work to prevent lions from combining with snakes and goats to form chimeras, since chimeras are in themselves impossible. Finally, in a third moment, God actually creates some, but not all of the things that could possibly be created. The reason there are no round squares or chimeras is that they can't exist; the reason I do exist and my sister doesn't is down to God's choice as a creator.

And make no mistake, God does have a choice about what He creates. Scotus' idea of simultaneously open possibilities is meant to apply to God's freedom as much as to ours. This is despite the fact that God is a necessary being. Scotus, being Scotus, in fact has a clever and complicated proof of God's necessary existence.[13] I'll avoid the complicated bits and cut straight to the most brilliant part. After a lot of work, Scotus is able to demonstrate to his own satisfaction that there could possibly be a cause for all other things, which is first and therefore uncaused. In other words, God *might* exist. From this Scotus thinks he can immediately infer that God *does* exist. For just consider: obviously a first cause does not come to exist by being caused to exist by something else. So the only way for such a cause to exist is by being necessarily actual. But we know that there is a way for the cause to exist, since we established that it might exist. Therefore, the cause is necessarily actual, so God does in fact exist. As Scotus notes himself, his proof is reminscent of earlier attempts to demonstrate the existence of God. The move from God's possible existence to His actual existence may remind us of the move at the center of Anselm's ontological argument (Chapter 8).[14] Scotus' proof also recalls Avicenna, and his idea of God as a necessarily existing first cause.[15]

Unlike Avicenna, though, Scotus thinks that God's actions as a Creator are contingent even if God exists necessarily. It may seem that, with Henry of Ghent's help, he has already shown us how this could be so. God chooses only some possible creatures for actual existence. But, as Hamlet might say, not so fast. Even granted that there are a variety of ways for God to make the world, isn't He required to choose the *best* of those ways? After all, He is perfectly good and benevolent. So, when God considered whether to create lions, He presumably had to consider whether a world with lions is better than a world without lions. Apparently, He decided the answer was yes, though giraffes might beg to differ with this decision. This isn't quite how the medievals typically saw things, though.[16] Aquinas and Bonaventure denied that it even makes sense to talk about a "best of all possible worlds." Any created world is infinitely inferior to God Himself, so that no matter what world God creates, there will be an infinite amount of room for improvement. In a sense our actual world is perfect because it is internally well ordered, but there is no point comparing this world to other worlds that might have entirely different sorts of creatures in them.

Scotus likewise focuses on the question of whether things could be better arranged given the natures that actually exist, rather than the question of whether a whole different set of natures might be preferable. He says that our world is perfect as it is, but for a different reason, namely that *whatever* God does is perfect just by definition. God's goodness does not consist in His choosing the best out of available options. Rather, it consists in conferring goodness on whichever option He does choose. To put it another way, if God had decided to arrange things differently, then that different arrangement would be the best. This is a rather surprising conclusion. To understand it more fully we're going to have to address the question of just what Scotus understands by goodness. Would he agree with Hamlet that "There is nothing either good or bad, but thinking makes it so?" Yes, if the one doing the thinking is God.

50

ON COMMAND
SCOTUS ON ETHICS

My parents knew a minister who spent a week living on a few dollars a day to draw attention to the plight of the poor. A member of the parish approached her at church and said she had been shocked by a picture of the minister's family having dinner. "Why shocked?" inquired the minister. The parishioner's response: "No matter how poor one is, or is pretending to be, one can still serve one's ketchup from a *bowl*." You have to admire this sort of unwavering commitment to right and wrong. Some things are just not acceptable under any circumstances. Perhaps serving ketchup out of a bottle is not one of them. But what about killing your own child? I'm glad to say my parents don't have a story about that. There is one in the Bible, though. In chapter 22 of the Book of Genesis, we are told how God instructed Abraham to sacrifice his son Isaac on a mountaintop. Abraham dutifully obeys and prepares his son upon an altar. But just as he is grasping hold of the knife to do the terrible deed, an angel is sent to tell Abraham to stop. He has passed the test and need not kill his son after all.

Despite the happy ending, this passage can easily provoke theological and philosophical perplexity. How can the same God who sent down the Ten Commandments, including "Thou shalt not kill," demand that Abraham slay his own son? If we accept that Abraham was right to obey God, does that show that any action, even the murder of one's own family members, could be righteous in sufficiently extreme circumstances? The mere thought may seem to throw the whole of morality into question. To see how, go have a look at Kierkegaard's *Fear and Trembling*. He uses the case of Abraham and Isaac to show that we may have duties higher than the requirements of ethics. Within the ethical realm it is wrong to kill one's child, but a divine command can trump ethical considerations. Another way of thinking about it might be that the rule against killing still holds, but not under all circumstances. Think back to our discussion of medieval just war theory (Chapter 40), when we saw the medievals explaining exactly that thou shalt sometimes go ahead and kill after all, and this on supposedly good Christian principles.

There is yet another way of thinking about the Abraham case, and it's this third way I want to talk about here. Instead of seeing instruction from God as an extraordinary event that overrides or changes our moral duty, we might see divine commands as the source of all moral obligation. We should do whatever God wants us to do, *because* He wants us to do it. Even if you don't find this a particularly tempting idea, you can probably see why medievals would be attracted to it. We've regularly seen them saying that God is the highest good and source of all good, just as He is the highest being who is the source of all being and highest truth who is the source of all truth. At the very least medievals would find it plausible that our knowledge of moral duty comes from God, since on the popular "illumination" theory *all* our knowledge comes from God. Thus, we find Hugh of Saint Victor saying that our understanding of good and evil "is a kind of command given to the heart of man."[1] Of course, the Bible itself might also encourage this way of thinking. Abraham is praised for his willingness to sacrifice his son if it is the will of God, and all of us are bound by the Ten Commandments given to Moses.

Modern-day philosophers call this the "divine command theory of ethics." According to this view, God is a kind of moral legislator whose decrees establish right and wrong. The implication is that, had God legislated differently, right and wrong would be different. He does not look to some objective set of ethical standards when He tells us what to do but makes up His own divine mind what He wants us to do. Within a religious framework this actually makes a lot of sense. It would explain obligations to follow certain dietary laws or to carry out certain rituals in certain ways. One might be able to come up with independent reasons for going on pilgrimage to Mecca, avoiding pork, or remaining chaste outside the bounds of marriage. But it's far simpler for believers to say that they do these things because God told them to. So why not just say that we are likewise to avoid murder and theft because God's commandments forbid them? The downside is that, if God commands us to commit murder, as He did with Abraham, then we will have a moral duty to perform an apparently immoral action. Yesterday's wrong will be today's new right.

Even if we suppose that God never actually changes the moral laws, the mere fact that He could do so is already quite troubling. It seems irresistible to think that in such a case God would be evil. Just consider how you would react to the Abraham story if God had let him go ahead and kill Isaac. Could you really believe that this was the right thing for Abraham to do, and could you really believe that God was being just rather than cruel and tyrannical? Maybe you could if you were Duns Scotus. We can see immediately why he might like the divine command theory. As we've just seen, Scotus is a voluntarist who lays great emphasis on God's untrammeled freedom. Even the natures of things are for him ultimately grounded in God's will: the possibility and actual reality of, say, giraffes presuppose His having created giraffe in "intelligible being." So even when we are doing non-moral reasoning, as when we undertake scientific inquiry into the nature of giraffes, in a sense we are just exploring the choices made by God. It wouldn't be at all surprising if Scotus thought the same is true of moral reasoning.

And this is indeed pretty much what he thinks. Earlier thinkers such as Philip the Chancellor had made moves in the direction of ethical voluntarism or divine command theory.[2] But Scotus' new ideas about the contingency of the created order allow him to develop such a theory with unprecedented sophistication. God could have created the world differently, so that there might have been no giraffes or so that murder might have been morally acceptable (it's hard to see which of those would be more horrifying). You won't be surprised to learn that Scotus develops this idea by drawing a subtle distinction. In this case he contrasts the "absolute" and "ordained" power of God.[3] God's absolute power is His ability to do anything whatsoever that can be done. On Scotus' understanding of possibility, this means that God has the power to do anything that is not "repugnant" to itself, or self-contradictory. We can see immediately why this fits the divine command theory. Since there is no contradiction in, say, allowing sex outside of marriage, God could have allowed it had He chosen to do so. Once God has laid down a natural and moral order, He can continue to act within that order without violating it. Because it involves adhering to such an established order, this is called "ordained" power.[4]

So far it sounds like morality for Scotus would be determined solely by God's choices, with no constraints whatsoever on those choices. But this isn't quite right. For one thing, there is the constraint I just mentioned. God's absolute power doesn't enable Him to do, or command, things that are outright incoherent. We've already seen that God cannot create a round square or chimera because such things are intrinsically impossible. Similarly, Scotus believes that God cannot release us from the responsibility to love Him. This is because God is the highest good, and what is good is intrinsically lovable. So a kind of contradiction would be implied if God told us to hate Him. This emerges in Scotus' discussion of the Ten Commandments, a key text for his moral theory.[5] He thinks that the commandments of the first table, namely the first four which regard our duties to God, are just a spelling out of the inevitable requirement to love God.[6] The remaining commandments have to do with our relations to created things, and these are subject to God's will.

With this move, Scotus has radically reworked the traditional idea of natural law.[7] Prominently mentioned in Gratian's *Decretum*, the concept of natural law had been expounded by numerous thirteenth-century theologians, including Aquinas (see Chapter 39). For him, morality is "promulgated" by being written into our very nature, giving us the ability to use our inborn reason to discern right from wrong. This means that for Aquinas too the moral law derives ultimately from God, but only in the sense that it is God who created us and gave us our human nature and capacity for reasoning. For Scotus natural law in the strict sense includes much less. In fact, it includes *only* the inevitable requirement to love God and the further obligations that stem directly from this, such as not worshipping graven images (the third commandment). The remaining commandments are "consonant" with this fundamental moral principle but do depend on God's voluntary decree. This is why they can be revoked, as when Abraham was commanded to kill.

Here we come to another constraint on what God can command. We may be able to accept that He can change the rules and tell Abraham to sacrifice his son. But surely God cannot command Abraham both to kill *and* not to kill. That would be another case of incoherence or self-contradiction. The same applies to the moral order more generally. The laws must be coherent. Indeed, that's why they merit the name of an "order." This could help Scotus respond to an obvious complaint against his ethical voluntarism: if God just freely decides what is good and what is bad, then there will be no point at all in moral reasoning. All we could do is consult Scripture and follow the rules. But if the moral order is consistent and coherent, as Scotus insists, then there is a place for such reasoning after all. Once God has laid down the contingent order that prevails in our world, it is possible for us to study that order and understand our place within it.[8] This is an eminently rational enterprise, not unlike what we do in natural science, where we use reason to understand the created world that God chose to bring into existence.

Still, Scotus is departing radically from the sort of ethical doctrine we find in Aquinas, and above all in Aristotle. In Aristotelianism human nature is the foundation of ethics. To be a good person is to be an excellent human, which means making excellent use of reason, the distinctively human faculty. The habit of excellent reasoning that gives rise to excellent action is virtue. For an Aristotelian, virtue is like a "second nature," an acquired disposition to do the right thing in each circumstance. Thus, a person who has the virtue of generosity will, upon seeing someone in need, judge that they are to be helped and perform a generous act, by giving them money or perhaps recommending a good philosophy book. Moreover, someone who really has this virtue is going to have other virtues as well, like courage, temperance, and wisdom. All the virtues are bound together by a capacity for good practical reasoning or "prudence" (*phronesis*, in Latin *prudentia*). Last but not least, for Aristotle having and exercising the virtues is what makes humans happy, the end towards which his entire ethics is directed. This ultimate end of happiness moves us to act as we pursue the most excellent and blessed life possible.

Scotus modifies or rejects every aspect of this Aristotelian picture.[9] For starters, human nature cannot be the ultimate ground of ethics, because human nature itself is contingently created by God. Furthermore, while Scotus agrees that virtue is the disposition to choose well, he denies that virtue explains morally good *choice*. This is because virtue always points the way towards the good. In this sense virtue is not a properly "rational" cause, which has the ability to choose between different alternatives, but like a "natural" cause such as fire, which always gives rise to heat. If choice is involved, then we need more than virtue: we need the will. Even if you have the virtue of easily and consistently discerning the right thing to do, your will must still make the right choice on each occasion. And, of course, good actions are not good *because* they proceed from virtuous dispositions, as an Aristotelian might think, or even because they conform to the ends of human nature. A good action is good because God commanded it.

Scotus is no more satisfied with the Aristotelian account when it comes to prudence and the unity of the virtues. He thinks it's obvious that you can have some virtues and lack others. For one thing, you might find yourself in a situation where you cannot practice or exercise virtue in a certain sphere. A person who grows up stranded on a desert island might be resourceful, moderate, and wise, but is not going to have much chance to work on generosity or sociability. In any case, the will's inviolable power to choose well or badly on each occasion means that there is no guarantee that tending to choose well in one sphere will mean doing so in another. For the same reason Scotus cannot accept the notion that good practical reasoning, or prudence, will guarantee good action. For prudence belongs to the intellect, not the will. Someone might understand perfectly well that they should not commit adultery but go ahead and do it anyway.[10]

A final (in every sense of the word) disagreement with the Aristotelians concerns the question of happiness. We saw that Albert the Great and Thomas Aquinas, seeking to retain as much of Aristotle's ethical teaching as they could, distinguished two types or levels of happiness. We can attain a degree of fulfillment in this life through virtuous activity, with a higher beatitude secured through a vision of God in the afterlife. In both cases we are moved by the final end of happiness. Scotus thinks this is wrong.[11] Surely we are not "moved" by any end to choose that end, not even by God. For Scotus, the will must be a self-mover, since otherwise our willing would be constrained and unfree. Besides, no human activity can secure happiness, since we can be happy only through the greatest of goods, which is God. Though it may be reasonable to pursue created goods in this life, we can never be satisfied with them, nor should we forget that "Everything other than God is good because it is willed by God, and not vice versa."[12] This God-centered moral theory may sound like a reassertion of Augustine against Aristotle. It certainly banishes any prospect that we might naturally attain (or "merit") happiness and salvation, and in that respect Scotus is on the same page as Augustine. But Scotus disagrees with Augustine on a different point. Having demoted natural virtue so far, he has no problem with the idea that we can be naturally virtuous without the help of God, something Augustine denied. For similar reasons he has no use for Aquinas' idea that there are divinely infused, as well as natural virtues.

All of this may seem to leave a gap in Scotus' moral theory, and you know how I feel about gaps. If virtue doesn't, as it were, spontaneously give rise to good action, then how and why do we act rightly? Of course, part of the answer is that we choose to do so through the will. But on what basis? Is it just random luck? Here Scotus looks back to an early medieval predecessor. He adopts Anselm's idea that we have two kinds of motivation, which often come into conflict with one another (see Chapter 7). On the one hand, we want what is useful to ourselves; on the other hand, we have an inclination towards justice that remains intact even in a state of original sin. Though prudence doesn't guarantee our choosing justice over advantage, it has an important role to play nonetheless, by helping us to see which actions are and are not just. When you deliberate about the right thing to do, you are engaging in this kind of reasoning. And thanks to your inborn affection for justice you have a motivation to choose in accordance with the advice that results, even if your freedom of will means that there is no guarantee you will do so.

One lesson to draw from all this might be that morality really has to do *only* with the choices made by the will. If you choose in accordance with the moral law laid down by God, then you have acted rightly. The action that results from the choice would really be only a by-product, with the moral value residing solely with the choice. This was the view of Peter Abelard, who taught that actions in themselves are neither good nor bad (Chapter 11). Goodness and badness would reside in the *intention* to perform an action, as shown by the fact that one and the same action can be performed for good reasons or bad: I might donate money to charity to help others or to impress my friends. While Scotus' voluntarism might seem to fit nicely with this idea of Abelard's, he doesn't go as far as he might have in this direction. For that we have to wait for William of Ockham, who also enthusiastically embraces voluntarism and does say that morality concerns only the "interior act" of the soul which gives rise to an outward, physical action.

So, for example, Ockham will say that God rewards and punishes people for their interior choices, and not what they actually do (see Chapter 57). Scotus takes a more moderate view.[13] He certainly agrees that interior choices can be morally good or bad. But, following other Franciscan thinkers like Bonaventure and Richard of Middleton, he also emphasizes that the outward act acquires a moral character of its own by flowing from a good or bad choice. This helps him explain something else about the biblical commandments. If you read through the list (it won't take long, there are only ten of them), you might notice that we are instructed not to covet another person's spouse and *also* not to commit adultery. On a view like Abelard's or Ockham's this could seem redundant. The problem should be the coveting, not the adulterous act to which the coveting leads. For Scotus, by contrast, the exterior act of adultery has a wrongness of its own despite being caused by an act of will that is already wrong in and of itself. Thus, he wouldn't entirely agree with Abelard on this issue. But he's a lot closer to him here than he will be when it comes to our final topic in Scotus' philosophy: the problem of universals.

51

ONE IN A MILLION
SCOTUS ON UNIVERSALS
AND INDIVIDUALS

"Roses are red, violets are blue, sugar is sweet, and so are you." This charming traditional poem may be suitable for a declaration of love between 7-year-olds. Yet upon closer inspection it proves to be rather perplexing. For one thing, surely violets are violet, not blue. For another thing, what exactly does it mean to say that all roses are red? The poem doesn't say that this or that rose is red, but that *all* roses are red. Actually, of course, it's also not true that all roses are red; the author of this poem clearly wasn't much of a gardener. But let's leave that aside and focus on making philosophical rather than botanical sense of the remark. It takes us back to a set of puzzles we met in the twelfth century, when Peter Abelard and his rivals disputed the question of universals (Chapter 9). Abelard was a nominalist: he held that there is no real, universal nature that belongs to all roses and is responsible for their being roses, nor is there any universal nature of redness that belongs to all red things. For Abelard all real things are individuals, and when we call a given individual "red" or "rose," we are simply applying general names that apply in virtue of the similarity between things. It's because this individual flower is like that one that we do not call this rose by any other name, regardless of whether it would smell as sweet. Opponents of Abelard like William of Champeaux were realists, meaning that they took the universal nature of roses to be something real that is present in each and every single rose, and likewise for redness in each red thing.

And there is another puzzle lurking here too. (It's really a remarkably complex poem!) I have in mind the problem of individuation. Again, this is a difficulty we encountered in the twelfth century, in this case with Gilbert of Poitiers, who wondered what makes each thing an individual (Chapter 16). Though we treated these two philosophical issues separately, they obviously make a good pair. The problem of universals is about what things in a given class have in common with one another: what makes all roses roses? The problem of individuation is what makes a member of a given class different from the other members of that class:

what makes the rose in my lapel to be a unique rose distinct from all the other roses in the world? These problems were certainly discussed by earlier thirteenth-century thinkers like Aquinas. But in this chapter I want to look at how Scotus, our final thinker of the century, rose to the challenge of solving both puzzles and in so doing set the terms of the later debate.[1]

Let's start with Abelard's central idea, the one that really led him to his nominalist position: everything that is real is one individual. On the face of it, this looks plausible, or even obvious. How can a thing exist without being just the one thing that it is? Just cast your mind back to one more previous medieval discussion, about the doctrine of transcendentals (Chapter 25). According to that doctrine, everything that has being also has unity; in other words, everything that is, is one. Scotus readily agrees with this. All real things are one and unity is a transcendental, that is, a feature of all things with a scope equal to that of being. But he denies that whatever is one is an *individual*. His way of putting the point uses traditional Aristotelian language to express a novel idea. He says that there is a kind of unity that is "less than numerical unity." This lesser sort of unity is the kind possessed by common natures shared among multiple things, as all roses share the nature of being a rose. Since common natures have a degree of unity, they also have a degree of reality or being.

So it would be tempting to label Scotus as a realist within the debate over universals. He is, after all, saying that shared natures are real. But just as every rose has its thorn, there's a sting in every tale told by Scotus. He strenuously *denies* that universals exist in external reality.[2] For him universality is a feature of our mental life. We have a general or universal understanding of roses that we abstract from all our encounters with particular roses, but there is no such thing as a universal nature of rose that exists by itself out there in the world. That, at least on his understanding, would amount to the Platonic theory of Forms, a theory he thinks is obviously false.[3] To say that there is a Form of Rose would be like saying that the very nature of roses is itself a separate individual, which is not just false but in fact rather silly. Nor is the nature of the rose a full-blown individual thing that is a part of each individual rose, like an individual person might be part of the crowd at a botanical garden. So when Scotus asserts that the common nature of roses is real, he sees himself as offering a moderate view between realism about universals and the sort of position adopted by Abelard, which ascribes no reality to common natures at all. Against the nominalists, he claims that common natures are indeed real. Against the realists, he claims that common natures are not in themselves universal, and that they have a lesser degree of unity and reality that that possessed by more familiar things like particular roses, which are individuals.

Needless to say, Scotus has clever arguments for all this. It's easy for him to show that the common nature is not a full-blown individual. If that were the case, then the nature of roses would be numerically only one thing. The result would be that there could only ever be one rose, a result whose absurdity will be evident to anyone other than Saint-Exupéry's character the Little Prince. It's more difficult to show that common natures are not only in the mind, where they are grasped universally, but also out there in the real world. Well, it would be difficult for most people, but this is Scotus. He's able to produce several arguments to prove the reality of shared natures. For one thing, we need them to account for causation.[4] In most cases we see that causes pass on some kind of shared nature to their effects: humans generate humans; sugar makes things sweet; and maybe roses germinate further roses, though I'm not much of a gardener either, so I wouldn't swear to it. For another thing, and more importantly, we grasp things out there in the world by subsuming them under general concepts. This doesn't mean that there is anything universal out there, as there is in the mind. But our universal notion of roses must be latching onto a common nature that is somehow actually in all roses. Otherwise, universal concepts like *rose* or *flower*, which are examples of the species and genera so beloved of medieval logicians, would be pure fictions.

Scotus thus signals his agreement with Avicenna, who stated that "Horseness is just horseness."[5] What this means, at least on Scotus' understanding, is that one and the same common nature appears both in particular horses and in the universal idea of horse. The nature is neither universal nor particular in itself.[6] We make it universal by thinking about it, as when we make a universal judgment such as "Horses like eating roses." The nature can also be part of a real individual in the world, and it's this that justifies such general judgments. When I think that horses enjoy a nice rose now and, again, I'm thinking about all the individual things that share the nature of horseness. This is, of course, just to say that I am thinking about all the individual horses. Notice, though, that, just as horseness is unaffected by whether it appears in a universal thought or a particular horse, so it is unaffected by belonging to any particular horse. As Scotus puts it, it is "accidental" to horseness that it belong to exactly the horses that exist now or to all the horses that ever have existed or will exist.[7] And this makes sense. Suppose God had decided not to create Secretariat, so that that particular horse never existed. This would make a big difference to the history of horseracing, but no difference at all to the nature of horses.

So that's Scotus' explanation of how horses are horses, roses are roses, and nominalists and Platonists are both wrong. What about our second problem of how individual horses and roses are individuals? Scotus' account may seem to make this problem worse, because he's insisting that the nature of roseness or horseness in an individual rose or horse is not in itself individual. Remember that the nature in itself has "less than numerical unity": it remains common or shared even when it is part of a given individual. Evidently, then, it is nothing about the nature of roses that makes this rose the particular rose that it is. No surprise there, Scotus would say. Again, if the very nature of rose were responsible for individuality, there could only ever be one individual rose. Clearly, we're going to need a different explanation of how things become individuals.

In fact, there were several explanations available to Scotus, which were being defended by various contemporaries. We've already met one of them, in the context of the 1277 condemnations and the debate over how angels become individuated (Chapter 41). As you might recall, Thomas Aquinas thought that things of the same kind are individuated by matter. One rose is distinct from another rose because it is made of different material stuff. Aquinas was forced to conclude that each angel is unique in its species; even God cannot make two distinct immaterial things of the same kind. It's in the context of this very same question about angels that Scotus takes up the problem of individuation in his early *Lectura*. In typical scholastic fashion he considers a series of proposals about how individuation occurs, and refutes each of them.[8]

Scotus makes several rather convincing points against the idea that matter individuates. For starters, matter is supposedly that which survives when something is destroyed. When a rose dies, its lifeless corpse might be put into the compost which is then used to grow another bed of roses. In this scenario a given bit of matter might belong first to one rose and then another rose, and obviously one and the same matter can't be responsible for distinguishing one rose from another. Then too, even if we granted that matter makes the rose individual, what makes the matter individual? Matter doesn't seem to be just intrinsically individual, given that all sorts of different individual things are made of it. So in order to use Aquinas' explanation, we actually need a further explanation of how this matter that constitutes this rose became *this* bit of matter rather than some other bit.

This is only one of the theories Scotus wants to refute. Another is that put forth by Henry of Ghent. He had the rather curious idea that individuation can be explained negatively, or rather by a double negation. What makes something an individual is that it is not identical with other members of the same species and that it is not divided into further individuals. In other words, our rose would be an individual because it is distinct from other roses and because the things that make it up are parts, not whole entities. Scotus gives this answer short shrift. We don't want to hear what individuals are not, but what they are. We want a positive account of individuation and, in this case, two negatives don't make a positive. I think Scotus is right to criticize Henry here, or at least to criticize Henry as Scotus is understanding him. The fact that one rose is not identical to another is precisely what needs to be explained; it's not the explanation.

So far, though, Scotus himself has only told us two ways *not* to explain individuation. We are still waiting for the right answer. To get our heads around that right answer, it might help to go back to what we were just saying about matter. If a thing is individuated by its matter, Scotus argued, that matter would itself need to be individuated by something else. This kind of problem bedevils many attempts to explain individuality, as we saw when looking at Gilbert of Poitiers. If a thing is individuated by its place, say, or by its accidents, then what individuates the place or the accidents? What we need is a principle of individuation that is, unlike matter or the common nature, *itself individual*. We need a nature that is singular rather than common, that belongs to only one thing, and can belong only to that thing.[9]

Such a singular nature is called a *haecceity* or "thisness," from the Latin word *haec* ("this"). It is a word still used by metaphysicians nowadays, so that this concept constitutes one of Scotus' most prominent and long-lasting contributions to later philosophy (actually he made many such contributions, but this one is more obvious than most). Scotus hardly ever uses the word *haecceitas* himself, though it was enthusiastically bandied about by his followers.[10] He prefers such phrases as "form of the individual (*forma individualis*)," "lowest-level form (*ultimus gradus formae*)," or "difference of the individual (*differentia individualis*)." That last expression is particularly illuminating, because Scotus explains the singular nature by drawing an analogy to the difference that picks out one species from other species in the same genus. From among the large class *flowers* the specific difference of roses will be whatever distinguishes roses from other flowers. Let's suppose for the sake of argument that the species of rose is distinguished from all other flowers by the possession of thorns.[11] In just the same way, according to Scotus, Secretariat would be distinguished from other members of the species of horse by Secretariat's singular essence or haecceity.

The upshot is that individuals are made up of two aspects or parts. Firstly, each thing has its common nature, which makes it like other things. Secondly, it has its singular essence, which makes it be a specific individual. Secretariat is thus made up of both horseness and Secretariat-ness, as the species of rose is made up of the genus of flower and the specific difference of having thorns. In a way, therefore, Scotus agrees with that assumption that drove Abelard to his nominalism: everything that exists is individual. Officially, he, of course, denies that everything real is an individual, since common natures are real. But common natures don't just hang around on their own, as the Platonist claims. They are only ever found conjoined to, or "contracted by," the haecceities that make things individual, or when we universalize the common natures in our minds. To put it another way, full-blown reality always involves numerical unity, that is, individuality. Indeed, the two natures in each thing, one common and one singular, are said to be only formally distinct, in the latest deployment of what may be Scotus' favorite distinction.

While all of this is clearly quite clever, it is also rather unsatisfying. It sounds as if Scotus' solution boils down to saying that what makes me individual is just... whatever makes me individual. It's hardly helpful to say that I am Peter Adamson thanks to my Peter-Adamson-ness. The analogy to the specific difference is a bit more illuminating. But it doesn't really help me envision what that feature could be that makes me the individual I am, distinct from other humans, the way that having thorns might make *rose* the species it is, distinct from other kinds of flower. There's a good reason for this, though. Scotus thinks that in our current embodied life, the singular essence is not something we can grasp. God understands haecceities but in this life, at least, humans cannot do the same, something Scotus blames on either original sin or our dependence on sensation. This turns out to be helpful for Scotus in wriggling out of an exegetical embarrassment. Aristotle says quite clearly that individuals have no essences (*Metaphysics* 1039b), whereas Scotus is insisting that they do. He avoids outright contradiction with Aristotelian metaphysics by saying that, when Aristotle denied that there are individual essences, he just meant that there are no such essences that *we* can know.

This interpretive move is not very persuasive, but Scotus has achieved resounding agreement with Aristotle on a different point. In Aristotle's theory of knowledge, scientific understanding is said to involve universal judgments. Scotus can now explain why. It's because singular essences are unknowable for us, even though they are real. We infer their reality only by an indirect argument, on the basis that if there were no haecceities, nothing could be an individual, something the Scotus scholar Peter King has compared to postulating the existence of an unseen planet on the basis of its effects on other heavenly bodies.[12] But having ratified the traditional Aristotelian doctrine that science must be universal, Scotus characteristically makes yet another departure from Aristotle. Of course, it takes the form of a distinction. The sort of understanding involved in Aristotelian science is universal and abstractive cognition. But there is another mode of grasping available to the intellect, which Scotus calls "intuitive cognition."[13]

The phrase can be misleading for the modern reader. We typically use the word "intuition" to mean something like instinctive or inspired insight, as in the tacitly sexist phrase "women's intuition." This is not what Scotus means by it. He has in

357

mind something like direct acquaintance with a thing, as opposed to the sort of cognition involved when you make a judgment about that thing or use general concepts abstracted from sense experience. Obviously, it is the latter "abstractive" sort of cognition that is involved in Aristotelian science and analyzed in medieval logic. And this is the kind of activity that medievals usually took to be characteristic of the human mind. The intellect grasps roses universally, by means of a general, abstracted concept of roses. But Scotus insists that the intellect is also capable of grasping an individual object, simply because it is present to us in existence. Actually "insists" is a bit strong. He does make the claim forcefully in some passages, but in other places says that intuitive cognition is impossible for us in this life, just like understanding of haecceities.

Still, when he speaks in favor of the idea, he gives compelling arguments and examples. For one thing, clearly sensation is able to engage in intuitive cognition. Seeing or smelling a rose would be a paradigm case for this kind of intuition: the particular rose simply presents itself to sensation. But intellect is better than sensation, so how can it be incapable of something that sense perception does all the time? For another thing, if we assume that the intellect can grasp individuals intuitively, this would explain how it is able to apply its universal ideas to particulars. In order to judge that Secretariat is a horse and therefore likes eating roses, the intellect had better be able to able to grasp Secretariat somehow! Then there is the phenomenon of self-awareness.[14] In this case too the intellect is having an "intuition," since it is grasping itself as present to itself, not using some kind of abstract concept of itself.

Fourteenth-century thinkers like Ockham are going to use this idea of intuitive cognition too, and with less hesitation than Scotus, which exemplifies his far-reaching influence. You may notice that I have devoted a lot of attention to Scotus. This is in part because he is just so brilliant, but also because he sets the stage for the next several generations of philosophers. Many of the main themes we'll be looking at in chapters to come revolve around Scotus' ideas. Vigorous debate was sparked by his voluntarism in psychology and ethics, and by his realism about common natures. Some of his signature distinctions, such as the contrast between absolute and ordained power and the contrast between real and formal distinctions, became common currency. Since Scotus was a Franciscan, his ideas were especially influential among thinkers of this order, even if they were not always accepted. We'll see a fine example of this when we get to his fellow Franciscan, William of Ockham, himself the rare prominent thinker in an unjustly ignored period of philosophy: the fourteenth century.

PART III
THE FOURTEENTH CENTURY

52

TIME OF THE SIGNS
THE FOURTEENTH CENTURY

If asked to name my favorite century, I would probably go with the twentieth, which gave us Buster Keaton, the Marx Brothers, Stevie Wonder, *and* Reese's Peanut Butter Cups. (Beat that, twenty-first century!) Most other historians of philosophy, being more serious-minded, would probably choose either the fourth century BC, the time of Plato and Aristotle, or the seventeenth century, which can boast Descartes, Spinoza, Leibniz, and Margaret Cavendish, to name just a few. Aficionados of medieval thought might however be tempted to go for the thirteenth century, when you had the rise of the universities, the recovery of Aristotle, Albert the Great, Bonaventure, Aquinas, and Scotus. It's a real embarrassment of riches. In comparison, the fourteenth century looks to be a plain old embarrassment. A popular book about the history of the period labels it as "calamitous,"[1] and here's a two-word phrase that will probably tempt you to agree immediately: "Black Death." On the philosophical front, it's one of those eras people tend to skip, going straight from high scholasticism to the Renaissance and Reformation or indeed vaulting all the way to the aforementioned glories of the Enlightenment.

But this is a big mistake. For one thing, you can't understand the philosophical developments of the Renaissance and Reformation without knowing what happened in the fourteenth century. Of course, you'd expect me to say this, given that the whole point of this book series is to show how each stage in the history of philosophy builds upon the previous stages. But it's particularly true in this case. The word "Renaissance" suggests a break with what came before, but in fact scholastic philosophy continued to flourish in the fifteenth and sixteenth centuries, when we see the emergence of factions or "schools" following the lead of Scotus, Ockham, and others. The name of Ockham also reminds us that, historical influence aside, the fourteenth century did have its share of famous names. In the scholastic context, Ockham and Buridan are probably the best-known figures. But specialists in medieval philosophy know that there are many others who deserve to be better known, like Peter Auriol, Gregory of Rimini, Adam Wodeham, Walter Burley, Thomas Bradwardine, Nicholas of Autrecourt, and Nicole Oresme. It has to be said that these are mostly figures of the early or mid-fourteenth century, though Oresme didn't die until 1382. Later in the century, after the Black Death and during the Hundred Years War, fewer stars seem to shine in the scholastic firmament. But there are exceptions, such as the controversial John Wyclif, who died around the same time as Oresme and helped to set the agenda for fifteenth-century thought.

It would be another big mistake to think that fourteenth-century philosophy is just the story of scholasticism. Here's a selective list of figures from this period who were active outside the university context, and who we'll be covering in the remainder of this book: Marguerite Porete, Dante Alighieri, Geoffrey Chaucer, and Julian of Norwich. Admittedly, none of them are usually seen primarily as philosophers. Dante and Chaucer are stars in a different firmament, being respectively the greatest figures in Italian and English medieval literature. It's easy to make a case for including Dante, though. His *Divine Comedy* has much to say about philosophy and he wrote two treatises on philosophical topics, the *Convivio* and *On Monarchy*. Chaucer, meanwhile, was interested in scholasticism and reflects on its ideas in his poems. As for Marguerite and Julian, they are more usually categorized as mystics. But by this stage you should be comfortable with the idea that the line between philosophy and mysticism is at best a blurry one. We'll be seeing that fourteenth-century mystical texts dealt with a range of issues in epistemology, metaphysics, and ethics, easily warranting their inclusion in our story. The same case can be made for Meister Eckhart, who did work in a scholastic context but also wrote in the vernacular and contributed greatly to the history of mysticism.

That's just a thumbnail sketch of what happened in the history of philosophy during the 1300s. Before getting into more detail, let's have a quick look at the wider historical context. As I've already mentioned, it was a rough century. Even aside from the Black Death—which first struck in 1347 and in several waves of infection reduced populations across Europe by something like one-third—there were plenty of other disasters to contend with. It seems that population growth had already slowed towards the end of the thirteenth century, and terrible weather in 1315 and 1316 caused harvests to fail, with widespread famine the inevitable result. Average temperatures also cooled in the so-called "little ice age," following a warming period that had prevailed in Europe in the previous centuries. While the people suffered, their leaders squabbled. As we'll see, a question that much occupied political thinkers of the time was the relative authority of Church and State. Positions were adopted all along the spectrum here, with Aquinas' disciple Giles of Rome making a strong case for the supremacy of the Pope, and Marsilius of Padua going just as far in a secularist direction. This was not just an abstract theoretical dispute, but a reaction to current events. We'll see this in Dante, too. He scatters political observations, predictions, and outright character assassinations throughout his *Divine Comedy*, reserving a special place in hell (quite literally) for Pope Boniface VIII.

The papacy in this period was embattled, and not just because of insolent Italian vernacular poets. Early in the century King Philip IV of France came into conflict with this same pope, Boniface VIII, who threatened him with excommunication. Philip had the Pope taken prisoner, and the pontiff died soon after. His immediate successors fell under the influence of the French Crown, one symptom being the relocation of the Pope's residence to Avignon. It would remain there for more than seventy years, a matter of annoyance to Italians, who expressed their dismay by complaining of the debauchery of the papal court; Petrarch called it the "sewer of the world."[2] To the modern ear, the name "Avignon" immediately conjures up the schism within the Church, with one pope there and another in Rome. This situation began in 1378 and persisted into the fifteenth century. We'll be looking at an agonized reaction to this state of affairs in the prolific schoolman and preacher Jean Gerson.

Worldly rulers too were causing their fair share of mischief. Particularly important for our story is the Hundred Years War between France and England, because Paris and Oxford are the main centers for scholastic philosophy in this period. This "war" was more a matter of intermittent hostility, beginning in 1337, when Edward III of England entered into conflict with Philip VI of France. The English made significant advances, culminating in the capture of the French king, John, and his son at the Battle of Poitiers in 1356. But the French clawed back territory under Charles V, who ruled until 1380. All of this naturally made it more difficult for ideas and scholars to pass freely between the English and French spheres. Already, earlier in the century, we see a dramatic reduction in the number of Englishmen being trained in Paris. Arguably, the war between the two states simply perpetuated the autonomy of Oxford from Paris, albeit without entirely preventing schoolmen at one university from following developments at the other.[3]

This is among the biggest changes in the university culture of the period. Over the previous hundred years Paris had been the center of the scholastic world, but modern-day historians usually see Paris as surrendering its leading role to Oxford in the fourteenth century. In his book on the topic William Courtenay says that "by 1345 Paris was captivated by English thought as if little else existed."[4] Parisian scholars begin to cite English contemporaries like Ockham, Walter Burley, and Adam Wodeham, and the English don't return the favor. We shouldn't exaggerate here, though. Parisian scholars did continue to do sophisticated and innovative work, for instance on the problem whether God's knowledge of the future has deterministic consequences (Chapter 61).[5] Something else to bear in mind is that scholasticism was able to develop outside of Oxford and Paris. The famous William of Ockham is a good example. Though he did study theology at Oxford, his early education and the highpoint of his writing career were both at the Franciscan house ("Greyfriars") in London. For reasons we'll get into later, he spent his final years at Avignon and then Munich. Scholasticism itself followed Ockham's example by moving all over Europe. Marsilius of Inghen, who, as it happens, also followed Ockham on philosophical matters, went from Paris to Heidelberg late in the century. By the time the 1300s draw to a close, scholasticism will be a pan-European phenomenon, with places like Prague and Padua giving the older universities a run for their money.

Not everyone was enthusiastic about the ideas being put forward by Ockham and others. Wyclif, whose ideas would be influential at Prague, decried the men he called the "doctors of signs" and sneered at the sort of logical exercises that, he said, amused the university scholars at Christmas.[6] Why "doctors of signs"? Wyclif was alluding to a philosophical teaching that became dominant in the first half of the century, concerning the problem of universals. We've just seen Scotus defending a moderate realism according to which true universals are only in the mind, yet enable us to grasp real common natures out in the world. So an individual giraffe like Hiawatha has a real giraffe nature, which is shared with other giraffes. Scotus took great pains to distinguish his own position from the more extreme realism he associated with Platonism, but that did not stop Ockham and others from attacking his view. For Ockham and then a whole range of other fourteenth-century thinkers, such as Buridan and Marsilius of Inghen, a common name is nothing but a "sign" that stands for a range of individuals out in the world. There is no shared giraffe nature, never mind a Platonic Form of giraffes. The name "giraffe" simply signifies all the particular giraffes.

When we met this attitude before in the work of Peter Abelard, we called it "nominalism," a word that is also routinely used for the position of Ockham, Buridan, and their philosophical allies. But we need to be careful here. For one thing, they did not call themselves "nominalists." The title was applied to them only in retrospect. For another thing, "nominalism" has come to be used for a whole collection of philosophical theses that hang together nicely and seem to be characteristic of much fourteenth-century thought.[7] By denying real common natures, the nominalist raises a doubt as to whether our ideas mirror reality the way that Scotus and others assumed. Certainly, we do have ideas that we apply to many things in common, but this is only a feature of our mental life and language. There is nothing common or shared out there in reality. From here you might worry that other aspects of our thought may be misleading or fail to capture reality fully.

You could also start to question philosophical science itself, at least as Aristotle understood it. In the Aristotelian tradition scientific judgments were thought to be universal in scope and to lay hold of necessary truths about nature. But now we're being told that there is nothing universal in nature. Furthermore the nominalist tends to doubt that anything in nature is really necessary. This is because, while the nominalist disagrees with Scotus about the common features of things, he is ready to make common cause with Scotus' voluntarism. He showed how God's absolute freedom could be understood as the power to choose between mutually exclusive alternatives. God has an "absolute power" to do anything that isn't self-contradictory. Taking this idea seriously, the nominalist concludes that the whole created world is fundamentally contingent. It could have been otherwise, because God could have created a very different universe.

The upshot is a double assault on the confident rationalism of Aristotelian philosophy. Though reason can still rule out some things as impossible—there can be no round squares, chimeras, or dry water—the scope of God's freedom means that nothing in our world is truly necessary, as all things depend on His untrammeled will. Then, too, the way we speak and think about those things might be quite misleading, as when we grasp a universe of individuals by means of universal terms and concepts. Some pretty radical thoughts are lurking here. If our mind and language do not match the structure of the world, why not give in to a thoroughgoing skepticism? Though we'll see hints in that direction in the fourteenth century, the nominalists found ways to avoid such a radical result. The fact that language and thought are not structured *exactly* as the world is does not imply that language and thought entirely misrepresent the world. More common will be a tendency simply to restrict the scope of what reason can achieve. In theology, faith and revelation are on hand to fill the gap, leading to a less rationalist and Aristotelian approach in religious and ethical matters than we saw with figures like Aquinas and Scotus. But contrary to what you might expect, these same ideas can be seen as fruitful for science. If we cannot simply reflect on our universal ideas to discern invariable necessities of nature, then the only way to learn about the world is to go look at it. Thus, the nominalists also have a fairly well-deserved reputation for empiricism, and are often credited with taking important steps in the direction of modern science. One particularly crucial insight will be that mathematical concepts and tools can be applied to topics in natural philosophy (see Chapter 63).

Again, though, we should avoid exaggerating. The so-called "nominalists" certainly did not agree with one another about everything, and throughout the century there were plenty of realists fighting the nominalist tide. In Ockham's own day Walter Burley continued to fly the flag for realism, and a generation or so later

Wyclif's snide reference to the "doctors of signs" already tells you where he stood. Eventually, this confrontation will crystallize into the fifteenth-century *Wegestreit*, a German word that literally means "dispute over methods." The battle lines will be drawn between the so-called *via antiqua* and *via moderna*: the "ancient" approach is traditional Aristotelianism, the "modern" approach that of the nominalists. Thus, a document written at Cologne in 1425 contrasts Thomas Aquinas, Albert the Great, "and other *antiqui*" with "the modern masters" John Buridan and Marsilius of Inghen, two famous nominalists.[8] Like the word "nominalist" itself, though, this contrast between "ancient" and "modern" is not yet used by the fourteenth-century thinkers themselves.[9]

Whatever terms we use, we should not read back into the fourteenth century the fifteenth- and sixteenth-century tendency to divide scholastics into "schools of thought," like Ockhamists, Thomists, and Scotists. This is another point made by the aforementioned William Courtenay. He admits that there were brief periods where Oxford may have seen a wave of enthusiasm for Aquinas or Scotus. But these were usually short-lived, and for a reason that may surprise us. We tend to think of medieval philosophers as being beholden to authority, as innovating only by mistake or because they could see no other way to find agreement between their various sources. But in fact there were good career reasons for a master to show how clever and original he was.[10] The game was to be innovative, but not so innovative that one ran into trouble with the Church.

Of course, leading scholastics like Scotus and Ockham did exert tremendous influence on other thinkers, but usually by setting the terms of further debate rather than replacing such debate with school allegiance. Take, for instance, Scotus' distinctive idea of the "formal distinction," meaning a real difference between two aspects of one and the same thing. In subsequent generations, some scholastics adopted it as a useful tool, especially for explaining the divine Trinity. But even proponents of Scotus' idea went beyond him by providing their own justifications for his distinction. Other scholastics rejected Scotus' proposal. One of them was Peter Auriol, who offered a subtle exploration of the formal distinction but ultimately dismissed it on the basis that such a distinction between the trinitarian Persons would undermine divine simplicity.[11]

In the fifteenth century the humanists will enjoy mocking this sort of hair-splitting and distinction-mongering, much as some observers nowadays decry the apparently pointless and technical work done by analytic philosophers. Yet some of the greatest literary minds of the age were very interested in the output of the university schoolmen. I've already mentioned Dante and Chaucer as examples. But they also exemplify something else, something that will ultimately pose an even greater challenge to the intellectual hegemony of the scholastics: the use of vernacular language. Philosophical learning was steadily becoming more available to those who couldn't read Latin. In a sense this was nothing new. It goes back at least as far as the ninth-century English translation of Boethius credited to King Alfred, and we saw thirteenth-century examples like Mechthild of Magdeburg and Hadewijch or the *Romance of the Rose*. But it's in the fourteeenth century that medieval philosophy really starts to feature lay authors and vernacular languages,[12] something we will begin to explore in Chapter 53.

AFTER VIRTUE
MARGUERITE PORETE

Who is the medieval version of Socrates? Perhaps Albert the Great, a famous philosopher who had an even more famous philosopher for a student? Or actually any number of scholastics, since they all loved a good disputed question. Or how about Peter Olivi, champion of voluntary poverty? You might also think of Roger Bacon because he was sent to prison for his teachings. But if we're thinking along these lines, then the medieval thinker with the best claim to the title might be Marguerite Porete. Like Socrates, she was executed after courageously refusing to recant her convictions. Rather than being allowed a final chat about the immortality of soul with friends followed by a bowl of hemlock, Marguerite was burned to death. It didn't come without warning. Years earlier she had been arrested after a book she had written came to the attention of the bishop of Cambrai. The book was destroyed before her very eyes, and she was warned never again to disseminate such heresy, on pain of execution.

Marguerite didn't let this stop her. She was evidently a woman of means and some social standing, since she could afford to have several copies of her book made—keeping one herself, as she admitted, and having her ideas written down and passed to others including another bishop. In 1308 she was arrested and excommunicated. A protracted period of imprisonment followed. The inquisitor William of Paris couldn't even get this stubborn woman to take an oath so that a trial could begin. Finally he gave up trying to extract her cooperation. A panel of Parisian theologians was assembled, and they agreed that her book was heretical. She was handed over to the secular authorities and executed in Paris on June 1, 1310.[1] The book for which she died fared somewhat better. It is called *The Mirror of Simple, Annihilated Souls and Those Who Only Remain in Will and Desire of Love* (*Le Mirouer des simples âmes anienties et qui seulement demeurent en vouloir et désir d'amour*). Without Marguerite's name attached, it enjoyed a fairly wide dissemination, being translated into Latin and Middle English, and also reworked into Middle French on the basis of the original Old French version.[2] It may already have influenced Meister Eckhart, a contemporary of Marguerite's.[3]

From among earlier thinkers, the most obvious comparison is, of course, not really to Socrates but to earlier women mystics, such as Hildegard of Bingen, Hadewijch, and Mechthild of Magdeburg. Her similarity to the Beguine mystics Hadewijch and Mechthild seems especially strong (see Chapter 32). Several medieval authors refer to Marguerite as a Beguine, which makes it tempting to connect her persecution to the increasing disquiet caused by the Beguine movement in the early fourteenth century. This culminated in a condemnation at the Council of Vienne in 1312, only two years after Marguerite was killed. But several scholars now doubt that she was a Beguine,[4] so we probably shouldn't push this connection too far. Still, we can compare her to the two Beguines insofar as Marguerite too wrote in a vernacular language, and because her central concern is union with God. Some of her favorite metaphors, such as the image of "melting away," can also be found in their works.[5] She even uses a central trope taken from the courtly love literature that inspired Hadewijch and Mechthild. Her work is effectively a three-way dialogue between her own soul, Love, and Reason; occasionally other characters appear, like Temptation and Truth. This is a clear echo of the allegorical dialogues we find in such works as the *Romance of the Rose*, where Love and Reason are shown debating the merits of romantic entanglements.

Yet Marguerite's writing does not display the eroticism we find in Hadewijch and Mechthild. When set alongside their writings, her *Mirror* seems far closer to being something we might call a philosophical treatise.[6] Her central character of Love has a clear agenda, and sets out the bold philosophical and theological claims that made this book so shocking to the bishop and the inquisitors. It's clear that Marguerite knew she was quite literally playing with fire. There's nothing quite as blunt as Mechthild of Magdeburg's mention of a threat to burn her book, but Marguerite alludes frequently to the controversial nature of her ideas. The purpose of the character of Reason in the book is, in part, to express reluctance or outright opposition to the teachings of Love. Reason thus speaks for the reader who may have trouble accepting Marguerite's teaching. This character points out apparent contradictions in that teaching and issues warnings against straying into dangerous territory (§35, 86–7). At one point Marguerite anticipates that the Church will be "astonished" by one of her core ideas, namely that soul can free itself of any need to use the virtues (§19). She was right to worry. Precisely this doctrine was among those condemned by her inquisitors and used as proof of her heresy.

Or perhaps "worry" is the wrong word. Marguerite seems to have known she was courting controversy and not minded doing so. She provocatively refers to the religious institutions of her day as "Holy Church the lesser" in contrast to the greater church of the souls who have been freed by love for God (§43, 49), and mentions that such souls no longer even need to pray (§51, 136). Clearly, Marguerite was well aware of the daring nature of her teaching. And in general the *Mirror* is a highly self-conscious work, something else it shares in common with the *Romance of the Rose*. The *Mirror* wears its artifice on its sleeve and several times offers so-called "glosses" on its own contents, so that it is a book that includes its own commentary (§77, 82, 84). She makes the point emphatically in a prologue which also reveals her dependence on earlier literary models. Playing on an earlier "romance" about Alexander the Great by Alexander of Bernai, she tells the story of a princess who falls in love with King Alexander but lives far away from him. The princess gains solace by commissioning a painting of the king. In the same way, Marguerite says that her own book is a representation of her soul's love for God. A character named "Soul" then appears throughout the text in discussion with Reason and Love. This device is much like the character of the lover in the *Romance of the Rose*. Like Jean de Meun, Marguerite takes on the dual roles of author and character. Yet the character's point of view is more limited than that of the author: Marguerite depicts the growing understanding of her own soul.[7]

What is it that the soul and the reader too must come to understand? Ultimately, something that cannot be put into words, since the peace of divine life "cannot be thought or written" (§93). Like the painting of the beloved king that would be discarded if the king himself were present, Marguerite's book points beyond itself towards an unmediated encounter between the soul and God. I said above that the *Mirror* reads somewhat more like a philosophical treatise than do the writings of Hadewijch and Mechthild. Though that is true, Marguerite is far more forthright than they were in her critique of human reason, as should already be clear from her decision to include Reason as a character and depict her as having a decidedly limited perspective. Hadewijch in particular was full of praise for reason and depicted reason as being guided by love. For Marguerite, Reason's task is instead to be transcended.

In part this is a critique of book learning, the sort of expertise taught at the universities and the sort of expertise boasted by the theologians who will have Marguerite put to death. So it's a kind of anticipatory revenge when Marguerite announces the death of Reason partway through her book (§87). Already in the prologue, she writes, "Men of theology and scholars such as they will never understand this writing properly...you must let love and faith together be your guides to climb where reason cannot come." Later she adds that the soul "does not seek for knowledge of God among the teachers of this world" (§5), and that Love's teaching is found "in no book" (§7). Reason herself is called "one-eyed" (§43, 116), and in what looks like a rather frank insult aimed at the experts of book learning,

Marguerite says, "it is plainly seen from Reason's disciples that an ass would achieve nothing which was willing to give them ear" (§84). Still, we shouldn't exaggerate her anti-rationalism. After all, being one-eyed is not the same as having no eyes at all, and Reason does come to accept something of the teachings of Love, even if she does so imperfectly and reluctantly. Eventually she pledges her allegiance to the Soul, now apparently converted to seeing things more or less in Marguerite's way (§39). On the other hand, it's remarked that the book could have been much shorter if Reason wasn't so slow on the uptake (§53). Again, the idea seems to be that Reason can slowly make some progress, but that the full truth is beyond her.

This interpretation of Marguerite's critique of human reason is confirmed by her notorious remarks on the subject of virtue. In one of the poems scattered through the work,[8] Marguerite writes: "Virtues, I take my leave of you...there was a time I was your serf, all of my heart was set on you. And the great Lord above I thank, now I have left your bondage" (§6). Like the inquisitors at Paris, Reason is appalled by these remarks and tries to poke logical holes in them (§21). No surprise here, since for Marguerite living in accordance with Reason goes hand in hand with living virtuously. Hildegard and Hadewijch would have agreed with that, but they do not dare to suggest that virtue is something the soul needs to transcend. Marguerite dares to do more than suggest it: she states it clearly and repeatedly, as when she writes that the soul "experiences no grace, she feels no longings of the spirit, since she has taken leave of the virtues" (§8), a passage later quoted by her inquisitors as proof of heresy. With chilling prescience, Marguerite at one point allows the Virtues to speak for themselves and to complain that anyone who holds them in such little regard is "a heretic and a bad Christian" (§56).

In a typical reversal, she, however, argues that having left the virtues behind, this pure soul is the most virtuous of all. It's been observed that this looks more like "piling a paradox upon a scandal"[9] than like defusing the explosive implications of what she's said. But let's see whether we can contain the philosophical damage. For starters, Marguerite is certainly not recommending that we all immediately give up on virtue. This is no triumph of mysticism over morality. She makes it clear that the virtues have an important preparatory role in bringing us closer to God. They are like messengers sent by Love to call us away from our own limited concerns so that we may be freed "from the burden of ourselves," as Marguerite nicely phrases it (§77–8). As with her treatment of Reason, her attitude towards virtue is that it has real, but limited value and use. So she has harsh words for those who content themselves with living virtuously. They too are "one-eyed," comparable to a mother owl who thinks no birds are finer than her own brood (§55).

Here she has in mind people who immerse themselves in heroic asceticism and charitable deeds, as if such acts of self-abnegation were the highest possible goal we might have. Ascetics are doomed to remain lost because they have an unfulfilled desire to reach God, something that cannot be attained through worldly virtue. Here we might detect an echo of those who criticized the voluntary poverty of the mendicant orders (Chapter 31), or a rebuke to the many medieval authors, both male and female, who fused mysticism with asceticism. Marguerite has tried this path herself and found it inadequate. Even those who live in virtue while realizing there could be something higher are "slaves" and "merchants" because of their lowly point of view (§57, 63), a good example of her tendency to apply the class distinctions of medieval society to grades of enlightenment. To transcend this forlorn state the soul should not, of course, engage in sin or vice, but neither should she concern herself with the virtues of asceticism. She "takes leave" of the virtues in the sense that she no longer makes any use of them (§8).

Up to this point, Marguerite's ethical teaching is strikingly reminiscent of late ancient Platonism. Plotinus especially is noted for identifying "civic" virtue (that is, acting virtuously in the world of the senses) as a mere preparatory stage, a step along the ladder towards purification and intellectual understanding.[10] The parallel is close enough to suggest that Marguerite is yet another medieval figure to be influenced by Neoplatonism, however indirectly. Still, she develops the idea of transcending virtue in a way that is, whatever her accusers may have thought, distinctively Christian. For Marguerite, what comes after virtue is nothing other than a higher, more important virtue, namely humility, which she styles "mother of the virtues."[11] Humility does not consist in obsessive attention to our own desires or actions, however well-intentioned. It consists in giving up on our desires, on acting to achieve some purpose. It consists, in fact, in giving up one's self and identity completely by letting one's will dissolve into the will of God.

We have here come to the core of Marguerite's thought, the idea of the soul's "annihilation."[12] It is the annihilated soul that Love praises throughout the book and that no longer devotes itself to action, virtuous or otherwise. This is also the soul that has transcended Reason; yet it's in explaining this very concept that Marguerite makes her most significant contributions to philosophy. She is making a novel claim about the workings of the human will, which echoes the "voluntarism" we've seen in Scotus and Henry of Ghent but goes beyond it.[13] She holds not only that the will takes us beyond the workings of reason, but also that the soul's highest attainment is to cease willing entirely, cease even willing to have a will (§12). Or, as today's philosophers might put it, the annihilated soul has neither first- nor second-order desires: it wants nothing and wants to want nothing. So intimate is the relationship between soul and will that this can be achieved only when the soul is "humbled" to the point that it is extinguished, something Marguerite describes as a kind of "death" (§44). For, as soon as the soul expresses itself as a being distinct from God, it must exercise its will, so even willing things for God's sake prevents one from achieving complete union between one's own will and God's.

To which you might say: what's so great about that? Of course, a medieval reader might be happy to take it for granted that we should strive to eliminate any distance between our own wills and the divine will, even if few such readers would have been happy to pursue the line of thought as far as Marguerite does. But she can offer a further rationale, which is that the extinction of will guarantees the extinction of unsatisfied desire. After all, you can't be unhappy about lacking things you don't want. The annihilated soul "lacks nothing, since she wishes for nothing" (§45; cf. §79 for the "freedom of wishing for nothing"). Furthermore, in accepting her own annihilation, the soul is actually coming to understand her metaphysical situation more accurately. For, according to Marguerite, the soul's infinite inferiority to God means that it has really always been nothing. So her recommendation is not so much that the soul should steadily work to eliminate her own reality, but that she should see through the illusion that she was ever anything and thus come to know her own nothingness (§34, 45, 47). Marguerite sums it up better than I can: "God is so great that [the Soul] can comprehend nothing of Him; and on account of this nothingness she has reached the certainty of knowing nothing and of wishing for nothing" (§81).

Marguerite still has a few more paradoxes to add on to this scandalous teaching. She makes the point that God cannot *force* the soul to give up on her will. The gift of a free will was inalienable, because the whole nature of a free will is to be independent of any constraint (§91, 104). Therefore, just as the soul and no one else can be responsible for her own sin (§103), so the soul alone can choose to submit her will to that of God. To bring out the paradox more clearly, we might say that the soul must use will to abandon her will. And here's another paradox: though the soul is nothing, she is a recipient of God's love. God has loved her eternally, which means that soul has *always existed* to the extent that we can say she exists at all (§35). This idea of an eternally preexisting soul is rather outrageous, something Marguerite acknowledges by having Reason protest when it is first proposed. But she refuses to back away from it, insisting that in the soul's original state with God, she was "simple." Thus, the *Mirror of Simple Souls* ends by reflecting upon the fact that, in returning to God, the simple soul returns to itself (§138).

TO HELL AND BACK
DANTE ALIGHIERI

You never forget your first love. And that goes for intellectual loves too. Mine was Dante Alighieri, whose marvelous poem the *Divine Comedy* entranced me so much when I was about 19 years old that it got me into the study of medieval intellectual culture. From there I got curious about medieval philosophy in both Latin Christendom and the Islamic world, and the rest is history—or at least history of philosophy. It was an unusual way to get into the philosophy business, but I'm confident that Dante himself would have approved. He made a concerted effort to spread philosophical knowledge to as wide a readership as possible by writing in Italian. Dante himself was an outsider to the world of the so-called "clerk" or "cleric" (*clericus*). He did, however, possess enough Latin, and sufficient knowledge of scholasticism, to engage with its teaching in a vernacular language, not least in the *Divine Comedy*.[1]

Philosophy was only Dante's second love, though. His first was Beatrice. The poems she inspired are gathered in Dante's first major work *La vita nuova* or *The New Life*, written in 1292, two years after Beatrice's tragic early death. *La vita nuova* also offers a running commentary on its own poems, marked by an obsession with numerical structure that will stay with Dante throughout his career. He associates Beatrice with the number nine and later constructs his *Comedy* in light of numerological structures (for example, it has a total of one hundred chapters or cantos, with lengths that are sometimes symmetrically arranged).[2] Dante's fusion of the personal with the poetic is also common to both *La vita nuova* and the later *Comedy*, as is his justified confidence in his own genius. That confidence is on full display in the rather pedantic commentary he devotes to his own poems in *La vita nuova*, a technique he will use again in the *Convivio* (*Banquet*).

It is here that Dante reveals how he fell in love all over again, with the new object of his affections being Lady Philosophy (§2.15).[3] Already in *La vita nuova*, Dante mentioned a "gracious lady (*donna gentile*)" who caught his eye after Beatrice's death. There, this new lady seemed to be a distraction from Dante's pure and faithful love for the departed Beatrice. In the *Convivio* Dante again suggests that there has been a struggle for his affections (§2.2, 2.12), with his new enthusiasm for philosophical learning pushing all other considerations from his mind. Many scholars have seen this as a passing phase, with Dante later repudiating philosophy in favor of a higher pursuit: a poetical theology personified yet again by Beatrice. It is she who sends the ancient poet Virgil to guide Dante through Hell in *Inferno* (2.70), the first of the three canticles of the *Comedy*, and then appears in person to show Dante through the spheres of the heavens in *Paradiso*.[4]

We'll return below to the question of whether Dante came to regret his flirtation with philosophy.[5] But first, let's help ourselves to some of the morsels served at Dante's *Convivio*. You can hardly miss its philosophical mission, given that he starts the work by quoting the famous beginning of Aristotle's *Metaphysics*, "By nature, all humans desire to know" (§1.1). You'll usually see this translated as "By nature, all *men* desire to know," but Dante most definitely has women in mind. They form a significant section of his intended audience, since they are shut out of the learned discourse conducted in Latin by the schoolmen (§1.9, 3.7). Yet women and others unversed in Latin share the universal human appetite for knowledge. Dante wants to help them to satisfy that hunger; he compares himself to someone providing crumbs of bread fallen from the table of the wise.[6] Hence his decision to write the poems and commentary of the *Convivio* in Italian, something he says he has done out of "compassion" for a relatively "uneducated" audience (§1.1, 1.7). This is something Dante feels he must defend, and for good reason. Just consider a story preserved in the thirteenth-century Italian collection called the *Novellino*, in which a vernacular author dreams that the Muses appear to accuse him of prostituting himself.[7] Anticipating such concerns, Dante goes on at some length justifying his use of Italian in the *Convivio*.

Here he is venturing into territory explored in another work, *On the Eloquence of the Vernacular*, which Dante chose to write in Latin. There he goes so far as to praise vernacular language as being in some respects better than Latin. Effectively, Latin has become an "artificial" language, more a "grammar" than a real, natural language like Italian. Latin has become universal and unchanging, a kind of antidote to the multiplying of human languages after the Tower of Babel. But Dante prefers his mother tongue, or rather a loftier version of it (the *vulgare illustre*) suited to such exalted topics as human virtue.[8] This would be a sort of idealized discourse to be used by all Italians, with a purity that raises it above their local dialects. Ironically, the *Convivio*, which is actually in Italian, shows less confidence in the superiority of the vernacular. Dante remarks that if he had written a Latin explanation for his Italian poems, then the commentary would be more "noble" than the poems they comment upon, whereas in fact the commentary should serve the text it expounds

(§1.5). Later on he does mention the idea that language should match the theme at hand, clearly a fundamental assumption of his literary aesthetics. But in this case, he explains to the reader that his writing is deliberately "harsh" because of the serious-ness of his philosophical theme (§4.2).

That theme is the exalted topic of virtue. The *Convivio* is sadly unfinished, but it was probably supposed to go through the virtues one by one; what remains is really only the discussion of virtue in general. Dante has good reasons for his choice of topic. Traditionally, Aristotelians had taken metaphysics to be chief among the human sciences. For Dante this place is instead assumed by ethics.[9] It directs us to pursue the other sciences by teaching us that we ought to pursue rational perfection. Even in the grip of his philosophical enthusiasm, though, Dante is convinced that reason can take us only so far. We cannot come to know God in this life by engaging in philosophical theory. Such knowledge would constitute perfect happiness reached through contemplation (§3.15). Since that sort of ultimate bliss is unattain-able for now, we have to make do with the lesser, practical happiness attained through ethical virtue. This should sound familiar. Dante is reiterating the two-level theory of happiness we found in Albert the Great and Thomas Aquinas. But he goes further by making ethics completely central to the sort of philosophy possible for human reason. This goes hand in hand with Dante's decision to speak to a "unlearned" audience. The rarefied truths of contemplative, theoretical philosophy are beyond our earthly reach. So if philosophy here and now is mostly about being ethically virtuous, and if we are all potentially virtuous, then why not think that philosophy is for everyone?[10] Yet Dante also gives voice to elitism of a different sort. Those who refuse to be guided by reason are bound to remain vicious, and are no better than animals; his words are not directed to such reprobates (§4.7).

Given Dante's fascination with virtue and vice, with sorting the pure wheat from the rotten chaff, what could be a more natural project for him than a vast poem in the vernacular language describing the fates of those who have been good and evil in this life? That is, of course, what we get in the *Divine Comedy*. As you probably know, in the *Comedy* Dante depicts himself as a "pilgrim" traveling through the three realms of the afterlife, Hell, Purgatory, and the heavenly Paradise. We've seen this sort of device before. Jean de Meun in his *Romance of the Rose* and Marguerite Porete in her *Mirror of Simple Souls* both adopted the dual roles of author and protagonist. Dante exploits the resulting ironic distance, as when he has a character in Paradise predict what is in store for Dante the pilgrim by naming events that have already befallen Dante the author by the time he is writing his poem (*Par.* 17). My favorite example of this sort of thing comes in *Inferno* 15. Here Dante the pilgrim expresses shock upon finding his mentor Brunetto Latini being eternally punished for sodomy—the decision to put him there having, of course, been taken by Dante the author (*Inf.* 15.30).

It's not the only case in which Dante the pilgrim feels sympathy for those damned by God. He even swoons in a faint out of pity for the star-crossed lovers Paolo and Franscesca (*Inf.* 5.139–42). What Dante the author thinks, or wants us to think, about such sympathetic sinners is a difficult question. For us the most relevant such case comes when Dante visits Limbo, the first circle of Hell, which is reserved for virtuous people who were pagans or unbaptized (*Inf.* 4.34–6). Their plight is made more vivid by the fact that Dante's guide at this stage is Virgil, himself a pagan and thus a resident of Limbo when he is not taking Italian poets on a tour of the afterlife. While the denizens of Limbo are spared the horrific punishments the pilgrim will see later in Hell, like being turned into bleeding trees, having their bodies torn asunder, or being embedded in ice, the virtuous pagans do suffer from their unfulfilled longing for God. This, of course, fits perfectly with the *Convivio*: the perfect happiness envisioned there is forever forbidden to the unbaptized.

The roll call of disappointed spirits in Limbo reads like a list of highlights from this book series. Dante mentions the pagans Socrates, Plato, Democritus, Diogenes, Empedocles, Zeno, Thales, Anaxagoras, Heraclitus, Seneca, Ptolemy, Hippocrates, and Galen, as well as the Muslim thinkers Avicenna and Averroes ("who wrote the great commentary," *Inf.* 4.144). Pride of place is, however, given to the man described simply as "the master of those who know (*maestro di color che sanno*)" (*Inf.* 4.131), who is, of course, Aristotle. Despite this praise, the knowledge attained by Aristotle and the rest was insufficient. Dante speaks of "the fruitless longing of those men who would – if reason could – have been content, those whose desire eternally laments: Aristotle and Plato, and many others" (*Purg.* 3.40–4). This may seem rather unfair. How can it be just for God to punish pagans for not embracing Christ, when they lived centuries before Christ was even born? Dante is sensitive to the problem.[11] In *Paradiso*, he considers the fate of the man "born on the banks of the Indus River," who has no way of knowing about Christianity (*Par.* 19.70–2). It's a problem that will seem yet more urgent in coming centuries, when Europeans grapple with the discovery of previously uncontacted peoples in the New World.

The scene in Limbo is not the only philosophical gathering in the *Divine Comedy*. Much later, as Dante is ascending through the celestial spheres on his tour of Paradise, he reaches the circle of the sun. This is the section of the poem most frequently discussed by historians of philosophy, in part because Dante makes Bonaventure and Thomas Aquinas the two chief spokesmen of this circle. Dante puts a speech of praise for St. Francis into the mouth of the Dominican theologian Aquinas, while the Franciscan Bonaventure speaks of the virtues of St. Dominic (*Par.*

11–12). The rivalry between the orders on earth is replaced by harmony and mutual admiration here in Paradise. Both Aquinas and Bonaventure are accompanied by other spirits who appear as dancing lights in two rings. They include such familiar medieval figures as Anselm, Peter Lombard, Gratian, and Hugh of Saint Victor. But one name has raised the eyebrows of many a reader: Siger of Brabant. Dante has Aquinas introduce him with the words, "This is the everlasting light of Siger, who when he lectured in the Street of Straw, demonstrated truths that earned him envy (sillogizzò invidiosi veri)."

What is this notorious so-called "Averroist" doing in Paradise, and why is it Aquinas of all people who is made to present him to Dante? It clearly fits with the broader harmonizing theme of the circle of the sun. Here, whether we are Dominicans or Franciscans, moderate or radical followers of Aristotle, we can all finally get along. Aquinas' heavenly reconciliation with Siger is matched by Bonaventure's introduction of Joachim of Fiore, a controversial twelfth-century thinker who commented on the Book of Apocalypse and looked ahead to the coming of the Antichrist. In real life he was powerfully criticized by Bonaventure, just as Siger was attacked by Aquinas.[12] Many have, however, suspected that Dante's choice to include Siger may be more than an instance of heavenly reconciliation. Might it be a sign of his deeper intellectual sympathies? Was Dante himself attracted by the radical teachings of the Averroists?[13] It's certainly plausible that he knew about their ideas. Guido Cavalcanti, Dante's friend and fellow exponent of the "sweet new style" in poetry, could have been a conduit for radical ideas from Paris.[14]

We've already seen that in both the Convivio and the Divine Comedy, Dante places limits on what pure reason can achieve. He sounds more like Aquinas than like Boethius of Dacia when he emphasizes that perfect happiness is achieved only through a contemplation of God that is impossible in this life. Yet the place of honor given in Paradise to Siger and his controversial "demonstrated truths" suggests that Dante did think there is a place for pure rational inquiry outside of theology. On both counts Dante's attitude in the Convivio seems to be retained in the Divine Comedy. Reason can tell us a great deal, but it can't tell us everything or make us completely happy. The influential French scholar of medieval philosophy Étienne Gilson wrote that Siger appears in Paradise to "symbolize the independence of a definite portion of the temporal order, that portion which we call philosophy." For Gilson, Dante's choice has to do only with the role of reason in general, not with specific Averroist teaching.[15]

Yet there are signs that Dante may have flirted with at least one notorious teaching associated with the so-called Averroists: the unity of the intellect.[16] In the Convivio, Dante says quite clearly that each individual human has his or her own potential intellect, which he understands as a power for receiving understanding through an illumination from God (§4.21). Then in *Purgatorio*, he has the ancient poet Statius tell Dante the pilgrim that Averroes' theory, according to which there is only one potential intellect for all of humankind, is in error (*Purg.* 25.62–6). Yet Statius also admits that it was an easy mistake for Averroes to fall into, and refers to the great Muslim commentator as "one wiser than you are." Quite a contrast to the invective aimed at Averroes and his theory by Aquinas and others!

But the plot doesn't really thicken until we turn to Dante's treatise on political rule, *On Monarchy*.[17] Written at about the same time Dante was working on the *Divine Comedy*, this is a defense of the idea of a unified and universal political rule. As he elaborates on this idea, Dante explains that the fulfillment of intellectual potential is something the whole human race must do together. He speaks as if it is a single power that is being exercised not individually, but collectively. Given his rejection of Averroes' theory in the *Comedy*, most interpreters have taken this to be merely a loose way of speaking. But John Marenbon has argued that, for Dante, rational argument left to its own devices would confirm that Averroes was right. It seems that since there is no bodily organ for intellective thought, such thought cannot belong to one individual at a time but must be universal and shared by all. There are sound theological reasons to reject the idea, though. In light of these concerns, Averroes' theory of the single shared human mind must in the end be abandoned, even if it makes sense within the confines of the Aristotelian system.

This is the philosophical issue that seems most telling when it comes to determining Dante's attitude towards Averroism, but it is far from the only philosophical issue explored in the *Comedy*. There is, for instance, a discussion of free will in *Purgatorio*, which affirms that the heavenly bodies do have influence on human affairs but do not constrain our freedom (16.73–81). Dante also has much to say about the heavens in *Paradiso*, which only stands to reason, given that the celestial realm serves as the setting of this final part of the poem. While visiting the sphere of the moon, Dante is treated to a discussion of Plato's idea that souls go to be with the stars after the death of the earthly body (*Par.* 4.49–60). Echoing twelfth-century interpreters who sought to put the most favorable possible interpretation on Plato's *Timaeus*, Beatrice suggests that Plato's words are not literally true but may be valid in an allegorical sense.[18]

Elsewhere in *Paradiso*, Beatrice adds some further thoughts on free will (*Par.* 5.19–84), brings the pilgrim to the so-called "Empyrean," an immaterial realm beyond the heavens where blessed souls dwell (*Par.* 30; cf. *Convivio* 2.3), and even describes a kind of scientific experiment involving candles and mirrors while refuting the pilgrim's idea that spots on the moon are caused by variations in density (*Par.* 2, 61–148).[19] Such disquisitions are a characteristic feature of this part of the poem.[20] They make *Paradiso* a rich source for Dante's philosophical ideas, even if most readers seem to prefer reading about the sadistic tortures meted out to the damned in *Inferno*.[21] The *Paradiso* also has quite a bit to say about political philosophy. For this topic, though, the really essential reading is *On Monarchy*, on the strength of which we can say that in the firmament of authors who wrote on politics in the fourteenth century, Dante was one of the brightest stars.

55

OUR POWER IS REAL
THE CLASH OF CHURCH
AND STATE

A t the turn of the fourteenth century, Giles of Rome found himself on the wrong side of history. He was a steadfast supporter of Boniface VIII, the Pope who fought a losing political battle with the French king, Philip IV, known as Philip the Fair. It's safe to say that it wasn't Boniface who gave him that nickname. Reacting to the taxes levied on church property by Philip and also the English Crown, Boniface issued what I can't resist calling an angry papal bull. Or even a whole herd of bulls, a series of documents commanding secular kings to bend to the authority of the papacy.[1] In 1301 he wrote that as Pope he was "placed above kings and kingdoms," with the responsibility and right "to uproot and destroy, to disperse and scatter, to build and to plant." Invoking the familiar biblical metaphor Boniface argued that the Church is given two swords, of spiritual and temporal power. If kings wield temporal power, it is on behalf of the Church and "at the command and by the permission of the priest." Philip was not impressed. As one of his representatives put it when speaking to the Pope, "your [power] is verbal; ours, however, is real (*vestra est verbalis, nostra autem realis*)." The king showed this power by having Boniface arrested, which led to the Pope's death in 1303. It was commented that Boniface took the papacy like a fox, ruled like a lion, but died like a dog.

It may surprise you to hear that in the deeply religious medieval age it was possible for kings to stand up to a pope like this, and come out as victors into the bargain. We are apt to think of the separation of Church and State as a distinctively modern idea. But the medievals would need no lessons from us on this score. At the turn of the fourteenth century the Church and the medieval states were not just separate: they were at each others' throats. We know from our earlier discussion of the clashing of these "two swords" that this struggle was a constant of medieval culture (Chapter 17), and really an inevitable one, given the substantial involvement of clerics in the temporal sphere, with vast landholdings and military forces at their command. Besides, the whole point of being a king or an emperor is that you don't answer to anyone. A monarch is the supreme authority in his sphere of action. Remember that this was even used to explain why wars must be fought: because there is no higher court of appeal to resolve conflicts between rulers (Chapter 40). When a pope said to these rulers that they answered to him, that their otherwise supreme power was exercised at his behest and at his discretion, they were hardly going to respond with meek acquiescence.

For the secular theorists in the debate the problem was saying where royal power and authority *did* come from, if not from the Pope. Their answer was that such authority is granted directly by God. This is the kind of historical irony I really cherish. The idea that kings have a "divine right" to rule seems an obvious example of the way that religion and politics were intertwined in earlier times. Yet the idea was, to no small degree, put forward in order to resist the rival claims of the Church. Which is not to deny that compromise positions were available. A figure often seen as a moderate in the debate was John of Paris, whose *On Royal and Papal Power* was written at the height of the confrontation between Pope Boniface and King Philip.[2] John resists the urge to subordinate one power to the other. For him, the secular ruler and the Pope receive their authorities separately from God, having dominion over temporal and spiritual concerns respectively. Each must take the lead within its own sphere. This may sound closer to the secularist position, since it would mean that the Pope should stay out of temporal affairs.[3] Yet John also points out that each of the two powers is subject to correction by the other. A king might depose a wicked pope, a pope excommunicate a wicked king.

Like an unenthusiastic accountancy student, Giles of Rome had no interest in such checks and balances. His treatise *On the Power of the Church* is as forthright a defense of the Pope's position as you could hope to read, which is not particularly surprising, given that it was dedicated to Boniface himself.[4] Giles explicitly aims to prove the superiority of the spiritual order to the temporal order (§1.1.3), and hence of the Pope to all secular rulers (§1.2.7). The Pope wields both "swords," though he allows secular rulers to use the sword of temporal authority at his command (§1.8.2; cf. 2.13). Giles sees here a parallel to the relationship between soul and body. It is because of our dual nature, both spiritual and physical, that we fall under two kinds of authority, spiritual and temporal. But the Church has spiritual authority over all human souls (§1.3.3–6), and the temporal order is subordinate to spiritual authority just as a human's body is subordinate to that human's soul (§1.7, 3.5.12). After all, the soul rules the body, with the limbs moving as the soul dictates (§2.4.7–8).

In Aristotelian terms, Giles is here suggesting that church authority is an efficient cause of temporal affairs: it sets them in motion much as the soul moves the body. But final causality is also relevant. Our ultimate goal as humans is a spiritual one, namely the soul's ultimate beatitude. Here Giles is recalling a doctrine of his teacher Thomas Aquinas and putting it to political ends. Our final end is contemplation of God, and obviously it is not any secular king but the head of the Church who guides us towards that end. On this basis Giles also rejects any notion that there could be two parallel orders that operate independently of one another. We have only one final end, not two, and all temporal goods must be used in pursuit of the single spiritual goal shared by all humankind (§2.4.3–6). An Aristotelian example might be that we should value money, a temporal good, only because it helps us display virtues like generosity. But the implications of Giles' theory might better be illustrated with a case like the Crusades, where the military might of kings was used to achieve an objective set by the papacy, and the soldiers were promised a heavenly reward, namely the remission of their sins. The chance of seizing a few temporal goods in the shape of land holdings or booty was, in theory at least, merely a welcome bonus.

Giles' defense of papal supremacy invokes another idea familiar from Aquinas: the subordination of the sciences. We saw that, for Aquinas, theology is the highest of all disciplines and gives principles to lower, philosophical sciences. Giles has a similar idea, which he applies especially to the philosophy of nature (§2.13.15–17; cf. § 2.6.24). Physics is a lower science than metaphysics because it is more restricted in its scope. The student of nature studies only bodily things, whereas the metaphysician studies all things, both spiritual and bodily. In much the same way, the concerns and the authority of secular kings are particular and parochial, whereas the concerns and authority of the Pope is universal (§2.6.16). Giles goes so far as to suggest that the Pope's universal rule over humankind is like God's rule over the created universe. God rules over all things and natural causes are inferior to the supreme divine cause (§1.5.8–11).

In fact, a natural cause like fire, or an animal that generates another animal, involves what we might call "delegated" power. This is secondary causation (§3.1.9), which derives ultimately from God's primary causal power and is always subject to being overturned by that power, which is what happens in a miracle (§3.9.5). Just so, the Pope may frequently allow secular affairs to proceed *as if* they were independent, but he can always assert his ultimate authority if he wishes. We see this when he refrains from intervening in secular court cases even though he does have final authority which could be brought to bear when answering an appeal from a temporal judge (§3.2.19). Just as God voluntarily restricts His own absolute power by (usually) exercising His power within an ordained set of natural laws, so the Pope lays down laws and statutes for the running of the Church and voluntarily obeys these laws. Really, though, he is above their jurisdiction, because of what Giles explicitly calls his "absolute power" (§3.7.7).

But, one can't help wondering, what if the Pope is a complete jerk? Do we really want to put ourselves in a position where a vicious man can exercise such untrammeled and unchallenged authority? Giles confronts this question and in so doing makes a point of perennial relevance. We should distinguish between the moral standing of a person and the moral standing of the position of authority that a person may occupy (§1.2.4–5). In other words, even if the current Pope is a vicious man, the papacy as such retains its supremacy. Conversely, the fact that some other person may have great moral virtue does not give that person spiritual authority. As Giles says, being a great singer doesn't by itself make you the cantor in your local church; you have to be awarded the office (§2.12.5). Here Giles may seem too relaxed about handing great power to wicked men. In a slightly earlier work called *On the Abdication of the Pope* (*De renuntiatione papae*) Giles had argued that popes are given their position through election by the cardinals and thereafter can be removed only voluntarily, that is, by abdication. The sole exception would be the Pope who falls into heresy. Still, Giles' comments on separating the dignity of the office from the moral status of the office holder can be read as a refreshing change from much ancient and medieval political writing, which tends to emphasize above all the moral character of the ideal ruler.

Giles was himself a significant contributor to that moralizing tradition. Years prior to his defense of papal authority, he had written a work called *On the Government of Princes* (*De regimine principum*). This became a hugely popular text, translated into numerous European vernacular languages and preserved in about three hundred manuscripts.[5] It is an example of the so-called "mirror for princes" genre, texts that give moral and practical advice to rulers and aspiring rulers. Drawing extensively on Aristotle's ethical and political writings,[6] this earlier treatise sees Giles arguing for the supreme rule of the *secular* monarch. This isn't necessarily in direct contradiction with the later treatise *On the Power of the Church*, since there Giles will recognize that the king is at the top of the temporal hierarchy, even if that whole hierarchy is subordinate to spiritual authority (§1.5.12). But in a third work, his commentary on the *Sentences*, Giles makes some remarks that cast doubt on the moralizing project of his mirror for princes.[7] In our fallen state of sin, he says, all secular authority is inevitably coercive in character. If a temporal ruler claims to rule with a view to the common good, this is always a pretense, since postlapsarian humans are inevitably selfish in their motives. By contrast, before the fall, Giles contends, Adam was in position of rule (*dominium*) over Eve, because men are superior to women, but this rule was based on mutual love and so involved no coercion.

For a far more optimistic attitude towards secular rule we can turn back to Dante Alighieri. Dante's political theory is diametrically opposed to what we have just seen. Where Giles championed the cause of Boniface VIII, Dante condemned this Pope to hell; where Giles placed secular rule under the universal authority of the papacy, Dante puts all his trust in the universal temporal rule of an emperor. His arguments to this end are presented in a work composed in Latin, *On Monarchy* (*De monarchia*).[8] As one scholar wrote shortly after World War II, in this work "the rights of the secular state as against Vatican direction are maintained with an emphasis that would have shocked Aquinas, but was destined to be quoted with many a chuckle by Benito Mussolini."[9] Dante hoped that his theory would find historical embodiment in the person of Henry VII of Luxembourg, a Holy Roman emperor whose invasion of Italy was greeted with great enthusiasm by Dante. In *Paradiso* he would immortalize Henry, and lament the ultimate failure of imperial rule in Italy, by having Beatrice say that in heaven "shall sit the soul of noble Henry: he shall show Italy the righteous way, but when she is unready (*a drizzare Italia verrà in prima ch'ella sia disposta*)" (3.136–8).

The contrast between Giles of Rome and Dante gives us a nice example of the fact that the same premise can be used to reach very different conclusions. Like Giles, Dante avails himself of the idea that humankind in general shares a single end, the perfection of our intellectual capacities. Since we all have this goal in common, there should be a single political order which seeks to help us along to reach our shared objective (§1.3). This means that we should have a single ruler whose imperial authority should ideally stretch over the entire earth, "bounded only by the ocean." Like Giles, Dante sees a parallel here to the providential rule of the one God over the universe (§1.7). There are many advantages to be expected from this political arrangement. Peace will reign, without multiple political entities competing for domination (§1.10). The sole ruler will also be without greed, because his power will be so supreme that there will be nothing left for him to desire (§1.11, 13). And there are more abstract, dare I say philosophical, justifications for single *imperium*. Dante refers to the theory of transcendentals, reminding us of the scholastic teaching that unity correlates to goodness, which shows that a single rule is also the best rule (§1.15). Furthermore, he cites the Neoplatonic *Book of Causes* for the idea that the higher a cause, the further its reach should be. It follows that the highest political rule must reach to all things (§1.11).

Dante thinks that Aristotle would agree with him about all this (§1.5), which is less than entirely convincing, given that Aristotle conceived of politics within the context of a city state or *polis*, a far smaller political entity than a world-spanning empire. For Dante the real ancient model is, of course, not Athens but Rome. He thinks that divine providence settled on Rome as the center of imperial authority, something shown even by the fact that King David was (supposedly) born at the same time as Aeneas (supposedly) founded the city of Rome (*Convivio* §4.5). You might object that Rome was for many centuries a republic and not the seat of empire. To this Dante would triumphantly remind you that Christ himself was born during the reign of the first Roman emperor, Augustus Caesar (*On Monarchy* §1.16, 2.11). What could be a greater indication of God's approval?[10]

On the last page of *On Monarchy* Dante somewhat grudgingly admits that the emperor owes respect and deference to the Pope, as a son does to his father. But apart from this, ecclesiastical power appears in the work solely as an undesirable obstacle to the imperial project (as at §3.3). Dante here reflects on the tensions between the papacy and secular rule in his own lifetime. He rejects the biblical interpretation that has "two swords" being put in the hands of the Church (§1.9), and denies that political authority was ever in the gift of the Church, either by nature or by divine command (§1.14). Where Giles of Rome referred to Old Testament passages to prove that kings were invested with their office by priests among the Hebrews (*On the Power of the Church* §1.6.2), Dante points out that the Christian Church arose only *after* the establishment of the Roman Empire under Augustus (*On Monarchy* §1.13). This obviously shows that imperial authority cannot derive from the command of the popes, given that the Church didn't even exist when imperial authority was originally, and most successfully, exercised.

Just as there has been scholarly controversy as to whether the philosophical ideas of the *Convivio* are retained in the *Divine Comedy*, so interpreters don't agree about the relationship between the Dante of *On Monarchy* and the Dante of the *Comedy*. It's been proposed that *On Monarchy* represented a passing phase of enthusiasm for secular rule, with a more theological attitude emerging in the famous poem.[11] But there are numerous signs that Dante's political attitudes remained fairly constant throughout his career. He champions the Roman Empire in the *Convivio* as well, and in both *On Monarchy* (3.10) and the *Comedy* (*Inf.* 19.115–18) decries the idea that the Emperor Constantine placed the Western realms of Christendom under the power of the papacy. Even if Constantine did this, he had no legitimate standing to do so, since the realms of the empire must remain united and under a sole temporal ruler. Dante even has Constantine appear in Paradise to admit his error (*Par.* 20). And just in case we're not yet sure how Dante feels about the medieval papacy, canto 19 of *Inferno* predicts the damnation of Boniface and treats us to the spectacle of another Pope being punished for simony by being buried head down in the earth, with his legs and feet writhing as they are burned by flames.[12] It would be hard to imagine anyone taking a firmer stance against the misdeeds of the Church—but we're about to meet another Italian who gave it a good try.

56

RENDER UNTO CAESAR
MARSILIUS OF PADUA

Political rulers should govern in the interest of their subjects, not in their own interests. It's a common enough sentiment, even if it is a guideline more honored in the breach than in the observance. Already Plato, in the first book of his *Republic*, has Socrates argue that rulers must look after the welfare of the citizens the way that shepherds look to the welfare of their flocks. Medieval thinkers in both the Islamic and Latin Christian worlds followed a similar line inspired by Aristotle: a state should be governed in such a way that the citizens of the state become virtuous. It's on this basis that al-Fārābī distinguished what he called the "virtuous city" from other cities in which citizens seek lower ends like pleasure or honor.[1] Aquinas likewise took the purpose of laws to be the training of citizens in virtue (Chapter 39), and we've just seen Dante justifying the idea of universal rule in terms of the universal, shared goal of humankind to achieve the contemplative virtue of intellectual perfection.

All these highminded recommendations provoke a pretty obvious response: easier said than done. It's one thing to say how rulers *should* govern and with what end in view, another to ensure that they *do* govern in this way. Much ancient and medieval political philosophy is disappointingly sketchy when it comes to that question. It's all well and good to envision an ideal state led by the virtuous and even by philosophers, but it smacks of utopianism. Plato already recognized this, contenting himself with showing that it is just about possible for philosopher-kings to come to power, albeit very unlikely. In general, one gets the impression that political thinkers were resigned to the fact that rulers would come to power by chance, through military conquest or inheritance. They optimistically hoped, in the face of a staggeringly large amount of evidence to the contrary, that God was providentially appointing the right men (and occasionally women) to sit on the thrones. And they wrote works of moral exhortation for rulers, like Giles of Rome's *On the Government of Princes*, in hopes that good advice would be taken to heart.

But at least one medieval thinker did more than that, by defining the conditions under which political rule is legitimate. His name was Marsilius (or Marsiglio) of

Padua. Like Giles of Rome, he responded to the struggle between papacy and secular princes that raged in the early fourteenth century. But unlike Giles he was very much on the secular side. Marsilius' masterpiece, the *Defender of the Peace*,[2] makes direct reference to the ambitious clerics whom he identified as the chief cause of political unrest and conflict in his age. He condemned the Popes Boniface VIII and John XXII for standing in the way of the rightful rule of kings and emperors. It was a polemic he waged at considerable personal cost. After initially being educated in his home-town of Padua, Marsilius moved back and forth between there and Paris, where he wrote the *Defender of the Peace* in the year 1324.[3] Perhaps because of his controversial writings, Marsilius left (or, more dramatically, fled) from Paris with a colleague named John of Jandun.[4] They traveled to the court of Ludwig of Bavaria, an ideal host for Marsilius, since Ludwig embodied the idea that secular rulers can and should wield power independently of the papacy. He invaded Italy and had himself crowned emperor at Rome in 1328 in a ceremony involving compliant bishops who were enemies of Pope John XXII, as well as representatives of the Roman aristoc-racy. The Pope was, it goes without saying, not best pleased. By this time he had already made it clear what he thought of Marsilius, naming both him and John of Jandun as heretics and excommunicating them in 1327. Ludwig returned the favor the next year by declaring the Pope deposed. As with the earlier struggle between Philip the Fair and Pope Boniface, these events meant that the debate over papal and princely sovereignty was far from theoretical. It addressed the burning political question of the day.

Given that he was such a partisan of Emperor Ludwig, you might think that Marsilius would seek to establish his patron's legitimacy by appealing to God's providence. This is what Dante had done in celebrating the Roman Empire and his own imperial hope Henry VII. But for Marsilius, God establishes legitimate rulers only through the actions of individual human communities (§1.9.2). If divine providence takes a hand in our political affairs, it is by guiding the people to choose the best rulers, not by bestowing victory in war or a favorable birth. The rightful ruler is determined by an "election" on the part of either "the universal body of the citizens, or the prevailing part (*valentior pars*)" (§1.12.3). Of course, he is not envisioning here something like a modern-day representative democracy. He excludes slaves and women, along with foreigners and children, from the ranks of citizens (§1.12.5). Marsilius is imagining an assembly along the lines of the noble electors whose support was in fact needed by German rulers like Ludwig. This was an ancient practice that goes back to Carolingian times, and even to the traditions of Germanic tribes.

So why have I described Marsilius as such a pioneering political theorist? Because he tries to explain *why* kings or emperors must be chosen through election. He appeals to a principle of Roman law, taken over by the medieval canonists, stating that "what affects all likewise should be approved by all (*quod omnes similiter tangit, ab omnibus comprobetur*)" (§1.12.7, 1.15.2). On this basis Marsilius reasons that the citizens must express their consent if the ruler is justly to rule over them. This is achieved through the process of election. The assembly of citizens is a legislative body and retains its standing even after having chosen a ruler. In fact, the ruler doesn't even need to be a single person, though Marsilius does insist, following a traditional analogy we've seen in earlier medieval authors like John of Salisbury (Chapter 17), that political rule should flow from a single person or group as an animal is ruled from a single organ, namely the heart (§1.17.8).[5]

Nor is this just going to be a rubber-stamping procedure, where the strongest strongmen or bluest blue bloods can assume that the nobles will acclaim them as kings or councillors. Marsilius explicitly mentions, as an advantage of the elective process, that it has the best chance of putting virtuous men in charge (§1.9.7). This is to be a genuinely representative government, with the representing to be done by those whom the citizens choose. The chosen virtuous ruler is not to pass authority on to his children. Instead, a new election must be held to appoint the successor (§1.16.11). This is to safeguard against the possibility of a vicious son taking the throne from a virtuous father (aficionados of Roman history will think immediately of Marcus Aurelius' son, Commodus). Marsilius does allow that the son of a virtuous monarch is likely to be virtuous too, having been raised by such an outstanding father (§1.16.13), and one gets the sense that in his ideal scenario inherited rule would still be frequent. Still, the point stands that inheritance in no way legitimates the ruler. Legitimacy of government comes only from the consent of the governed.

Marsilius thus provides exactly what we found missing in earlier political theorists. He reasons that, if the common good of the citizens is really the purpose of governance, then the citizens should have a say in deciding how their common good is best achieved. Power does not flow downwards from God through a divinely anointed king or pope, but flows upward from the people.[6] Marsilius is not quite expressing a thought that might seem natural for us, namely that consent of the governed is required because it is an intrinsic requirement of justice. Rather, he sees consent as a useful device, a mechanism by which the governed secure whatever is in their best interests.[7] On the other hand, the reason why we need rulers in the first place is that the people may not all agree on what is most beneficial. Hence the title of Marsilius' book. The elected ruler is the "defender of the peace" because the citizens consent to be governed by that ruler rather than coming into conflict with one another. The whole citizenry, or its prevailing part, is in the best position to judge the best person or persons who should be nominated to secure the best overall results. Marsilius is strikingly optimistic about this. In sharp contrast to the elitism of a Plato or an al-Fārābī, he argues that the people as a whole will make better choices than a select group of wise men (§1.13.4). We can see how seriously Marsilius takes this by noting his answer to an argument in favor of hereditary rule. One might suppose that under that system the people would be more docile, just accepting each ruler as anointed thanks to their family ties. To this Marsilius responds that, on the contrary, the people would be *more* likely to rebel against automatically inherited rule, and rightly so, since they would realize that they are being governed by men who are inferior to themselves.

Perhaps understandably Marsilius does not belabor the notion that all the hereditary rulers in Latin Christendom could rightfully be deposed if they did not come to their position through a new valid election. In any case, his chief target is not rule by inheritance, though he does oppose that practice. It is above all the Church that he accuses of disrupting the peace. This, Marsilius wryly remarks, is a source of dissension that was unknown to Aristotle, who never had the dubious privilege of experiencing the grasping greed and temporal ambitions of the Christian Church (§1.1.3 and 7). In fact, one can describe the *Defender of the Peace* as an update of Aristotle's *Politics* that takes account of the new dangers posed by clerical authority. Aristotle could not have foreseen the depredations of the popes or, as Marsilius likes to call them, the "Roman bishops." But no one who reads Marsilius will be in any doubt as to the dangers they pose.

He systematically deprives the popes and the Church more generally of any right to interfere in the temporal order. The priesthood has the sole purpose of seeing to our spiritual needs, which means looking to the eternal life and not the affairs of this world (§1.6.8). Priests do play an important role in administering the sacraments and thus helping us free ourselves of sin (§2.6.6–7). But apart from that they should mind their business. In this they would be following the example of Christ, who disavowed temporal rule (§2.4.3 and 6) saying "My kingdom is not of this world" and, of course, "Render unto Caesar that which is Caesar's" (John 18:36 and Luke 20:25, quoted at §2.4.4 and 9). But surely the medieval Church at least has the responsibility of enforcing orthodox Christian belief? Not exactly. The priesthood may have the role of identifying heretics but has no right to punish them. Consider the analogous case of a doctor who diagnoses leprosy. The doctor advises the secular authorities, and it is they who undertake appropriate measures like a quarantine (§2.10.9). Priests, whether popes or not, who think that they have an authority over any aspect of the temporal order should again look to the example of Christ, who, after all, allowed himself to be judged by a secular official, Pontius Pilate (§2.9.8).

Having taken away their political influence, Marsilius now really hits the priests where it hurts: in their pocketbooks. Again referring to the example of Christ and the Apostles, he argues that poverty is inextricably bound up with the Christian moral ideal. Predictably he quotes Jesus' advice from the Bible: "Sell all that you have and give to the poor, and you shall have treasure in heaven" (Luke 18.22, at §2.11.3). Here we come again to the bitter controversy over the mendicant orders and the ideal of poverty. We saw how Peter Olivi, Bonaventure, and others had defended that ideal in the thirteenth century (Chapter 31). In the early 1320s the dispute reached a new intensity thanks to Pope John XXII, who declared the vow of poverty irrational and therefore even heretical, insofar as the Franciscans and other mendicants were ascribing the supposed perfection of absolute poverty to Christ and the Apostles. The Pope's rejection of the mendicant vow ran along lines familiar to us. Even if the Franciscans could reasonably decline to own things like houses, they must at least use things like the food they eat; otherwise, they would starve themselves to death, thereby committing the sin of suicide. It makes no sense to say you use but do not own the bread you eat, given that you destroy the thing in the process of using it.

In the thirteenth century the mendicants had been able to rely on papal support and could take refuge in the argument that the things they used in fact belonged to the Pope. Now the sitting Pope was refusing to acknowledge this and in fact condemning the whole notion of voluntary absolute poverty. Marsilius' response is a furious one, accusing the Pope himself of being a heretic for his stance. This, by the way, is a constant refrain of his strictures against papal overreach, that popes might be and indeed have recently been heretical, so one cannot entrust them with a power such as excommunication or with a special right to determine the meaning of Scripture (§2.20.6, 2.21.9). In responding to Pope John's arguments Marsilius develops an innovative conception of ownership and more generally individual legal rights.[8]

An important step in Marsilius' argument is his definition of the Latin term *ius*, often translated into English as "right" (§2.12.3–12). In one sense though, *ius* simply means whatever is determined by laws or by legal commands and prohibitions; one could perhaps still speak here of what is "legally right." Scholars have found Marsilius' remarks here intriguing, because he seems to be saying that *whatever* a legal authority decides should be "right" becomes right, a position called legal "positivism."[9] It would contrast sharply with a theory of law like the one we found in Aquinas, where human laws must be grounded in the natural law and are in a sense just a more precise application of that law. Marsilius really has no use for the concept of natural law, because for him the realm of the legal is subject to human decision.[10] On the other hand, the positivist tendencies in Marsilius come with a significant qualification. As we saw earlier, laws do need to look to the common advantage of the citizens, which constrains the range of legitimate choices open to the legislator. An unfair or unjust law may count as no true law at all, as might a law that contravenes divinely ordained commands.[11]

In addition to this first sense of the word *ius*, Marsilius recognizes a second meaning: a *ius* or "right" is whatever is allowed to us within the scope of the law. To see what he has in mind here, let's take as an example your right to say that Buster Keaton's silent films aren't funny. For you to say this would certainly be erroneous, but you have the right to do it. There is no law requiring people to appreciate Keaton's films (despite the letters I keep sending to Congress). Your right to insult Buster Keaton is just one of many such rights. In general we are all permitted to do anything not forbidden by the law. In addition, we have certain positive rights, such as my right to bring you to court if you steal the Buster Keaton poster hanging over the desk where I'm writing this. This shows that ownership (*dominium*) is closely connected to the concept of a "right." Indeed, ownership is really a kind of right, the right to decide whether others can use the things you own.

Now Marsilius is just about ready to clarify what is happening with voluntary poverty. He observes that rights in general and the right of ownership in particular are voluntarily exercised (§2.12.13). The fact that you have the *right* to lament the supposed unfunniness of Keaton, or even of silent comedy in general, doesn't mean you have to be obnoxious enough to go and do it. Just so, you can have ownership rights over something without exercising those rights. Suppose a noblewoman donates bread to a Franciscan house. She can allow the friars to use the bread by eating it without transferring ownership to them. The fact that you can voluntarily let someone else use your possessions shows that the right of use is distinct from the right of ownership (§2.13.3). The noblewoman might also renounce her ownership of the bread so that if someone stole it from the Franciscans' pantry, she couldn't take the thief to court. But even that wouldn't mean that the mendicant friars are forced to assume ownership of the bread (§2.13.8, 2.14.20). The bread has come into their possession and they intend to use it, but they do not own it and have no legal claim to the bread.

So if the noblewoman renounces ownership and the friars don't accept ownership, then who does own the bread? Nobody, says Marsilius. He invokes the Roman concept of a *res nullius*, something owned by no one,[12] giving the nice example that a mendicant could catch and eat a fish without the fish ever passing into his ownership (§2.14.20). One implication is that, legally speaking, you can just take things from mendicants, because it isn't stealing. If you are standing on a river bank feeling hungry, see a Franciscan grilling a fish he just caught, and grab it out of his hands to eat it yourself, then the Franciscan has no legal recourse against you. The fish didn't belong to him: after all, he was just using it. The bad news is that you've committed a grave sin, breaking divine law rather than human law (§2.14.19).

For us, the reason all this is important is perhaps not so much the legitimization of poverty, as the theory of rights Marsilius has developed along the way. As Brian Tierney has written, "The argument that members of a spiritual elite could renounce their rights implied that, in the ordinary course of events, persons did possess rights and that normally they could be asserted."[13] In true "without any gaps" spirit, let's look quickly at how this sort of idea was developed by a far more obscure fourteenth-century author, William of Pagula.[14] In the early 1330s he wrote another one of those "mirrors for princes," or works of moral and practical advice, in this case dedicated to the English king, Edward III. Its theme is the practice of "purveyance," a custom in which the Crown could requisition goods from the king's subjects and just stipulate the price to be paid. In other words, if you were a peasant and the king came along and demanded you sell him your pig for one copper coin, you would have to do it. William of Pagula decries this practice. It is unjust to pay less than what he calls the "true price," meaning the price reached through negotiation and agreed by both parties. It's unjust not simply because the low price is hard on the already poor peasant, but because even peasants have rights of ownership over their possessions. These include the right to sell, or to refuse to sell, depending on whether the owner is happy with the price on offer.

You should by now be convinced that the first half of the fourteenth century was something of a high point in the history of political philosophy. Yet we still haven't even looked at the most famous political thinker of the period. Like Marsilius, that thinker took refuge with Ludwig of Bavaria after getting in trouble with the Church; and, like Marsilius, he was a devout defender of the ethic of poverty and a major figure in the development of political philosophy. Most would recognize him as the most significant scholastic thinker of the fourteenth century, and with all due respect to William of Pagula, just about everyone would admit that he was the most significant medieval philosopher named William.

DO AS YOU'RE TOLD
OCKHAM ON ETHICS AND
POLITICAL PHILOSOPHY

The medieval world was a world of hierarchies. Landholding and military service were organized through feudalism, with every man but the king having to fulfill obligations to his lord. The Church too was hierarchically arranged, with the Pope at its apex. Philosophy and theology were no exception. As they moved through the stratified educational system of the university, scholastics would speculate about angels arranged in descending ranks, about the subordination of all human sciences within a single system, and about the created universe itself, seen as a hierarchically ordered cosmos ruled by God. Yet, as we've been seeing, it was also a time of dissension and schism. There was rivalry between hierarchies, with the popes and emperors contending to be the truly supreme representatives of God on earth. And there was tension within hierarchies, too, as when nobles resisted the demands of their kings or clerics protested at the conduct or decrees of wicked popes. How could such dissent be justified? How could the leaders of institutions be rejected without rejecting the legitimacy of the institutions themselves?

A number of scholars came to grips with this question in the Middle Ages, none with more seriousness or subtlety than William of Ockham. In fact, he is sometimes called the "more than subtle doctor" to indicate that he surpassed the "subtle doctor" Duns Scotus. In his later years Ockham devoted himself to polemics against a pope whom he considered to be a heretic, and in the process developed something like a theory of principled disobedience. This is rather ironic, given that his earlier scholastic work features an ethical theory which takes obedience as its core idea. Like the merely subtle Scotus, Ockham was inclined to think that right and wrong are generated by divine commands. Under certain circumstances you may encourage people to depose a wicked pope. But if the ruler you're dealing with is God, you should just do as you're told.

We can divide Ockham's career into two parts.[1] Appropriately enough, the life-changing event that marks the division in his biography took place in a city indelibly associated with schism: Avignon. He went there in 1324 to defend himself against charges of heresy. Prior to that, he received his training at Greyfriars in London and then pursued a degree in theology at Oxford. But he returned to London without becoming a master of theology, which is why he is sometimes also called the "venerable inceptor," surely the least catchy nickname in all of medieval philosophy (it just means that he remained a "beginner"). Still, his time at Oxford did give him the chance to lecture on the *Sentences* of Peter Lombard, and we have written records of these lectures as well as many of his disputed questions and writings on logic. The genres within which Ockham was working are familiar to us, but his ideas were sufficiently daring that they provoked intense opposition. Ockham frequently developed his ideas by criticizing Scotus, spurring Scotus' followers—like William of Alnwick and John of Reading—to defend their master. It may have been John of Reading who asked the papal court to look into the orthodoxy of Ockham's teachings on such issues as the Eucharist.[2]

While Ockham's views were criticized at Avignon, he was not actually pronounced a heretic. Yet it was not his fate to return to his native England. Instead, he was swept up in the highly political clash between the Franciscan mendicants and Pope John XXII over the advisability and possibility of absolute poverty. Ockham threw in his lot with the head of the Franciscan order, Michael of Cesena, and having taken up a position in defiance of the Pope, they fled from Avignon in 1328. These renegade Franciscans found sanctuary with Ludwig of Bavaria, the same man who gave patronage and protection to Marsilius of Padua. From this point until his death in 1347, Ockham devoted his writing to political topics.

As just mentioned, however, Ockham was a controversial figure long before he got to Munich. One of the teachings that raised eyebrows in Avignon gives us some insight as to how radical and uncompromising he could be and how willing he was to follow his principles to their conclusions. He claimed that God could, if He so wished, require us to commit adultery or steal, and that if He did so, it would be right for us to obey. He even speculated about God commanding us to hate Him, something that was picked out by the Avignon commission as particularly problematic.[3] Here, he was following the logic of voluntarism, the view developed by Henry of Ghent and Duns Scotus, which insisted that both divine and human will are capable of uncaused decision-making unconstrained by any outside necessity. Ockham follows in the footsteps of Scotus by making moral laws subject to God's will. It's only a natural inference from this that, if God did tell you to commit adultery, it would become morally right for you to do so. Of course, Ockham doesn't dream that God will actually issue any such command. It's just that in principle He *could*.

There's a scholarly controversy lurking here. It's clear enough that Ockham ascribes God great latitude in fashioning the moral law. But is it really the case that we ought to, for instance, avoid committing adultery simply because He has told us that adultery is wrong? If so, then Ockham would simply be taking forward Duns Scotus' "divine command theory" of ethics. But interpreters have pointed to passages in Ockham's work that suggest a more complicated position. For one thing, he often invokes the role of "right reason" and "conscience" in morality.[4] He goes so far as to say, in fact, that no action can be virtuous unless it is guided by right reason.[5] If you just spontaneously and unthinkingly help an old lady across the street, give money to the poor, or recommend this book to someone in dire need of philosophical inspiration, it doesn't count as a morally virtuous act. You have to do these things because they are the right thing to do, and only for this reason.[6]

This may seem unnecessarily strict. So long as the old lady gets across the street, who cares what is going on in your mind when you offer her assistance? Isn't helping her just an intrinsically good thing to do? Not according to Ockham. He insists that any action, considered in itself, is morally neutral.[7] He gives the example of walking to church. Someone might set out towards church because of religious devotion but along the way begin to fantasize about seducing one of the other churchgoers. Here, the very same journey is at first motivated by love of God, then by adulterous lust. So this one act thus starts out as morally praiseworthy but becomes wicked partway through. And things could go the other way around. Ockham asks us to consider someone who commits suicide by jumping off a cliff. Since suicide is wrong, this counts as a sinful act. But if the person changes his mind halfway down, his continued fall is no longer sinful because it no longer stems from his will. The conclusion can be generalized. Since any action can be done out of a variety of motives, a virtuous action gets its character only from the process of practical reasoning and volition that gave rise to it.

There's a further reason for Ockham to stress the role of natural reasoning in ethics: somehow people do manage to act well despite being ignorant of divine revelation. The pagans who lived before Christ seem, in some cases, to have been downright heroic. Just consider Socrates or Cato the Younger, both widely admired for their bravery in resisting tyranny. Such characters obviously represent a serious difficulty for any divine command theory of ethics. Somehow the virtuous pagans managed to play the game of morality expertly despite never having learned the rules laid down by God. Ockham resolves the difficulty by pointing to the importance of practical rationality in our moral lives. Since pagans were often quite good at reasoning, they frequently managed to discern the right thing to do. But we should not be misled by this into thinking that virtuous actions are good *because* they are identified as such by reason. Only God's command makes something good. If a pagan manages to distinguish good from bad, it is because she is picking up clues to God's will by examining the created world. Ockham even speaks here of "self-evident" moral principles, for instance that the needy should be helped. This is the principle that inspires you to help the old lady. But it is only evident to you (or to a pre-Christian pagan) because you live in a world with a particular moral order that was ordained by God. He might have laid down a very different order, in which case the conclusions of right reason would have to be correspondingly different.[8] It follows from this that, even if pagans sometimes made the right choices, they never really understood why their choices were right. For Ockham, morality ultimately remains a matter of obeying God.

This may sound rather arbitrary. Why should I do something just because God tells me to? To avoid punishment? That would be like following the laws of a king out of fear rather than an appreciation of the justice of the laws, a rather unattractive view. Yet Ockham doesn't emphasize the dire consequences that face the sinner so much as the positive consideration that we should love God, and want to do as He commands. Some interpreters even think that for Ockham this is *why* we should do as God commands, that love for Him is the source from which all moral motivation must flow.[9] A test case considered by Ockham is the one that shocked the commission at Avignon: what if God commands us to hate Him, or simply neither to love nor to hate Him?[10] Ockham argues that this command would yield a kind of contradiction, in which we would need to hate God, or fail to love Him, precisely out of our love for Him. Thus, the commanded act of will is actually impossible.

By now it is clear that Ockham's moral theory is all about what is happening within the soul of the agent. Good people perform actions that we can all observe, but the business end of their virtue is on the inside, where good reasoning and free volition form the real basis of morality. This has obvious consequences for politics. For one thing, it tends to push Ockham away from the Aristotelian idea that the state's primary aim should be training and conditioning its citizens to be good. Virtue is ultimately a matter of free choices, which can never be determined by external influence. So it makes sense that Ockham has a rather limited conception of the role of the state in our practical lives. Government can give people the opportunity to live good lives by maintaining order, but this is largely a matter of removing practical obstacles rather than positively encouraging us to strive for virtue.[11] For another thing, it makes perfect sense that Ockham would emphasize the role of individual conscience in political life. You should do things because you understand them to be good, just as you believe things because you have good reason for thinking they are true. The responsibility is yours, and you cannot simply outsource your decisions or beliefs to external authorities.

With admirable consistency Ockham held himself to this demanding and individualistic ethic, spending about two decades of his life in exile as a conscientious objector to the Pope's rejection of the Franciscan ethic of poverty. We don't need to go through the arguments for and against the mendicants' stance again (instead, see Chapter 31). Suffice it to say that like Peter Olivi, Bonaventure, and his own contemporary Marsilius of Padua, Ockham was a fierce proponent of absolute poverty. But the political writings of his later career add something else that is worth discussing: a sustained justification of dissidence against papal authority.[12] For a man like Marsilius, this posed relatively little difficulty. As a secular polemicist, he argued that the Pope has no coercive authority in the first place, not over temporal rulers and not even over other clerics. Ockham, by contrast, was no secularist. He had a deep respect for the papacy and thought that a pope's authority could be resisted only in special and extreme circumstances.

In holding that a king or emperor can act against a wicked pope, the late medieval secularists drew on principles that had been familiar for generations, at least since that indispensable legal thinker Gratian, whose ideas were developed by the canonist Huguccio.[13] According to this legal tradition, the Pope's position within the spiritual realm is supreme. Medievals often spoke of him as possessing a "plenitude of power," which can be challenged by no one. So just as secular monarchs must resort to war to settle their differences because there is no human authority above them, likewise there is no court that can sit in judgment on a pope. This may seem to rule out any accusation of heresy in his case. But there is one exception. A pope might explicitly embrace a teaching that had already been established as heretical earlier in church history. In this case, no court or trial would be needed, since the prior decision of the Church can justify action against him. In fact, a pope in this position is really no pope at all, having surrendered his spiritual authority by falling into unbelief.

This was exactly the situation facing Ockham, or so he believed. The Church had somewhat grudgingly approved of absolute poverty in the thirteenth century. Now John XXII was overturning this decision and thus adopting a view that had already been established as false. Worse, he was clinging obstinately to this falsehood. For Ockham, this is part of what it means to be a heretic: in addition to holding a wrong belief, you have to insist on holding that wrong belief, even in the face of convincing arguments against it. For Ockham all of us, even popes, have a kind of moral responsibility for our own beliefs. We need to take criticism and refutation seriously and change our minds if we are given good reason to do so. There is a powerful anti-authoritarian message here, insofar as reasons for abandoning a falsehood could in principle come from anywhere.[14]

To take a far from hypothetical example, suppose you are a pope and a lowly Franciscan friar presents you with sound arguments that absolute poverty is conceptually possible and spiritually admirable. It's no good pulling rank on the friar or ignoring him. You have to engage in an honest attempt to discern the truth and change your mind if the opponent's view is more compelling. Which is not to say that you have to spend your whole life weighing up all rival opinions, no matter how outrageous they may seem to be. But neither should you bow to others because they hold a position of authority. If a single individual's views receive special consideration, this is "not especially because of his greater position" but "because he has a better account to give for himself, because of his better life, because he is better instructed about the case, or for some similar reason."[15]

On this basis Ockham thought that, in principle, any Christian could in good conscience oppose a heretical pope, indeed that one actually ought to do so. Of course, a lowly friar like himself did not pose much threat to papal power, though Ockham did his best by wielding his pen in a series of polemical documents. Sadly, despite rumors to the contrary the sword is quite a bit mightier than the pen. So effective resistance would have to come from rulers like Ludwig. Ockham supported him and other such rulers, arguing along with Marsilius that they do have an independent authority of their own rather than being subordinate to the Church. Legitimacy stems from consent of the people, and once granted, it cannot be withdrawn; the people just have to put up with the rulers they have chosen.[16] Still, Ockham did not go quite so far in the secularist direction as Marsilius. He wanted the temporal and spiritual powers to keep out of each other's way, rather than demanding that the papacy be placed under the imperial thumb. An emperor can depose a pope only in the unusual crisis posed by papal heresy, and, correspondingly, popes can intervene in temporal affairs only in a dire situation where no other power is adequate to the task. Otherwise the two powers are separate and equal, simply because both are unchallenged in their own respective spheres. All of this is, of course, subject to the caveat that God has decreed it to be so. It is because God wills it that people may rightly choose to be ruled by a non-spiritual power. As usual, Ockham remains consistent, applying his divine command theory to politics as well as ethics.

58

A CLOSE SHAVE
OCKHAM'S NOMINALISM

As we've just seen William of Ockham devoted the last two decades of his life to defending the Franciscan ideal of absolute poverty; the first part of his career was also about making do with less. In the works he wrote before his fateful trip to Avignon, he wrote about a wide range of issues in theology and logic, in which he defended an ontology that was deliberately impoverished.[1] He sought to eliminate the unnecessary entities postulated by other scholastics, especially Duns Scotus. Ockham's very name is synonymous with this endeavor. Even people who know nothing about medieval philosophy will probably be familiar with "Ockham's Razor," by which people usually mean that we should not provide complex explanations when simpler ones will do. Ockham formulates the principle in several ways, for instance "Plurality is not to be posited without necessity."[2] If you think about it, crediting this to Ockham as if it were a brilliant innovation is a bit odd. It's not as if philosophers before his time had revelled in deliberately postulating as many entities as possible for no good reason. Admittedly, some thinkers, like the late antique Neoplatonists, seem to have had a taste for the baroque. But even they were at pains to give arguments for each entity they introduced into their system. As for Ockham's contemporaries, they would readily have agreed with him that it is bad philosophical policy to posit superfluous principles or beings. In fact, John of Reading, whom we've met as an opponent of Ockham and follower of Duns Scotus' teachings, called this guideline "Scotus' rule."[3]

Yet Ockham deserves his reputation. His expert metaphysical trimming showed contemporaries the austere countenance of nominalism. Scotus' signature move was the drawing of subtle distinctions to show that there are more things than might meet the eye. Thus, the individual substance was revealed, on closer inspection, to consist of a common nature contracted by a particularizing singularity, the so-called "haecceity." Ockham's signature move is the reverse: show how to get equally good results with fewer metaphysical assumptions. This despite the fact that, for the most part, he is trying to achieve the same results as his realist opponents. For instance, he is not out to unmask universal generalizations as mere illusions.

Like other scholastics, he embraces the Aristotelian principle that science establishes universal truths. His point is just that we can account for such truths without postulating any universal things or common natures. The world is made up of individuals and nothing else.

Ockham even thinks that he can get by with a reduced number of individuals. Medieval scholastics cut their teeth on Aristotle's introductory logical treatise, the *Categories*, from which they took the doctrine that individual entities fall under all ten categories named by Aristotle. There would be not only individual substances like Groucho Marx, but also individual qualities like the black of his mustache, individual quantities like the length of his cigar, individual places like his location in Fredonia, individual actions like the waggling of his eyebrows, individual relations like his being Harpo's brother, and so on. Ockham's masterpiece, the *Summa logicae*, devotes great effort to demolishing this picture (§1.40–62).[4] For him, the world consists of nothing but singular substances and their qualities; nowadays we might instead say "things and their properties." Of course, we talk as if there were quantities, actions, places, relations, and so on, but we can always translate such talk into statements about substances and qualities.

Not to be outdone by Scotus, Ockham introduces a distinction of his own to show how this can be done, contrasting "absolute" with "connotative" names (§1.10).[5] An absolute name signifies something directly and unproblematically. Ockham's example is that "animal" refers to all animals. A connotative name by contrast refers to two things, one directly and one indirectly. His example is "white," which refers primarily to a thing that has whiteness in it and secondarily to the whiteness in the thing. In English, a better example might be calling Groucho's cigar a "Cuban" because it comes from Cuba. You name it after a relation it bears to its country of origin; yet you are still just talking about a substance, namely the cigar. Ockham's strategy, then, is to show that expressions in all ten categories apart from substance and quality are connotative terms. When we speak of a cigar as "long," it may seem that there must be a real "length" in the cigar. This would be an individual that falls under the category of quantity. But in fact, speaking of "quantity" just means that the parts of a substance are at a certain distance from one another. It would be a hassle to go around saying things like "One end of Groucho's cigar is distant from the other end," so we save time by using the connotative term "long" to refer to the disposition of its parts.

This is a nice illustration of the razor principle at work. Ockham hasn't argued here that it is absurd to posit a really existing length in the cigar that is distinct from the cigar itself. He's just showed us that we don't *need* to. That said, Ockham does also give arguments against accepting individuals in the categories apart from substance and quality. Take the category of relation. He does apply the razor strategy here, explaining how we can get by without relations. Suppose that, thinking of the mirror scene from *Duck Soup*, we say that Groucho and Harpo look quite similar. Ockham would say that we don't need to postulate a separate relation of "similarity" here. We can just say they both have qualities of the same type. But he also gives an argument against the very coherence of existing relations.[6] If the relation of brotherhood between Groucho and Harpo is a real thing, then it stands to reason that God, in His omnipotence, could create this relation without creating Groucho and Harpo. Their relation of brotherhood would then exist in the absence of the brothers, which is clearly absurd. Actually, Ockham concedes that we do need really existing relations for certain theological purposes, notably to account for the Trinity. But within the natural order, we can do without them—an interesting example, by the way, of a medieval philosopher *refusing* to tailor his general metaphysics to fit Christian doctrine.

With these arguments Ockham has shaved away most of the individuals recognized in previous scholastic metaphysics. But when we call him a "nominalist," it's really because of his mission to remove universals from the face of the earth. Ockham considered a belief in universals to be a crass mistake, in fact "the worst error in philosophy."[7] If there were a universal humanity in all four Marx Brothers, for instance, then it would have to be in more than one place at the same time (§2.2). Also, it would be impossible for God completely to destroy Groucho Marx, and not just because of his immortal place in the history of cinema. If God tried to annihilate him, the part of Groucho that is universal humanity would have to survive (§1.15). Thus, Ockham proclaims his agreement with Avicenna, who had insisted that natures are "universal" only in the mind. Now, Scotus claimed to agree with Avicenna too. Characteristically, he drew a distinction between the universal humanity in our minds and the common nature that is shared by all humans, and is contracted to be individual in each of them. Ockham is not impressed. He thinks Scotus' proposal boils down to saying that one and the same thing can be both common and individual, which is absurd (§1.16).

But Ockham's realist opponents had good reasons for their view. One of the most important had to do with knowledge. There do seem to be features shared in common by all humans and when we have knowledge of these features, our understanding is not directed at any particular human. To grasp that humans are rational is not to think that Groucho is rational, that Chico is rational, or (least of all) that Harpo is rational. It is to think that rationality belongs to human nature itself. Again, it is not Ockham's mission to deny the possibility of universal knowledge. He just thinks that it is unnecessary to postulate real universals or common natures to explain such knowledge. Here he recalls another distinction from Scotus, this time between two ways of grasping things. On the one hand, there is "intuitive" cognition, which is the sort involved when you grasp a particular thing, as when seeing a particular human like Groucho. On the other hand, there is "abstractive" cognition, which, as its name implies, requires abstracting away from any particular human to a general idea of humanity.

For the realists, abstractive cognition is what allows us to have knowledge of the common features of things. When you grasp humanity as a general idea, you do so by having what was standardly called an "intelligible species," a representation in the mind of humanity as such. This should remind us of Roger Bacon and his use of "species" to explain vision and other forms of sensation (Chapter 28). There too we were said to grasp things through the possession of a species that represents the things we are seeing. Intelligible species perform the same role at the level of universal thought. When you consider human nature in itself, you are enabled to do so by having the intelligible species of humanity in your mind, as you see a human by having a visual species in your eye. Intelligible species were regularly invoked in scholastic epistemology, by Aquinas, Scotus, and others. Despite retaining the contrast between intuitive and abstractive cognition, Ockham is going to reject this whole picture.[8]

For starters, he dispenses with the idea that we need to have a "species" of whatever we understand. Like his fellow Franciscan Peter Olivi (Chapter 30), Ockham worries that the use of such species would obstruct our direct access to the things we know. Even when I do something like remember seeing Groucho yesterday, I am not somehow using a mental picture of Groucho but thinking of him directly.[9] Furthermore, if I needed to use a representative image or species to think about something, how could I ever be sure that the image accurately represented the thing I want to think about?[10] But what happens when we are thinking of humans in general, rather than of Groucho in particular? Scotus had argued that we need to have an intelligible species in the mind in order to do this. Otherwise, we would have only our remembered images of individual humans and could only think about Groucho, Chico, Harpo, and so on, never universally about human nature as such. Ockham, of course, disagrees.[11] For him, *all* cognition involves grasping particulars. When you engage in abstractive cognition—in other words think at a universal level—you are simply thinking "indifferently" of all the individual humans.

This actually seems pretty plausible. If I say, "The Marx Brothers are hilarious," I am not postulating some common nature (we could call it "Marxism" if that name weren't already taken) and saying that it is part and parcel of this nature to be hilarious. I just mean that each of the Marx Brothers, taken singly, is hilarious (well, maybe not Zeppo). Just so, when I entertain the familiar example of a true proposition in Aristotelian science, "Human is rational," I am just thinking that each particular human is capable of reason. Ockham would caution us not to be misled by the surface grammar of the statement into thinking that there is such a thing as humanity which has a special relationship with rationality. Rather there are just particular humans. Since he develops his theory against the background of terminist logic, Ockham puts the point by insisting that the word "human" in a sentence like "Human is rational" just stands in ("supposits") for individual humans. In fact, it stands for all individual humans, past, present, and future.

This brings us to another difference between intuitive and abstractive cognition. Suppose I see that Groucho is shooting an elephant in his pajamas (how it got in his pajamas, I'll never know). Here I am having an intuitive cognition which, among other things, involves judging that Groucho exists. But abstractive cognition is entirely silent on the question of existence. Thinking about the nature of humans doesn't involve judging that there are any humans, though, of course, you wouldn't be in a position to think about human nature if you had never had any direct acquaintance with really existing humans. To put the same point in Ockham's terms, abstractive cognition depends on first having had some relevant intuitive cognitions.

One reason that there is such a close connection between intuitive cognition and existence is that each intuition is the intuition that it is simply because it is caused by something out in the world. Seeing Groucho counts as an intuition of Groucho because it was caused by him. At least, that's usually the case. Ockham does recognize deviant cases of intuition that are not caused by existing things.[12] For one thing, he suggests that we could be directly aware that something does not exist—a thesis heavily criticized by several later scholastics. For another thing, always mindful of God's untrammeled omnipotence, it occurs to Ockham that God could give someone intuitive cognition of something that is not really present. He could make you see Groucho Marx in front of you right now, even though Groucho has been dead for decades. This, however, is the exception that proves the rule, since the cognition you have in such a case is, miraculously, the same as the one you would have if Groucho *were* in front of you, that is, the one that would be caused by the real Groucho.

In the normal situation, though, it is through encounters with real individual things that we build up our store of general concepts. Having experienced particular humans, I construct for myself a general notion of humanity. Ockham's views about the status of these general concepts developed over the course of his career.[13] To understand his earlier view, we need to look at one last bit of scholastic terminology, which unfortunately is rather confusing for a speaker of modern English. The scholastics referred to things that have real existence out in the world as being "subjective" and things represented in the mind as "objective"—pretty much the reverse of how we would use these terms. Back when we looked at Anselm, we saw a nice anticipation of this distinction (Chapter 8).[14] To prepare us for his ontological argument he asked us to compare the idea of a painting in the artist's mind with the same painting existing in reality. In the later scholastic terminology, the idea in the artist's mind would be the painting as "objectively" existent, whereas the real painting would exist "subjectively." While the painting might exist in both ways, some things have only objective existence in the mind and no subjective or real existence.

For Ockham, these unreal things would include universals, since there is no common or universal nature of humanity out in the world. In his early works he expresses this with the notion of a *fictum* (in plural, *ficta*). The *ficta* are mental constructs or representations which we generate for ourselves after encountering things in the world. The mistake of Scotus and others was to think that common natures are real things, whereas, in fact, they are unreal *ficta*. Of course, the idea of something that exists in a way, but without being real, is rather strange. If Ockham was willing to postulate such items early on, it was because he thought they were absolutely needed to explain the way that we reason. After all, I must be thinking about something or other when I think that humans are rational. Since I am not thinking about any humans in particular, I must be thinking about my concept of humans, which is one of these *ficta*.

But Ockham was about to be shaved with his own razor. Another scholastic thinker, a fellow student named Walter Chatton, convinced Ockham that the *ficta* are superfluous.[15] We can do without them by saying that the act of cognition itself serves as the concept. And you can see why Ockham was willing to be convinced by Chatton's proposal. His early theory of cognition involved three kinds of entities: mentally constructed concepts or *ficta*, the things in the world that prompted us to form these concepts, and acts of cognition. With Chatton's help, Ockham now gets this down to just two items: things in the world and mental acts. Even better, the item that has been eliminated is the one that looked rather fishy, metaphysically speaking, with the odd status of being "objectively existent" but unreal. Mental acts by contrast are perfectly respectable entities. They are just individual qualities belonging to the mind, and, as we know, Ockham is happy to admit the real existence of individual qualities. The question is whether it makes sense to say that concepts are just mental acts. For the later Ockham, the answer is an emphatic yes. Mental acts "signify" and "resemble" things in the world, just as *ficta* were supposed to do in the earlier theory. And mental acts can just be brought together to form the propositions studied in logic. But this may seem to present a difficulty. How can logic, which analyzes the relations between bits of language like terms and propositions, apply to these so far rather mysterious mental acts? Very nicely, as it turns out. Logic is directly relevant to the realm of the mental, according to Ockham, because for him thought itself is linguistic.

59

WHAT DO YOU THINK?
OCKHAM ON MENTAL LANGUAGE

It's a good thing that I didn't read Mark Twain's essay "The Awful German Language" before learning German myself. Otherwise, I probably wouldn't have bothered to try. He laments the German habit of building extremely long compound words (*Generalstaatsverordnetenversammlungen*) and the use of grammatical case endings: "When a German gets his hands on an adjective, he declines it, and keeps on declining it until the common sense is all declined out of it." Then, there is Twain's criticism of German nouns. As he says, every noun is either masculine, feminine or neuter, and this has to be learned by heart, since the genders seem to have been assigned more or less at random. Twain remarks:

> In German, a young lady [*das Mädchen*] has no sex, while a turnip [*die Rübe*] has. Think what overwrought reverence that shows for the turnip, and what callous disrespect for the girl. See how it looks in print—I translate this from a conversation in one of the best of the German Sunday-school books:
>
> SRETCHEN: Wilhelm, where is the turnip?
> WILHELM: She has gone to the kitchen.
> GRETCHEN: Where is the accomplished and beautiful English maiden?
> WILHELM: It has gone to the opera.

I'm with Twain on this. When I speak German, I can just about bring myself to refer to knife, spoon, and fork as "it, he, and she"—whether this is more revealing of German attitudes towards gender or tableware, I've never been sure—but in my mind I'm thinking of them as "it, it, and it." The language of my thought is more sensible, stripped clean of such idiosyncrasies as grammatical gender, case, and umlauts. But is there really such a thing as a "language of thought"? As an American, do I not just think in English? For that matter, do I really think in language at all? Many philosophers have thought so, beginning with Plato, who said that thinking is the soul's talking to itself (*Theaetetus* 189e). But it was William of Ockham who offered the first really well-worked-out theory of mental language, and how it relates to spoken and written language.[1]

In developing this theory, he takes his cue from Aristotle. At the beginning of *On Interpretation* Aristotle wrote that whereas spoken and written signs are different for different people, "affections (*pathemata*) in the soul are the same for all (16a)." What he seems to have in mind is this. A German may call something *Löffel*, whereas I call it "spoon," but we both have the same idea in our minds. Ockham would say that the two different spoken expressions are "subordinated" to one and the same thing, namely a term in mental language. At the level of thought, the German and I are speaking the same language, and if we were telepaths or angels, we could even communicate in that language. In order to communicate in the more usual fashion, the German and I would formulate the same sentence mentally and would then express that sentence differently in speech or in writing (*Summa logicae* §1.12).

We call English and German "natural" languages, but according to Ockham it is really mental language that is natural. He distinguishes between two kinds of sign, natural and conventional. In the case of conventional signs, a deliberate choice has been made, yielding an agreement to use the sign to bring something else to mind (§1.1). The sign needn't be a word. Ockham uses the example of a barrel hoop hanging outside a tavern to indicate that wine may be purchased inside. Spoken languages, with the possible exception of onomatopoeias like "bang" or "woof," are obviously conventional in this sense. According to Ockham, the signs of mental language are, by contrast, natural. They are the same for everyone and can signify things without depending on agreed practices or the voluntary imposition of meaning. One consequence of this is that mental language lacks the sorts of idiosyncrasies I just mentioned. For instance, nouns at the level of thought have no grammatical gender (§1.2), so in this respect English is closer to mental language than German, or for that matter Latin. Then, too, even if mental language did involve grammatical gender, you still wouldn't have to refer to a fork in thought as "she," because mental language has no pronouns either. In general, mental terms will have only the features that are needed in order to signify, that is, to be meaningful.[2] Thus, while the gender of a Latin noun may fall away in the language of thought, Ockham holds that its grammatical case would remain, because its case affects the meaning of a sentence containing the word. Consider the difference between the function of "spoon" in "The spoon is on the table" (nominative case) and "I admire the spoon's fine polish" (genitive case). So that's a small victory for German.

But why insist that there is mental language at all? Again, Aristotle provides an important part of the answer.[3] In his theory of demonstration he insisted that true scientific understanding always involves necessary and universal truths, and Ockham is at pains to ensure that our knowledge can satisfy Aristotle's constraints.

Clearly, particular things out in the world, like an individual spoon or Harpo Marx, cannot be objects of scientific demonstration, since these are neither necessary nor universal. When I do science, I am grasping the conclusions of demonstrative proofs, and it is these that are the objects of our thought. It might seem that these conclusions could be spoken or written sentences, though. Why not just say that an English-speaking biologist has demonstrative understanding of the English sentence "Humans are animals," while a German one understands the sentence *Menschen sind Tiere*? Ockham insists that only mental sentences can do the job, and for a reason we've already seen: spoken and written language is conventional. So it can hardly offer the sort of fixed target needed for scientific understanding. Just consider the innocuous remark "Your gift was a wonderful surprise." That sentence would not be true if the English word "gift" shifted from its present meaning and acquired the meaning it has in German, where *Gift* means "poison." Mental language doesn't have this problem, since it consists of natural signs whose signification is unchanging.

To all this one might raise the following objection. Ockham's own voluntarism implies that science does not grasp necessary truths, because nothing about the created world is necessary. Take the sentence "Humans are animals." Ockham thinks that God could have chosen not to create humans, in which case there would be no humans to be animals. So the sentence would not seem to be necessarily true. Yet Ockham thinks that this sentence does express a general truth which would hold even in a world without humans. In a world without humans it would remain true that *if* there were any humans, they would be animals. This gives us another reason to doubt that the objects of scientific knowledge are always existing entities in the world as God has created it. Rather, Aristotle's theory of demonstration can be retained only if we assume that the objects of demonstrative, scientific knowledge are mental sentences.

Ockham's position was controversial in his own time. Realist thinkers like Scotus and Walter Burley, of course, held that the objects of general scientific understanding are common or universal things out in the world. But his theory was also criticized by a fellow nominalist, Walter Chatton, who was not prepared to admit that whenever we grasp a truth, we are apprehending bits of language, mental or otherwise.[4] This does happen occasionally, for instance when I grasp that "'Human' is a noun," since in that case I am grasping something about the term "human." When I judge that humans are animals, though, I am grasping something about individual humans, not about the term "human." For Ockham, though, the judgment applies to individuals only indirectly. Since we are in the first instance making a judgment of truth, and only sentences can be true (as he puts it, one cannot "assent to a rock or a cow"), individual things will come into the story only insofar as the sentences are themselves about things in the world, namely the things to which the terms in the sentences refer.

Of course, this all depends on Ockham's idea that a term in mental language, just as much as a spoken word, can indeed be a sign that refers to something else. This may strike us as strange. What could make one thought be the sign of a spoon, another thought the sign of a fork? This is no problem in the case of things like the barrel hoop outside the tavern or the spoken word "spoon," since, as we saw, these signify thanks to agreed conventions about meaning. But Ockham has already told us that convention plays no role in determining the signification of a mental term. What else might do the job? Two things, according to Ockham. Firstly, a mental term is *caused* by the thing it signifies. It is through encounters with spoons that we got to have the term for spoon in our mental language. Secondly and rather mysteriously, the mental term *resembles* the thing it signifies. Of course, it might resemble some other things too; perhaps the mental term for spoon is also a lot like a ladle. But it resembles spoons more than it resembles anything else.

One consequence of this explanation for mental signification is that you cannot have exact synonyms in mental language.[5] Each mental sign is the sign that it is because it is caused by a certain sort of thing in the world and resembles that sort of thing. There can be only one mental term that is caused by spoons and resembles spoons. By contrast, in conventional languages there can be more than one word that signifies the same thing: not just in two different languages as with *Löffel* and "spoon," but also within one and the same language as with "gift" and "present." Assuming that these are perfect synonyms, it is one and the same mental term that I express in conventional language in uttering both words (§1.13). The reason English has two terms here, where mental language has only one, is, according to Ockham, just a matter of stylistic ornamentation.[6] In this case a better explanation, as often with English synonyms, would be that the two words have respectively a Germanic and a Latin etymology. But obviously that would have nothing to do with signs at the level of thought either.

Another problem arises for Ockham's view right about here.[7] Suppose that I meet an amusing man at a party who introduces himself to me as "Julius." After the party I remark to my friend, "There was this hilarious fellow at the party, who was wisecracking and smoking a big cigar. Actually, he reminded me of Groucho Marx." At which point, my friend says, "You idiot, that *was* Groucho Marx! His real first name is Julius. You should have gotten an autograph." In this case, it seems that I was having two different thoughts, one of Julius, whom I met at the party, another of Groucho Marx, the movie star. I would even be willing to make contradictory assertions about them. Until my friend disabuses me, I would believe that I have met Julius from the party, while also believing that I have never had the honor of meeting Groucho Marx. But Julius just is Groucho Marx. So it seems clear that I have one thought of Groucho and another different thought of Julius from the party, and these must be synonymous, since they are caused by and resemble the same person out in the world. Yet Ockham has insisted that there are no synonyms in mental language. It's not clear how he could solve this problem, apart from insisting that in thinking of Groucho and Julius, I am (unbeknownst to myself) actually having one and the same thought.

If synonymy is ruled out in the language of thought, what about equivocation, where we have a single term with more than one meaning? Obviously, this does happen in conventional language, as the word "bank" has different meanings in the phrases "bank account" and "river bank." (German offers more spectacular examples: as Mark Twain writes, in German "the same sound, *sie*, means 'you,' and it means 'she,' and it means 'her,' and it means 'it,' and it means 'they,' and it means 'them.' Think of the ragged poverty of a language which has to make one word do the work of six—and a poor little weak thing of only three letters at that.") Ockham's explanation for synonyms was that two different signs in conventional language might express the same sign in mental language. With equivocation, the reverse happens. One and the same conventional sign, like "bank," expresses two distinct thoughts. Immediately, then, we may suspect that mental terms cannot be equivocal. After all, there is no further sort of discourse to which mental language is subordinated, so equivocation at the level of mental language could never be resolved by disambiguating at a higher level, the way we disambiguated "bank" by referring to two distinct thoughts.[8]

This is basically Ockham's view. He thinks that most equivocation is caused by vagaries of convention and would disappear in mental language. But there is an exception. As we saw when discussing terminist logic (Chapter 22), there are different ways that a term can refer to, or "supposit for," things. When you just refer to a thing normally, as when saying "I dropped my spoon," this is personal supposition. But you can also use the word "spoon" to refer to the very notion or mental concept of spoons; this is simple supposition. Or you can make observations about the *word* "spoon," as when you say "'Spoon' is a noun," which is material supposition. So the English word "spoon" can signify in all three ways, and this sort of ambiguity is one that Ockham is prepared to admit in mental language too (§1.64). In other words, it is one and the same thought of *spoon* that appears in the mental equivalents of the English sentences "I dropped my spoon" and "'Spoon' is a noun," even though in the first case I am thinking of a real spoon out in the world (personal supposition), but in the second case thinking about the uttered word "spoon" (material supposition).

Clearly, it is no easy matter to say how exactly mental language lines up with conventional language. We would like for Ockham to go systematically through the features of spoken and written language, telling us which of these features occur in mental language and which don't. Although he does make a few remarks in this direction, it seems that he may not have worked out the theory in full detail. A good example is the "connotative term." As just mentioned in Chapter 58, this is a term that refers primarily to one thing and secondarily to another, as when Groucho's cigar is called a "Cuban" with reference to the island where it was made. Ockham has quite a lot to say about connotative terms, since they help him to eliminate so much of the clutter from traditional scholastic metaphysics. Yet it has taken the modern scholar Claude Panaccio to show that there are indeed connotative terms in Ockham's mental language.[9]

Or to take another example, what about syncategorematic terms? These are the bits of a sentence that help establish its meaning but without playing the role of subject or predicate in a sentence. Thus, in the statement "All spoons are metal or wooden," the words "all" and "or" are syncategorematic. Here the problem isn't whether such terms would appear in mental language at all. Clearly they would, since they affect the signification of the other terms and the meaning of the sentence as a whole. The problem is that it's hard to see how syncategorematic terms get into our mental language in the first place. Remember, our thoughts are caused by things in the world. And there doesn't seem to be anything out there in the world that might cause the thoughts that play a syncategorematic role. As Ockham scholar Calvin Normore has nicely put it, "The world doesn't contain 'ifs' and 'cans' the way it does pots and pans."[10] Early in his career Ockham seems to have thought that we extract such terms from conventional language.[11] This sounds fairly plausible: by seeing how adults use words like "all" and "if," children learn to think by using such terms. But that would be a remarkable inversion of the normal order of priority between mental and conventional language. Usually mental language leads the way, and the job of speaking and writing is just to express what has already been thought. Another option would be that syncategorematic thinking is just innate. We might be "hardwired" to think using "if," "and," and "but," and this would not be a function of the conventional language you speak. Germans would have the same hardwiring, but express the same thoughts by saying *wenn*, *und*, and *aber*.

The fact that Ockham says less than he might about the nature of mental language has led some to argue that we exaggerate its importance in his philosophy.[12] I think it more likely that these are the teething problems that often come along with a theory that is more or less new. I say "more or less" new, because Ockham was certainly not the first to associate mental life with language. In addition to the aforementioned passages in Plato and Aristotle, there was the medieval depiction of the human mind as an image of the Trinity (Chapter 47). Following Augustine, scholastics like Aquinas and Henry of Ghent proposed that the mind forms a "word" within itself when it understands something, which for them is a reflection of the second Person of the Trinity. For Aquinas, such a "mental word" can be simple or complex, just as spoken language can consist of single words or full sentences. So Ockham was not engaging in radical innovation with his theory of mental language. Still, his approach was very different. For him, the crucial issues concern logic and meaning, not a theological approach to the human mind.[13] This is why he paid unprecedented attention to the question of whether thought really has all the structures and features we find in conventional language, even if he paid somewhat less attention to that question than we might like.

60

KEEPING IT REAL
RESPONSES TO OCKHAM

What does it mean to be an influential philosopher? The obvious answer would be that influential philosophers have followers, card-carrying members of traditions whose cards were stamped with the names of the founders. There have been Platonists of one sort or another more or less continuously since his lifetime; the Epicureans still celebrated the great man's birthday centuries after his death; and to this very day Germany has its fair share of Kantians and Heideggerians. But influence doesn't need to work that way. Philosophers can make their mark on history by attracting thoughtful critique, as Plato provoked Aristotle and Kant provoked Hegel. William of Ockham was certainly influential in the first way, in that many self-styled nominalists have looked to him for inspiration down to modern times. But among his contemporaries his impact was mostly a matter of inspiring criticism. Fellow nominalists disputed the fine points of his thought, while others mounted a spirited defense of realism, insisting that he had cut too deeply with his famous razor.[1]

One particularly important critic was a man we have already met: Walter Chatton, who was at Oxford at the same time as Ockham. His objections seem to have had an unparalleled influence on Ockham himself. We saw that Chatton convinced his more famous Franciscan colleague to give up the theory that universals are *ficta*, and that was only one of several cases in which his arguments persuaded Ockham to change his teachings. Chatton and Ockham were in turn important influences on Adam Wodeham, another Franciscan and nominalist, who studied with both men. Though Wodeham did not adopt Ockham's views across the board, he seems to have been the closest Ockham had to a faithful adherent. His debates with John of Reading effectively carried on the Ockham–Scotus debate into the next generation.[2] All these figures were active in England, but they also paid some attention to developments from across the channel at the University of Paris.

This is well illustrated by a controversy concerning a central idea in the epistemology of both Scotus and Ockham, namely intuitive cognition, in which we grasp particular things directly, prompting us to make judgments about the world around us.[3] This includes judgments about which things exist. When a damsel in distress is tied to the train tracks and looks up to see a locomotive about to run her over, that is an intuitive cognition and it causes her to judge that the train, unfortunately for her, is very much existent. By contrast, when, after freeing herself from her bonds at the last moment, she goes back to her day job comparing the energy efficiency of steam- and coal-powered engines, that is abstractive cognition because it involves making general judgments. So far, so straightforward. But there were doubts about the range of intuitive cognitions we can enjoy, and about their exact nature. Ockham thought that one can intuitively cognize non-existing things. God might make a non-existing thing appear to you, just as if it did exist, giving you an intuitive cognition of it. This was among the teachings of Ockham criticized by Walter Chatton, and it was rejected even by Ockham's closest follower, Adam Wodeham. Chatton complained that it came perilously close to the theory of another thinker of Ockham's generation: Peter Aureol.

Aureol was yet another Franciscan, and the most influential figure of the time to work on the Continent. He taught in Bologna, Toulouse, and Paris, and died in 1322, shortly after being made an archbishop in Provence. Aureol made a controversial proposal about human cognition.[4] He agreed with Ockham that only individual things exist in the outside world. To explain how it is that we nonetheless arrive at universal concepts in abstractive cognition, he suggested that the individual exists in our minds in a special way, which he called "apparent being (*esse apparens*)." This idea can also be applied to our intuitive cognitions. You know how, when you're sitting on a train that is stopped at a station and the train on the next platform starts to move, you have the sensation that your own train is moving? For Aureol, this would be an example of the way that individual things in the outside world can be grasped as having apparent properties, in this case motion. He gives the similar example of trees on a riverbank seeming to move because you are on a boat moving down the river.

For Chatton, both Ockham and Aureol were undermining the very foundations of human knowledge. He complains that if Ockham were right that we can have intuitive cognitions of things that don't even exist, then "All human certainty would perish."[5] As for phenomena like the apparently moving trees, these are not cases where sensation misleads us by actually presenting an unmoving thing to us as if it were moving. Rather, a higher faculty of the soul collects together successive cognitions of the trees, and on this basis we judge falsely that the trees are moving. A broadly similar explanation is offered by Wodeham. The senses are not to blame. You aren't literally feeling your own train start to roll or seeing the trees move, even if it is all but irresistible to experience them as doing so. In a striking passage,

Wodeham illustrates the point by referring to an ancient teaching that denies the revolution of the heavens above us. Rather, it could be the earth that turns with us on it, creating the illusion that the celestial bodies move.[6]

The debate may seem rather technical, but is of great philosophical and historical importance: it shows how the seeds of later worries about skepticism were already being planted in the fourteenth century. Aureol assumed that some cognitions are true and some not, even if they involve only "apparent being." But as his opponents hastened to point out, it sounds as if it would be impossible for us to know which cognitions are the true ones. Despite these high stakes, the controversy was largely one waged among like-minded philosophers. Like Ockham, Auriol and Wodeham were nominalists who thought that everything outside the mind is an individual. Indeed, given that nominalism was such a prominent feature of fourteenth-century thought, you could be forgiven for thinking that all scholastic philosophers of the time shared this approach. But that's rarely the way things work in the history of philosophy. More usually, new intellectual movements are opposed by spirited defense, and revision, of more traditional ways of thinking. And so it was here. Even as nominalist allies like Wodeham were tinkering with the train of Ockham's thought, others were trying to derail it completely.

The chief engineer of this development was Walter Burley.[7] He hailed originally from Yorkshire and was educated at both Oxford and Paris, where he apparently was able to study under Duns Scotus. Later in life he joined a group of scholars gathered around the bishop of Durham, who helped get him out of jail when he was arrested for having trees cut down without permission. (I like to think that he did it because he was annoyed at the way they seemed to be moving every time he sailed past in a boat.) Despite the connection to Scotus, in his early career Burley championed not Scotus' subtle theory of common natures and individuation, but a form of realism closer to what we find in thirteenth-century thinkers like Aquinas. According to this realist view, universals *actually* exist only in the mind, yet correspond to shared features that are present in particular things. Thus, the universal *tree* would be fully abstracted in the mind, but the same nature would also be a part of each tree, a third item alongside the matter and form that combine to produce that tree. The common nature out in the world that answers to our universal idea of a tree is identical with all the particular trees, given that it is found in each of them.[8]

In due course Burley became aware of Ockham's vigorous attack on this form of realism. Ockham showed the awkwardness of claiming that common natures are part of, or identical with, their instances. Aside from making the obvious complaint that the same thing cannot be universal and particular, common and individual, he pointed out that in destroying a particular thing one would also destroy the common nature in that thing. When Burley chopped down a tree in the forest, he would be eliminating the very nature of tree-ness, which would nonetheless survive in all other trees. All of this is absurd. For Ockham the lesson was clear: nothing outside the mind can be universal in any way. But Burley saw that another solution was available. If it is incoherent to suppose that the universal out in the world is real by being identical with its particulars, why not say that it is real but *distinct* from its particulars?[9]

Burley began to develop this solution in a commentary on Aristotle's *Physics*, which he wrote in 1324. In this and other works he adopts a position that is diametrically opposed to Ockham's and, furthermore, directs personal abuse at his opponent. He sarcastically remarks that Ockham claims to know more about logic than any other mortal, calls him a "beginner in philosophy" and, for good measure, a heretic.[10] More importantly, he meets Ockham's nominalist polemic with a defense of wholehearted realism. The common nature of trees is no longer a part of particular trees and so in some sense identical with each tree. It has a full-blown and distinct reality of its own. This is why it can survive destruction at the hands of a forest fire or an axe-wielding scholastic philosopher, the way that individual trees cannot. Burley's view is sometimes compared to Platonism, but he himself would deny the parallel. For him, the real universal tree never exists completely separate and unrelated to individual trees, as Plato apparently wanted. Rather, it is a special kind of thing that exists wherever there are trees and "in" each tree without being a part of it.

To understand what Burley has in mind, it will help to see how he responds to nominalist arguments. Ockham claimed that, for a realist, universals would have to be in more than one place at the same time and would need to have contradictory properties. Thus, when Socrates is asleep in front of us, while Plato is walking around in Rome, the universal *humanity* would be in two different places at the same time, and both at rest and in motion. To this Burley retorts:

> This species, humanity, is the same in Socrates and Plato. If it is said that the same thing is both here and in Rome, and simultaneously moving and at rest, we may respond that this species humanity is one thing as a species (*secundum speciem*), and there is no absurdity in something that is one as a species being both here and in Rome, or simultaneously moving and at rest.[11]

Ockham's mistake is the same as the one made by other less radical realists, including Burley himself at a younger age. Both the nominalist and the moderate realist assume that the only way for a universal to be real is for it to be identical with, or part of, a particular. In reality, though, a universal nature like tree-ness or humanity plays by different rules.

Of course, Ockham will here want to apply the razor, asking what could justify the apparently gratuitous assumption of such universal things outside the mind. An answer comes in Burley's commentary on Porphyry's *Isagoge*.[12] His main argument for realism has to do with knowledge. Aristotle tells us that proper scientific understanding is universal in character. Surely, then, there must be real universal objects for us to grasp. After all, it can hardly be that knowledge requires us to grasp all the particulars that fall under a given universal. Otherwise, as Burley puts it, we would need to know every last peasant in India before we can know the nature of humanity. Aristotle also says that individuals cannot be defined. "Human" and "giraffe" would have entries in the ideal scientific dictionary, but "Socrates" and "Hiawatha" would not. So if the nominalists were right, then neither knowledge nor definitions would latch onto things as they really are. As we know, Ockham would have replies for these arguments. He thinks that knowledge and definitions have as their target concepts that we derive from individual things in the world, not real universals in the world. Yet Burley has put his finger on a key potential weakness of the nominalist project. Admitting a mismatch between universal ideas and particular reality does give a foothold to skepticism, as we just saw with Aureol's idea of "apparent being."

Burley's position may seem to be fatally undermined by depending too heavily on ancient ideas about knowledge. He grounds his argument for realism on the assumption that science and definitions are universal in character. Granted, his opponent Ockham adhered to this same Aristotelian doctrine, so the assumption was dialectically effective. Still, it would not command widespread agreement nowadays, which may make Burley's realism seem outmoded and poorly justified. Fortunately, Burley does have points to make in favor of realism that we might find more convincing. In his *Physics* commentary he points out that we often have desires that are not directed at any particular object. When I'm hungry, I just want food, not some particular food. The same is true in commerce. If I have contracted to sell you a horse and you have already paid me, I can satisfy our agreement by giving you any one of the horses in my possession.[13] Another consideration has to do with language. When we first begin to use a word in a certain way, as when applying "tree" to trees, we do not have in mind any specific tree but are envisioning an open-ended use of this word for all trees in the future.[14] So it isn't only Aristotelian science that has universals as its target. Universals also explain such pervasive features of everyday life as desires, promises, and language use.

Nonetheless, there is no denying that Burley's realism is motivated in large part by fidelity to Aristotle; it has been said that his goal "is to be sound rather than striking or original."[15] Predictably, then, he takes further umbrage at Ockham's attempt to reduce the ten Aristotelian categories to a mere two, which, by the way, was not unique in this period: the aforementioned Peter Aureol thought he could get the list down to five. Against such attempts at reduction Burley argues for the reality and distinctness of all ten categories.[16] They are nothing less than the ten classes into which the real universals are divided. The categories do also apply to our mental concepts and language, but this is simply because our thoughts and language have the ten types of universals as their target. So Ockham's attempt to reduce all properties to substances and qualities is a flagrant departure from Aristotle's teaching and a failure to understand the structure of reality. And according to Burley, there is a further type of entity in the real world that is unjustly eliminated by Ockham's nominalism. Categorial terms pick out simple items like one quality, place, time, or action, but there are also more complex items out there. One can know not only tree-ness, or greenness, but also that trees are green. Modern-day philosophers might classify such things as "states of affairs" or "facts." True to form, Burley thinks that they too have distinct reality, on the basis that they can be grasped by the mind and expressed in language. Ultimately, it is the real fact that trees are green that is signified by the sentence "Trees are green."[17]

But it would be unfair simply to say that Burley thinks that Ockham is entirely wrongheaded when it comes to metaphysics; he thinks that Ockham is wrong about lots of other things too. To give just one other example, he rejects Ockham's analysis of the process by which we sin.[18] We saw that, for Ockham, morality has to do solely with the "interior act" by which we choose to perform our outward actions (Chapter 57). This is of a piece with his voluntarism. It is not really in acting, but in willing to act, that we do right and wrong. It's also of a piece with Ockham's rejection of more intellectualist approaches to sin, which would make moral evil the result of bad reasoning. By contrast, Burley carries forward ideas from thirteenth-century intellectualism, sounding more like Aquinas than like his own voluntarist contemporaries. For Burley, we may often do wrong, even when we know what is right, not by a perverse act of will but because we deliberate badly, as when our reasoning processes are overwhelmed by the strength of our desires. Of course, like Aquinas, Burley still retains a place for the will. Our reasoning can be only a partial cause of action, and an exercise of the will is always required to bring the act to fruition.

But with this further disagreement between Burley and Ockham we are only skimming the surface of deep and troubled waters. Moral responsibility was a prominent topic of debate in the early fourteenth century. These same thinkers we've just been discussing tried to establish the conditions under which humans can do good and ultimately merit salvation. The radical voluntarism of Ockham and his allies led them into dangerous territory: if the human will is genuinely free, then do we really need God's help in order to avoid sin? On the other hand, if God is genuinely free, can we have any confidence about whether and how He will offer us an eternal reward? For some contemporaries, notably Thomas Bradwardine, Ockham did indeed go too far with his voluntarism, so far that he undermined the fundamental principles of the Christian teaching on grace. It was a theological debate with philosophical implications, including the question of whether we retain our freedom even if God knows in advance what we will do.

61

BACK TO THE FUTURE
FOREKNOWLEDGE AND
PREDESTINATION

Suppose you and I are arguing about the outcome of an upcoming election. I think that candidate A will prevail over candidate B, and have good reasons for my view. All the polls suggest that candidate A has an insurmountable lead, and candidate B is manifestly unfit for office. You, however, insist that candidate B may just spring a surprise victory. When the vote is held, candidate B does indeed win the election. In addition to my dismay at the outcome, I must shoulder the additional burden of admitting that you were right and I was wrong. Or perhaps not. I might say to you: "Look, when you predicted the outcome of the election, the result was still open. The voters still had the capacity to choose between both candidates. So it cannot already have been true *then* that candidate B would win. That only became true once the election was actually held. So in fact, when you and I were having our argument, neither of us was right, because there was as yet no truth of the matter."

If you are a faithful reader of this book series, my argument will probably remind you of a passage in Aristotle.[1] In the ninth chapter of his logical work *On Interpretation*, Aristotle presented an argument for determinism, using the example of a sea battle. The argument goes that, if it is now true that there will be a sea battle tomorrow, then the sea battle's occurrence is already guaranteed. So there is no point deliberating about whether to fight the battle: the present truth shows that it is already settled that it will happen. The same pattern of argument can be used for any future event. Since there are present truths about all the things that will happen in the future, all things will happen necessarily. Of course, this conclusion is unproblematic for certain cases. No one will mind it being true now, and thus unavoidable, that one plus one will still equal two tomorrow, and Aristotle at least would have no objection to saying that the sun will necessarily rise tomorrow. The argument is disturbing only when it comes to what philosophers call "future contingents," that is, future events that seem as though they may or may not happen, like the outcome of an election or the waging of a sea battle. As Aristotle points out, these future contingents are exactly the things we ponder and deliberate about, as if more than one option were still open.

It is not entirely clear how Aristotle intended to avoid the problem, but in the fourteenth century it was generally accepted that his solution was simply to deny that there are present truths about future contingents. We find this in Ockham's commentary on Aristotle's *On Interpretation*, for instance.[2] This is the response I just proposed taking in the example of the election. Before the vote is held there is no truth one way or another about its outcome, since that outcome remains open. But the medievals could not easily take this simple way out. If there are no present truths about future contingents, then it would seem that God cannot know the future, and admitting this would mean denying His omniscience. Actually the Parisian scholastic Peter Auriol did stick to (what he took to be) Aristotle's solution here, arguing that God's knowing in advance what we will do would render our actions necessary. But he was the exception. Most philosophers of the period felt the need to explain how God can know what will happen without rendering future events necessary.

A traditional solution was to follow the late ancient thinker Boethius. He proposed that the way in which God knows things might be different from the way those things are in themselves. Thus, God could eternally know things that happen in time, and necessarily know things that are contingent. Thomas Aquinas adopted a version of this response to the problem, explaining that the contingency of things has to do with the contingency of their immediate causes, not any uncertainty or contingency in God's ultimate causation or in His knowledge. Thus, the voters, in their limited wisdom, would contingently determine that candidate B wins the election, whereas God, in His infinite wisdom, would have eternal and necessary knowledge of the outcome. But in the early fourteenth century this view came under fire. It was rejected by Scotus and also by Ockham's teacher Henry of Harclay, who insisted that God's perfect knowledge must involve knowing things as they are. We may use immaterial psychological powers to grasp a stone; yet we grasp the stone as material. In the same way God can be said to know all things necessarily but know the contingent things as contingent.[3]

It was, however, open for thinkers in this generation to abandon the Boethian solution because of the new advances made by Scotus in thinking about possibility. Remember that for him, a freely choosing agent—whether human or divine—can choose to do a certain thing while in that same moment retaining the possibility of choosing differently. Even as I stand in the ballot box putting down my vote for A, there is an unrealized, yet still real possibility that I vote for B. When we looked at Scotus' theory of possibility, we thought about it in this context of divine and human freedom. But it's obviously relevant to the problem of future contingents too.[4] The reason that I can be free to choose B even while choosing A is that, for Scotus, a thing remains possible or contingent so long as it implies nothing contradictory. Clearly, no contradiction follows from supposing that there will be a sea battle tomorrow, nor does a contradiction follow from supposing that there will be no sea battle tomorrow. Thus, both are possible. In light of this Scotus can and does resolve the problem by saying that when it is presently true that there will be a sea battle tomorrow, it remains possible that there will not be a sea battle. Just as my choice of A doesn't make it impossible that I choose B, a proposition about the future can be true while possibly being false.

But one thing about determinists is that they are very determined. They will stubbornly insist that the problem is not really yet resolved, and point out that *past* events are necessary. And this makes sense. If an election has already been held and produced a clear result, we don't argue about what the outcome was, though we might disagree about why the voters chose as they did, and no one deliberates about whether to have a sea battle yesterday. Past events are not open but decided or determined, so it is natural to think that they are necessary. The reason this is problematic is that, if we admit against Aristotle and Peter Auriol that there are present truths about the future, then how can we resist thinking that there were also past truths about the future? Just as it is true now that a sea battle will occur tomorrow, so it was already true yesterday that the sea battle will occur tomorrow. So if everything in the past is necessary, the truth of this proposition is necessary after all.

To avoid this problem the scholastics extended the new theory of possibility even to facts about the past. In general, truths may be either "determinate" or "indeterminate," meaning that they may or may not exclude their contraries. Thus, the statement "There will be a sea battle on Monday" is "indeterminately" true, since it is true even though it could have been false. By contrast the statement "One plus one equals two" is determinately true: it is true and can never be false. In a reminder of the value of anonymous material from the scholastic tradition, this idea is first found in a manuscript of unknown authorship.[5] And in a reminder of the value of identified but fairly obscure medieval thinkers, it is embraced by such non-household names as Arnold of Strelley and Richard Campsall.[6] According to this way of thinking, even truths about the past can be indeterminate, which is often expressed by saying that, despite being true, they can always have been false. In light of this, we can say that God has always known that candidate B would win the election. Since this is a contingent event, His knowledge still leaves it possible that candidate A will win, and even possible that it could always have been true that candidate A will win, despite the fact this is and has always been false. All of this is just a spelling out of what it means for something to be true, but contingently or "indeterminately" true rather than necessarily true.

Unsurprisingly, one of the most sophisticated treatments of this issue is found in William of Ockham. In his treatise *On Predestination* he sets out the implications of his voluntarism for the problem of divine foreknowledge.[7] Like Scotus and others, he argues that God can know something to be true without its contrary being impossible, so that the truth He knows "could never have been true" (§1E). Admittedly, we do say that God necessarily has knowledge of everything. But it is only necessary *that* He knows, without *what* He knows being necessary. As Ockham puts it, "For example, 'God knows that this person will be saved' is true and yet it is possible that He will never have known that this person will be saved. And so that proposition is immutable and is nevertheless not necessary but contingent" (§1F; see also §2L). But what about the problem that if propositions were already true in the past, they will be necessarily true because the past is necessary? Ockham concedes that, in general, past things are necessary. But he denies that there are necessary past truths about future things (§1C, 1N). It is misleading to say that if it was true yesterday that there will be a sea battle tomorrow, then the truth about the sea battle is a fact about the way things were in the past. Rather, it was a fact about the future, and remains so until the sea battle occurs. This solves the problem, because, as we've just seen, facts about the future are contingent.

Someone might raise the following worry here (§2C). Suppose that God knows in advance that I will vote for candidate A. According to Ockham, God's knowing this leaves it still possible that I vote for candidate B, as I can still freely choose when I enter the voting booth. But then it looks as if it is in my power to make God be wrong: it is open for me to act in a way contrary to what He predicts. This objection, thinks Ockham, is a mistake (§2D). God knows I will vote for candidate A, since this is how I will choose. If I were to choose candidate B, then God would always have known this instead.[8] He compares the objection to denying that when Socrates is sitting, it is possible for Socrates to be standing. Of course, it is possible for Socrates to be standing now even when he is sitting. What is impossible is that he be standing *on the assumption* that he is sitting, that is, that he be sitting and standing at the same time. So it is with God's knowledge. It's possible that He knows I will choose A, and possible that He knows I will choose B, because either option is open to me. What is not possible is that God knows I will choose B while also knowing that I will choose A.

With these distinctions Scotus, Ockham, and the other fourteenth-century voluntarists have offered a powerful and, in fact, I think correct solution to the age-old dilemma of future contingents. With the exception of Auriol, they are driven to admit that there are present and past truths about the future because they don't want to give up on divine omniscience. But this is also the right move for purely philosophical reasons. Once we have a grip on contingency as Scotus understands it, such truths can be acknowledged without any deterministic consequences. Indeed, the whole issue gives us a nice example of the fact that theological considerations could prompt genuine philosophical advances, advances that should be welcomed even by staunch atheists. Unfortunately, there was another theological difficulty lurking here, one that would not be so easy to solve.

This is a problem we saw much earlier in medieval history, back in the ninth century with Eriugena and his opponents in the predestination debate (Chapter 3). If we need God's grace to be saved, then are we still free? The debate over this question erupted with new force in the first half of the fourteenth century, perhaps in part because it could now be posed with unprecedented clarity. According to Scotus and other voluntarists, a free agent is one who can choose between genuinely possible alternatives. But in the case of a human action there are two free agents involved and not just one: God and the human who performs the action. So long as *someone* freely chooses what will happen, contingency is safeguarded. But it is not much comfort to be told that my action is contingent if it was chosen by God instead of by me. It was felt that Scotus might have fallen into this trap, since he speaks as if it is God's will alone that selects from all possible things which ones will happen, and which will not.[9]

The way out of the difficulty may seem obvious. Why not just say that it is up to us to choose what to do, for instance whether to commit a sin or not, with God knowing what we will do but not choosing or willing it? After all, we would hope that God always wills for all of us to be perfectly good, but all too often the attractions of sin prove too powerful (just ask candidate B). Unfortunately, philosophical and theological considerations made this solution at least problematic and possibly heretical. On the philosophical front, we might hesitate to say that a creaturely act could affect God, by making Him know something (namely, that we in fact do what we choose to do). On the theological front, in one of the more decisive moments in the history of Christian belief, Augustine had prevailed against the followers of Pelagius, who held that it is in the power of humans to be good and thus merit salvation. No, Augustine replied: God's grace is needed if we are to be saved. Following Augustine most medievals felt constrained to admit that God somehow "predestines" both the elect and the damned, freely choosing to offer grace to the former and not to the latter.[10]

If that is the whole story, then it looks like all the good philosophical work done by our voluntarists in solving the problem of future contingents has done nothing to safeguard human freedom. God does not just know what we will do, He also forces us to do it or even chooses for us. Not only would this deprive us of freedom: it would make God responsible for sin. To avoid this disappointing result, several voluntarists argued that God helps those who help themselves. A good example is the Dominican thinker Durandus of St. Pourçain.[11] He considers that, even though a human cannot merit salvation all on her own, she can at least try to be good. When she sincerely wills goodness, this natural and free act of willing prepares the way for God's grace, which is then infused as the theological virtue of charity. God's freedom to predestine the elect is not compromised, since He is entirely free in bestowing grace upon those who will be saved. Durandus compares this to the way a king might voluntarily gift a horse to one of his knights to reward the knight for good service. Ockham takes a broadly similar approach, making the merit that yields salvation a kind of joint product of divine and human action. While God's involvement is absolutely needed, the starting point lies with the human agent's initial choice to will goodness.

Durandus, Ockham, and other scholastics who adopted this theory of cooperative grace believed they had avoided the Pelagian heresy by stressing God's freedom to bestow grace. God owes us nothing, so it is up to Him whether or not to come to our assistance even once we show that we deserve it. But not everyone was impressed. A thunderous condemnation of their position was presented by Thomas Bradwardine, a remarkable thinker who studied at Oxford and became archbishop of Canterbury shortly before dying of the Black Death in 1349. For him, the theory of grace found in Durandus, Ockham, and others was nothing but rank Pelagianism, since it took the initiative for salvation out of God's hands. Instead, we must admit that nothing can happen in the created world without God's willing it: He is the "co-mover" of every motion.[12] And this must apply even to determinations of the human will. Even when someone simply tries to be good, this too requires God's freely offered assistance and involvement.

With Bradwardine we have a good example of voluntarism that roots all contingency in God's untrammeled freedom. Of course, this view is not without its drawbacks. While it is evident that Bradwardine is no Pelagian, it isn't so clear how he can account for our moral responsibility. After all, if God is responsible (or "co-responsible") for everything I do, then isn't God to be blamed for my sins just as He is to be credited with bestowing merit and grace? Here Bradwardine takes recourse to the quite literally ancient expedient of saying that evil is nothing but a privation of good, a theory first articulated by the late ancient Platonist Plotinus and then embraced by Augustine. Since sin is a privation or deficiency of goodness, it is not something God actually has to create and its presence in our world is ultimately due to human frailty. Sadly, this is not very persuasive. Bradwardine wants to have things both ways. He argues that God is intimately implicated in everything we do, speaking of God's agency as being co-effective, simultaneous, and mixed (*coeffector, simul, mixtum*) with human agency.[13] Yet he still wants to ascribe sin to human will and not divine will.

As God already knew in the fourteenth century, the debate between Bradwardine and his so-called "Pelagian" opponents would not be the end of the story. Bradwardine offered a striking anticipation of what we will find in the Protestant Reformation, to the point that we even find him saying that God eternally predestines a specific number of elect who will receive salvation. As with the emergence of secularist political theories and philosophy in vernacular languages, developments we associate with the fifteenth and even sixteenth centuries are already to be found here in the later medieval period. Another such development, as we'll see shortly, was a step in the direction of early modern science. And among the men responsible for that was none other than Thomas Bradwardine. First, though, let's turn to yet another area where Bradwardine was an important contributor: logic.

62

TRIVIAL PURSUITS
FOURTEENTH-CENTURY LOGIC

When I started out as a philosophy graduate student, I was asked to take a course on formal logic. I'll admit that I had some mixed feelings about it. On the one hand, I appreciated that logic is foundational to philosophy. It was with good reason that the medievals made their "trivium" of logical and linguistic arts foundational to university study. You can't do philosophy without reasoning well, and how can you do that without knowing the rules of reasoning? On the other hand, I couldn't help feeling that if I had wanted to take courses involving proofs and blackboards full of symbols, I could just have studied math instead. I suspect some readers may feel the same and are wondering whether they should just skip to Chapter 63. So let me offer the reassuring observation that, in a way, we've already been exploring medieval logic in considerable depth without even realizing it. When we examined the debate between Ockham's nominalism and Burley's realism, discussed mental language, and asked whether acknowledging truths about the future leads to determinism, we were discussing problems raised in treatises on logic. Take the nominalism-realism debate. This was really a controversy about such logical issues as the categories, universals, and supposition theory. We were trying to decide whether general terms in our language, and especially in the propositions that make up a valid syllogism, stand (or "supposit") for something real in the external world or merely universal concepts.

But, of course, supposition theory was not devoted only to this sort of question, which we today would consider as belonging to metaphysics rather than logic. What our medieval logicians really wanted was to determine the range of things a given term might stand for.[1] Sometimes, of course, this is quite straightforward. In the sentence "Groucho smoked cigars," the term "Groucho" stands for Groucho Marx. But we need only go as far as the rest of the sentence to see that things can get trickier. What does the term "cigars" stand for? The particular cigars that Groucho in fact smoked during his life? Or perhaps cigars in general? To say nothing of sentences like "Every farmer who has a donkey beats it," a famous example found in Walter Burley and still discussed by philosophers of language today (who call a whole class of propositions "donkey sentences" in honor of Burley's example). Again the statement looks straightforward at first glance. But what does the word "it" refer to at the end of the sentence? Let's imagine a farmer who has two donkeys. It follows from our sentence that this farmer must beat at least one of them. But it seems to be an open question what the word "it" refers to. Would the sentence be true if the farmer only beats one donkey and leaves the other alone or must both donkeys be subject to the abuse?

The lurking threat here is ambiguity. To avoid it, the medievals distinguished different types of supposition, as I've mentioned numerous times already: a word like "cigar" might be said to supposit "personally" when it stands for a specific cigar, and "simply" when it stands for the very notion of cigar. So to understand how the word "cigar" supposits in a sentence, we need to look to the context. The point of this, in turn, is to avoid making fallacious inferences. For instance, you might reason, "Groucho is a human; human has five letters; therefore Groucho has five letters." This sophistical argument trades on the ambiguity of "human," which in the first premise has personal supposition, since it stands for Groucho, but in the second premise has material supposition, since it standing for the word "human."

Sensitivity to ambiguity is also important in the interpretation of texts, including authoritative texts such as the writings of the church fathers or the Bible itself. This is one topic on which Burley and Ockham agreed. They both contrasted the use of words in their strict meaning (*de virtute sermonis*) with using figures of speech or other kinds of equivocation. So common did this technique become that, in 1340, a statute was passed in Paris forbidding instructors from condemning an authoritative text as false according to strict meaning without carefully explaining the alternative interpretation on which the text turns out to be true.[2] Are there no limits to the significations that a given word can take on, over and above its strict meaning? Consider that in the 1980s the word "bad" was used to mean something pretty close to the usual meaning of "good" (when Michael Jackson sang, "I'm bad, I'm bad, you know it," this was not an expression of low self-esteem). Yet there must be some constraints to the meanings of terms, if communication is to be possible. John Buridan achieved this with his proposal that signification is determined not only by the intention of the speaker, but by a convention agreed between two or more speakers in a given context. If you intend to mean "good" when you say "bad," that is fine so long as the person you're talking to is up to speed on 1980s slang.

Such concerns had already animated terminist logic in the thirteenth century. Indeed, figures like Burley and Ockham looked back to terminism more than to the modism of the speculative grammarians in the late thirteenth and early fourteenth centuries. There was, however, a shift insofar as fourteenth-century logic was especially concerned with ambiguity at the level of entire propositions and not just individual terms.[3] The mid-century logician William Heytesbury wrote a whole treatise exploring this topic.[4] Some of his examples will remind us of our discussions about contingency and free will. Take a sentence like "Elvis can be alive and dead." To decide whether this is true or false, we have to tease apart its two possible meanings. If it means that the sentences "Elvis is alive" and "Elvis is dead" can both be true at the same time, it is false. But if it just means that at one and the same time, either "Elvis is alive" could be true or "Elvis is dead" could be true, then this is perfectly unobjectionable.

Having noticed that propositions, just like individual terms, can be ambiguous, we might wonder whether entire propositions can have a signification just as terms do. If the word "Groucho" in "Groucho smoked cigars" signifies Groucho Marx, what does the whole sentence signify? We mentioned before that Walter Burley answered this question with his typical realist approach, arguing that there is something out there in the outside world, a state of affairs that the proposition represents.[5] A similar view was taken by Ockham's student Adam Wodeham, who was troubled by Ockham's idea that when we know something, what we are knowing is simply the true proposition that we affirm. Wodeham thought that this cannot be right. If I know that Groucho smoked cigars, the target of my knowledge is not a proposition but Groucho and a fact about him.[6]

This suggestion was taken up by Gregory of Rimini, a theologian of the Augustinian Order and another figure who worked in the middle of the century, dying in 1358. Gregory was active in Paris and Italy but responded to the English philosophers who have dominated our last several chapters, weighing in on such debates as the problem of divine foreknowledge.[7] He also had a distinctive view on this question of the proposition, holding that there is a "complex object of signification (*complexe significabile*)" which is a real and even eternal thing.[8] The idea here then is that Groucho's smoking cigars is an abstract state of affairs that may or may not be realized at some point in the history of the world. When it does come about, because Groucho is alive and habitually smokes cigars, the proposition "Groucho smokes cigars" is true. It signifies that that state of affairs is currently actual. Needless to say, thinkers of a more nominalist bent, like John Buridan, were stridently opposed to this; yet it's a proposal that has found adherents among some modern-day philosophers.

Another interesting point made by Gregory, which also has its roots in earlier debates, concerns the intellectual act by which we grasp a proposition.[9] The question here is, how many things are we doing with our mind when we assent to a sentence? Durandus of St. Pourçain believed that the mind can only do one thing at a time. Just as nothing can be simultaneously hot and cold, so the human intellect cannot simultaneously have two acts, one that grasps heat and another that grasps coldness. So we must have a single holistic grasp of each sentence when we think about it. This view was, however, criticized by another scholastic named Thomas Wylton, who pointed out that when we draw the conclusion of an argument, we cannot be thinking only about the conclusion but must also still bear in mind the premises of the argument. Otherwise, we would not be drawing the conclusion on the basis of those premises, and would just be making an unjustified assertion. Thus, the mind must simultaneously have different acts directed towards the premises and the conclusion. Gregory of Rimini comes down on Durandus' side of the debate, on the basis that the intellect is immaterial and hence simple. A piece of paper is a physical object, so when you write down a sentence on it, you can distribute the terms across different parts of the paper. But the intellect has no distinct parts and must therefore grasp each whole proposition all at once.

With this debate we're moving on from individual terms and propositions to the complexities of entire arguments. Starting in the early fourteenth century, logicians began to write treatises about the inferences we make when we produce such arguments. They called this branch of logic the study of "consequences," because the conclusion of an argument is the consequence of, or follows from, its premises. We can capture this relation of "consequence" by saying, with John Buridan, that a valid argument is one in which it is "impossible for the antecedent to be true while the consequent is false."[10] In other words, the truth of the premise or premises guarantees the truth of the conclusion. The easiest case is where the basis of the inference is obvious and explicit, as with the classic (and thanks to the citizen jurors of Athens, empirically verified) example "Socrates is a human; all humans are mortal; therefore Socrates is mortal."

But you can bet that our medieval logicians have thought about more difficult cases too. For starters, inferences may be good even if not everything is explicitly spelled out. Take the simpler argument "Socrates is human; therefore Socrates is mortal." By Buridan's definition, this is a valid inference, because if it is true that Socrates is human, then it cannot be false that he is mortal. It's just that the linking premise of the inference—that all humans are mortal—is not stated explicitly. Thomas Bradwardine, whom we just met in the context of the predestination debate, went so far as to say that each proposition signifies *everything* that it implies, because as soon as you accept that the proposition is true, all its consequences may be validly inferred.[11] In some cases you can validly draw conclusions that seem entirely irrelevant to the stated premises. Ockham and others accept inferences like "Some human is immortal; therefore Groucho doesn't smoke cigars," because once you assume that something impossible is true, anything will follow. Conversely, we may also reason, "Groucho smokes cigars; therefore humans are mortal," because humans are necessarily mortal, and a necessary truth may validly be affirmed from any premises.[12]

Other logical writings explored the so-called *insolubilia* and *sophismata*, meaning respectively paradoxical arguments and arguments that look valid, but in fact are not. Bradwardine's name comes up again here, because he offered an influential solution to the famous "paradox of the liar" in his work on insolubles.[13] The paradox arises with sentences like "What I am saying right now is false." As a moment's reflection shows, this sentence would seem to be true if it is false, and vice versa. Bradwardine's solution is worthy of Duns Scotus in its subtlety: he carefully defines the notions of "true" and "false" so as to prevent the problem from arising. A proposition is "true" if it signifies "only as is the case (*tantum sicut est*)"; a false proposition by contrast signifies "otherwise than is the case." The key here is the word "only" in his definition of "true." A true sentence must signify *only* as is the case, whereas a false sentence is under no such constraint. Thus, the liar statement cannot be true, on Bradwardine's definitions. For suppose that it were true: then the statement would signify that it is true, which would be the case, but *also* that it is not true, which would not be the case. Conversely, there is no such problem with its being false, since false statements are allowed to signify both otherwise than is the case *and* as is the case.

All these logical methods and distinctions come together in a fascinating and somewhat mysterious activity pursued at the universities, a game called "obligations."[14] Several of the authors we have discussed wrote about obligations, including, notably, Walter Burley. So did a couple of authors not yet mentioned: Richard Kilvington and Roger Swineshead, both active in the 1330s. The game was already played in the thirteenth century, as we know from numerous treatises on the topic. Some are by unnamed authors, yet another example where anonymous works are among the most important ones to survive today. A game of obligations goes as follows. There are two players, the "opponent" and "respondent." In the most common version of the game, the opponent proposes something, which the respondent should assume is true until the round is over (unless it is something impossible, in which case he should deny it). Then the opponent keeps offering more propositions, trying to get the respondent to make a mistake by contradicting himself, admitting something he should deny, or viceversa. So, to take a simple case, if the respondent is sitting down, the opponent might start by getting him to say he is standing, then ask him whether or not he admits "Either you are standing or the king of France is in the room." The respondent should admit this, on his former assumption, even though he is sitting down and there is no royal presence.

Though it would be an exaggeration to say that all of fourteenth-century logic was just intended to help scholastics win at this game, sometimes you do almost get that impression. The terminology of obligations is pervasive in discussion of other questions, including theological debates. Being able to distinguish between different sorts of supposition, and to disambiguate between the possible interpretations of a given sentence, was crucial for the respondent, as was recognizing when the opponent might be leading him into a paradoxical or sophistical trap. But surely being good at obligations was not an end in itself? Why were these scholars spending so much time on this logical game? It's a question much debated by modern-day scholars. One idea is that it was just a way of exploring the topic of inferences; an anonymous author of the thirteenth century suggests as much.[15] But in the fourteenth century there was a whole other genre of logical work devoted especially to inferences, the aforementioned works on "consequences," so this seems an inadequate explanation.[16]

Another possibility is that the scholastics wanted to explore what is nowadays called "counterfactual reasoning." The opponent gets the respondent to assume something false in the first move, and thereafter the conversation simply discovers what would lead from this false assumption. (This is another reason the respondent shouldn't agree to suppose anything impossible in the first move, since, as we've already seen, you can infer anything you like from an impossible proposition.) But a close look at the work on obligations by Kilvington shows him making the point that we would actually have to *change* the rules of the game if we want to do this.[17] He gives the following example. Let's say I am opponent and you are respondent. As my opening move, I get you to assume, falsely, that you are in Rome. You should agree, since this is not impossible. Next, I ask you to agree to the proposition "Either you are not in Rome or you are a bishop." In fact, this is true, because in real life you aren't in Rome, and by normal obligational rules you should admit anything that is true if it doesn't contradict what you have already agreed to. Next, I point out that these two premises prove that you are a bishop. So the whole argument would go like this:

You are in Rome.
Either you are not in Rome or you are a bishop.
Therefore you are a bishop.

And this doesn't look like a good example of counterfactual reasoning: no one would think that if I were in Rome, it would follow that I am a bishop! Kilvington thus says that if we want to restrict ourselves to the counterfactual implications, the respondent should be allowed to refuse the second premise even though it is true. Effectively, the respondent would pretend to inhabit a counterfactual situation where he is in Rome, and should give all his answers supposing that he lives in that alternative world rather than in the real world.

The foregoing should give you a sense of why the medievals were interested in bad arguments as well as good ones. The study of "sophistry," as they called deceptive argumentation, can reveal much about good reasoning. It can help you avoid making philosophical mistakes, and help you diagnose the mistakes of others. In this the medievals were, as so often, following the lead of Aristotle, who had written a logical work called *Sophistical Refutations*. Yet the medieval genre of *sophismata* differed from Aristotle's treatment in at least one surprising way. It became a context for pioneering work in physics, the discussion of which will have us doing some mathematics after all.

63

QUADRIVIAL PURSUITS
THE OXFORD CALCULATORS

I f you opened a work on physics in antiquity or at a medieval university and compared it to a physics textbook from the modern day, the first big difference that would strike you would be, well, that the ancient or medieval text is in Greek or Latin. But the second big difference would be that the modern textbook is full of mathematics, with formulas and numbers strewn across every page. Not so with works on natural philosophy written in antiquity or the thirteenth century. I didn't need to remind you of ideas from high school math class when discussing the natural philosophy of Richard Rufus or Albert the Great. It may seem obvious nowadays that physics should involve doing calculations and solving equations, but the earlier history of physics suggests that this approach is far from evident. Any shepherd will readily think to use numbers to keep track of the size of the flock. But it took scientists a long time to realize that it would also make sense to use numbers to keep track of how fast a sheep is working its way across the meadow as it grazes, or to compare the speed of that motion to its motion when it runs away from a wolf. This is to say nothing of applying mathematics to more subtle sorts of change, like the rate at which the grass in the meadow is turning brown in autumn or warming up on a summer's day.

In the popular imagination the breakthrough came when early modern scientists first merged the study of mathematics with the study of nature. But, in fact, certain natural phenomena, notably the motions of the stars and the harmonic ratios we use to produce music, had fallen under the study of mathematics since antiquity. The medievals too dealt with these phenomena in the so-called "quadrivium" of liberal arts: arithmetic, geometry, music, and astronomy. We've also seen how these arts were used in applied sciences such as optics, a specialty subject of Grosseteste and Bacon in the thirteenth century. As for the application of mathematical concepts to spatial motion and changes in quality, like color or temperature, we do not need to wait for the early moderns. This step was already taken in the fourteenth century by a group of thinkers at the University of Oxford (especially Merton College) whom historians call the "Calculators."[1]

We've already met most of them. One key figure, as in logic and the debate over predestination, was Thomas Bradwardine. Most professional philosophers have not even heard of Bradwardine; yet it should now be clear that he was a truly pivotal figure in medieval thought who made crucial contributions in a number of different fields—another sterling example of why it makes sense to study the history of philosophy "without any gaps." In his own day, he was more appreciated: the philosopher Ralph Strode called him "the prince of the modern philosophers of nature."[2] In a work written in 1328 and devoted to the "proportions" of motion, Bradwardine set forth an influential mathematical analysis of the relationship between the force applied to a moving body, the resistance the body encounters, and the velocity of the motion that will result. Also significant was that champion of realism Walter Burley, who, in addition to writing on Aristotle's *Physics*, composed treatises analyzing qualitative change. Other Calculators included Richard Kilvington and Roger Swineshead, whom we just met in our discussion of the game of obligations, as well as another Swineshead whose first name was Richard and who actually wrote a treatise called *Book of Calculations* (disappointingly, they were called "Swineshead" not as a comment on their personal appearance, but because they came from the same town). Other "Calculators" included John Dumbleton and William Heytesbury (disappointingly, not named for his dislike of soft fruits).

There were good reasons for medieval thinkers *not* to do what the Calculators finally did by pursuing a mathematical approach to physics. Crucial mathematical tools were still lacking. True, algebra had been invented by the ninth-century Muslim scholar al-Khwārizmī and passed into Latin in the twelfth century. (The word betrays this cultural origin: "algebra" comes from the Arabic *al-jabr*.) But calculus was still centuries away from being discovered. Then, too, there were doctrinal reasons to think that mathematical techniques would be out of place in discussions of physical change. In Aristotelianism, such items as the color of grass or the warmth of a sunny day belong to the category of quality. The category of quantity takes in an entirely different range of properties, like length. So applying numbers to colors and temperatures would require contemplating a categorial monstrosity, the quantity of a quality.[3]

Worse still, Aristotle gave explicit instructions that we are not to engage in what he called *metabasis*, or "crossing" from one scientific field to another, except under certain rather strict conditions. Basically, he allows it only when one of the sciences in question is subordinated to the other. That is, it must take its principles from the other science, as we saw Aquinas thinking that theology takes its principles from the knowledge (*scientia*) of God (Chapter 36). So, to take results from mathematics and apply them in natural philosophy seemed to contravene Aristotelian methodology.[4]

The Calculators were aware of the problem. Bradwardine argued that his procedure was justified, since we can speak in a broad sense of "proportion" whenever there is a question of "more" and "less." Grass can be more or less green and a motion can be more or less fast, licensing the application of the mathematics of proportion to these things.

Possibly the context of contemporary nominalism played a role too. Consider that, for Ockham, knowledge or science operates at the level of propositions. So long as we don't engage in outright equivocation—that is, use the same term in two different senses—it should be possible to combine true propositions into valid arguments so long as they share terms, whether or not these propositions were proven true in the same or in difference sciences. Also, nominalism readily grants that important scientific concepts, like universals, may be only in the mind. Thus, the Calculators lived at a time when introducing a mathematical abstraction like "velocity" may have seemed less problematic. Doing so need not imply the existence of a real thing out there in the world to which the word "velocity" applies.[5]

Given all this, we can hardly be surprised that in earlier medieval philosophy, there had been no tradition of applying numbers to qualitative changes and motions. When the Calculators ventured to do so, even they did it only in a rather abstract fashion. They used variables, as in "Suppose a motion moves A in time B," or simple numbers, "Suppose a motion moves 2 in one hour." There is no idea here of actually going out to measure real motions or to contrive units for the measurement of things like force, acceleration, resistance, and velocity.[6] Instead, the Calculators' arguments move at the level of intuition and what they took to be common sense. Furthermore, when we talk about their "mathematical" approach, we should not imagine that there are formulas or equations scattered through the manuscripts of their works, as in the modern-day physics textbook. Instead, everything is spelled out in Latin prose apart from the letters used as variables.

In this respect the Calculators' discussions of motion read very much like works on scholastic logic. There's a good reason for this: these discussions often appear in works on scholastic logic. As just mentioned, these Calculators were the same men who were writing about sophisms, obligations, and so on. They often took up the topic of change and motion when discussing sophistical arguments. Consider the following rather strange sentence: "Socrates is whiter than Plato begins to be white."[7] It is the first item considered by Richard Kilvington in his work about sophisms. What he has in mind is that Socrates is completely white, whereas Plato is not white but is just becoming white. Hence the sophistical sentence: Plato is just turning white while Socrates is completely white, and so is now whiter than Plato is beginning to be. Kilvington considers a potential problem with this sentence, namely that there are an indefinite number of shades of white between Plato's still dusky color and Socrates' brilliant, pure whiteness. Doesn't that mean that Socrates is infinitely whiter than Plato? No, says Kilvington. Though there are indeed an infinite number of degrees of whiteness between not-white and white, nothing can be infinitely white. We might say that pure white is the limit of the process of whitening. As something whitens, it goes through an indefinite number of degrees of whiteness along the way, just as something moving in a straight line can be thought of as moving across all the points on that line.

For a nice example of a sophism concerning spatial motion, we can turn to Heytesbury, who considers the following puzzle.[8] Suppose that Socrates moves distance B over the course of day A (notice that, as promised, he uses generic variables rather than concrete units). On the same day, Plato moves exactly the same distance. But whereas Socrates is moving at a constant rate, Plato starts slowly and speeds up as he goes, like a hare gradually accelerating to catch a tortoise that is plodding steadily along. Plato catches up with Socrates only at the very end of the day. So here comes the sophistical sentence: can we say that "Socrates and Plato will begin to move equally fast"? It may seem so, since they covered the same ground in the same time. But Heytesbury denies this, since Plato is not moving at the same *speed* as Socrates. Rather, as the Calculators would put it, Socrates and Plato have the same "total velocity,"[9] meaning that the complete distance and time of the motion are equal. But their velocities at each moment are different, except for the one moment when the slow Socrates is moving at the same rate as the increasingly speedy Plato.

Given their fascination with logical puzzles, we might suppose that the Calculators chose to explore motion in such depth simply to handle these and similar sophistries. Maybe they just didn't want to get caught out in a game of obligations after admitting that Plato is moving or turning white? But there was more to it than that. There were good theological reasons to worry about change, including the need to account for the Eucharist, which, as we've seen, was a topic that elicited deep reflection on qualities and the way that they alter (Chapter 47). The problem also came up when discussing the increase of divinely given grace in a human being. Yet again we see that the theological context of medieval thought, far from precluding scientific advance and inquiry, often provoked it. These theological worries seem to have been on the mind of Walter Burley when he wrote his treatises on change, for example.[10]

In these treatises Burley wanted to explain in greater depth what happens when something or someone is turning white, or when water heats until it turns into air (or a person grows in grace, but he uses the more mundane examples in his discussion). He considers the theory of an unnamed opponent, perhaps Thomas Wylton, that the process of change always involves a mixture of two contrary qualities. Thus, something that starts out cold and is becoming hot would have a certain ratio of cold to hot in it. We can even assign numbers to the ratio. Starting out from zero degrees of heat, water might advance to six degrees, at which point it would transform into air. Halfway through this process, it would have three degrees of cold and three of heat; hence we could say that its temperature would result from the "mixture" of qualities. Now, Burley has no quarrel with the basic idea of degrees of heat and cold. This notion could have come to the scholastics through the medical tradition.[11] The ancient doctor Galen and, following him, Muslim thinkers whose works were translated into Latin, like al-Kindī and Averroes, had assigned degrees of these basic qualities to drugs in their works on pharmacology. The same background helps to explain why Burley and the other Calculators speak of the "latitude" of a quality, meaning the range of intensity that a feature like white or heat may have. In medical texts by Galen and Avicenna health is described as a state with a certain "latitude," meaning that the human body can be more or less hot or cold, dry or moist, while still remaining healthy.

While Burley is happy to think of qualities in these terms, he rejects the theory of mixed qualities. Instead, he believes that qualitative change involves a succession of different qualitative forms in the changing thing. Something that is heating up has a form of heat that is slightly more intense than the one it had a moment ago, and slightly less intense than the one it will have a moment from now. On this account we can again think of qualitative change as being very much like spatial motion, a successive passage through an indefinite intensities. The analogy between motion and a change in quality means that the methods applied to one should apply to the other. Just as we can introduce quantitative measures to talk about degrees of heat or white, and even assign these degrees numbers, so we should be able to assign numbers to the intensity of a motion.[12] And that is exactly what we find the Calculators doing.

Here the most important contributions were made by Bradwardine and Heytesbury. In the aforementioned treatise on proportions, Bradwardine offers a new and influential mathematical analysis of spatial motion. Aristotle had argued that the speed of such a movement would be inversely proportional to the resistance offered by a medium. This is why you would need to exert much more force to walk through water than through air at the same speed. From this, Aristotle had drawn the conclusion that motion in a void would be impossible, because it would offer zero resistance, implying that an infinite speed would result. By the fourteenth century this argument against void had frequently been criticized, including in late antiquity by John Philoponus and in the Islamic world by several thinkers such as Ibn Bājja, Abū l-Barakāt al-Baghdādī, and Fakhr al-Dīn al-Rāzī.[13] They all made roughly the same complaint, which is that resistance only slows down the intrinsic speed of a motion. In a void there would be no slowing effect at all, so the motion would simply have its instrinsic speed, which, of course, would be finite. A number of Latin Christian thinkers likewise accepted that void is possible at least in theory, and that bodies could move in a void.[14] The 1277 condemnations may have helped popularize this view, since they discouraged the notion that God would be unable to create empty space should He choose to do so.

Bradwardine would agree that void is in principle possible. He devises a telling objection to Aristotle's argument, namely that if motion in a void were really infinite in speed, but a minimal resistance would make the speed finite, then adding just a small amount of resistance to a void space would somehow cause an infinite reduction in speed. Furthermore, he observes that increasing resistance more and more doesn't just make things move more and more slowly. At some point, the motion will grind to a halt completely. Imagine walking through a medium whose density is increasing. First it is like walking through air, then through water, then yogurt, then molasses, and so on. Eventually you would be unable to move at all, rather than merely slowing down. This is unexplained by Aristotle's simple theory that there is an inverse relation between speed and resistance.

Instead, Bradwardine offers a new account centering on what is in effect a new formula, though, of course, he presents it in Latin sentences and not symbols. To understand it, you will now need to dust off some of that high school math. Following earlier medieval ideas about proportions, he says that to double a speed, you don't halve the resistance or double the force applied to the moving body. Rather you have to take the ratio of the force to the resistance and multiply this by itself—in other words, you have to square the ratio. To triple the speed, you would need to cube that same ratio, or multiply it by itself three times. Thus, if a ratio of force to resistance is 3 to 2, and this yields a certain speed, then to triple that speed you would need a ratio of force to resistance of 27 to 8 (that is, 3^3 to 2^3). Bradwardine does not back this up with empirical proof and, in fact, it has some counterintuitive results, as pointed out by other fourteenth-century thinkers like Nicole Oresme.[15] But the other Calculators liked it, in part because the speed is now calculated as a function of the extent to which the force is in excess of the resistance. If the ratio of the force to resistance is 1:1 or even less, then the speed will be zero. This is why you can't walk through molasses, as people learned in Boston in the year 1919 (search online for the phrase "great molasses flood" to see what I mean).

Unlike those Bostonians, the Calculators continued to make progress with another breakthrough, first explained in writing by Heytesbury. Think back to our earlier example of Plato and Socrates moving the same distance in the same time but at varying speeds, because Plato starts slowly and accelerates while Socrates moves at a constant rate. (The Calculators would say that Socrates' steady motion is "uniform," while Plato's speeding up makes his motion "difform.") It is pretty easy to work out how far something will move in a given time if its speed is constant. But it is not so easy to work it out if the speed is varying. What we would like to do is find a way to reduce the case of accelerated motion to the simpler case of motion with constant speed. Heytesbury accomplishes this by announcing what is now known as the "mean speed theorem." It states that if a body is moving while changing speed, it will cover the same distance in a given time that it would have covered if it moved for that same time with its *mean* speed. Suppose a sheep moves for an hour across a meadow, slowing down and speeding up as it does so, first grazing and then lurching into the ovine version of a sprint when it sees a wolf in the next field. The different speeds can then be averaged—you might take its speed at every minute, then divide by sixty to get the average speed—and the distance it moves will be the same as the distance it would have moved if it had been going at that rate constantly the whole hour.

This is good work on Heytesbury's part, and not only because he's right. Also because to conceptualize the situation like this he needs to use the Calculators' new idea of a speed *at a time*. It's a notion we find obvious, living as we do in an age where we can just look at the speedometer of the car to see how fast we are going right this moment. But like so many apparently obvious ideas, it needed to be discovered. It has to be admitted that Heytesbury didn't actually *prove* the mean speed theorem. He only articulated it and left it to the reader to see that it makes intuitive sense. Before long though, something like a proof was offered by Nicole Oresme, who modeled the situation of the accelerating motion using geometrical diagrams. These diagrams anticipate the geometrical approach to these and related topics later taken by Galileo. If you're still not impressed, no less a figure than Leibniz—who, of course, is going to help introduce the much-needed tools of calculus—was aware of the fourteenth-century thinkers and praised their pioneering work.[16] And if even that doesn't impress you, then just turn the page.

GET TO THE POINT
FOURTEENTH-CENTURY PHYSICS

It's a bit misleading to talk about "Aristotelian physics." Not that Aristotle was uninterested in physics. To the contrary, he quite literally wrote the book on the subject. Already in late antiquity and still in the medieval worlds of Islam, Byzantium, and Latin Christianity, his *Physics* was the fundamental source for natural philosophy (the word "physics" comes from the Greek *physis*, meaning "nature"). What I mean is rather that, in a way, Aristotle had not one but *two* "physics," one for the terrestrial world and one for the heavens. Down here in the region where we live, often called the "sublunary" realm because it is situated below the sphere of the moon, all things are made of the four elements air, earth, fire, and water. They have natural tendencies to move in straight lines up or down, that is to say, away from or towards the center point of the universe. This is because they are trying to reach what Aristotle calls their "natural places." Thus, fire tries to occupy the region just below the sphere of the moon, while earth tries to work its way towards the center of the cosmos, which is why flames flicker upwards and stones fall downwards.

The reason the four elements do not follow this natural tendency to separate from one another is that they are bound together into composite substances, something that Aristotelians across the ages tended to explain with reference to heavenly movement. It is because the heavens revolve around us that our world is so complex and varied. And revolve around us they do. In the celestial world things move in perfect circles instead of straight lines. This, according to Aristotle, shows that heavenly bodies are made of a different kind of matter, not the four sublunary elements but an ungenerated indestructible fifth element called *aither*. So distinctive are the nature and physics that govern this celestial realm that Aristotle devoted a separate treatise to it, *On the Heavens*. For him, the visible planets and fixed stars are seated upon transparent spheres made of the fifth element, which concentrically surround the likewise spherical terrestrial realm.

If Aristotle gave the medievals their cosmology, then Ptolemy gave them their astronomy.[1] His system had first been passed on to the Islamic world, something you can see in the title still used for Ptolemy's massively influential treatise *Almagest* (that *Al-* at the beginning is just the Arabic definite article).[2] Astronomical treatises of the Islamic world were in turn enormously influential on Latin Christendom, which borrowed everything from terminology, like *zīj* for an astronomical table, to instruments like the astrolabe. Such Latin works as *On the Sphere*, written in the first half of the thirteenth century by John of Sacrobosco, offered textbooks for the university students who studied astronomy as part of the quadrivium. As we move into the fourteenth century, we see that the story of astronomy and cosmology runs parallel to the story of philosophy. We have a similar trend towards use of vernacular languages. Nicole Oresme translated and commented on Aristotle's *On the Heavens* in French,[3] and a work on the use of the astrolabe was written in English by none other than Geoffrey Chaucer. Much as nominalism and voluntarism were putting pressure on various long-held Aristotelian presuppositions, so the science of the stars was increasingly subjected to doubt. We've already seen that one key aspect of Aristotle's cosmology, the eternity of the celestial bodies and hence of the cosmos as a whole, led to intense controversy in the thirteenth century (Chapter 43). Eternalism was widely rejected, even by the hardline Aristotelians of the Parisian arts faculty. Now in the fourteenth century, the Aristotelian-Ptolemaic worldview received more detailed criticism. In 1364 a Parisian master named Henry of Langenstein argued that the perfect spheres envisioned in that worldview could make sense only as a mathematical model, not as a real physical cosmology.[4]

Other authors toyed with revisions to the Aristotelian system, though without necessarily embracing these revisions. Mightn't it be that the earth rotates under an unmoving heaven, instead of the other way around? Could we even tell the difference? We saw in passing that Adam Wodeham mentioned this hypothesis to illustrate the notion of an apparent property, a cosmic version of the case of trees on a riverbank seeming to move when you are on a boat (Chapter 60). John Buridan and Nicole Oresme also discussed the possibility. Buridan decided against it on the grounds that, if the earth were turning, a projectile like an arrow fired straight up should fall some distance away, because the ground would turn beneath it during its flight. Oresme disagreed: if someone on a moving boat fires an arrow straight up, the arrow will fall back down onto the same spot in the boat because it will retain its lateral motion while flying.[5] Ultimately, Oresme stopped short of embracing the idea of a turning earth, but not without first having established it as a serious possibility.

Another innovative natural philosopher active in the fourteenth century was Francis of Marchia. Like Ockham, he was a Franciscan who came into conflict with the Pope over the principle of voluntary poverty; unlike Ockham, he was ultimately brought to trial to answer for his defiance. Marchia was a pioneer of the impetus theory, which we'll get to shortly. First, I want to mention his views on another matter, namely, whether there is in fact another matter aside from the elements that exist in the terrestrial realm.[6] Was Aristotle right to hold that the celestial bodies are made from a special kind of stuff, indestructible and uniquely suited for permanent circular motion? Here Marchia offers what you might call an internal critique of Aristotelian physics. On the traditional understanding of Aristotle's view, the most fundamental sort of matter is nothing but pure potentiality. It survives through all change, even change between the elements. Marchia points out that this sort of underlying prime matter is just as indestructible as the heavens, in that it cannot be generated or annihilated by any natural power. In this sense, matter is the same for the whole created universe, both sublunary and heavenly. It can be admitted that the celestial spheres, with their perfect rotations, are bodies of a different kind than we find here in our earthly realm. But this is due to their different forms, not the matter from which they are made.

Where Marchia cast doubt on the radical contrast between celestial and terrestrial physics, others questioned the causal connections that were supposed to obtain between the two realms. This was problematic, because taking the idea of celestial influence really seriously in the 1300s was a bit like taking disco culture really seriously in the 1970s: it might lead you to embrace astrology. It was a highly contentious discipline, enthusiastically endorsed by some medievals such as Roger Bacon, criticized harshly by others, like the author of a work called *Errors of the Philosophers*.[7] Bradwardine too was fiercely opposed to any suggestion of astrological determinism.[8] A compromise view could be that the heavens do influence things down here and that astrologers might sometimes be able to discern this. But heavenly influence should not be the sole causal factor determining the events in our lives. At the very least, human free will should also play a part. The stars were also invoked to explain such phenomena as magnetism and even the impossibility of empty space, since a void would be a place where celestial influence could not reach.[9]

Again, though, all this came under scrutiny in the fourteenth century.[10] Already the condemnations in Paris in 1277 had censured the thesis that "If the heaven should stand still, fire would not [burn] because nature would cease to operate." A couple of generations on, Buridan and Oresme question whether natural processes really depend on causal influence from the heavens. They point to the fact that the biblical prophet Joshua commanded the sun and moon to stand still in the sky (Joshua 10:12–13), which did not result in a collapse in all natural processes, only a collapse in the enemies arrayed against the Israelite army. Buridan explains that without any help from the heavens, the four sublunary elements could simply interact with one another so as to yield indefinite change and mixture. The traditional recipe had celestial influence ensuring that fire keeps turning into air; for Buridan, you can just add water.

As Francis of Marchia pointed out in his argument for the commonality of celestial and terrestrial matter, Aristotelian doctrine had it that matter is bare potentiality. Anything made of this matter will occupy space—without any gaps, if you'll pardon the expression, since void is impossible. Also, all material things are indefinitely divisible, meaning that in principle you can take any continuous body and cut it in half, cut one of the resulting halves in half, cut one of the resulting quarters in half, and so on, forever. You might imagine doing this with a cake, taking off ever thinner slices. Aristotle put this conception forward against the atomists who had lived around the time of Socrates, who believed that every body is made up of smallest indivisible parts.

Most scholastics agreed with Aristotle about this, albeit with occasional modifications. Duns Scotus, for one, forthrightly rejected atomism but held that the infinite number of parts that can possibly be isolated in a body are all *actually* present, not just potentially present.[11] Ockham agreed with Scotus, since he could make no sense of a thing that exists merely potentially. If a whole body is real and it is made of parts, then its parts must be real too.[12] Ockham's argument for this illustrates his penchant for transposing metaphysical issues to the propositional level.[13] For him talk of "potential being" is just talk of negation plus possibility. Hence, if you say "This body potentially has parts," you can only mean "This body has no parts, though it could," which is false, since bodies do have parts. The parts are, however, not separated from one another as atoms would need to be, and in fact they overlap: half the cake includes two quarters of the cake as its subparts. Another point made by Scotus, and later by Francis of Marchia, is that the same amount of stuff (what Scotus calls "quantity of matter") can be packed into a greater or lesser volume. Here our medieval thinkers are getting at the notion that will later be called "mass."[14]

A more radical break with Aristotle's theory of matter was contemplated by Ockham's teacher, Henry of Harclay, and also by Ockham's intellectual sparring partner, Walter Chatton. Both were ready to admit that material things are, after all, made up of atoms, though not of the sort envisioned by ancient atomists. Instead, there would be actual *points* in a line or a body.[15] Given that, as we just saw, Scotus and Ockham accepted that all the parts of a whole are actually present, you might expect them to be happy with this. After all, isn't a line just made up of an infinite number of parts, which are indivisible points? Not according to Ockham.[16] He argued that an actual point is always the termination of a line; or, rather, speaking of a "point" is simply observing that the line ends. As a result, not even God can create a point existing all by itself.[17]

Yet Harclay and Chatton offered a powerful consideration for the reality of real, discrete points. They ask us to imagine a sphere approaching a plane. We might picture a billiard ball approaching a tabletop, with the ball and the table both envisioned as being geometrically flawless. Actually, to eliminate the imperfections that would arise in a real case, Chatton asks us to imagine that it is God who creates the situation in all its geometrical perfection. Our medieval atomists now argue that when the sphere first touches the plane, it will contact it at only a single point. This thought experiment provoked responses from Ockham, Wodeham, and Buridan.[18] I think the most clever answer is the one given by Wodeham. He imagines trying to isolate the part of the sphere touching the plane by slicing away upper portions of the sphere. You could start by cutting away the top hemisphere, then take off further layers as you work your way down. If you cut down so far that only the point of contact is left, the sphere will be gone completely. This shows that any constitutive part of the sphere that is really touching the plane must be extended.

Further thought experiments, both possible and impossible, played a role in the most famous development of fourteenth-century physics: the theory of impetus. It is associated especially with John Buridan but first appears in Francis of Marchia.[19] In another case of theological discussion prompting scientific progress, Marchia takes up the issue while discussing the way that the power of grace is instilled in the sacraments. He draws an analogy between this miraculous case and the mundane fact that a power for motion may be implanted in bodies, as when you throw a projectile like a javelin. Why does the javelin keep moving once it has left the hand of the thrower? For Marchia, the answer lies in what he calls *virtus derelicta*, or "remaining power." Buridan will call it *impetus*.

The theory of impetus is usually seen as a complete departure from Aristotle's theory of motion, perhaps in part because it was already proposed in late antiquity by John Philoponus, a stern critic of Aristotelian physics. For Marchia, though, it is just an elucidation of what Aristotle must have meant in the passages of his *Physics* that analyze motion.[20] To Aristotle's mind there must be something that causes the javelin to carry on moving. Since it can no longer be the thrower's hand once the javelin is in flight, he appeals to the air around the javelin. As it hurtles onward, the javelin displaces the air in front of it, and this displaced air is pushed behind the javelin, which gives it an onward shove. If your name is John, history suggests that you won't find this persuasive. Both John Philoponus and John Buridan pointed out the ridiculous consequences of Aristotle's theory, for instance that people on a boat sailing swiftly down a river would feel wind at their backs and not in their faces. Marchia more respectfully admitted that the medium may play a part in moving the body, while insisting that the "remaining power" given to the javelin by the thrower also helps to explain its tendency to keep moving, until the power is expended.

Not everyone was persuaded by the new idea. Ockham said that "It would be amazing if my hand caused some power (*virtus*) in the stone by touching it."[21] Impetus theory has clear advantages over Aristotle's account, though. As Richard Rufus had pointed out in the early thirteenth century (Chapter 23), it explains why you can throw rocks further than feathers: thanks to its size and density, a rock is able to take on a greater impetus. It also accounts for the acceleration of falling objects, so that a rock dropped off a building will kill you, whereas a rock dropped from one inch above your head will merely bruise you. As the rock falls, its impetus constantly builds thanks to its weight. Note, incidentally, that this is not the same as the later scientific concept of inertia. Neither Marchia nor Buridan claims that all moving bodies continue moving by default, slowing or stopping only when impeded. Rather, the idea is that a body can be invested with a power that will make it tend to move—like the attractive power in a magnet that moves it towards metal—but this tendency will always be brought to an end. Buridan is still committed to the Aristotelian idea that *something* must be causing motion whenever motion happens.

The heavens are quite literally the exception that proves this rule. There is a passage in Buridan where he speculates that celestial rotation can in principle go on forever.[22] In this respect it is unlike the motion of the sublunary elements, which travel along straight lines and thus must always stop. Earth will stop if it reaches an obstacle or, failing that, its "natural place" at the center of the cosmos. A heavenly sphere by contrast can keep going round and round, as there is no hindrance and no termination of its path. Yet this is *not* because the sphere just keeps spinning without any causal influence, the way we would think about a wheel that turns forever so long as it encounters no friction. Rather, the sphere is moved by an externally imposed force, namely the impetus given to it by God or an angel. (I realize that sounds strange, but we'll see why Buridan invokes an angel in Chapter 70.) Thus, even in the perfect, obstacle-free realm of the stars, there is no inertia, only the implanted power of impetus.

Let's conclude by stepping back from all these theories and asking about the methods that gave rise to them. The frequent appeals to concrete cases, all those thrown projectiles, boats, and falling rocks, may suggest that we are here seeing the rise of science based on observation. But rarely, if ever, do we get the sense that authors like Marchia, Ockham, or Buridan made a special effort to observe such phenomena, never mind carefully measuring them. Like the advances made by the Oxford Calculators, these were conceptual breakthroughs, not triumphs of experiment.[23] Indeed fourteenth-century physics often involves thought experiments that could never be conducted in real life. Appeal was made to God's absolute power, that is, the divine capacity to bring about any logically possible state of affairs, like the perfect sphere touching the perfect plane. These discussions of motion, divisibility, matter, and so on made constant reference to Aristotle by way of his greatest commentator, Averroes. But my hunch is that a different Muslim thinker helped inspire the use of this sort of thought experiment: Avicenna. His famous "flying man" argument, much discussed in Latin Christendom, asks us to suppose that God creates a mature human in midair.[24] Perhaps medieval science owed as much to Avicenna's startling method of argument as it did to the astronomical tables and astrologers of the Islamic world.

65

PORTRAIT OF THE ARTIST
JOHN BURIDAN

Can a medieval philosopher be fashionable? We'll probably never see Hildegard of Bingen's music feature in the pop charts, or teenagers ensuring that #HenryofGhent trends on Twitter. But even among scholars of medieval philosophy there are trends and fashions. As I've mentioned, Thomas Aquinas is nowadays like a television sitcom that has been running for too many seasons: still beloved but overly familiar. Who then is the hipster's scholastic philosopher? Actually, Henry of Ghent is a candidate, and certainly Scotus has received a lot of attention in recent scholarship. But as far as I can tell, the most fashionable choice these days is John Buridan. The last few chapters have already given a sense of why this should be. His name has come up numerous times as we've looked at fourteenth century developments in logic and natural philosophy. But there's more at play here than historical importance. Buridan speaks to the concerns of today's analytic philosophers, who for better or worse are today's arbiters of what counts as cool in the history of philosophy.[1] He shares their technical virtuosity, their enthusiasm for empirical science and equal impatience for extravagant metaphysics. And perhaps most importantly, his philosophy seems to be resolutely non-religious.

Obviously, Buridan was no atheist, and theological issues inevitably come up in his works from time to time. Usually, though, he mentions such issues simply to explain that they are above his pay grade, because he is not a theologian but a master of arts. As far as we know,[2] Buridan never even attempted to get a higher degree, and remained a teacher in the arts faculty in Paris for about forty years, from the 1320s until his death around 1361. One might wonder whether Buridan lacked ambition or perhaps fell foul of some sort of political intrigue? Apparently not the latter, as he was supported with numerous stipends during his time at Paris. Rather, it seems that the faculty of arts suited Buridan's interests, which lay with the study of logic and the other sciences covered by Aristotle, like natural philosophy and ethics. At one point he asks why the arts faculty is lower than those of theology, medicine, or law. His answer is a pointed one: the arts faculty may have less money but it studies more fundamental things, since logic and natural philosophy provide the principles for the higher disciplines.[3]

Because Buridan did not become a theologian we have no lectures from him on the *Sentences* of Peter Lombard, as we do for other major late medieval thinkers like Scotus and Ockham. But there is plenty to read nonetheless, starting with numerous commentaries on Aristotle, including the *Physics* and *Ethics* as well as all the logical treatises. These systematic accounts of Aristotle were extremely influential in subsequent generations, not only in Paris but also at the new universities that emerged in Central and Eastern Europe (Chapter 76). Equally important was the work that must count as Buridan's greatest achievement, the massive *Compendium of Dialectic* (*Summulae de dialectica*).[4] A substantial reworking and expansion of an earlier logical compendium written by Peter of Spain about a century earlier, Buridan's *Compendium* would become a standard textbook of logic in the medieval university. It epitomizes what would come to be called the *via moderna*, the nominalist approach to logic and philosophy as a whole.

For Buridan's young students, learning logic was probably like being made to eat their vegetables. But for Buridan himself, logic is a nourishing meal in itself, served in nine courses. This is the number of treatises in his *Summulae*, devoted to the various branches of logic we've already discussed, like category theory, supposition theory, consequences, demonstrations, sophisms, and so on. For Buridan, logic as a whole is a practically oriented discipline with two aspects. First, there is what he calls "theoretical logic (*logica docens*)," from which we learn how to put together arguments in principle. Second, there is "applied logic (*logica utens*)," where logic is actually being deployed to argue for a given conclusion.[5] So the logic student is acquiring a skill (a *habitus*) that will serve him in good stead, no matter what kind of discourse he may want to interpret or produce.

In keeping with this practical conception of logic, Buridan is keenly interested in the way language is actually used in real texts and arguments. It's in part on this basis that he rejects the approach of the speculative grammarians (the *modistae*) who had dominated this subject a couple of generations before and were still active in his day (Chapter 44). It's futile to infer the function of a word from its grammatical form, because natural languages just don't work that way. Buridan gives the nice example of verbs that are grammatically active, yet passive in meaning, like "to receive."[6] One response might be to purify natural language, working with an ideal version of Latin free of such unfortunate deviations from true logical form. This is not Buridan's way, and for good reason. He thinks that language is thoroughly conventional, with meaning determined by the intentions of language users.

He defends this picture of language in a number of ways. One of the more spectacular is a thought experiment. Suppose that there were a cataclysm in which our language is entirely lost. A new language might then arise in which the word "donkey" is used to refer to animals in general. In this situation—probably the least frightening post-apocalyptic scenario ever envisioned—it would be true to say "A human is a donkey," because "donkey" would mean what "animal" means now.[7] Buridan also considers more realistic cases, as when language is used metaphorically or ironically. (If you want to hear terms being used to supposit in an unusual way, just hang out with teenagers.) This is not to say that language is a free-for-all where every term acquires its meaning anew on each occasion of use. Normally, when we say "donkey," we are referring to donkeys, and this normal or "proper" use needs to be explained somehow. Buridan's suggestion is one case where his ideas resonate with modern-day proposals. Like some contemporary philosophers of language, he thinks that words initially receive their meaning in a kind of "baptism" in which a word is initially imposed on a certain thing. The clearest case would be giving a proper name to an individual, as parents do when a baby is born. Even in this case, meaning is set by the intentions of language users, in this case the parents. To this extent, the assignment of a word's primary meaning is like "deviant" cases, as when a teenager is asked how she is doing and grunts "Fine." Here, too, the teenager's intention determines the word's meaning, namely that it is none of your business.

Buridan avails himself of Ockham's idea that the same mental concepts can be expressed in different conventional signs. Regarding the example of the language apocalypse, he says that the word "donkey" would come to represent the same thing at the mental level as the word "animal" represents now. While this does sound very much like Ockham, Buridan is less inclined to think of concepts in strictly linguistic terms.[8] For him, language is conventional, whereas our minds latch onto things in the world via a natural process of concept formation. Buridan's explanation of how this occurs is thoroughly nominalistic.[9] As he puts it, "Whatever exists outside the soul does so in reality as an individual, that is, distinct from all else." Our access to those things outside the soul is through sensation of individual things, which is why it makes sense to speak of Buridan as an "empiricist." Once you have encountered individual donkeys, your mind can entertain a "singular concept" of each specific donkey, and also form a universal concept of donkeys in general.

It may seem that the nominalist's main problem is to account for the latter phenomenon. If there are no real universals, then how do we form universal concepts? But Buridan actually thinks this is quite straightforward. Individual donkeys obviously resemble one another: the long ears, the big dark eyes, the rich and distinctive scent. To form a notion of donkeys, we simply "abstract" these shared features, ignoring the properties that belong to only one donkey, like your donkey's name, its location in your barn, or its tendency to step on your foot. A realist like Scotus or Burley would, of course, insist that the similarity between donkeys is the result of their having a real common nature. Buridan dismisses this idea, though. If mere likeness is enough to justify positing a common nature, then such natures will proliferate uncontrollably. Suppose your donkey does step on your foot. In the moment it does so, it becomes like everything else that steps on anyone's foot. But surely this is not in virtue of some real common nature.

He (Buridan, not the donkey) finds it somewhat more puzzling how we can have *singular* concepts. This is because we are not completely reliable in reidentifying individual things. If I snuck into your barn and replaced your donkey with mine, you might not notice it until the donkey failed to step on your foot all the time. Or you might run into my identical twin brother and apply your concept of me to him. As far as I know, Buridan didn't have a twin brother, but he gives an equally compelling example. Suppose you are at sea and fall asleep. Upon waking, you will not be able to see that the ship has drifted, because you cannot tell one part of the water from another.[10] In light of this, Buridan thinks that a singular concept can only ever be tied to an individual upon actually sensing that individual. As he puts it, the thing must be "in the prospect (*in prospectu*)" of the cognizing person. This means that if you have not had an individual be in your physical presence, you can only ever grasp them under a description that could in theory apply to other individuals. It's only in this weaker sense that we have a "singular concept" of Buridan, for example, since none of us has ever met him.

The realist will, of course, find this whole account inadequate. Here's one reason why. Buridan has said that we grasp things universally simply by focusing on features found in many individuals; outside the soul, it is only the individuals that are real. But in that case, can't we just divide up the world however we like? Instead of contrasting donkeys with humans, we could contrast those creatures that step on people's feet with those that don't. The former may be a more useful kind of classification but it would be no more rooted in the common natures of things, because things have no real common natures. Furthermore, doesn't this undermine Aristotelian science? According to Aristotle, a proper demonstration that yields true understanding must be universal in scope and must also get at *essential* properties. How can we retain this idea if we accept that our universal concepts are just based on any old likenesses?

In discussing this challenge, Buridan expert Gyula Klima has contrasted realist essentialism with what he calls "predicate essentialism."[11] He explains that, for Buridan, an "essential predicate" will be a feature that things must have in order to keep existing. Thus, all donkeys need to have the predicates "living" and "non-rational" if they are to remain the same individuals as they are now. By contrast "stepping on someone's foot" is a property that a given donkey can have and then lose, much to the relief of its victim. This is why we will never encounter a donkey that is not alive or that is rational, whereas we occasionally encounter donkeys that are not stepping on anyone's foot. Hence the universality of a statement in Aristotelian science, such as "All donkeys are alive." In Buridan's technical terms, this is a matter of "ampliation." By speaking of *all* donkeys, we "ampliate" the word "donkey" so that it refers to every individual donkey that exists now, that ever has existed, or ever will exist. Every one of these donkeys is alive and non-rational, and must remain so if it is to avoid being destroyed. For Buridan, this is all we mean by the contrast between essential and accidental predicates, and it is enough to suit the requirements set down in Aristotle's philosophy of science.

All this talk of donkeys will probably put you in mind of the most famous idea ascribed to Buridan. Where Ockham had a razor, Buridan had an ass. He is famous for devising the example of a hungry donkey or ass that is presented with two equally tempting bales of hay. Would the donkey be able to choose arbitrarily between the two bales? Or would it just stand there starving to death? Obviously the latter answer is, well, asinine. Surely the donkey would indeed just choose some hay and start eating. But how is this possible? It would seem, after all, that we choose to do one thing rather than another precisely because we judge it to be preferable. In the case of the donkey, this explanation is not available—neither bale of hay can be preferred to the other—yet choice seems to occur nonetheless. It's unfortunate that Buridan is so famous for having invented this intriguing puzzle, because in fact he didn't. For one thing, it was invented quite a bit earlier, by the Muslim theologian al-Ghazālī. Admittedly, his version of the problem is donkey-free, and instead asks us to imagine a human choosing between two equally appealing dates.[12] For another thing, the donkey example actually never appears in Buridan's writings. It was used by later authors when they discussed his position on free will.

Let's take a look then at what Buridan does say about human freedom.[13] He tends to break with the voluntarism of Scotus and Ockham, returning to a more "intellectualist" account like that we found in Aquinas. According to this position, choice is simply the will's execution of a judgment reached by the intellect. That seems true to our experience of making decisions, where we do usually choose what seems upon reflection to be the best course of action. Yet it seems that, sometimes, the will fails to follow the dictates of reason. Or does it? Buridan thinks that it can, but only in a very limited way. One cannot simply reject one's own overall best judgment about what to do and do something different. When your will seems to be overwhelming your capacity for judgment, it is actually that capacity for judgment that is causing the problem. Suppose that, despite being an animal lover, you give in to anger and beat your donkey because it steps on your foot. Here your judgment that it would be good to seek revenge has temporarily overwhelmed your general conviction that animals should be treated with kindness.

But Buridan does make an important exception. The will can "defer" following reason in cases where the situation seems uncertain. Suppose you see a succulent apple on a shelf. You are hungry and judge that it would be good to eat the apple. But you might wait before eating it, just in case. Perhaps the apple has a worm in it; perhaps it is really a ceramic apple that would break your teeth; perhaps some other more tempting food will come along soon; perhaps your donkey will be hungry and your donkey loves apples. You needn't have just one specific belief that undermines the judgment in favor of eating an apple. Indeed, if you did, then that would be a case where reason judges that the apple should *not* be eaten. Rather, you hold off because your will is adopting a cautious "wait and see" attitude. The rational judgment is not rejected but filed under things to be done later when the time seems right. The will might also do this when the thing that seems best to the intellect is particularly daunting and difficult. So now we can see why the donkey and the bales of hay would be a puzzle worth putting to Buridan, or even a mockery of his position: put in that situation, would the donkey just "defer" acting indefinitely? Presumably his answer would simply be that if donkeys had reason and free choice (in fact, he thinks they don't), then the donkey would simply judge that it should pick one bale of hay at random and start eating. Nothing in Buridan's view would seem to foreclose this rather banal response.[14]

Buridan's treatment of freedom is unusual in another respect: he feels the need to respond to skeptical worries about whether we are indeed capable of free choice. Denying this would, he thinks, be pernicious in religious, scientific, and moral terms.[15] He also considers it simply evident from experience that we do make choices all the time. Nonetheless, Buridan admits, it is not possible to *prove* that we are free. Sometimes medieval thinkers say that a certain proposition is unprovable precisely because it is so obvious. As Aristotle observed, demonstrations should use more obvious ("better-known") premises to establish less obvious conclusions. It is at best pointless and at worst methodologically incoherent to try to prove something blindingly obvious. But that doesn't seem to be quite what Buridan means here. Though he considers it evident that we are free, he also considers this an "exalted" topic of inquiry that may elude our capacity for scientific demonstration.

This slightly uncomfortable combination—confidence in what seems evident to us, coupled with an awareness of the fallibility of human reasoning—also characterizes Buridan's response to his fellow Parisian Nicholas of Autrecourt. Nicholas mounted a case for skepticism that was unprecedented in the medieval period, for both its sophistication and its potentially far-reaching implications. Answering this challenge, Buridan decides to move the epistemological goalposts. He argues that we can consider ourselves to be capable of certain knowledge, so long as we have a properly modest understanding of what "certainty" involves. As we'll see, Buridan's vocation as an arts master will be relevant here. Confronted with skeptical arguments that appeal to God's power to deceive us and confound our expectations, he simply says that such worries are not his concern. Of course, God can perform miracles, but that is a matter Buridan is happy to leave to the theologians.

66

SEEING IS BELIEVING
NICHOLAS OF AUTRECOURT'S
SKEPTICAL CHALLENGE

Is having knowledge more like being pregnant or more like being hungry? Pregnancy is an all or nothing affair, like being alive or being located above the equator. Either you are or you aren't. Being hungry, by contrast, admits of degrees, taking in everything from Winnie the Pooh's hankering for a little something to the ravenous and permanently unquenched appetite of the Cookie Monster. If knowing is like this, then you could have more or less certain knowledge of things. You would presumably be prepared to say that you know how old you are. But if pushed, you might admit that while you do know this, you aren't as absolutely certain about it as you are about, say, the fact that two plus two equals four. After all, one could devise remotely possible scenarios according to which your actual age is different. Perhaps in your first year of life you were mixed up with another baby who had a different birthday, or perhaps your parents are spies who falsified your birth certificate. If you start taking such scenarios really seriously, you might conclude that you don't really know how old you are after all. Then you would be starting to think that knowing is like being pregnant. Real knowledge would require the highest degree of certainty, and if this sort of certainty is absent, then knowledge too would be lacking.

Often it is the skeptic who insists that knowledge is like this. The philosopher who leaps to mind immediately is Descartes. In his *Meditations* he famously subjected all his beliefs to rigorous doubt, inspecting them to see whether any of them rose to the level of absolute certainty. But Descartes was not the first to advance such a demanding test for knowledge. It was a challenge already issued by the Academic Skeptics in antiquity.[1] They took their cue from the Stoics, who assumed that knowledge is indeed like pregnancy, an all-or-nothing cognitive state that rules out all possibility of error. The Academics argued that no belief has guaranteed certainty, so by the Stoics' demanding epistemological standards we should admit that we know nothing (as Socrates did). Though a work by the later ancient Skeptic

456

Sextus Empiricus was translated into Latin around the turn of the fourteenth century, it doesn't seem to have had much impact, and we might easily suppose that the religious confidence of the medievals would have prevented them from seriously exploring skepticism anyway. But if we did suppose this, we ourselves would fall into error. In fact a number of fourteenth-century thinkers mounted serious skeptical challenges, albeit without necessarily embracing skepticism in the end.[2]

Among them was Nicholas of Autrecourt. Born around 1300, he was a contemporary of John Buridan at Paris, lecturing on theology there around the 1330s. He provides us with another entry in our melancholy list of medieval thinkers who were condemned for their teachings. This occurred in 1346, with Nicholas retracting his problematic theses in 1347. It's an interesting and rather ironic case of condemnation. Typically, we assume that philosophers ran into trouble for embracing Aristotelian doctrines too enthusiastically, as with the Parisian masters targeted in 1277. But Nicholas' unacceptable teachings were part of his polemic *against* Aristotelianism. In the prologue of his late work *Exigit ordo executionis*, also known as the *Universal Treatise*,[3] he complained bitterly about scholastic contemporaries who endorsed every claim in Aristotle and Averroes as if it were a self-evident truth. Nicholas sought to undermine these pretensions and in so doing suggested that almost nothing can be known with certainty.

The occasion for this onslaught on scholastic theories of knowledge was an exchange of letters with a certain Bernard of Arezzo. Two of the nine letters Nicholas wrote to Bernard survive.[4] In the first letter, Nicholas draws out what he sees as the consequences of Bernard's own ideas about knowledge. These include the now familiar notion of "intuitive cognition," the sort of direct apprehension of something that we have in sensation, on the basis of which we judge that things exist. But, Bernard admitted, it could happen that we have an intuitive cognition of something that doesn't exist (§I.2). What he must have had in mind is a scenario like the one that worried Ockham. God might create in someone the impression that they are seeing something that isn't there, like by miraculously making me see Groucho Marx even though he is long dead. Ockham foresaw the potential of such hypothetical cases to undermine our knowledge. So he insisted that genuinely intuitive cognitions do not give rise to false beliefs. In the scenario just described, if I am really having an intuitive cognition of a nonexistent Groucho, that could only mean seeing Groucho while understanding that he is nonexistent. Thus, intuitive cognitions are reliable, and can still serve as the foundations of all our knowledge.[5]

But there is an obvious complaint to be made here, which duly came from that specialist in complaining about Ockham, Walter Chatton. He pointed out that if

God wants to, He can create in me the experience of seeing a nonexistent Groucho that is just like the impression I would have if I really saw Groucho. Thus, if we admit that such a miraculous event could involve an intuitive cognition, then we have to admit that such cognitions can be misleading after all. This is the scholastic version of later skeptical puzzles, like Descartes' evil demon hypothesis or, more recently, the cinematic scenario in which all of our experiences are in fact a computer generated alternate reality called the Matrix. Since the illusion case is indistinguishable from the case where we are having a normal experience, shouldn't we admit that all our normal experiences are, as far as we know, illusions?

We don't have wait for Descartes or Keanu Reeves to find an affirmative answer to this question. It is precisely what Nicholas of Autrecourt says in his letter to Bernard. We cannot infer with certainty that Groucho is really in front of us when we see him unless we assume that our experience is arising normally, and not thanks to a supernatural intervention or other deviant source. And since that assumption is not one we can make with certainty, we cannot ever be certain that what we are seeing is real (§1.6–7). Nicholas is not shy in pointing out the pervasive skepticism that is looming here. If intuitive cognitions give us no certainty about the existence of the things they report, then his correspondent Bernard cannot know whether the Pope exists or even whether he has a head. Nor could the Apostles have been sure that Christ was crucified or rose from the dead (§1.14). Seeing is believing, but it isn't knowing.

Is there anything of which we could still be certain in the face of these sweeping skeptical worries? Nicholas addresses himself to this question in a second letter, which offers a still more penetrating critique of Aristotelian epistemology. Aristotle and the tradition he inaugurated were committed to what is nowadays called "foundationalism," that is, the idea that all our knowledge rests on indubitable first principles. This must be so, since otherwise we would always need to justify every proposition we assert with reference to some further proposition, and this process would go on indefinitely.[6] Nicholas is ready to agree with the Aristotelians that there is one principle that is genuinely certain. He formulates it as follows: "Contradictories cannot be true at the same time (*contradictoria non possunt simul esse vera*)" (§2.2). Thus, while I might not be sure whether Groucho exists, I can at least be sure that Groucho does not both exist and not exist, or that he cannot be both pregnant and not pregnant (the latter would be the better bet here).

It's at this point that Nicholas shows himself to be a proponent of the all-or-nothing understanding of certain knowledge. Having granted the absolute certainty of this first principle of reasoning, he says that if anything else is to be genuinely certain, it must have the same status as that principle. Anything less certain than it will fall short of being completely evident. But this is an extraordinarily high standard for certainty. It means, as Nicholas points out, that nothing is certain unless supposing it to be false entails a contradiction (§2.3). Indeed, it might seem that nothing at all could be certain in this sense, apart from the very principle that contradictories cannot both be true. However, Nicholas concedes that there may be other truths that are, as he puts it, "reduced" to this first principle (§2.6).[7] These would be propositions where the subject and the predicate are somehow "really the same (*idem realiter*)" (§2.9). For example, if "human" is defined as "rational animal," it could be completely certain that humans are animals, since to deny this would be to contradict oneself. It would amount to saying that rational animal is not animal. Similarly he admits that from "A house exists" one can infer with total certainty that "A wall exists," since there can be no house without a wall (§2.17).

The catch is that, as we know from the first letter to Bernard, we can never have this level of certainty concerning the existence of any given house or any given human. The things we know for sure derive simply from the meanings of words. They never include anything that could on any scenario, no matter how far-fetched, be false. Nicholas' anti-Aristotelian motives become clearer as he spells out the consequences. For one thing, we cannot be sure that there are substances underlying the accidents of which we are aware.[8] It's natural to assume that there is a substance, namely a human, underlying the sounds and visible shapes we see when we are aware of Groucho. But it is not a straightforward contradiction to suppose that accidents exist in the absence of any substance to which they belong (§2.22, 4.13). Here it may be on Nicholas' mind that accidents do supposedly survive without their original substance in the case of the Eucharist, where the color and taste of bread persist even though the bread has miraculously become the body of Christ (see Chapter 47). So this is not just a bizarre, yet theoretically possible scenario. According to the Christian faith, it actually happens. For another thing, we cannot be sure about necessary causal connections between things (§4.14). Obviously, we are accustomed to expecting that fire will heat things up, but if this should fail to occur, no contradiction would result. Thus, our belief that a fire will heat a stone brought near to it falls short of true certainty, the certainty possessed by the first principle about contradictories. The upshot, as Nicholas gleefully remarks, is that all of Aristotle's physics and metaphysics is entirely deprived of certainty (§II.23).

But was Nicholas really seeking to replace the confident convictions of Aristotelian science with thoroughgoing skepticism? Apparently not. At the end of his first letter Nicholas mentions briefly that in disputations at the Sorbonne in Paris, he has affirmed the evident certainty of the deliverances of the senses and of our own actions (§1.15). It would have been nice to hear more about this. But it seems at least to indicate that Nicholas is far from embracing the skeptical implications he has just outlined. His point is rather that Bernard's more traditional scholastic position would lead to those disastrous implications. In fact, when Nicholas was later attacked for his teachings, he did emphasize that everything stated in his letters to Bernard was intended only as a dialectical refutation, not as a statement of his own views. Yet we may still wonder: in the face of his arguments, how could any confidence in our everyday beliefs be restored?

One obvious way out would be to reject Nicholas' assumption about the all-or-nothing nature of knowledge and certainty. This is how supporters of Aristotelian orthodoxy responded. A certain Master Giles wrote a letter to Nicholas in which he insisted that certainty does come in degrees (§3.13). Here we are back to the idea that knowledge is like being hungry, in that it admits of more and less. As Giles points out, Aristotle himself said that in a proper demonstration we should be more confident about our premises than the conclusion, since we are trying to reason from what we know better to what is as yet unknown. Yet the conclusion may, nonetheless, be certain, having been established through this very demonstration. Another, more subtle way to reply to Nicholas might be to say that whether one counts oneself as "certain" depends on context. The standards of certainty appropriate to mathematics are not the same as those appropriate to knowing how old I am. In mathematics all the certain truths are full-blown logical necessities. It would be unreasonable to demand that our everyday beliefs need to meet that standard.

A version of this answer was put forward by John Buridan.[9] He agreed that some principles are certain because denying them would involve embracing a contradiction. These would include such things as saying that human is animal. But not everything of which we are certain has certainty in this strongest degree. When we are doing natural philosophy, we should seek, and accept, the type of certainty relevant to natural things. This means that we are allowed to exclude the occurrence of miraculous examples like the ones that worried Ockham and Chatton. Sure, God can make accidents exist with no substance, prevent fire from burning things, or cause something to appear to exist when it does not. But when we are doing natural philosophy this is irrelevant, because the conclusions reached in that context are certain under the proviso that the causes involved are indeed natural, not supernatural.

Buridan's solution hearkens back to the stance of Boethius of Dacia, one of the so-called "Latin Averroists," in the thirteenth century. He too claimed the right to set aside theological possibilities while doing physics. Thus, he could show that the world is eternal because no natural motion can arise from nothing, while admitting that this conclusion is overturned once we take into account supernatural creation by God (Chapter 43). This sort of response is actually one that Nicholas anticipated himself. He pointed out that certainty about the deliverances of the senses can be secured so long as one assumes that no miracle is taking place, but, with his typically demanding approach, added that that assumption is itself uncertain. I tend to think that Buridan is right, though. The best way to answer the skeptic is not to show that our knowledge can survive radical scenarios, like miracles, evil demons, or the Matrix. It is to say that that test is too demanding, and that our beliefs can count as knowledge even if we cannot absolutely rule out the possibility that the beliefs are false.

Nicholas himself seems to have realized this. In the aforementioned *Universal Treatise*, he too lowers the bar for human knowledge, albeit in a different way than Buridan.[10] Here Nicholas still insists that complete certainty is nearly impossible to achieve. He even goes so far as to say that the principle about contradictories, acknowledged in his second letter as the sole example of absolute certainty, may not be so certain after all. He imagines someone being habituated to suppose that two contradictory things could both be true. Instead of embracing radical skepticism, though, he admits that we may not need absolute certainty anyway. We should instead accept that our grasp of the truth is, as Nicholas puts it, merely "probable." This means that we have better reason to affirm the belief than deny it, perhaps much better reason, without being able actually to prove it beyond all possible doubt. The human mind is able to find itself "at rest" in endorsing such beliefs, confident of being right while still accepting the theoretical possibility of being wrong.

But if we are expecting Nicholas to restore the teachings of Aristotelian scholasticism, with the sole caveat that they are probable rather than certain, we have another thing coming. We've seen other scholastics of this period flirting with the idea that there could be atoms, indivisible components of which perceptible bodies are made. Nicholas doesn't just flirt with this idea: he asks it to come home with him for the night and makes it breakfast in the morning. In themselves, he argues, the components of the universe are eternal. When we seem to see substances being generated and destroyed, in fact we are seeing eternal atoms combining and separating. This revisionary account of physical change goes nicely with his continued doubts about the causes invoked by Aristotelian thinkers. Like al-Ghazālī before him and David Hume after him, Nicholas suggests that experience of the connection between events only yields an expectation that things will be similar in the future. His examples here are well chosen: the way that magnets attract iron and the efficacy of medicine. In these cases the medievals had no clear understanding of the relation between cause and effect, only a habit of expecting the iron to move towards the magnet and of the disease to be cured.[11]

Nicholas of Autrecourt was not the only one to voice skeptical ideas around the middle of the fourteenth century.[12] Similar worries about causation can be found in John of Mirecourt, another Parisian thinker who was censured in 1347, the same year that Nicholas was forced to recant his views. For John, too, the knowledge that a cause will yield an effect lacks the certainty possessed by a certain first principle. In England similar concerns were raised by Robert Holcot, who emphasized the absolute power of God to stop causes from working normally. Even when heat does follow fire, this does not prove that fire caused it, any more than the fact that people get afraid in the dark shows that darkness is the cause of fear. More radical still was the Oxford theologian Nicholas Aston. For him, we can never be certain about anything unless it is necessarily true, and nothing outside of God is necessary. In theory at least, this banishes all common-sense belief from the realm of genuine knowledge. Aston gives some memorable examples, for instance that there is no outright contradiction involved in the same person being in two places at the same time. If this is possible, then it should also be possible for a person to walk up to another version of himself and cut off his own head! Aston also addressed himself to a question raised long before by Peter Damian (Chapter 6), asserting that God can change the past, since no necessary truths would be violated were He to do so.[13]

What accounts for this spread of skeptical concerns in the fourteenth century? The most obvious explanation is that scholastics were impressed by God's power to do anything that is logically possible. With this threat lurking in the background, all knowledge about the created world would seem to be, as it were, marked with an asterisk. It may be true that fire heats, that substances underlie accidents, and that people can't be in more than one place at a time, but all of these truths presuppose that God is not overturning them by performing a miracle. On the other hand, it's not as if God's omnipotence was only discovered in the fourteenth century. Earlier medievals likewise asserted that God can do anything that is logically possible, without then engaging in the sort of skeptical worries we've just been discussing.[14] Remember, too, that Nicholas' skeptical challenge was incited by a more technical and specific doctrine, namely the idea that an intuitive cognition can have a non-existent object. So, while late medieval skepticism did involve allusions to miracles, it may have had its roots more in the epistemology of the time than in any fear that the good Christian God could sometimes act like Descartes' evil demon.

67

ON THE MONEY
MEDIEVAL ECONOMIC THEORY

S uppose you are a medieval merchant, traveling with a wagonload of grain to a town where grain is in short supply. Given the circumstances, you know that you'll be able to sell your goods for a high price, perhaps double or triple the usual going rate. You also happen to know that, only one day's travel behind you, another much larger shipment of grain is headed towards the same city. Do you have the obligation to reveal this to your customers, forgoing your advantage and selling at the normal price? Your answer might depend on whether you've read Thomas Aquinas. In his *Summa theologiae* he asks what a merchant in this situation ought to do (2.2 Q77 a3 obj 4). His answer is that the bounds of justice do not require divulging information that would reduce the price, even though it would be particularly admirable were the merchant honest enough to do so. A similar example is considered by Henry of Ghent, who allows someone to buy a horse and then sell it in the same city at a higher price only one hour later, if in the intervening time all other horses on the market have been taken away from the city on ships.[1]

Awareness of the phenomenon goes back to the dawn of Greek philosophy. A story about the Pre-Socratic philosopher Thales has him buying up all the olive oil presses to reap a windfall from a bumper crop of olives he had predicted. We know that anecdote because it is mentioned in Aristotle's *Politics* (1259a) in the midst of a discussion of financial exchange, to illustrate the concept of a monopoly. It's a text that left the medievals with complicated feelings on the subject of money and money-making. While Aristotle recognizes what he calls a "natural" art of dealing with money, which needs to be practiced by householders and politicians, he is disdainful of the "unnatural" pursuit of boundless wealth and of those who see money as an end in itself (1257b–58a). Rather, as Aristotle had already explained in the *Ethics*, money is really an instrument of exchange that allows us to trade very different goods—Aristotle's example is shoes and houses—by introducing a common measure of value. The exchange between buyer and seller will be "just" when that exchange is equal, with both sides getting something equivalent in value to what they give up (*Ethics* 1133a).

This may seem like no more than common sense. If I persuade you to sell me your house in exchange for a single shoe, then surely I have behaved unjustly, if not illegally (come to think of it, maybe the old woman who lived in a shoe was the victim of this very scam). But the cases described by Aquinas and Henry show that things must be more complicated. It seems strange that a horse could be equal in value to one gold coin at noon and to five gold coins an hour later only because the other horses have departed on ships. Or consider the following scenario. You have a horse, and a farmer needs a horse to bring in his harvest. So in exchange for one gold coin you let the farmer use the horse for a week. At the end of the bargain, you have a gold coin and the horse you started with, whereas the farmer has none of your property. That doesn't look like an equal exchange; yet the farmer doesn't feel cheated in any way.

Or imagine that you are a moneychanger who greets people as they come over the border from Germany into France. Let's say that you are exchanging German currency for French coins of equivalent value, because the German coins are not legal tender in France. It seems a valuable service and your customers are perfectly willing to avail themselves of it, even though you take a small profit on each trade, receiving a hundred gold German coins and paying out only ninety-nine French coins. The exchange is evidently not equal, because you hand over less money than you took. But does that mean an injustice was committed? Or, finally, take a case of what the medievals called "usury." You need to pay your rent so you borrow some money from your friend the farmer. The farmer agrees to lend you ten gold coins for a month, at the end of which you should pay him eleven gold coins. In this case, the farmer gives you ten coins and after a month's wait gets eleven back. It's a clear case of injustice by Aristotle's definition. And in his *Politics* he does not hesitate to condemn it, saying that it is like breeding "offspring" (*tokos*, also the Greek word for "interest") from something that is, in fact, barren, and adding that usury is the most unnatural of all ways to make money (1258b).

The scholastics gave careful thought to these matters, and not only because they were in the business of commenting on Aristotle. The medieval university was itself a business, with the relation between teacher and student involving monetary exchange. Certain positions at the university could bring with them further financial obligations. For instance, Nicole Oresme, who is going to feature towards the end of this chapter, was made grand master of his college at the University of Paris in the 1350s, a role which would have involved dealing with the college's expenditures. Oresme was also one of the thinkers who pioneered the use of mathematics to analyze motion, quality, and other physical phenomena (Chapter 63). It's been speculated that daily involvement in finance could even have been a spur to such breakthroughs.[2] After all, once you are used to using the abstract numerical measure of money to express the value of horses and ships, houses and shoes, it might seem all but obvious to apply numerical measures to motions and qualities.

You might be skeptical of this, on the grounds that money had been there all along. As we just saw, Aristotle already discussed it in some detail. Fair enough, but in the days of the scholastics there was a lot *more* money than there had been in the past. This is true in a quite literal sense: in England, there was thirty times as much currency in circulation in 1300 as there had been in the late eleventh century.[3] The "monetization" of medieval culture went hand in hand with the rise of market towns and growth of cities, which unfolded through the later Middle Ages. The universities emerged at the same time, part of that same story of urbanization. The scholastics duly brought to their reading of Aristotle a considerable awareness of the realities of economic life. This is evident in their handling of the problem we started with: what determines the value of the goods in an economic exchange?[4]

Aristotle had stated in his *Ethics* that justice is achieved when buyer and seller both get equal value out of the deal, and that money is used to facilitate such equal exchanges. This is compatible with the idea that everything you can buy or sell has an absolute, intrinsic value. A horse might be worth one hundred shoes, for instance. Aristotle seems to teach that if the ship has sailed with all the other horses and you demand the value of three hundred shoes for the horse, you might be able to extract this exorbitant amount from a customer, but you would be doing them an injustice. Yet the medievals could find a rather different idea in the *Digest* of Justinian, one of the main sources for their legal thinking. There, we read that the correct price of something is simply whatever the market will bear. This suggests that Aristotle was wrong. Things have no determinate value, and if you can get someone to trade you a house for a single shoe, then on that occasion the house and the shoe have the same value. Roman law complicated matters further, though, by allowing for legal redress if something is sold for less than half of its worth. That brings us back to the idea that commodities do have a "true value" independent of what they fetch on any given occasion.

The problem was solved, or at least mitigated, by medieval legal commentators like Accursius. When he came to the *Digest*'s remark that "A thing is worth what it can be sold for (*res tantum valet quantum vendi potest*)," he added the phrase "that is, commonly (*scilicet communiter*)."[5] So here we are getting to the fundamental insight that correct price is determined by the market in general and not by intrinsic equality or agreement in a one-off trade between two individuals. We might still wonder, though, what leads the market to converge on a thing's price. If a horse costs one hundred times as much as a shoe in medieval France, does that mean that the medieval French thought that horses are one hundred times better than shoes? Not quite, as Aquinas points out by using an example taken from Augustine: in the true order of things a mouse is worth much more than a pearl, because a mouse is a living creature, whereas a pearl is inanimate. Yet no one would accept a mouse in exchange for a pearl (unless they were a cat). So market price clearly does not reflect the genuine intrinsic value of things.

Rather, Aquinas suggests, it reflects people's need (*indigentia*) for the thing being sold. He makes this point in his commentary on Aristotle's *Ethics*, which already mentioned that money is somehow a measure of need or demand for a certain thing (1133a). Aquinas' teacher Albert had connected this to the behavior of society as a whole, rather than a given individual's need for something on a given occasion, saying that money is a measure of something's value "insofar as it is useful to the community."[6] Another thirteenth-century thinker, Peter Olivi, observed that price fluctuates in response to supply as well as demand. This is why air is free despite our constant and urgent need for it, and why grain prices shoot up during times of shortage and fall after a plentiful harvest.[7] Hence the cases I mentioned at the start of this chapter, like the high price of grain in a starving city. Such cases show that the "just price" of something may vary considerably depending on circumstances, so that something's "usefulness to the community" is not just a timeless abstraction. A more fine-grained attitude towards demand is also found in John Buridan, who astutely noticed that a person's "need (*indigentia*)" for something can be relative to that person's economic situation. A nobleman who cannot afford a fine new warhorse is hardly suffering from deprivation, but is still in a sense "poor" relative to his perceptions of his own needs. The leading historian of medieval economic theory, Odd Langholm, pointed out that with this observation Buridan was getting close to the modern-day notion of "effective demand."[8]

There is yet another factor that determines the price of things. In addition to supply and demand—of the whole market or only a part of it—there is the "added value" involved in bringing the goods to market in the first place. Grain needed to be harvested, prepared, and transported to those market towns, and when luxury goods reached Latin Christendom from the Islamic or Byzantine worlds, the costs of transport were much higher. These costs had to be factored into the price. The scholastics noticed this too. Duns Scotus defended the idea that merchants do earn the profits they take on trading precisely because of the risk and labor they have invested.[9] Thus, medieval analysis of justice in economic life led to a gradual softening of attitudes towards the life of money-making. It had long been a commonplace to say that the very existence of private property was a result of humanity's fall from grace. Were it not for original sin, things would be shared peacefully in common. Aquinas spelled out the consequences with a remark about human nature that Communists 650 years later would have done well to heed: were all things held in common, "everyone would avoid doing any work and leave to others that which concerns the community" (ST 2.2, Q66 a2).

Given the connection between economics and human frailty, it's hardly surprising to find Christian texts from late antiquity onwards warning that the life of the merchant is unusually liable to sin. It is much like the life of the soldier, except that the merchant's sins have to do with greed and dishonesty rather than violence. Here, for once, there seemed to be a perfect fit between church teaching and Aristotle, since, as we saw, he inveighed against the "unnaturalness" of building up wealth, and especially any practice that tries to make a profit from money itself. From a modern-day point of view, this seems completely wrongheaded. We understand that banks need to charge interest on loans and that it will cost us a bit of money to exchange currencies. Again, the medievals were not totally blind to this fact. A remarkable discussion of profit on loans is found in Durandus of St. Pourçain. He realized that moneylending is actually quite useful, yet still feels it is a rather squalid business. So he suggests that the state could appoint an official moneylender to play this role for the whole community, something Langholm calls "a bit of wishful thinking which for a moment shatters the boundaries of medieval thought about money and credit."[10]

The reason that medievals were so reluctant to concede the right to make money from loans is that it constitutes usury, considered an abomination by both Aristotle and Christian doctrine—the religious injunction traces back to biblical passages like Luke 6:35, "lend, hoping for nothing again." So it was uncontroversial that usury was wicked. The question was why. Aquinas defines usury as a case in which someone sells somebody else "something that does not exist (id quod non est)" (ST 2.2 Q78 a1). What he means is that money is a so-called "fungible" commodity, which is used up when it is spent, just as food is used up when it is eaten. Normally, if you lend someone a fungible good, then the lender has to return it or an equivalent. If you borrow a loaf of bread from me, you owe me a loaf of bread later, not a loaf of bread plus a blueberry muffin. Analogously, it is unjust to lend someone money and expect back the same money plus a fee.[11] Another argument had it that the usurer is actually selling something, namely time. The point here is that if you borrow ten coins for a year, after which you owe eleven coins, then you have paid one coin for the year during which you had the money. But if time belongs to anyone, it is God and certainly not the usurer.

There is an obvious problem here, namely that usury is incredibly useful and even essential to a well-run economy. As you probably know, Jews were grudgingly allowed to step into the gap, since they were under no religious injunction to avoid lending on interest, at least to non-Jews.[12] The implications for the history of anti-Semitism in Europe were, of course, vast (just think of Shakespeare's character Shylock). Still, given the careful attention the scholastics were paying to the function of money and markets, it was all but inevitable that they would at least begin to qualify their own injunction against moneylending. Here, a major advance was made by Gerald Odonis, who became head of the Franciscan order in 1329.[13] He realized that someone who lends money is actually giving up more than just the sum that has been borrowed. He is taking a risk that it will not be returned. Then, there is the profit the lender could have made off the money by putting it to work during the time it was lent out. The key insight here is that the usurer is not selling time, but the *use* of the money during the time of the loan. Thus, the so-called "usurer" is justified in charging interest to cover his risk and the profit he has forgone. This leaves Odonis in the awkward position of having to explain why usury is forbidden at all. Of course, we can still say that it is wrong to charge interest *in excess* of the hidden costs of lending. But also, Odonis added, the exchange involved in usury is not really a case of mutual consent. The borrower does enter into the contract voluntarily, but would much rather have been able to use the money without the added fee. So, in this sense, there is still some compulsion involved. Of course, this is patently unconvincing. It would be like saying that I exert compulsion on you when selling you a horse for money, since you would rather have had it for free.

Despite Odonis' nuanced discussion, it remained the case that just about the worst thing you could say about an economic transaction was to compare it to usury. A good illustration can be found in what may be the most extraordinary medieval text on economics, the first treatise on the nature of money itself: Nicole Oresme's diatribe against the debasement of currency.[14] This was a depressingly common feature of medieval life in general and fourteenth-century France in particular. The king would repeatedly call in the old currency and replace it with new coins, which would contain a smaller proportion of gold and silver. This would allow the state to profit by keeping the extra precious metal for itself. For Oresme, currency debasement is indeed like usury because it tries to generate something from what is itself barren (§16). Actually, it is even worse, because at least the usurer gets his victim to agree to a contract, whereas the king debases the currency without the consent of the community (§17). It violates the very nature of money, which is an "instrument of trade" (§3) owned in general by the whole community, and in particular by the person who earned a given quantity of money (§6). It is not the king's to do with as he will.

Oresme's defense of the integrity of money is remarkable in at least two ways. First, there is his extremely positive attitude towards money itself. While it can be put to perverted uses by the greedy, it is vital to the maintenance of society. He even ascribes to divine providence the existence of gold and silver, which are so perfect for turning into coins. Precious metal is durable, portable, and rare enough to retain its value, something ensured by nature herself when she thwarts the attempts of alchemists to make gold (§2). Second, there is Oresme's penetrating analysis of the drawbacks of debasement. He sees that currency itself can become a sort of commodity whose value is sensitive to market forces. At one point he even anticipates the law that "Bad money drives out good," called "Gresham's law" after an advisor to Queen Elizabeth I who hit upon a similar realization. The version of the problem noticed by Oresme is that when currency is debased, older coins are hoarded or taken abroad, because they have more gold and silver in them than the new coins despite their identical face value (§20).[15] The observation is remarkable in part because Oresme does not complain about the citizens who engage in hoarding and speculation. Rather, he blames the king, who should anticipate such consequences and avoid creating conditions where such speculation is bound to ensue.

This treatise would by itself justify Nicole Oresme's claim to be among the more interesting thinkers of the mid-fourteenth century. He showed that theoretical discussions of money could play a role in guiding government policy: a sound currency depends on a sound understanding of currency. But Oresme had still more to offer. We've already seen that he contributed to the scientific advances of the period, and he was also a key figure in another important development of the fourteenth century, the emergence of vernacular languages as a context for philosophy. Oresme translated his own treatise on money into French, and also rendered Aristotle's *Ethics* and *Politics* into this language for the French king, Charles V. We've met vernacular authors in previous chapters, like Marguerite Porete, Dante, Hadewijch, and Mechthild of Magdeburg. In the rest of this book non-Latin literature is going to resurface as a major theme, beginning with writers who wrote in the "awful German language."

DOWN TO THE GROUND
MEISTER ECKHART

Mark Twain's essay on the awfulness of German concludes with proposals for reform and, failing that, the suggestion that it "ought to be gently and reverently set aside among the dead languages, for only the dead have time to learn it." If you've ever tried to render the different pronunciations of the verbs "push (*drücken*)" and "print (*drucken*)" in German while a native speaker repeatedly tells you that you're doing it wrong, you will probably sympathize with him. In comparison Latin is a beautifully logical and rational language whose structures map on perfectly to the nature of reality itself, at least according to the medieval speculative grammarians. Yet it was still a major advance when philosophers who were rough contemporaries of those grammarians began writing in German. Among them, the most famous is Meister Eckhart.

No other figure represents the interaction of Latin and vernacular culture as well as he does. Unlike Dante, Mechthild, and Marguerite Porete, Eckhart was no outsider to scholasticism. This is captured even in the title by which he is still known today. *Meister* is the German word for "master," the honorific an allusion to the fact that he became a master of theology in Paris in 1302.[1] He was a member of the Dominican order and moved back and forth between the university setting at Paris and "provincial" postings, working for the order in Erfurt, Strasbourg, and Cologne. His literary output is similarly double, having been written with these two contexts in mind. The "scholastic" side of his thought is represented by biblical and theological commentaries in Latin, while the pastoral and provincial side is captured in a series of powerful sermons and works of instruction composed in German.[2]

Do we have two significantly distinct bodies of work here or do all his writings put forth a single set of themes in two different languages?[3] Probably the right answer lies somewhere in the middle. His choice to write in German may have been in part a matter of audience, but even this is not so simple. It's been stressed by some scholars that he preached to non-Latin speaking female audiences, namely the nuns of convents incorporated into the Dominican order.[4] Yet he also wrote in German for male Dominican colleagues who would have known Latin.[5] Certainly, his

German works do develop a rich and idiosyncratic vocabulary for capturing his ideas, but those ideas can frequently be found in his Latin treatises too. A good example is his insistence that God's creatures are in themselves "nothing," something he explores by engaging with the scholastic theory of the transcendentals, as we'll see shortly.

Meanwhile, perusal of the German works shows that, within them, Eckhart combines more "popular" and pastoral themes with the challenging metaphysics for which he is best known. Consider his *Book of Consolation* (*Daz Bouch der goetlîchen troestunge*), a short treatise about how to cope with suffering.[6] This includes some advice that wouldn't be out of place in a modern-day advice column: if you have one hundred gold marks and lose forty, just remember that plenty of people would do anything to own the sixty marks you still possess (60–1). Eckhart is here working in a register like that of Boethius, that other great exponent of philosophical consolation, and, like Boethius, is following in the footsteps of the Roman Stoics. (Eckhart even quotes Seneca by name.) Yet there are also ideas here that you might more expect to find in a scholastic theological treatise, such as that the soul is in itself outside time and space (57) or that the good person is "uncreated" insofar as that person is good, because the word "good" refers to nothing but pure goodness (*blôze und lûter güete*), namely God Himself (56).

Eckhart warns his listeners that such statements may be easily misunderstood: "I declare by eternal wisdom that if you do not yourself become the same as that wisdom of which we wish to speak, then my words will mean nothing to you" (203). He was right to worry. Two fellow Dominicans who were themselves under suspicion for bad behavior brought an accusation of heresy against Eckhart. We have a document prepared by Eckhart for his defense in 1326, and he later declared his innocence in a public forum in 1327. The eventual upshot was condemnation by Pope John XXII, who declared twenty-eight of Eckhart's statements either heretical or suspect in 1329. By that time, Eckhart was already dead, having passed away in early 1328.[7] Among the theses he discussed in his public defense is the one I just mentioned, namely that the soul is in some sense "uncreated." While stressing that he was ready, even eager, to give up any beliefs he might hold that are in fact contrary to the faith, Eckhart saw himself as the victim of just the sort of misreading he warned against in his sermons. Of course the soul is created, but there is also a sense in which it is uncreated, insofar as the just or good soul participates in eternal, uncreated justice and goodness.

Here, as promised, we get back to the idea of the transcendentals, which, as you'll recall, are properties thought to belong to all existing things, including God (Chapter 25). The standard list would include goodness, being, oneness, and truth.

A prologue to Eckhart's ambitious Latin treatise, the unfortunately incomplete *Three-Part Work* (*Opus tripartitum*), adds wisdom (*sapientia*) to these four transcendentals and explains that they are not accidental properties but are "prior to all else in things."[8] Created things, as we might expect, receive being and the other transcendental properties from God, who is identical to being itself (*esse est deus*). For Eckhart, this is the meaning of the famous biblical passage (Exodus 3:14) where God says of Himself, "I am who am." Now, so far, what Eckhart is saying sounds a lot like what we found in Thomas Aquinas (Chapter 48). According to his theory of analogy, God is pure being and thus the primary referent of the word "being," with all other things receiving being from Him by a kind of participation. Eckhart is indeed indebted to his fellow Dominican on this score and even speaks explicitly of "analogy," but he puts the idea to a more radical use.[9] In the prologue to the *Three-Part Work* Eckhart observes that if God is being, then created things, insofar as they are distinct from God, are nothing at all.[10] Equally, insofar as they do have being or the other transcendentals, they are nothing *other* than God, and are eternal in Him.

In other words, where Aquinas recognized that creatures have a limited or reduced form of being and goodness which they receive from God, Eckhart's theory makes them quite literally all or nothing. Insofar as they are "in" God, creatures share in His perfection and timelessness; insofar as they are outside Him, they have no being or goodness whatsoever. In one of his biblical commentaries,[11] Eckhart explains what he has in mind using an illustration that may sound familiar from our discussions of philosophy of language in the fourteenth century. Ockham mentioned the barrel hoop that conveys the welcome message that wine is on sale (Chapter 59). Eckhart gives the same example, though with a wreath of leaves instead of a barrel hoop, to illustrate the relationship between creatures and God. Again, his point would seem to be that creatures are merely "signs" or representations of God's being but have no being in themselves, just as a wreath signifies that wine is for sale but is not in itself wine.

Eckhart also appealed to the analogy theory when he defended himself against the charge of heresy. His more daring pronouncements, which seem to suggest that the human soul is identical with God, are only one half of a double approach to creatures, which, as he warned, can easily be misunderstood. According to this twofold understanding, creatures are true beings in God but nothing in themselves because they only "borrow" their being from Him.[12] This is a nice example of the continuity between Eckhart's Latin and German works. The passages I've just been quoting are from Latin sources, but in his pastoral sermons he frequently advises his listeners to "take leave of nothingness and grasp perfect being" (173). More startlingly, he insists that our souls are eternal and uncreated, or even their own creators:

"When I existed in my first cause, I had no God and I was my own cause. I willed nothing and desired nothing, for I was naked being and I knew myself by the savor of truth" (204).

With this we have arrived at one of Eckhart's most characteristic teachings, which centers on an example of the special terminology he developed in his German writings, the term "ground (grunt)."[13] His idea is that the soul's ultimate origin is the most foundational aspect of God, the "ground" of all divinity which is in some sense prior even to God when He is understood as being identical to the transcendentals, in terms of the Trinitarian Persons, or as the Creator of the universe. The ultimate "ground" is the same for both soul and God, and it is at this level that the soul and God are one. Eckhart thus writes that in our quest the soul is "satisfied neither with goodness nor wisdom nor with truth nor even with God Himself. In truth, it is as little satisfied with God as with a stone or a tree. It never rests, but breaks into the divine ground where goodness and wisdom begin, before the divine acquires a name" (214).

I was just saying that, according to Eckhart, God is being and creatures are nothing. But now that Eckhart has pushed forward to the ultimate "ground" of the divine, he describes God—and our souls insofar as they are in God—as nothing, or as "naked." Whereas his theory of analogy and the transcendentals made God the true referent of words like "being" and "goodness," in the passages on God as ground he embraces negative theology. Here Eckhart is indebted to two previous masters of the negative approach to God, both of whom he explicitly cites in his works: the anonymous late ancient Christian Platonist we call the Pseudo-Dionysius and the twelfth-century Jewish thinker Maimonides.[14] Thus, he quotes Dionysius for the idea that "They speak most beautifully of God who can maintain the deepest silence concerning Him" (46). Or, as he puts it elsewhere, "If God is not goodness, nor being, nor truth, nor one, what is He then? Nothing at all (nihtes niht)."[15] And if God is at His "ground" ultimately "nothingness," a "wasteland" or "desert," as Eckhart sometimes says, then it is precisely in admitting and even embracing our own "nothingness" as creatures that we achieve unity with God. Eckhart has a further array of metaphors to capture this realization, describing it rather Neoplatonically as a "flowing back" into the source from which we first "flowed forth" (208), when God "boiled over" and poured out the rest of things. The soul in seeking union is "raised up" by God or alternatively "sinks down" to meet God's nothingness. As he puts it in a characteristic paradox, "the deeper and lower the ground, the higher...the height" (46).

Another analogy Eckhart uses frequently is one we already saw briefly, with his reference to the soul in God as "naked being." He often speaks of the soul's needing to "strip" itself bare, seeking to possess nothing other than God (48, 71). This gives him an original approach to the familiar topic of voluntary poverty, as pursued by the Dominicans and other mendicants. His sermons usually expound a biblical passage, and one of them (202–9) is devoted to the famous text "Blessed are the poor in spirit, for theirs is the kingdom of heaven" (Matthew 5:3). Eckhart, of course, encourages us to embrace poverty, but not merely in the literal sense of owning no physical possessions. Rather, our goal is to will nothing at all, not even to have knowledge or to carry out God's will. True poverty is to "be so free of our own created will as we were before we were created" (204)—again, the idea of taking the soul back to its "ground" at the stage of uncreatedness. This radical poverty is union with God, who likewise is "free of all things, which is why He *is* all things" (206).

That might sound like just another paradox, but it is actually a further clue to resolving the puzzle as to why Eckhart would both identify God with being and say that He is nothing. To some extent we already have the answer: God as the negatively understood "ground" is distinct from God as being, as good, as Creator, and so forth. But even without delving into the most negative depths of Eckhart's theology, we can make sense of his idea that God is both all things and none of them. Eckhart occasionally says that God is being of a very special kind, which he calls "indistinct" (25).[16] Since God is timeless, He (and the soul, when unified with Him) exists in an eternal, unchanging "now (*nû*)" that includes all things simultaneously. They are contained in him as "virtual being (*esse virtuale*)," not in the sense we use the word "virtual" to refer to 3D video games but with its original Latin meaning: contained in some power (*virtus*), in this case that of God.[17]

All of this may seem rather abstract and metaphysical. But, as so often in medieval philosophy, the abstract and the metaphysical have implications for how we live our lives. We've already seen that Eckhart's *Book of Consolation* touches fleetingly on his more radical teachings in order to explain why we shouldn't mourn the loss of things that only serve to divide us from God. These same teachings are at the core of an equally radical ethical theory, which, surprisingly (given how different they are as thinkers), echoes ideas we saw in Abelard and Ockham. For Eckhart, as for them, it is the interior activity or state of the person that matters and not so much the exterior action we perform. External virtue is not to be condemned, of course, but it is really the good or just *person* who partakes in God's goodness and even is, as we saw earlier, identical with God insofar as he or she is good. Eckhart's bracingly irreverent approach to what we might call "exterior ethics" extends to the monastic life itself. In almost mocking terms he dismisses as misguided the impulse to withdraw from society and seek seclusion, reminding us that if we possess God, we have Him wherever we go (9).

This idea that we might be able to "transcend" practical virtue is one of several that connect Meister Eckhart to one of the aforementioned champions of vernacular thought, his somewhat earlier contemporary Marguerite Porete. Was Eckhart aware of her *Mirror of Simple Souls*, or her ideas more generally?[18] Some have deemed this possible, on the basis that records about Marguerite should have been available to him in Paris. Certainly, the parallels are striking. Apart from the point about virtue, Marguerite also demands of us that we abandon our will, and speaks of God as a kind of "abyss," which sounds quite a bit like Eckhart's notion of "ground" (even closer is Hadewijch, who used the word *gront*).[19] And, of course, both Marguerite and Eckhart were ultimately deemed too daring by the Church of their time. While the link between the two remains somewhat uncertain and obscure, we can at the very least say that both figures represent a broader wave of daring late medieval mysticism expressed in vernacular language. But there is another way to contextualize Eckhart: as part of a movement within the German Dominican community.

69

MEN IN BLACK
THE GERMAN DOMINICANS

Nowadays, when you meet a man dressed in black, you might guess that you are confronted with an undertaker, a chimney sweep, or a goth. But in the fourteenth century, when it was about seven hundred years too early to meet a modern-day goth and about seven hundred years too late to meet the original version, the men in black were the Dominicans, whose distinctive black cloaks distinguished them from members of other orders, such as the grey-clad Franciscans. Hence the answer to a question I used to ponder when I lived in London: where does the name of Blackfriars Bridge come from? It is named after a Dominican monastery that stood nearby. The Franciscans likewise established Greyfriars in London, which hosted several philosophers who have featured in this book. Ockham, Wodeham, and Chatton were all there at the same time. Among Dominicans, a more important city, philosophically speaking, was Cologne. The order established a *studium* there in 1248 and, from this center, the Dominicans became a dominant force in the intellectual life of Germany.[1]

Like a goth with a weakness for show tunes, the story of the Dominicans in this period combines a cliché with a surprise twist. The cliché is the story of medieval philosophy as you might have thought of it before reading this book, where a single dominant figure loomed over all others in the shape of Thomas Aquinas. And he was indeed influential among fourteenth-century Dominicans.[2] The order affirmed Aquinas' special authority in 1313, and ten years later he was canonized. Enthusiasm for Thomistic teachings is evident in an author like John Picardi, a Dominican who studied at Paris in 1305–7. He defends Aquinas' views on several controversial topics, including the will, regarding which he upholds Thomistic intellectualism against Henry of Ghent's voluntarism, and the unity of form in substance. Like Aquinas, Picardi thinks that the forms of the material constituents that make up a substance are only "virtually" present in that substance. Thus, the earth and water that make up a corpse were not yet actual constituents of the body before death. Picardi unflinchingly accepts this Thomistic conclusion, whereas most contemporary thinkers thought it absurd. And there was considerable pressure on Dominicans like Picardi to follow Aquinas' teachings. Failure to do so could cause controversy, with Durandus of St. Pourçain in particular being criticized on this score.

The surprise twist is that, pressure notwithstanding, some of the most interesting Dominican thinkers in this period were not particularly and certainly not exclusively Thomistic. Our story, in fact, has its real starting point with the first notable member of the order to work at Cologne, Albert the Great.[3] He made great use of ideas from late ancient Platonists like the Pseudo-Dionysius and Proclus, the latter mostly by way of the Arabic-Latin version of Proclus called the *Book of Causes*. These same authors were important for Aquinas too. But we find a more wholehearted appropriation of Platonism amongst a group of Dominicans who worked in Germany. Because of the connection to Cologne, scholars have sometimes spoken of "Rhineland mysticism."[4] I'm going to refer more cautiously to "German Dominicans," without, of course, suggesting that all the figures who fall under this heading adopted a single body of teachings.[5]

Only one of these Dominicans can plausibly be described as "famous," and we just covered him: Meister Eckhart. But it's worth having a broader look at the movement, to put Eckhart himself in context and to demonstrate the diversity of philosophy in the fourteenth century. The German Dominicans offer a striking contrast to the logical and empiricist orientation of scholastics like John Buridan. Not for them the abstemious, clean-shaven metaphysics of nominalism. The Dominicans could instead be described as "ultra-realists"[6] who hold that created things, including the human soul, have their true being in divinity. When Eckhart put forward that idea, he was drawing on his slightly earlier Dominican colleague Dietrich of Freiberg.[7] A treatise by Dietrich called *On the Intellect and the Intelligible* embraces the classically Neoplatonic idea that God's creation of things is an overflowing of divine superabundance (§1.9).[8] Like Eckhart, he uses the image of boiling water to express this idea of a cause giving forth its effects from within its own nature (§1.5).

For Dietrich, as for the pagan Platonists, the first thing to emerge from God is the intellect. He envisions a whole procession of intellects associated with the heavenly spheres, closely following Avicenna on the mechanism of this emanative process (§1.11). As Dietrich goes on to explain the relationship between intellect and being, we see him aligning himself with full-fledged Neoplatonism rather than the Platonically tinged Aristotelianism of Aquinas. For Aquinas, God is primarily a cause of existence, and creation is the association of existence with essences—itself an idea taken from Avicenna. Working years before the canonization of his Dominican colleague, Dietrich feels free to reject this teaching, denying that there is any cogent distinction between essence and existence.[9] For him, being is not a neutral kind of existence that belongs to a given thing, but is rather the essential being of that thing.

Thus, for a horse, "to be" means being a horse, whereas, for a human, it means being a human.

Of course, the distinction between essence and existence was controversial, and Dietrich was not the only one to deny it. More unusual was his attempt to seek a foundation for metaphysics in the intellect itself, with the notion of "being at the level of conception (*ens conceptionale*)" (§3.8). For the nominalists, that phrase would evoke an attenuated, merely mental phenomenon that may or may not correspond to the way things really are. As they never tired of pointing out, we mentally grasp things under universal concepts even though in reality all things are particular. But, as I say, Dietrich was no nominalist. For him, the intellect contains "a likeness of the whole of being as being, and holds in its compass the universe of beings" (§2.26). The intellect does not abstract intelligible being from sensory experiences, but establishes and constitutes the essences through its own activity.[10] To underscore the way that this activity is internally active and not passively caused by an experience of things, Dietrich offers a creative etymology (not original with him) of the word *intelligere*, meaning "to understand": it comes from *legere*, "to read," and *intus*, "internally" (§3.17). All this applies in the first instance to the cosmic intellects that emerge from God, but it also goes for our own human intellects. Again, in stark contrast to Aquinas, Dietrich does not see the human mind as a mere power or faculty of the soul. It is rather the cause and very essence of soul (§2.2, 2.7), even though it is nothing at all until it becomes identical with its intelligible objects (§3.3).[11]

For this heady account of the intellect and its role in both the cosmos and our lives, Dietrich depends on a wide range of authors, among them Proclus. Thanks to William of Moerbeke's translation of Proclus' *Elements of Theology*, it was known that the *Book of Causes* was in fact derived from this treatise by a late ancient pagan. This seems not to have bothered Dietrich much. Still less did it trouble the next Dominican we need to discuss, Berthold of Moosburg. The successor of Eckhart as Dominican lector at Cologne, Berthold wrote a massive and highly learned commentary on Proclus' *Elements*. It represents something of a high-water mark for the medieval reception of Proclus, reminiscent of an earlier wave of enthusiasm for his writings that crested in the Byzantine Empire in the eleventh century.[12] Berthold is careful to say that Proclus' approach to theology is that of a philosopher working with the resources of natural reasoning, rather than that of a theologian who benefits from revelation. But having given this caveat, he goes on to praise Proclus as the greatest of the followers of Plato. Proclus alone unveils the true Platonic teachings, so often covered in the cloak ("integuments") of figurative language.

Berthold's project can be seen, on the one hand, as a revival of the sort of effusive Platonism that had rarely been seen since the days of Eriugena back in the ninth century. A looser comparison might be drawn with the members of the school of Chartres in the twelfth century—looser because they were inspired more by Plato's *Timaeus* than by pagan Neoplatonism. Yet Berthold also responds to current events. He is wrestling with the controversy around, and eventual condemnation of, the teachings of Eckhart.[13] His metaphysics thus takes inspiration from both ancient sources and his immediate predecessor at Cologne. Like Dietrich, who was a strong influence on Berthold's commentary, Berthold envisions the intelligible realm as the domain of true being. This evokes Eriugena's claim that all things are first of all made by God in the so-called "divine primordial causes," a version of Platonic Forms that equates the Forms with ideas in God's mind. Yet it is also reminiscent of Eckhart's notion that things have their true being in God, so that the just person is in a sense identical with the justice of God and the soul's ground is the same as the divine ground. Berthold also seems to see a connection between the negative theology of Proclus and Pseudo-Dionysius, on the one hand, and, on the other hand, the mystical teachings of his fellow Dominican Eckhart. Repeating a classic ploy of Dionysius and Eriugena and anticipating a classic ploy of DC Comics, Berthold makes use of the prefix "super-." He coins the idea of *supersapientia*, or "transcendent wisdom," as a label for the highest insight that grasps the ultimate reality of things in God. What could be more Eckhartian than to identify the world of the intellect as the seat of being, and then to push on further in an effort to grasp God's transcendent negativity, uniting with the exalted nothingness that is, as Berthold puts it, "beyond the mind (*super mentem*)"?

Well, probably nothing could be more Eckhartian, but that isn't going to stop two more Dominicans from trying. John Tauler and Henry Suso were contemporaries, and both carried on aspects of Meister Eckhart's intellectual mission, notably by writing in German rather than the Latin used by Dietrich and Berthold. With Suso, the connection with Eckhart is clear, enough so that his contemporaries did not fail to notice it. Suso defied authority by defending Eckhart from his accusers, even though those accusers included the Pope. Probably as a result, Suso was demoted from his position as Dominican lector. In an autobiographical work, he speaks of having been unjustly accused of "heretical obscenities (*kezerliche unflat*)."[14] We can see why by turning to his most famous treatise, the *Small Book of Truth*,[15] which explicitly mentions several of Eckhart's condemned theses in order to explain and justify them. Eckhartian themes, and even language, are present from the outset. Suso explains that the soul can achieve blessedness and truth only through inner *gelazenheit* (§1). This distinctive word, borrowed from Eckhart, means (as Suso explains later) that one must stop paying attention to one's own self (§5), ceasing to have any will distinct from God's (§6).

Though Suso's book is indeed small, it offers something like a greatest hits of medieval mysticism. One chapter begins by relating a vision and then offering explanatory commentary (§6), a structure reminiscent of the writings of Hildegard of Bingen. Yet, like Marguerite Porete, Suso composes his work in the form of a dialogue between himself, cast as a questioning beginner in wisdom, and an allegorical figure, in this case Eternal Truth. Later on, another character appears, "the nameless wild one (*daz namelos wilde*)." He seems to stand in for those who would take a heretical message from Eckhart's writings, as if Eckhart's own warnings that he may be easily misunderstood have been given concrete form. By introducing this character, Suso is able to distinguish a true from a false, or "disorderly," interpretation of *gelazenheit*. Whereas the historical reception of Eckhart's ideas was contentious and complex, in Suso's literary version the debate is resolved quickly. The "wild one's" complaints are easily answered and thus silenced. Speaking of silence, the negative theology we have seen in other German Dominicans is found in Suso as well, as is a balance between such negativity and a more positive understanding, according to which God is pure mind. Suso explicitly cites Dionysius for the idea that God is "nonbeing" and "eternal nothing" (*nit wesen, ewiges niht*: §2; cf. §6). He adds, though, that we must describe God somehow, and for this purpose should call Him "living, being rationality (*lebendú wesendú vernúnftikeit*)." Suso is also careful to incorporate material from figures like Bernard of Clairvaux, the better to show that Eckhart's apparently daring doctrines are in fact fully in agreement with the authorities of the Church.[16]

The *Small Book of Truth* has a unique place in the generation after Eckhart because of its all but explicit defense of Eckhart's legacy. Still, Suso was not the only Dominican thinking along these lines, as we can see from the career of John Tauler. We have a number of his sermons, which like Eckhart's were written in German and respond to a daily reading from the Bible. Despite the pastoral nature of these works, Tauler locates himself in the intellectual tradition we've been discussing throughout this chapter. In one sermon he quotes Albert the Great, Dietrich of Freiberg, and Eckhart, and for good measure cites Proclus, whom he would have known through the work of Berthold.[17] Like Berthold, Tauler is especially inspired by the idea that our grasp of God is mystical in the sense that it transcends intellect or rationality, and involves an inexpressible union with divine nothingness.

On the basis of the manuscript tradition of Eckhart's own vernacular works, it has been argued that the Church managed to prevent his ideas from being disseminated amongst a lay audience.[18] But Suso and Tauler would have spread his ideas among just such an audience, in part through the spiritual guidance they offered to women; our written records of their vernacular sermons were also likely made by women. Both men ministered to female convents attached to the Dominican order. Tauler corresponded with fellow German mystic Margaret Ebner and was connected to Henry of Nördlingen, who was responsible for the translation of Mechthild of Magdeburg into Middle High German that I mentioned when discussing her. We also have fairly extensive evidence of Suso's mentoring of Elsbeth Stagel, whom he called his "spiritual daughter."[19] Suso speaks admiringly of her enthusiasm for a life of asceticism, which is a major theme for both authors. In a typical passage, Tauler allegorizes the flight of Mary and Joseph as representing the soul's attempt to flee from the desires of the flesh.

Of course, the combination of philosophical mysticism and asceticism is nothing new. But in the German Dominicans it finds a new and distinctive intellectual justification. Alain de Libera, a leading historian of medieval philosophy in general and German mysticism in particular, remarks that their most central doctrine is this: in its very core, or "ground," the soul is unchanging and even uncreated and divine, forever identical with its source in God.[20] This explains the asceticism: concern with the things of this world simply prevents your realization of your deepest identity. It explains the epistemology too: the soul's task is to rise to the level of intellect, and then further to the nothingness that is God's and its own ground. It even explains the Dominicans' enthusiasm for the Neoplatonic sources that had inspired Albert the Great. In Proclus they could find the idea that there is a kind of image within each of us of the True One, the divine first principle, in the form of the so-called "one of the soul (*unum animae*)." That idea is taken up in one way or another by all of our Dominicans, in Tauler's case as an improvement on Thomas Aquinas' more Aristotelian attempt to locate the image of God in each human by pointing to a trinity of powers within the soul.[21]

While the German Dominicans do recall the earlier medieval Neoplatonism of Eriugena and, above all, Albert, they also seem to point forward. Tauler, in particular, would be rather influential in the coming centuries. His writings found approval with Martin Luther, thanks to whom Tauler had an afterlife among Protestant readers. The others fell into obscurity more quickly, with some exceptions: the major Renaissance thinker Nicholas of Cusa had cautious admiration for Berthold of Moosburg. In a more general sense, though, these Dominicans undermine an assumption we might otherwise have had about late medieval philosophy and the way it contrasts with Renaissance philosophy. The prominence of scholastics like Scotus, Ockham, and Buridan makes it easy to think that pagan Platonism had faded utterly as an intellectual force until it was rediscovered by Renaissance figures such as Cusa or Marsilio Ficino. In fact, Neoplatonism was like God's creative power according to Dietrich and Eckhart: a powerful force constantly boiling under the surface, ever ready to express itself.

70

A WING AND A PRAYER
ANGELS IN MEDIEVAL
PHILOSOPHY

O f all the lyrics in the Elvis Presley songbook, the most puzzling is the one that begins his 1963 single "Devil in Disguise," in which an affronted Elvis complains that his sweetheart is not nearly as sweet as she first seemed to be. He sings, "You look like an angel, walk like an angel, talk like an angel, but I got wise: you're the devil in disguise." Surely angels are immaterial beings, so they don't "look" like anything. Even if they did have bodies, they would have wings, so they wouldn't need to "walk" anywhere. Besides which, these are purely intellectual beings, so it seems hard to believe that they "talk" either. But perhaps I am only puzzled because I've been reading medieval philosophy—something Elvis never got around to, having died so young. The scholastics loved to think about angels, with pretty much every figure we've covered having something to say on the subject.

It can be hard to relate to this feature of medieval thought. Like the spectacular caped suits of Elvis' Vegas period, the intricate scholastic discussions of angels have not dated well, with exquisite ornament and filigreed detail being lavished upon something that was arguably a pretty bad idea to begin with. Hence scholastic philosophy has famously been mocked as dealing with questions like how many angels can dance on the head of a pin. But I'd like to persuade you that medieval angelology was more like the leather outfit Elvis wore for the '68 "comeback special": possessing a relevance as timeless as angels themselves. You don't have to believe in angels yourself to see their philosophical appeal. The medievals found them fascinating for theological and doctrinal reasons, no doubt, but also for the way that angels can be used to address an astonishingly wide range of philosophical topics. If angels really lack bodies then how can they be individual substances? If they can walk and talk after all, or at least engage in motion and communication, what does this mean for physics and the philosophy of language? Are angels really timeless, and, if so, what does timeless existence even mean? What does the hierarchical society of angels tell us about ideal political structures? What might reflection on their exalted minds reveal about our lesser mental lives?

In grappling with such questions, the medievals drew on conflicting sources of ideas about angels.[1] Obviously, angels feature throughout the Bible, often bearing messages from God (this is actually the meaning of the word "angel," which comes from the Greek word for "messenger"). This is still probably the first thing to come to mind when you think about angels: winged messengers announcing the coming of Christ to astonished shepherds, or Gabriel informing Mary she is with child. The messages could go the other way too. Though it was considered inappropriate to "worship" angels, since that should be reserved for God, one could ask them to pray on one's own behalf or to bear one's prayers up to God. Particularly important angels were known by name—Gabriel, Michael, and so on—and celebrated on feast days. Medievals also believed that they were protected by guardian angels and subject to temptation or other malign influence from fallen or rebel angels, who took over the place occupied by demons (*daimones*) in pagan imagination. As noted by Elvis, a seeming angel may be a devil in disguise. The Bible speaks of Satan himself posing as an "angel of light" (2 Corinthians 11:14).

So, to the medieval mind, both good and evil angels were beings whose influence is pervasive in everyday life. They serve as conduits between the spiritual and material realms. Your average believer would presumably have imagined them as having bodies and certainly had no trouble accepting that they could leave traces of themselves in the physical world. One medieval church had a piece of marble in which one could see the footprint of the angel Gabriel. Against all this, though, stood another tradition of thought stemming from ancient philosophy and the Islamic world. The Koran too mentions angels. Indeed, Muhammed's prophecy begins when an angel appears to him and commands "Recite!" (While we're in an etymological mood, this is where the title *Qur'ān* comes from: it means "recitation.") Philosophers of the Islamic world, like al-Fārābī and Avicenna, identified the angels of the Abrahamic tradition with the celestial movers of the Aristotelian tradition. According to Aristotle, there are dozens of pure intellects that explain the different motions of heavenly bodies, with God simply the highest such intellect. On this conception, angels are definitely incorporeal. The whole point of the philosophical account is that only a purely immaterial, intellective being can be an "unmoved mover," as demanded by Aristotelian cosmology.

The topic of angels thus turns out to be a beautiful illustration of the way that the recovery of Aristotle and influence from the Islamic world shaped philosophy in Latin Christendom. Up until the twelfth century even schoolmen tended to think of angels as having bodies, but this became a minority view in the thirteenth century. Some thinkers embraced the identification of angels with intellectual movers, a leading example being Thomas Aquinas (who incidentally bears the honorific "angelic doctor"!). His teacher, Albert the Great, was more cautious. For him, there are two ways of thinking about angels, the philosophical one found in figures like Avicenna and the theological one we know through revelation. A more aggressive tone was taken by Peter Olivi, who complained that the pagans and Muslims spoke of angels as if they were minor gods, rather than created beings, and refused to identify them with pure intellects.[2]

Other thinkers of the late thirteenth century were not so ready to abandon the old Neoplatonic idea of pure intellectual beings who mediate between God and physical creation, yet shared Olivi's misgivings about identifying the angels of the Bible with such intelligences. One solution was simply to accept the existence of both intel-lective celestial movers and angels while refusing to identify the two. This is what we find in Dietrich of Freiberg.[3] For him, angels are more like humans than divinities, though he does try to justify the fact that pagan authorities called them "gods."[4] Angels are not the intelligences spoken of by these pagans.[5] Rather, while angels do have intellects, they are capable of imagination and of making mistakes, which is how some angels could have made the tragic error of rejecting God's grace. Yet Dietrich also echoes the Platonist doctrine that the heavens have their own minds and souls. These celestial intelligences take up a further place alongside angels in the cosmological hierarchy.

Dietrich also contributed to a heated debate concerning the individuation of angels, that is, the question of how there are many angels, whereas there is only one God. The problem here is that, according to yet another teaching that can be traced to the Islamic world (and Avicenna in particular), individuation is caused by matter. There is only one human species, but many humans who exist at different times and places, something made possible by the different parcels of matter of which the humans are made. Imagine, if you are old enough to remember this technology, a factory pressing records with Elvis Presley's latest smash hit. The individual disks are distinguished not by their shape or the pattern of grooves cut into them, but by being made of different bits of vinyl. Clearly, though, this explanation is not available in the case of angels, once we accept that they have no bodies. As I mentioned when discussing the condemnations issued at Paris in 1277 (Chapter 41), it was forbidden to assert what Aquinas said on this issue, namely that each angel must just be unique in its species because not even God can make two immaterial things that are the same in species.

That left other thinkers to sort out how angels *are* differentiated from one another, without straying into forbidden territory. One solution, which had been adopted by Bonaventure, was simply to admit that angels are made of matter. He argued for this on the basis that all creatures must have a certain potential for non-existence, having been created from nothing by God. And that potential being is seated in matter. As Giorgio Pini has pointed out, this means that Bonaventure has a unified account of individuation: all things other than God Himself come to be singular entities by being made of matter.[6] Unfortunately, as I also mentioned when we looked at the condemnations, the Parisian edict actually requires the university masters to admit that God can create two angels of the same species even if they are utterly immaterial. Dietrich of Freiberg's solution would fit this bill. In a version of the old idea that accidental features can individuate the substances to which they belong, he says that there is no need for matter in angels, since the angels can be distinguished by the activities they perform.[7]

As metaphysics developed in the fourteenth century, other solutions became available. We saw that, for Duns Scotus, common essences are "contracted" by being joined to individual natures (Chapter 51). This explanation will work just as well for an immaterial angel as it will for a physical being like a rose or a human. Which is to say that this explanation won't work at all, at least according to the nominalist critics of Scotus who come along in the fourteenth century. A nice example is provided by Durandus of St. Pourçain, for whom the whole scandal over angelic individuation was the result of a simple misunderstanding.[8] Aquinas was driven to suppose that angels are unique in their species because he thought that matter is needed to render each thing an individual. But this is a crass error, in Durandus' view. Aquinas' problem is that he thinks essences are somehow universal by default, whereas actually it is only the process of mental abstraction that yields universality. To the nominalist way of thinking, things in themselves are always individuals, whether they are immaterial or not. That is just a brute fact about them that needs no explanation.

Having explained how there can be a multiplicity of angels, we might next wonder how many there are. The classic Aristotelian view would have assigned an angel to each simple heavenly motion. There might be several angels whose combined efforts result in the complex path a certain planet seems to travel when viewed from the earth. Aristotle himself was unsure how many movers there need to be, and advises us to go ask a mathematician, but it is somewhere around sixty. As Roger Bacon noted, this is far short of what Christianity licenses us to believe: "We know by the faith of the Church, by Scripture, and the saints that there are tens of hundreds of thousands, innumerable to us."[9] For a better sense of the population and structure of the angelic realm, the medievals turned to a work called the *Celestial Hierarchy*, written by the Pseudo-Dionysius.

In this book Dionysius has mostly figured as a hero of negative theology, but his influence in the area of angelology was also profound. You might recall that, in the

Carolingian period, John Scotus Eriugena ushered the works of Dionysius into the Latin realm. Other early medieval thinkers enthusiastically repeated the details of the angelic ranks described by Dionysius and accepted a parallel he suggested between the hierarchy of angels and that of the Church. The parallel could be extended to the political realm. Just as the angels are ruled by God and the Church by the Pope, so the secular realm has at its head the king (I mean an actual monarch, not Elvis). An elaborate version of this is found in William of Auvergne, who explains that the orders of seraphim, cherubim, and thrones correlate to royal advisors, lawmakers, and judges. The parallel goes both ways. It's been said that "William portrays heaven as a throbbing court busy with both the tasks of government and the settlement of legal disputes,"[10] with Christ advocating on behalf of the human race before the divine tribunal. Bonaventure follows suit, describing Christian society as an image of the angelic society with the highest rank of the seraphim mirrored among humans by—you'll never guess—mendicant friars. You know, like St. Francis and Bonaventure himself.

Our next question about angels is one that I'd imagine quite a few members of medieval society asked about mendicant friars: what do they do all day? Actually, we should start with the question of whether they have "days" at all. Are angels subject to time, or do they live in a timeless eternity like God? Yet again, views on this diverged.[11] A common view was that they occupy a special temporal duration called the *aevum*, which is basically a middle ground between normal time and God's eternity. It means that duration does pass for the angels but without their actually changing. Hence Aquinas, for whom angels are pure intellects, thinks that these are minds created with all the knowledge they will ever have. If they experience duration, it is simply because they focus on different things they know at different moments. Bonaventure makes a similar point by contrasting a river with a sunbeam. Angelic existence is not a part-by-part process like that of a river, but occurs "all at once." Scotus agrees, though for him this suggests that the *aevum* is not really a temporal duration at all. Other scholastics are happy to suppose that angels are subject to time and even that they can learn new things during their life, for instance as they see the choices made by free humans. William of Ockham falls into this camp, holding that angels increase in knowledge as they observe the course of the world, something Martin Lenz has called "angelic empiricism."[12]

If angels can learn, can they also tell one another what they have found out? This brings us back to our Elvis-inspired question of whether angels can walk and talk. Given the aforementioned role of angels as messengers, it would be pretty disappointing if it turned out that they cannot communicate. One way they might do so would be to assume a physical body, even if they are in themselves immaterial. Here it's worth mentioning Bonaventure again. He describes angels doing exactly this, though he hastens to add that an angel cannot actually "unify" with a body the way the human soul can. Indeed, the capacity to form a unity with the body is what distinguishes souls from angels.[13] If we are to imagine Gabriel appearing to Mary in the form of a luminous winged man, then we should realize that Gabriel would be using that body in something like the way a puppeteer would use a doll.

Presumably, this isn't how angels communicate with each other. Dionysius never mentions in the *Celestial Hierarchy* that the seraphim and cherubim are getting together for costume parties. Instead, the scholastics try to understand how purely mental beings could transmit knowledge to one another.[14] For the most part, it was assumed that angels would not need to use "signs" to communicate, the way that we do. Instead, Aquinas thinks that an angel can simply will to reveal its thoughts, opening the book of its mind to its celestial companions. Scotus thinks the angel needs to do something a bit more metaphysically aggressive, so to speak. It actually causes its thought to appear in another angelic mind, not so much a case of mind-reading as mind-writing. As so often, Ockham reacts critically to this proposal of Scotus', pointing out that if an angel could do that, it would presumably be able to modify the will of another angel too, something he takes as an absurd consequence. For Ockham himself, the problem is easy to solve. Given his theory of mental language, the angel's thoughts are already in just the right form to be communicated.

That's talking. What about walking, or at least moving? Again, there was a heated debate over whether and how an angel can move around and occupy space.[15] And again, you can see why this is an interesting philosophical issue, beyond the need to sort out angelology. Just as worrying about angelic communication was a chance to think about language and how it relates to thought, the puzzle about angelic location is really just a version of the more general question how an immaterial thing can be present to any place at all. God is immaterial, yet omnipresent, and my soul is immaterial, yet in my body and not in yours. How is this to be explained? In the case of angels, the task was yet again bedeviled by those problematic condemnations passed down in 1277. They ruled out of bounds the account offered by Aquinas, according to which the angel is present at a given location simply by exerting influence at that location, as when it causes heavenly motion. He compared this to the way the king is present throughout his kingdom by dint of exercising jurisdiction there (*ST* I Q8 a3).

The committee who wrote the condemnations were unwilling to accept this, in part on the grounds that it would mean an inactive angel is nowhere. Henry of Ghent, who was actually on that committee, subsequently admitted that he was perplexed about just how angels are indeed present in a given place. We aren't allowed to say that it is by causal action, but neither does it seem that an immaterial angel has location by its very nature. Scotus rose to the challenge by suggesting that the angel must first of all have spatial location *before* it can act within that location, and furthermore proposing that the angel just "overlaps" or "interpenetrates" with whatever else is found in that same place. This is an interesting idea, since it implies that several things can share a single location, at least if all but one of the things in question are incorporeal.

What conclusions can we draw from all these controversies and puzzles? It would be an exaggeration to say that you can tell the whole story of medieval philosophy just by talking about angels, but not much of an exaggeration. We have seen problems about angels turning up in many areas of philosophy, as promised. And with good reason. Thinking about angels helped the medievals to think about non-angelic cases, much as philosophers nowadays use extreme thought experiments to elicit and test intuitions about more everyday cases. Reflecting on immaterial entities was an excellent way to figure out whether matter individuates things that are *not* immaterial, or how a being could sin despite having no bodily temptations (remember Anselm's discussion of this problem, as discussed in Chapter 7). We've also seen that the history of philosophy about angels is the history of scholastic philosophy itself, but in miniature. It shows us the effect of the Latin translation movement, as ideas from Aristotle and Avicenna were applied in angelology. It shows how tensions between these new ideas and older conceptions led some to contrast a "theological" and a "philosophical" approach to the topic. And it shows too how debates changed with the rise of nominalism. Some apparently insoluble problems became nearly trivial, as with Ockham's solution to angelic communication or Durandus' explanation of how angels are individuated. This is why I wanted to cover it before stepping outside the context of scholastic philosophy as we'll be doing in chapters to come, as we continue to examine philosophy in late medieval vernacular literature.

71

ALLE MANER OF THYNG
SHALL BE WELLE
ENGLISH MYSTICISM

The late fourteenth century was a watershed in the history of English literature, the time of Chaucer's *Canterbury Tales* and Langland's *Piers Plowman*. Of course, the "Middle" English of these texts is not quite the same as the language you're reading now. There are unfamiliar words, and familiar words used in unfamiliar ways. Still, for the most part it's surprisingly comprehensible. It reads like modern English typed by someone with unrestrained enthusiasm for the silent e and a keyboard whose y key has gotten stuck. The corpus of Middle English literature also includes several classics of Christian spirituality, which sometimes drew on the same sources that inspired scholastic thinkers, yet were produced outside of a scholastic context.[1] The decision to write in English is symptomatic of that fact. These writings do not aim at schoolmen, but at a wider readership hungry for spiritual guidance. Already in the first half of the century, a religious hermit named Richard Rolle wrote treatises of religious devotion as well as liturgical commentary.[2] His lead was followed by Walter Hilton, who died at the close of the century in 1396. Close to him in time and in thought is the anonymous author of *The Cloud of Unknowing*. Hilton has even been identified as a possible author of the *Cloud*, though scholars generally reject this proposal.[3] Both Hilton and the *Cloud* author move away from Rolle's "affective" mysticism towards a more abstract approach that has less to do with embodiment.

Most intriguing, more famous, and more inclined to adopt something like Rolle's "affective" mystical approach are the women mystics who wrote in English. Rolle and Hilton provide a context for understanding how this was possible, as both composed works aimed at a female audience. The key figure here is Julian of Norwich, author of the *Book of Showings*, in which she recounts and interprets a series of visions she experienced while suffering from a nearly fatal illness. It is tempting to lump both the male and female figures together as a kind of counter-cultural movement. They were isolated, sometimes quite literally when they lived as hermits and anchorites, and also in the sense that they were outside the main intellectual currents of the fourteenth century. Even the obvious precedents for a figure like Julian would not have been available as an encouraging model. The writings of female mystics were more widely disseminated and read on the Continent than in England. An exception that proves the rule is the *Mirror of Simple Souls* by Marguerite Porete (Chapter 53). Her book was translated into Middle English, and circulated in the same spiritualist circles as the works of these English mystics, but it did so anonymously. On the other hand, we should avoid exaggerating the outsider status of the English mystics. Rolle and Hilton both wrote in Latin as well as English, and, unlike Marguerite, these authors—even the rather daring Julian—were careful to adhere to the teachings of the Church. Nor should we exaggerate the similarity between these authors. The fact that they all wrote works of spiritual devotion in English does not mean that they agreed about everything.[4]

Indeed we can find plenty of disagreements between the two most famous works produced by the English mystics, which will be the focus of this chapter: the *Cloud of Unknowing* and Julian's *Book of Showings*. Of the two, the *Cloud* is slightly more likely, though still not very likely, to feature in histories of philosophy less broadminded than this one.[5] This is because it draws on a source that has been influencing medieval thinkers from the Carolingian period onwards, from Eriugena to Albert the Great, from Aquinas to Meister Eckhart. This source is the writing of the Pseudo-Dionysius, pioneering negative theologian and among the first to integrate Neoplatonic ideas into Christianity (he is mentioned explicitly in the *Cloud of Unknowing* at §70). The anonymous author of the *Cloud* is especially inspired by the negative theology, as the title of his devotional treatise already suggests.

He is offering advice to a younger recipient, explaining to him the best path to follow when devoting oneself to God. We begin in a "derknes" which is the eponymous "cloude of unknoying," a failure to grasp God that we can never overcome, since He transcends the light of reason (§3). Instead, we should add a further "clowde of foryetyng," that is, strive to forget all created things to focus on God alone (§5). God is and will remain ungraspable to our mind, but not to our love. This is apt to remind us of Marguerite, and before her the Beguine mystics Hadewijch and Mechthild. All these female authors believed that love is the ladder that takes us up to God. Hence their appropriation of courtly love literature, borrowing the trope of longing and suffering to convey the soul's desperate hope for a glimpse of God.

Despite his discouraging remarks about knowledge and the human mind, the author of the *Cloud* prefers a more abstract approach. He recognizes two paths to

God, which he calls "active" and "contemplative." Each path can be pursued in a lower or higher way. The lower path of active devotion consists in, basically, leading a good life: performing acts of mercy and charity (§8). The author's attitude towards this sort of life is reminiscent of Marguerite's remarks on virtue, though his statements are far less provocative. Virtuous actions are admirable, but the true devotee of God cannot be satisfied with them. A superior method is the higher active path, which is one and the same as the lower path of contemplation. It consists in meditating on one's own smallness in comparison to God, on the suffering of Christ on the cross, and so on. As we'll see, this path is the one followed by Julian of Norwich. But our anonymous author thinks that we can do better still. The higher path of contemplation is the one symbolized by the "cloud of forgetting." We should leave behind even such exalted objects of contemplation as the angels and saints, focusing on nothing but God Himself (§9).

It's a rather paradoxical instruction, given that God entirely transcends any means we might have of grasping Him. The author's advice is to use meditational techniques that sound strikingly like practices found in other cultures. For example, one might repeat a single word to oneself again and again, like "sin" or the name "God" (§37–40)—something that may call to mind the use of mantras in Tantra or the recitations involved in Jewish Kabbalah. As we do so, we should work to turn our will and our knowledge away from the self, indeed away from any created thing. The author makes the nice point that acknowledging other things implicitly involves acknowledging oneself as their knower, so that concentration on any created thing leads back to the self (§43). Instead, we should choose to be blind rather than have knowledge (§34). Another passage that is strikingly reminiscent of Marguerite explains why we should be seeking union with God in the first place, rather than pursuing the classically philosophical project of knowing the self. Each of us was created from nothing, and we are still nothing in comparison to God, to whom we are infinitely inferior (§67).

The author of the *Cloud* also worries that the sort of "inward-turning" practiced by other mystics could make one vulnerable to demonic influence (§52). If you are granted a vision, how are you to know whether it comes from God or the devil? Perhaps by taking advice from your neighborhood necromancer. The author relies on experts in demonology for the observation that the devil always shows himself as having a single nostril (§55). You may snort through both nostrils at this, but in this period the phenomenon of the divine, or apparently divine, vision was widely accepted. It was especially common among cloistered women, as is clear from a story of the German nun Christine Ebner, who was taken aback when told that one of her sisters had never enjoyed a visionary experience![6] The *Cloud* author was not the only one to fret that apparently divine visions could, in fact, be the workings of madness or some other even more insidious influence.

The case of Julian of Norwich shows that such worries sometimes affected the visionaries themselves. After she was visited by a series of sixteen visions, she was at first afraid to embrace them as what she would later call "shewyings," or genuine revelations. Instead, she described them to others as ravings brought on by illness, something she later regretted as a kind of betrayal on her part. According to her later account in the *Book of Showings of Divine Love*,[7] she had, in fact, prayed for such an illness: "I desyrd to have all maner of paynes, bodily and ghostly, that I should have if I should have died, all the dreyds and temptations of fiendes, and all maner of other paynes, save the out passing of the sowle" (§2). The prayers were answered in May 1373, when Julian was struck down with a crisis that lasted three days. During this time she saw, with what she calls "spiritual" rather than bodily sight (§8–9, 73), such images as the bloody face of Christ, the crown of thorns, and the Devil (sadly, she doesn't mention how many nostrils he had). Yet she is clear that she had no desire to suffer for suffering's sake. She wished rather to commune in the passion of Christ.

The most striking passages in her book are the descriptions of these "showings." They are often horrific, always detailed and concrete (have a look at §17), and sometimes amplified with metaphors, as when she describes drops of blood shaped like the scales of fish and pouring down like water off a roof (§7). The physicality and frank violence of these passages may seem to betray a negative attitude towards things of the body. But Julian's central concern is not hatred of the body. It is the theological and philosophical problem of suffering.[8] This becomes clear from her own account of the meaning of her visions. Like Hildegard of Bingen, Julian presents herself as a visionary who is in the best position to expound the meaning of her own visions, despite the fact that she is, as she admits with a touch of false modesty, "a symple creature unlettyrde" (§2). Her *Showings* explain what she saw and also the point of what she saw, "according to [her] own understanding," as she often puts it (as at §6, 10). One passage epitomizes the way that female medieval mystics could assert authority over their own teaching without directly challenging contemporary assumptions about the inferiority of women:

> God forbid that you should say or assume that I am a teacher, for that is not and never was my intention; for I am a woman, ignorant, weak, and frail. But I know very well that what I am saying I have received by the revelation of Him who is the sovereign teacher...Because I am a woman, ought I therefore to believe that I should not tell you of the goodness of God, when I saw at that same time that it is His will that it be known?[9]

Yet Julian did not immediately understand the import of her own experience. To the contrary, after composing a short account of the visions, she spent years trying to decode the message she had received, finally setting down her conclusions in a far longer version with extensive interpretive material.[10] The difficulty that drove forward this protracted process was the aforementioned one of reconciling the existence of suffering with the mercy and providence of God. Even nowadays, the so-called "problem of evil" is often brandished by atheists as a powerful reason to reject the existence of God. Julian, of course, had no doubts on this score, but struggled to reconcile the reality of sin and suffering with divine benevolence. It was a particular challenge for her, because, in what has become the most famous moment of her visions, she heard God saying, "I can make alle thynge well. And I shalle make alle thynge well. And I wylle make alle thynge well. And thou shalt se thy selfe that alle maner of thyng shall be welle" (§31). Compounding the forthright optimism of these words was Julian's conviction that God is in all things and predestines all things. Nothing is "done by hap ne by aventure" because all things are ultimately done by God and all that He does is "welle done" (§11).

One explanation of how this can be so, despite the evident reality of sin, is the traditional account of evil that goes back to the late ancient Platonist philosopher Plotinus by way of Augustine. Evil is in itself nothing, so does not need to be created by God. Or, as Julian puts it, "synne is no deed" (§11). Yet her answer to the puzzle goes considerably beyond this familiar response. She can point to her own experience, in which she took on suffering voluntarily in order to come closer to God, in an echo of God's generously suffering in human form to redeem humankind of sin. The Incarnation is at the heart of Julian's theodicy, since it provides the ultimate example of pain working towards good ends. Still, without sin, there would be no suffering. In fact, it is suffering that makes sin manifest to us. Because sin is nothing in itself, we can never be aware of it directly, but we do grasp it through its effects (§27). More original still is Julian's reconciliation of sin with divine benevolence. She claims that sin at first comes about through good, not bad intentions. She compares humankind to a servant who, rushing to carry out his master's will, falls into a ditch and suffers great agony before finally being rescued (§51). A similar analogy was given by Anselm, who, however, had emphasized the malevolent will of the servant; you might remember his struggle to understand the perverse choice that led to the fall of Satan (Chapter 7). Julian rejects the idea that we are being punished for perverse malevolence, instead seeing sin as the inevitable result of our vast inferiority to God.[11]

In a further unwitting echo of Plotinus, Julian thinks that there is a part of the soul that remains unfallen and perfect in its will. The soul's "godly will" ensures that it can never separate fully from God, but is permanently united to Him. As she puts it, "our soule is so fulsomely onyd to God of hys goodnesse that betwene God and our soule may be ryght nought" (§46). Our sinful nature, sadly, means that in addition to this perfect will we have a lower aspect, which she calls "sensualyte" (§55) or the "bestial" part that inevitably chooses sin. It has been said that this view seems to "teeter on the edge of heresy," given that grace may seem unnecessary if part of us remains always pure and good.[12] But Julian puts great emphasis on the unity of the human person, who is both body and soul. Being human quite literally involves taking the good with the bad. So there is no prospect that we can merit salvation without God's freely given assistance.[13]

Nonetheless, Julian worries that she risks contradicting authoritative Christian doctrine. Unlike the more provocative Marguerite, Julian is at pains to assure her reader that this is not the case. Her greatest worry again relates to God's promise that "alle maner of thyng shall be welle." This certainly seems to suggest that all souls are saved in the end; yet Julian knows this would be in flagrant contradiction to the view of the Church (§33, 45, 50). For this reason her idea of a perfect will that remains united with God is, officially at least, applied only to those souls that are predestined for salvation. Yet she can't help wondering whether God might offer some sort of mysterious, last minute redemption, and in general reminds us that, as creatures, we are never really going to understand why sin was allowed or how exactly it will be redeemed (§27). At the risk of making her sound heretical after all, it has to be said that Julian's solution to the problem of sin seems to resonate strongly with the ideas of the late ancient Christian thinker Origen, for whom souls fall away from God into sin, but are all eventually redeemed.[14]

SAY IT WITH POETRY
CHAUCER AND LANGLAND

I'm intrigued by the slogan "Say it with flowers," familiar from advertising for florists and as the title of a 1934 British film, because it seems to me that the range of things one can say with flowers is really pretty small. Beyond "I love you," "I'm sorry," and "I bear you seething resentment and happen to know that you're allergic to flowers," not much leaps to mind. But I like the idea of saying things in an unexpected way: the mafiosi in the *Godfather* who deliver messages in the form of a horse's head or a package of dead fish, or the Roman gods who made their will known through the movement of birds and behavior of sacred chickens. We tend to avoid such flights of fancy when it comes to philosophy, expecting philosophical ideas to be expressed straightforwardly in treatises and other didactic texts full of arguments. But a glance through history shows that philosophy has often traveled in other guises, often in works that can be classified as literature. From Plato's dialogues and the *Upaniṣads* to Nietzsche's *Thus Spoke Zarathustra* and the novels of Iris Murdoch, there have been works that could as naturally be studied in literature departments as in philosophy departments.

We're already familiar with this phenomenon in the medieval period. We just looked at the great work of literature that is Julian of Norwich's *Showings*, and previously we explored the philosophical ideas of Dante as well as allegorical works like the *Romance of the Rose* and Alan of Lille's *Lament of Nature*. These examples illustrated the wider cultural impact of philosophy as it was being pursued in the rarefied context of the schools and universities. We might ask more from literature, though. Could a novel, play, or poem express philosophical ideas in an original way, even a way that a treatise or textbook cannot? Now we're going to test that hypothesis by looking at two literary authors of the late fourteenth century, both of whom wrote in Middle English. The more famous of the two is Geoffrey Chaucer, who hardly needs me to introduce him. He is author of the *Canterbury Tales*, in which a group of pilgrims compete to win a free meal by telling a series of stories, and of several other works, including a romance called *Troilus and Criseyde*. The second author is William Langland, who wrote a long and complicated poem called *Piers*

Plowman.[1] It recounts a series of dreams in which a narrator meets a sequence of speechifying allegorical characters. That narrative frame is thus reminiscent of the *Romance of the Rose*, but *Piers Plowman* devotes itself to more exalted concerns than the eroticism of Jean de Meun. A central character named "Will" quests after spiritual improvement, trying to understand what it means to do well, do better, and do best ("dowel, dobet, dobest").

We have good reason to think that these two poets may be philosophically rewarding. In the fourteenth century England has emerged as a major force in scholastic thought thanks to the work done at Oxford and London Greyfriars, and the mystically oriented English writings we've just looked at were produced around the time of Chaucer and Langland. Furthermore, we know that both of them were acquainted with philosophical literature at least to some extent. Chaucer translated Boethius' *Consolation of Philosophy* into English,[2] and both he and Langland allude to the schoolmen, with mendicant friars and the so-called "clerks" featuring frequently in their writings. One of the stories in the *Canterbury Tales* is even narrated by such a "clerk." In the prologue to that tale the Clerk is said to "studie aboute som sophyme," a sign that we are dealing with a trained scholastic (5).[3] As for Langland, given his evidently wide reading, it's been argued that he himself was trained in the liberal arts at Oxford, though training at a cathedral school may be more likely.[4]

Accordingly there is a longstanding tradition of reading both authors within a philosophical frame. This is especially true of Chaucer. Already his contemporary Thomas Usk called him the "noble philosophical poete in Englissh," while his fifteenth-century editor William Caxton spoke of him as a "noble and grete philosopher." Modern-day scholars have made similar suggestions, detecting traces of voluntarism and nominalism in the *Canterbury Tales* and other Chaucerian works.[5] It's been proposed that one of the avian characters in his early *Parliament of Fowls* represents a voluntarist outlook on the will: a female eagle rejects the rational advice offered by Nature herself regarding the choosing of a mate. The thoughts of a knight in another work, the *Book of the Duchess*, are supposedly a depiction of the abstractive process of cognition we know from Ockham's philosophy of mind. Chaucer's portrayal of irreducibly individual characters, as in the famous prologue of the *Canterbury Tales*, where we meet the various pilgrims, has been deemed to evince a nominalist devotion to particulars over universal types.[6] A domineering husband in one of the *Tales* has been compared to the God of the voluntarists, who wields absolute power, in the face of which we can only be passively obedient. His long-suffering wife even seems, at one point, to think that her husband's inscrutable will makes things right or wrong (*Clerk's Tale* 649–53), as in Scotus' divine command theory of ethics.

That last suggestion is a bit more attractive than some of the others, since it concerns the tale told by the aforementioned Clerk, the one who is said to trade in sophisms. There is also evidence internal to the *Canterbury Tales* that Chaucer knew about voluntarism. He mentions Thomas Bradwardine in the *Nun's Priest's Tale* (3242) and in the *Man of Law's Tale* offers a rather nifty summary of the voluntarist idea that God's will is unknowable: "ofte, as knowen clerkis, dooth thyng for certein ende that ful derk is to mannes wit, that for oure ignorance ne konne nought knowe his prudent purveiance" (480–3). Indeed, if we are going to credit Chaucer with a serious interest in any philosophical question, it would be divine providence. Here his translation of Boethius' *Consolation* is relevant, since it contains a classic treatment of the issue.

Any skepticism that Chaucer would have carried over this material into a literary context can be answered by turning to *Troilus and Criseyde*, which, by the way, was dedicated to a schoolman and philosopher named Ralph Strode. It contains a lengthy passage in which the hero Troilus reprises Boethius' presentation of the problem, namely that if God knows in advance what we will do, then we are necessitated to act as He foresees.[7] Troilus even considers, and dismisses, a possible solution. Even if things are foreseen because they will happen, rather than happening because they are foreseen, nonetheless, once foreseen, they must occur, since otherwise God's providence would be falsified ("for although that for thing shall come, y-wis, therefore it is purveyed certeynly, not that it com'th for it perveyed is. Yet nathelees behov'th it needfully that thing to come be purvey'd trewely"). His worry is in keeping with other passages in the poem which show the characters giving in to a kind of determinism. As Chaucer scholar Jill Mann has written, the lovers "reinterpret previous events as part of the pattern of destiny, their significance ... now being established by the end that has been reached."[8]

Yet, unlike Boethius himself or any number of medieval scholastics, Chaucer offers no solution to the problem of divine foreknowledge. He allows Troilus to conclude on a fatalist note ("the befalling of thinges that ben wist before the tyde, they mowe not ben eschewed on no syde") and suggests that he has included the passage simply in order to depict the "heavinesse" of Troilus' heart and his ineffectual "disputing with himself in this matter."[9] This, I think, is typical of Chaucer's allusions to specific scholastic doctrines in his works. He includes them for the sake of characterization, often to underscore indecision and inaction. There is also an element of parody here. As a skeptical survey of philosophical material in Chaucer has pointed out, the *Nun's Priest's Tale* mentions Bradwardine, author of a vastly complex inquiry into human freedom and its place in the divinely decreed order of things, only for Chaucer to drop the subject of free will after a few paltry lines.[10]

But perhaps we have been going about this the wrong way. Instead of trying to detect concrete allusions to scholastic debates in Chaucer, we might open ourselves to the aforementioned idea that his works explore genuinely philosophical topics but in a distinctively literary way. Maybe he is trying to say it with poetry. To show how this might work, let's consider the two opening stories of the *Canterbury Tales*, the *Knight's Tale* and the *Miller's Tale*.[11] Both of them involve a beautiful woman who is pursued by more than one man, but the comparisons pretty much end there. The first tale has a classical setting, complete with pagan gods and their temples, and takes inspiration from courtly love literature, with two imprisoned knights pining away for a beautiful lady they see in a garden (she does not exchange a single word with them, but manages to speak volumes with flowers). The second tale is a bawdy and comic one told by a drunken miller, the contrast between the tales reflecting that between the social station of the two speakers.

So we are being presented here with two very different worldviews, and, in particular, two ways of understanding the role of desire in human life. The *Knight's Tale* depicts its two rival lovers as being at the mercy of their passions. They use their powers of reason only to scheme and to justify why they should be the one to capture the hand of the beloved. As the narrating Knight says, love rules over them as a kind of natural law, one great enough to overwhelm any human law ("positif lawe," 1167). The lovers are, therefore, compared to wild beasts, especially when they come to violent blows with one another for the right to wed a woman who quite literally doesn't know they exist (1809).[12] As a contrast case, we are offered King Theseus. Though he is not perfectly rational—he has something of a temper—he is largely presented as a wise and merciful monarch (as at 1774, 2563–4) who embodies the medieval notion that the human ruler is a kind of viceregent of God on earth.[13] This is underscored in his speech, which ends the tale and which draws again on Boethius for the Aristotelian idea of God as a "first mover" who stands at the top of a "fair chain of love" binding together all things in the universe (2987–8).

By the end of the *Knight's Tale* we might be convinced that Chaucer, like a latter-day Alan of Lille, is using poetry to convey to us his ideas about the well ordered cosmos and about the proper role of reason in ethical action. But then we turn the page to the *Miller's Tale*. Here sexual attraction does not lead to years of romantic, passionate pining: it leads to sex. Where the lady of the *Knight's Tale* is a passive and beautiful object of desire, the adulterous wife of the *Miller's Tale* acts on her own desires, in one famous scene offering her backside to a man who asks her for a kiss. The vulgarity is a rebuke to the storytelling Knight, as is the Miller's conception of human nature. For him, passion is not a distraction from the rationality that makes us truly human. Rather, the whole point of human life is to have desires and act on them, without getting bogged down too much in thinking about what might and should be the case. This is already made clear in the prologue to this tale, when the Miller says that he prefers simply to assume that his wife is faithful to him rather than ponder on the prospect of her possible infidelity. It's enough to appreciate the pleasures that God has given you. Or, as the Miller puts it with characteristically crude wordplay, a husband shouldn't be too inquisitive about God's private matters ("pryvetee"), nor those of his wife; so long as he finds God's abundance there, he needn't worry about the rest (3163–6).

The vivid contrast of the Knight and the Miller is comically effective, and also philosophically effective. As in a Platonic dialogue, the literary frame makes it possible to offer the reader two clashing perspectives on happiness and human nature, and, as with Plato, Chaucer is the author of both perspectives. This, I think, is one of the things that literature can do for philosophy. It can help us to inhabit more than one worldview and understand them from the inside out. As another Chaucer scholar has recently put it, for him "Philosophy is more a matter of probing a difficult and evolving set of problems than it is of laying out doctrines that can be neatly summarized and classified according to schools of thought."[14]

That sentiment may also apply to William Langland and his poem *Piers Plowman*. It can seem to be a series of false starts, with the main character Will (Is his name another allusion to voluntarism?) taking sometimes contrary moral and spiritual advice from a series of allegorical characters. The social satire we found in Chaucer is present here too, with frequent criticism of the greed and immoral conduct found among the clergy.[15] The poem makes interesting reading in light of our previous discussion of medieval economic theory (Chapter 67), since it betrays something of the same ambivalence towards money, which even appears as one of the allegorical characters. Langland allows that money has two aspects (3.231), beneficial insofar as it is given for honest work but pernicious when it leads to usury or is heaped up "without measure" (3.241, 246). In this sense, wealth can be a bar to entering heaven (10.332). He also recognizes what seems to be a higher moral law than that governing economic life, insofar as the dictates of "need" outweigh the concerns of property (20.18–20).

Langland's repeated attacks on the learned clerical class may suggest a certain anti-intellectualism on his part. There is some truth to that suspicion, but he would be no ally of Chaucer's Miller. Langland has the character Imagination discourage Will from disparaging learning (*clergie*), since knowledge (*kynde wit*) is akin to Christ Himself and offers guidance to both the unlettered and the literate (12.92–6). Part of his complaint about the "clerks" is that these supposed scholars actually lack a firm grounding in "philosophie and phisik" (15.382). Still, the poem warns that too much concern with the niceties of theology can distract one from learning how to do well or do best (10.372). We are also told that we can learn truth even from the vulgar or less learned folk (the "lewed," 11.95), and that clerks somehow seem to wind up sinning more than the unlearned (those of "litel knowyng," 10.471–4). Religious belief is of greater help to us in our spiritual goals than logic (11.218). The message is one familiar from other spiritually minded medieval authors, like Bonaventure. Langland shows us the spiritual guide Piers Plowman rejecting the value of all knowledge, save love (13.23–4).

Yet, as many scholars have argued, Langland used his poem as an opportunity to respond to contemporary debates among the scholastics. In particular, he seems to have been concerned with the problem of divine grace, and the question of whether it is in the power of humans to merit salvation. In one of the most famous scenes, Langland describes Piers Plowman receiving a kind of legal document from the character Truth, a "pardon" which promises redemption to all those who do good works (7.1–8).[16] Piers rather shockingly tears up the pardon. It's a matter of debate what Langland is trying to tell us here, but one explanation is that Langland is opposing a tendency towards Pelagianism among fourteenth-century scholastics. In other words, he is rejecting the notion that we can be saved merely by "doing well," in the sense that good works *must* be rewarded by God, as promised in the pardon. Rather, as voluntarists like Bradwardine argued, it lies with God alone to determine through His absolute power who will and will not be saved (Chapter 61).

Another reflection of Langland's interest in contemporary debates about grace is his engagement with the so-called "problem of paganism," that is, the question of whether virtuous pagans may be redeemed without having accepted Christ.[17] In *Piers Plowman* we are explicitly told that such figures as Solomon, Socrates, and Aristotle (the "grete clerk") may have been damned, despite their wisdom (10.381–4, 12.268–9). Conversely, we learn that the Roman emperor Trajan has been saved, despite his not having been baptized (11.153–4, 12.211–13, 12.281). If we are hoping for a nuanced theological explanation for this, we will be disappointed. Apart from crediting the salvation to Trajan's virtue in life and an intercession by a prayerful Pope Gregory, Langland simply appeals to the inscrutability of God's will, taking refuge in the Latin slogan *Quare placuit? Quia voluit*: "Why did it please Him? Because He willed it so" (12.216). This rings those voluntarist bells again, but may also be a reflection of legal practices at the time of Langland. He was well acquainted with the world of lawyers—another group that comes in for some bitter critique in the poem—and may be thinking of the fourteenth-century practice by which the king or Parliament could use discretion to mitigate judgments of the common law.[18]

Yet another aspect of *Piers Plowman* that connects it to earlier philosophical literature is its handling of nature, which forcefully recalls the treatment of the natural world in twelfth-century authors like William of Conches and, especially, Alan of Lille. Langland too portrays nature as a kind of subordinate principle to God, through which divine "werkmanship" is exercised to make humans and other creatures (9.45).[19] Unfortunately, at least in our fallen state, we humans cannot assume that nature will suffice to make us good. Again like Alan, Langland focuses in particular on sexual misconduct as a depressingly common feature of human life, one that our power of rationality should prevent but does not (11.372). This idea that sin has opened up flaws within the natural order in fact explains why pagans are, with some apparently fairly arbitrary exceptions, all damned. Operating with nothing but natural reason and knowledge ("kynde wit," "kynde knowyng"), the pagans could not hope to "do best" in the way that is possible for Christians.[20]

You may have noticed that love and sexuality have been recurring themes in the medieval texts we've considered that bring together literature with philosophy. In addition to Alan of Lille, Chaucer, and Langland, one might think of the *Romance of the Rose*, Dante's portrayal of Beatrice, and for that matter of the way that female mystics like Hadewijch adopted the tropes of courtly love poetry. Chaucer is also one of several fourteenth-century authors to address the question of gender explicitly, in a work I haven't yet mentioned: the *Legend of Good Women*. The scholastic thinkers too have things to say about these issues, even if they aren't necessarily things we're going to be happy to hear. Sex and the status of women are, of course, rarely considered to be central topics in medieval philosophy, but given the more open-minded approach we're taking in this book, we're not going to let that stop us.

THE GOOD WIFE
SEXUALITY AND MISOGYNY
IN THE MIDDLE AGES

Have you ever been tempted to describe retrograde views about gender and sexuality as being "medieval"? If so, you were more right than you probably knew. A particularly good example is the condemnation of homosexuality as immoral. Famously, the Greeks generally considered male-male sexual relationships to be acceptable, in some cases even noble, as with the Sacred Band of Thebes. Pederastic liaisons were seen as serving a potentially useful social function, with an older man inducting a teenage "boy" into political life.[1] As for the Romans, they did not divide erotic proclivities into the heterosexual and homosexual. Instead, they distinguished between the dominant masculine role of "penetrating" a partner, who might be either female or male, and the more shameful and passive role of being penetrated. Even lesbianism was understood along these lines. When the Romans were disturbed by it, this was not so much because both partners were women, but because of the inevitable implication of this, namely that one of the two women would have to play the active, penetrating role.

But surely moral condemnation of homosexuality as such goes back at least as far as the origins of the Christian religion? Not exactly. Late ancient Christians too lacked the concept of homosexuality, especially if we mean by this a settled sexual preference or identity. Sex between men, always of more concern to churchmen than lesbian sex, was certainly denounced by Augustine and others. But it did not emerge as a specific sin called "sodomy (*sodomia*)" until the eleventh century.[2] The term appears in Peter Damian as a neologism formed in imitation of the word "blasphemy (*blasphemia*)." Damian was a tireless crusader on behalf of the moralizing reform movement that swept across Christendom at that time (Chapter 6). This same reform movement, promoted by Pope Gregory VII, also resulted in a new demand for celibacy among clerics. That was not universally welcomed by the clerics themselves. In one case they burned a reformer alive for promoting this novel restriction.[3]

Already before the time of Damian and for a long time after him, sex between men was classified as just one example of a broader sin called *luxuria*. As the name may suggest to the English speaker's ear, this was the moral failing of being too susceptible to pleasure. The pleasure did not need to be sexual in nature; *luxuria* could even include a weakness for things like soft bedding and fine clothes. But there was a strong association between being "luxurious" and engaging in deviant sexual practices. What counted as deviant sex? According to some authors, pretty well any sexual activity apart from intercourse between a man and a woman in the missionary position. It was seen as "natural" because of the front-facing orientation of the genitals, or because it put the woman literally under the man in a reflection of their hierarchical relationship. Bestiality, masturbation, and even cannibalism were sometimes classified alongside sodomy as bestial or "luxurious" sins. If Damian was moved to draw particular attention to sodomy and give it a name, it was perhaps because this was the version of the sin most likely to be practiced by clerics and monks in their exclusively male environments. Still, in the thirteenth century, Albert the Great thought of sodomy as a form of *luxuria*, which he defined more narrowly as "an experience of pleasure according to the reproductive power that does not comply with law."[4]

To explain why exactly these sins are so sinful, medieval thinkers took up the tools of philosophy. One option was to draw on the scientific tradition. Avicenna's massively influential medical compilation, the *Canon*, includes a section on coitus which explained male desire for sex with other men in anatomical terms. But the Latin scholastics tended to favor psychological explanations. As Albert's definition suggests, he saw the problem primarily as an inability to resist the attraction of unlawful pleasures (likewise Aquinas, *ST* 2.1 Q31 a7). As for the reason why such pleasures are unlawful, the usual rationale was that non-reproductive sex constitutes a misuse of the generative power. Like their late ancient predecessors, the medievals had no concept of sexual identities, no division of people into "homosexuals" and "heterosexuals." So their rationale for what we would call "homophobia" was a fear of undermining fertility, not a fear of undermining the family, a consideration more likely to be mentioned by anti-homosexual bigots nowadays.[5] The medievals thus had the problem of explaining why, if the sexual faculty is exclusively for reproduction, couples known to be infertile should be allowed to marry and have sex.[6] This remains a difficulty for anyone who thinks that all morally licit intercourse must at least potentially issue in reproduction, an assumption that still today underlies religious strictures against contraception and homosexuality.

A rich source of information about medieval ideas of sexuality is the enormous body of penitential literature produced in the wake of the Gregorian reform.[7] That reform involved the institution of regular confession by believers, prompting the need for texts advising clerics on how to tend to their spiritual flocks. The penitential literature attempted to bring order to human disorder. Vices were listed and sorted into their various types with indications of the "tariff" of penance due for each sin. A potential danger here was that speaking too openly of sodomy or other sins could, to put it bluntly, give people ideas. Even worse, sodomites might realize that they were far from alone in their "perversion." Thus, the author of one penitential text, William Peraldus, recommended that "This vice is to be spoken of with great caution both in preaching and in confessional questioning, that nothing be revealed to men that might give them occasion to sin."[8] The penitentials also tell us a great deal about attitudes towards sexuality more generally, for instance that sex outside of marriage was popularly considered to be no big deal, to the frustration of church authorities.[9]

What we're seeing here is the (if you'll pardon the expression) penetration of scholastic and especially legalistic ways of thinking into the intimate lives of everyday people. Advice to confessors often drew on the great canonists like Gratian and Hortensius, who in turn looked back to older authors like Augustine and Isidore of Seville. Isidore encapsulated much medieval thought on sex and gender relations in his etymologies of "man" and "woman": "man (vir) is so named because there is greater force (vis) in him than in women...woman (mulier) gets her name from softness (mollities)...for the two sexes are differentiated in the strength and weakness of their bodies."[10] The standard view among intellectuals was that women's bodies are more moist, more cold, and hence "softer," which in turn gave rise to the notion that they are highly susceptible to a variety of sins ranging from avarice to sexual excess.

This attitude towards women was assumed as a matter of course by most schoolmen on the basis of Aristotelian natural philosophy and Galenic medicine. Not that women were a matter of much interest at the universities. Passages that mention them usually do so only in order to set up a good puzzle, as when Henry of Ghent asks whether a widow who remarries should go back to her first husband if he is raised from the dead. A review of such texts has concluded that the scholastics' failure to discuss the weakness of women in any depth was "not because they were gender-blind egalitarians, but because women simply were not interesting to them as women: they were not part of their intellectual world."[11] Still, it is easy to find what we would now describe as "misogynistic" statements in many a scholastic thinker.

To take only the most famous of those thinkers, we find Aquinas wondering why it made sense for God to create woman at all and answering that she was needed as help for man and specifically for the purpose of procreation (ST 1 Q92 a1). He elsewhere remarks that one should love one's father more than one's mother because the father is the active principle, the mother a "passive and material principle" (ST 2.2 Q26 a10). In still another passage he states that women should not speak publicly to the Church because "in general they are imperfect in wisdom" (ST 2.2 Q177 a2).[12] His student Giles of Rome similarly explains that "A woman ought naturally to be subject to a man because she is naturally inferior to the man in prudence."[13] On the bright side, Aquinas doesn't think that women should actually be *enslaved* to men. He explains that women's passivity does not make them subordinate to men in the fashion of slaves, but in the manner appropriate to the household or city (*subiectio oeconomica vel civilis*), in which the subject is ruled with a view to her own good (ST 1 Q92 a1 repl 2).[14]

One branch of medieval scientific literature that did focus on women was gynaecology, which offered extensive and often explicit information about women's bodies, including their genitals.[15] Gynaecological works were also widely translated into vernacular languages. One translator, sounding a bit like Dante at the beginning of his *Convivio*, even said that he was producing a Middle English version of a gynaecological work in order that it might be of use to a female audience that could not read Latin. Nonetheless, it would seem that such books were mostly written and read by men.[16] A scientific interest in women did not necessarily imply a friendly attitude towards them. We repeatedly find in such books the claim that menstrual blood is poisonous, with one commentator wondering why it doesn't kill the menstruating women. The great medieval defender of women, Christine de Pizan, to whom we'll be coming shortly, protested that one widely read gynaeco-logical work called *Secrets of Women* and falsely ascribed to Albert the Great was a "treatise composed of lies."

Of course, even medieval schoolmen did not think that all women are bad people. They knew well the stories of female saints, who were sometimes singled out for special praise because they had overcome their natural inferiority and risen to the heights of piety and virtue.[17] Since women were supposedly especially prone to strong sexual desires, it was all the more admirable if they refrained from sex out of piety. Even within marriage, chastity was valued, though it was reasoned that a wife who vowed abstinence should give up her vow if her husband ordered her to do so.[18] It may seem paradoxical that woman, who was purportedly created to help man with procreation, should ideally adopt virginity or chastity, but charac-teristically Aquinas is ready with a distinction that resolves the problem. Procreation is indeed good but it is a good of the body, whereas virginity is "ordered to the good of the soul in respect of the contemplative life," because the chaste person is devoted to thinking only of God (ST 2.2 Q152 a4).

Were any of the scholastics willing to entertain the possibility of a woman who is praiseworthy for her mind rather than for piety and submission to men? I said above that "most" schoolmen were deeply and, for the most part, unreflectively convinced of women's inferiority. One exception to this rule was Peter Abelard. As is clear from the letters he exchanged with Heloise, Abelard was impressed by and infatuated with her in large part because of her intellect. Perhaps for this reason, after they were parted, he went on to write one of the most impassioned defenses of women written in the Middle Ages. It is a treatise on the dignity of nuns like Heloise and her sisters, full of theological arguments for admiring and cherishing women. He reminds us that it was women who anointed Christ during his lifetime and argues that the original sin initiated by Eve has been compensated by the Virgin Mary. Even Abelard, though, couples his praise of women with an assumption of their inferiority: "Although women are the weaker sex, their virtue is more pleasing to God and more perfect."[19]

He was only one of many medieval authors who wrote on the "defense of woman" or who rebutted misogynist arguments.[20] The earliest example would seem to come in the late eleventh century with Marbod of Rennes, who wrote a poem attacking woman followed by a response in her praise. In the fourteenth century the case for women will be advanced by Jean Le Fèvre, who incidentally refers to Heloise and calls her *philosofesse*. He and other authors who defended women drew on biblical material, including the apocryphal books, and were at pains to list virtuous women from pagan history and among Christian saints.[21] Telling points made in such texts include the observation that men implicitly condemn their own mothers when they repeat misogynistic arguments, and a proof that woman is intended as a partner to man and not his inferior, on the grounds that Eve was made from the rib in Adam's side and not from his foot. It must, however, be said there is a good deal of praising with faint damn in the works written in defense of women. Le Fèvre, for instance, comments that woman is superior to man in her freedom because she has less reason and more will!

The masters of ambivalent praise of women were the fourteenth-century poets Boccaccio and Chaucer. Both composed works gathering together stories of good women, which sounds like a forthrightly feminist project. Yet highlighting exceptionally virtuous females can go hand in hand with lamenting the fact that most are far from exceptional. Thus, Boccaccio complained that women typically concern themselves only with sex and childrearing, despite having "the ability to do those things which make men famous, if only they are willing to work with perseverance."[22] As for Chaucer, he focused on famous women who suffered from the mistreatment of men. This is apt to provoke the reader's sympathy but also conveys the sense that women are inevitably passive, and frequently victimized by male deceptions because they are so easy to deceive.[23]

Chaucer's most fascinating and ambiguous text on women comes in his *Canterbury Tales* in the form of the Prologue of the *Wife of Bath's Tale*. Our protagonist Alisoun tells the satirical and frequently outrageous story of her five marriages. She minces no words about the pleasure she takes in sex, announcing that "in wifehood I will use my instrument as freely as my maker hath it sent" (149–50). She is willing to admit that virginity is admirable but stresses that it is not obligatory. She might almost be responding to Aquinas' remarks on this topic when she says that maidenhood may be preferred to marriage like gold spoons to wooden ones; yet "a lord in his household, he has not every vessel all of gold; some are of tree, and do their lord service" (99–101). Her unsentimental eye also discerns that marriage is a kind of economic exchange, in which sex is a "debt" paid by one partner to another, in her own case with little pleasure when she was married to older men.

This prologue also contains a remarkable reflection on the tradition of misogynist literature and its connections to the culture of "clerks." Alisoun's final husband, Jankyn, is such a clerk, who studied at Oxford (527). He reads from a book full of nasty remarks about women, compiled from a wide range of authors, including none other than Heloise (677), a surprising inclusion until we remember the diatribe against marriage in her letters to Abelard.[24] Scholars have eagerly sought to reconstruct this fictional miscellany of misogyny: Monica Green has quipped that the "'book of wikked wyves' might be the most thoroughly studied book that never existed."[25] When an outraged Alisoun tears pages from the book and slaps Jankyn, he retaliates with such force that she is knocked senseless and rendered temporarily deaf, a memorable portrayal of domestic violence.

The Wife is clearly a comic character, but the modern reader naturally sympathizes with her plight in this scene and more generally with her scathing critique of men, their violence and cruelty, their fecklessness and sexual inadequacy. But is this really what Chaucer wanted us to take from his poem? When you know about the sin of *luxuria*, you can't help noticing the delight the Wife of Bath takes in fine clothes as well as sex, or the suggestion that she uses religious pilgrimage as an opportunity for sexual adventure. On the other hand, when you're familiar with medieval misogyny, you can't help noticing how comprehensively she parodies and rebuts the typical accusations made against women. I tend to side with those who see Chaucer as using positive and negative sentiments towards women primarily as a tool for vivid characterization. Even as Alisoun debunks misogyny, she is herself being debunked.[26] Certainly, she is not recommended to us as a model of female virtue or as proof that women are truly equal to men.

This has been a pretty depressing chapter. We've seen medieval intellectuals unthinkingly embracing, or even actively arguing for, attitudes towards same-sex sexuality and women that led to many centuries of very real suffering, ranging from domestic violence to legal persecution of homosexuals. Even more depressing is the fact that these same attitudes live on today. But there is more to say. In Chapter 75 we'll be seeing how one remarkable woman took a stand against the kinds of misogynist views we've just surveyed. And in Chapter 74, we'll be seeing how some female thinkers responded to the common medieval association between women and the body. Rather than rejecting this association, they exploited it, and on the most powerful grounds imaginable: that God Himself had chosen embodiment when He was incarnated in human form.

74

SIGHS WERE HER FOOD
CATHERINE OF SIENA
AND AFFECTIVE MYSTICISM

W e probably imagine the typical medieval philosopher as a solitary figure removed from the rest of society, perhaps not in a literal ivory tower (too expensive), but scratching away on parchment in a scriptorium, university classroom, or monastic cell. Yet a number of personalities in this book belie that assumption. Among the politically engaged thinkers we've mentioned were Anselm, Robert Grosseteste, William of Ockham, and Nicole Oresme. Scholastics could be dragged into political affairs unwillingly, and often attained influence by holding church offices. Yet one of the most politically active thinkers of the fourteenth century was, as a woman, barred from such positions of authority. This was Catherine of Siena, who in hundreds of surviving letters corresponded with a range of notables, including two popes, the queen of Naples, the French king, and the count of Anjou. Her political platform had three main planks. She exhorted the popes to heal the Great Schism within the Church that began in 1378; she campaigned for reform of the Church, like a latter-day Peter Damian; and she called for the launching of a crusade.[1]

These three goals were in fact part of her overall aim, which was to work towards nothing less than peace and solidarity in Christian Europe. This obviously applies to her complaints about the schism, but also to her plea for church reform and a crusade: through these measures, she hoped, all Christians would rally and unite under the leadership of the papacy. Thus, she wrote to the powerful mercenary John Hawkwood, "Do not make war any longer against Christians, because in this you offend God, but go against the infidels." She backed up this advice with the traditional rationale for waging war in the name of the Christian faith (see Chapter 40 above): "The infidels have done us an injury, for they possess what is not theirs, but ours."[2] She worked to establish personal relationships with the potentates who received her letters, as when she addressed the Pope as *babbo* ("daddy"). But when the situation required, she could be rather more stern. One story has her meeting the Pope and being asked how she is so well informed about the situation at the papal court. Her forthright response: "Even while I was in my native city, I was more aware of the stench of the sins that are committed in the Roman curia than are even those who committed them and commit them now on a daily basis."[3] Catherine was particularly active in her native Siena, cultivating a spiritual relationship with the senators of that city and relentlessly supporting the interests of the papacy against the rebel cities of Tuscany, which she labeled as "rotten members" of the Christian community.

How was it possible for a woman to enter so fearlessly onto the normally all-male stage of fourteenth-century power politics? Not unlike Hildegard of Bingen two centuries earlier, Catherine achieved prominence and authority through her reputation for holiness, in part because of the mystical visions she enjoyed. Born in 1347, Catherine swore a life of chastity already at the age of 7 and later entered into a "mystical union" with God; only she could see a wedding band that appeared on her own finger. Her most famous miracle was the appearance of stigmata on her hands and feet, that is, wounds like the ones inflicted on Christ in the crucifixion. This would also become her most controversial miracle, because Franciscans were reluctant to admit that anyone but the founder of their order could be distinguished in this way. In 1470, almost a century after Catherine's death, the sitting Pope was even persuaded to forbid depicting her with the stigmata.

Catherine's political engagement unfolded side by side with a radical commitment to personal asceticism. This too may seem a paradox. When late antique Christians devoted themselves to lives of self-abnegation, they would typically withdraw from society.[4] Women took part in this movement, such as Syncletica in the fourth century, and a thousand years later women were still following this path, like the anchorite Julian of Norwich (Chapter 71). But Catherine managed to exercise influence in the world of men precisely because of her reputation for pious discipline. As reported in a hagiographical account of her life written by her "spiritual director" and confessor, Raymond of Capua, she effectively starved herself to death at the age of 33, going for long stretches of time where she ate nothing but the Eucharist. This has led some scholars to suggest that Catherine may have suffered from anorexia.[5] But for a full understanding of Catherine's "inedia" (that is, living without eating), we need to think more broadly about the role of food in medieval society and its remarkably consistent association with women.

Here we are taking up a theme explored in one of the most influential books in the field of medieval studies, Caroline Walker Bynum's *Holy Feast and Holy Fast*.[6] As Bynum pointed out, Catherine of Siena is only the most famous example of a medieval woman renouncing food, or nourishing herself solely from the consecrated host. This was a feat also performed by the self-explanatorily named Joan the

Meatless, and by Alpaïs of Cudot, who went forty years without eating anything else. Women also had visions of Christ offering them the host directly. Catherine and other women are said to have eaten the scabs of lepers and and drunk the pus from their sores. Mechthild of Magdeburg wrote of drinking the blood of Christ and imagined nursing souls in Purgatory with her own blood rather than milk. A passage in Catherine's writing sums up the theme nicely: "The pains are [the soul's] refreshment and the tears which it has shed for the memory of [Christ's] blood are its drink. And the sighs are its food."[7]

Bynum asked herself why so many miracles and images having to do with food appear in works by and about medieval women, and reached the following conclusions. Most obviously, food was associated more with women than men: it was their task to prepare meals for the family. Food was, therefore, unusual in being under the control of women, unlike land or money: it was something they could give up as an expression of pious asceticism, or donate as an act of charity. Equally obvious to us, given what we've seen in Chapter 73, is that women were associated with the passions and the body, rather than with the powers of reason that were exalted by so many medieval scholastics. Many have supposed that this is reflected in the physicality of the language used by medieval women mystics. Women were taught to think of themselves as embodied beings rather than as immaterial souls, and this shaped their religious, literary, and philosophical imagination. This would be a standard approach to what is often called "affective mysticism," as practiced by the Beguine mystics, Julian of Norwich, and Catherine of Siena, but also by plenty of male authors of the medieval period, like Bernard of Clairvaux. In fact, as Christina Van Dyke points out, this approach was actually dominant in mystical literature of the thirteenth and fourteenth centuries, even if more abstract language is found in "contemplative" mystical texts like the *Cloud of Unknowing* or the work of Walter Hilton, who disdained allusions to such bodily phenomena as the "sounding of the ear, or savoring in the mouth, or smelling at the nose."[8]

Bynum does not deny the cultural link between women and the body, but she points out that the use of this link by female authors had a very different significance in medieval religious culture than it might have today. When women spoke of milk, blood, tears, and so on, they were not grudgingly accepting an inferior role as inhabitors of the body while ceding the superior realms of the mind to their male contemporaries. Rather, they were treating the very fact of embodiment as an exalted "path to God."[9] At the core of affective mysticism was the Incarnation, in which God Himself saw fit to take on a human body and suffered unimaginably for our sins. Women could participate in Christ's sacrifice through their own unimaginable suffering, pursuing a rigorous asceticism that might involve outrageous feats of self-abnegation. Hence the refusal to eat, or the miraculous ability to refrain from doing so. As Bynum puts it, "In a religiosity where wounds are the source of a mother's milk, fatal disease is a bridal chamber, pain or insanity clings to the breast like perfume, physicality is hardly rejected or transcended. Rather, it is explored and embraced."[10]

The result is that, as Bynum says in the funniest sentence of her book, "Reading the lives of fourteenth and fifteenth century women saints greatly expands one's knowledge of Latin synonyms for whip, thong, flail, chain, etc."[11] Women who chastized their flesh were frequently praised for pursuing identification with Christ to its logical extreme; indeed, in most cases we know about women ascetics from admiring texts written about them by men. Yet extreme examples of female self-punishment also made male authors uncomfortable. We've already met Henry Suso (Chapter 69), a follower of Meister Eckhart, whose own ascetic practices are detailed in a hagiographic account of Suso's life; it may have been written by his spiritual daughter Elsbeth Stagel. While, of course, presenting Suso as a spiritual hero, the biography also seeks to discourage female readers from following his example.[12] The suggestion would seem to be that extraordinary, even life-threatening, self-abnegation is not necessarily a bad thing in itself, but is more appropriate for strong men than weak women.

Ambivalence greeted another noteworthy aspect of female asceticism, namely chastity. To follow the example of the so-called "desert mothers" of late antiquity and live chastely was to reject the role of wife and mother which was so central to Christian conceptions of the purpose of women. Precisely for this reason, families often opposed the pious calling of female daughters and wives. Catherine of Siena is again a famous example. We learn from her hagiography that she cut off her hair and swore marriage to Christ alone when she was young, perhaps in part in reaction to her sister's death in childbirth (it's worth bearing in mind that for medieval women, every pregnancy was a potential death sentence). Tellingly, the followers who gathered around Catherine were called her *famiglia*, suggesting that bonds of piety and holiness could replace and transcend those of blood. Another renowned case was Margery Kempe, a remarkable figure whose life was full of controversial exploits and travels, which included a pilgrimage to the Holy Land and even an inspirational face-to-face meeting with an elderly Julian of Norwich in the year 1413. After a negotiation with her husband, she agreed to give up fasting if he would live chastely with her.

This sort of thing elicited mixed feelings.[13] On the one hand, the monastic calling, with its renunciation of sexual pleasure, was, of course, considered to be praise-worthy. On the other hand, condemning sex as irretrievably sinful was the stuff of heresy. In the wake of extreme ascetic movements like Catharism, the Church moved increasingly towards valuing marriage as a good and honoring motherhood as the ideal to which women should aspire. In this respect, the female ascetics and affective mystics were far from passively internalizing Christian dogmas about their nature and limitations as women. If anything, they were going against the trend of church teaching. Nor was chastity within marriage—perhaps after having several children—necessarily encouraged by the Church, as we might have expected. Rather, both partners were instructed not to refuse sex to their spouse, so that at a minimum a chaste marriage needed to be mutually agreed by both husband and wife. Perhaps this was in part a way for the clergy to protect its own uniqueness.[14] It rather takes the shine off of being a celibate priest or monk when the local merchant and his wife are managing to live together in pious abstinence, especially when people like Bernard of Clairvaux were going around saying things like, "To be always with a woman and not have sexual relations with her is more difficult than to raise the dead."[15]

While Bynum's thesis has, as I say, been extremely influential and fruitful for subsequent studies in this field, it has not gone unchallenged. Amy Hollywood is another medievalist who has built on, but also sought to qualify, her conclusions. Hollywood drew attention to the way that the male hagiographers of holy women emphasize their "embodiment" more than the holy women themselves. She considers the case of Beatrice of Nazareth, who is unusual in that we have a work composed by her (a treatise called *Seven Manners of Loving*) as well as an account of her life written by a man.[16] Comparing these two texts, Hollywood finds that, whereas the biography emphasizes the bodily side of Beatrice's practices, Beatrice's own writing refuses to consider women's "bodies as the site of their sanctity." Rather, Beatrice emphasizes her own "interiorized, disembodied" self and subjecthood—much, we could add, as a typical (and, of course, male) scholastic at the medieval university might do, under inspiration from Platonist ideas about the immaterial, rational soul as the true self or core of each person.

The lesson to draw from this, I think, is firstly that women authors of the Middle Ages, including the mystical authors, in fact adopted a variety of approaches to embodiment and the self. The intense physicality of the imagery in Julian of Norwich is nothing like what we found in Marguerite Porete, for example. Secondly, even within the corpus associated with a single author, we may find affective mysticism alongside more abstract and "rationalist" elements of the sort that is usually associated with contemplative mysticism, and more likely to be taken seriously by historians of philosophy (when, that is, they take mysticism seriously at all). For an example of this we can turn finally to the work by Catherine of Siena most likely to turn up on the syllabus of a philosophy class, her *Dialogue*.[17]

In one of her visions Catherine was promised a "mouth and wisdom which none can resist," and not without reason. The *Dialogue*, written in Italian, is another star in our firmament of fourteenth-century vernacular works. In a manner reminiscent of Augustine's *Confessions*, Catherine wrote it as a dialogue between her own soul and God, though unlike in the *Confessions*, here it is God who does most of the talking. One way to read the *Dialogue* is as a long explanation of Catherine's own ascetic practices. For her, physical and mental suffering is the inevitable consequence of sin. No amount of agony can ever make good the wrong of defying God, since He is infinite goodness. And agony is very much called for: the reality of sin, both one's own and that of others, should inspire infinite suffering and dismay. To allow us to feel this pain more fully, God abandons the soul so that it may be confronted by its own weakness.

But as a balance to this idea of hopeless abandonment, which recalls the theme of *Verworfenheit* in Mechthild of Magdeburg, Catherine develops an account of love for God. In other writings, she fuses this idea with a highly charged eroticism. The most famous example is a letter recounting her encounter with a man named Niccolò di Toldo, whom she comforted as he was led to his execution on political charges.[18] In a remarkable gender inversion, the letter casts Niccolò in the role of a bride being led to marriage with Christ in the afterlife. As the two prepare for his date with death, Catherine writes: "He had his head resting on my breast. I sensed an intense joy, a fragrance of his blood, and it was not without the fragrance of my own, which I wait to shed for the sweet husband Jesus." This sort of thing is largely absent in the *Dialogue*, where Catherine speaks of weeping a "river of tears" but does not make much use of erotic language. This is a more psychological account of the gradual progress of the soul's progress from wicked self-love and love of pleasure to altruistic love of her neighbor, and then ultimately love for God. This treatise proves to be yet another document of fourteenth-century voluntarism, as Catherine puts emphasis above all on the agreement between the human will and the will of God. After death, once the blessed are in heaven and the damned in hell, it is too late to use one's freedom to love God. At that point, the will is "confirmed" in its orientation towards or away from infinite divine goodness. So everything depends on our use of the will in this life.

Again, this is relevant to the theme of suffering: one feels real pain only in cases of thwarted willing or unsatisfied desire. But insofar as the soul's will is aligned perfectly with God's, the soul is satisfied. Catherine's line of thought may distantly remind us of the Stoic proposal that we can secure perfect happiness by wholeheartedly accepting whatever divine providence ordains. More proximately, it recalls Marguerite Porete's idea of unifying our will with God's (Chapter 53). For Catherine, this is the purpose of the ascetic's war on her own wayward will. Penitential practices do not suffice in themselves, being only a means towards the ultimate goal of aligning the will with that of God. Though she echoes Marguerite's point that union with God is a higher objective than ordinary charity and virtue, Catherine makes this proposal in a far less provocative way and retains the idea that chastizing the body is a key part of the mystical path, something Marguerite came to reject.

But perhaps it is a mistake to read the *Dialogue* in a way that is so influenced by the accounts of Catherine's self-starvation and other punitive practices handed down by her biographer Raymond of Capua. Rather than understanding the soul's pain and suffering to be at the heart of her teaching, we might instead think of the *Dialogue* as an exploration of the self. As Christina Van Dyke has written, "Introspection into our limitations is meant to open us to a deeper awareness of God's unlimited attributes. In general, the idea is that the more conscious we are of our own failings and imperfections, the more we will notice God's ultimate perfection and appreciate God's unfailing love for us."[19] Like other mystics, whether affective or contemplative, Catherine of Siena was among other things pursuing that most Socratic of goals: self-knowledge.

THE MOST CHRISTIAN DOCTOR
THE *QUERELLE DE LA ROSE*
AND JEAN GERSON

O ur tour through medieval intellectual culture is reaching its final stops as we approach the year 1400, the date I've somewhat artificially chosen to mark the boundary between medieval and Renaissance philosophy. To make sure you realize how artificial that boundary is, in these last few chapters, I'll be looking at figures and movements that spanned the divide between the fourteenth and fifteenth centuries. We'll be seeing anticipations of Renaissance humanism and of the religious controversies that ultimately gave rise to the Protestant Reformation. But around 1400 people were also looking back. They continued to take inspiration from earlier scholastics like Aquinas, Scotus, and Ockham, and texts that were more than a century old were the late medieval equivalent of bestsellers. One of them was the *Romance of the Rose*.

Normally I would worry that readers might struggle to remember a topic covered about thirty chapters ago. But I suspect you'll have no trouble recalling this ironic, artful, and occasionally obscene production of the late thirteenth-century poet Jean de Meun. The occasional obscenity was one reason for the so-called *Querelle de la rose*, a famous debate that was sparked at the close of the fourteenth century. It involved about half a dozen members of the French aristocracy with various connections to the French court and, in the person of Jean Gerson, the chancellor of the University of Paris. He was scandalized by the poem's enthusiastic embrace of erotic conquest, and its use of naughty language and even naughtier metaphors to describe the sexual organs. Another of its detractors was Christine de Pizan, who complained especially of the misogyny running throughout the *Romance*.

I'm going to cover Christine properly in the next volume of this series. We'll see that she contributed significantly to political philosophy and established herself as a sort of figure unprecedented in the medieval period. She was an independent woman, neither ascetic nor nun, who participated in intellectual and literary discussions on an equal footing with scholars of her time. In the case of the *Querelle de la rose,* she initiated the discussion. She first expressed her disquiet about Jean de Meun's work in 1399, following this up with a series of letters in which she sharpened and extended her critique of the *Romance* and its pernicious effect on readers. What strikes the modern reader most is her spirited rebuke of those passages in the *Romance* which speak badly of all women, as when Jean has one character complain "You are all now, will be, and have been, whores, in deed or intention *(Toutes estes, serez et fustes, de fet ou de volenté, pustes)*" (38).[1] Christine was outraged by such statements. Certainly some women are wicked, but just as we don't say that all angels are evil because of the fall of Lucifer, neither should we condemn the whole sex for the sins of the few. As a female author, she had a personal stake in the defense of woman, something not lost on her opponents. Defenders of the *Romance* added insult to insult by implying that she had no business criticizing it. One of them, Jean de Montrueil, wrote: "Although she is not lacking in intelligence within the limits of her female capacity, it seemed to me nevertheless that I was hearing the Greek whore Leontium, who, as Cicero reports, 'dared to write against so great a philosopher as Theophrastus'" (103).

In response Christine modestly admitted to being "a woman of untrained intellect and uncomplicated sensibility" (50), while insisting that her voice should be heard nonetheless. Heroines of classical history and Christian religion show, she argued, that there is no cause to discount someone just because she is female (97). Besides, if the debate in part concerned women's virtue, then this was something to which she could speak with a certain authority, being a woman herself (60). Not that you need to be a woman to see the implausibility of saying that women are more wicked than men. After all, "Where are the countries or kingdoms that have been ravaged by women's great iniquities?" (57). Yet misogyny was only one of the accusations she lobbed in the direction of Jean de Meun. Like the "Foolish Lover" character in the *Romance* itself, she complained about the use of the dirty word "testicles" (52) and more generally worried that the *Romance* is liable, indeed purposefully designed, to urge its reader on to sin.

Jean de Meun's admirers responded with more than just sexist abuse of Christine. The most interesting voice on the other side was Pierre Col, who wrote a letter to Christine putting a case in favor of the *Romance.* Here we get into more obviously philosophical territory, as the debate begins to turn on questions of aesthetics and in particular the relation between fiction and the moral integrity of an author. Col urges us not to confuse the characters who speak in the *Romance* with Jean de Meun himself. Admittedly, figures like the Old Woman and the Jealous Man do have nasty advice for the character of the Foolish Lover, but these "evil words" are intended simply to prepare the reader, who is likely to encounter such arguments and attitudes in real life (149). According to Pierre Col, the attitude of Jean de Meun was quite different. He used to be a Foolish Lover himself but eventually came to his senses. It is thus a work of repentance and even of helpful warning for the reader not to give in to the irrationality of passionate love (137). Col even claims to know a man who was brought to his senses upon reading the *Romance* and recovered from a bout of foolish love (151).

In truth, this is a patently unconvincing reading of the *Romance*, and one wonders how seriously Col means what he is saying. A true follower of de Meun, Col indulges in his own literary games. As one interpreter has put it, "even in the midst of defending, Col appears all too often self-mocking and ironic...while preserving all the while a delightful, blithe air of naïve innocence."[2] Christine takes the whole business more seriously, responding that the detail and persuasiveness of the wicked speeches in the *Romance* go far beyond what would be needed to give warning. It would be like actually teaching someone to counterfeit money in the process of warning them about false currency (180). And for her, this is no game: to match Col's story about the friend who was cured of love, Christine tells of another man who beats his wife, having been turned misogynistic by this dangerous reading material (182).

As for Jean Gerson, he was somewhat more willing to play with literary artifice.[3] In a work of 1402 he had lampooned the *Romance* by describing a courtroom scene in which the character of the Foolish Lover (in other words, Jean de Meun) is accused in the presence of a personification of Justice. His ironically disapproving approach is already indicated by the detail that his own "vision" is related as something that happened when he was very much awake (*en mon veillant*), not dreaming like de Meun or for that matter like Langland in *Piers Plowman*. Despite his literary sensibility, he was no more impressed than Christine by the idea that we should carefully distinguish an author's own views from those of his characters. This does not give an author license to say just whatever he wants.[4] Clearly, it would be unacceptable for a Christian to preach on behalf of the Muslim faith but just for the sake of argument.[5] Besides, the *Romance* makes its speakers say things that are discordant with the concepts they personify; the character "Reason" is not very reasonable, for example. This betrays that the author is, in fact, putting his own words into the mouths of his characters, so that effectively everything is said "in his person (*en sa persone*)" (118). Yet both Gerson and Christine were still able to admire the aesthetic qualities of the poem. They admitted that it is well written and registered no objections to courtly love literature as such, even if Christine teasingly mocked some of its conventions: "I have never heard tell where the cemeteries are in which are buried those whom pure love has put to death" (46). Thus, Gerson was perfectly happy with the beginning of the *Romance* by Guillaume de Lloris (129). Only its scandalous continuation by Jean de Meun needed to be brought to court.

Though the work at the center of this debate is a quintessentially medieval one, the debate itself seems to belong more to the Renaissance. We have here reflection on the uses and abuses of literature in the vernacular, studded with frequent allusions to classical authors like Cicero and Seneca, far more salutary authors than Jean de Meun in the opinion of Christine and Gerson (62, 126). The defence of female virtue, already a feature of fourteenth-century literature with Boccaccio and Chaucer, would become a frequent topic of reflection in the fifteenth and sixteenth centuries. As we'll see when we come again to Christine, she returned to the subject in later works, notably her *City of Ladies*. A list of other Renaissance thinkers who took up the cause of women would include Henricus Cornelius Agrippa, Moderata Fonte, and Lucrezia Marinella. One may thus see both Gerson and Christine de Pizan as transitional figures, blurring the line between the Middle Ages and the Renaissance.

Indeed, few authors spanned these two periods like Jean Gerson. From a humble background, he rose to become a theologian at Paris in 1392 and, as already mentioned, the chancellor of the university. This made him a prominent individual, with the opportunity to comment on a wide range of topics ranging from the political to the pastoral to the philosophical. It has been proposed that he was among the first of Europe's "public intellectuals," and a leading exponent of the short topical treatise that was displacing older forms of writing at this period, like the commentary.[6] Among the topics he tackled in such texts were the question of tyrannicide, the validity of visions received by women, including Brigitte of Sweden and Joan of Arc, the goodness of celibacy, and the evil of the heresies taught by John Wyclif and Jan Hus. He often followed in the footsteps of his admired teacher at Paris, the theologian Peter d'Ailly, who was also involved in the debate over the *Romance of the Rose*.

For both d'Ailly and Gerson, a far more crucial dispute was the one that raged in the late fourteenth and early fifteenth centuries as a result of the schism in the papacy. The rift began in 1378 when cardinals decamped from Italy to Avignon in France, claiming that the election of Pope Urban VI had been forced upon them by the people of Rome. They nominated a new pope, Clement VII, beginning a decades-long period where there were two or even three rival popes. When popes died, the schism continued, with new candidates simply replacing them on both sides. It was a political conundrum that also posed grave spiritual difficulties. What were Christians to do in the face of conflicting decrees handed down by two different popes? Gerson offered a voice of calm guidance, reminding us of Peter

Abelard's ethics by suggesting that the main thing was to form an intention to be pious.[7] In the same optimistic spirit, he worked for years to encourage the so-called *via cessionis*, a solution by which all rival claimants to the papacy would voluntarily renounce their titles, paving the way for the election of a new and universally recognized candidate.

Ultimately, though, and, to be more specific, at the time of a pivotal council held in Constance from 1414 to 1418, Gerson became a key supporter of the *via concilii*. This alternative solution called for a church council that would impose a settlement of the issue. Peter d'Ailly and others, notably the early conciliarists Conrad of Gelnhausen and Henry of Langenstein (on whom, see Chapter 75), had already pressed for this outcome, and the addition of Gerson's voice helped to bring it about. If we think back to a writer like Giles of Rome, we can see why the conciliar approach was so controversial. Giles argued that the Pope possessed a "plenitude of power" from which all valid authority flowed, in spiritual matters, of course, but also in secular affairs (Chapter 55). For Giles, human society in general—and the Church in particular—was a rigid hierarchy with a single power at its peak, just as the universe has its single divine ruler. Taking inspiration from the works of the Pseudo-Dionysius, Giles compared the church hierarchy to that of the angels.

It was not easy for Gerson to resist this logic, since he too ascribed a "plenitude of power" to the papacy and saw the ecclesiastical hierarchy as an image of that in heaven.[8] Yet he rejected the absolutist conclusion drawn by the likes of Giles. The Pope may be the head of the Church but the head is only one part of the greater whole, whereas a council represents the whole Church.[9] So it is such a council and not the Pope that makes infallible judgments, and that has a power of obligation that no one may licitly refuse. For Gerson the Church is thus an example of the best political arrangement described in Aristotle's *Politics*, namely a "mixture" of other constitutional forms. It has a monarchial element in the person of the Pope, an oligarchic element with the council of bishops, and a democratic element insofar as the Church is universal among all the faithful.

It would probably be fair to say that Gerson came around to this position in part for pragmatic reasons, but his pragmatism was principled. He argued that a dispute like this would often need to be resolved through the application of practical legal judgment, what Aristotle called *epikeia*. The person in the best position to do this is not the canon lawyer but the trained theologian, who understands the divine law and can thus work towards the ends God intended for us.[10] With this point we see another key element of Gerson's intellectual profile. As the leading representative of the University of Paris, he was unstinting in defending the prerogatives of the trained theologian. His public interventions were often in this spirit. He called on his expertise to give advice to others, even to the French king (whom he encouraged to listen to his "daughter," the university), and frequently remonstrated with other theologians who strayed into error. This could occur because of an overly literal approach to Scripture, as with the heresies of Wyclif and Hus (Chapters 75 and 76), or, at the other extreme, because of excessively figurative readings. The latter was the case when the Parisian theologian Jean Petit argued that the murder of a wicked tyrant does not violate the commandment against killing. Gerson had no patience with this, insisting that here one should adhere to the plain letter of Scripture even if further symbolic interpretations may also be given.[11]

Actually, Gerson ran out of patience with quite a few of his colleagues. He lamented the scholastic tendency towards "curiosity" and "singularity," by which he meant overspecializing in narrow technical issues. What we now see as highlights of later medieval thought, such as the debate over universals, were for him little more than pointless distinction-mongering. He warned that unbounded philosophy would "dash itself upon the stone of error," and advised, "Let us learn not so much to dispute as to live."[12] This attitude finds its most eloquent expression in his sermons, many of which survive today. Here too he is at pains to avoid questions that are "abstruse and curious (*estrangez et curieuses*)." As Catherine Brown has remarked, "Although he admits that there is nothing wrong with scholastic theology *per se*, the impression is that one is really better off without it, especially if one wishes to attain the height of Christian wisdom."[13] His sermons thus concentrated on communicating important issues to a wide audience. Convinced that ignorance of sin is no excuse, he strove to offer moral advice and also consolation to the laity, and in particular to women.

This brings us full circle, back to Gerson's attitude towards women.[14] In several passages he seems to express the sort of misogyny he himself attacked in the debate over the *Romance of the Rose*. He agreed with the standard scholastic view that women should not speak publicly, and went so far as to say that any teaching put forth by a woman is automatically suspect. He was troubled by the heroic asceticism of certain women—here one might think of Catherine of Siena—which often came together with a degree of arrogance. On the other hand, he was critical of male mystics too, such as Jan van Ruysbroeck, who claimed that it is possible to achieve complete identity with God in mystical union. Then, too, he frequently spoke more positively of women, admiring their capacity for spiritual devotion and, towards the end of his life, expressing support for Joan of Arc. There is no inconsistency here. For Gerson, the unlettered simplicity and emotional nature of women helped them avoid the sort of overcomplicated approach to religion Gerson detected in his fellow schoolmen, and made them apt for true mystical experience.

Somewhat like Eckhart before him, albeit with far less daring, Gerson attempted to integrate mysticism into a worldview shaped by scholasticism. He wrestled with the question of whether union with God is primarily accomplished through intellectual understanding or through "affective" or emotional experience. Though he generally seems to have thought that both approaches have merit, he moved towards affective mysticism as his career progressed, coming to embrace the sort of sentiment we find in the *Cloud of Unknowing*: "God may well be loved, but not thought."[15] The appropriate stance for the one who "journeys" toward God (the so-called *viator*) is passionate yearning, waiting for an ultimately unknowable God to bestow the reward of mystical insight. Such union with God never amounts to a complete dissolving of the mystic in God's essence, as claimed by any number of medieval mystics who compared the process to dissolution or annihilation, like a complete mixing of two liquids. Rather the mystical theologian is like the polished glass that can receive a perfect reflection or like a statue that sculpts itself. The aspiring mystic works at removing everything that prevents him, or indeed her, from being a perfect image of God.[16]

MORNING STAR OF THE
REFORMATION
JOHN WYCLIF

A mong fourteenth-century scholastics, you'd be hard pressed to name two such dissimilar men as John Buridan and John Wyclif. Where Buridan was a prominent nominalist, Wyclif stated that "All envy or actual sin is caused by the lack of an ordered love of universals."[1] Where the eternal arts master Buridan steered clear of theological issues, Wyclif made daring pronouncements on such subjects as the sacraments and divine predestination. But the two do have one thing in common, apart from their given name: both are famous above all for something they never actually did. Just as Buridan did not in fact devise the thought experiment of a donkey choosing between two bales of hay, so Wyclif did not translate the Bible into English. In 1396 the chronicler Henry Knighton gave him credit for doing so, or rather the blame: "Because of him the content of Scripture has become more common and more open to laymen and women who can read than it customarily is to quite learned clerks of good intelligence, and thus the pearl of the gospel is scattered abroad and trodden underfoot by swine."[2]

Wyclif may indeed have inspired and helped guide the effort that produced the so-called "Wyclif Bible," but scholars are agreed that it was in fact the work of many hands. The association of Wyclif's name with the English Bible did it no favors, and helps to explain why it was banned in England in 1409. Wyclif was hated by the Church for his relentless attack on ecclesiastical wealth, and associated with the Peasants' Revolt of 1381, which involved the murder of an archbishop and rioting in London. It was not entirely fair to blame that event on him, given that the revolt was less an expression of his ideas than an angry backlash against tax policies and attempts to keep wages artificially low as the workforce shrank in the wake of the Black Death. Wyclif was also condemned for his unorthodox teachings numerous times, most memorably at a 1382 council which was interrupted by an earthquake, something his accusers hastily explained as a sign of Wyclif's hatefulness to God. Yet Wyclif did have his supporters. Called Lollards—the term probably a derogatory reference to their senseless speech—they were preachers inspired, if not actually organized, by Wyclif and they spread his teachings around England.[3] A Lollard uprising centered around the nobleman John Oldcastle failed in 1414, and the threat posed by Wyclif's sympathizers receded. In the end, it was less earthquake than tremor.

But if so, it was one that anticipated the earth-shattering events of the Protestant Reformation. Martin Luther—famous above all for nailing ninety-five theses to the door of a church, which he didn't really do either—would champion an ideology that had much in common with Wyclif's. For this reason, the Protestant John Bale called Wyclif the "morning star of the Reformation," while David Hume remarked in his *History of England* that Wyclif was "the first person in Europe, that publicly called in question those principles, which had universally passed for certain and undisputed during so many ages." But to repeat a cliché, Wyclif was simultaneously the evening star of medieval thought. He took up many of the themes we have been pursuing throughout this book, including the problem of universals, the value of poverty, the compatibility of freedom with predestination, the nature of legitimate political power, the relation of body and soul, and the sacraments.

You might see his career as divided into two parts, first evening star of scholasticism and then morning star of reform.[4] The early Wyclif was a technically brilliant schoolman who was trained at Oxford and achieved his doctorate in theology in 1372. But his works became increasingly contentious and political. He entered into the service of John of Gaunt, an unpopular son of the king (that's three Johns so far in this chapter). In this capacity Wyclif went on a diplomatic mission to Bruges in 1374, representing the Crown. But, as would soon become obvious, he was anything but diplomatic. We've seen other writers of the period, like Langland, critiquing the Church for its overweening temporal power and wealth. This was not enough for Wyclif. He went so far as to declare that the Church should own no property at all. That got him and John of Gaunt, as the protector of this apparent heretic, hauled before a church tribunal in 1377, an event that ended in chaos and acrimony. Papal condemnation followed. Despite the controversy, Wyclif retained sufficient political protection to avoid imprisonment or execution, and ultimately managed to die of natural causes in 1384.

Let's take our cue from Wyclif himself and consider first his views on universals, given his warning that error on this topic is the root of all "envy and actual sin." The main thing to know here is that according to him universals are real. As with other realists, his main rationale is that our thought evidently gets hold of common or general features of the world. Thus, we would be subject to pervasive falsehood if universals were only fictions of the mind. Sometimes Wyclif has been depicted as a kind of "ultrarealist," but this is not how he saw himself.[5] Rather, he claimed to occupy a middle ground between nominalists like Ockham and Buridan and realists like Walter Burley. While agreeing with Burley that the universals are real, he stops short of saying that they exist as realities separate from particulars. Instead, the universal just is the individual considered in terms of its common nature, a now familiar application of Scotus' "formal distinction." This may be nicely illustrated by my promise to give you one of the two coins in my hand. I am offering you something shared in common by both of them, namely "a coin in my hand," without promising to hand over either coin in particular. So, in this case, the general can be distinguished from the individual. Yet I obviously cannot fulfill my general promise without handing you a particular coin.[6]

Wyclif's position on universals is, then, more or less what we've seen from other fourteenth-century realists. Less familiar to us will be his realism about entire *propositions*, which for him are just identical with things in the world.[7] That coin in my hand is in itself just a state of affairs in which the predicate "coin" belongs to a subject, namely the individual coin. This shows just how serious he is about making the world out there correspond to our minds. True thoughts are bits of mental language that perfectly mirror external things in structure and content. Of course, our minds are posterior to those things. I don't make something be a coin by thinking about it: rather, the coin's being a coin produces my thought of it. By contrast, God's mind is causally prior to things in the world. Indeed, all universals are grounded in God's ideas, which are universals or common natures that serve as the principles of created things. Here we may begin to understand Wyclif's dramatic claim that sin is caused by error about universals. In the same passage where he says that, he goes on to add that sin consists in "a will preferring a lesser good to a greater good, whereas in general the more universal goods are better." In keeping with this, he routinely invokes his theory of universals in theological disputes, as when he says that we need to concede the reality of the common nature of *humanity* if we are to understand the Incarnation, and if we are to grasp how the sin of the particular human Adam can have plunged the whole human race into a fallen state.

Wyclif retained his realist commitments when he started to write about overtly political topics such as the nature of legitimate authority, or as he would put it, "dominion."[8] Here he takes inspiration from another scholastic, named Richard Fitzralph,[9] who should first of all be congratulated for not being named John. Also, he came up with a new idea in the bitter contest between the papacy and secular rulers. Rather than granting either of these authorities supreme power in any given sphere, Fitzralph suggested that all true dominion is granted, or really only "loaned," to humans by God. Thus, power is exercised justly only when it is an expression of divine grace. Wyclif takes over and radicalizes this doctrine. Echoing Augustine's contrast between the "city of God" and the city here on earth, he proposes that the true Christian community is simply that group of people who have been given grace. They are God's instruments for good in the world and are predestined to be saved. A legitimate king is one whose actions are motivated by charity, a selfless channel for the manifestation of God's providential benevolence.

According to Wyclif the king has one particularly important function, namely the defense of the community that enjoys grace. That would mean protecting the Church, but not exactly the Church as it exists in Wyclif's day and certainly not the temporal property owned by that Church. To the contrary, Wyclif encourages secular monarchs to do the Church a favor by taking away all of its possessions, since concern with wealth distracts the clergy from their proper, spiritual tasks. In a state of grace before original sin, there was no private property and Christ's restoration of human nature offers us the chance to live again with all things shared in common, something embraced by the Apostles, who led lives of poverty. The Church of Wyclif's own day was obviously failing rather spectacularly to follow suit. He traces the parlous state of affairs to the Donation of Constantine, in which land was supposedly granted to the papacy by the emperor. Within a few generations this will be shown to have been based on a forgery, which would have delighted Wyclif no end had he lived to see it.[10]

Wyclif was staging a double assault on the Church. He offered an intellectual rationale for depriving the Church of its assets, and more subtly, he distinguished between the Church as an institution and the true Christian community, which consists simply of those who are given grace. Furthermore, in another striking anticipation of ideas we usually associate with the Reformation, Wyclif asserted that we have no way of identifying those who are among the predestined. We cannot know, for example, whether the Pope himself is sanctified and thus whether he is a member of the true Church.[11] So in addition to arguing that the Church should be deprived of its nice things, he was questioning the spiritual position of the clergy, all the way to the top. In place of their religious authority, Wyclif instructed his readers to take instruction from the one source they could certainly trust: the word of God Himself. So you can see why he would have thought it important for more people to have access to the Bible. When you aren't sure whether you can rely on the Church, you have to be your own theologian.

Unsurprisingly, all this caused outrage among the clergy, who responded in an equally unsurprising way by accusing him of heresy. One charge leveled at Wyclif was that he was falling into the teaching of Donatism refuted in antiquity by Augustine. This heresy maintained that priests in a state of sin cannot administer the sacraments effectively. In fact, Wyclif was careful not to say this, but he was less cautious in putting forth his ideas on another dangerous topic, namely the Eucharist.[12] As we've seen (Chapter 47), no ingenuity was spared by the scholastics in trying to explain how the host becomes Christ's body in this ritual. Yet Wyclif was unsatisfied with the resulting consensus. He found it preposterous to say, as Pope Innocent III had declared and as had been reasserted by many scholastics, that accidental features like the color, shape, and taste of bread can remain when the substance of the bread is no longer present. Wyclif thought it obvious that the bread should remain and be present together with the body of Christ in one and the same place.

Again, this connects to his cherished teaching on universals, and for several reasons. Most obviously, we have Christ's nature being somehow present in common to many particular pieces of bread upon different altars. Also, there is an argument Wyclif gives against those who assert transubstantiation. The nature of bread cannot actually be destroyed and replaced by Christ's body, since God never annihilates anything. He cannot, because the reality of all things is grounded in Him, in divine ideas that are eternal and indestructible. This incidentally gives us an insight into how Wyclif would respond to an argument against realism given by Ockham, namely that if the common nature of *humanity* were present in Socrates, it would, absurdly, be destroyed if God were to annihilate Socrates. Wyclif would agree that this consequence is absurd, but not in the way Ockham is thinking. The mistake here is not admitting that *humanity* is real, but supposing that God would or indeed could annihilate Socrates or anything else. For Socrates is in some sense identical to the common nature of *humanity* that is present in God Himself as one of His ideas.

If you're wondering how Wyclif can say that the body of Christ and the substance of bread can be in the same place, you aren't alone. His opponents certainly didn't think he offered a satisfactory account of this, and about the best he came up with was the insistence that Christ is "sacramentally" present to each point within the bread.[13] That may be theologically unsatisfying, but it's philosophically exciting, because of the reference to points. Which takes us to another aspect of his thought: his atomism.[14] Wyclif maintained the standard Aristotelian doctrine that each thing is made of matter and form, but thought that the most fundamental constituents of things are atoms, in which an elemental form is predicated of an unextended bit of prime matter. These elemental atoms are then composed into homogeneous materials like flesh or bone, which are then further combined to make up complex substances like the human body.

An obvious implication is that each human must have many forms at different levels of material composition. Against defenders of the unity of substantial form, like Aquinas, Wyclif held that all these forms are really present. Again, he thinks his position is just obviously true, since we can see that decomposing bodies break down into more basic ingredients which must have been there right along. Furthermore, the form that animates the human body needs to be distinguished from the immaterial rational soul, a mind that is connected to the animate body only through divine will and that can, of course, survive bodily death. This is about as far from Aquinas' teaching on the human person as one can get, at least in a medieval context. But apart from the atomism it is not much different from what other form pluralists had been saying since Aquinas' day.

In conclusion, it might be worth comparing Wyclif to another great scholastic, his younger contemporary Jean Gerson. He was a far less radical thinker, of course, and was staunch in his criticism of Wyclif and his followers. But on at least one topic the two were not so far apart: predestination and grace. Both of them worked in the wake of Bradwardine's thunderous condemnation of scholastics who came too close to a "Pelagian" view of grace by suggesting that God gives grace to those who, under their own power, make a sincere effort to be good. Bradwardine went in the other direction, effectively making God responsible for every step in the process of salvation, even our attempts to deserve His mercy. Gerson and Wyclif sought to split the difference. With his typical emphasis on personal spirituality, Gerson proposed that even if the sinner can do nothing to merit salvation, he can commit himself to complete humility in obedient and patient hope of being redeemed. Hence Gerson's stress, in his pastoral works, on the idea of the penitent Christian seeking God's grace while knowing he or she is unworthy of it.[15]

As for Wyclif, he insisted that human freedom is just as real as, say, universals. God foreknows what we will choose; yet our choices remain contingent since they could always have been different. This is, of course, just a version of the standard solution to the problem of divine foreknowledge developed earlier in the fourteenth century (Chapter 61). Also traditional is his asymmetrical treatment of sin and merit: humans can be wicked on their own, but need God's help to be good. For once Wyclif was not particularly radical on this score. His view became distinctive, and dangerous, only once he stressed the unknowability of grace and the consequences of that fact for human society. Both Gerson and Wyclif, in their own ways, were pushing Christendom towards a more individual approach to spirituality, in which confidence that the Church and its sacraments will offer a heavenly reward is replaced by humble uncertainty. They offered hope of predestined salvation, but it was a hope not far from despair, because of the fear that one has already been chosen to be among the damned.

THE PRAGUE SPRING
SCHOLASTICISM ACROSS EUROPE

When I took up my job teaching philosophy at the Ludwig Maximilian University in Munich, there were three things I wanted to know: who was Ludwig, who was Maximilian, and where is my new office? The answers stretch back over the last half millennium and more. The university was originally founded by Duke Ludwig IX in 1472. At the start, it was based in Ingolstadt, not Munich. From there the institution was moved to Landshut in 1800 by King Maximilian I of Bavaria. Only in 1826 did it come to Munich, thanks to another Ludwig, King Ludwig I of Bavaria, which is why my office is conveniently located here and not in Ingolstadt or Landshut. It's a long and storied history; yet by the standards of German universities you could argue that the LMU is a latecomer. The University of Heidelberg was founded about a century earlier, in 1386, part of a movement that swept across Europe in the fourteenth century. Between the years 1300 to 1425, no fewer than thirty-two universities were founded, about one every four years.[1]

The older scholastic centers at Oxford, Cambridge, Paris, and Bologna faced competition from these brash new arrivals. A telling, though admittedly not unbiased remark was made by Henry of Langenstein, a theologian who trained and taught at Paris before moving to the new university at Vienna. "Behold the universities of France are breaking up, the sun of wisdom is eclipsed there. Wisdom withdraws to light another people. Are not three lamps of wisdom now lit among the Germans, that is three universities (*studia generalia*) shining with rays of glorious truth?"[2] These three lamps were the universities at Prague, Heidelberg, and, of course, Henry's own Vienna. The story of how he came to teach there is, to continue his metaphor, an illuminating one. Scholasticism spread across Europe because well trained masters decamped from the traditional places of learning to new institutions that were well funded by local nobility.

The scholars needed good reasons to move, since they would be giving up access to book collections and a reliable stream of qualified students.[3] In the case of Langenstein, his motive for leaving Paris was the papal schism. He was one of numerous scholars whose sympathy for the Roman Pope led him to abandon France, which was under the sway of Avignon. As for the sponsoring role of the nobility, in the first, but certainly not the last, case where the Habsburg family enters our history of philosophy, the University at Vienna was founded in 1365 with the support of Duke Rudolph IV. Greater "Germany" and Italy provided ideal conditions for the creation of such institutions because of the independent power of local aristocrats, who had an interest in promoting the economy and prestige of their home cities. They had freedom to do so because in Italy there was no effective central authority, while in Germany the Holy Roman emperor did not exercise sufficient control to stop this sort of thing from happening.[4] All a late fourteenth-century noble needed was funding and permission from the Pope. And conveniently, there was even more than one pope to choose from!

Which is not to say that the new universities always succeeded. Vienna needed some years to flourish, as did the university at Erfurt. Others failed completely. In Würzburg, a university was introduced just after 1400 but fizzled out quickly. The city would have to wait until the late sixteenth century for a refounding. In England there was a similarly abortive attempt to create a northern rival to Cambridge and Oxford at Stamford. Such initiatives were often resisted by the old guard, as when Bologna required its newly minted doctors to promise not to teach elsewhere for two years. Despite their position as rivals, the new universities gave the old ones the sincerest form of flattery by imitating them shamelessly. They modeled their structure and even their curricula on the older seats of learning, typically choosing either the pattern of Bologna, where law was the primary discipline, or that of Paris, where theology was the most powerful faculty. In Prague, problems were caused by an attempt to combine both models, since it led to clashes between the law and theology faculties.[5] Some schools carved out other specialisms. Erfurt was known for expertise in astronomy and in grammar, while the masters at Padua were quick to adopt the breakthroughs in physics from the Oxford Calculators (Chapter 63) and combined inquiry into natural philosophy with the study of medicine.[6]

Padua is also a good illustration for something else we should bear in mind, which is that universities were not the only context for scholasticism. As we've seen, friars of the various orders established their own bases for teaching. Think of Ockham at London Greyfriars or Albert the Great and other Dominicans in Cologne, where there would not be a university until 1388. The general term *studium* was applied quite liberally, basically to any grouping of teachers able to attract students. This applied to Padua already in the 1220s, even though we do not hear of a "university" with an arts faculty until 1262.[7] The first outstanding intellectual based in Padua came several decades later. This was Peter of Abano, an expert in medicine and astrology. As so often with the leading masters at smaller universities, he trained at one of the more established schools, in this case, Paris.

It's been suggested that an important feature of Italian scholastic culture in the Renaissance can be traced back to Peter of Abano: a tendency to adopt the controversial doctrines found in Averroes' commentaries on Aristotle. Here we might also think of Dante, another Italian and contemporary of Peter who was arguably influenced by Averroism. Or we might move ahead to the greatest figure of late medieval philosophy in Italy, Paul of Venice. He too studied at an older university, in his case, Oxford. He then toured the schools of Italy, teaching in Padua, Siena, and Bologna. Where Peter of Abano's focus was natural philosophy, Paul of Venice's contribution was especially in logic and metaphysics.[8] He too was powerfully influenced by Averroes, to the point that in commenting on Aristotle he was sometimes effectively writing supercommentary on Averroes, though interpretations that have him adopting the notorious Averroist theory of a single mind for all humans seem to be misplaced. And in the most prominent dispute of the late fourteenth century, between realism and nominalism, he was above all a follower of the British realists Duns Scotus and John Wyclif, indeed only one of several Italian scholars who defended what has been called "Oxford realism."[9]

Like Wyclif, Paul of Venice held that a universal is a real thing out in the world but not something that exists independently of its instances, so that the universal *human* and individual humans are only formally distinct. Paul offers a clever twist on this theory when he comes to explain how exactly a universal like *human* comes to reside in one particular human, like Groucho Marx. He combines elements from two very different theories, those of Thomas Aquinas and Duns Scotus. For Aquinas, Groucho gets to be an individual by being made of some particular chunk of matter. For Scotus, Groucho's individuality is instead caused by a so-called "haecceity," the distinctive feature that belongs only to Groucho and picks him out as a particular human, much as rationality distinguishes humans from other animal species. Paul of Venice avails himself of *both* explanations. When a human form is joined to a parcel of matter, the matter's reception of that form produces the distinctive haecceity envisioned by Scotus. This might seem like metaphysical overkill, since it could sound as if everything is individuated twice over, once by matter and then again by the haecceity. But it has advantages over both older theories. Unlike Aquinas, Paul does not have to say that Groucho's individuality is just borrowed from the individuality of Groucho's matter, as if being a particular human is nothing more than being made out of *this* flesh and bone rather than *that* flesh and bone. It is the individuating feature that guarantees Groucho's particularity. But unlike Scotus, Paul can explain how that distinctive feature came to belong to Groucho in the first place: by being associated with his particular matter. In this sense, matter is still the "principle of individuation."

Another scholastic thinker who worked in Italy, and, like Paul of Venice, was a member of the Augustinian order, was Gregory of Rimini.[10] Following the familiar pattern, he studied in Paris before serving the Augustinians in Bologna, Padua, and Perugia, finally becoming head of the order in 1357 and dying in Vienna in 1358. We met Gregory briefly before, when we talked about his idea that states of affairs are "complex objects of signification" (Chapter 62). This is indeed his signature view, or at least one of them. It constitutes another step in the direction of realism, since for Gregory such states of affairs are real things which we can signify or express with propositions. In fact, we can distinguish three levels of reality, where a strict nominalist like Ockham would only want one, the level of concrete individual objects. The weakest sort of reality recognized by Gregory belongs to states of affairs that may or may not be realized, like Groucho's smoking a cigar. More real than this is a state of affairs that is in fact realized, as when Groucho in fact smokes the cigar. Yet such a realized state of affairs is still not as real as the concrete individuals that realize them, like Groucho himself or his cigar.

Gregory can also be contrasted with Ockham when it comes to ethics. Again, the notion of a state of affairs is relevant here. Gregory uses this notion to absolve God of responsibility for creating evils. The fact that something bad happens, or that a sin is committed, is not one of the fully real things created by God, as Groucho is. It is only a "complex object of signification," a state of affairs brought about by the human sinner. Furthermore, these states of affairs have an intrinsic badness that is not decided only by God's legislating will. Here Gregory moves away from the voluntarism of Scotus or Ockham, arguing that "even if God did not exist (*etiamsi deus non daretur*)," certain states of affairs would still be evil, because they would be in conflict with reason. This allows Gregory to do what he usually wants to do, as a member of the Augustinian order: validate the judgments of Augustine himself, who in this case had said that sin is a "violation of right reason."

Let's now turn our attention north to Germany, and in particular to Heidelberg, where nominalism was finding a more favorable reception. This was especially thanks to Marsilius of Inghen (not to be confused with the pioneering political thinker Marsilius of Padua, discussed in Chapter 56). Like Henry of Langenstein, Gregory of Rimini, and Peter of Abano, he was responsible for exporting Parisian scholastic thought to new territories. Also like Henry of Langenstein, Marsilius may have left Paris because of the tensions surrounding the papal schism. This was much to the benefit of the new university at Heidelberg, which he helped found and served numerous times as rector.[11] Especially influenced by John Buridan in natural philosophy and by Ockham and Gregory of Rimini in logic and its application to theological questions, Marsilius' thought is not easy to encapsulate briefly. But a good example of his approach can be found in his solution to the much-discussed problem of future contingents (Chapter 61).[12] Like other scholastics, he wanted to safeguard human freedom in the face of God's certain awareness of what we will do, before we do it and, indeed, before we even exist. He was, however, reluctant to admit that humans actually cause God already to have known what we will do. This is not so much for the reason we might expect—namely that this would involve us exerting causal influence on the past—but because God should not be subject to causal influence from His creatures at all. Marsilius is generally skeptical about using the techniques of logic to understand God's nature. It is one thing to show how it may be contingently true that I perform a given action, another to say that God is made to know that truth by my action.

A rather similar debate was unfolding at the same time in Austria at the University of Vienna.[13] Here too the nominalists were in favor, with Ockham, Wodeham, Buridan, and Marsilius himself on the reading lists. But the Vienna schoolmen had trouble deciding how far to follow Ockham on one particular point. He had argued vehemently against Scotus' use of the formal distinction, the very distinction that was being used to defend realism by Wyclif in England and by Paul of Venice in Italy. For Ockham there is only one context in which we can recognize two genuinely different, yet also somehow identical, things. It applies in the case of the Trinity, where the Father, Son, and Holy Spirit are all one God, yet three different Persons. Gregory of Rimini pointed out the problematic implication. If the formal distinction is generally unacceptable, yet allowable in this one case, doesn't that show that our normal canons of logic and metaphysics break down in the case of God? And doesn't that show that theology is, well, irrational?

We find engagements with this problem by two leading masters of Vienna, both named Henry. First there was Henry of Oyta, who made the following cunning observation. For him, as a good nominalist, the sort of realism endorsed by Platonists and men like Walter Burley is false. But it is not completely irrational! One can imagine that there could be a paradigmatic universal *human* which stands over all individual humans: it is just that there are good arguments to show that we do not need to posit such a Platonic Form. Thus, it would be in harmony with reason to posit an overarching nature in God, which stands over the three Persons the way that the supposed universal *human* stands over the three Marx Brothers. A different view was taken by another Henry, the aforementioned Henry of Langenstein. Or actually I should say that he took two different views. At first he accepted Ockham's teaching that the formal distinction can be allowed in the one special case of the Trinity. But then he changed his mind. Like Marsilius worrying about the application of philosophical tools to God's knowledge, Henry of Langenstein suddenly began to argue that Aristotelian philosophy is simply inadequate for grasping the Trinity. Much as Aristotle's natural philosophy is rendered incomplete, or worse, by our belief that God can create from nothing, so Aristotle's logic cannot provide the resources we need in theology. No surprise there, he observed, given that even the study of logic outside of theological contexts shows that it cannot solve certain problems, namely such "insoluble" puzzles as the liar paradox (see Chapter 62).

Some have proposed that the dissemination of nominalist thought across greater Germany was the work of a "school of Buridan," with first- and second-generation students carrying John Buridan's logic and natural philosophy to these new universities. Though this is probably an exaggeration,[14] it is certainly true that his commentaries on Aristotle's *Physics* and his logical writings were widely read. One of his main inheritors in physics was Albert of Saxony, who is not to be confused with his fellow German, Albert the Great. But this Albert was not so bad either, noteworthy for his application of ideas from both Ockham and Buridan in natural philosophy.[15] He has also been hailed for his contributions in epistemology, because of his penetrating critique of the tendency of other nominalists to think that we grasp things through an intermediary, namely a "concept." Thus, if I see Groucho smoking a cigar, Buridan would say that I am grasping Groucho as cigar-smoking by forming an appropriate proposition about him in my mind. In other words, I represent him to myself at the level of concepts. Instead, Albert of Saxony thinks that we can just immediately grasp the external object.[16] The only thing here that has the status of a "concept" is the very act by which the mind grasps Groucho. Here we may be reminded of similar debates from the thirteenth century, as in Peter Olivi's epistemology of direct perception which he put forward as a critique of theories like that of Roger Bacon, who thought we perceive things through an intermediary image called a species (Chapter 30).

Let's finish this tour around late medieval Europe by going to Prague. Here too the works of nominalists like Buridan and Marsilius were influential, but it was the ideas of John Wyclif that triggered the most intense debate.[17] His views on universals and the sacraments were already known in Prague by the 1370s; two early adherents were Stanislav of Znojmo and Stephen Páleč. Stanislav was forced to recant his adherence to Wyclif's teaching on the Eucharist, but this was nothing compared to the trouble that awaited two other figures at the university, Jerome of Prague and Jan Hus. Jerome had visited England and picked up knowledge of Wyclif's doctrines there, while Jan Hus wrote a set of glosses to Wyclif in 1398. These include the remark "Out, Germans, out!"[18]—a manifestation of the Czech nationalism that Hus was fusing together with daring adherence to Wyclif's critique of the Church and Eucharistic theology. As the historian František Šmahel has written, the Wycliffites "presented their dispute over Wyclif to the Czech public as part of the struggle for the fulfillment of the natural rights 'of the holy Czech nation' within the university, in Prague, and in the whole kingdom."[19] The controversy over Wyclif's teachings came to a head in 1409, when the opponents of those teachings left the university in protest at being required to attend disputations held by masters they considered to be heretics. Within the space of a few years Wyclif's books would be burned, and Jan Hus and Jerome of Prague would be executed as an outcome of the Council of Constance. In the short run, then, this particular attempt to export scholastic ideas was a failure, as realism itself came to be tainted by association with insurrectionary nationalism. But in the longer run it's clear that Prague was a harbinger of things to come: a reformation before the Reformation.[20]

RENAISSANCE MEN
RAMON LLULL AND PETRARCH

I n my first week of graduate school I found myself at a gathering of philosophers, explaining how I developed an interest in medieval philosophy thanks to my enthusiasm for Dante. A professor of logic who was present said, "But Dante wasn't medieval: he was Renaissance!" Good grief, I thought, I've only been here for a few days and already they've realized I don't know what I'm talking about. I muttered something about Dante having worked in the early fourteenth century, which sounds pretty medieval. But I also knew what he meant. Given his admiration for classical literature and his brilliant use of the vernacular, Dante can seem to be not of his time, a Renaissance man trapped in the Middle Ages. Nor was he alone in this respect. In these past few chapters we've been considering figures who prepared the way for the Renaissance and the Reformation, but who were still recognizably "medieval" in their approach. For all their theological innovations, Jean Gerson and John Wyclif were above all scholastics. Now though, I want to look at two authors who were outsiders to the world of scholasticism. Culturally, they seem to belong to the Renaissance, and were, in fact, very influential in the fifteenth century; yet they wrote respectively in the thirteenth and fourteenth centuries.

The first is Ramon Llull, who might even be described as the outsider artist of medieval philosophy. And I do mean "artist." He developed a stunningly original method for doing philosophy and science, and called this universal method an "Art." It could, Llull thought, free humankind from suffering and unite them all under the banner of a single truth; along the way he would solve all the questions being discussed at the universities and more problems besides. Yet in the short run his hopes were largely disappointed. He was unable to persuade the schoolmen of Paris to adopt his Art as their new method, and his teachings would be banned twice towards the end of the fourteenth century, condemned by the inquisitor at Aragon in 1376 and banned at Paris in 1390 thanks to none other than Jean Gerson. This is not to say that Llull had no adherents in the fourteenth century.[1] His philosophy was promoted especially by his associate Thomas le Myésier, who helped him by posing a series of questions on which to test the Art, and also by undertaking to produce a systematic anthology culled from Llull's vast and varied output. Yet Llull's thought would prove to be more at home in the Renaissance and early modern Europe, when its adherents would include Nicholas of Cusa, Giordano Bruno, and even Leibniz, who admired both the universal ambitions of Llull and the clever system of combinations that drove his method. Inauthentic works ascribed to Llull also made him into a forerunner of Renaissance alchemy and Kabbalastic speculation.

Llull's unusual position outside the intellectual mainstream owed something to his origins.[2] He was born in 1232 on the island of Majorca, which had only recently been seized from the Muslims by the kingdom of Aragon. The multicultural setting of Llull's birthplace would be reflected in his life's work. By his own account, Llull's early years were misspent, but when he experienced visions of Christ on the cross, he changed his ways, "converting to penitence," as he put it. He made it his mission to establish definitively the truths of Christianity and thus persuade members of other faiths to convert. In order to speak to a non-Christian audience he learned Arabic from a slave, and composed works of his own in this language while also drawing on knowledge of Arabic philosophical literature, as in an early work on logic based on al-Ghazālī's *Aims of the Philosophers*.[3] He wrote this in the Catalan language. Though Llull did write in Latin as well, he did so as an autodidact whose style could seem rebarbative to readers who had a more standard education.[4] His use of Catalan makes him another founding figure of vernacular literature, the Dante of the Balearic Islands, if you will.[5]

A pivotal event in Llull's long and eventful life was his visit to Paris in the late 1280s. Here he had the chance to give public lectures displaying his Art to a scholastic audience. It was only part of a concerted campaign to persuade the Parisians of his orthodoxy and, hopefully, his genius. Towards this end Llull also joined in the attacks on the radical Aristotelians dubbed "Averroists," and even went so far as to write a treatise in defense of the 1277 condemnations. Yet his reception was not a warm one. It's been nicely remarked that in Paris "his Art met with neither comprehension nor approval."[6] Decades later, in 1309, he would make a more successful trip to Paris. On that occasion he found a more appreciative audience and was given official confirmation of his orthodoxy. But by then Llull was a very old man, so that he spent most of his career being kept at arm's length by the scholastic establishment. This was a matter of no little frustration to him; he commented at one point, "My books are appreciated little, and I can assure you that plenty of people think me a fool."[7]

Llull's response to the incomprehension that greeted his Art was to produce a simpler presentation of the system, in what he called a concession to the "weakness of the human intellect." For this reason, modern-day scholars offering an overview of the Art are obligated to summarize it twice, going over the more complex, so-called "quaternary" version, and then explaining the changes made to get to the stripped down, "ternary" presentation of the Art.[8] I'm not going to attempt anything that expansive here, but will just try to explain the basics of the method. Overall, the point is to relate certain general concepts by means of a systematic combinatorial procedure, so as to generate philosophical questions and answers in a novel method of proof. The later and simpler version is the one set out in his most influential presentation, the *Ars Brevis*.[9] Here and in other treatises Llull makes extensive use of an alphabetic notation, in this case consisting of nine letters (it's the prominence of multiples of three that gives this system the name "ternary"). These letters can be used to represent each of the elements of the whole system (299).

They are first used to label a series of nine properties that confer perfection on things, sometimes called by Llull "dignities," but here in the *Ars Brevis* called "principles." They include goodness, greatness, truth, power, and so on. The first figure of the Art has these arranged around the circumference of a circle, with each property given its letter label, and lines drawn between the properties to indicate that each of them is convertible with the others (300). Thus, something that is perfect in goodness will also be perfect in greatness, truth, power, and all the remaining principles. A second figure introduces relations that can obtain between properties, such as difference, causation, or equality (302). These are tagged with the same letters used in the first figure. Further chapters, often with accompanying diagrams or tables, explain the definitions of these concepts, their possible combinations, the questions that can be posed about them in light of these combinations, topics to which the Art can be applied, and so on.

The upshot of all this is to provide a system with four features.[10] The Art is "inventive," because it can generate questions by asking about combinations of the concepts, like "Is goodness great?" or "What is good greatness?" (319). It is "general," because the topics it covers include all existing things, God and every one of His creatures. It is "compendious," because the number of possible combinations is absolutely enormous, in just a few pages giving the reader a basis for generating an almost indefinite number of philosophical queries. Finally, it is "demonstrative," because it does not just pose such queries, but also answers them. The way that it does so would be surprising for a scholastic thinker schooled in Aristotle and, given the reception Llull received in Paris, apparently unsatisfying as well. The Aristotelians thought that demonstration always proceeds by discovering causes. Llull does include causation in his system, but it is not the engine of his demonstrations. This allows him to avoid a problem of Aristotelian scientific theory, namely that there can be no demonstrations concerning God, as God has no cause.[11]

In place of this, Llull devises a method of proof which he calls demonstration *per aequiparantiam*, which basically means showing that two concepts are equivalent in the sense of being extensionally identical. For instance, greatness is equivalent to goodness, because whatever is good is thereby also great. A nice example of this method, and the way it can address central questions in the scholastic culture of his day, would be his proof that the universe is not eternal. He argues that it cannot be, on the grounds that something eternal would be maximally great, and would thus produce maximal good and thus exclude evil; yet we see that the universe contains evil.[12] Thus, Llull manages, by presupposing the equivalence of eternity, greatness, and goodness, to prove that the universe is created—precisely on the grounds of the presence of evil, which has led many to doubt the existence of God! Another unusual feature of Llull's system, also illustrated by this same argument about eternity, is his idea that it is distinctive of goodness to produce good, and hence of maximal goodness to produce maximal good. In fact, he *defines* goodness in these terms, stating that "Goodness is that thing by reason of which good does good" (309). Again, this would strike an Aristotelian as methodologically suspect, because it sounds circular. (As Llull might say, a circular definition is one that defines something circularly.) But he is trying to express the idea that each of his principles, indeed everything in his whole system, is distinguished by its action. For a thing to exist, according to Llull, is for it to produce that which is in accordance with its nature. Thus, he also defines "human" as "that which makes human," as in generating children.

Obviously, this is all very different from what we find in other thirteenth- and early fourteenth-century thinkers; yet certain aspects of the Art ring familiar bells. His list of principles sounds very much like a theory of transcendentals, those properties that are found in all existing things (Chapter 25). Meanwhile, Llull's treatment of God as the maximal case of such perfections or "dignities" may evoke Anselm's approach to proving God as a maximally perfect being.[13] But Llull's Art is not just a reworking of scholastic ideas. It is a genuinely new system, whose mechanism of correlative terms and combinatorial possibilities is very different from the categorial logic of the schoolmen of his day. The novelty of the method was in keeping with the novelty of his ambition: he wanted to produce a system that could appeal to any intellectual, including the elite among Jews and Muslims whom he hoped to convert. And he did see conversion mostly in these intellectualist terms. Though he supported the Crusades, he thought that such a military undertaking was simply paving the way to conversion through rational persuasion. As one scholar has commented, "Having witnessed only the combination of cultural difference and violence, Llull did not believe that cultural difference and peace could ever coexist; since peace was his overriding goal, universal assimilation was the only real option."[14] And, of course, Llull's own Art was the means by which universal conversion could best be achieved.

This attitude is most eloquently captured in a work called *The Book of the Gentile and the Three Wise Men*.[15] It is a dialogue in which a man without religion, who loves only this world and thus lives in fear of death (86, 91–2), meets three scholars, a Jew, a Muslim, and a Christian. These three learned men use arguments based on the Art, here allegorically represented as trees bearing flowers, to convert the gentile to monotheism (96–7.) Each of the three then attempts to persuade him of the truth of their own particular religion. Here Llull is, for the most part, remarkably even-handed. Though Judaism and Islam come in for a degree of criticism, all three scholars are shown as being scrupulously rational and as adept practitioners of the Art, so that the Jew is allowed to prove God's uniqueness on the basis that His greatness requires infinity and that there cannot be two infinite beings (100). In a surprising conclusion, we do not discover which religion has captured the allegiance of the gentile, a striking contrast to similar texts of interreligious debate like those written by the Jewish author Judah Hallevi and by Peter Abelard.[16] For Ramon Llull, the hope of peace on earth lies in the civil exchange of rational discourse motivated by a feeling of mutual love between humans,[17] and the basis of that discourse is provided by his Art.

Where Llull spent much of his life trying to impress the Aristotelian scholastics at Paris with his innovative system, our second author was distinctly unimpressed by those very scholastics. This was Francesco Petrarca, usually called Petrarch in English. Again and again he complains that Aristotle leaves him cold, writing, for instance, that this man whom the scholastics honored as "the Philosopher" was in fact "so completely ignorant of true happiness that any devout old woman, or any faithful fisherman, shepherd, or peasant, is happier, if not more subtle, in recognizing it."[18] Upon reading Aristotle's *Ethics*, Petrarch remarked, "I know slightly more than I did before. But my mind is the same as it was; my will is the same; and I am the same." By contrast, the great Roman authors Cicero and Seneca "pierce our vitals with the sharp, burning barbs of their eloquence."[19] This will become a familiar refrain in the fifteenth century, as the humanists celebrate the rhetorical excellence and spiritual impact of classical literature and spurn what they see as the dry technicalities of scholasticism.

Indeed, the humanists themselves saw Petrarch as their founding father.[20] Especially the scholars of Petrarch's home city of Florence extolled him as a pioneer, like

Leonardo Bruni or Gianozzo Manetti, whose *Lives of Three Illustrious Florentine Poets* was devoted to Dante, Boccaccio, and Petrarch. The idea that it was Petrarch in particular who "initiated" humanism is not implausible. He already had the literary tastes typical of the humanists and also philological expertise, as shown by an edition of Livy he produced early in his career. Modern-day scholars have questioned this to some extent.[21] They have pointed out that there was a tradition of rhetorically skilled secretaries and notaries, the so-called *dictatores*, running back to the twelfth century, and that a number of other figures were reviving the study of the Classics before Petrarch, like the Paduan scholar Albertino Mussato, who drew on the ancient historians and the tragedies of Seneca. If the Renaissance humanists insisted on seeing Petrarch alone as the founder of their enterprise, it was perhaps because it was Petrarch who first championed philology and eloquence as a full-blown ideology.

This ideology is on display in one of his more philosophically oriented works, the *Secret Book*.[22] It is a dialogue whose dramatic setting is by now familiar: as in Boethius, Alan of Lille, or Marguerite Porete, a fictional version of the author is confronted by the female personification of an abstract idea, in this case Truth. But she doesn't have much to say. Mostly Truth just presides over a dialogue between the autobiographical character Francesco and Augustine, another of Petrarch's favorite classical authors.[23] Indeed, the *Secret Book* is inspired especially by Augustine's own dialogues, while the character of Francesco seems to be modeled on the young Augustine of the *Confessions*, riven by doubt and seeking spiritual peace. In Petrarch's dialogue, Augustine teaches Francesco that only virtue leads to happiness, and that since virtue and sin are always subject to our will, unhappiness is actually voluntary (§1.3.1). This teaching sounds very much like that of the ancient Stoics, a debt Petrarch explicitly recognizes in the dialogue.

Augustine now diagnoses Francesco's weaknesses in regard to the seven deadly sins. Fans of Hellenistic philosophy, or of Augustine himself, will thrill at the psychological insight and nuance of these sections. Petrarch notes the perverse pleasure one may take in one's own depression (§2.13.1–2) and is forthright in lamenting his own tendencies towards pride (§2.2.8) and ambition for literary glory (§3.14.1). This is also one of those rare philosophical dialogues that is genuinely a dialogue. Francesco is depicted as spiritually imperfect, but also allowed to push back against Augustine's unrelenting morality with points that the reader is apt to find persuasive. This is especially so in a section on love, in particular Petrarch's love for Laura, the muse who inspired his writings in much the way that Beatrice inspired Dante (appropriately to Petrarch's highly developed sense of literary artifice, scholars disagree about whether Laura was a real person). When Augustine rails against lust and attachment to mortal beings, Francesco insists that it is Laura's virtuous soul that he loves and not her body (§3.3.11). It's not an easy point for Augustine to resist, given his own praise of virtue and emphasis on the concerns of the soul over those of the body (§1.8.3). Nonetheless, he argues, it is God alone and no creature who is the correct object of our love, a position for which Augustine is indeed the most appropriate possible mouthpiece (§3.5.2).

Another reminiscence of Hellenistic thought is Petrarch's vision of philosophy as a kind of medicine for the soul rather than the body (§2.16.2–3, 3.8.5, 3.9.4).[24] Being Petrarch, he sees books as the most powerful source of treatment. But which books? He is refreshingly dismissive of the philosophical bromides that have appeared so often in ancient and medieval literature, for example the slogan that the earth is like a tiny point in the context of the vast universe (§3.15.3). Francesco does not find that meditating on this impedes his desire for worldly fame, as it is meant to. It helps more to read his beloved Seneca and Cicero, but even here the effect is temporary. He finds himself sliding back into bad ways of thinking (*perversam opinionem*, §2.14.13) as soon as he closes the books (§2.15.9; cf. §3.12.8). Augustine recommends taking careful notes while reading, advice that Petrarch in fact followed himself, as we know from the marginal annotations from still surviving manuscripts that belonged to his library. Here we have a typically medieval practice of caring for the soul by meditating on texts; yet the texts in question are those of Roman pagans rather than the Bible.[25]

Or, as that professor at Notre Dame might have put it, Petrarch was not medieval: he was Renaissance. He gives us a final illustration of a point I've been making, if not belaboring, in the closing chapters of this book. Even as typically medieval phenomena like scholasticism carried on into the fifteenth century with figures like Jean Gerson, so the currents of thought and literature we associate with the Renaissance already appeared with Llull, Petrarch, Boccaccio, and, yes, Dante. Remember too that some scholars see figures of the twelfth century as anticipating the Renaissance. The humanist values of Petrarch were, to no small degree, already espoused by John of Salisbury (Chapter 17). So often hailed as a new beginning in philosophy, as in art and literature, the rebirth of classical culture in the fifteenth century was also a continuation of the medieval age. But that is a story whose full telling belongs in a future volume of the *History of Philosophy without Any Gaps*.

NOTES

Preface

1. J. Courtenay, *Parisian Scholars in the Early Fourteenth Century: A Social Portrait* (Cambridge: 1999), 20.

Chapter 1

1. See further G. W. Trompf, "The Concept of the Carolingian Renaissance," *Journal of the History of Ideas* 34 (1973), 3–26.
2. Even so, we won't even touch on the vast majority of known medieval thinkers. To get an impression of just how many there were simply at the Arts Faculty in Paris in the thirteenth century, page through P. Glorieux, *La Faculté des Arts et ses maîtres au XIIIe siècle* (Paris: 1971), which names 469 individuals—and bear in mind too that many extant manuscripts are also anonymous!
3. See *Philosophy in the Hellenistic and Roman Worlds*, ch.48.

Chapter 2

1. Solution: the man drinks 36 l of coffee each year (250 ml × 3 cups × 48 chapters = 36,000 ml), so it will take him approximately 644,444 years, which coincidentally is also the length of time I project for completing this book series.
2. Alcuin, *Epistle* 170, cited in D. A. Bullough, *Alcuin: Achievement and Reputation* (Leiden: 2004), 436.
3. Translated in J. Hadley and D. Singmaster, "Problems to Sharpen the Young," *The Mathematical Gazette* 76.475 (1992), 102–26.
4. Each of the sons is both the nephew and the uncle of the other.
5. See *Philosophy in the Hellenistic and Roman Worlds*, ch.52.
6. As argued in I. Hadot, *Arts libéraux et philosophie dans la pensée antique* (Paris: 2005).
7. S. A. Barney et al. (trans.), *The Etymologies of Isidore of Seville* (Cambridge: 2006). Cited below by section number from this translation. On Isidore, see further J. Henderson, *The Medieval World of Isidore of Seville: Truth from Words* (Cambridge: 2007).
8. P. E. Prill, "Rhetoric and Poetics in the Early Middle Ages," *Rhetorica* 5 (1987), 129–47, at 134.
9. M. T. Gibson, "Boethius in the Carolingian Schools," *Transactions of the Royal Historical Society*, 5th series, 32 (1982), 43–56, at 47.
10. J. Moorhead, *Gregory the Great* (London: 2005), 21. On Gregory, see further N. Bronwen, *A Companion to Gregory the Great* (Leiden: 2013); R. A. Markus, *Gregory the Great and his World* (Cambridge: 1987); C. Straw, *Gregory the Great: Perfection in Imperfection* (Berkeley, CA: 1988).
11. See *Philosophy in the Hellenistic and Roman Worlds*, ch.45.

12. P. Godman, *Alcuin: The Bishops, Kings and Saints of York* (Oxford: 1982). His praise of Bede is quoted in by D. Dales, *Alcuin: Theology and Thought* (Cambridge: 2013), 23.

13. Prill, "Rhetoric and Poetics in the Early Middle Ages," 139.

14. Here I'm thinking especially of the debate settled at the Synod of Whitby in Northumbria, in 664. This took place shortly before the birth of Bede, a main source of information about the event.

15. For what follows I rely on Bullough, *Alcuin: Achievement and Reputation*; he makes the point about Alcuin's brief time with Charles at 435.

16. W. S. Howell, *The Rhetoric of Alcuin and Charlemagne* (Ithaca, NY: 1959).

17. Dales, *Alcuin: Theology and Thought*, 142–3.

18. Bullough, *Alcuin: Achievement and Reputation*, 348.

19. Textual references are to the English translation in J. J. M. Curry, "Alcuin, *De Ratione Animae*: A Text with Introduction, Critical Apparatus, and Translation" (unpublished PhD thesis, Cornell University, 1966).

20. *Phaedo* 82e.

21. See Augustine's *On the Trinity*, discussed in *Philosophy in the Hellenistic and Roman Worlds*, ch.51.

22. This text is related to the icon controversy by Dales, *Alcuin: Theology and Thought*, 58.

23. Dales, *Alcuin: Theology and Thought*, 92.

24. Dales, *Alcuin: Theology and Thought*, 87; see also 65, 78.

25. This figure is cited by G. W. Trompf, "The Concept of the Carolingian Renaissance," *Journal of the History of Ideas* 34 (1973), 3–26, at 20.

Chapter 3

1. She was introduced in *Philosophy in the Islamic World*, ch.17.

2. A good collection of papers on this is M. McCord Adams and R. H. Adams (eds), *The Problem of Evil* (Oxford: 1990).

3. For this criticism, see the texts quoted by D. Ganz, "The Debate on Predestination," in M. T. Gibson and J. L. Nelson (eds), *Charles the Bald: Court and Kingdom* (Aldershot: 1990), 283–302, at 287–8, and in the same volume J. Marenbon, "John Scottus and Carolingian Theology: From the *De Praedestinatione*, its Background and its Critics, to the *Periphyseon*," 303–25, at 305.

4. Discussed in *Philosophy in the Hellenistic and Roman Worlds*, ch.43.

5. I have discussed this point in "Freedom and Determinism," in R. Pasnau (ed.), *The Cambridge History of Medieval Philosophy*, 2 vols (Cambridge: 2010), vol.1, 399–413.

6. John Scottus Eriugena, *Treatise on Divine Predestination*, trans. M. Brennan (Notre Dame, IN: 1998); quoted by section number from this translation.

Chapter 4

1. Eriugena, *Periphyseon (The Division of Nature)*, trans. I.-P. Sheldon-Williams and J. J. O'Meara (Montreal: 1987). Cited by section number from the *Patrologia Latina* edition; these are also given in Sheldon-Williams' Latin and English facing-page edition, published by the Dublin Institute for Advanced Studies.

2. On this, see W. Otten, "The Dialectic of the Return in Eriugena's *Periphyseon*," *Harvard Theological Review* 84 (1991), 399–421.

3. See *Philosophy in the Hellenistic and Roman Worlds*, ch.48.

4. Trans. in A. B. Schoedinger, *Readings in Medieval Philosophy* (Oxford: 1996), 275–9. On this, see J. Marenbon, *From the Circle of Alcuin to the School of Auxerre* (Cambridge: 1981), 62–3; M. L. Colish, "Carolingian Debates over *Nihil* and *Tenebrae*: A Study in Theological Method," *Speculum* 59 (1984), 757–95.

5. Augustine, *De magistro* §2.3, translation at P. King (trans.), *Augustine: On the Teacher* (Indianapolis: 1995), 98.

6. See Chapters 68 and 71, and for the topic in the *Periphyseon* itself D. F. Duclow, "Divine Nothingness and Self-Creation in John Scotus Eriugena," *Journal of Religion* 57 (1977), 109–23.

7. Eriugena is also drawing here on Greek theologians, and in particular on the Cappadocians, who argued against the heterousian theologian Eunomius that substance or essence (*ousia*, a Greek word also used for the category of substance by Eriugena) in itself is unknowable. On this, see *Philosophy in the Hellenistic and Roman Worlds*, ch.42.

Chapter 5

1. My thanks to Bernard Colbert for suggesting that I mention the poem.

2. J. J. Contreni, *Carolingian Learning: Masters and Manuscripts* (Aldershot: 1992), §IX, 766.

3. Contreni, *Carolingian Learning*, §VIII, 63–4.

4. J. Marenbon, *From the Circle of Alcuin to the School of Auxerre* (Cambridge: 1981), 88–105.

5. Marenbon, *From the Circle of Alcuin*, 123–6, and 69, for the "hyper-realist" position described further below.

6. Contreni, *Carolingian Learning*, §IV, 85.

7. Here I draw on the studies of Mariken Teeuwen. See her *Harmony and the Music of the Spheres: The Ars Musica in Ninth-Century Commentaries on Martianus Capella* (Leiden: 2002); "Marginal Scholarship: Rethinking the Function of Latin Glosses in Early Medieval Manuscripts," in P. Lendinara et al. (eds), *Rethinking and Recontextualizing Glosses* (Porto: 2011), 19–37; and M. Teeuwen and S. O'Sullivan (eds), *Carolingian Scholarship and Martianus Capella* (Turnhout: 2011).

8. This point is made by R. W. Southern, *Scholastic Humanism and the Unification of Europe. Vol. 1: Foundations* (Oxford: 1995), 9.

9. The following information is drawn from C. E. Lutz, *Schoolmasters of the Tenth Century* (Hamden, CT: 1977).

10. Contreni, *Carolingian Learning*, §XII, 385.

11. Lutz, *Schoolmasters of the Tenth Century*, 132, for the criticism of Gerbert, 8–9, for the poet's remark about Martianus. C. J. Mews, *Abelard and Heloise* (New York: 2005), 105, for Manegold and Wolfhelm.

12. H. E. J. Cowdrey, *Lanfranc: Scholar, Monk, and Archbishop* (Oxford: 2003), 47. On him, see also M. Gibson, *Lanfranc of Bec* (Oxford: 1978).

13. For a brief overview of these activities, see S. Gersh, "Anselm of Canterbury," in P. Dronke (ed.) *A History of Twelfth-Century Western Philosophy* (Cambridge: 1988), 255–78, at 256.

14. Cowdrey, *Lanfranc: Scholar, Monk, and Archbishop*, 68–9.

15. Quoted by D. Knowles, *The Evolution of Medieval Thought* (New York: 1964), 95.

Chapter 6

1. The example is from Ulpian, *Digest* 9.1.1.10. My thanks to Caroline Humfress for the reference, and for discussion of the possible connection to medieval speculations.

2. For the first example, see J. Marenbon, *The Philosophy of Peter Abelard* (Cambridge: 1997), 179. I owe the second, which is discussed by the fourteenth-century thinker Robert Holcot, to Christophe Grellard. See further M. V. Dougherty, *Moral Dilemmas in Medieval Thought from Gratian to Aquinas* (Cambridge: 2011).

3. R. W. Southern, *Scholastic Humanism and the Unification of Europe. Vol. 1: Foundations* (Oxford: 1995), 152.

4. I. M. Resnick, "Attitudes Towards Philosophy and Dialectic During the Gregorian Reform," *Journal of Religious History* 16 (1990), 115–25, at 117.

5. For Peter's life and career, see I. M. Resnick, *Divine Power and Possibility in St. Peter Damian's De Divina Omnipotentia* (Leiden: 1992), ch.2; P. Ranft, *The Theology of Peter Damian* (Washington DC: 2012).

6. See *Philosophy in the Hellenistic and Roman Worlds*, ch.45.

7. For a thorough discussion of these aspects of Damian's works, see Ranft, *The Theology of Peter Damian*.

8. In Jerome's *Letter to Eustochius*, §5. For Damian's letter, see A. Cantin (ed. and trans.), *Pierre Damien: Lettre sur la toute-puissance divine* (Paris: 1972), cited by section number from his edition and also the sections from the *Patrologia latina* which are reproduced in the margins of Cantin's Latin edition.

9. See for this issue D. Frede, "Omne quod est quando est necesse est esse," *Archiv für Geschichte der Philosophie* 54 (1972), 153–67.

10. Resnick, *Divine Power and Possibility*, 59.

11. J. A. Endres, "Die Dialektiker und ihre Gegner im 11. Jahrhundert," *Philosophisches Jahrbuch* 19 (1906), 20–33. For a strident argument against this reading, see L. Moonan, "Impossibility and Peter Damian," *Archiv für Geschichte der Philosophie* 62 (1980), 146–63.

12. P. Remnant, "Peter Damian: Could God Change the Past?" *Canadian Journal of Philosophy* 2 (1978), 259–68.

13. L. Moonan, "Impossibility and Peter Damian," *Archiv für Geschichte der Philosophie* 62 (1980), 146–63.

14. An interpretation turning on this notion has been put forward in various places by T. J. Holopainen, including his *Dialectic and Theology in the Eleventh Century* (Leiden: 1996), ch.2.

15. R. Gaskin, "Peter Damian on Divine Power and the Contingency of the Past," *British Journal for the History of Philosophy* 5 (1997) 229–47; Resnick, *Divine Power and Possibility*, 105.

16. *Why God Became Man*, 2.17, in B. Davies and G. R. Evans (eds), *Anselm of Canterbury: The Major Works* (Oxford: 1998).

Chapter 7

1. For Anselm's life, see R. W. Southern, *Saint Anselm: A Portrait in a Landscape* (Cambridge: 1991); and G. R. Evans, "Anselm's Life, Works and Immediate Influence," in B. Davies and B. Leftow (eds), *The Cambridge Companion to Anselm* (Cambridge: 2004), 5–31.

2. This point is made by Evans, "Anselm's Life," 16.

3. Prologue to the *Monologion*, in B. Davies and G. R. Evans (eds), *Anselm of Canterbury: The Major Works* (Oxford: 1998). Citations in the main text are to section numbers from this volume.

4. As shown in E. C. Sweeney, *Anselm of Canterbury and the Desire for the Word* (Washington DC: 2012).

5. A point made by M. McCord Adams, "Anselm on Faith and Reason," in B. Davies and B. Leftow (eds), *The Cambridge Companion to Anselm* (Cambridge: 2004), 32–60, at 46.

6. In what follows I am broadly in agreement with the account given in S. Visser and T. Williams, "Anselm's Account of Freedom," in B. Davies and B. Leftow (eds), *The Cambridge Companion to Anselm* (Cambridge: 2005), 179–203; and ch.11 of S. Visser and T. Williams, *Anselm* (New York: 2009). See further C. G. Normore, "Picking and Choosing: Anselm and Ockham on Choice," *Vivarium* 36 (1998), 23–39; K. A. Rogers, *Anselm on Freedom* (Oxford: 2008).

7. W. J. Courtenay, "Necessity and Freedom in Anselm's Conception of God," in *Analecta Anselmiana* 4.2 (Frankfurt am Main: 1975), 39–64, reprinted in Courtenay, *Covenant and Causality in Medieval Thought* (London: 1984).

8. This idea is Augustinian. See Augustine, *On Free Choice of the Will*, trans. T. Williams (Indianapolis, IN: 1993), §2.2.

Chapter 8

1. For Plantinga's version, see A. Plantinga, *The Nature of Necessity* (Oxford: 1974); M. Tooley, "Plantinga's Defence of the Ontological Argument," *Mind* 90 (1981), 422–7.

2. Again, citations in the text are to the section numbers of the translations in B. Davies and G. R. Evans (eds), *Anselm of Canterbury: The Major Works* (Oxford: 1998).

3. For the parallel to Anselm, see P. Adamson, "From the Necessary Existent to God," in P. Adamson (ed.), *Interpreting Avicenna* (Cambridge: 2013), 170–89.

4. This same assumption about the unity of a concept is made concerning justice and truth at Anselm's *On Truth*, §13.

5. For more on this problem, see G. R. Evans, *Anselm and Talking about God* (Oxford: 1978).

6. Here and in what follows I am largely in agreement with the analysis given in T. Williams and S. Visser, *Anselm* (New York: 2009), ch.5.

7. N. Malcolm, "Anselm's Ontological Arguments," *Philosophical Review* 69 (1960), 41–62, sees this section as articulating the real reasoning that lies behind the whole proof.

8. *Critique of Pure Reason*, B667.

Chapter 9

1. See, for instance, Aristotle, *Metaphysics* 1039a30–31.

2. Translation in P. V. Spade (trans.), *Five Texts on the Mediaeval Problem of Universals: Porphyry, Boethius, Abelard, Duns Scotus, Ockham* (Indianapolis, IN: 1994). I refer to section numbers from Spade's translation throughout the main text of this chapter.

3. See *Classical Philosophy*, ch.31.

4. C. J. Mews, "Nominalism and Theology before Abaelard: New Light on Roscelin of Compiègne," *Vivarium* 30 (1992), 4–33, at 30. I follow Mews' account of Roscelin's project in what follows.

5. J. Marenbon, "Vocalism, Nominalism and the Commentaries on the Categories from the Earlier Twelfth Century," *Vivarium* 30 (1992), 51–61, at 53.

6. Mews, "Nominalism and Theology before Abaelard," 21.

7. For Abelard's theory, see J. Marenbon, *The Philosophy of Peter Abelard* (Cambridge: 1997), ch.8; P. King, "Metaphysics," in J. E. Brower and K. Guilfoy, *The Cambridge Companion to Abelard* (Cambridge: 2004), 65–125.

8. In real life Harpo was not mute; this was just part of his stage persona. He did, however, genuinely like to chase women.

Chapter 10

1. See the judicious discussion in J. Marenbon, *The Philosophy of Peter Abelard* (Cambridge: 1997), 82–93. More controversial has been Constant Mews' claim in *The Lost Love Letters of Heloise and Abelard* (New York: 1999) to have uncovered further correspondence between the two; this claim has been rejected in D. Luscombe (ed.), *The Letter Collection of Abelard and Heloise* (Oxford: 2013). For a more recent contribution by Mews, see "Between Authenticity and Interpretation: On The Letter Collection of Peter Abelard and Heloise and the Epistolae Duorum Amantium," *Tijdschrift voor Filosofie* 76 (2014), 823–42.
2. The most elaborate case for this thesis has been made in C. J. Mews, *Abelard and Heloise* (New York: 2005).
3. B. Radice and M. T. Clanchy, *The Letters of Abelard and Heloise* (London: 2003), 10. Hereafter cited by page number in the main text.
4. Mews, *Abelard and Heloise*, 12.
5. See further *Philosophy in the Hellenistic and Roman Worlds*, ch.25.
6. Mews, *Abelard and Heloise*, 58–9.
7. C. J. Martin, "The Development of Logic," in R. Pasnau (ed.), *The Cambridge History of Medieval Philosophy*, 2 vols (Cambridge: 2010), vol.1, 129–45, at 133. For more on this, see K. Jacobi, "Philosophy of Language," in J. E. Brower and K. Guilfoy, *The Cambridge Companion to Abelard* (Cambridge: 2004), 126–57.
8. As pointed out by Mews, *Abelard and Heloise*, 152.
9. M. T. Clanchy, *Abelard: A Medieval Life* (Oxford: 1997), 169.
10. Translated in Radice and Clanchy, *The Letters of Abelard and Heloise*.
11. Mews, *Abelard and Heloise*, 200.
12. Mews, *Abelard and Heloise*, 147.
13. Mews, *Abelard and Heloise*, 127.

Chapter 11

1. English translation in P. V. Spade (trans.), *Peter Abelard: Ethical Writings* (Indianapolis, IN: 1995). Cited by section number from this translation in the rest of the chapter.
2. A good overview of Abelard's arguments is offered in P. King, "Abelard's Intentionalist Ethics," *The Modern Schoolman* 72 (1995), 213–32.
3. This implication has been pointed out by King, "Abelard's Intentionalist Ethics," 217, albeit only as one that Abelard comes "dangerously close" to endorsing.
4. Some of the objections I consider in what follows are set out in I. P. Bajczy, "Deeds without Value: Exploring a Weak Spot in Abelard's Ethics," *Recherches de Théologie et Philosophie Médiévale* 70 (2003), 1–21.
5. See *Philosophy in the Greek and Roman Worlds*, ch.13.
6. J. Marenbon, *The Philosophy of Peter Abelard* (Cambridge: 1997), 256.
7. Bajczy, "Deeds without Value," 1; Marenbon, *The Philosophy of Peter Abelard*, 253.
8. See, for instance, D. E. Luscombe, *The School of Peter Abelard* (Cambridge: 1970), 18; C. J. Mews, *Abelard and Heloise* (New York: 2005), 158.
9. I am quoting, with modification, the translation in B. Radice and M. T. Clanchy, *The Letters of Abelard and Heloise* (London: 2003), 53.

10. I here agree with Marenbon, *The Philosophy of Peter Abelard*, 92. For further discussion of the general issue, see B. H. Findley, "Does the Habit Make the Nun? A Case Study of Heloise's Influence on Abelard's Ethical Philosophy," *Vivarium* 44 (2006), 248–75.

Chapter 12

1. See *Philosophy in the Hellenistic and Roman Worlds*, ch.41.
2. For this emphasis on history, see P. Rorem, *Hugh of Saint Victor* (New York: 2009), 20, drawing on the much earlier study by G. Zinn, "*Historia Fundamentum Est*: The Role of History in the Contemplative Life according to Hugh of St Victor," in G. H. Shriver (ed.), *Contemporary Reflections on the Medieval Christian Tradition* (Durham, NC: 1974), 135–58.
3. These examples are mentioned in Rorem, *Hugh of Saint Victor*, 148; and P. McElroy Wheeler, "The Twelfth-Century School of St Victor" (PhD Thesis, University of Southern California, 1970), 64.
4. J. Taylor (trans.), *The Didascalicon of Hugh of St. Victor* (New York: 1961). Citations in the text of this chapter are to section numbers from this translation.
5. Actually it isn't totally certain that he was Hugh's direct student. For references on this, see B. T. Coolman and D. M. Coulter (eds), *Trinity and Creation: A Selection of Works of Hugh, Richard and Adam of St Victor* (Hyde Park, NY: 2002), 198.
6. E. T. Healy (trans.), *Works of Saint Bonaventure. Vol. 1: De Reductione Artium ad Theologiam* (Saint Bonaventure, NY: 1940), §5.
7. The analogy reappears at §V.2, VI.3, and was already used in a letter written to William of Champeaux encouraging his founding of the Abbey: see Wheeler, *The Twelfth-Century School of St Victor*, 10.
8. Rorem, *Hugh of Saint Victor*, 44.
9. E. Gibbon, *Decline and Fall of the Roman Empire*, ed. J. B. Bury (Cambridge: 2013), vol.5, 286.
10. Wheeler, *The Twelfth-Century School of St Victor*, 10–11. Incidentally, this letter also uses the aforementioned honeycomb analogy for the spiritual life.
11. For this and what follows, see B. T. Coolman, *The Theology of Hugh of St Victor* (Cambridge: 2010).
12. Coolman, *The Theology of Hugh of St Victor*, 146.
13. Coolman, *The Theology of Hugh of St Victor*, 16, 28, 51.
14. See also Hugh's *Sentences on Divinity*, in Coolman and Coulter (eds), *Trinity and Creation*, 141.
15. See *Philosophy in the Hellenistic and Roman Worlds*, ch.34.
16. R. J. Deferrari (trans.), *On the Sacraments of the Christian Faith (De Sacramentis)* (Cambridge, MA: 1951).
17. *On Sacraments* §I.9.2, quoted at Rorem, *Hugh of Saint Victor*, 80.
18. Coolman, *The Theology of Hugh of St Victor*, 170.
19. G. A. Zinn (trans.), *Richard of St. Victor: The Twelve Patriarchs, the Mystical Ark, Book Three of The Trinity* (New York: 1979).
20. G. Constable, *The Reformation of the Twelfth Century* (Cambridge: 1996), 6. Cited by Coolman, *The Theology of Hugh of St Victor*, 7.

Chapter 13

1. See *Philosophy in the Hellenistic and Roman Worlds*, ch.51.
2. *Epistle* 190; quotation taken from J. R. Sommerfeldt, *Bernard of Clairvaux on the Life of the Mind* (New York: 2004), 126.

3. On Bernard's criticisms, see, e.g., D. E. Luscombe, *The School of Peter Abelard* (Cambridge: 1970), ch.4; G. R. Evans, *The Mind of St. Bernard of Clairvaux* (Oxford: 1983), ch.3.

4. B. Radice and M. T. Clanchy, *The Letters of Abelard and Heloise* (London: 2003), 25.

5. Evans, *The Mind of St. Bernard of Clairvaux*, 96, 141, 144 (he was "at home with the talk of the schools"). See further M. A. Doyle, *Bernard of Clairvaux and the Schools* (Spoleto: 2005), part 2, for his relation to the Victorines.

6. In what follows I draw on the lucid account in J. E. Brower, "Trinity," in J. E. Brower and K. Guilfoy, *The Cambridge Companion to Abelard* (Cambridge: 2004), 223–57.

7. Luscombe, *The School of Peter Abelard*, 4. He also discusses the anonymous works I go on to mention here.

8. Evans, *The Mind of St. Bernard of Clairvaux*, 169.

9. See part 3 of Hugh's *Sentences on Divinity*, translated in B. T. Coolman and D. M. Coulter (eds), *Trinity and Creation: A Selection of Works of Hugh, Richard and Adam of St Victor* (Hyde Park, NY: 2002), 155–60. This volume also contains Richard of Saint Victor's *On the Trinity*, which is cited by section number in what follows.

10. Luscombe, *The School of Peter Abelard*, 123–4, 166.

Chapter 14

1. D. D. McGarry (trans.), *John of Salisbury: The Metalogicon. A Twelfth-Century Defense of the Verbal and Logical Arts of the Trivium* (Philadelphia, PA: 2009). Cited by section number in the main text.

2. P. E. Dutton, *Bernard of Chartres: Glosae super Platonem* (Toronto: 1991), who makes the point about supplanting Calcidius at 69.

3. A. Somfai, "The Eleventh-Century Shift in the Reception of Plato's *Timaeus* and Calcidius' Commentary," *Journal of the Warburg and Courtauld Institutes* 65 (2002), 1–21, with a chart of manuscripts at 8. For more on Calcidius, see *Philosophy in the Hellenistic and Roman Worlds*, ch.52.

4. See D. B. George and J. R. Fortin (trans.), *The Boethian Commentaries of Clarembald of Arras* (Notre Dame, IN: 2002).

5. See the republished version of his original argument, with responses to critics, in R. W. Southern, *Scholastic Humanism and the Unification of Europe. Vol. 1: Foundations* (Oxford: 1995). For responses, see P. Dronke, "New Approaches to the School of Chartres," *Anuario de Estudios Medievales* 6 (1969), 117–40; N. M. Häring, "Chartres and Paris Revisited," in J. R. O'Donnell (ed.), *Essays in Honor of Anton Charles Pegis* (Toronto: 1974), 268–329; J. Marenbon, "Humanism, Scholasticism and the School of Chartres," *International Journal of the Classical Tradition* 6 (2000), 569–77.

6. K. M. Fredborg, *The Latin Rhetorical Commentaries by Thierry of Chartres* (Toronto: 1988), 7.

7. Indeed, this period of thought has often been called a renaissance too, as in the title of C. H. Haskins, *The Renaissance of the Twelfth Century* (Cambridge, MA: 1927).

8. This theme is discussed extensively in W. Wetherbee, *Platonism and Poetry in the Twelfth Century* (Princeton, NJ: 1972), from which I draw the following examples. For further discussion, see B. Stock, *Myth and Science in the Twelfth Century: A Study of Bernard Silvester* (Princeton, NJ: 1972).

9. Wetherbee, *Platonism and Poetry*, 41–2.

10. The development of his position is summarized in R. W. Southern, *Scholastic Humanism and the Unification of Europe. Vol. II: The Heroic Age* (Oxford: 2001).

11. Wetherbee, *Platonism and Poetry*, 123.

12. For what follows, see Dutton, *Bernard of Chartres*, 70–96.

13. N. M. Häring, *Life and Works of Clarembald of Arras: A Twelfth-Century Master of the School of Chartres* (Toronto: 1965), 30. See also N. M. Häring, "The Creation and Creator of the World according to Thierry of Chartres and Clarenbaldus of Arras," *Archives d'Histoire Doctrinale et Littéraire du Moyen Âge* 22 (1955).

14. I. Ronca and M. Curr (trans.), *William of Conches: A Dialogue on Natural Philosophy (Dragmaticon Philosophiae)* (Notre Dame, IN: 1997). Cited by chapter and section number in what follows.

15. I take this point from J. Cadden, "Science and Rhetoric in the Middle Ages: The Natural Philosophy of William of Conches," *Journal of the History of Ideas* 56 (1995), 1–24.

16. See H. R. Lemay, "Science and Theology at Chartres: The Case of the Supracelestial Waters," *British Journal for the History of Science* 10 (1977), 226–36.

Chapter 15

1. John Spencer, *A Discourse Concerning Prodigies* (1665), 2nd edn, Preface. The Latin in the middle means "There is no blemish in the book of nature." My thanks to Robert Yelle for bringing the passage to my attention. It should be noted that Spencer did recognize that miracles have been sent by God, but such events had ceased long ago, in antiquity.

2. Quoted by P. Rorem, *Hugh of Saint Victor* (New York: 2009), 63.

3. For instance in *Confessions* §13.15. For more on the metaphor, see A. Vanderjagt, *The Book of Nature in Antiquity and the Middle Ages* (Leuven: 2005); D. Hawkes, *The Book of Nature and Humanity in the Middle Ages and the Renaissance* (Brepols: 2013).

4. Useful reading here is provided by D. C. Lindberg and M. J. Shank (eds), *The Cambridge History of Science. Vol. 2: Medieval Science* (Cambridge: 2013).

5. Quoted by C. Burnett, "Scientific Speculations," in P. Dronke (ed.) *A History of Twelfth-Century Western Philosophy* (Cambridge: 1988), 151–76, at 152.

6. For this and what follows, see T. Stiefel, "The Heresy of Science: A Twelfth-Century Conceptual Revolution," *Isis* 68 (1977), 346–62; for the wax nose analogy, see 359.

7. Lindberg and Shank, *Medieval Science*, 291.

8. Stiefel, "The Heresy of Science," 350.

9. A. Speer, "The Discovery of Nature: The Contribution of the Chartrians to Twelfth-Century Attempts to Found a *Scientia Naturalis*," *Traditio* 52 (1997), 135–51, at 140. See also B. Stock, *Myth and Science in the Twelfth Century: A Study of Bernard Silvester* (Princeton, NJ: 1972), 240.

10. J. Jolivet, "Les *Quaestiones Naturales* d'Adélard de Bath ou la nature sans le Livre," *Études de civilisation médiévale* (Poitiers: 1974), 437–46.

11. Note that the title playfully resonates with that of Boethius' *Consolation of Philosophy*. I cite the *Cosmographia* by page number from the English version in W. Wetherbee, *The Cosmographia of Bernardus Silvestris* (New York: 1973), and the *Lament of Nature* from W. Wetherbee (trans.), *Alan of Lille: Literary Works* (Cambridge, MA: 2013), by chapter and section number.

12. Boethius, *Theological Tractates and Consolation of Philosophy*, trans. H. F. Stewart et al. (London: 1973); *Consolation* I, prose 1.

13. Quoted by Stock, *Myth and Science*, 46. My translation.

14. Stock, *Myth and Science*, 114–17.

15. I. Ronca and M. Curr (trans.), *William of Conches: A Dialogue on Natural Philosophy (Dragmaticon Philosophiae)* (Notre Dame, IN: 1997), §2.4.1.

16. Stock, *Myth and Science*, 27.

17. For the theme of nature as a book, see also Alan of Lille's poem beginning *omnis mundi creatura quasi liber*, edited and translated at 544–7 in Wetherbee, *Alan of Lille*.

18. For the contrast between "soft" and "hard" astrology, which respectively make the stars mere signs and actual causes of earthly events, see *Philosophy in the Hellenistic and Roman Worlds*, ch.28.

19. On this, see J. Bardzell, *Speculative Grammar and Stoic Language Theory in Medieval Allegorical Narrative: From Prudentius to Alan of Lille* (London: 2009), 97; M. D. Jordan, *The Invention of Sodomy in Christian Theology* (Chicago: 1997), 79, 82.

Chapter 16

1. For what follows, and indeed this entire chapter, I have drawn extensively on J. J. E. Garcia, *Introduction to the Problem of Individuation in the Early Middle Ages* (Munich: 1988).

2. This is more or less Porphyry's way of explaining accidents in his *Isagoge* (*Introduction*), in P. V. Spade (trans.), *Five Texts on the Mediaeval Problem of Universals: Porphyry, Boethius, Abelard, Duns Scotus, Ockham* (Indianapolis, IN: 1994), §57–9. A note of caution: in the Aristotelian tradition one also sees reference to "essential accidents," which involves a broader use of the term "accident" to mean just any property, whether essential or "accidental" in the narrower sense.

3. Porphyry, *Introduction*, §36, in Spade, *Five Texts*.

4. Text quoted at Garcia, *Introduction to the Problem of Individuation*, 91.

5. I take this point in particular from Garcia, *Introduction to the Problem of Individuation*, for instance at 125.

6. On this, see L. O. Nielsen, *Theology and Philosophy in the Twelfth Century* (Leiden: 1982), 57–69; Garcia, *Introduction to the Problem of Individuation*, 155–78; C. Erismann, "Explaining Exact Resemblance: Gilbert of Poitiers's *Conformitas* Theory Reconsidered," *Oxford Studies in Medieval Philosophy* 2 (2014), 1–24.

7. What Gilbert is proposing here is known in contemporary philosophy as a "trope" theory. For an introduction to this, see M. J. Loux, *Metaphysics: A Contemporary Introduction* (London: 1998), 79–87.

8. This is of, course, not to say that they are on a par in every respect. As Erismann, "Explaining Exact Resemblance," 11, points out, Gilbert would still accept a "core" of essential features that account for a thing's species membership (e.g. it is by being alive, rational, animal, etc., that Groucho is a human).

9. See the text quoted at Nielsen, *Theology and Philosophy*, 60.

10. This has been stressed by J. Marenbon, "Gilbert of Poitiers," in P. Dronke (ed.) *A History of Twelfth-Century Western Philosophy* (Cambridge: 1988), 328–52.

11. Quoted (in Latin) at Nielsen, *Theology and Philosophy*, 34.

Chapter 17

1. This point is well made by B. Tierney, *The Crisis of Church and State 1050–1300* (Toronto: 1988), 2. In the first part of this chapter citations in the main text are to the primary texts provided by Tierney.

2. See *Philosophy in the Hellenistic and Roman Worlds*, ch.46.

3. Alcuin, *Epistle* 171, quoted at J. H. Burns, *The Cambridge History of Medieval Political Thought c. 350–c.1450* (Cambridge: 1988), 303; for the following quotations from Alcuin, see 221 and 289.

4. See Burns, *Cambridge History*, 297–8.

5. U. R. Blumenthal, *The Investiture Controversy: Church and Monarchy from the Ninth to the Twelfth Century* (Philadelphia, PA: 1988), 89–90.

6. On him, see R. W. Southern, *Scholastic Humanism and the Unification of Europe. Vol. 1: Foundations* (Oxford: 1995), 252–61.

7. R. Ziomkowski (trans.), *Manegold of Lautenbach: Liber contra Wolfelmum* (Paris: 2002). Cited by chapter.

8. For readers of this book series who are keeping track of memorable dates, this is eleven years after the death of al-Ghazālī in 1111.

9. For his biography, see the relevant sections of both volumes of Southern, *Scholastic Humanism and the Unification of Europe*.

10. Cited by book and chapter number from the selective translation in C. J. Nederman (trans.), *John of Salisbury: Policraticus* (Cambridge: 1990).

11. For the Ciceronian and Aristotelian aspects, see C. J. Nederman, "Nature, Sin and the Origins of Society: The Ciceronian Tradition in Medieval Political Thought," *Journal of the History of Ideas* 49 (1988), 3–26, and C. J. Nederman, "The Aristotelian Doctrine of the Mean and John of Salisbury's Concept of Liberty," *Vivarium* 24 (1986), 128–42.

12. See P. Adamson, "State of Nature: Human and Cosmic Rulership in Ancient Philosophy," in B. Kellner and A. Höfele (eds), *Menschennatur und politische Ordnung* (Paderborn: 2015), 79–94.

13. On this, see C. J. Nederman, "A Duty to Kill: John of Salisbury's Theory of Tyrannicide," *Review of Politics* 50 (1988), 365–89, which refers to the extensive further literature.

14. For more on this, see C. J. Nederman and C. Campbell, "Priests, Kings and Tyrants: Spiritual and Temporal Power in John of Salisbury's *Politicratus*," *Speculum* 66 (1991), 572–90.

Chapter 18

1. R. W. Southern, *Scholastic Humanism and the Unification of Europe. Vol. 1: Foundations* (Oxford: 1995), 305.

2. Quoted by J. A. Brundage, "The Teaching and Study of Canon Law in the Law Schools," in W. Hartmann and K. Pennington (eds), *The History of Medieval Canon Law in the Classical Period, 1140–1234* (Washington DC: 2008), 119. For the tradition more generally, see J. A. Brundage, *Medieval Canon Law* (London: 1995).

3. Translation, modified, taken from A. Thompson (trans.), *Gratian: The Treatise on Laws* (Washington DC: 1993). The *Decretum* has a very complex structure with subdivisions of the distinctions, but I will keep things simple by just quoting the relevant distinction number.

4. The concept does have roots in antiquity, especially in the Stoics. On this, see P. Mitsis, "Natural Law and Natural Right in Post-Aristotelian Philosophy: The Stoics and their Critics," *Aufstieg und Niedergang der römischen Welt* 36.7 (1994), 4812–50.

5. On this question, see J. Porter, "Custom, Ordinance and Natural Right in Gratian's *Decretum*," in A. Perreau-Saussine and J. B. Murphy (eds), *The Nature of Customary Law* (Cambridge: 2007), 79–100.

6. See F. H. Russell, *The Just War in the Middle Ages* (Cambridge: 1975), ch.3.

7. For this and other aspects of the reception of the *Sentences*, see the concluding chapter of P. W. Rosemann, *Peter Lombard* (New York: 2004).

8. For an overview of these authors as background to the *Sentences*, see M. L. Colish, *Peter Lombard*, 2 vols (Leiden: 1994), vol.1, ch.2. Lombard's approach is also compared to that of Hugh and others in P. W. Rosemann, *Peter Lombard* (New York: 2004), ch.3. It should also be noted that Greek authors had already produced comprehensive works of theology, notably *On the Orthodox Faith* by John of Damascus, which was itself influential in Latin translation, including on Peter Lombard.

9. Colish, *Peter Lombard*, vol.1, 78.

10. Rosemann, *Peter Lombard*, 64–5.

11. The relevant sections can be found in vol.3 of Peter Lombard, *The Sentences*, trans. G. Silano, 4 vols (Toronto: 2007–10). I will cite by distinction, chapter, and section number; all references are to book 3. A useful discussion of Lombard's treatment of the Incarnation is Colish, *Peter Lombard*, ch.7.

12. See *Philosophy in the Hellenistic and Roman Worlds*, ch.44.

13. Rosemann, *Peter Lombard*, 131–3.

14. See Colish, *Peter Lombard*, e.g. at vol.1, 84–5, for an argument against the assumption that Lombard was actually an anti-philosophical thinker.

Chapter 19

1. *Physics* 8.10, 267b. On this, see P. Adamson and R. Wisnovsky, "Yaḥyā Ibn ʿAdī on the Location of God," *Oxford Studies in Medieval Philosophy* 1 (2013), 205–28.

2. References in the main text of this chapter are to page number of M. Atherton (trans.) *Hildegard of Bingen: Selected Writings* (London: 2001).

3. S. Flanagan, *Hildegard of Bingen 1098–1179: A Visionary Life* (London: 1998), 4. This very useful book gives an overview of Hildegard's life and the main themes of her work, and I have drawn on it throughout this chapter.

4. On whom, see A. Clark, *Elisabeth of Schönau: A Twelfth-Century Visionary* (Philadelphia, PA: 1992).

5. This point is emphasized by Flanagan, *Hildegard of Bingen*, 41–4.

6. This comparison is made by J. Stover, "Hildegard, the Schools and their Critics," in B. M. Kienzle, D. Stoudt, and G. Ferzoco (eds), *A Companion to Hildegard of Bingen* (Leiden: 2014), 109–35, at 127. On the same topic, see C. Mews, "Hildegard and the Schools," in C. Burnett and P. Dronke (eds), *Hildegard of Bingen: The Context of her Thought and Art* (London: 1998), 89–110.

7. Flanagan, *Hildegard of Bingen*, 175.

8. Stover, "Hildegard, the Schools and their Critics," 120.

9. For an illustration, see Flanagan, *Hildegard of Bingen*, 151–2.

10. Indeed, she says elsewhere that the cosmos is spherical, for instance at *Selected Writings*, 153.

11. A point made by Flanagan, *Hildegard of Bingen*, 187.

Chapter 20

1. See further *Philosophy in the Islamic World*, ch.3.

2. C. Burnett, "Humanism and Orientalism in the Translations from Arabic into Latin in the Middle Ages," in A. Speer and L. Wegener (eds), *Wissen über Grenzen: arabisches und lateinisches Mittelalter* (Berlin: 2006), 22–31, at 28.

3. C. D'Ancona Costa, *"Cause prime non est yliathim: Liber de causis* prop. 8 [9]. Le fonti e la dottrina," *Documenti e Studi sulla Tradizione Filosofica Medievale* 1 (1990) 327–51.

4. C. Burnett and D. Jacquart, *Constantine the African and Alī ibn al-Abbās al-Majūsī: The Pantegni and Related Texts* (Leiden: 1994); P. O. Kristeller, "The School of Salerno," *Bulletin of the History of Medicine* 17 (1954), 138–94.

5. I. Ronca and M. Curr (trans.), *William of Conches: A Dialogue on Natural Philosophy (Dragmaticon Philosophiae)* (Notre Dame, IN: 1997), 6.18.4.

6. C. Burnett, *Arabic into Latin in the Middle Ages* (Farnham: 2009), §VII, 257–8. On Adelard in general, see J. Kraye and W. F. Ryan (eds) *Adelard of Bath* (London: 1987); L. Cochrane, *Adelard of Bath: The First English Scientist* (London: 1994); and C. Burnett, *Adelard of Bath: Conversations with his Nephew* (Cambridge: 1998).

7. Burnett, *Arabic into Latin*, §III, 104–5.

8. For what follows, see Burnett, *Arabic into Latin*, §VII; and D. N. Hasse, "The Social Conditions of the Arabic-(Hebrew-)Latin Translation Movements in Medieval Spain and in the Renaissance," in A. Speer and L. Wegener (eds), *Wissen über Grenzen: arabisches und lateinisches Mittelalter* (Berlin: 2006), 68–86.

9. See the text quoted at Burnett, *Arabic into Latin*, §VII, 255.

10. Covered in *Philosophy in the Islamic World*, ch.31.

11. D. N. Hasse, *Avicenna's De Anima in the Latin West: The Formation of a Peripatetic Philosophy of the Soul, 1160–1300* (London: 2000), 7.

12. On whom, see Burnett, *Arabic into Latin*, §VIII; and L. Thorndyke, *Michael Scot* (London: 1965).

13. John of Salisbury, *Metalogicon*, trans. D. D. McGarry (Philadelphia, PA: 2009), IV.6.

14. Stephen of Antioch, quoted at Burnett, "Humanism and Orientalism," 30, concerning a medical treatise.

15. V. A. Guagliardo et al. (trans.), *St. Thomas Aquinas: Commentary on the Book of Causes* (Washington DC, 1996).

16. Burnett, *Arabic into Latin*, §VII, 260, 264.

17. See the prologue of John of Salisbury, *Policraticus*, trans. C. J. Nederman (Cambridge: 1990); probabilist skepticism will ultimately return in the fourteenth century, as we'll see in Chapter 66.

Chapter 21

1. A point made by O. Pedersen, *The First Universities: Studium Generale and the Origins of University Education in Europe* (Cambridge: 1997), 122; Pedersen's book is one of several sources I have drawn on in this chapter, along with F. C. Ferruolo, *The Origins of the University: The Schools of Paris and their Critics, 1100–1215* (Stanford, CA: 1985); H. de Ridder-Symoens (ed.), *A History of the University in Europe. Vol. 1: Universities in the Middle Ages* (Cambridge: 1992); and I. P. Wei, *Intellectual Culture in Medieval Paris: Theologians and the University, c. 1100–1330* (Cambridge: 2012). See also O. Weijers, *A Scholar's Paradise: Teaching and Debating in Medieval Paris* (Turnhout: 2015).

2. Ridder-Symoens, *A History of the University in Europe*, 112.

3. Pederson, *The First Universities*, 159.

4. Pederson, *The First Universities*, 243.

5. For a useful chart of the course of study, see J. Marenbon, *Later Medieval Philosophy (1150–1350)* (London: 1987), 21–2.

6. Ridder-Symoens, *A History of the University in Europe*, 202.

7. Pedersen, *The First Universities*, 254.
8. Pedersen, *The First Universities*, 262.
9. See B. C. Bazán et al. (eds), *Les Questions disputées et les questions quodlibétiques dans les facultés de théologie, de droit et de médicine* (Turnhout: 1985).
10. Quoted from Wei, *Intellectual Culture in Medieval Paris*, 94.
11. The arts curriculum is quoted in full at Pedersen, *The First Universities*, 278.
12. As pointed out in Ridder-Symoens, *A History of the University in Europe*, 27–8.

Chapter 22

1. As observed by H. Lagerlund, "The Assimilation of Aristotelian and Arabic Logic up to the Later Thirteenth Century," in D. M. Gabbay and J. Woods (eds), *Handbook of the History of Logic. Vol. 2: Mediaeval and Renaissance Logic* (Amsterdam: 2008), 281–346, at 281. An important caveat: great strides were also made independently in other, non-Western logical traditions, for example with the Nyāya school in ancient India.
2. D. D. McGarry (trans.), *John of Salisbury: The Metalogicon. A Twelfth-Century Defense of the Verbal and Logical Arts of the Trivium* (Philadelphia, PA: 2009).
3. For a recent discussion of the identity of this masked man, see D. Bloch, *John of Salisbury on Aristotelian Science* (Turnhout: 2012), appendix I.
4. Both are available in English: William of Sherwood, *Introduction to Logic*, trans. N. Kretzmann (Minneapolis, MN: 1966); Peter of Spain, *Language in Dispute*, trans. F. P. Dineen (Amsterdam: 1990). See also the texts available in N. Kretzmann and E. Stump (ed. and trans.), *The Cambridge Translations of Medieval Philosophical Texts. Vol. 1: Logic and the Philosophy of Language* (Cambridge: 1988).
5. See T. Parsons, "The Development of Supposition Theory in the Later 12th through 14th Centuries," in *Handbook of the History of Logic*, 157–280, at 158. For this kind of "regimentation" of Latin, see also A. Broadie, *Introduction to Medieval Logic* (Oxford: 1993), 42, 48, 69.
6. For the rules used to form the nicknames, see Peter of Spain, *Language in Dispute*, 4.13.
7. See *Classical Philosophy*, ch.30.
8. On this, see J. Spruyt, "Thirteenth-Century Discussions on Modal Terms," *Vivarium* 32 (1994), 196–226.
9. See Lagerlund, "The Assimilation," 341.
10. This is close enough for present purposes, but as P. V. Spade points out in N. Kretzmann, A. Kenny, and J. Pinborg (eds), *The Cambridge History of Later Medieval Philosophy* (Cambridge: 1982), at 188, we might in fact want to deny that signification is exactly the same as meaning, since "meaning" doesn't need to involve causation (e.g. of a thought in someone else's mind) in the way envisioned by the medieval logicians.
11. On these two options, see E. J. Ashworth, "Terminist Logic," in R. Pasnau (ed.), *The Cambridge History of Medieval Philosophy*, 2 vols (Cambridge: 2010), vol.1, 146–58, at 151.
12. For the contrast between signification and supposition, see William of Sherwood, *Introduction to Logic*, 5.1; Peter of Spain, *Language in Dispute*, 6.2–3.
13. See *Philosophy in the Hellenistic and Roman Worlds*, ch.48.
14. Parsons, "The Development of Supposition Theory," 201.
15. Parsons, "The Development of Supposition Theory," 198; cf. Broadie, *Introduction*, 32.
16. On this contrast, see A. de Libera, "The Oxford and Paris Traditions in Logic," in Kretzmann et al. (eds), *The Cambridge History*, 174–87.
17. See *Philosophy in the Hellenistic and Roman Worlds*, ch.8.

Chapter 23

1. On this issue, see R. Wood, "The Influence of Arabic Aristotelianism on Scholastic Natural Philosophy: Projectile Motion, the Place of the Universe, and Elemental Composition," in R. Pasnau (ed.), *The Cambridge History of Medieval Philosophy*, 2 vols (Cambridge: 2010), vol.1, 247–66.
2. For his commentary, see R. Wood (ed.), *Richard Rufus of Cornwall: In Physicam Aristotelis* (Oxford: 2003); R. Wood, "Richard Rufus of Cornwall and Aristotle's Physics," *Franciscan Studies* 52 (1992), 247–81; P. Raedts, *Richard Rufus of Cornwall and the Tradition of Oxford Theology* (Oxford: 1987).
3. F. W. Zimmermann, "Philoponus' Impetus Theory in the Arabic Tradition," in R. Sorabji (ed.), *Philoponus and the Rejection of Aristotelian Science* (London: 1987), 121–9. See also *Philosophy in the Hellenistic and Roman Worlds*, ch.38.
4. Wood, *Richard Rufus of Cornwall: In Physicam Aristotelis*, 9–10 and §8.3.1. For further developments in the understanding of projectile motion, see also Chapter 64 below.
5. See *Classical Philosophy*, ch.7.
6. *Physics* 3.1, 200b–201a.
7. The same example (without the baseball) is used to illustrate this point in C. Trifogli, "Change, Time, and Place," in Pasnau, *Cambridge History*, vol.1, 267–78, at 270.
8. C. Trifogli, *Oxford Physics in the Thirteenth Century (ca. 1250–70): Motion, Infinity, Place and Time* (Leiden: 2000). For the critiques of Averroes on motion mentioned just below, see 58 and 60.
9. E. J. McCullough, "St. Albert on Motion as *Forma Fluens* and *Fluxus Formae*," in J. A. Weisheipl (ed.), *Albertus Magnus and the Sciences* (Toronto: 1980), 129–53; S. Baldner, "Albertus Magnus and the Categorization of Motion," *The Thomist* 70 (2006), 203–35.
10. See *Philosophy in the Hellenistic and Roman Worlds*, ch.47.
11. *Physics* 4.14, 223a.
12. Trifogli, *Oxford Physics*, 221–2 (again, without the baseball), with the English commentators' responses at 224–30.
13. For what follows, see Trifogli, *Oxford Physics*, ch.2.
14. *Physics* 4.4, 212a.
15. Trifogli, *Oxford Physics*, ch.3.

Chapter 24

1. R. C. Dales, *The Problem of the Rational Soul in the Thirteenth Century* (Leiden: 1995), 32.
2. Section numbers from R. J. Teske (trans.), *William of Auvergne: The Soul* (Milwaukee, WI: 2000).
3. See *Philosophy in the Hellenistic and Roman Worlds*, ch.31.
4. As documented in D. N. Hasse, *Avicenna's De Anima in the Latin West* (London: 2000).
5. Hasse, *Avicenna's De Anima*, 21. In what follows, citations in the main text are to section numbers of D. A. Callus and R. W. Hunt (ed.), M. W. Dunne (trans.), *John Blund: Treatise on the Soul* (Oxford: 2013).
6. See *Philosophy in the Islamic World*, ch.29.
7. These positions are detailed by Dales, *The Problem of the Rational Soul*. For Bacon, see T. Crowley, *Roger Bacon: The Problem of the Soul in his Philosophical Commentaries* (Louvain: 1950), 82.
8. Again, this is cited by section number from Teske (trans.), *William of Auvergne: The Soul*.
9. See *Philosophy in the Hellenistic and Roman Worlds*, ch.51.

10. Discussed in *Philosophy in the Islamic World*, ch.19. For the Latin reception of the thought experiment, see also Hasse, *Avicenna's De Anima*, 87–92.

11. For theories of self-awareness in the thirteenth century, see T. Cory, *Aquinas on Human Self-Knowledge* (Cambridge: 2013), ch.1.

12. See also R. J. Teske, "William of Auvergne on the Individuation of Human Souls," *Traditio* 49 (1994), 77–93, reprinted in R. J. Teske, *Studies in the Philosophy of William of Auvergne, Bishop of Paris (1228–1249)* (Milwaukee, WI: 2006).

13. J. Laumakis, "The Voluntarism of William of Auvergne and Some Evidence of the Contrary," *Modern Schoolman* 76 (1999), 303–12.

Chapter 25

1. The passage is cited as a source for the medieval discussion of transcendentals by J. J. E. Gracia, "The Transcendentals in the Middle Ages: An Introduction," *Topoi* 11 (1992), 113–20, at 117.

2. The same observation was made in late antiquity by Plotinus. See *Philosophy in the Hellenistic and Roman Worlds*, ch.30.

3. For a contrast between William and the subsequent discussions on transcendentals, see S. MacDonald, "Goodness as a Transcendental: The Early Thirteenth-Century Recovery of an Aristotelian Idea," *Topoi* 11 (1992), 173–86. For the inspiration in Boethius, see S. MacDonald, "Boethius's Claim that all Substances are Good," *Archiv für Geschichte der Philosophie* 70 (1988), 245–79; and *Philosophy in the Hellenistic and Roman Worlds*, ch.53.

4. For the origins of the doctrine in Plotinus, see *Philosophy in the Hellenistic and Roman Worlds*, ch.32.

5. MacDonald, "Goodness as a Transcendental," 177.

6. J. A. Aertsen, *Medieval Philosophy and the Transcendentals: The Case of Thomas Aquinas* (Leiden: 1996), 34.

7. Aertsen, *Medieval Philosophy and the Transcendentals*, 94.

8. Aertsen, *Medieval Philosophy and the Transcendentals*, 46.

9. Thomas Aquinas, *On Truth* §21.1, cited at Aertsen, *Medieval Philosophy and the Transcendentals*, 100.

10. MacDonald, "Goodness as a Transcendental," 178.

11. Aertsen, *Medieval Philosophy and the Transcendentals*, 80. For Avicenna, see T. Koutzarova, *Das Transzendentale bei Ibn Sina: zur Metaphysik als Wissenschaft erster Begriffs- und Urteilsprinzipien* (Leiden: 2009).

12. J. Aertsen, *Medieval Philosophy as Transcendental Thought: From Philip the Chancellor (ca. 1225) to Francisco Suárez* (Leiden: 2012).

13. Here I draw on J. A. Aertsen, "Beauty in the Middle Ages: A Forgotten Transcendental?" *Medieval Philosophy and Theology* 1 (1991), 68–97, which is the basis for ch.8 of Aertsen, *Medieval Philosophy and the Transcendentals*. On the topic, see also U. Eco, *The Aesthetics of Thomas Aquinas*, trans. H. Bredin (Cambridge, MA: 1988); M. D. Jordan, "The Evidence of the Transcendentals and the Place of Beauty in Thomas Aquinas," *International Philosophical Quarterly* 29 (1989), 393–407; C. S. Sevier, *Aquinas on Beauty* (Lanham, MD: 2015).

14. A good thirteenth-century example is Bonaventure's *Journey of the Mind to God* §2.6.

15. *Confessions* §10.27, cited by M. Carruthers, *The Experience of Beauty in the Middle Ages* (Oxford: 2013), 166; what follows is based on the argument of this book.

16. Isidore, *Etymologies* §10.203, cited by Curruthers, *The Experience of Beauty*, 182.

Chapter 26

1. See M. Frede, *A Free Will: Origins of the Notion in Ancient Thought* (Berkeley, CA: 2011).
2. They circulated as two texts, the *Ethica Vetus* (books 2–3) and *Ethica Nova* (book 1). For details, see G. Wieland, *Ethica-scientia practica: die Anfänge der philosophischen Ethik im 13. Jahrhundert* (Münster: 1981).
3. V. A. Buffon, "The Structure of the Soul, Intellectual Virtues and the Ethical Ideal of Masters of Arts in Early Commentaries on the *Nicomachean Ethics*," in I. P. Bejczy (ed.), *Virtue Ethics in the Middle Ages: Commentaries on Aristotle's Nicomachean Ethics, 1200–1500* (Leiden: 2008), 13–30, with the key passage from Avicenna at 23.
4. For the following, see I. Zavattero, "Moral and Intellectual Virtues in the Earliest Latin Commentaries on the *Nicomachean Ethics*," in Bejczy, *Virtue Ethics*, 31–54; A. J. Celano, "The Relation of Prudence and *Synderesis* to Happiness in Medieval Commentaries on Aristotle's Ethics," in J. Miller (ed.), *The Reception of Aristotle's Ethics* (Cambridge: 2012), 125–54.
5. Buffon, "The Structure of the Soul," 16.
6. M. J. Tracey, "*Virtus* in the Naples Commentary on the *Ethica Nova*," in Bejczy, *Virtue Ethics*, 55–74, at 60; Celano, "The Relation of Prudence and *Synderesis*," 133–5. See also A. J. Celano, "The Understanding of the Concept of *felicitas* in the Pre-1250 Commentaries on the *Ethica Nicomachea*," *Medioevo* 12 (1986), 29–53.
7. Discussion and texts in T. C. Potts, *Conscience in Medieval Philosophy* (Cambridge: 1980). Citations in the main text are to page numbers of Potts' translations.
8. For the etymology, see Potts, *Conscience in Medieval Philosophy*, 10.
9. He's also been credited with anticipating the development of ethical voluntarism. See C. McCluskey, "The Roots of Voluntarism," *Vivarium* 39 (2001), 185–208.
10. I take the phrase from Celano, "The Relation of Prudence and *Synderesis*," 136.
11. D. Langston, "The Spark of Conscience: Bonaventure's View of Conscience and *Synderesis*," *Franciscan Studies* 53 (1993), 79–95. I take the phrase "applied conscience" from him (81).
12. Celano, "The Relation of Prudence and *Synderesis*," 147.

Chapter 27

1. *Philosophy in the Islamic World*, ch.44.
2. *Philosophy in the Hellenistic and Roman Worlds*, ch.48.
3. For an overview of his life, see J. McEvoy, *Robert Grosseteste* (New York: 2000).
4. For a recent argument to this effect, see N. M. Schulman, "Husband, Father, Bishop? Grosseteste in Paris," *Speculum* 72 (1997), 330–46, responding to R. Southern, *Robert Grosseteste: The Growth of an English Mind in Medieval Europe* (Oxford: 1986).
5. This is the contention of McEvoy, *Robert Grosseteste*, 114.
6. On which, see J. Hackett, "Robert Grosseteste and Roger Bacon on the *Posterior Analytics*," in M. Lutz-Bachmann et al. (eds), *Knowledge and Science: Problems of Epistemology in Medieval Philosophy* (Berlin: 2004), 161–212; D. Bloch, "Robert Grosseteste's *Conclusiones* and the Commentary on the *Posterior Analytics*," *Vivarium* 47 (2009), 1–23.
7. J. McEvoy, *The Philosophy of Robert Grosseteste* (Oxford: 1982), 327–8. See further C. Van Dyke, "The Truth, the Whole Truth, and Nothing but the Truth: Robert Grosseteste on Universals (and the *Posterior Analytics*)," *Journal of the History of Philosophy* 48 (2010), 153–70.
8. As pointed out by S. Oliver, "Robert Grosseteste on Light, Truth, and Experimentation," *Vivarium* 42 (2004), 151–80; see 179 for the following quotation.

9. As he observes in a work called *On Truth*: see McEvoy, *The Philosophy of Robert Grosseteste*, 323.

10. S. P. Marrone, *The Light of thy Countenance: Science and Knowledge of God in the Thirteenth Century. Vol. 1: A Doctrine of Divine Illumination* (Leiden: 2001), 39, 58. Marrone points out that the same applies to William of Auvergne, another early proponent of divine illumination.

11. I cite it by line number from the new Latin edition by C. Panti in J. Flood et al. (eds), *Robert Grosseteste and his Intellectual Milieu: New Editions and Studies* (Toronto: 2013). This volume also offers an English translation by N. Lewis, which supersedes earlier versions such as C. C. Riedl, *Robert Grosseteste: On Light* (Milwaukee, WI: 1942).

12. *Philosophy in the Islamic World*, ch.11.

13. McEvoy, *The Philosophy of Robert Grosseteste*, 160.

14. McEvoy, *The Philosophy of Robert Grosseteste*, 178.

15. Oliver, "Robert Grosseteste on Light, Truth, and Experimentation," 160.

16. McEvoy, *The Philosophy of Robert Grosseteste*, 204; McEvoy, *Robert Grosseteste* 94–5.

17. B. S. Eastwood, "Robert Grosseteste's Theory of the Rainbow: A Chapter in the History of Non-Experimental Science," *Archives Internationales de l'Histoire des Sciences* 19 (1966), 313–32.

18. D. C. Lindberg, "Roger Bacon's Theory of the Rainbow: Progress or Regress?" *Isis* 57 (1966), 235–48.

19. B. S. Eastwood, "Medieval Empiricism: The Case of Robert Grosseteste's Optics," *Speculum* 43 (1968), 306–21.

20. McEvoy, *The Philosophy of Robert Grosseteste*, 18. For a recent critique of Crombie, see E. Serene, "Robert Grosseteste on Induction and Demonstrative Science," *Synthese* 40 (1979), 97–115.

Chapter 28

1. J. Hackett, "*Scientia Experimentalis*: From Robert Grosseteste to Roger Bacon," in J. McEvoy (ed.), *Robert Grosseteste: New Perspectives on his Thought and Scholarship* (Dordrecht: 1995), 89–120.

2. R. Lemay, "Roger Bacon's Attitude towards the Latin Translations and Translators of the Twelfth and Thirteenth Centuries," in J. Hackett (ed.), *Roger Bacon and the Sciences* (Leiden: 1997), 25–47.

3. Lemay, "Roger Bacon's Attitude," 27.

4. J. Hackett, "Roger Bacon on Astronomy-Astrology: The Sources of the *Scientia Experimentalis*," in Hackett (ed.), *Roger Bacon and the Sciences*, 175–98, at 177.

5. For the full story, see T. Crowley, *Roger Bacon: The Problem of the Soul in his Philosophical Commentaries* (Louvain: 1950), ch.1, J. Hackett, "Roger Bacon: His Life, Career and works," in Hackett (ed.), *Roger Bacon and the Sciences*, 9–23; A. Power, *Roger Bacon and the Defense of Christendom* (Cambridge: 2012).

6. G. Molland, "Roger Bacon and the Hermetic Tradition in Medieval Science," *Vivarium* 31 (1993), 140–60, at 148.

7. As mentioned in *Philosophy in the Islamic World*, ch.28.

8. Crowley, *Roger Bacon: The Problem of the Soul*, ch.4.

9. J. Hackett, "Roger Bacon on *Scientia Experimentalis*," in Hackett (ed.), *Roger Bacon and the Sciences*, 277–315, at 291.

10. *Philosophy in the Hellenistic and Roman Worlds*, ch.48.

11. References in what follows are to section numbers of T. S. Maloney (trans.), *Roger Bacon: On Signs* (Toronto: 2013). For further discussion, see T. S. Maloney, "The Semiotics of Roger Bacon," *Mediaeval Studies* 45 (1983), 120–54; T. S. Maloney, "Roger Bacon on Equivocation," *Vivarium* 22 (1984), 84–112; I. Rosier-Catach, "Roger Bacon and Grammar," in Hackett (ed.), *Roger Bacon and the Sciences*, 67–102.

12. Citations in what follows are to section and Latin line number of *On the Multiplication of Species*, in D. C. Lindberg, *Roger Bacon's Philosophy of Nature* (Oxford: 1983).

13. *Philosophy in the Islamic World*, ch.11; and on Bacon, see D. C. Lindberg, "Roger Bacon on Light, Vision and the Universal Emanation of Force," in Hackett (ed.), *Roger Bacon and the Sciences*, 243–75.

14. D. C. Lindberg, *Theories of Vision from al-Kindi to Kepler* (Chicago: 1976).

15. Partial translation available in P. Adamson and P. E. Pormann (trans.), *The Philosophical Works of al-Kindī* (Karachi: 2012).

16. W. R. Newman, "An Overview of Roger Bacon's Alchemy," in Hackett (ed.), *Roger Bacon and the Sciences*, 317–36, at 327.

17. J. Kupfer, "The Father of Empiricism: Roger not Francis," *Vivarium* 12 (1974), 52–62.

Chapter 29

1. *Classical Philosophy*, ch.22.

2. C. M. Cullen, *Bonaventure* (Oxford: 2006), 22.

3. S. P. Marrone, *The Light of thy Countenance: Science and Knowledge of God in the Thirteenth Century. Vol. 1: A Doctrine of Divine Illumination* (Leiden: 2001), 114–15.

4. Trans. by E. T. Healy in vol.1 of P. Boehner and M. F. Laughlin (eds), *Works of Saint Bonaventure*, 15 vols (Saint Bonaventure, NY: 1955–2010). Cited by section number.

5. For Philo of Alexandria as an ultimate source, see A. Heinrichs, "Philosophy, the Handmaiden of Theology," *Greek, Roman and Byzantine Studies* 9 (1968), 437–50.

6. For more on the question of whether Bonaventure should be considered a "philosopher," see A. Speer, "Bonaventure and the Question of a Medieval Philosophy," *Medieval Philosophy and Theology* 6 (1997), 25–46.

7. Trans. by Z. Hayes in vol.4 of the *Works of Saint Bonaventure*. Cited by page number. See further A. Speer, "Illumination and Certitude: The Foundation of Knowledge in Bonaventure," *American Catholic Philosophical Quarterly* 85 (2011), 127–41; and Marrone, *The Light of thy Countenance*, part two.

8. Marrone, *The Light of thy Countenance*, 163.

9. Trans. by P. Boehner in vol.2 of the *Works of Saint Bonaventure*. Cited by section number.

Chapter 30

1. *Enneads* §1.4.10.

2. For a detailed overview of his life and controversies, see D. Burr, "The Persecution of Peter Olivi," *Transactions of the American Philosophical Society* 66 (1976), 1–98.

3. R. Pasnau, *Theories of Cognition in the Later Middle Ages* (Cambridge: 1997), 130; cf. Burr, "Persecution," 56; J. Toivanen, *Perception and the Internal Senses: Peter of John Olivi on the Cognitive Functions of the Sensitive Soul* (Leiden: 2013), 135. For Olivi's attitude in general, see also D. Burr, "Petrus Ioannes Olivi and the Philosophers," *Franciscan Studies* 31 (1971), 41–71.

4. R. Pasnau, "Olivi on the Metaphysics of Soul," *Medieval Philosophy and Theology* 6 (1997), 109–32, at 114 and 119. On the topic, see also Toivanen, *Perception*, part one.

5. Toivanen, *Perception*, 47, who points out that the image is not necessarily put forward as Olivi's own view but probably captures his attitude well enough.

6. Pasnau, "Olivi on the Metaphysics of Soul," 124–5.

7. This point is made by R. Pasnau, "Olivi on Human Freedom," in A. Boureau and S. Piron (eds), *Pierre de Jean Olivi (1248–1298): pensée scolastique, dissidence spirituelle et société* (Paris: 1999), 15–25, who emphasizes the difficulty of seeing exactly what is at issue in the clash between Olivi and Aquinas.

8. For what follows, see Toivanen, *Perception*, part two; and for the broader issues raised, see D. Perler (ed.), *Ancient and Medieval Theories of Intentionality* (Leiden: 2001) and H. Lagerlund (ed.), *Representation and Objects of Thought in Medieval Philosophy* (Aldershot: 2007).

9. J. F. Silva and J. Toivanen, "The Active Nature of the Soul in Sense Perception: Robert Kilwardby and Peter Olivi," *Vivarium* 48 (1010), 245–78, with this terminology noted at 256.

10. Silva and Toivanen, "The Active Nature," 269; Toivanen, *Perception*, 156–7.

11. Pasnau, *Theories of Cognition*, 171.

12. My thanks to Juhana Toivanen for helpful advice on this chapter.

Chapter 31

1. G. E. M. Gasper and S. H. Gullbekk, *Money and the Church in Medieval Europe, 1000–1200: Practice, Morality and Thought* (Farnham: 2015), 124–5.

2. An early text on Francis, the *Sacrum Commercium*, even has him and his brethren enjoying a visionary experience where they are visited by Lady Poverty herself.

3. V. Mäkinen, *Property Rights in the Late Medieval Discussion on Franciscan Poverty* (Leuven: 2001), 25.

4. One contemporary author who lamented the viciousness of the dispute was Roger Bacon, who complained that the two sides called one another "heretics and disciples of the Antichrist": *Compendium studii philosophiae*, ed. J. S. Brewer (London: 1859), 429.

5. For an overview of their case, see Mäkinen, *Property Rights*, 34–53. William's downfall gives us a hint of another long-running tension, in this case within the established church. In general, bishops resisted the centralization of power in the papacy, and in particular, disputes over the university often pitted the bishop of Paris against the Pope, with the bishop tending to side with the secular masters and the Pope with the mendicants.

6. D. Burr, *Olivi and Franciscan Poverty: The Origins of the Usus Pauper Controversy* (Philadelphia, PA: 1989), 9.

7. J. De Vinck and R. J. Karris (trans.), *Works of Saint Bonaventure. Vol. 15: Defense of the Mendicants* (Saint Bonaventure, NY: 2010); K. L. Hughes, "Bonaventure's Defense of Mendicancy," in J. M. Hammond, J. A. Wayne Hellmann, and J. Goff (eds), *A Companion to Bonaventure* (Leiden: 2014), 509–42.

8. J. V. Fleming, *An Introduction to the Franciscan Literature of the Middle Ages* (Chicago: 1977), 87.

9. See the discussion of Jerome's library in *Philosophy of the Hellenistic and Roman Worlds*, ch.46.

10. Mäkinen, *Property Rights*, 69–70, and 73, for the case of books.

11. Mäkinen, *Property Rights*, part III.

12. D. Flood, "Poverty as Virtue, Poverty as Warning, and Peter of John Olivi," in A. Boureau and S. Piron (eds), *Pierre de Jean Olivi (1248–1298): Pensée scolastique, dissidence spirituelle et société* (Paris: 1999), 157–72. His apocalyptic tendencies are also visible in his biblical commentaries,

as shown by K. Madigan, *Olivi and the Interpretation of Matthew in the High Middle Ages* (Notre Dame, IN: 2003).

13. D. Burr, "The Persecution of Peter Olivi," *Transactions of the American Philosophical Society* 66 (1976), 1–98, at 12.

14. Burr, *Olivi and Franciscan Poverty*, ix.

15. E. Petroff, "A Medieval Woman's Utopian Vision: The Rule of St. Clare of Assisi," in *Body and Soul: Essays on Medieval Women and Mysticism* (New York: 1994), 66–79. See further I. Brady (trans.), *Legend and Writings of Saint Clare of Assisi* (Saint Bonaventure, NY: 1953).

Chapter 32

1. See further R. Imbach, *Laien in der Philosophie des Mittelalters* (Amsterdam: 1989).

2. B. McGinn, "The Changing Shape of Late Medieval Mysticism," *Church History* 65 (1996), 197–219, at 198; B. McGinn, *The Varieties of Vernacular Mysticism 1350–1550* (New York: 2012).

3. For useful surveys, see P. Dronke, *Women Writers of the Middle Ages* (Cambridge: 1984); and A. Minnis and R. Voaden (eds), *Medieval Holy Women in the Christian Tradition c.1100–c.1500* (Turnhout: 2010).

4. Dronke, *Women Writers of the Middle Ages*, 75.

5. The etymology of "Beguine" is a matter of debate, but in the Caribbean it came to mean a girl or girlfriend, and then the name of a dance. Hence the title of the Cole Porter song "Begin the Beguine," which I have borrowed for this chapter. It's also worth noting that there was a parallel movement for men, called the "Beghards."

6. I take the phrase "grey zone" from U. Wiethaus, "Sexuality, Gender and the Body in Late Medieval Women's Spirituality: Cases from Germany and the Netherlands," *Journal of Feminist Studies in Religion* 7 (1991), 35–52.

7. Collected in C. Hart (trans.), *Hadewijch: The Complete Works* (New York: 1980), from which I cite in what follows.

8. I have used the edition and modern German translation in G. Vollmann-Profe (trans.), *Mechthild von Magdeburg: das fließende Licht der Gottheit* (Berlin: 2010), quoted in my translations and cited by book and section number. For an English version, see F. Tobin (trans.), *Mechthild of Magdeburg: The Flowing Light of the Godhead* (New York: 1998).

9. Here I follow the lead of I. Mandrella, "Meisterinnen ohne Schüler: Philosophierende Frauen im Mittelalter," in A. Speer and J. Baumbach (eds), *Schüler und Meister* (Berlin: 2016), 135–56. My thanks to Professor Mandrella for discussion of the topic.

10. For a good discussion of *minne* in Hadewijch, see B. McGinn, *The Flowering of Mysticism: Men and Women in the New Mysticism, 1200–1350* (New York: 1998), 201–22. See also B. Newman, *God and Goddesses: Vision, Poetry, and Belief in the Middle Ages* (Philadelphia, PA: 2003), ch.4.

11. McGinn, *The Flowering of Mysticism*, 214–15, citing Vision 4.

12. A. Hollywood, *The Soul as Virgin Wife: Mechthild of Magdeburg, Marguerite Porete and Meister Eckhart* (Notre Dame, IN: 1995), 62. Hollywood suggests (73–7) that Mechthild's ideas on the body may have evolved, with an early emphasis on the hindrances of body giving way to an appreciation of bodily suffering as an echo of Christ's suffering.

13. This idea that the Beguines offered a counterweight to the Cathars is made by D. Elliott, "Flesh and Spirit: The Female Body," in *Medieval Holy Women*, 13–46, at 25.

14. Elliott, "Flesh and Spirit," 23.

Chapter 33

1. *Philosophy in the Islamic World*, ch.32; and ch.35 for the "Maimonides controversy" that led to the burning of his books.
2. *On Imagination* §98, in A. Broadie (trans.), *Robert Kilwardby: On Time and Imagination* (Oxford: 1993).
3. For his work in logic, see H. Lagerlund, *Modal Syllogistics in the Middle Ages* (Leiden: 2000), ch.3; P. Thom, *Logic and Ontology in the Syllogistic of Robert Kilwardby* (Leiden: 2007). For what follows, see C. H. Kneepkens, "Robert Kilwardby on Grammar," and P. Thom, "Robert Kilwardby on Syllogistic Form," both in H. Lagerlund and P. Thom (eds), *A Companion to the Philosophy of Robert Kilwardby* (Leiden: 2013), 17–64 and 131–61.
4. For more on this issue, see Chapter 44 below.
5. This way of speaking can be traced back to antiquity. See T.-S. Lee, *Griechische Tradition der aristotelischen Syllogistik in der Spätantike* (Göttingen: 1984), ch.2, and for the issue in general, see C. Dutilh Novaes, "The Different Ways in which Logic Is (Said to Be) Formal," *History and Philosophy of Logic* 32 (2011), 303–32, and "Form and Matter in Later Latin Medieval Logic: The Cases of *Suppositio* and *Consequentia*," *Journal of the History of Philosophy* 50 (2012), 339–64.
6. Actually Kilwardby would say that the placeholder variables here (A, B, and C) are themselves a kind of matter; see Thom, "Robert Kilwardby on Syllogistic Form," 140.
7. Trans. in Broadie, *Robert Kilwardby: On Time and Imagination*, cited by section number below. See further C. Trifogli, "Robert Kilwardby on Time," in Lagerlund and Thom, *A Companion to the Philosophy of Robert Kilwardby*, 209–38.
8. See *Philosophy in the Hellenistic and Roman Worlds*, ch.47.
9. J. F. Silva, *Robert Kilwardby on the Human Soul: Plurality of Forms and Censorship in the Thirteenth Century* (Leiden: 2012).
10. S. Donati, "Robert Kilwardby on Matter," in Lagerlund and Thom, *A Companion to the Philosophy of Robert Kilwardby*, 239–73, at 248.
11. Silva, *Robert Kilwardby on the Human Soul*, 56.
12. Donati, "Robert Kilwardby on Matter," 246.
13. Silva, *Robert Kilwardby on the Human Soul*, 105–15.
14. Silva, *Robert Kilwardby on the Human Soul*, 94.
15. This idea is also used by Bonaventure, as noted in Chapter 70.
16. Citations in the following are section numbers in *On Imagination*, in Broadie, *Robert Kilwardby: On Time and Imagination*. For a comparison of his view to that of Olivi, see J. F. Silva and J. Toivanen, "The Active Nature of the Soul in Sense Perception: Robert Kilwardby and Peter Olivi," *Vivarium* 48 (1010), 245–78.
17. For this aspect of the prohibition, see S. L. Uckelman, "Logic and the Condemnations of 1277," *Journal of Philosophical Logic* 39 (2010), 201–27.
18. Here I follow Silva, *Robert Kilwardby on the Human Soul*, 261.

Chapter 34

1. J. M. G. Hackett, "The Attitude of Roger Bacon to the *Scientia* of Albertus Magnus," in J. Weisheipl (ed.), *Albertus Magnus and the Sciences: Commemorative Essays 1980* (Toronto: 1980), 53–72.
2. For his life, see J. Weisheipl, "Albert the Great and Medieval Culture," *Thomist* 44 (1980), 481–501.

3. For this topic, see K. Reeds (note the appropriate name), "Albert on the Natural Philosophy of Plant Life," and J. Stannard, "Albertus Magnus and Medieval Herbalism," both in J. Weisheipl (ed.), *Albertus Magnus and the Sciences: Commemorative Essays 1980* (Toronto: 1980), 341–54 and 355–77; M. de Asúa, "Minerals, Plants and Animals from A to Z. The Inventory of the Natural World in Albert the Great's *philosophia naturalis*," in O. P. Senner et al. (eds), *Albertus Magnus: zum Gedenken nach 800 Jahren. Neue Zugänge, Aspekte und Perspektiven* (Berlin: 2001), 389–400; G. Wöllmer, "Albert the Great and his Botany," in I. M Resnick (ed.), *A Companion to Albert the Great* (Leiden: 2013), 221–67.

4. Wöllmer, "Albert the Great and his Botany," 231–4.

5. B. Barker Price, "The Physical Astronomy and Astrology of Albert the Great," in *Albertus Magnus and the Sciences*, 155–85, at 181.

6. P. Kibre, "Albertus Magnus on Alchemy," in *Albertus Magnus and the Sciences*, 187–202.

7. For this, see I. M. Resnick, *Albert the Great: On the Causes of the Properties of the Elements* (Milwaukee, WI: 2010), book 1, treatise 2.

8. The treatise has been translated into English: D. Wyckoff, *Albertus Magnus: Book of Minerals* (Oxford: 1967). See also J. M. Riddle and J. A. Mulholland, "Albert on Stones and Minerals," in *Albertus Magnus and the Sciences*, 203–34.

9. L. Demaitre and A. A. Travill, "Human Embryology and Development in the Works of Albertus Magnus," in *Albertus Magnus and the Sciences*, 405–40, at 411. See further H. Anzulewicz, "Albertus Magnus und die Tiere," in S. Obermaier (ed.), *Tiere und Fabelwesen im Mittelalter* (Berlin: 2009), 29–54.

10. See R. Kruk, "Ibn Sīnā on Animals: Between the First Teacher and the Physician," in J. Janssens and D. De Smet (eds), *Avicenna and his Heritage* (Leuven: 2002), 325–41.

11. Cited by Latin page number from H. Anzulewicz and J. R. Söder (trans.), *Albert the Great: Über den Menschen (De homine)* (Hamburg: 2004). On the topic, see L. Ducharme, "The Individual Human Being in Saint Albert's Earlier Writings," in F. Kovach and R. Shahan (eds), *Albert the Great: Commemorative Essays* (Norman, OK: 1980), 131–60; S. Baldner, "St. Albert the Great on the Union of the Human Soul and Body," *American Catholic Philosophical Quarterly* 70 (1996), 103–20; S. Lipke, "Die Bedeutung der Seele für die Einheit des Menschen nach *De homine*," in *Albertus Magnus: zum Gedenken nach 800 Jahren*, 207–19; H. Anzulewicz, "Anthropology: The Concept of Man in Albert the Great," in *A Companion to Albert the Great*, 325–46.

12. J. A. Weisheipl, "Albertus Magnus and Universal Hylomorphism: Avicebron," in *Albert the Great: Commemorative Essays*, 239–60.

13. K. Krause, "Albert the Great on Animal and Human Origin in his Early Works," *Lo Sguardo: Rivista di Filosofia* 18 (2015), 205–32.

Chapter 35

1. *Philosophy in the Islamic World*, ch.21.

2. A. Bertolacci, "The Reception of Avicenna's *Philosophia Prima* in Albert the Great's *Commentary on the Metaphysics*: The Case of the Doctrine of Unity," in O. P. Senner et al. (eds), *Albertus Magnus: zum Gedenken nach 800 Jahren. Neue Zugänge, Aspekte und Perspektiven* (Berlin: 2001), 67–78; A. Bertolacci, "The Reception of Avicenna in Latin Medieval Culture," in P. Adamson (ed.), *Interpreting Avicenna: Critical Essays* (Cambridge: 2013), 242–69.

3. T. Bonin, *Creation as Emanation: The Origin of Diversity in Albert the Great's On the Causes and the Procession of the Universe* (Notre Dame, IN: 2001), 5–7.

4. On this and other changes to Proclus in the translation, and on the reception of the *Book of Causes* in Latin, see C. D'Ancona Costa, *Recherches sur le Liber de Causis* (Paris: 1995). An English translation of the Latin version can be found in V. A. Guagliardo et al. (trans.), *St. Thomas Aquinas: Commentary on the Book of Causes* (Washington DC: 1996). For the point that being is the first effect, see Proposition 4.

5. For all this, see *Philosophy in the Islamic World*, ch.17.

6. For what follows, see Bonin, *Creation as Emanation*, as well as L. Sweeney, "*Esse primum creatum* in Albert the Great's *Liber de Causis et Processu Universitatis*," *The Thomist* 44 (1980), 599–646; L. Sweeney, "The Meaning of *Esse* in Albert the Great's Texts on Creation in the *Summa de Creaturis* and *Scripta super Sententias*," in F. Kovach and R. Shahan (eds), *Albert the Great: Commemorative Essays* (Norman, OK, 1980), 65–95; and R. E. Vargas, "Albert on Being and Beings: The Doctrine of *Esse*," in I. M Resnick (ed.), *A Companion to Albert the Great* (Leiden: 2013), 627–48.

7. Bonin, *Creation as Emanation*, 87.

8. J. A. Aertsen, "Die Frage nach dem Ersten und Grundlegenen: Albert der Große und die Lehre von den Tranzendentalien," in *Albertus Magnus: zum Gedenken nach 800 Jahren*, 91–112; J. A. Aertsen, "Albert's Doctrine on the Transcendentals," in *A Companion to Albert the Great*, 611–19.

9. Cited by J. Marenbon, *Pagans and Philosophers: The Problem of Paganism from Augustine to Leibniz* (Princeton, NJ: 2015), 133, quoting from Albert's *On Generation and Corruption*.

10. T. B. Noone, "Albert the Great on the Subject of Metaphysics and Demonstrating the Existence of God," *Medieval Philosophy and Theology* 2 (1992), 31–52; M. D. Jordan, "Albert the Great and the Hierarchy of Sciences," *Faith and Philosophy* 9 (1992), 483–99; H. Anzulewicz, "Metaphysics and its Relation to Theology in Albert's Thought," in *A Companion to Albert the Great*, 553–61.

11. J. Hergan, *St. Albert the Great's Theory of the Beatific Vision* (New York: 2002), which quotes the relevant texts; K. Krause, "Albert and Aquinas on the Ultimate End of Humans: Philosophy, Theology, and Beatitude," *Proceedings of the American Catholic Philosophical Association* 86 (2012), 213–29. My thanks to Katja Krause for her advice on this topic and the chapter generally.

12. M. Führer, "Albertus Magnus' Theory of Divine Illumination," in *Albertus Magnus: zum Gedenken nach 800 Jahren*, 141–55.

Chapter 36

1. On his life, see K. Foster (ed.), *The Life of Thomas Aquinas: Biographical Documents* (London: 1959); J. A. Weisheipl, *Friar Thomas d'Aquino: His Life, Thought and Works* (Washington DC: 1974); and J.-P. Torrell, *Saint Thomas Aquinas: The Person and his Work* (Washington DC: 1996).

2. Translated in A. C. Pegis et al., trans., *Thomas Aquinas: Summa contra Gentiles* (Notre Dame, IN: 1975). Discussion in M. D. Jordan, "The Protreptic Structure of the *Summa contra Gentiles*," *The Thomist* 50 (1986), 173–209; and R. A. de Velde, "Natural Reason in the *Summa contra Gentiles*," in *Thomas Aquinas: Contemporary Philosophical Perspectives*, 117–40.

3. For this approach, see N. Kretzmann, *The Metaphysics of Theism: Aquinas's Natural Theology in Summa contra Gentiles I* (Oxford: 1997).

4. First proposed by M.-D. Chenu; for a critical response, see R. de Velde, *Aquinas on God: The "Divine Science" of the Summa Theologiae* (Aldershot, 2006), ch.1. See also B. Johnsone, "The Debate on the Structure of the *Summa Theologiae* of St. Thomas Aquinas from Chenu

(1939) to Metz (1998)," in P. van Geest et al. (eds), *Aquinas as Authority* (Leuven: 2002), 187–200.

5. A. Maurer (trans.), *St Thomas Aquinas: Faith, Reason and Theology. Questions I–IV of his Commentary on the De Trinitate of Boethius* (Toronto: 1987). On this work, see D. C. Hall, *The Trinity: An Analysis of St. Thomas Aquinas' Expositio of the De Trinitate of Boethius* (Leiden: 1992).

6. De Velde, *Aquinas on God*, 39. It should be noted that elsewhere, as in *Summa contra gentiles*, Aquinas offers much more detailed versions of the proofs; for instance, his discussion of the proof of motion there shows how to rule out an infinite series of movers, unlike the version here in the *Summa theologiae*.

7. On the five ways, see, e.g., A. Kenny, *The Five Ways* (London: 1969); J. Owens, *St Thomas Aquinas on the Existence of God* (Albany, NY: 1980); F. van Steenberghen, *Le Problème de l'existence de Dieu dans les écrits de S. Thomas d'Aquin* (Louvain-la-Neuve: 1980); F. Kerr, "Ways of Reading the Five Ways," in F. Kerr, *After Aquinas: Versions of Thomism* (Malden, MA: 2002), 52–72.

8. Notice by the way that Aquinas thinks that God's being necessary doesn't imply that His existence is self-evident, at least not self-evident for us.

9. The phrase was used by A. J. Lovejoy, *The Great Chain of Being: A Study of the History of an Idea* (Cambridge, MA: 1936). For discussion of its relevance in medieval thought, see S. Knuuttila, *Modalities in Medieval Philosophy* (London: 1993).

10. As does J. F. Wippel, "The Five Ways," in *Thomas Aquinas: Contemporary Philosophical Perspectives*, 159–225.

11. B. Davies, *The Thought of Thomas Aquinas* (Oxford: 1992), 26.

Chapter 37

1. As emphasized in B. Davies (ed.), *Thomas Aquinas: Contemporary Philosophical Perspectives* (Oxford: 2002). On the history of Aquinas' reception, see B. McGinn, *Thomas Aquinas's Summa Theologiae: A Biography* (Princeton, NJ: 2014), chs.4–5.

2. Aquinas discusses these matters in various texts; two of the most useful are his *Disputed Questions on the Soul* (cited in this chapter as *DQS*) and the so-called *Treatise on Human Nature*, which refers to questions 75–89 of the first part of the *Summa theologiae*. On the latter, see R. Pasnau, *Thomas Aquinas on Human Nature: A Philosophical Study of Summa Theologiae 1a 75–89* (Cambridge: 2002).

3. For more on debates in psychology, see D. A. Callus, "The Problem of the Unity of Substantial Form and Richard Knapwell, O.P.," in *Mélanges offerts a Étienne Gilson* (Toronto: 1959), 123–60; B. C. Bazán, "Pluralisme de formes ou dualisme de substances?" *Revue Philosophique de Louvain* 67 (1969), 30–73; R. Pasnau, *Metaphysical Themes 1274–1671* (Oxford: 2011), ch.25; S. W. de Boer, *The Science of the Soul: The Commentary on Aristotle's De Anima c.1260–c.1360* (Leuven: 2013). For Aquinas' supporters more generally, see F. J. Roensch, *Early Thomistic School* (Dubuque, IA: 1964).

4. For a lengthy and detailed discussion, see F. Amerini, *Aquinas on the Beginning and End of Human Life*, trans. M. Henninger (Cambridge, MA: 2013). Pasnau, *Thomas Aquinas on Human Nature*, ch.4, sees sharp disagreement between Aquinas and the contemporary Catholic teaching.

5. For some interpreters, Aquinas actually accepts that the soul is destroyed and returns only at the time of the resurrection. See P. Toner, "Personhood and Death in St. Thomas Aquinas," *History of Philosophy Quarterly* 26 (2009), 121–38; and "St. Thomas Aquinas on

Death and the Separated Soul," *Pacific Philosophical Quarterly* 91 (2010), 587–99; T. C. Nevitt, "Survivalism, Corruptionism, and Intermittent Existence in Aquinas," *History of Philosophy Quarterly* 31 (2014), 1–19. Against this "corruptionist" account, "survivalists" assume, as I have here, that Aquinas does think the soul would continue to exist in the meantime without its body. See, for instance, E. Stump, "Resurrection and the Separated Soul," in B. Davies and E. Stump (eds), *The Oxford Handbook of Aquinas* (New York: 2012), 458–66.

6. This is not to say that it is *guaranteed* to survive. As pointed out by B. Davies, *The Thought of Thomas Aquinas* (Oxford: 1992), 216, it is up to God whether to preserve the soul after death. All we can show using philosophical argument is that this is not impossible.

7. On the evolution of Aquinas' thought on this matter, see G. Pini, "The Development of Aquinas's Thought," in B. Davies and E. Stump (eds), *The Oxford Handbook of Aquinas* (Oxford: 2011), 491–510.

8. On whom, see E. Gilson, "Roger Marston: Un cas d'augustinisme avicennisant," *Archives d'Histoire Doctrinale et Littéraire du Moyen Âge* 8 (1933), 37–42.

9. A point made by Pasnau, *Thomas Aquinas on Human Nature*, 308.

Chapter 38

1. See further J. Marenbon, *Pagans and Philosophers: The Problem of Paganism from Augustine to Leibniz* (Princeton, NJ: 2015), with the cases of Holcot and Dante mentioned at 183 and 189 respectively.

2. Marenbon, *Pagans and Philosophers* 101, and 34 for Augustine on Cato.

3. S. B. Cunningham, *Reclaiming Moral Agency: The Moral Philosophy of Albert the Great* (Washington DC: 2008), 65.

4. See *Classical Philosophy*, ch.37.

5. For what follows, see Cunningham, *Reclaiming Moral Agency*; S. B. Cunningham, "Albertus Magnus and the Problem of Moral Virtue," in *Vivarium* 7 (1969), 81–119; J. Müller, *Natürliche Moral und philosophische Ethik bei Albertus Magnus* (Münster: 2001); M. J. Tracy, "The Moral Thought of Albert the Great," in I. M Resnick (ed.), *A Companion to Albert the Great* (Leiden: 2013), 347–80.

6. There are several pieces on medieval ethics and confession in P. Biller and A. J. Minnis (eds), *Handling Sin: Confession in the Middle Ages* (New York: 1998).

7. For a translation of the relevant section of the *Summa*, see T. Williams (trans), *Thomas Aquinas: The Treatise on Happiness. The Treatise on Human Acts* (Indianapolis, IN: 2016). A useful comparison of Albert and Aquinas on happiness is J. Müller, "*Duplex Beatitudo*: Aristotle's Legacy and Aquinas's Conception of Human Happiness," in T. Hoffmann, J. Müller, and M. Perkams (eds), *Aquinas and the Nicomachean Ethics* (Cambridge: 2013), 52–71. Recent studies of the topic in Aquinas include two articles by J. Stenberg, "Aquinas on the Relationship between the Vision and Delight in Perfect Happiness," *American Catholic Philosophical Quarterly* 90 (2016), 665–80; and "*Considerandum quid sit beatitudo*: Aquinas on What Happiness Really Is," *Res Philosophica* 93 (2016), 161–84.

8. A. J. Celano, "Robert Kilwardy on the Relation of Virtue to Happiness," *Medieval Philosophy and Theology* 2 (1999), 149–62.

9. R. Konyndyk DeYoung, C. McCluskey, and C. Van Dyke, *Aquinas's Ethics: Metaphysical Foundations, Moral Theory, and Theological Context* (Notre Dame, IN: 2009), 147–8.

10. In what follows I quote from E. M. Atkins and T. Williams (eds and trans.), *Aquinas: Disputed Questions on the Virtues* (Cambridge: 2005). Hereafter cited as *DQV*.

11. Actually the quote is spurious, but Aquinas thinks it is genuine and it does express Augustine's true view fairly well; authentic Augustinian passages are cited in other objections to the same article.

12. On this, see DeYoung et al., *Aquinas's Ethics*, 142.

13. For Aquinas, see *ST* 1.2 Q3 a5 resp (Osterle trans.): "imperfect happiness, such as can be had in this life, consists principally in contemplation, but secondarily in the operation of the practical intellect directing human actions and passions."

14. See R. Konyndyk DeYoung, "Power Made Perfect in Weakness: Aquinas's Transformation of the Virtue of Courage," *Medieval Philosophy and Theology* 11 (2003), 147–80; J. A. Herdt, "Aquinas's Aristotelian Defense of Martyr Courage," in Hoffmann et al. (eds), *Aquinas and the Nicomachean Ethics*, 110–28.

Chapter 39

1. Mentioned by J. Lepore, "The Rule of History," *New Yorker*, April 20, 2015.

2. J. H. Burns, *The Cambridge History of Medieval Political Thought c. 350–c.1450* (Cambridge: 1988), 431.

3. Burns, *Cambridge History*, 427–8.

4. Burns, *Cambridge History*, 429.

5. See P. Adamson, "State of Nature: Human and Cosmic Rulership in Ancient Philosophy," in B. Kellner and A. Höfele (eds), *Menschennatur und politische Ordnung* (Paderborn: 2015), 79–94.

6. Some texts take the concept to apply more broadly. In the legal writings gathered under Justinian the medievals could read that "natural law (*ius naturale*) is that which nature has taught to all animals; for this law is not specific to mankind but common to all animals, which are born in land and sea, and also to birds...because we see that other animals, wild beasts included, are rightly understood to be acquainted with this law," *Corpus iuris civilis. Vol. 1: Digesta*, ed. T. Mommsen (Berlin: 1908), §1.1.1.3–4.

7. B. Tierney, *Liberty and Law: The Idea of Permissive Natural Law 1100–1800* (Washington DC: 2014), 51–7.

8. See also S. B. Cunningham, *Reclaiming Moral Agency: The Moral Philosophy of Albert the Great* (Washington DC: 2008), 222, 231, 236–7.

9. The relevant questions are translated in R. J. Henle (ed. and trans.), *St Thomas Aquinas: The Treatise on Law* (Notre Dame, IN: 1993); and R. J. Regan (trans.), *Thomas Aquinas: Treatise on Law* (Indianapolis, IN: 2000).

10. See D. M. Nelson, *The Priority of Prudence: Virtue and Natural Law in Thomas Aquinas and the Implications for Modern Ethics* (University Park, PA: 1992), 177.

11. On the importance of this idea, see M. M. Keys, *Aquinas, Aristotle and the Promise of the Common Good* (Cambridge: 2006).

12. This innovative idea of "determiniation" has been stressed by J. Finnis, *Aquinas: Moral, Political, and Legal Theory* (Oxford: 1988), 266–7.

13. I owe the reference to Henle, *Treatise on Law*, 329.

14. *On the Rule of Princes (De Regimine Principium)*, translated in R. W. Dyson, *Aquinas: Political Writings* (Cambridge: 2002). See page xix for Dyson's explanation of the consensus regarding authenticity.

15. For these Aristotelian ideas, see *Classical Philosophy*, ch.40.

16. As noted by Nelson, *The Priority of Prudence*, 122.

17. For an overview of this debate and a defense of a more "essentialist" view, see A. Lisska, *Aquinas' Theory of Natural Law: An Analytic Reconstruction* (Oxford: 1996). See also F. Kerr, "Natural Law: Incommensurable Readings," in B. Davies (ed.), *Aquinas's Summa Theologiae: Critical Essays* (Lanham, MD: 2006), 245–63, which rightly points out (254) that since the natural law is grounded in the eternal law, it must on any interpretation be understood within Aquinas' theological presuppositions.

Chapter 40

1. For the problem of just war in general, see, e.g., R. Sorabji and D. Rodin (eds), *The Ethics of War: Shared Problems in Different Traditions* (Aldershot: 2007), and from a historical perspective J. T. Johnson, *Ideology, Reason and Limitation of War: Religious and Secular Concepts, 1200–1740* (Princeton, NJ: 1975) and *The Just War Tradition and the Restraint of War* (Princeton, NJ: 1981).
2. J. D. Tooke, *The Just War in Aquinas and Grotius* (London: 1965), 3–5.
3. Johnson, *Ideology*, 36.
4. F. H. Russell, *The Just War in the Middle Ages* (Cambridge: 1975), 5. I draw on this book extensively in what follows.
5. D. S. Bachrach, *Religion and the Conduct of War c.300–1215* (Woodbridge: 2003); D. Whetham, *Just Wars and Moral Victories: Surprise, Deception and the Normative Framework of European War in the Later Middle Ages* (Leiden: 2009).
6. Russell, *The Just War*, 216–17, and 140, for Johannes de Deo.
7. Russell, *The Just War*, 256.
8. As pointed out by Whetham, *Just Wars and Moral Victories*, 47.
9. Russell, *The Just War*, 229.
10. Russell, *The Just War*, 89.
11. Russell, *The Just War*, 297.
12. Russell, *The Just War*, 122.
13. Tooke, *The Just War in Aquinas and Grotius*, 170.
14. Russell, *The Just War*, 259.
15. G. E. M. Anscombe, "Medalist's Address: Action, Intention and 'Double Effect,'" in P. A. Woodward (ed.), *The Doctrine of Double Effect* (Notre Dame, IN: 2001), 50–66, at 64–5, argues that this passage does not really express the doctrine, despite the presence of the phrase *duplex effectus*, because this article is really about responding *proportionally* to aggression. She instead points to *ST* 1.2 Q20 a5 (cited below) which asks about the bearing of an action's consequences for its moral standing.
16. For a good discussion of the challenges, see N. Davis, "The Doctrine of Double Effect: Problems of Interpretation," in Woodward (ed.), *The Doctrine of Double Effect*, 119–42.

Chapter 41

1. Contrary to what is often believed, this seems to have been far less true under Islam, as I have noted in *Philosophy in the Islamic World*, ch.44. On the situation in Latin Christendom and at Paris in particular, see W. J. Courtenay, "Inquiry and Inquisition: Academic Freedom in Medieval Universities," *Church History* 58 (1989), 168–81; L. E. Wilshere, "The Condemnations of 1277 and the Intellectual Climate of the Medieval University," in

N. Van Deusen (ed.), *The Intellectual Climate of the Medieval University* (Kalamazoo, MI: 1997), 151–93; J. Thijssen, *Censure and Heresy at the University of Paris 1200–1400* (Philadelphia, PA: 1998); L. Bianchi, *Censure et liberté intellectuelle à l'université de Paris (XIIIe–XIVe siècles)* (Paris: 1999).

2. J. A. Aertsen, *Medieval Philosophy and the Transcendentals: The Case of Thomas Aquinas* (Leiden: 1996), 28.

3. For the 1270 list, see M. Hille, *Die Pariser Verurteilung vom 10. Dezember 1270* (Leipzig: 2005); English translation in J. F. Wippel and A. B. Wolter (trans.), *Medieval Philosophy: From St. Augustine to Nicholas of Cusa* (New York: 1969), 366. For the 1277 list, see D. Piché (ed. and trans.), *La Condamnation parisienne de 1277* (Paris: 1999); and, for commentary, R. Hissette, *Enquête sur les 219 articles condamnés à Paris le 7 mars 1277* (Louvain: 1977). English translation in R. Lerner and M. Mahdi, *Medieval Political Philosophy: A Sourcebook* (Glencoe, NY: 1963), 335–54. I use the numbering from the latter translation in referring to the articles.

4. Hille, *Die Pariser Verurteilung*, 68–70; F. van Steenberghen, *Maître Siger de Brabant* (Louvain: 1977), 33–46 and 102–14; J. F. Wippel, "Thomas Aquinas and the Condemnation of 1277," *Modern Schoolman* 72 (1995), 233–72, at 237.

5. K. Emery and A. Speer, "After the Condemnation of 1277: New Evidence, New Perspectives, and Grounds for New Interpretations," in J. A. Aertsen, K. Emery, and A. Speer (eds), *After the Condemnation of 1277: Philosophy and Theology at the University of Paris in the Last Quarter of the Thirteenth Century* (Berlin: 2001), 3–19, at 6.

6. Hille, *Die Pariser Verurteilung*, 43 n. 234.

7. Here I follow Wippel, "Thomas Aquinas and the Condemnation of 1277." See also C. G. Normore, "Who Was Condemned in 1277?" *Modern Scholasticism* 62 (1995), 273–81; Bianchi, *Censure et liberté*, 212–13.

8. E. P. Mahoney, "Reverberations of the Condemnation of 1277 in Later Medieval and Renaissance Philosophy," in Aertsen, Emery, and Speer, *After the Condemnation of 1277*, 902–30, at 909.

9. L. Bianchi, "1277: A Turning Point in Medieval Philosophy?," in J. A. Aertsen and A. Speer (eds), *What is Philosophy in the Middle Ages?* (Berlin: 1998), 90–110, at 96.

10. Mahoney, "Reverberations," 927.

11. See Bianchi, "1277: A Turning Point," 94–6, on the goal of restricting teaching and the question of whether Tempier's declaration actually counted as a "condemnation" in the strict sense. On the relevance of university debates over "doubtful propositions," see also D. Calma, "Du Bon Usage des grecs et des arabs: Réflexions sur la censure de 1277," in L. Bianchi (ed.), *Christian Readings of Aristotle from the Middle Ages to the Renaissance* (Turnhout: 2011), 115–84.

12. M. de Mowbray, "The *De Aeternitate Mundi* of Boethius of Dacia and the Paris Condemnation of 1277," *Recherches de Théologie et Philosophie* 73 (2006), 201–56, at 234.

13. For the following, see G. Pini, "The Individuation of Angels from Bonaventure to Duns Scotus," in T. Hoffman (ed.), *A Companion to Angels in Medieval Philosophy* (Leiden: 2012), 79–115. For more details, see Chapter 70 below.

14. E. Grant, "The Condemnation of 1277, God's Absolute Power, and Physical Thought in the Late Middle Ages," *Viator* 10 (1979), 211–44. For further discussion, see also J. E. Murdoch, "1277 and Late Medieval Natural Philosophy," in Aertsen and Speer (eds), 111–21; and Mahoney, "Reverberations."

15. Bianchi, "1277: A Turning Point," 103.

Chapter 42

1. Trans. from R. Lerner and M. Mahdi, *Medieval Political Philosophy: A Sourcebook* (Glencoe, NY: 1963), 337.

2. Quoted and cited by section number from R. McInerny (trans.), *Aquinas against the Averroists on There Being Only One Intellect* (West Lafayette, IN: 1993).

3. For references to earlier works discussing the supposed doctrine, see R. C. Dales, "The Origin of the Doctrine of the Double Truth," *Viator* 15 (1984), 169–79, at 169 n. 4. The idea that Siger and Boethius were "Latin Averroists" was expounded by the French scholars Ernest Renan and Pierre Mandonnet. For references and a critical summary of their views, see R. Imbach, "L'Averroïsme latin du XIIIe siècle," in *Gli studi di filosofia medievale fra Otto e Novocento*, ed. R. Imbach and A. Maierù (Rome: 1991), 191–208. This material is also surveyed in J. Marenbon, "Latin Averroism," in *Islamic Crosspollinations: Interactions in the Medieval Middle East*, ed. A. Akasoy et al. (Cambridge: 2007), 135–47, which makes a case that the phrase "Latin Averroism" could still be profitably used and may also apply to the later thinkers Dante and Jean of Jandun.

4. This is the analysis of F. van Steenberghen, *Maître Siger de Brabant* (Louvain: 1977); much turns here on his dating of Siger's works. One might worry about a certain circularity in van Steenberghen's reconstruction, in that works with bolder philosophical claims are assumed, in part for this very reason, to come earlier in Siger's career. Still, the overall picture presented by van Steenberghen remains fairly compelling.

5. For more details, see *Philosophy in the Islamic World*, ch.26.

6. Here I follow L. Bianchi, *Censure et liberté intellectuelle à l'université de Paris (XIIIe–XIVe siècles)* (Paris: 1999), 180–1, and his nuanced response to the view of F.-X. Putallaz and R. Imbach, *Profession: Philosophe. Siger de Brabant* (Paris: 1997).

7. In his *Commentary on the Book of Causes*, cited by van Steenberghen, *Maître Siger*, 241.

8. Bianchi, *Censure et liberté*, 184; the same goes for Siger, see van Steenberghen, *Maître Siger*, 242. It's worth noting that Averroes himself would have been totally opposed to the twofold truth doctrine; see *Philosophy in the Islamic World*, ch.25. For further discussion, see also A. Akasoy, "Was Averroes an Averroist? The Problem, the Debate, and its Philosophical Implications," in A. Akasoy and G. Giglioni (eds), *Renaissance Averroism and its Aftermath: Arabic Philosophy in Early Modern Europe* (New York: 2013), 321–47.

9. Translated in J. F. Wippel (trans.), *Boethius of Dacia: On the Supreme Good, On the Eternity of the World, On Dreams* (Toronto: 1987); cited by page number from this translation.

10. Bianchi, *Censure et liberté*, 192.

11. See Dales, "The Origin of the Doctrine of the Double Truth," 170–1; Dales traces the methodological point to Maimonides.

12. Translated in Wippel (trans.), *Boethius of Dacia*; see further A. J. Celano, "Boethius of Dacia: On the Highest Good," *Traditio* 43 (1987), 199–214. While this idea may readily be associated with the intellectualism of Averroes, it may instead (or also) be derived from Byzantine commentators on Aristotle's *Ethics*. See M. Trizio, "From Anna Komnene to Dante: The Byzantine Roots of Western Debates on Aristotle's *Nicomachean Ethics*," in J. M. Ziolkowski (ed.), *Dante and the Greeks* (Washington DC: 2014), 105–39.

13. As has been forcefully argued by G. Klima, "Ancilla Theologiae vs Domina Philosophorum: Thomas Aquinas, Latin Averroism and the Autonomy of Philosophy," in J. A. Aertsen and A. Speer (eds.), *Was ist Philosophie im Mittelalter?*, Berlin 1998, 393–402.

Chapter 43

1. *Philosophy in the Hellenistic and Roman Worlds*, ch.38.
2. For extensive discussion, see *Philosophy in the Islamic World*; and Chapter 21 for the point that most philosophers did not accept the eternity thesis, as is often assumed. For yet more details, see P. Adamson, "Eternity in Medieval Philosophy," in Y. Melamed (ed.), *Eternity: A History* (Oxford: 2016), 75–116.
3. Aristotle, *Topics* 104b16, cited at *ST* I Q46 a1 resp.
4. For translation of the relevant texts, see C. Vollert, L. H. Kendzierski, and P. M. Byrne (trans.), *St Thomas Aquinas, Siger of Brabant, St Bonaventure: On the Eternity of the World* (Milwaukee, WI: 1984). On his view, see also B. Bonansea, "The Impossibility of Creation from Eternity according to St Bonaventure," *Proceedings of the American Catholic Philosophical Association* 48 (Washington DC: 1974), 121–35; B. Bonansea, "The Question of an Eternal World in the teaching of St Bonaventure," *Fransiscan Studies* 34 (1974), 7–33; F. J. Kovach, "The Question of the Eternity of the World in St. Bonaventure and St. Thomas: A Critical Analysis," *Southwestern Journal of Philosophy* 5 (1974), 141–72; A. Zimmermann, "Mundus est aeternus? Zur Auslegung dieser These bei Bonaventura und Thomas von Aquin," in *Die Auseinandersetzungen an der Pariser Universität in XIII. Jahrhundert* (Berlin: 1976), 317–30.
5. Also translated in Vollert et al., *On the Eternity of the World*. See on this P. Porro, "The Chicken and the Egg (*suppositis fundamentis Philosophi*): Henry of Ghent, Siger of Brabant and the Eternity of Species," in L. Bianchi (ed.), *Christian Readings of Aristotle from the Middle Ages to the Renaissance* (Turnhout: 2011), 185–210, on which I draw in what follows. I assume that Henry is responding to Siger, though, as Porro points out, neither the chronological sequence nor Siger's authorship is certain.
6. Again, see the translations in Vollert et al., *On the Eternity of the World*. In what follows *Aet.* refers to Aquinas' treatise on the eternity of the world, cited by section number. On this text, see J. F. Wippel, "Did Thomas Aquinas Defend the Possibility of an Eternally Created World?" *Journal of the History of Philosophy* 19 (1981), 21–37; J. Weisheipl, "The Date and Context of Aquinas' De aeternitate mundi," in L. P. Gerson (ed.), *Graceful Reason* (Toronto: 1983), 239–71.
7. This is in the disputed questions *On Power*, as discussed by J. A. Aertsen, "The Eternity of the World: The Believing and the Philosophical Thomas. Some Comments," in J. B. M. Wissink (ed.), *The Eternity of the World in the Thought of Thomas Aquinas and his Contemporaries* (Leiden: 1990), 9–19.
8. For F. van Steenberghen, *Thomas Aquinas and Radical Aristotelianism* (Washington DC: 1970), 12, these are Aquinas' real targets in the treatise, not the so-called "Averroists."
9. I. M Resnick (ed.), *A Companion to Albert the Great* (Leiden: 2013), 206–9.
10. On Aquinas' conception of timeless eternity, see D. B. Burrell, "God's Eternity," *Faith and Philosophy* 1 (1984) 389–406; B. J. Shanley, "Eternity and Duration in Aquinas," *The Thomist* 61 (1997) 525–48; B. Leftow, "Aquinas on Time and Eternity," *American Catholic Philosophical Quarterly* 64 (1990), 387–99; N. Wandinger, "Der Begriff der *aeternitas* bei Thomas von Aquin," *Zeitschrift für Katholische Theologie* 116 (1994), 301–20.
11. A further question raised by Aquinas' position is this: given that God had the choice whether to make a finite or eternal world, why did He do the former and not the latter? Aquinas thinks we can only guess, but he proposes that God's power is better manifested to His creatures by bringing the world to be after it did not yet exist.
12. Translated in J. F. Wippel (trans.), *Boethius of Dacia: On the Supreme Good, On the Eternity of the World, On Dreams* (Toronto: 1987). For discussion, see M. de Mowbray, "The *De*

Aeternitate Mundi of Boethius of Dacia and the Paris Condemnation of 1277," *Recherches de Théologie et Philosophie* 73 (2006), 201–56.

Chapter 44

1. As mentioned in *Philosophy in the Hellenistic and Roman Worlds*, ch.21 (which also discusses the contributions of ancient grammarians) and ch.38.
2. For the development of speculative grammar, see J. Pinborg, *Die Entwicklung der Sprachtheorie im Mittelalter* (Münster: 1967), J. E. Ashworth, *The Tradition of Medieval Logic and Speculative Grammar from Anselm to the End of the Seventeenth Century* (Toronto: 1977), K. M. Fredborg, "Speculative Grammar," in *A History of Twelfth-Century Philosophy*, ed. P. Dronke (Cambridge: 1988), 177–95; and S. Ebbesen (ed.), *Sprachtheorien in Spätantike und Mittelalter* (Tübingen: 1995). For further bibliography, see also F. Pironet, *The Tradition of Medieval Logic and Speculative Grammar: A Bibliography (1977–1994)* (Turnhout: 1997).
3. M. Hertz (ed.), *Priscian: Institutiones grammaticae*, 2 vols (Leipzig: 1855–9), §2.18.
4. Pinborg, *Die Entwicklung der Sprachtheorie*, 57.
5. For summary accounts, see Pinborg, *Die Entwicklung der Sprachtheorie*, 41, 71; G. L. Bursill-Hall, *Speculative Grammars of the Middle Ages: The Doctrine of partes orationis of the Modistae* (The Hague: 1971), 72–3.
6. For details, see A. M. Mora-Márquez, *The Thirteenth-Century Notion of Signification* (Leiden: 2015). Here I would also like to record my gratitude to Ana María Mora-Márquez for her valuable advice on this chapter.
7. See J. Toivanen, "Marking the Boundaries: Animals in Medieval Philosophy," in *Animals: A History*, ed. P. Adamson and G. F. Edwards (Oxford: 2018), 121–50.
8. Pinborg, *Die Entwicklung der Sprachtheorie*, 43; Bursill-Hall, *Speculative Grammars*, 43.
9. Bursill-Hall, *Speculative Grammars*, 136.
10. S. Ebbesen, "The Man who Loved Every: Boethius of Dacia on Logic and Metaphysics," in *Collected Papers of Sten Ebbesen*, 2 vols (Aldershot: 2008–9), vol.2, 163–77, at 175.
11. Bursill-Hall, *Speculative Grammars*, 125.
12. See M. Sirridge and K. M. Fredborg, "*Demonstratio ad Oculum* and *Demonstratio ad Intellectum*: Pronouns in Ps.-Jordan and Robert Kilwardby," in J. L. Fink, H. Hansen, and A. M. Mora-Márquez (eds), *Logic and Language in the Middle Ages: A Volume in Honour of Sten Ebbesen* (Leiden: 2013), 199–220.
13. For this continuity between terminism and modism, see I. Rosier-Catach, "Modisme, pré-modisme, proto-modisme: Vers une définition modulaire," in S. Ebbesen and R. L. Friedman (eds), *Medieval Analyses in Language and Cognition* (Copenhagen: 1999), 45–82, at 70.
14. S. Ebbesen, "Radulphus Brito, the Last of the Great Arts Masters. Or: Philosophy and Freedom," in *Collected Papers of Sten Ebbesen*, vol.2, 179–96, at 182–3.
15. Bursill-Hall, *Speculative Grammars*, 47 and 151; S. Ebbesen, "Concrete Accidental Terms: Late Thirteenth-Century Debates about Problems Relating to Such Terms as *Album*," in *Collected Papers of Sten Ebbesen*, vol.2, 109–51; S. Knuttila, "Concrete Accidental Terms," in Fink et al. (eds), *Logic and Language in the Middle Ages*, 273–86.
16. See Ebbesen, "The Man Who Loved Every"; L. Cesalli, A. de Libera, and F. Goubier, "Does Loving Every Mean Loving Every Every, Even Non-Existent Ones? Distribution and Universals in the *Opus Puerorum*," in Fink et al. (eds), *Logic and Language in the Middle Ages*, 305–36; A. M. Mora-Márquez, "Boethius of Dacia (1270s) and Radulphus Brito (1290s) on the Universal Sign 'Every'," *Logica Universalis* (2015), 193–211.

Chapter 45

1. *De amore* §1.1: *Amor est passio quaedam innata procedens ex visione et immoderata cognitione formae alterius sexus*. The word *passio* could mean simply "being affected" (like Greek *pathos*), but Andreas makes clear in what follows that he means it involves suffering (he connects love especially to fear). As we'll see, Jean de Meun also took it in a rather pejorative sense.

2. Translation from F. Horgan (trans.), *The Romance of the Rose* (Oxford: 1994). Cited by page number from this version. The standard edition is F. Lecoy (ed.), *Le Roman de la rose*, 3 vols (Paris: 1965–70).

3. For discussions of his sources, see, e.g., W. Wetherbee, "The Literal and the Allegorical: Jean de Meun and the *de Planctu Naturae*," *Mediaeval Studies* 33 (1971), 264–91; K. A. Ott, "Jean de Meun und Boethius," in U. Schwab and E. Stutz (eds), *Philologische Studien: Gedenkschrift für Richard Kienast* (Heidelberg: 1978), 193–227.

4. That said, Guillaume too does refer to philosophical literature and ideas, for example in an apparent reminiscence of the discussion of time in Augustine's *Confessions* (3).

5. For an example of me gratuitously doing the same thing, see the previous note.

6. On this possible relationship, see F. W. Müller, *Der Rosenroman und der lateinische Averroismus des 13. Jahrhunderts* (Frankfurt am Main: 1947).

7. On this theme, see C. Dahlberg, "Love and the *Roman de la Rose*," *Speculum* 44 (1969), 568–84, at 573.

8. S. Huot, "Sexuality and the Subversion of Order in Jean de Meun's *Roman de la Rose*," *The Modern Language Review* 95 (2000), 41–61. Others who take a broadly "theological" approach include D. W. Robertson, *A Preface to Chaucer: Studies in Medieval Perspectives* (Princeton, NJ: 1962); J. V. Fleming, *The Roman de la Rose: A Study in Allegory and Iconography* (Princeton, NJ: 1969).

9. Cited from D. F. Hult "Language and Dismemberment: Abelard, Origin and the *Romance of the Rose*," in K. Brownlee and S. Huot (eds), *Rethinking the Romance of the Rose: Text, Image, Reception* (Philadelphia, PA: 1992), 101–30, at 105.

10. As pointed out by Ott, "Jean de Meun und Boethius," 211.

11. G. D. Economou, "The Character Genius in Alan de Lille, Jean de Meun, and John Gower," *The Chaucer Review* 4 (1970), 203–10.

12. Indeed, the passage is taken this way by Huot, "Sexuality and the Subversion of Order," 59. See further C. Dahlberg, "Love and the *Roman de la Rose*," *Speculum* 44 (1969), 568–84; and, with great panache and detailed readings of Jean and his sources, J. V. Fleming, *Reason and the Lover* (Princeton, NJ: 1984).

13. On this, see Hult "Language and Dismemberment"; and J. Mann, "Jean de Meun and the Castration of Saturn," in J. Marenbon (ed.), *Poetry and Philosophy in the Middle Ages* (Leiden: 2001), 309–26.

14. J. M. Fyler, *Language and the Declining World in Chaucer, Dante, and Jean de Meun* (Cambridge: 2007), 77.

15. As noted by Mann, "Jean de Meun and the Castration of Saturn," 319–20.

16. For the double meaning of "gloss," see Hult, "Language and Dismemberment," 122–3; Mann, "Jean de Meun and the Castration of Saturn," 317.

17. M. Franklin-Brown, *Reading the World: Encyclopedic Writing in the Scholastic Age* (Chicago: 2012) argues that, "destabilized by her eclectic education, Jean's Nature has lost the poise and decorum that Alan had attributed to Natura" (193), and cites the animal passage as an example (194–5).

Chapter 46

1. Thus S. Brown, "Henry of Ghent's *De Reductione Artium ad Theologiam*," in D. M. Gallagher (ed.), *Thomas Aquinas and his Legacy* (Washington DC: 1994), 194–206, at 194, contrasting him with Godfrey of Fontaine, who instead criticized Aquinas from an Aristotelian point of view.

2. G. A. Wilson, *A Companion to Henry of Ghent* (Leiden: 2011), 13.

3. For this topic, see S. Brown, "Henry of Ghent's Criticism of Aquinas' Subalternation Theory and the Early Thomistic Response," in R. Työrinoja et al. (eds), *Knowledge and the Sciences in Medieval Philosophy* (Helsinki: 1990), vol.3, 337–45. For relevant texts on the issue, see Henry of Ghent, *Summa of Ordinary Questions: Articles Six to Ten on Theology*, trans. R. J. Teske (Milwaukee, WI: 2011), cited by page number in what follows.

4. M. Pickavé, *Heinrich von Gent über Metaphysik als erste Wissenschaft* (Leiden: 2007); for a briefer discussion in English, see M. Pickavé, "Henry of Ghent on Metaphysics," in G. A. Wilson, *A Companion to Henry of Ghent* (Leiden: 2011), 153–79.

5. On this, see S. P. Marrone, *Truth and Scientific Knowledge in the Thought of Henry of Ghent* (Cambridge, MA: 1985); M. L. Führer, "Henry of Ghent on Divine Illumination," *Bochumer philosophisches Jahrbuch für Antike und Mittelalter* 3 (1998), 69–87.

6. B. Goehring, "Henry of Ghent on the *Verbum Mentis*," in Wilson, *A Companion to Henry of Ghent*, 241–72.

7. G. Pini, "Henry of Ghent's Doctrine of *Verbum* in its Theological Context," in G. Guldentops and C. Steel (eds), *Henry of Ghent and the Transformation of Scholastic Thought* (Leuven: 2003), 307–26.

8. M. Laarmann, "God as *Primum Cognitum*: Some Remarks on the Theory of Initial Knowledge of *Esse* and God according to Thomas Aquinas and Henry of Ghent," in W. Vanhamel (ed.), *Henry of Ghent: Proceedings of the International Colloquium on the Occasion of the 700th Anniversary of his Death* (Leuven: 1996), 171–91, at 185.

9. *Quodlibet* 9, Q15, cited by Marrone, "Henry of Ghent's Epistemology," 237.

10. On this, see S. P. Marrone, "Henry of Ghent and Duns Scotus on the Knowledge of Being," *Speculum* 63 (1988), 22–57; and Laarmann, "God as *Primum Cognitum*."

11. For texts, see Henry of Ghent, *Quodlibetal Questions on Moral Problems*, trans. R. J. Teske (Milwaukee, WI: 2005); the *Quaestio* I go on to discuss here is at 29–32. On the issue, see R. Macken, "Henry of Ghent as a Defender of the Personal Rights of Man," *Franziskanische Studien* 73 (1991), 170–81; B. Tierney, "Natural Rights in the Thirteenth Century: A *Quaestio* of Henry of Ghent," *Speculum* 67 (1992), 58–68.

12. For texts, see Henry of Ghent, *Quodlibetal Questions on Free Will*, trans. R. J. Teske (Milwaukee, WI: 1993), cited by page number in what follows. The literature on this topic is rather large; see, for example, R. Macken, "La Volonté humaine, faculté plus élevée que l'intelligence selon Henri de Gand," *Recherches de Théologie Ancienne et Médiévale* 42 (1975), 5–51; R. Macken, "Heinrich von Gent im Gespräch mit seinen Zeitgenossen über die menschliche Freiheit," *Franziskanische Studien* 59 (1977), 125–82; J. Müller, "Willensschwäche im Voluntarismus? Das Beispiel Heinrichs von Gent," *Archiv für Geschichte der Philosophie* 89 (2007), 1–29; R. J. Teske, "Henry of Ghent on Freedom of the Human Will," in Wilson, *A Companion to Henry of Ghent*, 315–35.

13. Here the literature is even more vast, but see, for instance, E. Stump, "Aquinas's Account of Freedom: Intellect and Will," *The Monist* 80 (1997), 675–97.

14. R. J. Teske, "Henry of Ghent's Rejection of the Principle *Omne Quod Movetur ab Alio Movetur*," in Vanhamel, *Henry of Ghent*, 279–308.

Chapter 47

1. I will not in this chapter tackle a third obvious topic, the aforementioned issue of the Incarnation. For this, see Chapter 73 below and R. Cross, *The Metaphysics of the Incarnation: Thomas Aquinas to Duns Scotus* (Oxford: 2005).
2. See *Philosophy in the Hellenistic and Roman Worlds*, ch.51.
3. See, e.g., H. McCabe, "Aquinas on the Trinity," *New Blackfriars* 80 (1999), 268–83; J. C. Flores, *Henry of Ghent: Metaphysics and the Trinity* (Leuven: 2006); G. Emery, *The Trinitarian Theology of St Thomas Aquinas*, trans. F. A. Murphy, (Oxford: 2007).
4. Flores, *Henry of Ghent*, 97.
5. See Flores, *Henry of Ghent*, 55.
6. See *Philosophy in the Hellenistic and Roman Worlds*, ch.54.
7. For more details, see C. Luna, "Essenza divina e relazioni trinitarie nella critica di Egidio Romano a Tommaso d'Aquino," *Medioevo* 14 (1988), 3–69.
8. On this debate, see R. L. Friedman, *Medieval Trinitarian Thought from Aquinas to Ockham* (Cambridge: 2010). At 171–3 he provides a useful overview of the central points in the debate.
9. Friedman, *Medieval Trinitarian Thought*, 27–30.
10. R. Cross, *Great Medieval Thinkers: Duns Scotus* (New York: 1999), 66.
11. Friedman, *Medieval Trinitarian Thought*, 46–7. A reductive reading along these lines has, however, been ascribed to Aquinas himself: see T. M. Ward, "Relations without Forms: Some Consequences of Aquinas's Metaphysics of Relations," *Vivarium* 48 (2010), 279–301; see also M. Henninger, "Thomas Aquinas on the Ontological Status of Relations," *Journal of the History of Philosophy* 25 (1987), 491–515. For Henry's application of "relational being" to the createdness of things other than God, see J. Decorte, "Relation and Substance in Henry of Ghent's Metaphysics," in G. Guldentops and C. Steel (eds), *Henry of Ghent and the Transformation of Scholastic Thought* (Leuven: 2003), 3–14. For more on theories of relations, see M. Henninger, *Relations: Medieval Theories, 1250–1325* (Oxford: 1989); J. Decorte, "Giles of Rome and Henry of Ghent on the Reality of a Real Relation," *Documenti e Studi sulla Tradizione Filosofica Medievale* 7 (1996), 183–21; R. Cross, "Relations and the Trinity: The Case of Henry of Ghent and John Duns Scotus," *Documenti e Studi sulla Tradizione Filosofica Medievale* 16 (2005), 1–21.
12. For a clear explanation of this, see P. King, "Scotus on Metaphysics" in T. Williams (ed.), *The Cambridge Companion to Duns Scotus* (Cambridge: 2003), 15–68, at 22–5. For longer studies, see A. B. Wolter, "The Formal Distinction," in A. B. Wolter, *The Philosophical Theology of John Duns Scotus* (Ithaca, NY: 1990), 27–41; and S. Dumont, "Duns Scotus's Parisian Question on the Formal Distinction," *Vivarium* 43 (2005), 7–62.
13. For a comprehensive discussion, see M. McCord Adams, *Some Later Medieval Theories of the Eucharist* (Oxford: 2010).
14. J. Goering, "The Invention of Transubstantiation," *Traditio* 46 (1991), 147–70. For more background, see G. Macy, *The Theologies of the Eucharist in the Early Scholastic Period* (Oxford: 1984).
15. McCord Adams, *Some Later Medieval Theories of the Eucharist*, 99, and 118–19; for the following points about Scotus. For this, see also Cross, *Duns Scotus*, 143–4.
16. A. Côté, "Siger of Brabant and Thomas Aquinas on Divine Power and the Separability of Accidents," *British Journal for the History of Philosophy* 16 (2008), 681–700.

Chapter 48

1. Like Scotus (see the end of this chapter), Fakhr al-Dīn al-Rāzī also held that being is univocal and is divided by disjunctive predicates like contingent-or-necessary. Another parallel is a point we'll see below in Godfrey of Fontaines, and found in numerous Muslim thinkers, that a real distinction between essence and existence would require essence to exist prior to receiving existence. See further *Philosophy in the Islamic World*, ch.47, and for a very detailed account F. Benevich, "The Essence-Existence Distinction: Four Elements of the Post-Avicennian Metaphysical Dispute (11–13th Centuries)," *Oriens* 45 (2017), 203–58.

2. See *Philosophy in the Islamic World*, ch.17.

3. J. F. Wippel, "Essence and Existence," in R. Pasnau (ed.), *The Cambridge History of Medieval Philosophy*, 2 vols (Cambridge: 2010), vol.2, 622–34, at 624–5.

4. In Latin *De ente et essentia*; Germans are occasionally disappointed to learn that it is not about ducks. For an English translation, see A. Maurer (trans.), *St. Thomas Aquinas: On Being and Essence* (Toronto: 1968); cited by section number.

5. *On Being and Essence* §4.6. He actually mentions not triangle but human and the phoenix, Avicenna's example of a thing that does *not* exist. See T.-A. Druart, "Avicennan Troubles: The Mysteries of the Heptagonal House and of the Phoenix," *Tópicos* 42 (2012), 51–74.

6. P. W. Nash, "Giles of Rome on Boethius' *Diversum Est Esse et Id Quod Est*," *Mediaeval Studies* 12 (1950), 57–91.

7. This, for Giles, is the difference between creation and the production of the trinitarian Persons, which involves no delimitation by essences. See G. Pini, "Being and Creation in Giles of Rome," in J. A. Aertsen, K. Emery, and A. Speer (eds), *Nach der Verurteilung von 1277: Philosophie und Theologie an der Universität von Paris im letzten Viertel des 13. Jahrhunderts* (Berlin: 2001), 390–409, at 406–8.

8. See *On Being and Essence* §5.1.

9. See further R. McInerny, *Aquinas and Analogy* (Washington DC: 1996), with a partial rebuttal in E. J. Ashworth, "Aquinas on Analogy," in J. Hause (ed.), *Debates in Medieval Philosophy* (New York: 2014), 232–42. See also E. J. Ashworth, *Les Théories de l'analogie du XIIe au XVIe siècle* (Paris: 2008).

10. See S. MacDonald, "The *Esse/Essentia* Argument in Aquinas's *De Ente et Essentia*," *Journal of the History of Philosophy* 22 (1984), 157–72.

11. The following is based on J. F. Wippel, "Godfrey of Fontaines and the Real Distinction between Essence and Existence," *Traditio* 20 (1964), 385–410. See also J. F. Wippel, *The Metaphysical Thought of Godfrey of Fontaines: A Study in Late Thirteenth-Century Philosophy* (Washington DC: 1981) and "The Relationship Between Essence and Existence in Late Thirteenth-Century Thought: Giles of Rome, Henry of Ghent, Godfrey of Fontaines, and James of Viterbo," in P. Morewedge (ed.), *Philosophies of Existence, Ancient and Medieval* (New York: 1982), 131–64.

12. This is arguably something to which Avicenna would agree, since he also believes that all knowable essences must exist at least mentally.

13. For a comparison between these two notions, see A. B. Wolter, "The Formal Distinction," in A. B. Wolter, *The Philosophical Theology of John Duns Scotus* (Ithaca, NY: 1990), 27–41, at 31. Effectively, the difference is that Scotus stresses that a formal distinction needs to be a sort of conceptual distinction grounded in non-identical features of an external object; otherwise, it will be only a "fiction of the mind."

14. R. Cross, "Duns Scotus on Essence and Existence," *Oxford Studies in Medieval Philosophy* 1 (2013), 172–204, at 202.
15. For the following, see, e.g., P. King, "Scotus on Metaphysics," in T. Williams (ed.), *The Cambridge Companion to Duns Scotus* (Cambridge: 2003), 15–68; and several contributions in L. Honnefelder, R. Wood, and M. Dreyer (eds), *John Duns Scotus: Metaphysics and Ethics* (Leiden: 1996).
16. G. Pini, "Scotus on Doing Metaphysics *in Statu Isto*," *Archa Verbi: Subsidia* (2009), 29–53.
17. See further S. P. Marrone, "Henry of Ghent and Duns Scotus on the Knowledge of Being," *Speculum* 63 (1988), 22–57.
18. For a debate concerning whether Scotus' view on this matter changes across his career, see the contrary views of R. Wood and H. Möhle in L. Honnefelder et al. (eds), *Johannes Duns Scotus 1308–2007: die philosophischen Perspektiven seines Werkes* (Münster: 2010). For passages relevant to the issue, see A. Wolter (trans.), *Duns Scotus: Philosophical Writings* (Indianapolis, IN: 1987), §I.

Chapter 49

1. On the other hand, he elsewhere says that, for instance, when you are standing, it is false that you are not standing, yet not impossible (*On the Heavens* 281b). See, on the problem, C. Kirwan, "Aristotle on the Necessity of the Present," *Oxford Studies in Ancient Philosophy* 4 (1986), 167–87.
2. For an overview, see A. B. Wolter, "Reflections on the Life and Works of Scotus," *American Catholic Philosophical Quarterly* 67 (1993), 1–36, reprinted in A. B. Wolter, *Scotus and Ockham: Selected Essays* (Saint Bonaventure, NY: 2003); T. Williams, "Introduction: The Life and Works of John Duns Scotus," in T. Williams (ed.), *The Cambridge Companion to Duns Scotus* (Cambridge: 2003), 1–14.
3. For the former issue, see S. P. Marrone, "Revisiting Duns Scotus and Henry of Ghent on Modality," in L. Honnefelder et al. (eds), *John Duns Scotus: Metaphysics and Ethics* (Leiden: 1996), 175–89. For the latter, see S. D. Dumont, "Did Duns Scotus Change his Mind on the Will?" in J. A. Aertsen et al. (eds), *After the Condemnation of 1277: The University of Paris in the Last Quarter of the Thirteenth Century* (Berlin: 2000), 719–94; M. B. Ingham, "Did Scotus Modify his Position on the Relationship of Intellect and Will?" *Recherches de Théologie et Philosophie Médiévales* 69 (2002), 88–116.
4. See *Classical Philosophy*, ch.39.
5. Cited from A. B. Wolter, "Duns Scotus on the Will as Rational Potency," in A. B. Wolter, *The Philosophical Theology of John Duns Scotus* (Ithaca, NY: 1990), 163–80, at 165.
6. For passages on this, see A. B. Wolter (ed. and trans.), *Duns Scotus on the Will and Morality* (Washington DC: 1986), 145–73. See further T. Hoffmann, "The Distinction between Nature and Will in Duns Scotus," *Archives d'Histoire Doctrinale et Littéraire du Moyen Âge* 66 (1999), 189–224.
7. Cited from Wolter, "Duns Scotus on the Will," 178.
8. This story has been explored especially by Simo Knuuttila. See, e.g., his "Time and Modality in Scholasticism," in S. Knuuttila (ed.), *Reforging the Great Chain of Being: Studies in the History of Modal Theory* (Dordrecht: 1981), 163–257; S. Knuuttila, *Modalities in Medieval Philosophy* (London: 1993).
9. Cited from Marrone, "Revisting Duns Scotus," 176. A good text for Scotus' ideas on possibility is A. Vos et al. (trans.), *John Duns Scotus: Contingency and Freedom. Lectura I, 39* (Dordrecht: 1994).

10. Another important forerunner was Olivi, as argued by S. D. Dumont, "The Origin of Scotus's Theory of Synchronic Contingency," *Modern Schoolman* 72 (1995), 149–67.

11. See J. F. Wippel, "The Reality of Nonexisting Possibles according to Thomas Aquinas, Henry of Ghent, and Godfrey of Fontaines," *Review of Metaphysics* 34 (1981), 729–58; R. Cross, "Henry of Ghent on the Reality of Non-Existing Possibles—Revisited," *Archiv für Geschichte der Philosophie* 92 (2010), 115–32.

12. See A. B. Wolter, "Scotus on the Divine Origin of Possibility," *American Catholic Philosophical Quarterly* 47 (1993), 95–107; T. Hoffmann, "Duns Scotus on the Origin of the Possibles in the Divine Intellect," in S. F. Brown et al. (eds), *Philosophical Debates at Paris in the Early Fourteenth Century* (Leiden: 2009), 359–79; and the contributions of Knuuttila, Normore, and Marrone in Honnefelder et al. (eds), *John Duns Scotus: Metaphysics and Ethics*. Scotus' position remained a subject of controversy also in much later philosophers who followed his teaching. See J. Coombs, "The Possibility of Created Entities in Seventeenth-Century Scotism," *Philosophical Quarterly* 43 (1993), 447–57.

13. For which, see R. Wood, "Scotus's Argument for the Existence of God," *Franciscan Studies* 47 (1987), 257–77; A. B. Wolter, "Duns Scotus and the Existence and Nature of God," in A. B. Wolter, *The Philosophical Theology of John Duns Scotus* (Ithaca, NY: 1990), 254–77; R. Cross, *Duns Scotus on God* (Aldershot: 2005).

14. Scotus says in the report of his lectures at Paris that Anselm's proof just needs to be "touched up (*colarari*)" in order to be rendered more persuasive. For the passage and its meaning, see W. J. Courtenay, *Schools and Scholars in Fourteenth-Century England* (Princeton, NJ: 1987), 344 n. 40.

15. T.-A. Druart, "Avicenna's Influence on Duns Scotus' Proof for the Existence of God in the *Lectura*," in J. Janssens and D. De Smet (eds), *Avicenna and his Heritage* (Leuven: 2002), 253–66.

16. For the following, see G. Pini, "Scotus on the Possibility of a Better World," *Acta Philosophica* 18 (2009), 283–306. See also R. Cross, "Duns Scotus on Goodness, Justice and what God Can Do," *Journal of Theological Studies* 48 (1997), 48–76; T. Williams, "A Most Methodical Lover? On Scotus' Arbitrary Creator," *Journal of the History of Philosophy* 38 (2000), 169–202.

Chapter 50

1. Citation from A. B. Wolter, "Native Freedom of the Will as a Key to the Ethics of Scotus," in A. B. Wolter, *The Philosophical Theology of John Duns Scotus*, ed. M. McCord Adams (Ithaca, NY: 1990), 148–62, at 160.

2. C. McCluskey, "The Roots of Ethical Voluntarism," *Vivarium* 39 (2001), 185–208.

3. For a translation of relevant passages, see A. B. Wolter (ed. and trans.), *Duns Scotus on the Will and Morality* (Washington DC: 1986), 255–61

4. Francis Oakley has written extensively on the contrast between absolute and ordained power. See, e.g., his *Omnipotence, Covenant, and Order: An Excursion in the History of Ideas from Abelard to Leibniz* (Ithaca, NY: 1984) and *Omnipotence and Promise: The Legacy of the Scholastic Distinction of Powers* (Toronto: 2002). See also W. J. Courtenay, *Covenant and Causality in Medieval Thought* (London: 1984) and *Capacity and Volition: A History of the Distinction of Absolute and Ordained Power* (Bergamo: 1990); H. A. Oberman, *The Harvest of Medieval Theology: Gabriel Biel and Late Medieval Nominalism* (Cambridge, MA: 1963).

5. In *Ordinatio* III d.37, in T. Williams (trans.), *John Duns Scotus: Selected Writings on Ethics* (Oxford: 2017), 248–58.

6. For the distinction between the two tables, see Exodus 31:18.

7. H. Möhle, "Scotus's Theory of Natural Law," in T. Williams (ed.), *The Cambridge Companion to Duns Scotus* (Cambridge: 2003), 312–31.

8. Möhle, "Scotus's Theory of Natural Law," 321. On the role of reason in his ethics, see also T. Williams, "Reason, Morality, and Voluntarism in Duns Scotus: A Pseudo-Problem Dissolved," *The Modern Schoolman* 74 (1997), 73–94.

9. On virtue, see B. Kent, "Rethinking Moral Dispositions: Scotus on the Virtues," in T. Williams (ed.), *The Cambridge Companion to Duns Scotus* (Cambridge: 2003), 352–76. For prudence, see S. Dumont, "The Necessary Connection of Moral Virtue to Prudence according to John Duns Scotus—Revisited," *Recherches de Théologie Ancienne et Médiévale* 55 (1988), 184–206, and the contributions of Adams and Ingham in L. Honnefelder, R. Wood, and M. Dreyer (eds), *John Duns Scotus: Metaphysics and Ethics* (Leiden: 1996).

10. For medieval views on this phenomenon of "weakness of will" or *akrasia*, see J. Müller, *Willensschwäche in Antike und Mittelalter* (Leuven: 2009).

11. T. Williams, "How Scotus Separates Morality from Happiness," *American Catholic Philosophical Quarterly* 69 (1995), 425–45, and also his "From Metaethics to Action Theory," in T. Williams (ed.), *The Cambridge Companion to Duns Scotus* (Cambridge: 2003), 332–51.

12. *Ordinatio* III d.19 n.7, cited from A. B. Wolter, "Native Freedom of the Will as a Key to the Ethics of Scotus," in A. B. Wolter, *The Philosophical Theology of John Duns Scotus*, ed. M. McCord Adams (Ithaca, NY: 1990), 148–62, at 157.

13. For the contrast, see T. M. Osborne, "The Separation of the Interior and Exterior Acts in Scotus and Ockham," *Mediaeval Studies* 69 (2007), 111–39.

Chapter 51

1. For a primary text (*Ordinatio* II, d3 part 1 Q1–6) in English translation, see P. V. Spade (trans.), *Five Texts on the Mediaeval Problem of Universals: Porphyry, Boethius, Abelard, Duns Scotus, Ockham* (Indianapolis, IN: 1994). For a good overview of Scotus' position, see A. B. Wolter's entry on Scotus in J. J. E. Gracia (ed.), *Individuation in Scholasticism: The Later Middle Ages and the Counter-Reformation, 1150–1650* (Albany, NY: 1994), 271–98; and for more detailed discussions, see P. King, "Duns Scotus on the Common Nature and the Individual Differentia," *Philosophical Topics* 20 (1992), 50–76, and T. B. Noone, "Universals and Individuation," in T. Williams (ed.), *The Cambridge Companion to Duns Scotus* (Cambridge: 2003), 100–28. T. Bates, *Duns Scotus and the Problem of Universals* (London: 2010) argues for the viability of Scotus' position within the context of modern-day debates over universals.

2. As emphasized by G. Pini, "Scotus on Universals: A Reconsideration," *Documenti e Studi sulla Tradizione Filosofica Medievale* 18 (2007), 395–409.

3. See Bates, *Duns Scotus and the Problem of Universals*, 77.

4. For this argument, see Pini, "Scotus on Universals," 403.

5. M. E. Marmura (ed. and trans.), *Avicenna: The Metaphysics of the Healing* (Provo, UT: 2005), §5.1.5, For discussion, see S. Menn, "Avicenna's Metaphysics," in P. Adamson (ed.), *Interpreting Avicenna* (Cambridge: 2013), 143–69, at 157.

6. Notice that this is similar to what Scotus said about being, which had disjunctive properties like infinite-or-finite and necessary-or-possible. In both cases Scotus is inspired by Avicenna.

7. See Wolter in *Individuation in Scholasticism*, 277.

8. The explanation in terms of matter was also the topic of a debate between Scotus and a follower of Aquinas, named William Peter Godinus; see C. Stroick, "Eine Pariser Disputation vom Jahre 1306: die Verteidigung des thomistischen Individuationsprinzip gegen Johannes Duns Scotus durch Guillelmus Petri de Godino, O.P.," in W. P. Eckert (ed.), *Thomas von Aquino: Interpretation und Rezeption, Studien und Texte* (Mainz: 1974).

9. P. King, "Duns Scotus on Singular Essences," *Medioevo* 30 (2005), 111–37.

10. Wolter in *Individuation in Scholasticism*, 290.

11. Not only is this not true, but apparently botanists insist that those sharp things on roses should in fact be called "prickles." So much for every rose having its thorn.

12. P. King, "Duns Scotus on Singular Essences," *Medioevo* 30 (2005), 111–37.

13. On this, see R. Pasnau, "Cognition," in T. Williams (ed.), *The Cambridge Companion to Duns Scotus* (Cambridge: 2003), 285–311; and R. Cross, *Duns Scotus' Theory of Cognition* (Oxford: 2014), ch.2. An older study is S. Day, *Intuitive Cognition: A Key to the Significance of the Later Scholastics* (Saint Bonaventure, NY: 1947). As Pasnau points out, Scotus was not the first thinker to use the idea of intuitive cognition, but it is a notion that has been associated especially with him, both in the fourteenth century and in modern scholarship.

14. For thirteenth-century discussions of this phenomenon, see F.-X. Putallaz, *La Connaissance de soi au XIIIe siècle de Matthieu d'Aquasparta à Thierry de Freiberg* (Paris: 1991); T. Cory, *Aquinas on Human Self-Knowledge* (Cambridge: 2013).

Chapter 52

1. B. W. Tuchman, *A Distant Mirror: The Calamitous 14th Century* (New York: 1978).

2. As mentioned by B. Tierney and S. Painter, *Western Europe in the Middle Ages, 300–1475* (New York: 1992), 536.

3. W. J. Courtenay, *Schools and Scholars in Fourteenth-Century England* (Princeton, NJ: 1987), 347.

4. Courtenay, *Schools and Scholars*, 164.

5. C. Schnabel, "Paris and Oxford between Aureoli and Rimini," in J. Marenbon (ed.), *The Routledge History of Philosophy: The Middle Ages* (London: 1998), 386–401, names this (at 390) as a topic that showcases the Parisian contribution.

6. Courtenay, *Schools and Scholars*, 327, 352.

7. For this idea and a number of caveats to it, see W. J. Courtenay, "Nominalism and Late Medieval Religion," in C. Trinkhaus and H. A. Oberman (eds), *The Pursuit of Holiness* (Leiden: 1974), 26–59.

8. M. J. F. M. Hoenen, "Via Antiqua and Via Moderna in the Fifteenth Century: Doctrinal, Institutional and Political Factors in the *Wegestreit*," in R. Friedman and L. O. Nielsen (eds), *The Medieval Heritage in Early Modern Metaphysics and Modal Theory, 1400–1700* (Dordrecht: 2005), 9–36 at 15.

9. At least not with quite this meaning, as shown by W. J. Courtenay, "Antiqui and Moderni in Late Medieval Thought," *Journal of the History of Ideas* 48 (1987), 3–10.

10. Courtenay, *Schools and Scholars*, 189–92.

11. T. B. Noone, "Ascoli, Wylton and Alnwick on Scotus's Formal Distinction: Taxonomy, Refinement, and Interaction," in S. Brown, T. Dewender, and T. Kobusch (eds), *Philosophical Debates at Paris in the Early Fourteenth Century* (Leiden: 2009), 127–49.

12. This theme has been explored especially by Ruedi Imbach. See his *Laien in der Philosophie des Mittelalters: Hinweise und Anregungen zu einem vernachlässigten Thema* (Amsterdam: 1989); *Dante, la philosophie et les laïcs* (Fribourg: 1996); *Le défi laïque: Existe-t-il une philosophie de laïcs au Moyen Âge?* (Paris: 2013).

Chapter 53

1. For detailed information, see P. Verdeyen, "La Procès d'inquisition contre Marguerite Porete et Guiard de Cressonessart (1309–1310)," *Revue d'Histoire Ecclésiastique* 81 (1986), 47–94. The inquisitorial documents are translated as an appendix in J. Maguire Robinson, *Nobility and Annihilation in Marguerite Porete's Mirror of Simple Souls* (Albany, NY: 2002).

2. R. E. Lerner, "New Light on *The Mirror of Simple Souls*," *Speculum* 85 (2010), 91–116, concludes that the version closest to what Marguerite wrote is actually the Middle English version and that the French version is to some extent "watered down" in its contents.

3. M. Lichtmann, "Marguerite Porete and Meister Eckhart: *The Mirror of Simple Souls* Mirrored," in B. McGinn (ed.), *Meister Eckhart and the Beguine Mystics* (New York: 1994), 65–86.

4. For instance E. Colledge, J. C. Marler, and J. Grant (trans.), *Marguerite Porette: The Mirror of Simple Souls* (Notre Dame, IN: 1999), 48; M. G. Sargent, "Marguerite Porete," in A. Minnis and R. Voaden (eds), *Medieval Holy Women in the Christian Tradition c.1100–c.1500* (Turnhout: 2010), 291–309, at 303.

5. J. Marin, "Annihilation and Deification in Beguine Theology and Marguerite Porete's *Mirror of Simple Souls*," *Harvard Theological Review* 103 (2010), 89–109, at 93–6.

6. Cited by chapter number; quotations from the translation in Colledge et al., *The Mirror of Simple Souls*. For another translation, see E. Babinski (trans.), *Marguerite Porete: The Mirror of Simple Souls* (New York: 1993).

7. For an exploration of this aspect, see A. Hollywood, *The Soul as Virgin Wife: Mechthild of Magdeburg, Marguerite Porete and Meister Eckhart* (Notre Dame, IN: 1995), ch.4.

8. Note the choice to mix prose and poetry in a single work, which has been used earlier by Boethius, Dhuoda, and the school of Chartres among others.

9. D. Kangas, "Dangerous Joy: Marguerite Porete's Good-Bye to the Virtues," *The Journal of Religion* 91 (2011), 299–319, at 307.

10. See *Philosophy in the Hellenistic and Roman Worlds*, ch.32.

11. Kangas, "Dangerous Joy," 308.

12. On this, see, e.g., Robinson, *Nobility and Annihilation*; Marin, "Annihilation and Deification;" M. G. Sargent, "The Annihilation of Marguerite Porete," *Viator* 28 (1997), 253–79; B. Newman, "Annihilation and Authorship: Three Women Mystics of the 1290s," *Speculum* 91 (2016), 591–630.

13. For the primacy she places on reason, see C. Van Dyke, "Mysticism," in R. Pasnau and C. Van Dyke (eds), *The Cambridge History of Medieval Philosophy* (Cambridge: 2010), 720–34.

Chapter 54

1. On this project and its context, see R. Imbach, *Dante, la philosophie et les laïcs* (Fribourg: 1996).

2. See C. S. Singleton, *Dante's Commedia: Elements of Structure* (Cambridge, MA: 1954) and J. Ferrante, "A Poetics of Chaos and Harmony," in R. Jacoff (ed.), *The Cambridge Companion to Dante* (Cambridge: 1993), 153–71.

3. English translation in C. Ryan (trans.), *Dante: The Banquet* (Saratoga: 1989). Cited in the main text by chapter and section number. On this work, see P. Dronke, *Dante's Second Love: The Originality and the Contexts of the Convivio* (Exeter: 1997), whose title I have shamelessly appropriated earlier in this paragraph.

4. There are many English translations of the *Comedy*; I quote below from the well-thumbed copy I used in college, which is A. Mandelbaum (trans.), *The Divine Comedy of Dante Alighieri*, 3 vols (Berkeley, CA: 1980–84). Cited by canto and line number.

5. For this interpretation, see, e.g., J. Freccero, "Casella's Song," in R. Jacoff (ed.), *Dante: The Poetics of Conversion* (Cambridge, MA: 1986), 186–94; for a contrary view, see, e.g., J. A. Scott, "Dante and Philosophy," *Annali d'Italianistica* 8 (1990), 258–77; J. Aleksander, "Dante's Understanding of the Two Ends of Human Desire and the Relationship between Philosophy and Theology," *Journal of Religion* 91 (2011), 158–87.

6. For this metaphor, see L. Bianchi, "*Noli Comedere Panem Philosophorum Inutiliter*: Dante Alighieri and John of Jandun on Philosophical 'Bread'," *Tijdschrift voor Filosofie* 75 (2013), 335–55.

7. This has been used to illustrate the background of Dante's project by J. A. Scott, "The Unfinished *Convivio* as a Pathway to the *Comedy*," *Dante Studies* 113 (1995), 31–56, at 52 n. 3. See also C. Greyson, "Latin and Vernacular in Dante's Thought," in *Centenary Essays on Dante* (Oxford: 1965), 54–76.

8. See G. C. Alessio, "A Few Remarks on the *Vulgare Illustre*," *Dante Studies* 113 (1995), 57–67. On the relation between the two works, see A. R. Ascoli, "The Unfinished Author: Dante's Rhetoric of Authority in *Convivio* and *De Vulgari Eloquentia*," in R. Jacoff (ed.), *The Cambridge Companion to Dante* (Cambridge: 1993), 45–66.

9. A theme explored by E. Gilson, *Dante and Philosophy*, trans. D. Moore (London: 1948), 99–112, followed by Aleksander, "Dante's Understanding," 164.

10. This point is made well by Bianchi, "*Noli comedere*," 353.

11. On this, see J. Marenbon, *Pagans and Philosophers: The Problem of Paganism from Augustine to Leibniz* (Princeton, NJ: 2015), ch.10. The problem is also mentioned in Dante's *On Monarchy*, §2.7.

12. The parallel is noted by Gilson, *Dante and Philosophy*, 263.

13. For discussion of this question, see, in addition to studies cited above, B. Nardi, "Dante e la filosofia," *Studi Danteschi* 25 (1940), 5–42; M. Corti, *Dante a un nuovo crocevia* (Florence: 1982) and *La felicità mentale* (Turin: 1983); G. B. Stone, "Dante's Averroistic Hermeneutics (On 'Meaning' in the *Vita Nuova*)," *Dante Studies* 112 (1994), 133–59; J. Marenbon, "Dante's Averroism," in J. Marenbon (ed.), *Poetry and Philosophy in the Middle Ages* (Leiden: 2001), 349–74.

14. As suggested by Corti, *Dante a un nuovo crocevia*. On him, see A. Gagliardi, *Guido Cavalcanti: Poesia e filosofia* (Alessandria: 2001); he is praised in the *Comedy* at *Purg.* 11.97–8.

15. Gilson, *Dante and Philosophy*, 257 and 275.

16. For what follows, see Marenbon, "Dante's Averroism."

17. Translation in H. W. Schneider, *Dante: On World-Government* (New York: 1957), cited by book and chapter number.

18. This resonance has been noted by J. Freccero, "*Paradiso X*: The Dance of the Stars," *Dante Studies* 86 (1968), 85–111, at 88.

19. On the latter, see J. Kleiner, "The Eclipses in the *Paradiso*," in *Stanford Italian Review* 9 (1990), 5–32; and on the Empyrean, see C. Moevs, *The Metaphysics of Dante's Divine Comedy* (Oxford: 2005), ch.1.

20. As emphasized by R. Hollander, "Dante's *Paradiso* as Philosophical Poetry," *Italica* 86 (2009), 571–82, at 574.

21. For a discussion of how these torments can be consistent with God's love and goodness, see E. Stump, "Dante's Hell, Aquinas's Moral Theory, and the Love of God," *Canadian Journal of Philosophy* 16 (1986), 181–98.

Chapter 55

1. For the following passages, see the introduction to R. W. Dyson (trans.), *Giles of Rome's On Ecclesiastical Power: A Medieval Theory of World Government* (New York: 2004), ix and xi.
2. See J. A. Watt (trans.), *John of Paris: On Royal and Papal Power* (Toronto: 1971). On him, see G. Heiman, "John of Paris and the Theory of the Two Swords," *Classica et Mediaevalia* 32 (1980), 324–47; J. Coleman, "Medieval Discussions of Property: Ratio and Dominium according to John of Paris and Marsilius of Padua," *History of Political Thought* 4 (1983), 209–28; J. Coleman, "Dominium in Thirteenth- and Fourteenth-Century Political Thought and its Seventeenth-Century Heirs: John of Paris and Locke," *Political Studies* 33 (1985), 73–100.
3. On the question of property, John is even more plausibly taken to be on the secularist side of the debate, since he denies that the Church as such can possess property at all, instead holding certain temporal goods on behalf of all Christians.
4. Cited by section number from Dyson, *Giles of Rome's On Ecclesiastical Power*. Some of what follows summarizes the argument of P. Adamson, "*Interroga Virtutes Naturales*: Nature in Giles of Rome's *On Ecclesiastical Power*," *Vivarium* 57 (2019), 1–31.
5. On its reception, see C. F. Briggs, *Giles of Rome's De Regimine Principum: Reading and Writing Politics at Court and University, c. 1275–c.1525* (Cambridge: 1999).
6. See R. Lambertini, "The Prince in the Mirror of Philosophy: About the Use of Aristotle in Giles of Rome's *De regimine principum*," in B. C. Bazán, E. Andújar, and L. G. Sbrocchi (eds), *Moral and Political Philosophies in the Middle Ages* (New York: 1995), 1522–34.
7. For the following, see G. McAleer, "Giles of Rome on Political Authority," *Journal of the History of Ideas* 60 (1999), 21–36.
8. Cited by section number from H. W. Schneider, *Dante: On World-Government* (New York: 1957). For studies, see A. P. d'Entrèves, *Dante as a Political Thinker* (Oxford: 1952); U. Limentani, "Dante's Political Thought," in U. Limentani (ed.), *The Mind of Dante* (Cambridge: 1965), 113–37; J. M. Ferrante, *The Political Vision of the Divine Comedy* (Princeton, NJ: 1984).
9. H. L. Stewart, "Dante and the Schoolmen," *Journal of the History of Ideas* 10 (1949), 357–73, at 368.
10. See further C. T. Davis, *Dante and the Idea of Rome* (Oxford: 1957).
11. D'Entrèves, *Dante as a Political Thinker*, a reading rejected by C. T. Davis, "Dante and the Empire," in R. Jacoff (ed.), *The Cambridge Companion to Dante* (Cambridge: 1993), 67–79. A "non-theological" reading of *On Monarchy* can also be found in A. C. Mastrobuono, *Essays on Dante's Philosophy of History* (Florence: 1979), 38, which complains that Dante here deduces the need for imperial power on solely rational grounds, which is inconsistent with the contingency of divine will and its providential support for any given political arrangement.
12. Ferrante, *Political Vision*, 89, makes the nice point that this image is echoed by the sight of Lucifer's legs seen upside down at the end of *Inferno*.

Chapter 56

1. See *Philosophy in the Islamic World*, ch.10.
2. Cited by book, chapter, and section numbers, which are given in both of the following English translations: A. Gewirth (trans.), *Marsilius of Padua: The Defender of the Peace* (New York: 1956), A. Brett (trans.), *Marsilius of Padua: The Defender of the Peace* (Cambridge: 2006).

3. For his life, see F. Godthardt, "The Philosopher as Political Actor—Marsilius of Padua at the Court of Ludwig the Bavarian: The Sources Revisited," in G. Moreno-Riaño (ed.), *The World of Marsilius of Padua* (Turnhout: 2006), 29–46; and by the same author "The Life of Marsilius of Padua," in G. Moreno-Riaño and C. J. Nederman (eds), *A Companion to Marsilius of Padua* (Leiden: 2012), 13–55.

4. The dramatic flight is typically assumed by scholars but doubted by Godthardt, "The Life of Marsilius," 23–7, which argues that the *Defensor pacis* did not come to the attention of church authorities until after John and Marsilius were already at Ludwig's court. Incidentally, John is a figure who would really deserve more coverage than I am giving him. He is often seen as a representative of "Averroism" and commented extensively on Aristotle. See, for example, on his reception of Averroes' theory of intellect, J.-B. Brenet, *Transferts du sujet: La noétique d'Averroès selon Jean de Jandun* (Paris: 2003).

5. On Marsilius' use of this "organic" metaphor, see B. Koch, "Marsilius of Padua on Church and State," in Moreno-Riaño and Nederman (eds), *Companion to Marsilius*, 139–79, at 151–2.

6. W. Ullmann, *Principles of Government and Politics in the Middle Ages* (London: 1966), 269–79.

7. C. J. Nederman, "Community and Self-Interest: Marsiglio of Padua on Civil Life and Private Advantage," *Review of Politics* 65 (2003), 395–416.

8. On this topic, see, e.g., B. Tierney, "Marsilius on Rights," *Journal of the History of Ideas* 52 (1991), 3–17; A. Brett, *Liberty, Right and Nature: Individual Rights in Later Scholastic Thought* (Cambridge: 1997); A. Brett, "Politics, Right(s) and Human Freedom in Marsilius of Padua," in B. Mäkinen and P. Korkman (eds), *Transformations in Medieval and Early-Modern Rights Discourse* (Dordrecht: 2006), 95–116; A. Lee, "Roman Law and Human Liberty: Marsilius of Padua on Property Rights," *Journal of the History of Ideas* 70 (2009), 23–44; J. Coleman, "Medieval Discussions of Poverty: *Ratio* and *Dominium* according to John of Paris and Marsilius of Padua," *History of Political Thought* 4 (1983), 209–28.

9. The positivist reading of Marsilius is set out in A. Gewirth, *Marsilius of Padua and Medieval Political Philosophy* (New York: 1951); see further E. Lewis, "The 'Positivism' of Marsiglio of Padua," *Speculum* 38 (1963), 541–82.

10. Tierney, "Marsilius on Rights," 9. See further H. Hamilton-Bleakley, "Marsilius of Padua's Conception of Natural Law Revisited," in Moreno-Riaño, *The World of Marsilius*, 125–42.

11. C. J. Nederman, "Nature, Justice and Duty in the *Defensor Pacis*: Marsiglio of Padua's Ciceronian Impulse," *Political Theory* 18 (1990), 615–37, at 639–40; G. Moreno-Riaño and C. J. Nederman, "Marsilius of Padua's Principles of Secular Politics," in Moreno-Riaño and Nederman (eds), *Companion to Marsilius*, 117–38.

12. Lee, "Roman Law and Human Liberty," 38.

13. Tierney, "Marsilius on Rights," 16.

14. For what follows, see C. J. Nederman, "Property and Protest: Political Theory and Subjective Rights in Fourteenth-Century England," *Review of Politics* 58 (1996), 323–44.

Chapter 57

1. For good surveys of Ockham's life and the political contexts of his work, see W. J. Courtenay, *Ockham and Ockhamism: Studies in the Dissemination and Impact of his Thought* (Leiden: 2008), ch.6; and A. S. McGrade, *The Political Thought of William of Ockham* (Cambridge: 1974), 4–28.

2. For details, see D. Burr, "Ockham, Scotus, and the Censure at Avignon," *Church History* 37 (1968), 144–59; see also C. J. Chambers, "William of Ockham, Theologian: Convicted for Lack of Evidence," *Journal of the History of Philosophy* 7 (1969), 381–9.

3. See D. Clark, "William of Ockham on Right Reason," *Speculum* 48 (1973), 13–36, at 30.
4. On this topic, see Clark, "William of Ockham on Right Reason"; P. King, "Ockham's Ethical Theory" and M. McCord Adams, "Ockham on Will, Nature and Morality," both in P. V. Spade (ed.), *The Cambridge Companion to Ockham* (Cambridge: 1999), 227–44 and 245–72.
5. See, e.g., R. Wood, *Ockham on the Virtues* (West Lafayette, IN: 1997), 121.
6. King, "Ockham's Ethical Theory," 233–4.
7. For the following examples, see P. Boehner (ed. and trans.) and S. F. Brown (rev.), *Ockham: Philosophical Writings* (Indianapolis, IN: 1990), 144–7.
8. Here I follow the line taken by T. M. Osborne, "Ockham as a Divine-Command Theorist," *Religious Studies* 41 (2005), 2–11.
9. Clark, "William of Ockham on Right Reason," 35; King, "Ockham's Moral Theory," 239. Osborne, "Ockham as a Divine-Command Theorist," rejects this interpretation.
10. See, e.g., A. J. Freddoso and F. E. Kelley, *William of Ockham: Quodlibetal Questions* (New Haven, CT: 1991), 213–14.
11. McGrade, *The Political Thought of William of Ockham*, 189.
12. On Ockham's political ideas the most important publication remains McGrade's *The Political Thought of William of Ockham*. But see also P. Boehner, "Ockham's Political Ideas," *Review of Politics* 5 (1943), 462–87; C. C. Bayley, "Pivotal Concepts in the Political Philosophy of William of Ockham," *Journal of the History of Ideas* 10 (1949), 199–218; A. S. McGrade, "Ockham and the Birth of Individual Rights," in B. Tierney and P. Lineham (eds), *Authority and Power: Studies on Medieval Law and Government* (Cambridge: 1980), 149–65; J. Kilcullen, "The Political Writings," in *The Cambridge Companion to Ockham*, 302–25.
13. For what follows, see B. Tierney, "Ockham, the Conciliar Theory and the Canonists," *Journal of the History of Ideas* 15 (1954), 40–70.
14. McGrade, *The Political Thought of William of Ockham*, 57.
15. Quoted from McGrade, *The Political Thought of William of Ockham*, 71.
16. Boehner, "Ockham's Political Ideas," 479.

Chapter 58

1. I steal this joke from Tim Noone.
2. For this and some other formulations, see P. V. Spade, "Ockham's Nominalist Metaphysics: Some Main Themes," in P. V. Spade (ed.), *The Cambridge Companion to Ockham* (Cambridge: 1999), 100–17, at 101. See also P. V. Spade, "Three Versions of Ockham's Reductionist Program," *Franciscan Studies* 35 (1975), 223–36.
3. R. Wood, *Ockham on the Virtues* (West Lafayette, IN: 1997), 20. Similarly, Ockham's intellectual rival William Chatton endorses the rule. See, for instance, K. Tachau, *Vision and Certitude in the Age of Ockham* (Leiden: 1988), 183.
4. Cited by section number throughout this chapter and Chapter 59. For translations of the first two parts of the *Summa*, see M. J. Loux, *Ockham's Theory of Terms: Part I of the Summa Logicae* (Notre Dame, IN: 1974); A. J. Freddoso and H. Schuurman (trans.), *Ockham's Theory of Propositions: Part II of the Summa Logicae* (Notre Dame, IN: 1980). The agenda of the *Summa* is well surveyed in P. King, "William of Ockham: Summa Logicae," in J. Shand (ed.), *Central Works of Philosophy. Vol. 1: Ancient and Medieval* (Aldershot: 2005), 242–69. For the reductive program, see G. Klima, "Ockham's Semantics and Ontology of the Categories," in Spade, *Cambridge Companion*, 118–42.

5. See P. V. Spade, "Ockham's Distinctions between Absolute and Connotative Terms," *Vivarium* 13 (1975), 55–76. For a critical response to Spade's influential analysis, see A. Goodu, "Connotative Concepts and Mathematics in Ockham's Natural Philosophy," *Vivarium* 31 (1993), 106–39.

6. For discussion of this, see G. Klima, "The Nominalist Semantics of Ockham and Buridan: A 'Rational Reconstruction'," in D. M. Gabbay and J. Woods (eds), *Handbook of the History of Logic. Vol. 2: Mediaeval and Renaissance Logic* (Amsterdam: 2008), 389–431, at 406.

7. Quoted from his commentary on *On Interpretation* by M. McCord Adams, "Ockham's Nominalism and Unreal Entities," *Philosophical Review* 86 (1977), 144–76, at 144.

8. See on this T. K. Scott, "Ockham on Evidence, Necessity and Intuition," *Journal of the History of Philosophy* 7 (1969), 27–49; M. McCord Adams, "Intuitive Cognition, Certainty and Skepticism in William of Ockham," *Traditio* 26 (1970), 389–98; J. Boler, "Ockham on Intuitive Cognition," *Journal of the History of Philosophy* 11 (1973), 95–106; E. Karger, "Ockham's Misunderstood Theory of Intuitive and Abstractive Cognition," in Spade, *Cambridge Companion*, 204–26; C. Panaccio, *Ockham on Concepts* (Aldershot: 2004), ch.1.

9. A. S. McGrade "Plenty of Nothing: Ockham's Commitment to Real Possibles," *Franciscan Studies* 45 (1985), 146–56, at 147.

10. E. Stump, "The Mechanisms of Cognition: Ockham on Mediating Species," in Spade, *Cambridge Companion*, 168–203, at 180.

11. See D. Perler, "Things in the Mind: Fourteenth-Century Controversies over 'Intelligible Species'," *Vivarium* 34 (1996), 231–53.

12. These cases are discussed by M. McCord Adams, "Ockham's Nominalism and Unreal Entities," *Philosophical Review* 86 (1977), 144–76; McGrade, "Plenty of Nothing"; K. H. Tachau, *Vision and Certitude in the Age of Ockham* (Leiden: 1988), ch.5; S. Brower-Toland, "Intuition, Externalism, and Direct Reference in Ockham," *History of Philosophy Quarterly* 24 (2007), 317–36.

13. As first established by P. Boehner, *Collected Articles on Ockham*, ed. E. Buytaert (Saint Bonaventure, NY: 1958). Further discussion in S. Read, "The Objective Being of Ockham's Ficta," *Philosophical Quarterly* 27 (1977), 14–31; R. Pasnau, *Theories of Cognition in the Later Middle Ages* (Cambridge: 1997), ch.8, part 3; Panaccio, *Ockham on Concepts*, ch.2.

14. For this connection, see Read, "Objective Being," 20.

15. For his debates with Chatton, see F. Kelley, "Walter Chatton vs Aureoli and Ockham regarding the Universal Concept," *Franciscan Studies* 41 (1981), 222–49; A. Maurer, "Ockham's Razor and Chatton's Anti-Razor," *Mediaeval Studies*, 46 (1984), 463–75; S. Brower-Toland, "How Chatton Changed Ockham's Mind: William Ockham and Walter Chatton on Objects and Acts of Judgment," in G. Klima (ed.), *Intentionality, Cognition and Mental Representation in Medieval Philosophy* (Fordham, NY: 2014), 204–34.

Chapter 59

1. This has generated a large secondary literature. For good overviews, see C. Normore, "Ockham on Mental Language," in J. C. Smith (ed.), *Historical Foundations of Cognitive Science* (Dordrecht: 1990), 53–70; C. Panaccio, "Semantics and Mental Language," in P. V. Spade (ed.), *The Cambridge Companion to Ockham* (Cambridge: 1999), 53–75; C. Panaccio, *Mental Language: From Plato to Ockham*, trans. J. P. Hochschild and M. K. Ziebart (New York: 2017).

2. P. V. Spade, "Synonymy and Equivocation in Ockham's Mental Language," *Journal of the History of Philosophy* 18 (1980), 9–22, at 10, refers to this as "Ockham's Criterion."

3. For what follows, see E. W. Hagedorn, "Ockham's *Scientia* Argument for Mental Language," *Oxford Studies in Medieval Philosophy* 3 (2015), 145–68.

4. S. Brower-Toland, "How Chatton Changed Ockham's Mind: William Ockham and Walter Chatton on Objects and Acts of Judgment," in G. Klima (ed.), *Intentionality, Cognition and Mental Representation in Medieval Philosophy* (Fordham, NY: 2014), 204–34.

5. For discussion of this issue, see P. V. Spade, "Synonymy and Equivocation in Ockham's Mental Language," *Journal of the History of Philosophy* 18 (1980), 9–22; D. Chalmers, "Is There Synonymy in Ockham's Mental Language?" in Spade, *Cambridge Companion*, 76–99.

6. See *Quodlibet* §5.8, quoted by Chalmers, "Synonymy," 86.

7. See D. J. Brown, "The Puzzle of Names in Ockham's Theory of Mental Language," *Review of Metaphysics* 50 (1996), 79–99.

8. Spade, "Synonymy and Equivocation," 17.

9. See C. Panaccio, "Connotative Terms in Ockham's Mental Language," *Cahiers d'Épistémologie* no. 9016 (Montreal: 1990); the problem is also dealt with in Panaccio, "Semantics and Mental Language," 57–8, and in Panaccio, *Mental Language*, ch.9.

10. Normore, "Ockham on Mental Language," 59.

11. M. Lenz, "Why is Thought Linguistic? Ockham's Two Conceptions of the Intellect," *Vivarium* 46 (2008), 302–17. William Chatton also insisted that we learn syncategorematic terms in this way. See H. Gelber, "I Cannot Tell a Lie: Hugh of Lawton's Critique of William of Ockham on Mental Language," *Franciscan Studies* 41 (1984), 141–79, at 152.

12. Spade, "Synonymy and Equivocation," 22.

13. This is the conclusion of C. Panaccio, "From Mental Word to Mental Language," *Philosophical Topics* 20 (1992), 125–47.

Chapter 60

1. W. Courtenay, *Adam Wodeham: An Introduction to his Life and Writings* (Leiden: 1978) surveys the lives and works of numerous figures in this period, as does F. Hoffmann, *Ockham-Rezeption und Ockham-Kritik im Jahrzehnt nach Wilhelm von Ockham in Oxford 1322–1332* (Münster: 1998).

2. Courtenay, *Adam Wodeham*, 62, and 162–3 for his studies with Ockham and Chatton.

3. Surveyed in great detail by K. Tachau, *Vision and Certitude in the Age of Ockham* (Leiden: 1988).

4. P. Boehner, "*Notitia Intuitiva* of Non Existents according to Peter Aureoli, O.F.M. (1322)," *Franciscan Studies* 8 (1948), 388–416; L. Lička, "Perception and Objective Being: Peter Auriol on Perceptual Acts and their Objects," *American Catholic Philosophical Quarterly* 90 (2016), 49–76.

5. Tachau, *Vision and Certitude*, 188, and 192 for the following response to Aureol.

6. Tachau, *Vision and Certitude*, 301.

7. For his biography, see J. Ottman and R. Wood, "Walter of Burley: His Life and Works," *Vivarium* 37 (1999), 1–23; M. Vittorini, "Life and Works," in A. D. Conti (ed.), *A Companion to Walter Burley, Late Medieval Logician and Metaphysician* (Leiden: 2013), 17–45. For critical reactions to Ockham by two lesser-known figures, see L. Cesalli, "Pseudo-Richard of Campsall and Richard Brinkley on Universals," in F. Amerini and L. Cesalli (eds), *Universals in the Fourteenth Century* (Pisa: 2016), 225–40. Cesalli also presents their views in his contribution to C. Rode and F. Amerini (eds), *A Companion to the Responses to Ockham* (Leiden: 2016).

8. A somewhat different view is found in the treatise *On Matter and Form* ascribed to Burley, which speaks of the universal existing in things in only a "habitual" way, in other words as needing to be made fully actual by abstractive cognition. On this and on the difference between the early and later Burley, see H. Shapiro, "A Note on Walter Burley's Exaggerated Realism," *Franciscan Studies* 20 (1960), 205–14; and E. Karger, "Walter Burley's Realism," *Vivarium* 37 (1999), 24–40.

9. For this way of framing his response, see A. D. Conti, "Ontology in Walter Burley's Last Commentary on the *Ars Vetus*," *Franciscan Studies* 31 (1971), 121–76, at 141; C. Dutilh Novaes, "The Ockham-Burley Dispute," in *A Companion to Walter Burley*, 49–84, at 60.

10. Ottman and Wood, "Walter of Burley," 13–14.

11. My translation from the Latin quoted at Conti, "Ontology," 143.

12. I have consulted the translation by P. V. Spade in his *History of the Problem of Universals in the Middle Ages: Notes and Texts*, which is freely available as an online text at www.pvspade.com/Logic/docs/univers.pdf, accessed 6 February 2019.

13. For these examples, see H.-U. Wöhler, "Universals and Individuals," in *A Companion to Walter Burley*, 167–89, at 176.

14. P. V. Spade, "Some Epistemological Implications of the Burley-Ockham Dispute," *Franciscan Studies* 35 (1975), 212–22, at 217.

15. E. D. Sylla, "Walter Burley's Practice as a Commentator on Aristotle's *Physics*," *Medioevo* 27 (2002), 301–71, at 324.

16. See A. D. Conti, "Ockham and Burley on Categories and Universals: A Comparison," *The Modern Schoolman* 86 (2008–9), 181–210; and by the same author, "Burley's Theories of Categories," in *A Companion to Walter Burley*, 191–222.

17. Conti, "Ontology," 126.

18. See R. Wood, "Willing Wickedly: Ockham and Burley Compared," *Vivarium* 37 (1999), 72–93. For the topic in general, see R. Saarinen, *Weakness of the Will in Medieval Thought: From Augustine to Buridan* (Leiden: 1994); J. Müller, *Willensschwäche in Antike und Mittelalter* (Leuven: 2009).

Chapter 61

1. *Classical Philosophy*, ch.30.

2. See the section translated as an appendix in M. McCord Adams and N. Kretzmann, trans., *William of Ockham: Predestination, God's Foreknowledge, and Future Contingents* (Indianapolis, IN: 1983), at 105.

3. M. H. Henninger, "Henry of Harclay's Questions on Divine Prescience and Predestination," *Franciscan Studies* 40 (1980), 167–243; and for more on the critique of Aquinas in this period, see J. Hause, "Thomas Aquinas and the Voluntarists," *Medieval Philosophy and Theology* 6 (1997), 167–82.

4. On this, see W. L. Craig, "John Duns Scotus on God's Foreknowledge and Future Contingents," *Franciscan Studies* 47 (1987), 98–122.

5. C. Normore, "Peter Aureoli and his Contemporaries on Future Contingents and Excluded Middle," *Synthese* 96 (1993), 83–92, at 84.

6. For Campsall, see Normore, "Peter Aureoli and his Contemporaries," 88; for Strelley, see H. G. Gelber, *It Could Have Been Otherwise: Contingency and Necessity in Dominican Theology at Oxford, 1300–1350* (Leiden: 2004), 236.

7. Cited by section number from the translation in Adams and Kretzmann, *William of Ockham: Predestination*.

8. For Scotus' similar solution, see Gelber, *It Could Have Been Otherwise*, 153–7.

9. See Craig, "John Duns Scotus on God's Foreknowledge," 113; Henninger, "Henry of Harclay's Questions," 186.

10. On this, see *Philosophy in the Hellenistic and Roman Worlds*, ch.49.

11. G. Leff, *Bradwardine and the Pelagians* (Cambridge: 1957), 165–87. On him, see further I. Iribarren, *Durandus of Pourcain: A Dominican Theologian in the Shadow of Aquinas* (Oxford: 2005).

12. Leff, *Bradwardine and the Pelagians*, 52 n.1.

13. Leff, *Bradwardine and the Pelagians*, 94.

Chapter 62

1. This point is well made by C. Dutilh Novaes, *Formalizing Medieval Logic: Supposition, Consequentia and Obligations* (Berlin: 2007), 17, arguing against attempts to see supposition theory as an account of reference.

2. See W. J. Courtenay, "Force of Words and Figures of Speech: The Crisis over *Virtus Sermonis* in the Fourteenth Century," *Franciscan Studies* 44 (1984), 107–28.

3. J. Pinborg, "The English Contribution to Logic Before Ockham," *Synthese* 40 (1979), 19–42, at 37; N. Kretzmann, "Medieval Logicians on the Meaning of the *Propositio*," *Journal of Philosophy* 67 (1970), 767–87, at 771.

4. On which, see N. Kretzmann, "*Sensus Compositus, Sensus Divisus*, and Propositional Attitudes," *Medioevo* 7 (1981), 195–229, with the following examples at 203.

5. See also L. Cesalli, "Le Réalisme propositionnel de Walter Burley," *Archives D'histoire Doctrinale et Littéraire du Moyen Âge* 68 (2001), 155–221; S. Meier-Oeser, "Walter Burley's *Propositio in Re* and the Systematization of the *Ordo Significationis*," in S. Brown, T. Dewender, and T. Kobusch (eds), *Philosophical Debates at Paris in the Early Fourteenth Century* (Leiden: 2009), 483–504.

6. J. Zupko, "How it Played in the *Rue de Fouarre*: The Reception of Adam Wodeham's Theory of the *Complexe Significabile* in the Arts Faculty at Paris in the Mid-Fourteenth Century," *Franciscan Studies* 54 (1994), 211–25. See also G. Gál, "Adam of Wodeham's Question on the *Complexe Significabile* as the Immediate Object of Scientific Knowledge," *Franciscan Studies* 37 (1977), 66–102.

7. See W. J. Courtenay, "John of Mirecourt and Gregory of Rimini on Whether God Can Undo the Past," *Recherches de Théologie Ancienne et Médiévale* 39 (1972), 224–56; 40 (1973), 147–74.

8. Kretzmann, "Medieval Logicians on the Meaning of the *Propositio*," 779.

9. For this, see R. Friedman, "On the Trail of a Philosophical Debate: Durandus of St-Pourçain vs. Thomas Wylton on Simultaneous Acts in the Intellect," in S. Brown et al. (eds), *Philosophical Debates at Paris in the Early Fourteenth Century*, 433–61; R. Friedman, "Mental Propositions before Mental Language," in J. Biard (ed.), *Le Language mental du Moyen Âge a l'Âge classique* (Louvain: 2009), 95–115.

10. Quoted at Dutilh Novaes, *Formalizing Medieval Logic*, 84.

11. See, e.g., E. J. Ashworth and P. V. Spade, "Logic in Late Medieval Oxford," in J. I. Catto and R. Evans (eds), *The History of the University of Oxford. Vol. 2: Late Medieval Oxford* (Oxford: 1992), 35–64, at 38; S. Read, "Inferences" in R. Pasnau (ed.), *The Cambridge History of Medieval Philosophy*, 2 vols (Cambridge: 2010), vol.1, 173–84, at 78.

12. C. Dutilh Novaes, "Logic in the 14th Century after Ockham," in D. Gabbay and J. Woods (eds), *The Handbook of the History of Logic* (Amsterdam 2008), vol.2, 433–504, at 474.

13. See P. V. Spade, *Lies, Language and Logic in the Late Middle Ages* (London: 1988), item IV; S. Read, "Paradoxes of Signification," *Vivarium* 54 (2016), 335–55, at 337.

14. The literature on this is rather vast. A good recent starting point is C. Dutilh Novaes and S. Uckelman, "*Obligationes*," in C. Dutilh Novaes and S. Read (eds), *Cambridge Companion to Medieval Logic* (Cambridge: 2016), 370–95. For an intimidatingly long footnote itemizing earlier work on obligations, see H. G. Gelber, *It Could Have Been Otherwise: Contingency and Necessity in Dominican Theology at Oxford, 1300–1350* (Leiden: 2004), 139 n.90.

15. M. Yrjönsuuri, "Obligations and Conditionals," *Vivarium* 53 (2015), 322–35, at 323.

16. So argues Spade, *Lies, Language and Logic*, item XVII, 2.

17. Here I follow S. Read, "Richard Kilvington and the Theory of Obligations," *Vivarium* 53 (2015), 391–404.

Chapter 63

1. For introductory overviews, see E. D. Sylla, "The Oxford Calculators," in N. Kretzmann, A. Kenny, and J. Pinborg (eds), *The Cambridge History of Later Medieval Philosophy* (Cambridge: 1982), 540–63; and W. R. Laird, "Change and Motion," in D. C. Lindberg and M. H. Shank (eds), *The Cambridge History of Science. Vol. 2: Medieval Science* (Cambridge: 2013), 404–35. The key studies of the Calculators are A. Maier, *Studien zur Naturphilosophie der Spätscholastik*, 5 vols (Rome: 1949–68); and E. D. Sylla, *The Oxford Calculators and the Mathematics of Motion* (New York: 1991).

2. In his *Insolubilia*, at ms Erfurt Amploniana Quarto 277, folio 3vb. I owe the reference to Stephen Read.

3. Sylla, *The Oxford Calculators*, 159–60.

4. For the problem and the following solutions, see S. J. Livesey, "The Oxford Calculatores, Quantification of Qualities, and Aristotle's Prohibition of *Metabasis*," *Vivarium* 24 (1986), 50–69; S. J. Livesey, "Science and Theology in the Fourteenth Century: The Subalternate Sciences in Oxford Commentaries on the *Sentences*," *Synthese* 83 (1990), 273–92.

5. See E. D. Sylla, "The Oxford Calculators' Middle Degree Theorem in Context," *Early Science and Medicine* 15 (2010), 338–70, at 364.

6. As pointed out by Maier, *Studien zur Naturphilosophie*, vol.1, 115.

7. Discussed by N. Kretzmann, "Socrates is Whiter than Plato Begins to Be White," *Nous* 11 (1977), 3–15.

8. Discussed by Sylla, "The Oxford Calculators' Middle Degree Theorem," 347–9.

9. For this concept, see Maier, *Studien zur Naturphilosophie*, vol.1, 118.

10. Sylla, *The Oxford Calculators*, 57, 73.

11. This connection is by proposed by Sylla, *The Oxford Calculators*, 116, 224–40, and 329–32. For a discussion of how such degrees could be combined mathematically, see al-Kindī's treatment of compound drugs, explained in P. Adamson, *al-Kindī* (New York: 2007), 161–6.

12. See further E. D. Sylla, "Medieval Quantifications of Qualities: The 'Merton School'," *Archive for History of Exact Sciences* 8 (1971), 9–39; E. D. Sylla, "Medieval Concepts of the Latitude of Forms: The Oxford Calculators," *Archives d'Histoire Doctrinale et Littéraire du Moyen Âge* 40 (1973), 223–83.

13. For Philoponus, see *Philosophy in the Hellenistic and Roman Worlds*, ch.38; for the others, see *Philosophy in the Islamic World* chs.24, 42.

14. See, e.g., R. Wood, "Walter Burley on Motion in a Vacuum," *Traditio* 45 (1989–90), 191–217; and for the broader history E. Grant, *Much Ado About Nothing: Theories of Space and Vacuum from the Middle Ages to the Scientific Revolution* (Cambridge: 1981), including a lengthy discussion of Bradwardine on void.

15. Maier, *Studien zur Naturphilosophie*, vol.1, 101–4.
16. As mentioned by Sylla, "The Oxford Calculators' Middle Degree Theorem," 362.

Chapter 64

1. See the overview in J. North, "Astronomy and Astrology," in D. C. Lindberg and M. J. Shank (eds), *The Cambridge History of Science. Vol. 2: Medieval Science* (Cambridge: 2013), 456–84.
2. For the full etymology, see *Philosophy in the Hellenistic and Roman Worlds*, 196–7.
3. See S. M. Babbitt, *Oresme's Livre de politiques and the France of Charles V* (Philadelphia, PA: 1985).
4. As noted by North, "Astronomy and Astrology," 471. I mention similar tendencies towards "instrumentalism" in *Philosophy in the Islamic World*, at 247.
5. E. Grant, *Physical Science in the Middle Ages* (New York: 1971), 66–7. See also S. Carotti, "Oresme on Motion (*Quaestiones super Physicam*, III, 2–7)," *Vivarium* 31 (1993), 8–36, at 30–1.
6. Here I follow M. Thakkar, "Francis of Marchia on the Heavens," *Vivarium* 44 (2006), 21–40.
7. J. Koch (ed.) and J. O. Riedl (trans.), *Giles of Rome: Errores Philosophorum* (Milwaukee, WI: 1944). The ascription to Giles of Rome is now considered doubtful.
8. See G. Leff, *Bradwardine and the Pelagians* (Cambridge: 1957), 88 and 93.
9. For magnetism, see E. Grant, "Medieval and Renaissance Scholastic Conceptions of the Influence of the Celestial Region on the Terrestrial," *Journal of Medieval and Renaissance Studies* 17 (1987), 1–23, at 9; for the denial of void, see R. W. Dyson (trans.), *Giles of Rome's On Ecclesiastical Power: A Medieval Theory of World Government* (New York: 2004), 337.
10. For the following, see Grant, "Medieval and Renaissance Scholastic Conceptions," 16–20.
11. R. Cross, *The Physics of Duns Scotus: The Scientific Context of a Theological Vision* (Oxford: 1998), 141.
12. J. E. Murdoch, "William of Ockham on the Logic of Infinity and Continuity," in N. Kretzmann (ed.), *Infinity and Continuity in Antiquity and Medieval Thought* (Ithaca, NY: 1982), 165–206, at 184–6.
13. A. Goddu, *The Physics of William of Ockham* (Leiden: 1984), 164–76.
14. Cross, *The Physics of Duns Scotus*, 166–9.
15. J. Murdoch and E. Synan, "Two Questions on the Continuum: Walter Chatton (?), O.F.M. and Adam Wodeham, O.F.M." *Franciscan Studies* 26 (1966), 212–88.
16. Buridan also denies this: see J. M. Thijssen, "Buridan on Mathematics," *Vivarium* 23 (1985), 55–78, at 67.
17. For a debate on Ockham's exact view, see Murdoch, "William of Ockham on the Logic of Infinity and Continuity," 175; and E. Stump, "Theology and Physics in *De Sacramento Altaris*: Ockham's Theory of Indivisibles," in Kretzmann, *Infinity and Continuity*, 207–30, at 217.
18. J. Zupko, "Nominalism Meets Individualism," *Medieval Philosophy and Theology* 3 (1993), 158–85.
19. Or even earlier precursors, as discussed in C. Schabel, "Francis of Marchia's *Virtus Derelicta* and the Context of its Development," *Vivarium* 44 (2006), 41–80. See also F. Zanin, "Francis of Marchia, *Virtus derelicta*, and Modifications of the Basic Principles of Aristotelian Physics," *Vivarium* 44 (2006), 81–95; and the fundamental study by A. Maier, *Studien zur Naturphilosophie der Spätscholastik*, 5 vols (Rome: 1949–68), vol.2: chs. 5, 6, and 7 on Marchia, Buridan, and Oresme respectively. An English translation of other work by Maier on impetus can be found in A. Maier, *On the Threshold of Exact Science: Selected Writings of Anneliese Maier on Late Medieval Natural Philosophy*, ed. and trans. S. D. Sargent (Philadelphia, PA: 1982). For translations of some of the primary texts, see E. Grant, *A Source Book in Medieval Science* (Cambridge, MA: 1974).
20. Maier, *Studien zur Naturphilosophie*, vol.2, 195.
21. Schabel, "Francis of Marchia's *Virtus derelicta*," 53.

22. For this, see Zanin, "Francis of Marchia," 95.
23. The contrast between this fact and the officially sensation-based method of Aristotelian science has been expressed by Edward Grant in the slogan "empiricism without observation." See the piece of that title reprinted in E. Grant, *The Nature of Natural Philosophy in the Late Middle Ages* (Washington DC: 2010).
24. See *Philosophy in the Islamic World*, ch.19.

Chapter 65

1. As noted by G. Klima, *John Buridan* (New York: 2008), 5 (Buridan was a "medieval analytic philosopher").
2. For this caveat, see W. J. Courtenay, "The University of Paris at the Time of Jean Buridan and Nicole Oresme," *Vivarium* 42 (2004), 3–17, at 16.
3. See the text quoted at J. Zupko, *John Buridan: Portrait of a Fourteenth-Century Arts Master* (Notre Dame, IN: 2003), 143.
4. G. Klima (trans.), *John Buridan: Summulae de Dialectica* (New Haven, CT: 2001).
5. For this contrast, see Klima, *John Buridan*, 13; Zupko, *John Buridan*, 29.
6. Zupko, *John Buridan*, 41. See also J. Biard, *Science et nature: La théorie buridanienne du savoir* (Paris: 2012), 99.
7. Klima, *John Buridan*, 16.
8. As pointed out by Zupko, *John Buridan*, 95.
9. For what follows, see P. King, "Buridan's Theory of Individuation," in J. E. Gracia (ed.), *Individuation and Scholasticism* (Albany, NY: 1994), 397–430; P. King, "John Buridan's Solution to the Problem of Universals," in J. M. M. H. Thijssen and J. Zupko (eds), *The Metaphysics and Natural Philosophy of John Buridan* (Leiden: 2001), 1–27, from which I take the following quote.
10. For this example, see J. Zupko, "Universal Thinking as Process: The Metaphysics of Change and Identity in John Buridan's *intellectio* Theory," in C. Bolyard and R. Keele (eds), *Later Medieval Metaphysics: Ontology, Language, and Logic* (New York: 2013), 137–60.
11. Klima, *John Buridan*, 260. See also P. King, "Jean Buridan's Philosophy of Science," *Studies in History and Philosophy of Science* 18 (1987), 109–32, which discusses the notion of ampliation.
12. For discussion, see *Philosophy in the Islamic World*, ch.21.
13. On this topic, see E. J. Monahan, "Human Liberty and Free Will according to John Buridan," *Mediaeval Studies* 16 (1954), 72–86; J. J. Walsh, "Is Buridan a Sceptic about Free Will?" *Vivarium* 2 (1964), 50–61; J. Zupko, "Freedom of Choice in Buridan's Moral Psychology," *Mediaeval Studies* 57 (1995), 75–99 (as well as Zupko, *John Buridan*, ch.15); F. Pironet, "The Notion of *Non Velle* in Buridan's Ethics," in Thijssen and Zupko, *The Metaphysics and Natural Philosophy*, 199–219.
14. Pironet, "The Notion of *Non Velle*," 204. My thanks to Jack Zupko for discussion of the relation between the thought experiment and Buridan's views on free will.
15. J. J. Walsh, "Is Buridan a Sceptic about Free Will?" *Vivarium* 2 (1964), 50–61, at 53; Zupko, *John Buridan*, 247.

Chapter 66

1. See *Philosophy in the Hellenistic and Roman Worlds*, ch.16.
2. Perhaps the only medieval thinker to do so was John of Salisbury, who was indeed influenced by ancient skepticism; see Chapter 17.

3. Edited in J. R. O'Donnell, "Nicholas of Autrecourt," *Medieval Studies* 1 (1939), 179–266; translated in L. A. Kennedy et al. (trans.), *Nicholas of Autrecourt: The Universal Treatise* (Milwaukee, WI: 1971).

4. Cited by section number from L. M. De Rijk (ed. and trans.), *Nicholas of Autrecourt: His Correspondence with Master Giles and Bernard of Arezzo* (Leiden: 1994).

5. See T. K. Scott, "Nicholas of Autrecourt, Buridan and Ockhamism," *Journal of the History of Philosophy* 9 (1971), 15–41, at 18.

6. See C. Grellard, "Scepticism, Demonstration and the Infinite Regress Argument (Nicholas of Autrecourt and John Buridan)," *Vivarium* 45 (2007), 328–42.

7. As explored in A. Krause, "Nikolaus von Autrecourt über das erste Prinzip und die Gewißheit von Sätzen," *Vivarium* 47 (2009), 407–20.

8. Similarly, around 1340, the anonymous Benedictine "black monk" (*monachus niger*) argued that we cannot know naturally that there are substances, as shown by the example of the Eucharist. See S. E. Lahey, *John Wyclif* (New York: 2009), 44.

9. On this, see P. King, "Jean Buridan's Philosophy of Science," *Studies in History and Philosophy of Science* 18 (1987), 109–32; J. Zupko, "Buridan and Skepticism," *Journal of the History of Philosophy* 31 (1993), 191–221.

10. Studied in J. R. Weinberg, *Nicholas of Autrecourt: A Study in 14th Century Thought* (Princeton, NJ: 1948). At 186–91 Weinberg gives a translation of the key conclusions drawn by Nicholas in the *Exigit*.

11. See further J. M. M. H. Thijssen, "John Buridan and Nicholas of Autrecourt on Causality and Induction," *Traditio* 43 (1987), 237–55.

12. For what follows, see L. A. Kennedy, "Philosophical Scepticism in England in the Mid-Fourteenth Century," *Vivarium* 21 (1983), 35–57; and for more on medieval skepticism, see D. Perler, *Zweifel und Gewissheit: skeptische Debatten im Mittelalter* (Frankfurt am Main: 2006); H. Lagerlund (ed.), *Rethinking the History of Skepticism: The Missing Medieval Background* (Leiden: 2010).

13. For more on this issue in the fourteenth century, see W. J. Courtenay, "John of Mirecourt and Gregory of Rimini on Whether God Can Undo the Past," *Recherches de Théologie Ancienne et Médiévale* 39 (1972), 224–56, and 40 (1973), 147–74.

14. A point made by Georgio Pini in his review of Lagerlund, *Rethinking the History of Skepticism*, on the online *Notre Dame Philosophical Review*.

Chapter 67

1. As mentioned by O. Langholm, *Economics in the Medieval Schools* (Leiden: 1992), 257.

2. This is the thesis of J. Kaye, *Economy and Nature in the Fourteenth Century: Money, Market Exchange, and the Emergence of Scientific Thought* (Cambridge: 1998), who mentions Oresme's financial responsibilities to illustrate the point at 30. He builds here on the work of Michael Wolff (see 123) who suggested an analogy between the implanting of an impetus for motion and the way that labor invests the product of the labor with value.

3. Kaye, *Economy and Nature*, 15 n. 2, citing the research of Nicholas Mayhew.

4. For medieval ideas of the just price, see R. De Roover, "The Concept of the Just Price: Theory and Practice," *Journal of Economic History* 18 (1958), 418–34; J. W. Baldwin, *The Medieval Theories of the Just Price: Romanists, Canonists, and Theologians in the Twelfth and Thirteenth Centuries* (Philadelphia, PA: 1959); O. Langholm, *Price and Value in the Aristotelian Tradition* (Bergen: 1979); O. Langholm, *Economics in the Medieval Schools* (Leiden: 1992); D. Wood, *Medieval Economic Thought* (Cambridge: 2004), ch.6.

5. Kaye, *Economy and Nature*, 92–3; Wood, *Medieval Economic Thought*, 136. Accursius also excludes fraudulent exchanges by pointing out that the buyer should be aware of the condition of the thing, and thus shows an awareness of the need for good information in economic exchange. See Langholm, *Economics in the Medieval Schools*, 94.

6. Langholm, *Economics in the Medieval Schools*, 184.

7. Wood, *Medieval Economic Thought*, 137.

8. Langholm, *Price and Value*, 126.

9. Langholm, *Economics in the Medieval Schools*, 411.

10. Langholm, *Economics in the Medieval Schools*, 485.

11. The argument is well explained at Wood, *Medieval Economic Thought*, 75. For more on the topic, see J. Noonan, *The Scholastic Analysis of Usury* (Cambridge, MA: 1957).

12. The cultural link between usury and Jews was so strong that one polemicist referred to all usurers (whatever their religion) under the protection of the French king as "his Jews," quoted at Wood, *Medieval Economic Thought*, 167. For theological views in both traditions, see A. Kirschenbaum, "Jewish and Christian Theories of Usury in the Middle Ages," *Jewish Quarterly Review* 75 (1985), 270–89. For the general topic, see, e.g., J. Shatzmiller, *Shylock Reconsidered: Jews, Moneylending, and Medieval Society* (Berkeley, CA: 1990).

13. On this, see Langholm, *Economics in the Medieval Schools*, ch.20.

14. For the Latin text and an English translation, see C. Johnson (trans.), *The De Moneta of Nicholas Oresme and English Mint Documents* (London: 1956). Cited by chapter number. See further D. Menjot, "La Politique monétaire de Nicolas Oresme," in P. Souffrin and A. P. Segonds (eds), *Nicolas Oresme: Tradition et innovation chez un intellectuel du XIVe siècle* (Paris: 1988), 179–93.

15. The comparison was already noted by T. W. Balch, "The Law of Oresme, Copernicus, and Gresham," *Proceedings of the American Philosophical Society* 47 (1908), 18–29.

Chapter 68

1. On his life and works, see the first four chapters of J. M. Hackett (ed.), *A Companion to Meister Eckhart* (Leiden: 2013). Other general studies include K. Ruh, *Meister Eckhart: Theologe, Prediger, Mystiker* (Munich: 1985); B. McGinn, *The Mystical Thought of Meister Eckhart: The Man from whom God Hid Nothing* (New York: 2001); and K. Flasch, *Meister Eckhart: Philosoph des Christentums* (Munich: 2010).

2. For the early period when he was a prior and then leader of the province of Saxony, see A. Speer and L. Wegener (eds), *Meister Eckhart in Erfurt* (Berlin: 2005). For the period in Strasbourg, see A. Quero-Sánchez and G. Steer (eds), *Meister Eckharts Straßburger Jahrzehnt* (Stuttgart: 2008).

3. For a survey of some views on this question, see McGinn, *The Mystical Thought*, 33.

4. See O. Langer, *Mystische Erfahrungen und spirituelle Theologie: zu Meister Eckharts Auseinandersetzung mit der Frauenfrömmigkeit seiner Zeit* (Munich: 1987).

5. As pointed out by Ruh, *Meister Eckhart*, 44.

6. I cite by page number from O. Davies, *Meister Eckhart: Selected Writings* (London: 1994). I have also consulted the medieval German and Latin texts, and modern German translations, in J. Quint et al. (ed. and trans.), *Meister Eckhart: Werke*, 2 vols (Frankfurt am Main: 1993).

7. On the trial, see Sennert's chapter in Hackett, *A Companion to Meister Eckhart*; H. Stirnimann and R. Imbach (eds), *Eckhardus Theutonicus homo doctus et sanctus: Nachweise und Berichte zum Prozeß gegen Meister Eckhart* (Fribourg: 1992); L. Sturlese, *Homo Divinus:*

philosophische Projekte in Deutschland zwischen Meister Eckhart und Heinrich Seuse (Stuttgart: 2007), 121–9.

8. The prologue is not included in Davies, *Meister Eckhart: Selected Writings*. See Quint, *Meister Eckhart: Werke*, vol.2, 468, for the passage.

9. On this topic, see A. de Libera, *Le Problème de l'être chez Maître Eckhart: Logique et metaphysique de l'analogie* (Geneva: 1980); F. Tobin, *Meister Eckhart: Thought and Language* (Philadelphia, PA: 1986); and B. Mojsisch, *Meister Eckhart: Analogy, Univocity and Unity*, trans. O. F. Summerell (Amsterdam: 2001).

10. Quint, *Meister Eckhart: Werke*, vol.2, 482.

11. From his *Second Lecture on Ecclesiastes*, ch.24; for translation and discussion, see Tobin, *Meister Eckhart: Thought and Language*, 44–5.

12. Ruh, *Meister Eckhart: Theologe, Prediger, Mystiker*, 85.

13. For extensive discussion of this concept, see McGinn, *The Mystical Thought of Meister Eckhart*.

14. See respectively *Philosophy in the Hellenistic and Roman Worlds*, ch.43, and *Philosophy in the Islamic World*, ch.33.

15. Quint, *Meister Eckhart: Werke*, vol.2, 270. On this theme, see D. Turner, *The Darkness of God: Negativity in Christian Mysticism* (Cambridge: 1995).

16. See also McGinn, *The Mystical Thought of Meister Eckhart*, 98.

17. Tobin, *Meister Eckhart: Thought and Language*, 60.

18. For a balanced discussion, see Wegener's contribution in Hackett, *A Companion to Meister Eckhart*; see also B. McGinn, *Meister Eckhart and the Beguine Mystics: Hadewijch of Brabant, Mechthild of Magdeburg and Marguerite Porete* (New York: 1994).

19. McGinn, *The Mystical Thought of Meister Eckhart*, 39.

Chapter 69

1. For the Dominicans generally, see W. A. Hinnebusch, *The History of the Dominican Order* (New York: 1966); for the background of earlier philosophy in Germany, see L. Sturlese, *Die deutsche Philosophie im Mittelalter: von Bonifazius zu Albert dem Großen* (Munich: 1989).

2. See the studies collected in M. J. F. M. Hoenen et al. (eds), *Deutsche Thomisten des 14. Jahrhunderts: Lektüren, Aneignungsstrategien, Divergenzen*, special issue of *Freiburger Zeitschrift für Philosophie und Theologie* (2010); the following remarks on Picardi are based on the papers of Beccarisi, Leone, and Benedetto.

3. As documented in M. J. F. M. Hoenen and A. de Libera (eds), *Albertus Magnus und der Albertismus: deutsche philosophische Kultur des Mittelalters* (Leiden: 1995).

4. For instance A. de Libera, *Introduction à la mystique rhénane* (Paris: 1999).

5. See the critique of such a monolithic approach in N. Largier, "Die 'deutsche Dominikanerschule': zur Problematik eines historiographischen Konzepts," in J. A. Aertsen and A. Speer (eds), *Geistesleben im 13. Jahrhundert* (Berlin: 2000), 202–13. For the movement in general, see K. Flasch, *Von Meister Dietrich zu Meister Eckhart* (Hamburg: 1987), K. Ruh, *Geschichte der abendländischen Mystik, 3. Band: die Mystik des deutschen Predigerordens und ihre Grundlegung durch die Hochscholastik* (Munich: 1993), L. Sturlese, *Homo Divinus: philosophische Projekte in Deutschland zwischen Meister Eckhart und Heinrich Seuse* (Stuttgart: 2007), with Italian versions of some of the same essays in L. Sturlese, *Eckhart, Tauler, Suso: Filosofi e mistici nella Germania medievale* (Florence: 2010).

6. This designation is applied to Dietrich by K. Flasch, *Dietrich von Freiberg: Philosophie, Theologie, Naturforschung um 1300* (Frankfurt am Main: 2007), 328.

7. On the relation between the two, see J. Halfwassen, "Gibt es eine Philosophie der Subjektivität im Mittelalter? Zur Theorie des Intellekts bei Meister Eckhart und Dietrich von Freiberg," *Theologie und Philosophie* 72 (1997), 338–60; L. Sturlese, "Dietrich di Freiberg lettore di Eckhart?" *Giornale Critico della Filosofia Italiana* 85 (2006), 437–53.

8. Cited by section number from M. L. Führer (trans.), *Dietrich von Freiberg: Treatise on the Intellect and the Intelligible* (Milwaukee, WI: 1992). On this work, see B. Mojsisch, *Die Theorie des Intellekts bei Dietrich von Freiberg* (Hamburg: 1977) and for documentation on Dietrich's career and writings, see L. Sturlese, *Dokumente und Forschungen zu Leben und Werk Dietrichs von Freiberg* (Hamburg: 1984).

9. A. Maurer, "The *De Quidditatibus Entium* of Dietrich of Freiberg and its Criticism of Thomistic Metaphysics," *Mediaeval Studies* 18 (1956), 173–203.

10. Flasch, *Dietrich von Freiberg*, 124; de Libera, *Introduction à la mystique rhénane*, 166–8.

11. See also Mojsisch, *Die Theorie des Intellekts*, 74–5.

12. See M. Führer and S. Gersh, "Dietrich of Freiberg and Berthold of Moosburg," in S. Gersh (ed.), *Interpreting Proclus: From Antiquity to the Renaissance* (Cambridge: 2014), 299–317; P. Adamson and F. Karfík, "Proclus' Legacy," in P. d'Hoine and M. Martijn (eds), *All from One: A Guide to Proclus* (Oxford: 2016), 290–321. My thanks to Evan King for help in understanding Berthold, including access to unpublished studies, and for further advice on this chapter.

13. For the importance of this context, see Sturlese, *Homo Divinus*, 138.

14. On this work, see Ruh, *Geschichte der abendländischen Mystik*, 445–68. Sturlese, *Homo Divinus*, 200, connects Suso's demotion to his defense of Eckhart.

15. Cited by chapter number from L. Sturlese and R. Blumrich (ed.), *Heinrich Seuse: das Buch der Wahrheit* (Hamburg: 1993).

16. Sturlese, *Homo Divinus*, 219–20.

17. Ruh, *Geschichte der abendländischen Mystik*, 503.

18. N. Bray "The Reception of Meister Eckhart in 14th-Century Germany," in J. M. Hackett (ed.), *A Companion to Meister Eckhart* (Leiden: 2013), 481–508, at 485.

19. Ruh, *Geschichte der abendländischen Mystik*, 450–1. On their relationship, see F. Tobin, "Henry Suso and Elsbeth Stagel: Was the *Vita* a Cooperative Effort?" in C. Mooney (ed.) *Gendered Voices: Medieval Saints and their Interpreters* (Philadelphia, PA: 1999), 118–35.

20. De Libera, *Introduction à la mystique rhénane*, 187.

21. Sturlese, *Homo Divinus*, 177.

Chapter 70

1. See D. Keck, *Angels and Angelology in the Middle Ages* (New York: 1998), and especially chs.8–9 for common medieval beliefs about angels. For earlier beliefs, see E. Muehlberger, *Angels in Late Ancient Christianity* (Oxford: 2013).

2. See Sylvain Piron's contribution in I. Iribarren and M. Lenz, *Angels in Medieval Philosophical Inquiry: Their Function and Significance* (Aldershot: 2008).

3. T. Suarez-Nani, *Les Anges et la philosophie* (Paris: 2002), 143–64. See also L. Sturlese, "Il *De animatione caeli* di Teodorico di Freiberg," in R. Creytens and P. Künzle (eds), *Xenia medii aevi historiam illustrantia oblata Thomae Kaeppeli OP* (Rome: 1978), 174–247; K. Flasch, *Dietrich von Freiberg: Philosophie, Theologie, Naturforschung um 1300* (Frankfurt am Main: 2007), 196–8.

4. M. L. Führer (trans.), *Dietrich von Freiberg: Treatise on the Intellect and the Intelligible* (Milwaukee, WI: 1992), §1.7. See also Flasch, *Dietrich*, 309.

5. Führer, *Dietrich von Freiberg: Treatise on the Intellect*, §1.12.

6. See Pini in T. Hoffmann (ed.), *A Companion to Angels in Medieval Philosophy* (Leiden: 2012), at 83, and for this topic, see in the same volume the contribution by Wippel.

7. Führer, *Dietrich von Freiberg: Treatise on the Intellect*, §2.26; Suarez-Nani, *Les Anges*, 61.

8. See Isabel Iribarren's contribution in Iribarren and Lenz, *Angels in Medieval Philosophical Inquiry*.

9. My translation from the Latin text of the *Opus tertium* quoted in R. J. Long, "Roger Bacon on the Nature and Place of Angels," *Vivarium* 35 (1997), 266–82, at 278 n.39.

10. The remark is from David Luscombe, in Iribarren and Lenz, *Angels in Medieval Philosophical Inquiry*, 23.

11. See Richard Cross' chapter in Hoffmann, *A Companion to Angels*.

12. In Iribarren and Lenz, *Angels in Medieval Philosophical Inquiry*, 156.

13. T. M. Osborne, "*Unibilitas*: The Key to Bonaventure's Understanding of Human Nature," *Journal of the History of Philosophy* 37 (1999), 227–50.

14. This is one of the most extensively researched aspects of medieval angelology, especially in Aquinas. See M. Raukas, "St. Thomas on the Speech of the Angels," *Freiburger Zeitschrift für Philosophie und Theologie* 43 (1996), 30–44; C. Panaccio, "Angel's Talk, Mental Language, and the Transparency of the Mind," in C. Marmo (ed.), *Vestigia, Imagines, Verba: Semiotics and Logic in Medieval Theological Texts, XIIth–XIVth Century* (Turnhout: 1997), 323–35; H. Goris, "The Angelic Doctor and Angelic Speech: The Development of Thomas Aquinas's Thought on How Angels Communicate," *Medieval Philosophy and Theology* 11 (2003), 87–105; I. Rosier-Catach, "Le Parler des anges et le nôtre," in S. Caroti et al. (eds), *Ad Ingenii Acuitionem: Studies in Honour of Alfonso Maierù* (Louvain-la-Neuve: 2006), pages 307–411; B. Roling, *Locutio angelica: die Diskussion der Engelsprache als Antizipation einer Sprechakttheorie in Mittelalter und früher Neuzeit* (Leiden: 2008).

15. See H. Lang's chapter "Duns Scotus: Putting Angels in their Place," in her *Aristotle's Physics and its Medieval Varieties* (Albany, NY: 1992), 173–87, and Cross' pieces in Iribarren and Lenz, *Angels in Medieval Philosophical Inquiry*, and in Hoffmann, *A Companion to Angels*.

Chapter 71

1. See D. Knowles, *The English Mystical Tradition* (London: 1961); N. Watson, "The Middle English Mystics," in *The Cambridge History of Medieval English Literature* (Cambridge: 1999), 539–65; and for Julian's place in this tradition, see D. N. Baker, "Julian of Norwich and the Varieties of Middle English Mystical Discourse," in L. Herbert McAvoy (ed.), *A Companion to Julian of Norwich* (Cambridge: 2008), 53–63.

2. On whom, see J. P. H. Clark, "Richard Rolle: A Theological Re-Assessment," *Downside Review* 101 (1983), 108–39; N. Watson, *Richard Rolle and the Invention of Authority* (Cambridge: 1991).

3. J. P. H. Clark, *The Cloud of Unknowing: An Introduction*, 3 vols (Salzburg: 1995–6), vol.1, 13–14, 86–92.

4. This point is made emphatically by Watson, "Middle English Mystics," who also rightly urges us to see the English mystics in the context of other contemporary literature in English, including Chaucer and Langland.

5. For the original text, see Clark, *The Cloud of Unknowing*, vol.2, translation in C. Wolters (trans.), *The Cloud of Unknowing* (London: 1961). Cited in the main text by chapter number from this translation.

6. N. Watson, "The Composition of Julian of Norwich's *Revelation of Love*," *Speculum* 68 (1993), 637–83, at 643.

7. Original text of both short and long versions edited in E. Colledge and J. Walsh, *A Book of Showings to the Anchoress Julian of Norwich*, 2 vols (Toronto: 1978); modern text in D. N. Baker (ed.), *The Showings of Julian of Norwich* (New York: 2005). Cited here in the main text by chapter number.

8. M. R. Lichtmann, "'I Desyred a Bodylye Sight': Julian of Norwich and the Body," *Mystics Quarterly* 17 (1991), 12–19.

9. This passage is from the short version of the *Showings*, and was deleted in the longer version. I take the translation from D. N. Baker, *Julian of Norwich's Showings: From Vision to Book* (Princeton, NJ: 1994), 135–6.

10. It is usually assumed that the short version was set down quickly after the visions, but this is questioned in N. Watson, "The Composition of Julian of Norwich's *Revelation of Love*," *Speculum* 68 (1993), 637–83.

11. For this contrast, see Baker, *Julian of Norwich's Showings*, 92, 99.

12. J. Ruud, "Nature and Grace in Julian of Norwich," *Mystics Quarterly* 19 (1993), 71–81, at 77. For other discussions of her theodicy, see S. Tugwell, "Julian of Norwich as a Speculative Theologian," *14th Century English Mystics Newsletter* 9 (1983), 199–209; B. Peters, "The Reality of Evil within the Mystic Vision of Julian of Norwich," *Mystics Quarterly* 13 (1987), 195–202.

13. Julian would also reject the "semi-pelagian" idea that we can provoke God into bestowing grace upon us; see Baker, *Julian of Norwich's Showings*, 74, and for this view Chapter 61.

14. See *Philosophy in the Hellenistic and Roman Worlds*, ch.41.

Chapter 72

1. For an introduction, see K. Kerby-Fulton, "*Piers Plowman*," in D. Wallace (ed.), *The Cambridge History of Medieval English Literature* (Cambridge: 1999), 513–38; or A. Cole and A. Galloway, *The Cambridge Companion to Piers Plowman* (Cambridge: 2014).

2. A. J. Minnes (ed.), *Chaucer's Boece and the Medieval Tradition of Boethius* (Cambridge: 1993).

3. I cite the *Tales* by line number; for an edition, see F. N. Robinson (ed.), *The Works of Geoffrey Chaucer* (Oxford: 1957).

4. See respectively D. C. Fowler, "Poetry and the Liberal Arts: The Oxford Background of Piers Plowman," in *Arts libéraux et philosophie au Moyen Âge* (Paris: 1969), 715–19; A. Galloway, "Piers Plowman and the Schools," *Yearbook of Langland Studies* 6 (1992), 89–107, at 92.

5. For the following, see R. Peck, "Chaucer and the Nominalist Questions," *Speculum* 53 (1978), 745–60; K. L. Lynch, "The 'Parliament of Fowls' and Late Medieval Voluntarism," *Chaucer Review* 25 (1990), 1–16 and 85–95; R. Stepsis, "*Potentia Absoluta* and the *Clerk's Tale*," *Chaucer Review* 10 (1975), 129–46; R. Delasanta, "Nominalism and the 'Clerk's Tale' Revisited," *Chaucer Review* 31 (1997), 209–31.

6. Similar, and to my mind similarly implausible, is the notion that Langland reflects a "nominalist" outlook by presenting abstract concepts like "doing well" as concrete characters, as proposed by D. Strong, "The Questions Asked, the Answers Given: Langland, Scotus and Ockham," *Chaucer Review* 38 (2004), 255–75, at 262. In fact, of course, this technique of personification was used by authors like Jean de Meun and Alan of Lille, who wrote before the rise of nominalism and who were models for both Chaucer and Langland.

7. J. Warrington (ed.), *Geoffrey Chaucer: Troilus and Criseyde* (London: 1974), book 4, verses 136–54 (the quote just below is from verse 151).

8. J. Mann, "Chance and Destiny in *Troilus and Criseyde* and the *Knight's Tale*," in P. Boitani and J. Mann (eds), *The Cambridge Companion to Chaucer* (Cambridge: 1986), 93–111, at 100.

9. *Troilus and Criseyde*, book 4, verse 155.

10. F. Michelet and M. Pickavé, "Philosophy," in S. Akbari (ed.), *The Oxford Handbook of Chaucer* (Oxford: forthcoming).

11. What follows is largely inspired by material in M. Miller, *Philosophical Chaucer: Love, Sex and Agency in the Canterbury Tales* (Cambridge: 2005).

12. One of the two lovers even seems to envy the status of animals at 1315–21.

13. For more on this theme, see S. H. Rigby, *Wisdom and Chivalry: Chaucer's Knight's Tale and Medieval Political Thought* (Leiden: 2009).

14. Miller, *Philosophical Chaucer*, 31.

15. A very frequent theme in the poem; see, e.g., Prol.58–67, 1.190–1, 3.35–50, 3.144–9, 5.642–3, 11.71–3, 13.73–6, 15.328–30. For an edition, see A. V. C. Schmidt (ed.), *William Langland: The Vision of Piers Plowman* (London: 1978); see also the version in modern English in A. V. C. Schmidt, *Piers Plowman: A New Translation of the B-Text* (Oxford: 2009). I will be quoting by *passus* and line number from the "B" text, the second of Langland's three different versions of the poem.

16. For this scene and its relation to scholastic theological debates, see J. Coleman, *Piers Plowman and the Moderni* (Rome: 1981), 103; D. N. Baker, "From Plowing to Penitence: *Piers Plowman* and Fourteenth-Century Theology," *Speculum* 55 (1980), 715–25.

17. Coleman, *Piers Plowman and the Moderni*, 108–46; J. Marenbon, *Pagans and Philosophers: The Problem of Paganism from Augustine to Leibniz* (Princeton, NJ: 2015), ch.11.

18. I take this suggestion from R. Davis, *Piers Plowman and the Books of Nature* (Oxford: 2016), 199.

19. Davis, *Piers Plowman and the Books of Nature*, 87. Davis however suggests a contrast between Nature in *Piers* as an immanent divine force and the earlier treatments of Nature as a more autonomous principle. For this theme in later medieval literature, see also K. Robertson, *Nature Speaks: Medieval Literature and Aristotelian Philosophy* (Philadelphia, PA: 2017).

20. See M. C. Davlin, "*Kynde Knowyng* as a Major Theme in *Piers Plowman B*," *Review of English Studies* 22 (1971), 1–19.

Chapter 73

1. For Plato's reflections on such practices, see *Classical Philosophy*, ch.27.

2. For details, see M. D. Jordan, *The Invention of Sodomy in Christian Theology* (Chicago: 1997), on which I draw in what follows. For sexuality in general, see, e.g., P. J. Payer, *The Bridling of Desire: Ideas of Sex in the Later Middle Ages* (Toronto: 1993); J. E. Salisbury, *Medieval Sexuality: A Research Guide* (New York: 1990); M. Green, "Female Sexuality in the Medieval West," *Trends in History* 4 (1990), 127–58; and works referred to below.

3. V. L. Bullough and J. A. Brundage (eds), *Handbook of Medieval Sexuality* (New York: 1996), 37.

4. Quoted at Jordan, *The Invention of Sodomy*, 126.

5. R. M. Karras, *Sexuality in Medieval Europe: Doing unto Others* (London: 2017), 28.

6. For the medieval discussion of the problem, see J. A. Brundage, *Law, Sex, and Christian Society in Medieval Europe* (Chicago: 1987).

7. See P. J. Payer, *Sex and the Penitentials: The Development of a Sexual Code, 550–1150* (Toronto: 1984).

8. Quoted at Jordan, *The Invention of Sodomy*, 151.

9. *Handbook of Medieval Sexuality*, 13, 42.

10. *Etymologies* §11.2.17, quoted from A. Blamires, K. Pratt, and C. W. Marx (eds), *Woman Defamed and Woman Defended* (Oxford: 1992), 43.

11. R. M. Karras, "Using Women to Think with in the Medieval University," in A. B. Mulder-Bakker (ed.), *Seeing and Knowing: Women and Learning in Medieval Europe 1200–1550* (Turnhout: 2004), 21–33, at 28.

12. Similarly Gratian instructs his readers, "Woman's authority is nil; let her in all things be subject to the rule of men...And neither can she teach, nor be a witness, nor give a guarantee, nor sit in judgment." Quoted at E. A. Petroff, *Body and Soul: Essays on Medieval Women and Mysticism* (New York: 1994), 167.

13. *De regimine* §1.2.65, quoted by A. Blamires, *Chaucer, Ethics, and Gender* (Oxford: 2006), 72 n. 77.

14. Compare Aristotle, *Nicomachean Ethics* 8.10.

15. D. Jacquart and C. Thomasset, *Sexuality and Medicine in the Middle Ages* (Princeton, NJ: 1988)

16. See M. H. Green, *Making Women's Medicine Masculine: The Rise of Male Authority in Pre-Modern Gynaecology* (Oxford: 2008), 184, 196; see 218 and 133 for the following point about menstruation and the quotation from Christine.

17. A. Blamires, *The Case for Women in Medieval Culture* (Oxford: 1997), 133.

18. See D. Elliott, *Spiritual Marriage: Sexual Abstinence in Medieval Wedlock* (Princeton, NJ: 1993), and on medieval marriage in general, see H. A. Kelly, *Love and Marriage in the Age of Chaucer* (Ithaca, NY: 1975); and C. Brooke, *The Medieval Idea of Marriage* (Oxford: 1994). It should incidentally be noted that a husband was also meant to seek his wife's consent before swearing himself to chastity.

19. B. Radice and M. T. Clanchy, *The Letters of Abelard and Heloise* (London: 2003), 118.

20. As detailed in Blamires, *The Case for Women*, with discussion of Abelard especially at 201–7; I draw on this book for the following paragraph: see 19 for Marbod of Rennes; 52 for the Apocrypha; 39 and 238 for the two cited remarks by Le Fèvre.

21. See G. McLeod, *Virtue and Venom: Catalogs of Women from Antiquity to the Renaissance* (Ann Arbor, MI: 1991).

22. Quoted from Blamires, *The Case for Women*, 70.

23. As pointed out by J. Laird, "Good Women and Bonnes Dames: Virtuous Females in Chaucer and Christine de Pizan," *Chaucer Review* 30 (1995), 58–70.

24. In a letter to Abelard she also mentions the fact that women have often brought men to ruin. See Radice and Clanchy, *Letters of Abelard and Heloise*, 67, and 13–16 for Abelard's report of her arguments against marriage.

25. Green, *Making Women's Medicine*, 225.

26. S. H. Rigby, "The Wife of Bath, Christine de Pizan and the Medieval Case for Women," *Chaucer Review* 35 (2000), 133–65, at 154.

Chapter 74

1. On her political activity, see F. T. Luongo, *The Saintly Politics of Catherine of Siena* (Ithaca, NY: 2006).

2. Quotes taken from *Letter* 140 and 207, quoted by Luongo, *The Saintly Politics*, 84 and 170. For her correspondence, see S. Noffke, *The Letters of Catherine of Siena*, 2 vols (Tempe, AZ: 2000–1).

3. Translation from B. Beattie, "Catherine of Siena and the Papacy," in C. Muessig, G. Ferzoco, and B. M. Kienzle (eds), *A Companion to Catherine of Siena* (Leiden: 2012), 73–98, at 82–3.

4. See *Philosophy in the Hellenistic and Roman Worlds*, ch.45.

5. R. M. Bell, *Holy Anorexia* (Chicago: 1985).

6. C. W. Bynum, *Holy Feast and Holy Fast: The Religious Significance of Food to Medieval Women* (Berkeley, CA: 1987). See also her *Fragmentation and Redemption: Essays on Gender and the Human Body in Medieval Religion* (New York: 1992). For a study summarizing and building on Bynum's insights, see U. Wiethaus, "Sexuality, Gender and the Body in Late Medieval Women's Spirituality: Cases from Germany and the Netherlands," *Journal of Feminist Studies in Religion* 7 (1991), 35–52.

7. *Letter* 2, cited by Bynum, *Holy Feast*, 176.

8. C. Van Dyke, "Self-Knowledge, Abnegation, and Fulfillment in Medieval Mysticism," in U. Renz (ed.), *Self-Knowledge* (Oxford: 2017), 131–45, at 139. For the need to recognize embodied states as a dominant aspect of the mystical tradition, see also C. Van Dyke, "What Has History to Do with Philosophy? Insights from the Medieval Contemplative Tradition," in M. Van Ackeren (ed.), *Philosophy and the Historical Perspective* (Oxford: 2018), 155–70.

9. Bynum, *Fragmentation and Redemption*, 170.

10. Bynum, *Holy Feast*, 249–50.

11. Bynum, *Holy Feast*, 210.

12. W. Williams-Krapp, "Henry Suso's *Vita* between Mystagogy and Hagiography," in A. B. Mulder-Bakker (ed.), *Seeing and Knowing: Women and Learning in Medieval Europe 1200–1550* (Turnhout: 2004), 35–47.

13. For an informative discussion, see chapters 2 and 3 of R. M. Karras, *Sexuality in Medieval Europe: Doing unto Others* (London: 2017).

14. As suggested by Karras, *Sexuality in Medieval Europe*, 61.

15. Cited by Bynum, *Holy Feast*, 16.

16. See A. Hollywood, *Sensible Ecstasy: Mysticism, Sexual Difference, and the Demands of History* (Chicago: 2002), 247–66.

17. S. Noffke (trans.), *Catherine of Siena: The Dialogue* (New York: 1980).

18. *Letter* 273; I follow the discussion in Luongo, *The Saintly Politics*, ch.3, with the following quote taken from 99.

19. Van Dyke, "Self-Knowledge, Abnegation, and Fulfillment," 135. See also her "'Many Know Much, but Do Not Know Themselves': Self-Knowledge, Humility, and Perfection in the Medieval Affective Contemplative Tradition," in G. Klima and A. Hall (eds), *Consciousness and Self-Knowledge in Medieval Philosophy: Proceedings of the Society for Medieval Logic and Metaphysics*, vol.14, 89–106.

Chapter 75

1. Texts from the debate are cited from D. F. Hult (trans.), *Christine of Pizan et al.: Debate of the Romance of the Rose* (Chicago: 2010). For an alternative translation, see C. McWebb and E. J. Richards, *Debating the Rose: A Critical Anthology* (New York: 2007). For attitudes to the poem prior to Christine, see J. V. Fleming, "The Moral Reputation of the *Roman de la Rose* before 1400," *Romance Philology* 18 (1965), 430–5.

2. J. L. Baird, "Pierre de Col and the *Querelle de la Rose*," *Philological Quarterly* 60 (1981), 273–86, at 277.

3. For his intervention in the debate (and a useful summary of the whole affair), see R. Blumenfeld-Kosinski, "Jean Gerson and the Debate on the *Romance of the Rose*," in B. P. McGuire (ed.), *A Companion to Jean Gerson* (Leiden: 2006), 317–56.

4. See J. L. Baird and J. R. Kane, "*La Querelle de la Rose*: In Defense of the Opponents," *French Review* 48 (1974), 298–307, at 301.

5. Christine and Gerson also both mention the Quran as a paradigm case of pernicious literature (119, 177).

6. D. Hobbins, "The Schoolman as Public Intellectual: Jean Gerson and the Late Medieval Tract," *American Historical Review* 108 (2003), 1308–37.

7. B. P. McGuire, *Jean Gerson and the last Medieval Reformation* (University Park, PA: 2005), 89. For the topic in general, see also B. Tierney, *Foundations of the Conciliar Theory* (Cambridge: 1955); J. B. Morrall, *Gerson and the Great Schism* (Manchester: 1960).

8. For the latter point, see L. E. Pascoe, *Jean Gerson: Principles of Church Reform* (Leiden: 1973), 17–22 and 48; D. C. Brown, *Pastor and Laity in the Theology of Jean Gerson* (Cambridge: 1987), 30.

9. G. H. M. Posthumus Meyjes, *Jean Gerson: Apostle of Unity* (Leiden: 1999), 262, and 199 for the appeal to Aristotle's political theory (also 362 for an anticipation of this idea in d'Ailly).

10. Pascoe, *Jean Gerson*, 94–5.

11. For the exegetical dimension of the Petit affair, see D. Z. Flanagin, "Making Sense of it All: Gerson's Biblical Theology," in McGuire, *Companion*, 133–77. For this topic, see also A. Coville, *Jean Petit: La question du tyrannicide au commencement du XVe siècle* (Paris: 1932).

12. M. S. Burrows, *Jean Gerson and De Consolatione Theologiae* (Tübingen: 1991), 130; McGuire, *Jean Gerson and the Last Reformation*, 134–5.

13. Brown, *Pastor and Laity*, 186.

14. For a balanced and sympathetic assessment, see W. L. Anderson, "Gerson's Stance on Women," in McGuire, *Companion*, 293–315.

15. For the idea of a radical break in his mystical thought, see the classic A. Combes, *La Théologie mystique de Gerson: Profil de son évolution* (Paris: 1963–4), and for a more recent study of his mysticism, see M. Vial, *Jean Gerson: Théoricien de la théologie mystique* (Paris: 2006).

16. Brown, *Pastor and Laity*, 193.

Chapter 76

1. Quoted at S. E. Lahey, *Metaphysics and Politics in the Thought of John Wyclif* (Cambridge: 2003), 82.

2. Quoted at M. Dove, "Wyclif and the English Bible," in I. C. Levy (ed.), *A Companion to John Wyclif: Late Medieval Theologian* (Leiden: 2006), 365–406, at 378.

3. On them, see M. Aston, *Lollards and Reformers* (London: 1984); A. Hudson, *Lollards and their Books* (London: 1985); A. Hudson, *The Premature Reformation* (London: 1988); K. B. McFarlane, *Wycliffe and English Nonconformity* (London: 1972); R. Rex, *The Lollards* (Basingstoke: 2002).

4. For overviews of his life, see S. E. Lahey, *John Wyclif* (New York: 2009), ch.1; and Larsen's opening chapter in Levy, *A Companion to John Wyclif*.

5. As argued by P. V. Spade, "The Problem of Universals and Wyclif's Alleged 'Ultrarealism'," *Vivarium* 43 (2005), 111–23. See also A. D. Conti, "Analogy and Formal Distinction: on the Logical Basis of Wyclif's Metaphysics," *Medieval Philosophy and Theology* 6 (1997), 133–67.

6. See A. D. Conti, "Wyclif's Logic and Metaphysics," in Levy, *A Companion to John Wyclif*, 67–125, at 116; see also S. Read, "'I Promise You a Penny that I Do Not Promise': The Realist/ Nominalist Debate over Intensional Propositions in Fourteenth-Century Logic and its Contemporary Relevance," in O. P. Lewry, *The Rise of British Logic* (Toronto: 1985), 335–59.

7. L. Cesalli, "Le 'Pan-propositionnalisme' de Jean Wyclif," *Vivarium* 43 (2005), 124–55. Compare Gregory of Rimini's position on states of affairs, discussed in Chapter 76 below.

8. This is the argument of Lahey, *Metaphysics and Politics*, which I follow here.

9. On whom, see K. Walsh, *A Fourteenth-Century Scholar and Primate: Richard Fitzralph in Oxford, Avignon, and Armagh* (Oxford: 1981).

10. As pointed out by Lahey, *John Wyclif*, 215.
11. For the implications of this, see Shogimen's chapter in Levy, *A Companion to John Wyclif*.
12. See G. Leff, "Ockham and Wyclif on the Eucharist," *Reading Medieval Studies* 2 (1976), 1–13; and Penn's chapter in Levy, *A Companion to John Wyclif*.
13. See the quotation at Lahey, *John Wyclif*, 126. He stresses the connection between Wyclif's Eucharistic theology and his point-atomism.
14. On this, see E. Michael, "John Wyclif's Atomism," in C. Grellard and A. Robert (eds), *Atomism in Late Medieval Philosophy and Theology* (Leiden: 2009), 183–220; N. Kretzman, "Continua, Indivisibles, and Change in Wyclif's Logic of Scripture," in A. Kenny (ed.), *Wyclif in his Times* (Oxford: 1986), 31–65; and for the following implications regarding anthropology, see E. Michael, "John Wyclif on Body and Mind," *Journal of the History of Ideas* 64 (2003), 343–60.
15. M. S. Burrows, *Jean Gerson and De Consolatione Theologiae* (Tübingen: 1991), 174.

Chapter 77

1. J. Ijsewijn and J. Paquet (eds), *The Universities in the Late Middle Ages* (Leuven: 1978), 29.
2. Quotation taken from Shank, "Logic, University, and Society, 6.
3. As stressed by J. M. Fletcher, "University Migrations in the Late Middle Ages with Particular Reference to the Stamford Secession," in J. M. Kittelson and P. J. Transue (eds), *Rebirth, Reform and Resilience: Universities in Transition, 1300–1700* (Columbus, OH: 1984), 163–89. For more on the topic, see A. L. Gabriel, "'Via Antiqua' and 'Via Moderna' and the Migration of Paris Students and Masters to the German Universities in the Fifteenth Century," *Miscellanea Mediaevalia* 9 (1974), 439–83.
4. Fletcher, "University Migrations," 184.
5. F. Šmahel, *Die Prager Universität im Mittelalter: Charles University in the Middle Ages* (Leiden: 2007), 174.
6. N. Siriasi, *Arts and Sciences at Padua: The Studium of Padua before 1350* (Toronto: 1973), 64, 110; at 174 she mentions that in Padua medicine was seen as the "crown" of the arts curriculum.
7. Siriasi, *Arts and Sciences at Padua*, 18–22. Her book is also a good source of information on Abano; see 136, with further references, for the question of his "Averroism."
8. On this, see A. D. Conti, "Paul of Venice on Individuation," *Recherches de Théologie et Philosophie Médiévales* 65 (1998), 107–32; and several papers in A. Musco et al. (eds), *Universalità della ragione: Pluralità delle filosofie nel medioevo*, vol. II.2 (Palermo: 2012). In the latter volume, see the papers by Amerini and Conti for skeptical views about his Averroism on the intellect, and Galluzzo for his use of Averroes. See also A. Maierù (ed.), *English Logic in Italy in the 14th and 15th Centuries* (Naples: 1982).
9. The subject of numerous studies by A. D. Conti, including "Paul of Venice on Individuation," *Recherches de Théologie et Philosophie Médiévales*, 65 (1998), 107–32, which I summarize in the next paragraph; "Paul of Venice's Theory of Divine Ideas and its Sources," *Documenti e Studi sulla Tradizione Filosofica Medievale* 14 (2003), 409–48; and "Opinion on Universals and Predication in Late Middle Ages: Sharpe's and Paul of Venice's Theories Compared," *Documenti e Studi sulla Tradizione Filosofica Medievale* 18 (2007), 483–500.
10. For a useful summary of his views, see I. Mandrella, "Gregory of Rimini," in C. Rode (ed.), *A Companion to Responses to Ockham* (Leiden: 2016), 197–24. For a book-length study, see G. Leff, *Gregory of Rimini: Tradition and Innovation in Fourteenth Century Thought* (New York:

1961); and for a collection of studies H. A. Oberman (ed.): *Gregor von Rimini: Werk und Wirkung bis zur Reformation* (Berlin: 1981).

11. On him, see H. A. G. Braakhuie and M. J. F. M. Hoenen (eds), *Marsilius of Inghen* (Nijmegen: 1992); M. J. F. M. Hoenen and P. J. J. M. Bakker (eds), *Philosophie und Theologie des ausgehenden Mittelalters: Marsilius von Inghen und das Denken seiner Zeit* (Leiden: 2000).

12. M. J. F. M. Hoenen, *Marsilius of Inghen: Divine Knowledge in Late Medieval Thought* (Leiden: 1993).

13. For what follows, see M. H. Shank, *"Unless You Believe, You Shall Not Understand": Logic, University, and Society in Late Medieval Vienna* (Princeton, NJ: 1988).

14. As argued by J. H. M. M. Thijssen, "The Buridan School Reassessed: John Buridan and Albert of Saxony," *Vivarium* 42 (2004), 18–42.

15. See J. Sarnowsky, *Die aristotelisch-scholastische Theorie der Bewegung: Studien zum Kommentar Alberts von Sachsen zur Physik des Aristoteles* (Münster: 1989); J. Biard (ed.), *Paris-Vienne au XIVe siècle: Itinéraires d'Albert de Saxe* (Paris: 1991); J. Sarnowsky, "Place and Space in Albert of Saxony's Commentary on the *Physics,*" *Arabic Sciences and Philosophy* 9 (1999) 25–45.

16. M. J. Fitzgerald, "The Medieval Roots of Reliabilist Epistemology: Albert of Saxony's View of Immediate Apprehension," *Synthese* 136 (2003), 409–34.

17. See Šmahel, *Die Prager Universität*; H. Kaminsky, "The University of Prague in the Hussite Revolution: The Role of the Masters," in J. W. Baldwin and R. A. Goldthwaite (eds), *Universities in Politics: Case Studies from the Late Middle Ages and Early Modern Period* (Baltimore, MD: 1972), 79–106; A. Hudson, "From Oxford to Prague: The Writings of John Wyclif and his English Followers in Bohemia," *Slavonic and East European Review* 75 (1997), 642–57; and several studies by Vilém Herold, including "How Wycliffite Was the Bohemian Reformation?" *Bohemian Reformation and Religious Practice* 2 (1998), 25–37, and "The University of Paris and the Foundations of the Bohemian Reformation," *Bohemian Reformation and Religious Practice* 3 (2000), 15–24. My thanks to Stephen Lacey for advice on the topic.

18. On these glosses, see Šmahel, *Die Prager Universität*, 181, 260, 471.

19. Šmahel, *Die Prager Universität*, 476.

20. See H. Kaminsky, *A History of the Hussite Revolution* (Berkeley, CA: 1967); T. A Fudge, *Jerome of Prague and the Foundations of the Hussite Movement* (Oxford: 2016).

Chapter 78

1. J. N. Hillgarth, *Ramon Lull and Lullism in Fourteenth-Century France* (Oxford: 1971).

2. For a detailed account of his life, see A. Fidora and J. E. Rubio (eds), *Raimundus Lullus: An Introduction to His Life, Works and Thought* (Turnhout: 2008), part I. The main document for his life is an autobiography which is translated in A. Bonner (trans.), *Selected Works of Ramon Llull*, 2 vols (Princeton, NJ: 1985), at vol.1, 12–48; for a smaller selection, not including the autobiography, see A. Bonner (trans.), *Doctor Illuminatus: A Ramon Llull Reader* (Princeton, NJ: 1993).

3. On which, see M. D. Johnston, *The Spiritual Logic of Ramon Llull* (Oxford: 1987), ch.1. For his engagement with Islamic culture, see more generally D. Urvoy, *Penser l'islam: Les présupposes islamiques de l'Art de Lull* (Paris: 1980); G. B. Stone, "Ramon Llull," in M. R. Menocal (ed.), *The Cambridge History of Arabic Literature: The Literature of al-Andalus* (Cambridge: 2006), 345–57.

4. As noted by F. Domínguez in Fidora and Rubio, *Raimundus Lullus*, 125.

5. L. Badia et al., *Ramon Llull as a Vernacular Writer: Communicating a New Kind of Knowledge* (Woodbridge: 2016).

6. Fidora and Rubio, *Raimundus Lullus*, 63.

7. A quote from his *Tree of Science*, cited at Fidora and Rubio, *Raimundus Lullus*, 82.

8. For a detailed and clear account, see A. Bonner, *The Art and Logic of Ramon Llull: A User's Guide* (Leiden: 2007). See also F. A. Yates, *Lull and Bruno: Collected Essays I* (London: 1982); J. M. Ruiz Simon, *L'Art de Ramon Llull i la teoria escolàstica de la ciència* (Barcelona: 1999); P. Rossi, *Logic and the Art of Memory: The Quest for a Universal Language*, trans. S. Clucas (Chicago: 2000); F. Domínguez et al. (eds), *Arbor scientiae: der Baum des Wissens von Ramon Llull* (Turnhout: 2002). The article on Llull in the online *Stanford Encyclopedia of Philosophy* is also helpful, and includes images of the figures from the Art taken from Renaissance manuscripts.

9. Translated in Bonner, *Doctor Illuminatus*, 298–364, cited by page number in the main text.

10. Here I follow Bonner, *The Art and Logic of Ramon Llull*, 17.

11. As noted by Johnston, *The Spiritual Logic of Ramon Llull*, 308–12.

12. Bonner, *The Art and Logic of Ramon Llull*, 151.

13. The connection to trancendental theory is noted in passing by Johnston, *The Spiritual Logic of Ramon Llull*, 48. For a skeptical discussion of attempts to compare Llull to Anselm, see M. Colish, "The *Book of the Gentile and the Three Sages*: Ramon Llull as Anselm *Redivivus?*" in A. Musco et al. (eds), *Universalità della ragione: Pluralità delle filosofie nel medioevo*, vol.II.2 (Palermo: 2012), 1077–88. However, she focuses on their different approaches to logic, not the theology of perfect being.

14. Stone, "Ramon Llull," 346.

15. Selective translation in Bonner, *Doctor Illuminatus*, 85–171, cited by page number in the main text.

16. For Abelard's dialogue between a philosopher, Christian, and Jew, see P. V. Spade (trans.), *Peter Abelard: Ethical Writings* (Indianapolis, IN: 1995); for Judah Hallevi, see *Philosophy in the Islamic World*, ch.30.

17. Johnston, *The Spiritual Logic of Ramon Llull*, 140.

18. *On his Own Ignorance and that of Many Others* §49, in D. Marsh, *Francesco Petrarca: Invectives* (Cambridge, MA: 2003). On this work, see W. J. Kennedy, "The Economy of Invective and a Man in the Middle: *De Sui Ipsius et Multorum Ignorantia*," in V. Kirkham and A. Maggi (eds), *Petrarch: A Critical Guide to the Complete Works* (Chicago: 2009), 263–73.

19. *On his Own Ignorance* §107.

20. For what follows, see J. E. Siegel, *Rhetoric and Philosophy in Renaissance Humanism* (Princeton, NJ: 1968), ch.7; A. Mazzocco, "Petrarch: Founder of Renassance Humanism?" in A. Mazzocco (ed.), *Interpretations of Renaissance Humanism* (Leiden: 2006), 215–42; T. Kircher, "Petrarch and the Humanists," in A. R. Ascoli and U. Falkeid (eds), *The Cambridge Companion to Petrarch* (Cambridge: 2015), 179–90.

21. Especially R. G. Witt, *"In the Footsteps of the Ancients": The Origins of Humanism from Lovato to Bruni* (Leiden: 2000). I follow especially Mazzocco's interpretation here.

22. Cited in the main text by section number from N. Mann, *Francesco Petrarca: My Secret Book* (Cambridge, MA: 2016).

23. See A. Lee, *Petrarch and St Augustine: Classical Scholarship, Christian Theology and the Origins of the Renaissance in Italy* (Leiden: 2012).

24. G. Zak, *Petrarch's Humanism and the Care of the Self* (Cambridge: 2010).

25. Zak, *Petrarch's Humanism*, 113.

FURTHER READING

Further reading is suggested here for each of the main sections of the book, followed by recommendations for the topics of specific chapters. References on more specific topics and for primary literature in translation can be found in notes to the chapters of this volume.

In addition to the suggestions below, the online *Stanford Encyclopedia of Philosophy* has many pages on individual medieval thinkers. In this list I have mostly focused on English language publications, with some exceptions. It should, however, be noted that medieval philosophy is an area of scholarship where much important literature has been produced in French, German, Italian, and other European languages.

General Overviews

J. A. Aertsen and A. Speer (eds), *What is Philosophy in the Middle Ages?* (Berlin: 1998).

J. H. Burns (ed.), *The Cambridge History of Medieval Political Thought c.350–c.1450* (Cambridge: 1988).

J. Canning, *A History of Medieval Political Thought 300–1450* (London: 1996).

R. Cross, *The Medieval Christian Philosophers: An Introduction* (London: 2014).

J. E. Gracia and T. Noone (eds), *A Companion to Philosophy in the Middle Ages* (Oxford: 2003).

E. Grant, *God and Reason in the Middle Ages* (Cambridge: 2001).

D. Knowles, *The Evolution of Medieval Thought* (New York: 1964).

D. C. Lindberg and M. J. Shank (eds), *The Cambridge History of Science. Vol. 2: Medieval Science* (Cambridge: 2013).

A. S. McGrade (ed.), *The Cambridge Companion to Medieval Philosophy* (Cambridge: 2003).

J. Marenbon (ed.), *The Routledge History of Philosophy: The Middle Ages* (London: 1998).

J. Marenbon, *Medieval Philosophy: An Historical and Philosophical Introduction* (London: 2007).

R. Pasnau (ed.), *The Cambridge History of Medieval Philosophy*, 2 vols (Cambridge: 2010).

Anthologies of texts

R. N. Bosley and M. M. Tweedale (eds), *Basic Issues in Medieval Philosophy* (Ontario: 2006).

A. Hyman, J. Walsh, and T. Williams (eds), *Philosophy in the Middle Ages: The Christian, Islamic and Jewish Traditions* (Indianapolis, IN: 2010).

N. Kretzmann and E. Stump (ed. and trans.), *The Cambridge Translations of Medieval Philosophical Texts. Vol. 1: Logic and the Philosophy of Language* (Cambridge: 1988).

G. Klima (ed. and trans.), *Medieval Philosophy: Essential Readings with Commentary* (Oxford: 2007).

S. A. McGrade, J. Kilcullen, and M. Kempshall (ed. and trans.), *The Cambridge Translations of Medieval Philosophical Texts. Vol. 2: Ethics and Political Philosophy* (Cambridge: 2001).

R. Pasnau (ed. and trans.), *The Cambridge Translations of Medieval Philosophical Texts. Vol. 3: Mind and Knowledge* (Cambridge: 2002).

A. B. Schoedinger (ed.), *Readings in Medieval Philosophy* (New York: 1996).

Early Medieval

A. H. Armstrong (ed.), *The Cambridge History of Later Greek and Early Medieval Philosophy* (Cambridge: 1967).

I. Bajczy and R. G. Newhauser (eds), *Virtue and Ethics in the Twelfth Century* (Leiden: 2005).

P. Dronke (ed.), *A History of Twelfth-Century Western Philosophy* (Cambridge: 1988).

D. E. Luscombe, *The School of Peter Abelard* (Cambridge: 1970).

J. Marenbon, *Early Medieval Philosophy (480–1150): An Introduction* (London: 1988).

L. O. Nielsen, *Theology and Philosophy in the Twelfth Century* (Leiden: 1982).

R. W. Southern, *Scholastic Humanism and the Unification of Europe. Vol. 1: Foundations* and *Vol. 2: The Heroic Age* (Oxford: 1995 and 2001).

Thirteenth Century

H. Holzhey (ed.), *Grundriss der Geschichte der Philosophie: die Philosophie des Mittelalters, 13. Jahrhundert* (Basle: 2017).

N. Kretzmann, A. Kenny, and J. Pinborg (eds), *The Cambridge History of Later Medieval Philosophy* (Cambridge: 1982).

J. Marenbon, *Later Medieval Philosophy (1150–1350)* (London: 1987).

R. Pasnau, *Theories of Cognition in the Later Middle Ages* (Cambridge: 1997).

I. P. Wei, *Intellectual Culture in Medieval Paris: Theologians and the University, c.1100–1330* (Cambridge: 2012).

Fourteenth Century

S. Brown, T. Dewender, and T. Kobusch (eds), *Philosophical Debates at Paris in the Early Fourteenth Century* (Leiden: 2009).

W. J. Courtenay, *Schools and Scholars in Fourteenth-Century England* (Princeton, NJ: 1987).

W. J. Courtenay, *Changing Approaches to Fourteenth-Century Thought* (Toronto: 2007).

W. J. Courtenay, *Ockham and Ockhamism: Studies in the Dissemination and Impact of his Thought* (Leiden: 2008).

D. G. Denery, K. Ghosh, and N. Zeeman (eds), *Uncertain Knowledge: Scepticism, Relativism and Doubt in the Middle Ages* (Turnhout: 2014).

R. Friedman, *Intellectual Traditions at the Medieval University*, 2 vols (Leiden: 2013).

A. Hudson and M. Wilks (eds), *From Ockham to Wyclif* (Oxford: 1987).

G. Klima (ed.), *Intentionality, Cognition, and Mental Representation in Medieval Philosophy* (New York: 2015).

E. A. Moody, *Studies in Medieval Philosophy, Science, and Logic* (Berkeley, CA: 1975).

H. A. Oberman, *The Harvest of Medieval Theology: Gabriel Biel and Late Medieval Nominalism* (Cambridge, MA: 1963).

J. Verger, *Men of Learning at the End of the Middle Ages* (Notre Dame, IN: 2000).

A. B. Wolter, *Scotus and Ockham: Selected Essays* (St. Bonaventure, NY: 2003).

A. Zimmermann (ed.), *Antiqui und Moderni: Traditionsbewusstsein und Fortschrittsbewusstsein im späten Mittelalter* (Berlin: 1974).

The Carolingian Renaissance

D. A. Bullough, *Alcuin: Achievement and Reputation* (Leiden: 2004).

D. Dales, *Alcuin: Theology and Thought* (Cambridge: 2013).

L. A. J. R. Houwen and A. A. MacDonald, *Alcuin of York: Scholar at the Carolingian Court* (Groningen: 1998).

R. McKitterick, *Carolingian Culture: Emulation and Innovation* (Cambridge: 1994).

Eriugena

W. Beierwaltes (ed.), *Eriugena: Studien zu seinen Quellen* (Heidelberg: 1980).

D. Carabine, *John Scottus Eriugena* (Oxford: 2000).

D. Ganz, "The Debate on Predestination," in M. T. Gibson and J. L. Nelson (eds), *Charles the Bald: Court and Kingdom* (Aldershot: 1990), 283–302.

D. Moran, *The Philosophy of John Scottus Eriugena: A Study of Idealism in the Middle Ages* (Cambridge: 1989).

J. J. O'Meara, *Eriugena* (Oxford: 1988).

J. J. O'Meara and L. Bieler (eds), *The Mind of Eriugena* (Dublin: 1973).

The Roots of Scholasticism

J. J. Contreni, *Carolingian Learning: Masters and Manuscripts* (Aldershot: 1992).

M. Gibson, *Lanfranc of Bec* (Oxford: 1978).

C. E. Lutz, *Schoolmasters of the Tenth Century* (Hamden, CT: 1977).

J. Marenbon, *From the Circle of Alcuin to the School of Auxerre* (Cambridge: 1981).

Peter Damian

R. Gaskin, "Peter Damian on Divine Power and the Contingency of the Past", *British Journal for the History of Philosophy* 5 (1997) 229–47.

T. J. Holopainen, *Dialectic and Theology in the Eleventh Century* (Leiden: 1996).

P. Ranft, *The Theology of Peter Damian* (Washington DC: 2012).

I. M. Resnick, *Divine Power and Possibility in St. Peter Damian's De divina omnipotentia* (Leiden: 1992).

Anselm

B. Davies and B. Leftow (eds), *The Cambridge Companion to Anselm* (Cambridge: 2004).

G. R. Evans, *Anselm* (London: 1989).

J. Hopkins, *A Companion to the Study of St Anselm* (Minneapolis, MN: 1972).

K. A. Rogers, *Anselm on Freedom* (Oxford: 2008).

R. W. Southern, *Saint Anselm: A Portrait in a Landscape* (Cambridge: 1991).

E. Sweeney, *Anselm of Canterbury and the Desire for the Word* (Washington DC: 2012).

T. Williams and S. Visser, *Anselm* (New York: 2009).

The Ontological Argument

G. R. Evans, *Anselm and Talking about God* (Oxford: 1978).

J. Hick and A. C. McGill, *The Many-Faced Argument* (New York: 1967).

B. Leftow, "The Ontological Argument," in W. Wainwright (ed.), *The Oxford Handbook of Philosophy of Religion* (Oxford: 2005), 80–115.

N. Malcolm, "Anselm's Ontological Arguments," *Philosophical Review* 69 (1960), 41–62.

A. Plantinga (ed.), *The Ontological Argument* (Garden City, NY: 1965).

K. A. Rogers, *The Anselmian Approach to God and Creation* (Lewiston, NY: 1997).

The Problem of Universals

I. Iwakuma, "Vocales, or Early Nominalists," *Traditio* 47 (1992): 37–111.

A. de Libera, *La Querelle des universaux: de Platon à la fin du Moyen Âge* (Paris: 1996).

J. Marenbon, *Aristotelian Logic, Platonism and the Context of Early Medieval Philosophy in the West* (Aldershot: 2000).

P. V. Spade (trans.), *Five Texts on the Mediaeval Problem of Universals: Porphyry, Boethius, Abelard, Duns Scotus, Ockham* (Indianapolis, IN: 1994).

Heloise and Abelard

J. E. Brower and K. Guilfoy (eds), *The Cambridge Companion to Abelard* (Cambridge: 2004).

M. T. Clanchy, *Abelard: A Medieval Life* (Oxford: 1997).

D. E. Luscombe, *The School of Peter Abelard* (Cambridge: 1970).

J. Marenbon, *The Philosophy of Peter Abelard* (Cambridge: 1997).

J. Marenbon, *Abelard in Four Dimensions* (Notre Dame, IN: 2013).

C. J. Mews, *Peter Abelard* (London: 1995).

C. J. Mews, *Abelard and Heloise* (New York: 2005).

B. Wheeler (ed.), *Listening to Heloise: The Voice of a Twelfth-Century Woman* (New York: 2000).

The Victorines

R. Berndt (ed.), *Schrift, Schreiber, Schenker: Studien zur Abtei Sankt Viktor in Paris* (Berlin: 2005).

B. T. Coolman, *The Theology of Hugh of St Victor* (Cambridge: 2010).

C. S. Jaeger, "Humanism and Ethics at the School of St Victor in the Early Twelfth Century," *Mediaeval Studies* 55 (1993), 51–79.

P. Rorem, *Hugh of Saint Victor* (New York: 2009).

Philosophy at Chartres

J. Cadden, "Science and Rhetoric in the Middle Ages: The Natural Philosophy of William of Conches," *Journal of the History of Ideas* 56 (1995), 1–24.

P. Ellard, *The Sacred Cosmos: Theological, Philosophical and Scientific Conversations in the Twelfth-Century School of Chartres* (Scranton, PA: 2007).

J. Newell, "Rationalism at the School of Chartres," *Vivarium* 21 (1983), 108–26.

R. W. Southern, *Medieval Humanism and Other Studies* (Oxford: 1970).

W. Wetherbee, *Platonism and Poetry in the Twelfth Century* (Princeton, NJ: 1972).

Philosophy of Nature in the Twelfth Century

B. K. Balint, *Ordering Chaos: The Self and the Cosmos in Twelfth-Century Latin Prosimetrum* (Leiden: 2009).

P. Dronke, *Fabula: Explorations into the Uses of Myth in Medieval Platonism* (Leiden: 1974).

G. D. Economou, *The Goddess Natura in Medieval Literature* (Cambridge, MA: 1972).

G. R. Evans, *Alan of Lille: The Frontiers of Theology in the Later Twelfth Century* (Cambridge: 1983).

A. Speer, "The Discovery of Nature: The Contribution of the Chartrians to Twelfth-Century Attempts to Found a *Scientia Naturalis*," *Traditio* 52 (1997), 135–51.

B. Stock, *Myth and Science in the Twelfth Century: A Study of Bernard Silvester* (Princeton, NJ: 1972).

Gilbert of Poitiers on Individuation

L. M. de Rijk, "Semantics and Metaphysics in Gilbert of Poitiers: A Chapter of Twelfth-Century Platonism," *Vivarium* 26 (1988), 73–122 and 27 (1989), 1–35.

C. Erismann, "Explaining Exact Resemblance: Gilbert of Poitiers's *Conformitas* Theory Reconsidered," *Oxford Studies in Medieval Philosophy* 2 (2014), 1–24.

J. J. E. Garcia, *Introduction to the Problem of Individuation in the Early Middle Ages* (Munich: 1988).

H. C. Van Elswijk, *Gilbert Porreta: Sa vie, son œuvre, sa pensée* (Leuven: 1966).

Early Medieval Political Philosophy

C. J. Nederman and C. Campbell, "Priests, Kings and Tyrants: Spiritual and Temporal Power in John of Salisbury's *Politicratus*," *Speculum* 66 (1991), 572–90.

I. S. Robinson, *Authority and Resistance in the Investiture Contest* (New York: 1978).

B. Tierney, *The Crisis of Church and State 1050–1300* (Toronto: 1988).

M. Wilkes (ed.), *The World of John of Salisbury* (Oxford: 1984).

Gratian and Peter Lombard

M. L. Colish, *Peter Lombard*, 2 vols (Leiden: 1994).

W. Hartmann and K. Pennington (eds), *The History of Medieval Canon Law in the Classical Period, 1140–1234* (Washington DC: 2008).

C. Monagle, *Orthodoxy and Controversy in Twelfth-Century Religious Discourse: Peter Lombard's Sentences and the Development of Theology* (Turnhout: 2013).

P. W. Rosemann, *Peter Lombard* (New York: 2004).

P. W. Rosemann, *The Story of a Great Medieval Book: Peter Lombard's Sentences* (Ontario: 2007).

A. Winroth, *The Making of Gratian's Decretum* (Cambridge: 2000).

Hildegard of Bingen

C. Burnett and P. Dronke (eds), *Hildegard of Bingen: The Context of her Thought and Art* (London: 1998).

S. Flanagan, *Hildegard of Bingen 1098–1179: A Visionary Life* (London: 1998).

B. M. Kienzle, D. Stoudt and G. Ferzoco (eds), *A Companion to Hildegard of Bingen* (Leiden: 2014).

B. Newman (ed.), *Voice of the Living Light: Hildegard of Bingen and her World* (Berkeley, CA: 1998).

Translations into Latin

J. Brams, *La riscoperta di Aristotele in Occidente* (Milan: 2003).

C. Burnett, "Arabic into Latin: The Reception of Arabic Philosophy into Western Europe," in P. Adamson and R. C. Taylor (eds), *The Cambridge Companion to Arabic Philosophy* (Cambridge: 2005), 370–404.

C. Burnett, *Arabic into Latin in the Middle Ages* (Farnham: 2009).

D. N. Hasse, *Avicenna's De Anima in the Latin West: The Formation of a Peripatetic Philosophy of the Soul, 1160–1300* (London: 2000).

R. Pasnau, "The Latin Aristotle," in C. Shields (ed.), *The Oxford Handbook of Aristotle* (Oxford: 2012), 665–89.

The Rise of the Universities

A. B. Cobban, *The Medieval Universities: Their Development and Organization* (London: 1975).

W. J. Courtenay and J. Miethke (eds), *Universities and Schooling in Medieval Society* (Leiden: 2000).

F. C. Ferruolo, *The Origins of the University: The Schools of Paris and their Critics, 1100–1215* (Stanford, CA: 1985).

G. Leff, *Paris and Oxford Universities in the Thirteenth and Fourteenth Centuries: An Institutional and Intellectual History* (New York: 1968).

O. Pedersen, *The First Universities: Studium Generale and the Origins of University Education in Europe* (Cambridge: 1997).

H. de Ridder-Symoens (ed.), *A History of the University in Europe. Vol. 1: Universities in the Middle Ages* (Cambridge: 1992).

I. P. Wei, *Intellectual Culture in Medieval Paris: Theologians and the University, c.1100–1330* (Cambridge: 2012).

Thirteenth-Century Logic

A. Broadie, *Introduction to Medieval Logic* (Oxford: 1993).

D. M. Gabbay and J. Woods (eds), *Handbook of the History of Logic. Vol. 2: Mediaeval and Renaissance Logic* (Amsterdam: 2008).

L. M. de Rijk, *Logica Modernorum*, 2 vols (Assen: 1967).

J. Spruyt, "Thirteenth-Century Discussions on Modal Terms," *Vivarium* 32 (1994), 196–226.

J. Spruyt and C. Dutilh Novaes, "Those 'Funny Words': Medieval Theories of Syncategorematic Terms," in M. Cameron and R. J. Stainton (eds), *Linguistic Content: New Essays on the History of Philosophy of Language* (Oxford: 2015), 100–20.

Thirteenth-Century Physics

E. Grant, *Much Ado About Nothing: Theories of Space and Vacuum from the Middle Ages to the Scientific Revolution* (Cambridge: 1981).

A. Maier, *Studien zur Naturphilosophie der Spätscholastik*, 5 vols (Rome: 1949–55).

C. Trifogli, *Oxford Physics in the Thirteenth Century (ca. 1250–70): Motion, Infinity, Place and Time* (Leiden: 2000).

R. Wood, "Richard Rufus of Cornwall and Aristotle's Physics," *Franciscan Studies* 52 (1992), 247–81.

R. Wood, "Richard Rufus of Cornwall on Creation: The Reception of Aristotelian Physics in the West," *Medieval Philosophy and Theology* 2 (1992), 1–30.

R. Wood, "Richard Rufus: Physics at Paris before 1240," *Documenti e Studi sulla Tradizione Filosofica Medievale* 5 (1994), 87–127.

Thirteenth-Century Psychology

M. Bienak, *The Soul-Body Problem at Paris, ca. 1200–50: Hugo of St-Cher and his Contemporaries* (Leuven: 1974).

R. C. Dales, *The Problem of the Rational Soul in the Thirteenth Century* (Leiden: 1995).

S. W. de Boer, *The Science of the Soul: The Commentary Tradition on Aristotle's De anima, c.1260–c.1360* (Leuven: 2013).

E. A. Moody, "William of Auvergne and his Treatise *De Anima*," in E. A. Moody (ed.), *Studies in Medieval Philosophy, Science and Logic* (Berkeley, CA: 1975), 1–109.

R. J. Teske, *Teske, Studies in the Philosophy of William of Auvergne, Bishop of Paris (1228–1249)* (Milwaukee, WI: 2006).

The Transcendentals

J. A. Aertsen, "Beauty in the Middle Ages: A Forgotten Transcendental?" *Medieval Philosophy and Theology* 1 (1991), 68–97.

J. A. Aertsen, *Medieval Philosophy and the Transcendentals: The Case of Thomas Aquinas* (Leiden: 1996).

J. A. Aertsen, *Medieval Philosophy as Transcendental Thought: From Philip the Chancellor (ca. 1225) to Franciscio Suárez* (Leiden: 2012).

S. MacDonald (ed.), *Being and Goodness: The Concept of the Good in Metaphysics and Philosophical Theology* (Ithaca, NY: 1991).

S. MacDonald, "Goodness as a Transcendental: The Early Thirteenth-Century Recovery of an Aristotelian Idea," *Topoi* 11 (1992), 173–86.

Thirteenth-Century Ethics

I. P. Bejczy (ed.), *Virtue Ethics in the Middle Ages: Commentaries on Aristotle's Nicomachean Ethics, 1200–1500* (Leiden: 2008).

A. J. Celano, "The Understanding of the Concept of *Felicitas* in the Pre-1250 Commentaries on the *Ethica Nicomachea*," *Medioevo* 12 (1986), 29–53.

B. Kent, *Virtues of the Will: The Transformation of Ethics in the Late Thirteenth Century* (Washington DC: 1995).

D. Langston, "The Spark of Conscience: Bonaventure's View of Conscience and *Synderesis*," *Franciscan Studies* 53 (1993), 79–95.

J. Miller (ed.), *The Reception of Aristotle's Ethics* (Cambridge: 2012).

T. C. Potts, *Conscience in Medieval Philosophy* (Cambridge: 1980).

Robert Grosseteste

J. Flood, J. R. Ginther, and J. W. Goering (eds), *Robert Grosseteste and his Intellectual Milieu: New Editions and Studies* (Toronto: 2013).

J. McEvoy, *The Philosophy of Robert Grosseteste* (Oxford: 1982).

J. McEvoy (ed.), *Robert Grosseteste: New Perspectives on his Thought and Scholarship* (Dordrecht: 1995).

J. McEvoy, *Robert Grosseteste* (New York: 2000).

R. Southern, *Robert Grosseteste: The Growth of an English Mind in Medieval Europe* (Oxford: 1986).

C. Van Dyke, "The Truth, the Whole Truth, and Nothing but the Truth: Robert Grosseteste on Universals (and the *Posterior Analytics*)," *Journal of the History of Philosophy* 48 (2010), 153–70.

Roger Bacon

T. Crowley, *Roger Bacon: The Problem of the Soul in his Philosophical Commentaries* (Louvain: 1950).

J. Hackett, *Roger Bacon and the Sciences* (Leiden: 1997).

D. C. Lindberg, *Roger Bacon's Philosophy of Nature* (Oxford: 1983).
A. Power, *Roger Bacon and the Defense of Christendom* (Cambridge: 2012).

Bonaventure

J. G. Bougerol, *Introduction to the Works of Bonaventure* (New York: 1964).
C. M. Cullen, *Bonaventure* (Oxford: 2006).
E. Gilson, *The Christian Philosophy of St. Bonaventure*, trans. D. I. Trethowan and F. J. Sheed (London: 1940).
J. M. Hammond, J. A. Wayne Hellmann, and J. Goff (eds), *A Companion to Bonaventure* (Leiden: 2014).
A. Speer, "Illumination and Certitude: The Foundation of Knowledge in Bonaventure," *American Catholic Philosophical Quarterly* 85 (2011), 127–41.

Peter Olivi

A. Boureau and S. Piron (eds), *Pierre de Jean Olivi (1248–1298): Pensée scolastique, dissidence spirituelle et société* (Paris: 1999).
S. Brower-Toland, "Olivi on Consciousness and Self-Knowledge: The Phenomenology, Metaphysics, and Epistemology of Mind's Reflexivity," *Oxford Studies in Medieval Philosophy* 1 (2013), 136–71.
R. Pasnau, "Olivi on the Metaphysics of Soul," *Medieval Philosophy and Theology* 6 (1997), 109–32.
J. Toivanen, *Perception and the Internal Senses: Peter of John Olivi on the Cognitive Functions of the Sensitive Soul* (Leiden: 2013).

Franciscan Poverty

D. Burr, *Olivi and Franciscan Poverty: The Origins of the Usus Pauper Controversy* (Philadelphia, PA: 1989)
J. V. Fleming, *An Introduction to the Franciscan Literature of the Middle Ages* (Chicago: 1977).
K. L. Hughes, "Bonaventure's Defense of Mendicancy," in J. M. Hammond, J. A. Wayne Hellmann, and J. Goff (eds), *A Companion to Bonaventure* (Leiden: 2014), 509–42.
M. D. Lambert, *Franciscan Poverty: The Doctrine of the Absolute Poverty of Christ and the Apostles in the Franciscan Order 1210–1323* (London: 1961).
V. Mäkinen, *Property Rights in the Late Medieval Discussion on Franciscan Poverty* (Leuven: 2001).

Hadewijch and Mechthild of Magdeburg

P. Dronke, *Women Writers of the Middle Ages* (Cambridge: 1984).
A. Hollywood, *The Soul as Virgin Wife: Mechthild of Magdeburg, Marguerite Porete and Meister Eckhart* (Notre Dame, IN: 1995).
B. McGinn, *The Flowering of Mysticism: Men and Women in the New Mysticism, 1200–1350* (New York: 1998).
A. Minnis and R. Voaden (eds), *Medieval Holy Women in the Christian Tradition c.1100–c.1500* (Turnhout: 2010).
E. Petroff (ed.), *Medieval Women's Visionary Literature* (New York: 1986).
S. S. Poor, *Mechthild of Magdeburg and her Book: Gender and the Making of Textual Authority* (Philadelphia, PA: 2004).
F. Tobin, *Mechthild of Magdeburg: A Medieval Mystic in Modern Eyes* (Columbia, SC: 1995).

Robert Kilwardby

H. Lagerlund and P. Thom (eds), *A Companion to the Philosophy of Robert Kilwardby* (Leiden: 2013).

J. F. Silva, *Robert Kilwardby on the Human Soul: Plurality of Forms and Censorship in the Thirteenth Century* (Leiden: 2012).

P. Thom, *Logic and Ontology in the Syllogistic of Robert Kilwardby* (Leiden: 2007).

Albert the Great

T. Bonin, *Creation as Emanation: The Origin of Diversity in Albert the Great's* On the Causes and the Procession of the Universe (Notre Dame, IN: 2001).

S. B. Cunningham, *Reclaiming Moral Agency: The Moral Philosophy of Albert the Great* (Washington DC: 2008).

F. Kovach and R. Shahan (eds), *Albert the Great: Commemorative Essays* (Norman, OK: 1980).

A. de Libera, *Albert le Grand et la philosophie* (Paris: 1990).

G. Meyer and A. Zimmermann (eds), *Albertus Magnus, doctor universalis, 1280/1980* (Mainz: 1980).

I. M Resnick (ed.), *A Companion to Albert the Great* (Leiden: 2013).

O. P. Senner et al. (eds), *Albertus Magnus. Zum Gedenken nach 800 Jahren: Neue Zugänge, Aspekte und Perspektiven* (Berlin: 2001).

J. Weisheipl (ed.), *Albertus Magnus and the Sciences: Commemorative Essays 1980* (Toronto: 1980).

Thomas Aquinas

J. Brower, *Aquinas's Ontology of the Material World* (Oxford: 2014).

T. Cory, *Aquinas on Human Self-Knowledge* (Cambridge: 2013).

B. Davies (ed.), *The Oxford Handbook of Aquinas* (Oxford: 2012).

J. Finnis, *Aquinas: Moral, Political, and Legal Theory* (Oxford: 1988).

T. Hoffmann, J. Müller, and M. Perkams (eds), *Aquinas and the Nicomachean Ethics* (Cambridge: 2013).

J. Jenkins, *Knowledge and Faith in Thomas Aquinas* (Cambridge: 1997).

A. Kenny, *Aquinas on Mind* (New York: 1993).

N. Kretzmann, *The Metaphysics of Theism: Aquinas' Natural Theology in Summa Contra Gentiles*, 2 vols (Oxford: 1997 and 1999).

J. Owens, *St Thomas Aquinas on the Existence of God* (Albany, NY: 1980).

R. Pasnau, *Thomas Aquinas on Human Nature: A Philosophical Study of Summa Theologiae 1a 75–89* (Cambridge: 2002).

A. Pegis, *St. Thomas and the Problem of the Soul in the Thirteenth Century* (Toronto: 1934).

Just War Theory

J. T. Johnson, *The Just War Tradition and the Restraint of War* (Princeton, NJ: 1981).

G. M. Reichberg, *Thomas Aquinas on War and Peace* (Cambridge: 2016).

F. H. Russell, *The Just War in the Middle Ages* (Cambridge: 1975).

The Paris Condemnations

J. A. Aertsen, K. Emery, and A. Speer (eds), *After the Condemnation of 1277: Philosophy and Theology at the University of Paris in the Last Quarter of the Thirteenth Century* (Berlin: 2001).

L. Bianchi, *Censure et liberté intellectuelle à l'université de Paris (XIIIe–XIVe siècles)* (Paris: 1999).

K. Flasch, *Aufklärung im Mittelalter? Die Verurteilung von 1277* (Frankfurt: 1989).

R. Hissette, *Enquête sur les 219 articles condamnés à Paris le 7 mars 1277* (Louvain: 1977).

J. Thijssen, *Censure and Heresy at the University of Paris 1200–1400* (Philadelphia, PA: 1998).

J. F. Wippel, "The Condemnations of 1270 and 1277 at Paris," *Journal of Medieval and Renaissance Studies* 7 (1977), 169–201.

"Latin Averroists"

R. C. Dales, "The Origin of the Doctrine of the Double Truth," *Viator* 15 (1984), 169–79.

G. Klima, "*Ancilla Theologiae* vs *Domina Philosophorum*: Thomas Aquinas, Latin Averroism and the Autonomy of Philosophy," in J. A. Aertsen and A. Speer (eds.), *Was ist Philosophie im Mittelalter?* (Berlin: 1998), 393–402.

F.-X. Putallaz and R. Imbach, *Profession: Philosophe. Siger de Brabant* (Paris: 1997).

F. van Steenberghen, *Thomas Aquinas and Radical Aristotelianism* (Washington DC: 1970).

F. van Steenberghen, *Maître Siger de Brabant* (Louvain: 1977).

The Eternity of the World

R. C. Dales, *Medieval Discussions of the Eternity of the World* (Leiden: 1990).

M. de Mowbray, "The *De Aeternitate Mundi* of Boethius of Dacia and the Paris Condemnation of 1277," *Recherches de Théologie et Philosophie* 73 (2006), 201–56.

J. F. Wippel, "Did Thomas Aquinas Defend the Possibility of an Eternally Created World?" *Journal of the History of Philosophy* 19 (1981), 21–37.

J. B. M. Wissink (ed.), *The Eternity of the World in the Thought of Thomas Aquinas and his Contemporaries* (Leiden: 1990).

Speculative Grammar

J. E. Ashworth, *The Tradition of Medieval Logic and Speculative Grammar from Anselm to the End of the Seventeenth Century* (Toronto: 1977).

G. L. Bursill-Hall, *Speculative Grammars of the Middle Ages: The Doctrine of the Partes Orationis of the Modistae* (The Hague: 1971).

S. Ebbesen and R. L. Friedman (eds), *Medieval Analyses in Language and Cognition* (Copenhagen: 1999).

J. L. Fink, H. Hansen, and A. M. Mora-Márquez (eds), *Logic and Language in the Middle Ages: A Volume in Honour of Sten Ebbesen* (Leiden: 2013).

A. M. Mora-Márquez, *The Thirteenth-Century Notion of Signification* (Leiden: 2015).

J. Pinborg, *Die Entwicklung der Sprachtheorie im Mittelalter* (Münster: 1967).

I. Rosier, *La Grammaire spéculative des Modistes* (Paris: 1983).

The *Romance of the Rose*

N. Cohn, *The World-View of a Thirteenth-Century Parisian Intellectual: Jean de Meun and the Roman de la Rose* (Durham: 1961).

J. V. Fleming, *Reason and the Lover* (Princeton, NJ: 1984).

S. Kay, *The Romance of the Rose* (London: 1995).

M. Luria, *A Reader's Guide to the Roman de la Rose* (Hamden, CT: 1982).

J. Morton, *The Roman de la Rose in its Philosophical Context: Art, Nature, and Ethics* (Oxford: 2018).

Henry of Ghent

G. Guldentops and C. Steel (eds), *Henry of Ghent and the Transformation of Scholastic Thought* (Leuven: 2003).

S. P. Marrone, *Truth and Scientific Knowledge in the Thought of Henry of Ghent* (Cambridge, MA: 1985).

M. Pickavé, *Heinrich von Gent über Metaphysik als erste Wissenschaft: Studien zu einem Metaphysikentwurf aus dem letzten Viertel des 13. Jahrhunderts* (Leiden: 2007).

W. Vanhamel (ed.), *Henry of Ghent: Proceedings of the International Colloquium on the Occasion of the 700th Anniversary of his Death* (Leuven: 1996).

G. A. Wilson (ed.), *A Companion to Henry of Ghent* (Leiden: 2011).

The Trinity and the Eucharist

L. Bianchi (ed.), *L'eucaristia nella tradizione orientale e occidentale* (Venice: 2007).

D. Burr, *Eucharistic Presence and Conversion in Late Thirteenth-Century Franciscan Thought* (Philadelphia, PA: 1984).

G. Emery, *The Trinitarian Theology of St Thomas Aquinas*, trans. F. A. Murphy (Oxford: 2007).

J. C. Flores, *Henry of Ghent: Metaphysics and the Trinity* (Leuven: 2006).

R. L. Friedman, *Medieval Trinitarian Thought from Aquinas to Ockham* (Cambridge: 2010).

M. McCord Adams, *Some Later Medieval Theories of the Eucharist* (Oxford: 2010).

Duns Scotus

R. Cross, *The Physics of Duns Scotus: The Scientific Context of a Theological Vision* (Oxford: 1998).

R. Cross, *Duns Scotus* (New York: 1999).

R. Cross, *Duns Scotus on God* (Aldershot: 2005).

R. Cross, *Duns Scotus' Theory of Cognition* (Oxford: 2014).

L. Honnefelder, R. Wood, and M. Dreyer (eds), *John Duns Scotus: Metaphysics and Ethics* (Leiden: 1996).

G. Pini, "Scotus on Universals: A Reconsideration," *Documenti e Studi sulla Tradizione Filosofica Medievale* 18 (2007), 395–409.

M. M. Tweedale, *Scotus vs Ockham: A Medieval Dispute over Universals*, 2 vols (Lewiston, NY: 1999).

T. Williams, "The Libertarian Foundations of Scotus's Moral Philosophy," *The Thomist* 62 (1997), 193–215.

T. Williams (ed.), *The Cambridge Companion to Duns Scotus* (Cambridge: 2003).

A. B. Wolter, *The Philosophical Theology of John Duns Scotus*, ed. M. McCord Adams (Ithaca, NY: 1990).

Marguerite Porete

A. Hollywood, *The Soul as Virgin Wife: Mechthild of Magdeburg, Marguerite Porete and Meister Eckhart* (Notre Dame, IN: 1995).

D. Kangas, "Dangerous Joy: Marguerite Porete's Good-bye to the Virtues," *The Journal of Religion* 91 (2011), 299–319.

S. Kocher, *Allegories of Love in Marguerite Porete's Mirror of Simple Souls* (Turnhout: 2008).

J. Maguire Robinson, *Nobility and Annihilation in Marguerite Porete's Mirror of Simple Souls* (Albany, NY: 2002).

M. G. Sargent, "The Annihilation of Marguerite Porete," *Viator* 28 (1997), 253–79.

Dante Alighieri

E. Gilson, *Dante and Philosophy*, trans. D. Moore (London: 1948).

R. Imbach, *Dante, la philosophie et les laïcs* (Fribourg: 1996).

R. Jacoff (ed.), *The Cambridge Companion to Dante* (Cambridge: 1993).

C. Moevs, *The Metaphysics of Dante's Divine Comedy* (Oxford: 2005).

J. A. Scott, *Understanding Dante* (Notre Dame, IN: 2004).

Church and State

C. F. Briggs and P. S. Eardley (eds), *A Companion to Giles of Rome* (Leiden: 2016).

J. Canning, *Ideas of Power in the Late Middle Ages, 1296–1417* (Cambridge: 2014).

A. P. d'Entrèves, *Dante as a Political Thinker* (Oxford: 1952).

J. M. Ferrante, *The Political Vision of the Divine Comedy* (Princeton, NJ: 1984).

J. Miethke, *De potestate papae: die päpstliche Amtskompetenz im Widerstreit der politischen Theorie von Thomas von Aquin bis Wilhelm von Ockham* (Tübingen: 2000).

M. Wilks, *The Problem of Sovereignty in the Later Middle Ages* (Cambridge: 1963).

Marsilius of Padua

A. Brett, *Liberty, Right and Nature: Individual Rights in Later Scholastic Thought* (Cambridge: 1997).

G. Briguglia, *Marsilio da Padova* (Rome: 2013).

A. Gewirth, *Marsilius of Padua and Medieval Political Philosophy* (New York: 1951).

G. Moreno-Riaño (ed.), *The World of Marsilius of Padua* (Turnhout: 2006).

G. Moreno-Riaño and C. J. Nederman (eds), *A Companion to Marsilius of Padua* (Leiden: 2012).

C. J. Nederman, *Community and Consent: The Secular Political Theory of Marsiglio of Padua's Defensor pacis* (Lanham, MD: 1995).

William of Ockham

L. Freppert, *The Basis of Morality according to William of Ockham* (Chicago: 1988).

M. McCord Adams, *William Ockham*, 2 vols (Notre Dame, IN: 1987).

A. S. McGrade, *The Political Thought of William of Ockham* (Cambridge: 1974).

A. Maurer, *The Philosophy of William of Ockham in the Light of its Principles* (Toronto: 1999).

T. M. Osborne, "Ockham as a Divine-Command Theorist," *Religious Studies* 41 (2005), 2–11.

C. Panaccio, *Ockham on Concepts* (Aldershot: 2004).

P. V. Spade (ed.), *The Cambridge Companion to Ockham* (Cambridge: 1999).

Responses to Ockham

S. Brower-Toland, "How Chatton Changed Ockham's Mind: William Ockham and Walter Chatton on Objects and Acts of Judgment," in G. Klima (ed.), *Intentionality, Cognition and Mental Representation in Medieval Philosophy* (Fordham, NY: 2014), 204–34.

A. D. Conti (ed.), *A Companion to Walter Burley, Late Medieval Logician and Metaphysician* (Leiden: 2013).

W. Courtenay, *Adam Wodeham: An Introduction to his Life and Writings* (Leiden: 1978).

E. Karger, "Walter Burley's Realism," *Vivarium* 37 (1999), 24–40.

C. Rode (ed.), *A Companion to Responses to Ockham* (Leiden: 2016).

K. Tachau, *Vision and Certitude in the Age of Ockham* (Leiden: 1988).

Foreknowledge and Predestination

W. L. Craig, *The Problem of Divine Foreknowledge and Future Contingents from Aristotle to Suarez* (Leiden: 1988).

E. W. Dolnikowski, *Thomas Bradwardine: A View of Time and a Vision of History in Fourteenth-Century Thought* (Leiden: 1995).

H. G. Gelber, *It Could Have Been Otherwise: Contingency and Necessity in Dominican Theology at Oxford, 1300–1350* (Leiden: 2004).

G. Leff, *Bradwardine and the Pelagians* (Cambridge: 1957).

D. Perler, *Predestination, Zeit und Kontingenz* (Amsterdam: 1988).

C. Schabel, *Theology at Paris, 1316–1245: Peter Auriol and the Problem of Divine Foreknowledge and Future Contingents* (Aldershot: 2000).

Fourteenth-Century Logic

C. Dutilh Novaes, *Formalizing Medieval Logic: Supposition, Consequentia and Obligations* (Berlin: 2007).

C. Dutilh Novaes and S. Read (eds), *The Cambridge Companion to Medieval Logic* (Cambridge: 2016).

T. Parsons, *Articulating Medieval Logic* (Oxford: 2014).

S. Read (ed.), *Sophisms in Medieval Logic and Grammar* (Dordrecht: 1993).

P. V. Spade, *Lies, Language and Logic in the Late Middle Ages* (London: 1988).

M. Yrjönsuuri (ed.), *Medieval Formal Logic* (Dordrecht: 2001).

The Oxford Calculators

R. C. Dales, *The Scientific Achievement of the Middle Ages* (Philadelphia, PA: 1973).

A. Maier, *Studien zur Naturphilosophie der Spätscholastik*, 5 vols (Rome: 1949–68).

E. D. Sylla, *The Oxford Calculators and the Mathematics of Motion* (New York: 1991).

E. D. Sylla, "The Oxford Calculators' Middle Degree Theorem in Context," *Early Science and Medicine* 15 (2010), 338–70.

C. Wilson, *William Heytesbury: Medieval Logic and the Rise of Mathematical Physics* (Madison, WI: 1956).

Fourteenth-Century Physics

M. Clagett, *The Science of Mechanics in the Middle Ages* (Madison, WI: 1961).

A. Goddu, *The Physics of William of Ockham* (Leiden: 1984).

E. Grant, *The Nature of Natural Philosophy in the Late Middle Ages* (Washington DC: 2010).

C. Grellard and R. Aurélien (eds), *Atomism in Late Medieval Philosophy and Theology* (Leiden: 2009).

N. Kretzmann (ed.), *Infinity and Continuity in Antiquity and Medieval Thought* (Ithaca, NY: 1982).

A. Maier, *On the Threshold of Exact Science: Selected Writings of Anneliese Maier on Late Medieval Natural Philosophy*, ed. and trans. S. D. Sargent (Philadelphia, PA: 1982).

John Buridan

J. Biard, *Science et nature: La théorie buridanienne du savoir* (Paris: 2012).

G. Klima, *John Buridan* (New York: 2008).

J. Pinborg (ed.), *The Logic of John Buridan* (Copenhagen: 1976).

J. M. M. H. Thijssen and J. Zupko (eds), *The Metaphysics and Natural Philosophy of John Buridan* (Leiden: 2001).

J. Zupko, *John Buridan: Portrait of a Fourteenth-Century Arts Master* (Notre Dame, IN: 2003).

Nicholas of Autrecourt

C. Grellard, *Croire et savoir: Les principes de la connaissance selon Nicolas d'Autrécourt* (Paris: 2005).

H. Lagerlund (ed.), *Rethinking the History of Skepticism: The Missing Medieval Background* (Leiden: 2010).

E. A. Moody, "Ockham, Buridan, and Nicholas of Autrecourt," *Franciscan Studies* 7 (1947), 113–46.

D. Perler, *Zweifel und Gewissheit: skeptische Debatten im Mittelalter* (Frankfurt: 2006).

J. R. Weinberg, *Nicholas of Autrecourt: A Study in 14th Century Thought* (Princeton, NJ: 1948).

J. Zupko, "Buridan and Skepticism," *Journal of the History of Philosophy* 31 (1993), 191–221.

Medieval Economic Theory

B. Gordon, *Economic Analysis before Adam Smith* (London: 1975).

J. Kaye, *Economy and Nature in the Fourteenth Century: Money, Market Exchange, and the Emergence of Scientific Thought* (Cambridge: 1998).

O. Langholm, *Economics in the Medieval Schools* (Leiden: 1992).

J. Le Goff, *Your Money or Your Life: Economy and Religion in the Middle Ages* (New York: 1990).

D. Wood, *Medieval Economic Thought* (Cambridge: 2004).

Meister Eckhart

J. M. Connolly, *Living without Why: Meister Eckhart's Critique of the Medieval Concept of Will* (Oxford: 2014).

K. Flasch, *Meister Eckhart: Philosoph des Christentums* (Munich: 2010).

J. M. Hackett (ed.), *A Companion to Meister Eckhart* (Leiden: 2013).

B. McGinn, *The Mystical Thought of Meister Eckhart: The Man from whom God Hid Nothing* (New York: 2001).

K. Ruh, *Meister Eckhart: Theologe, Prediger, Mystiker* (Munich: 1985).

F. Tobin, *Meister Eckhart: Thought and Language* (Philadelphia, PA: 1986).

The German Dominicans

J. Biard, *Recherches sur Dietrich de Freiberg* (Turnhout: 2009).

K. Flasch, *Von Meister Dietrich zu Meister Eckhart* (Hamburg: 1987).

K. Flasch, *Dietrich von Freiberg: Philosophie, Theologie, Naturforschung um 1300* (Frankfurt am Main: 2007),

A. de Libera, *Introduction à la mystique rhénane* (Paris: 1999).

B. Mojsisch, *Die Theorie des Intellekts bei Dietrich von Freiberg* (Hamburg: 1977).

K. Ruh, *Geschichte der abendländischen Mystik, 3. Band: die Mystik des deutschen Predigerordens und ihre Grundlegung durch die Hochscholastik* (Munich: 1993).

L. Sturlese, *Eckhart, Tauler, Suso: Filosofi e mistici nella Germania medievale* (Florence: 2010).

Angels in Medieval Philosophy

M. L. Colish, "Early Scholastic Angelology," *Recherches de Théologie Ancienne et Médiévale* 67 (1995), 80–109.

T. Hoffmann (ed.), *A Companion to Angels in Medieval Philosophy* (Leiden: 2012).

I. Iribarren and M. Lenz, *Angels in Medieval Philosophical Inquiry: Their Function and Significance* (Aldershot: 2008).

D. Keck, *Angels and Angelology in the Middle Ages* (New York: 1998).

T. Suarez-Nani, *Les Anges et la philosophie* (Paris: 2002).

English Mysticism

L. Herbert McAvoy (ed.), *A Companion to Julian of Norwich* (Cambridge: 2008).

D. Knowles, *The English Mystical Tradition* (London: 1961).

S. J. McEntire, *Julian of Norwich: A Book of Essays* (New York: 1998).

J. M. Nuth, *Wisdom's Daughter: The Theology of Julian of Norwich* (New York: 1991).

Chaucer and Langland

D. N. Baker, "From Plowing to Penitence: *Piers Plowman* and Fourteenth-Century Theology," *Speculum* 55 (1980), 715–25.

P. Boitani and J. Mann (eds), *The Cambridge Companion to Chaucer* (Cambridge: 1986).

A. Cole and A. Galloway, *The Cambridge Companion to Piers Plowman* (Cambridge: 2014).

J. Coleman, *Piers Plowman and the Moderni* (Rome: 1981).

R. Davis, *Piers Plowman and the Books of Nature* (Oxford: 2016).

K. Kerby-Fulton, "*Piers Plowman*," in D. Wallace (ed.), *The Cambridge History of Medieval English Literature* (Cambridge: 1999), 513–38.

Sexuality and Misogyny in the Middle Ages

A. Blamires, *The Case for Women in Medieval Culture* (Oxford: 1997).

V. L. Bullough and J. A. Brundage (eds), *Handbook of Medieval Sexuality* (New York: 1996).

P. Dronke, *Women Writers of the Middle Ages* (Cambridge: 1984).

M. H. Green, *Making Women's Medicine Masculine: The Rise of Male Authority in Pre-Modern Gynaecology* (Oxford: 2008).

M. D. Jordan, *The Invention of Sodomy in Christian Theology* (Chicago: 1997).

R. M. Karras, *Sexuality in Medieval Europe: Doing unto Others* (London: 2017).

K. Pratt and C. W. Marx (eds), *Woman Defamed and Woman Defended* (Oxford: 1992).

Catherine of Siena and Affective Mysticism

C. W. Bynum, *Holy Feast and Holy Fast: The Religious Significance of Food to Medieval Women* (Berkeley, CA: 1987).

C. W. Bynum, *Fragmentation and Redemption: Essays on Gender and the Human Body in Medieval Religion* (New York: 1992).

C. Dinshaw and D. Wallace (eds), *The Cambridge Companion to Medieval Women's Writing* (Cambridge: 2003).

A. Hollywood, *Sensible Ecstasy: Mysticism, Sexual Difference, and the Demands of History* (Chicago: 2002).

F. T. Luongo, *The Saintly Politics of Catherine of Siena* (Ithaca, NY: 2006).

C. Muessig, G. Ferzoco, and B. M. Kienzle (eds), *A Companion to Catherine of Siena* (Leiden: 2012).

E. A. Petroff, *Body and Soul: Essays on Medieval Women and Mysticism* (New York: 1994).

C. Van Dyke, "Self-Knowledge, Abnegation, and Fulfillment in Medieval Mysticism," in U. Renz (ed.), *Self-Knowledge* (Oxford: 2017), 131–45.

Jean Gerson

D. C. Brown, *Pastor and Laity in the Theology of Jean Gerson* (Cambridge: 1987).

M. S. Burrows, *Jean Gerson and De Consolatione Theologiae* (Tübingen: 1991).

A. Combes, *La Théologie mystique de Gerson: Profil de son évolution* (Paris: 1963–64).

B. P. McGuire, *Jean Gerson and the last Medieval Reformation* (University Park, PA: 2005).

B. P. McGuire (ed.), *A Companion to Jean Gerson* (Leiden: 2006).

G. H. M. Posthumus Meyjes, *Jean Gerson: Apostle of Unity* (Leiden: 1999).

John Wyclif

A. Hudson, *The Premature Reformation* (London: 1988).

S. E. Lahey, *Metaphysics and Politics in the Thought of John Wyclif* (Cambridge: 2003).

S. E. Lahey, *John Wyclif* (New York: 2009).

I. C. Levy (ed.), *A Companion to John Wyclif: Late Medieval Theologian* (Leiden: 2006).

A. Kenny, *Wyclif* (Oxford: 1985).

A. Kenny (ed.), *Wyclif in his Times* (Oxford: 1986).

J. A. Robson, *Wyclif and the Oxford Schools* (Cambridge: 1961).

Scholasticism across Europe

M. J. F. M. Hoenen and P. J. J. M. Bakker (eds), *Philosophie und Theologie des ausgehenden Mittelalters: Marsilius von Inghen und das Denken seiner Zeit* (Leiden: 2000).

J. Ijsewijn and J. Paquet (eds), *The Universities in the Late Middle Ages* (Leuven: 1978).

M. H. Shank, *"Unless You Believe, You Shall Not Understand": Logic, University, and Society in Late Medieval Vienna* (Princeton, NJ: 1988).

N. Siriasi, *Arts and Sciences at Padua: The Studium of Padua before 1350* (Toronto: 1973).

F. Šmahel, *Die Prager Universität im Mittelalter: Charles University in the Middle Ages* (Leiden: 2007).

Ramon Llull

A. Bonner, *The Art and Logic of Ramon Llull: A User's Guide* (Leiden: 2007).

A. Fidora and J. E. Rubio (eds), *Raimundus Lullus: An Introduction to His Life, Works and Thought* (Turnhout: 2008).

M. D. Johnston, *The Spiritual Logic of Ramon Llull* (Oxford: 1987).

Petrarch

A. R. Ascoli and U. Falkeid (eds), *The Cambridge Companion to Petrarch* (Cambridge: 2015).

V. Kirkham and A. Maggi (eds), *Petrarch: A Critical Guide to the Complete Works* (Chicago: 2009).

N. Mann, *Petrarch* (Oxford: 1984).

A. Mazzocco, "Petrarch: Founder of Renassance Humanism?" in A. Mazzocco (ed.), *Interpretations of Renaissance Humanism* (Leiden: 2006), 215–42.

C. Trinkaus, *The Poet as Philosopher: Petrarch and the Formation of Renaissance Consciousness* (New Haven, CT: 1979).

G. Zak, *Petrarch's Humanism and the Care of the Self* (Cambridge: 2010).

PUBLISHER'S ACKNOWLEDGMENTS

We are grateful for permission to include the following copyright material in this book.

The poem about the cat Pangur, printed at the start of Chapter 5, is from Anon., 'The Monk and His Cat', trans. by W.H. Auden, in *A Thematic Catalogue of the Complete Works*, by Samuel Barber (2012). Reproduced with permission of Oxford University Press through PLSclear.
The verse about love which appears at the end of Chapter 19 is '[*Caritas abundat*] Psalm antiphon for the Holy Spirit as Divine Love' (D 157r, R466v) by Hildegard of Bingen. Latin collated from the transcription of Beverly Lomer and the edition of Barbara Newman; trans. by Nathaniel M. Campbell / International Society of Hildegard von Bingen Studies.

The publisher and author have made every effort to trace and contact all copyright holders before publication. If notified, the publisher will be pleased to rectify any errors or omissions at the earliest opportunity.

INDEX

Note: names are alphabetized according to our best guess at what readers will look up first, e.g. "William of Ockham" under "Ockham" but "William of Moerbeke" under "William." If you don't find it on the first try, look under the other option.

For the benefit of digital users, indexed terms that span two pages (e.g., 52–53) may, on occasion, appear on only one of those pages.

Abbo of Fleury 36, 101, 116
Abelard, Peter 5–6, 35, 40, 61–78, 80, 85–6,
 88–94, 96–7, 102, 112–13, 118, 122, 124–6, 131,
 136, 143, 148, 156, 158, 185, 190, 250, 262, 284,
 322, 326, 350–3, 356, 364, 474, 506–7, 520, 540
Abraham 345–8
Academic Skeptics 456–7
accidents 30, 63–5, 108–10, 305–6, 308–9, 330, 334,
 459, 484–5
Accursius 122, 270, 465
Adam 17–18, 50, 62, 83, 100, 108, 130, 196, 203–4,
 239–40, 384
Adam Wodeham 361, 363, 414–16, 430, 443, 446,
 476, 533
Adelard of Bath 102–3, 135, 137
adoptionism 15–16
Aeneas 97, 386
aesthetics 180–1, 375–6, 517–19
afterlife 6, 23, 147, 169–71, 183–4, 190–1, 203–4, 214,
 246, 251–2, 264–5, 290, 292, 349–50, 376–7,
 379, 514
Albert the Great 8, 140, 164, 187, 202, 230, 236–50,
 256, 264–5, 272, 285–6, 290, 295–6, 302, 317,
 349, 366, 368, 376, 435, 466, 477, 480–1, 484,
 490, 503, 505, 530
Albert of Saxony 534
Albertino Mussato 541
alchemy 200, 238–9, 469, 536–7
Alcibiades 94
Alcuin 4, 10–16, 19, 29, 34, 36, 99, 101, 115
Alan of Lille 102–5, 133, 312–13, 315, 495,
 498, 501, 541
Alexander of Aphrodisias 173, 189
Alexander of Bernai 370
Alexander the Great 195, 236, 370
Alexander of Hales 178, 180, 195, 204, 216,
 236, 271, 295
analogy 197–8, 334–6, 471–3
Anastasius 115
Anaximander 242
Andreas Capellanus 311
Andrew of Saint Victor 81

angels 6–7, 51, 109–10, 190, 207, 240–1, 288, 293,
 355, 447, 482–8, 520
Anselm of Canterbury 5, 35, 45–57, 61, 88,
 91, 135, 143, 322–3, 340, 350, 378, 405, 509, 539
Anselm of Laon 67, 71, 78, 94, 102, 117
Antony the Great 215
Aquinas, Thomas 5, 8–9, 52, 84, 98, 122, 125, 136,
 139–41, 147, 149, 179–81, 187, 201, 209–11,
 217, 229, 234, 236, 243, 247–67, 271–5,
 281–2, 285–6, 288, 291–3, 296, 299, 301–3,
 318–20, 325–35, 344, 348–50, 355, 361,
 365–6, 376–8, 383, 385, 387, 403, 413,
 416, 419, 422, 436, 449, 453, 463–7,
 472, 476–8, 481, 483–4, 486–7, 490,
 504–5, 516, 527–8, 531
Arnold of Strelley 423
asceticism *see* poverty
Arianism 327–9
Aristotle 3, 5, 8, 11, 12, 33, 35, 37, 48, 59–60, 67–8,
 74, 90, 96, 100, 105, 108, 110, 119, 128, 136–41,
 147–8, 153–7, 159–70, 172, 174, 177–80, 182–4,
 187–90, 192–3, 196, 201–2, 204–7, 209–10, 219,
 222, 229–31, 242–3, 245–6, 249–52, 254–6, 259,
 261, 264–7, 272–3, 275, 284–7, 290–303, 305,
 318, 320, 323, 326–7, 332, 334, 341, 348–50, 357,
 361, 365, 377–8, 384–5, 387, 390, 401, 408–9,
 413–14, 418–19, 423, 434, 436, 439–40,
 442–7, 452–3, 457–60, 463–7, 469, 483,
 485, 488, 500, 520, 531, 534, 540
 commentaries on 8–9, 59, 184, 201–2, 249, 417,
 450, 531, 534
 Categories 30, 67–8, 154–5, 332–3
 On Interpretation 12–13, 154–5, 177–8, 339–40,
 408, 421–2
 On Heavens 189–90, 442–3
 Metaphysics 175–6, 180, 243, 340, 375
 Nicomachean Ethics 140, 183–4, 189–90, 236–7,
 263–4, 450, 540
 Physics 417, 436, 446–7, 450
 On Plants 237
 Politics 390
 Posterior Analytics 139–41, 190, 251–2, 305, 333

Aristotle (cont.)
  Prior Analytics 154–5
  Sophistical Refutations 141, 154–5, 434
  On the Soul 189, 259–60, 291
  Topics 154, 298–9, 303
astrology 105, 199, 238, 444, 447–8, 530–1
astronomy 9–10, 34, 36, 101, 442–3, 447–8, 530
atheism 6–7, 17, 53, 252, 267, 449, 493
atomism 79, 99, 242, 445–6, 527
Augustus Caesar 386
Augustine 4–5, 8, 11, 15–19, 21–3, 28, 30, 33, 35, 37,
  47–8, 51, 71, 79, 87, 91, 101, 116–7, 122, 131–2, 136,
  147, 158, 164–5, 169–70, 172, 174, 176, 180, 182,
  188–9, 196, 201–2, 204–5, 207, 229–33, 246,
  249, 251, 253, 255, 260, 262–4, 278–81, 302,
  315–16, 318, 326, 350, 413, 425–6, 466, 493,
  502, 504, 514, 526, 532, 541–2
Avendauth (Abraham Ibn Daud) 138, 243
Averroes and Averroism 3, 136, 138–9, 141, 147,
  163–7, 170, 249, 256, 259, 285–6, 290–93,
  299–300, 306, 314, 377, 379, 438–9, 448,
  457, 531, 537
Avicenna 3, 36, 53–4, 57, 13–39, 141, 168, 170–3,
  172–3,179–80, 183, 198, 238–40, 243–4, 249,
  254, 260, 287, 298–9, 301, 313, 333, 336, 338,
  342, 344, 354, 402, 439, 448, 477, 483–4, 503
awareness 208, 213–14, 233, 336, 463; see also
  self-awareness

Bacon, Francis 200
Bacon, Roger 9, 141, 171, 192–200, 210, 212–13, 233,
  236–8, 289, 368, 435, 444, 485, 534
al-Baghdādī, Abū l-Barakāt 440
Beatrice of Nazareth 513
beauty 180–1, 192, 264–5
Becket, Thomas 81
Bede 13, 15, 32, 101
St Benedict 13, 89
being 33, 57, 93, 175–81, 244, 321–2, 332–8, 471–3;
  see also essence-existence distinction
  mental 55–6, 253, 343, 354, 364, 403–12,
  437, 478
Beguines 223–4, 227, 312, 369, 511
Berengar of Poitiers 91, 329
Berengar of Tours 37–8, 48, 116, 326
Bernard of Arezzo 457–8
Bernard of Clairvaux 67, 81, 86, 88–9, 91–3,
  113, 118, 125, 129, 131, 148, 227, 246, 480,
  511, 513
Bernard of Chartres 94–8, 109, 118, 154
Bernard Silvestris 95–7, 103–4, 131, 133
Berthold of Moosburg 478–81
Bible
  commentaries 13, 32–3, 70–1, 91, 138, 209,
  249–50, 470
  interpretations of 13, 27, 80–2, 84–5, 100,
  102–3, 131–3, 386, 429, 520–1
biology 237–9

Blund, John 170–3, 234, 240
Boccaccio 506, 519, 541–2
Boethius 4, 9, 11, 16, 21, 32, 34–5, 43, 59, 92, 98–9,
  103–4, 108–11, 136–7, 141, 147, 153, 159, 171,
  176–7, 223, 226, 250–2, 302, 312–13,
  327, 366, 422, 471, 496–8, 541
Boethius of Dacia 285, 290–1, 293–6, 303, 306, 309,
  378, 460
Bologna university 122, 142–5, 148, 415, 529–32
Bonaventure 8, 81, 85, 143, 181, 186, 196, 201–10,
  217–20, 250, 260, 285, 293–6, 299–302, 320,
  328, 344, 350–1, 361, 377–8, 391, 398, 484–7,
  499–500
Boniface VIII (Pope) 363, 381–2, 385–6, 388
Bradwardine, Thomas 361, 420
Brigitte of Sweden 519
Burgundio of Pisa 140, 183
Buridan, John 6–7, 155, 159, 255, 289, 361, 364,
  429–31, 443–55, 460–1, 477, 481, 516, 523,
  525, 533–4
Burley, Walter 361, 363, 365, 409, 416–9, 428–30,
  432–3, 436, 438–9, 451, 525, 533
Byzantine 3, 11, 15, 19, 137, 139–40, 190, 277,
  327, 478

Cabrol, John 256
Cajetan 256
Cathars 227, 277, 284, 512–13
Catherine of Siena 509–15, 521
Calcidius 95, 105
Calixtus II (Pope) 117
calendar 13–14, 36
Cambridge University 144, 529–30
Castro, Fidel 107, 111, 119
categories 29–30, 33, 67–8, 163, 179, 401,
  418–19, 436
causation 21, 26, 83–4, 180, 230–1, 241–4, 301–3,
  319, 341, 349, 382–3, 385, 444–5, 460–1, 473,
  477, 532–3, 538–9
Cavendish, Margaret 361
celestial bodies and intellects 79, 105, 173, 183, 192,
  238–9, 241, 247, 377–9, 435, 442–5, 447, 477–8,
  483–5
change 163–4, 438–9, 444, 461; see also
  transubstantiation
Charlemagne 4, 10–14, 19, 34, 115–16
Charles the Bald 19, 34, 37, 115
Chatton, Walter 405, 409, 414–5, 445–6, 457,
  460, 476
Chaucer 8, 224, 362, 366, 443, 495–9, 501,
  506–7, 519
choice 76, 124, 185, 211, 323, 340–2, 349, 453–4, 528;
  see also free will
Christ 3; see also Incarnation and Trinity
  as God's Wisdom or Intellect 25–6, 83–4, 88–9,
  92–3, 97–8, 320–1, 326–7, 412–13
  relation to God Father 15–16, 25–6, 73, 327–8
  sacrifice 15–18, 79–80

Christine de Pizan 315, 505, 516–19
Church
  Fathers 5–7, 21, 37, 121–2, 249–50, 278, 429
  authority of 9, 114–20, 123–4, 133, 217, 220–1,
    223, 227, 229, 270, 280–1, 284, 286–7, 289,
    362–3, 381–8, 390–1, 394, 398–9, 509–10,
    519–20, 526
Cicero 12, 16, 96, 105, 119, 143, 313, 519,
    540, 542
Clare of Assisi 221
Clarembald of Arras 95–6, 98, 109
Clement IV (Pope) 195
Clinton, George 168
Col, Pierre 315, 517–18
communism 218–19, 466–7
Conrad of Gelnhausen 520
conscience 182, 184–7, 220, 271–3, 396–8
Constantine the Great 386, 526
Constantine the African 136–7
counterfactuals 433–4; see also modalities and
  thought experiments
cosmology see natural philosophy and celestial
  bodies
creation 25–6, 29, 84, 191–2, 242, 244, 287, 294–5,
  297–303, 533–4
Crusades 89, 124, 277, 280–1, 284, 383,
  509–10

Dante 8, 222, 225, 255, 362, 366, 374–80, 384–8, 470,
  495, 501, 531, 536, 541–2
David (king) 14, 385
definition 33, 179–80, 418, 538–9
demonstration 141, 190–1, 250–1, 320, 408–9, 450,
  452, 454, 460, 538–9
Descartes 3, 8, 39, 52, 121, 172, 361,
  456, 458, 462
determinism 285, 339–42, 363–4, 421–8, 444, 494,
  497, 528
Devil 39, 49–51, 119, 483, 491–2
Dietrich of Freiberg 477–81, 484–5
Dhuoda 223
dialectic 34, 37, 43, 48, 67–8, 70–1, 153–4, 204, 249,
  298–9, 318, 432–3
dialogue 24–5, 49, 98–9, 102, 146, 317, 369, 499,
  514, 540–1
distinction, real vs. nominal 68–9, 90, 92, 177–9,
  244–5, 328–9, 333–6, 366, 524–5, 533, 539
divine command theory 346–7, 386, 394,
  395–7, 496
Dominicans 148–9, 201–2, 216, 223–4, 231, 236,
  239, 248, 256, 258, 279–80, 377–8, 425–6, 470,
  473–4, 476–81, 530–1
Dominicus Gundisalvi 137, 170
Donatism 116–18, 526–7
double effect theory 281–3
Dr Funkenstein see Clinton, George
Durandus of St Pourçain 426, 430–1, 467, 477,
  485, 488

Eadmer 47
Ebner, Margaret 481
economic theory 463–9, 499, 507
education and curriculum 10–12, 36–7, 39, 80–3,
  94–6, 137, 140–9, 195, 225, 284–5, 304–5, 435,
  442–3
elements 99–100, 105, 166, 191, 257, 302,
  442–5, 447
Elizabeth of Schönau 130
Elsbeth Stagel 481, 512
embryo 173–4, 232–3, 258, 283
Empedocles 242
empiricism 8–9, 102–3, 162, 190, 193, 195, 199–201,
  237–9, 260, 320, 365, 440, 447–9, 451,
  459–60, 486
Epictetus 76
Epicurean 79
Erasmus 3
Eriugena 5, 17–34, 37, 43, 49, 55, 63, 83, 137, 190, 243,
  322, 425, 478–9, 481, 486, 490
essence 27–8, 108–12, 127, 171, 287, 356–7,
  452–3, 485
  essence-existence distinction 244, 333–7, 477–8
eternity of the world 29, 138–9, 285–7, 290,
  294–303, 442–3, 539
ethics 51, 72–8, 80, 82, 85–6, 120, 133, 170, 182–7,
  220, 262–7, 322, 345–51, 371–3, 376, 384, 394–8,
  419–20, 492, 505, 519–20, 532, 540; see also
  good and sin
Euclid 41, 137, 193, 196
Eucharist 37, 84, 116–17, 227, 326, 329–31, 395, 438,
  459, 510, 527, 534–5
Evagrius 13, 41
Eve 17–18, 50, 62, 83, 100, 239, 384, 506
evil 17, 23, 42–3, 49, 104–5, 124, 131–2, 176–7, 180–1,
  426–7, 493, 532
exegesis see Bible: interpretations of
existence see also being and essence-existence
  distinction

al-Fārābī 36, 139, 141, 387, 389–90, 483
food 510–11
foundationalism 458
Francis of Assisi 194, 207, 215, 220–1,
  377–8, 486
Francis of Marchia 443–8
Franciscans 148–9, 162–3, 194, 196, 201–2, 208–9,
  215–328, 350–1, 358, 363–4, 391–3, 395, 398,
  414–15, 443–4, 467–8, 476, 510
free will 8, 17–18, 20–3, 49–51, 76, 89–90, 210–11,
  322–3, 339–44, 349–50, 373, 379–80, 397–8,
  425–7, 429–30, 444, 453–4, 497, 524, 528
Fredegisus 15, 29
Frederick II of Sicily 138–9
Frederick Barbarossa 145
Frege, Gottlob 153
future contingents 339–40, 363–4, 421–5, 497,
  532–3

Galen 438–9
Galileo 287, 441
Gaunilo 52–3, 55–7
Gelasius 115, 117
generation of animals 238, 241, 258, 300–1; *see also* biology
    spontaneous generation 102, 300–1
Geoffrey Plantagenet 99
Gerard of Abbeville 216
Gerard of Cremona 137–8, 140
Gerald Odonis 468
Gerbert of Aurillac (Silvester II) 36–7, 101, 136
Gersonides 3
al-Ghazālī 243, 298, 453, 461, 537
Gilbert of Poitiers 89, 95–6, 109–13, 118, 125–6, 132, 143, 146, 287, 352, 356
Gilbert of Tournai 223
Giles of Rome 285–6, 289, 328, 330, 333, 335–6, 362, 381–6, 505, 520
Giordano Bruno 537
giraffes 7, 33, 44, 48–9, 58–60, 68–9, 110, 143–4, 155–7, 159, 205–6, 230–1, 233–4, 241, 245, 291, 304–8, 320, 364; *see also* beauty, good, happiness, *and* best of all possible animals
Giver of Forms 135–6, 173, 260
God
    and being 33, 98, 171, 321–2, 333–8, 343–4, 471–3, 480
    attributes 53–4
    change in 21–2
    divine omnipotence 6–7, 40–5, 288–9, 297, 299–302, 347, 365, 383, 401–2, 404, 447–8, 460, 462, 500
    grace 6–7, 17–18, 20, 22, 48–9, 84–5, 88–9, 131, 267, 322–3, 419–20, 425–7, 438, 446, 466–7, 500, 528
    foreknowledge 21–2, 421–7, 430, 497, 528
    proofs for the existence of 5–6, 46, 52–7, 252–4, 297–8, 343–4
    simplicity of 21–2, 91–3, 132, 171, 326, 335, 366–7
    union with 27, 131, 183–4, 225–7, 369, 473, 479, 481, 491, 514–15, 521–2
    vision of 89, 203–5, 246–7
    will 41, 44–5, 49, 51, 79–80, 326–7, 344, 372, 425–7, 497, 514–15
Gödel, Kurt 52
Godfrey de Fontaines 219, 286, 328, 335–6
good 14, 49, 54, 73–4, 76–8, 176–7, 184, 262–3, 267, 319, 347, 471, 474–5, 539
Gottschalk 18–24
grammar 10, 35, 48, 62, 90, 96, 98, 105–6, 230–1, 304–10
Gratian 121–5, 144, 147, 195, 217, 269–71, 278, 280–1, 378, 398, 504
Gregory the Great 13, 16, 36–7, 92
Gregory of Nyssa 24
Gregory of Rimini 361, 430–1, 532–3
Gregory VII (Pope) 86, 114, 116–17, 502

Greyfriars 476, 496, 530–1
Grosseteste, Robert 140, 188–95, 198, 201, 204, 206, 215, 264, 435, 509
Guillaume de Lloris 312–14

Hadewijch 222–8, 312, 366, 369–71, 475, 490, 501
haecceity 356–8, 400–1, 485, 531–2
happiness 51, 264–5, 285, 295–6, 348–50, 376, 378, 499, 514–15, 541
Hedwig of St. Gall 36
Heloise 66–72, 78, 134, 190, 506–7
Henricus Cornelius Agrippa 519
Henry II of England 99
Henry III (emperor) 116
Henry IV (emperor) 114, 117–18
Henry V (emperor) 117
Henry VII (emperor) 385, 388
Henry of Ghent 219, 256, 287, 300, 318–28, 332, 336, 340–3, 355, 372, 395, 413, 449, 463, 476, 487–8, 504
Henry of Harclay 422, 445–6
Henry of Langenstein 443, 520, 529, 532–4
Henry of Oyta 533
Henry Suso 479–81, 512
Hercules 64
Heytesbury, William 430, 436, 438–9
Hildegard of Bingen 6, 128–34, 146, 181, 222, 239, 369, 371, 480, 492, 510
Hilduin (bishop of St. Denis) 24
Hilton, Walter 489, 511
Hincmar 19–20, 23–4, 116
history 13–14, 79–80, 84
Hobbes, Thomas 121
Holcot, Robert 262, 462
Holy Spirit 88–9, 92–3, 97, 225, 326–7
homosexuality 41, 103–6, 275, 376–7, 502–4
Horace 12, 32, 96, 119
Hortensius 504
Hrbanus Maurus 19, 23–4
Hrotsvitha 223
Hugh of St. Cher 279
Hugh of Saint Victor 80–5, 91–3, 99, 101, 103, 125–126, 132, 148, 202–3, 327, 346, 378
Huguccio 280–1, 398
Humbert (cardinal) 116
Hume, David 3, 8, 461, 524
humors 105, 198

Iamblichus 84
Ibn Bājja 440
Ibn Gabirol 171, 191, 232, 240, 287
Ibn al-Haytham 191, 199
Ibn Yūnūs, Kamāl al-Dīn 139
Ibn Khaldūn 195
icons 15
illuminationism 8, 184, 188–93, 196–9, 201–7, 233, 250–1, 260–1, 263, 320–1, 346, 378–9

immateriality 60–1, 82, 84, 92, 98, 135–6, 169,
171–2, 209–10, 214, 240–1, 259, 291–2, 482–3,
487, 513; *see also* soul and body
impetus 443–4, 446–7
Incarnation 6–7, 15–16, 26, 48, 79–80, 125–7,
202–3, 227, 232–3, 325, 493, 511–12, 525
individuation 107–13, 231–2, 287–8, 291–2, 354–8,
452, 484–5, 488, 531–2
inference 158–60, 429, 431–3
infinity 165–6, 192, 300, 437–40, 445–6
Innocent III (Pope) 527
intellect (mind) 14–15, 91–2, 99, 123, 131, 138–9,
169–70, 186, 189–90, 240–1, 259, 285–6,
290–2, 295–6, 300, 307–8, 322–3, 326–9,
340–1, 378–9, 430–1, 478, 531
universal or active 26–7, 104–5, 189–90, 243–4,
321, 477–8; *see also* Giver of Forms *and* Christ:
as God's Wisdom
intellectualism 187, 210–13, 225–6, 271–2, 323, 419,
453–4, 476–7
intentions 75–7, 88–9, 281–2, 322–3, 493,
519–20
Investiture Contest *see* Church: the authority of
Isidore of Seville 11, 16, 24, 35, 117, 147, 181,
278, 504
Islam 35–6, 79, 139, 277, 280–1, 298, 483–4,
518–19, 539–40
Ivo of Chartres 117, 121

James of Venice 139–40
Jan Hus 519, 521, 534–5
Jean de Meun (*Romance of the Rose*) 66, 311–12,
314–17, 366, 370, 376, 496, 501, 516–19
Jean de Montrueil 517
Jean Gerson 311, 363, 516, 528, 536, 542
Jean Le Fèvre 506
Jean Petit 521
Jerome (Church Father) 41, 184
Jerome of Prague 534–5
Joachim of Fiore 378
Joan of Arc 519, 521
John Dumbleton 436
John of Jandun 388
John of Mirecourt 462
John of Paris 382
John Picardi 476
John of Reading 395, 400, 414
John de la Rochelle 178, 271
John of Sacrobosco 443
John of Salisbury 35, 67, 94–6, 113, 118, 133, 139, 141,
143, 188, 389, 542
Judah Hallevi 540
Julian of Norwich 6, 362, 489, 491–2, 495,
510–13
Justinian 121, 217, 269, 465
Joan de Arc 129
John XXII (Pope) 219, 221, 388, 391, 395, 398, 471
John of Damascus 140

John de le Rochelle 178
Jokes
particularly bad ones 10–12, 17–18, 32, 36, 63–4,
109, 126–7, 134, 146–7, 156, 162, 177, 190, 196–7,
212, 236, 238, 248, 253–4, 278–9, 292, 301, 306,
362–3, 405–6, 416, 436, 445, 464, 469, 476,
486–7, 504
good ones 128
Judas 73–4
Judaism 13, 79, 131, 138, 171, 242, 249–50, 298–9,
467–8, 491, 539–40
Julius Caesar 114, 262

Kabbalah 8, 491
Kant, Immanuel 3, 52, 57, 74, 297
Keaton, Buster 52, 361, 392
Kepler, Johannes 199
Kierkegaard, Søren 325, 345
Kilwardby, Robert 183, 202, 229–35, 241, 246,
256–7, 265
al-Kindī 191, 199, 439
knowledge 8, 59–60, 83–4, 179–80, 184–5, 188–91,
196, 201, 203–6, 225–6, 233, 247, 250–2, 267,
320–321, 346, 357–8, 402–4, 414–16, 418, 437,
451, 456–62, 496; *see also* skepticism
reason, limits of 8, 15–16, 54–5, 85, 88, 131–2,
190–1, 246–7, 251, 298–9, 303, 320–1, 331, 337,
357, 365, 370–1, 376, 478–9, 490–1, 532–3
intuitive (direct) 357–8, 402–4, 414–15, 457–8,
462, 534
al-Khwārizmī 436

Lambert of Auxerre 155
Lanfranc of Bec 37–8, 47–8, 91, 117, 326
Langland, William 495–6, 499–501, 518, 524
language 7, 12–13, 28, 59–62, 68–9, 90, 157, 159,
177–8, 196–8, 230, 304–10, 316, 407–12, 450–1,
487; *see also* vernacular
Laurentius Hispanus 270
law 11, 39–41, 117, 121–4, 143, 148, 217, 219, 269–83,
388–9, 391–3, 465, 500; *see also* natural law
Leibniz, Gottfried Wilhelm von 5, 361, 441, 537
Leo (pope) 115
liar paradox 432
liberal arts *see* education and curriculum
Llull, Ramon 536–40, 542
logic 6–7, 10, 12–13, 36, 67–9, 108, 113, 141, 153–60,
202–3, 230–1, 290, 308, 405–6, 428–434, 437–8,
450, 533–4, 539–40
Lot 102
love 8–9, 14, 66, 69–70, 77–8, 88, 92–3, 225–7, 265,
311–17, 347, 369–73, 377, 397, 490, 499–501, 514,
516, 541–2
Lucan 12
Lucrezia Marinella 519
Lucretius 12
Ludwig of Bavaria (emperor) 388, 393, 395, 399
Luther, Martin 125, 481, 524

Machiavelli 3, 119
Macrobius 37, 104, 312, 316
Magna Carta 269
Magyars 36
Maimonides 3, 229, 249, 298–9, 473
Manegold of Lautenbach 37, 117–18, 120
Manicheans 217, 227
Marbod of Rennes 506
Marcus Aurelius 389
Margery Kempe 512
marriage 70, 84, 317, 504–5, 507, 512–13
Marsh, Adam 195
Marsilio Ficino 481
Marislius of Inghen 364, 366, 532
Marsilius of Padua 362–3, 38–93, 398
Marston, Roger 260
Martianus Capella 11–12, 34–7, 103–4, 143
Martin of Dacia 306–7
Martin of Laon 32
Martin Luther King Jr 274
Marx Brothers 24, 46, 58, 61, 64, 74, 87, 107, 111–2,
    287, 328, 361, 403–4, 533
Mary 481, 483, 486, 506
Master Giles 460
mathematics 9–10, 13–14, 36, 98, 102, 192–3, 196,
    312–13, 365, 374, 435–41, 443, 464–5
Matthew of Aquasparta 201, 206
matter 98–100, 103–5, 171, 191–2, 210, 230–2,
    238–41, 257, 287–8, 299–302, 330, 333–4,
    355–6, 442–6, 484–5, 527, 531–2
Maximus the Confessor 24
Mechthild of Magdeburg 8, 222–8, 312, 366,
    369, 470, 481, 490, 511, 514
medicine 9, 11, 82, 129–30, 136–7, 143, 148,
    200, 237, 282, 438–9, 449, 461, 503–4,
    530–1, 542
Meister Eckhart 8, 29, 222, 362, 368, 477, 479,
    490, 522
metaphysics, subject matter of 180, 245
Michael Scot 138–9
Michael the Stammerer 19
microcosm 103, 133
miracles 6, 13, 102, 295, 383, 454–5, 460–1
Moderata Fonte 519
modalities 5–7, 40, 42–4, 108, 156–7, 244, 254,
    288–9, 297–8, 313, 334, 339–43, 347, 365,
    421–5, 429–30, 462; see also future
    contingents
monasticism 13, 36, 41, 66, 69, 81, 85–6, 89, 143,
    183–4, 208–9, 215–21, 223–4, 271, 313–14, 505;
    see also poverty and asceticism
morality see ethics
Moses 79
motion 105, 162–5, 211, 230–1, 253–4, 294–5, 341,
    349–50, 436–42, 446–7, 483, 487
Muhammad 79, 100
murder 22, 75, 119–20, 273–4, 278, 281–3, 345,
    347, 521

music 10–11, 32–4, 129–30, 435
mysticism 6, 8, 85, 89, 129–31, 181, 190–1, 201,
    223, 225–8, 362, 369, 371–3, 478–81, 489–94,
    510–14, 521–2

nature 25, 29–30, 48–9, 85–6, 98, 101, 103–4,
    316–18, 501
  natural philosophy and science 9, 11–12, 36,
    98–106, 118, 131–3, 141, 161–7, 191, 198–9, 231,
    23–41, 302–3, 383, 391, 415–16, 435–48
  naturalism (in law and ethics) 122–30, 186,
    219–20, 263–8, 270–3, 275–6, 314, 317, 322,
    348–50, 386, 463, 498, 503, 532
  natural language 408–9, 450–1
necessity see modalities
negative theology 27–9, 33, 54–5, 328, 473, 478–80,
    485–6, 490
Neoplatonism 5, 19–20, 168, 226–7, 242–4,
    249–250, 400, 473, 477–9, 481
Newton, Isaac 46
Nietzsche, Friedrich 495
Nicholas III (Pope) 219
Nicholas Aston 462
Nicholas of Autrecourt 361, 454, 457–62
Nicholas of Cusa 481, 537
Nicholas of Damascus 237
Nicholas of Paris 155
Noah 80, 83, 85, 196, 207, 239
nominalism see universals
non-being 28–9, 33, 197, 304, 308, 404, 414–15,
    457, 462, 467, 470–2, 480
Normans 40–1
Notker Labeo 36–7

Ockham, William of 6–7, 125, 194, 350–1, 358,
    361, 363, 394–420, 424, 426, 428–30, 437,
    445–7, 450–1, 453, 457, 460, 474, 476, 481,
    486–8, 496, 509, 516, 525, 527, 530, 532–4
Odo of Soissons 132
Olivi, Peter 208–14, 217–18, 220–1, 229, 232–3,
    233, 241, 246, 289, 368, 391, 398, 403, 466,
    484, 534
omnipresence passim
optics 9, 192–3, 198–200, 251–2, 435
Oresme, Nicole 361–2, 440–44, 464, 468–9, 509
Origen 79, 278, 494
Otto (king) 36
Ovid 11–12, 32, 312
Oxford University 122, 140–5, 147–8, 155, 159,
    170, 189, 194–5, 200, 229–30, 234–5, 256–7,
    340, 363–4, 416, 426, 435, 462, 496, 507,
    524, 529

paganism 11–13, 19–20, 26–7, 34, 37, 76, 84, 93,
    96–97, 104, 114, 118, 196, 203, 262, 267, 298,
    313–314, 326, 377, 396–7, 477–8, 481, 483–4,
    498, 500–1, 542
Páleč, Stephen 534

Paul of Venice 531–3
Paris University 18, 95–6, 109–10, 113, 121–2, 125,
    140–9, 154–5, 159, 162–3, 176–9, 189–90, 195,
    201–4, 208–9, 216, 229–30, 235–7, 243,
    248–50, 256, 259, 270–1, 284–8, 290, 313, 318,
    340, 363–4, 378, 414, 416, 449, 459–60, 464–5,
    470, 519, 529–32, 537
Parmenides 28, 163, 304
patristic literature see Church Fathers
Pecham, John 201, 206, 258
Pelagius 18, 20, 22, 262, 262, 425, 500
Pepin 115
Peter (apostle) 37
Peter of Abano 530–32
Peter d'Ailly 519–20
Peter Aureol 415–6, 418–19
Peter Damian 39–46, 81, 116, 462, 502–3, 509
Peter Lombard 81, 121, 124–7, 144, 146–7, 184,
    186, 195, 209, 249, 263–5, 279, 286, 378,
    395, 450
Peter of Spain 155, 450
Petrarch 363, 540–2
Philip IV the Fair 363, 381–2, 388
Philip the Chancellor 171, 177, 185, 187, 189,
    210, 263–4, 347
Philo of Alexandria 13, 25
Philoponus, John 163, 298, 305, 440, 446–7
philosophy
    and religion 6–7, 20–1, 27, 37–8, 40–1, 43, 48, 71,
        79, 81–2, 84–5, 88–92, 100, 113, 118, 130, 138–9,
        148, 184, 203, 209, 229, 234–5, 249–52, 284–91,
        297–8, 303, 319–20, 325, 329, 331, 365, 368,
        377–8, 401–2, 449, 456–7, 467, 478,
        499–500, 503, 533–4
    and science 9, 17, 102, 161, 288–9, 295–6, 438,
        446, 536–7
    personification of 10, 103–4, 223, 225–6,
        374–5
physics see nature: natural philosophy
Pico della Mirandola 287
Plantinga, Alvin 52
place and space 109–10, 166–7, 297, 330, 356,
    445, 487–8
    natural 99–100, 166, 442, 447
Plato 3–4, 9, 12–15, 29, 35, 37, 40–1, 59, 67–8, 93–5,
    97, 99–100, 118, 141, 169–71, 188, 240–1, 255–6,
    298, 313, 316, 326, 361, 377, 379, 387, 389–90,
    407, 412–14, 417, 478, 481, 495, 499
Platonic Forms 25–6, 54, 59, 63, 67–8, 79, 83–4, 93,
    97–8, 190, 203–6, 260, 321, 353, 364, 430,
    478–9, 525, 533–4
Platonism 6, 11, 14–15, 26–7, 33, 54, 79–80, 82–4,
    96–9, 170, 201, 205, 240–1, 243, 249–50, 364,
    417, 477–8, 533–4
Plotinus 23, 84, 169, 208, 213, 243, 372, 426, 493
Plutarch 119
poetry 8–9, 13–14, 96–7, 103–4, 133, 180–1, 223,
    311–17, 362, 374–80, 495–6, 498

political philosophy 14, 119, 132–3, 176, 269–71,
    273–5, 279–81, 362–3, 379, 381–93, 398–9,
    485–6, 519–20, 524–6; see also Church: the
    authority of
Porete, Marguerite 6, 103–4, 222–3, 362, 368–73,
    376–7, 417, 470, 474–5, 489–91, 494, 513–15, 541
Porphyry 12, 59–63, 67–8, 84, 108–9, 418
possibility see modalities
poverty and asceticism 9, 13, 194, 208–9, 214–21,
    271, 313–14, 368, 372, 391–2, 395, 398–9, 443–4,
    473–4, 480–1, 510–21, 523–4, 526
predestination see free will and determinism
principle of non-contradiction 43, 45, 290, 294–6,
    342–3, 347–8, 365, 422–3, 458–9, 461
Priscian 62, 230, 305–6
probabilism 460–1
prophecy 79–80, 128–9
propositions 68–9, 154–60, 190–1, 206, 304,
    403–6, 422–4, 428–33, 437, 458–9, 525, 532
Protestantism 427, 481, 516, 524, 526
providence 101, 104–5, 385–6, 388, 469, 493, 497,
    514–15
Ptolemy 137, 377, 442–3
Pythagoras 40–1
Presocratics 25, 163, 242, 445
Proclus 84, 140, 243, 249, 298, 477–81
Pseudo-Dionysius 8, 19–20, 23–6, 54–5, 140, 188,
    190–1, 243, 249–50, 473, 477–9, 485–7,
    490, 520

Radulphus Brito 306, 309
Ralph Strode 436, 497
Ratramnus 37
al-Rāzī, Fakhr al-Dīn 332–3, 338, 440
redemption 27, 42, 79–80, 83, 88–9, 228, 500
Reformation see Protestantism
resurrection 169–70, 173, 258–9, 294
relations 325–30, 401–2
Remigius of Auxerre 34
Renaissance 3–5, 9, 94–6, 138–40, 222, 256, 361,
    481, 516, 519, 531, 536–42
    Carolingian 4, 10–16, 46
Richard Campsall 423–4
Richard Kilvington 432–3, 436–8
Richard of Middleton 351
Richard of Saint Victor 81, 85, 92–3, 103
Richard Rolle 489–90
Richard Rufus 162–3, 165, 199, 231, 435, 447
Roland of Cremona 279–80
(Holy) Roman Empire 4, 11, 16, 280, 384–6,
    529–30
Romauld of Ravenna 41
Roscelin 61–2, 67–8, 90
Ruysbroeck, Jan van 521

sacraments 84–5, 116, 389, 446, 524, 526–7; see also
    Eucharist
Satan see Devil

self-awareness 172, 479, 491
salvation *see* Christ's sacrifice
Sabellianism 327–8
sex 39–40, 50, 72, 75, 100, 104, 226–7, 314–17,
    498–9, 501–5, 512–13, 516
Seneca 70, 471, 519, 540–2
sense-perception 15, 99, 141, 181, 188–90, 196, 201,
    205–6, 212–14, 233–4, 246, 253–4, 357–8, 403,
    415–16, 457–61
Shakespeare, William 17
Siger of Brabant 149, 285–6, 290–1, 293–6,
    300, 303, 306, 331, 377
Siger of Courtai 306
signification 62, 157–8, 177–8, 196–8, 305–8, 332,
    335–6, 364, 401, 410–12, 418, 428–30, 450–1,
    532, 539
Simplicius 298, 305
sin 9, 14, 17–18, 21, 40, 42–3, 49–51, 74–5, 96–7, 116,
    218, 278–9, 322–3, 372, 377, 391–3, 419, 425–7,
    467, 488, 493, 501–4, 507, 514, 525
    original sin 17–18, 20, 27, 50, 79–80, 184, 314,
    350, 357, 384, 466–7, 525–6
skepticism 8, 71, 141, 309–10, 364–5, 403, 415–16,
    454–62
science 9, 141, 180, 193, 251–2, 319–20, 337, 357, 365,
    376, 383, 400–1, 408–9, 436–7, 452, 454, 458,
    460, 538–9; *see also* philosophy and science
    and demonstration
Scotus, John Duns 5–7, 124–5, 146, 194, 255–6,
    318–19, 322–3, 328–30, 33–58, 361–2, 364–5,
    372–3, 394–5, 400, 402–3, 405, 409–10,
    414–16, 422–5, 432, 445–6, 449–54, 466–7, 481,
    485, 487–8, 516, 524–5, 531–2
Sextus Empiricus 456–7
sophistry 434
Spencer, John 101
Socrates 67, 94, 262–4, 266, 296, 315, 368, 396–7,
    456–7, 500
Solomon 14, 196, 500
soul 26–7, 80, 82–3, 131, 168–74, 209–10, 226–7,
    231–4, 239–41, 257–9, 293, 369–70, 373, 471,
    493–4
    and body 14–15, 92, 96–7, 126, 168–73, 183–4,
    209–10, 214, 233, 240–1, 257–8, 291–2, 382,
    493–4, 511–13, 524
    and the state (parallel) 14–15, 188
    annihilation of 372–3
    faculties of 136–7, 168–70, 173–4, 209–10, 232–3,
    257, 326, 415–16, 478
    pre-existence of 97, 373, 471
    immortality of 168–9, 209, 239–40, 258–9, 368
    unity of 169–70, 210, 234, 241, 286, 493–4, 527–8
    world soul 97
Spinoza, Baruch 361
Stanislav of Znojmo 534
Starchild *see* Clinton, George
stars *see* astronomy, astrology, *and* celestial bodies
states of affairs 418–19, 430, 525, 532

Stoics 76, 135, 159–60, 188, 204, 232, 456, 471,
    514–15, 541
subjective and objective 404–5
substance 30, 60, 62–3, 67–8, 87, 92–3, 110–11,
    164, 171–2, 210, 230, 232, 257–8, 304–6, 308–9,
    327, 330, 334, 401, 459, 461, 476–7, 527–8
Suhrawardī 188
Sufism 6, 8
Swineshead, Roger 432, 436
Synclectica 510

teleology 48–9
Tempier, Stephen 235, 256, 284–8, 291, 295
textual traditions 16, 21, 32, 35, 125, 137–8, 140, 183,
    314; *see also* translations
Thales 463
theodicy 18, 21–3, 49–50, 346–7, 426–7, 532
Theodore of Antioch 139
Theodulf 15
Thierry of Chartres 95–6, 98, 102–3, 109–10, 118
Thomas Bradwardine 426–7, 431–2, 436–7,
    439–40, 444, 497, 500, 528
Thomas le Myésier 536–7
Thomas of Erfurt 306
Thomas Wylton 431, 439
thought 135–6, 172, 260, 287, 306–7, 407, 430–1
thought experiments 39–40, 172, 446–8, 450–1,
    488, 523
Trajan 119, 500
translations 5–6, 11, 19–20, 94–5, 102, 135–41, 177,
    229, 263–4, 368, 442–3, 462, 488, 496, 505, 523
Trinity 6–7, 14–15, 25–6, 68, 83–4, 87–93, 98, 118,
    132, 207, 225, 249–51, 313–14, 320–1, 325–9,
    366, 401–2, 473, 481, 533–4
transubstantiation 6–7, 329–30, 526–7
truth 48–9, 178–9, 205, 253, 290, 409–10, 421–5,
    429–30
Tauler, John 479–81
Tengswich of Andernach 133–4
Terence 37
Tertullian 278
time 164–5, 231, 297, 300, 441
    and eternity 21–2, 43–4, 302, 474, 486; *see also*
    eternity of the world
transcendentals 176–81, 192, 206, 244–5, 284,
    321–2, 333–4, 336–7, 353, 385, 470–2, 539–40

Ulpian 39, 269
universals 5–7, 33, 58–65, 107, 112–13, 127, 158–9,
    172, 190, 259–60, 305, 308–9, 352–4, 364–5,
    400–6, 416–18, 437, 450–2, 478, 485, 496, 521,
    5–NaN, 527, 531–4
universities 7, 34–5, 98–9, 122, 140–1, 142–8, 194,
    216, 250, 256, 284–5, 287, 297, 317, 361, 363–4,
    370–1, 432–3, 450, 464–5, 504, 529–35; *see also*
    Cambridge University, Oxford University, *and*
    Paris University
Upaniṣads 242, 495

al-Urmawī 139
usury 464–8, 499
utilitarianism 282, 350, 466

Varro, Marcus 11
vernacular 138, 222, 224–5, 310, 313, 362–3,
    366–7, 369, 374–7, 384, 427, 442–3, 469–70,
    480–1, 489–90, 505, 519, 537
vikings 19, 35–6
Virgil 12, 16, 37, 96–7, 105, 119, 143–54, 375, 377
virginity 40, 102
virtue 13, 74–6, 82–3, 88–9, 118, 127, 133, 183–4, 262–7,
    348–9, 369, 371–3, 375–6, 387, 474–5, 490–1, 541
Visigoths 11, 15
void 288–9, 439–40, 444–5
voluntarism 76, 174, 210–11, 346–7, 365, 372–3,
    395, 409, 419, 424–7, 453–4, 476–7, 496–7,
    499–500, 514, 532

war, just 9, 124, 277–83, 345, 382–3, 509–10
will 49, 51, 74–6, 174, 182, 184–7, 210–11, 266, 293,
    322–4, 326–9, 339–44, 349–50, 372–3, 395, 419,
    426–7, 453–4, 476–7, 496, 506, 541; see also free
    will and God's will
Wilde, Oscar 18

William II (king) 47
William of Alnwick 340, 395
William of Auvergne 168–9, 171–4, 182, 195, 228,
    232, 234, 246, 256, 333, 486
William of Auxerre 176–7, 271
William of Champeaux 62–3, 67, 80, 82, 85, 94, 96,
    143, 352
William the Conqueror 40
William de le Mare 258
William of Moerbeke 140, 195, 478
William of Pagula 393
William of St. Thierry 88–92, 131
William of Conches 95–100, 102–3, 105, 118,
    137, 501
William of Sherwood 155, 158, 307
William of St Amour 216, 218
Wittgenstein, Ludwig 304
Wolfhelm of Brauweiler 37
women 6, 8–9, 67, 70, 77–8, 100, 128–34, 145–6,
    315, 368–73, 375, 384, 388, 480–1, 501, 504–8,
    510–14, 516–19, 521
Wyclif, John 362, 364–6, 519, 521, 523–8, 531,
    533–6

Zeno of Elea 163